EXPLORING

Social Psychology

EXPLORING
Social Psychology
Fourth Canadian Edition

Robert A. Baron
Rensselaer Polytechnic Institute

Donn Byrne
State University of New York at Albany

Gillian Watson
University of British Columbia

PEARSON

Toronto

National Library of Canada Cataloguing in Publication

Baron, Robert A
   Exploring social psychology / Robert A. Baron, Donn Byrne, Gillian Watson.

4th Canadian ed.
Includes bibliographical references and index.
ISBN 0-205-40379-4

1. Social psychology. I. Byrne, Donn II. Watson, Gillian III. Title.

HM1033.B37 2005	302	C2003-905781-X

ISBN 0-205-40379-4

Vice President, Editorial Director: Michael J. Young
Acquisitions Editor: Ky Pruesse
Senior Marketing Manager: Judith Allen
Senior Developmental Editor: Lise Dupont
Production Editor: Richard di Santo
Copy Editor: Valerie Adams
Proofreader: Anne Borden
Production Manager: Wendy Moran
Permissions Manager: Susan Wallace-Cox
Literary Research: Beth McAuley
Photo Research: Alene McNeill
Page Layout: Laserwords
Art Director: Julia Hall
Interior and Cover Design: Gillian Tsintziras
Cover Image: Photonica/Ian Sanderson

Statistics Canada information is used with the permission of the Minister of Industry, as Minister responsible for Statistics Canada. Information on the availability of the wide range of data from Statistics Canada can be obtained from Statistics Canada's Regional Offices, its World Wide Web site at http://www.statcan.ca, and its toll-free access number 1-800-263-1136.

1 2 3 4 5   09 08 07 06 05

Printed and bound in Canada.

Contents

Preface

Continuity and Change: or "*Plus ca change, plus c'est la même chose*" (Alphonse Karr, 1849)

The fourth Canadian edition of *Exploring Social Psychology* marks its tenth anniversary since the publication of the first Canadian edition. Anniversaries often lead to reflection about the changes that have occurred in the interim. In this case, the reflection relates not only to the world in general, but also to social psychology and to our book in particular. In the past decade, we have crossed from the 20th to the 21st century, and some remarkable changes have occurred in our world. Just one example is the amazing expansion of internet use, which has transformed education and communication. In 1994, the use of computers in the classroom was a new initiative, and internet communication was not seen as a necessity. Today, our students are expected to have internet access and to own a computer. Communications have been transformed in the last ten years, enabling constant contact between people and easy access to information. This radical change in our lives over the past decade is one that is close to the heart of all academics who have been scrambling to keep up with the demands of technology.

With change comes a realization of an underlying continuity. What is the most common use of the internet? As always, the primary use of communication technology is *social*—email and cell phone contact with friends, family and acquaintances. But continuity may not always be so benevolent. For example, our shrinking planet now seems even smaller, and global warming has become widely acknowledged. Conflict and war has continued: The Gulf War of the 1990s was followed by the Iraq war in this decade. We in Canada continue to be affected by conflict around the world, from the 9-11 fallout to the deployment of our troops as peacekeepers. "*Plus ca change, plus c'est la même chose,*" as Alphonse Karr famously wrote—somehow, it seems that the more things change, the more they stay the same.

Social psychology has also changed and developed over the last decade. However, its relevance to our changing lives, whether for good or bad, has remained constant. Similarly, this text has strives to maintain its relevance to social psychology by providing a balance of both change and continuity: by representing new directions in the discipline while maintaining a commitment to its roots and the core literature.

Change

1. Recent Developments in Social Psychology

Just how have we represented change in the fourth Canadian edition of *Exploring Social Psychology?* Each chapter has been thoroughly updated, reflecting recent developments in our field. As a result, you will find literally hundreds of references from 2000–2003. Here are some of these new and updated topics:

Chapter 1: An ethno-cultural portrait of Canada; expanded coverage of the evolutionary perspective and emphasis on the parallel growth of cultural psychology.

Chapter 2: Using non-verbal cues to recognize deception; East Asian and North American differences in communication; the negativity bias in perception.

Chapter 3: Attitude ambivalence; wartime propaganda related to the Gulf and Iraq wars.

Chapter 4: A new section contrasting evolutionary and cultural explanations for the development of the self; research on the sexual self-schema.

Chapter 5: Implicit prejudice and stereotypes; hostile and benevolent sexism; role-congruity theory of prejudice to female leaders.

Chapter 6: New evolutionary research on the physical features of attraction in both males and females; recent challenges to the assumptions of sexual strategies theory; updated research on internet relationships.

Chapter 7: Extreme forms of social influence, including intense indoctrination; compensatory conformity in bicultural minority members.

Chapter 8: A new section on prosocial motivation, including evolutionary perspectives; bullying.

Chapter 9: The discontinuity effect in group competition; interpersonal justice in intimate relationships.

Chapter 10: Stress responses to 9-11; expansion of organizational citizenship behaviour research; guidelines for evaluating recovered memories of crimes.

2. The Expansion of Evolutionary Social Psychology

Perhaps one of the most startling developments in social psychology over the past decade has been the growth of a biological perspective. Ten years ago, most social psychologists were disinterested in, or even antagonistic to the idea of how biological processes and evolved tendencies could shape our social behaviour. Today, *evolutionary social psychology* is a major force in social psychology. This is reflected in nearly every chapter of this book. Here are just a few examples:

Chapter 1: A description of Darwin's theory of natural selection and how it relates to social behaviour.

Chapter 2: The evolutionary explanation for a negativity bias.

Chapter 4: Both historical and modern evolutionary perspectives on the nature of the self; the issue of whether a self-enhancement bias is pan-cultural.

Chapter 5: Evolutionary explanations for prejudice and xenophobia.

Chapter 6: Research on composite masculinized and feminized male faces; the waist-to-hip ratio and shoulder-to-hip ratio as they influence attractiveness in both males and females; evolutionary perspectives on jealousy.

Chapter 8: Kin selection and altruism; youth violence—the young male syndrome—as intrasexual competition.

Chapter 10: An evolutionary explanation for overeating.

Continuity

While there have been many changes in this text, our basic approach is still the same. We have striven to produce a readable book that represents modern social psychology and is relevant to Canadian students in a number of ways. First, as in previous editions, it features a wide range of Canadian content, both in its examples and by highlighting Canadian research. Second, it continues to reflect Canadian multiculturalism with a special emphasis on cultural issues and research. Third, it emphasizes the ways in which social psychology can be applied to an individual's life. Fourth, it draws attention to the roots of social psychology in sections focusing on classic research.

1. Canadian Content

We have tried to maintain Canadian content through the *Canadian Research: On the Cutting Edge* features, and through references to recent events and issues. However, Canadian research is not just confined to these special sections—it is represented throughout the book. A selection of this Canadian content is below:

Chapter 1: Roger Buehler and colleagues: overcoming the planning fallacy; Canadian culture: its impact on social behaviour.

Chapter 2: Noranzayan and colleagues: cultural differences in holistic and analytic thinking.

Chapter 3: Strahan and colleagues: the influence of subliminal priming on behaviour.

Chapter 4: Tafarodi: the negativity bias in paradoxical self-esteem; Heine: the cultural basis of self-enhancement.

Chapter 5: Song Hing & Zanna: challenging implicit prejudice through hypocrisy induction; Dion: the stress model of victim responses to prejudice.

Chapter 6: Dion & Dion: cultural factors in love relationships; changing patterns of common-law relationships in Canada.

Chapter 7: Janes & Olson: conforming in response to "jeer pressure."

Chapter 8: Pihl and colleagues: sex differences in response to alcohol and aggression.

2. Cultural Diversity

Recognition of the importance of Canada's cultural diversity has always been a mandate of this text and, in the ten years since our first edition, the cultural perspective has expanded considerably, especially since the idea that culture has a fundamental influence on social behaviour has been widely accepted. This edition has been updated with new cultural content in most of its chapters. A selection is provided below:

Chapter 1: An ethnocultural portrait of Canada; changing patterns of immigration to Canada.

Chapter 2: Cultural differences in analytic and holistic thinking; East Asian and North American difference in communication.

Chapter 3: The role of cultural values in attitude formation and change.

Chapter 4: The collective constructionist model of the development of the self; the self in East Asian and North American culture; self-enhancement and self-improvement in Western and East Asian cultures.

Chapter 6: Cultural factors in interpersonal attraction (e.g., body proportion); cultural differences in passionate love.

Chapter 7: Ethnic identity and compensatory conformity.

Chapter 8: Cultural norms in prosocial behaviour and aggression.

Chapter 10: Firearms availability and violence across cultures.

3. Applying Social Psychology

A central theme of this book has always been that social psychology can and should be applied to our daily lives. This theme continues in the current edition and comes to the fore in two features. First, *Ideas to Take with You*, a section located at the end of each chapter, is designed to highlight important concepts students should remember and use in their lives. Second, the *Social Psychology in Practice* features focus on how social psychology has been applied to real-world issues by researchers and others. A few topics covered in these sections are presented below:

Chapter 2: Cultural differences in styles of communication.

Chapter 3: Psychological warfare: persuasion and propaganda.

Chapter 5: Sexism and women in the workplace.

Chapter 6: The effect of internet relationships on our social lives.

Chapter 8: Bullying.

Chapter 9: Biased decision-making in juries.

Chapter 10: Research on the effects of weapons and the relationship of firearms availability to violence.

4. Classic Research in Social Psychology

A commitment to the roots of social psychology emerges through both historical references and the *Cornerstones* features, which highlight classical research in social psychology. A few examples of the topics discussed in these sections are Rosenthal's work on the self-fulfilling prophecy, LaPiere's classic study of attitudes and behaviour, Bem's work on psychology androgyny, Dutton and Aron's Capilano Bridge experiment, and Asch's famous conformity experiments.

Maintaining Pedagogical Features: Design and Supplements

A number of pedagogical features designed to make the text more readable and useful for students are continued in this edition:

Chapter Outline. Each chapter begins with an outline of the major topics covered.

List of Special Sections. Also featured at the beginning of each chapter is a list of the special sections and features presented.

Key Points. To help you understand and remember what you have read, each major section is followed by a list of *Key Points*, briefly summarizing main points. Each chapter also ends with a summary and review of these key points.

Key Terms. Key terms appear in boldface type in the text and are defined in the margin.

Cornerstones. These special sections describe truly classic studies in the field—ones that are fundamental to the development of major lines of research, and thus have exerted a lasting impact on social psychology.

On the Applied Side. These sections highlight the applicability of social psychology and demonstrate ways in which its knowledge and principles can be applied to a wide range of real-life issues and problems.

Canadian Research: On the Cutting Edge. These sections describe Canadian research that we believe is on the frontier of knowledge in social psychology.

Ideas to Take with You. Featured near the end of each chapter, these sections are designed to highlight important concepts you should remember—and use—long after this course is over.

Icons. Throughout the book, many sections illustrate differences across various cultures or between ethnic groups within a given society. To help you identify this material, these culture-related discussions throughout the main text are marked with the following symbol:

Social psychologists have recently shown increased interest in the potential role of biological or genetic factors in social behaviour. To help you identify these biological-related discussions, we have marked them with the following icon, designed to draw your attention to the evolutionary perspective:

At various points in this book, we juxtapose the evolutionary and cultural approach and compare their explanations. These sections will be highlighted with the by the following combination of the two symbols shown above:

Summary. Each chapter ends with a summary of major points in the chapter. Reviewing this section is an important first step in the study process.

For More Information. Annotated suggested readings appear at the end of each chapter. These readings will be useful to you as you study and prepare your essays and assignments.

Weblinks. Visit the relevant websites at the end of each chapter for additional information and assistance with the topics covered.

Supplements to the Text

Learning Aids for Students

Companion Website (www.pearsoned.ca/baronbyrne). The purchase of this book provides you with instant access to the Companion Website that accompanies the fourth Canadian edition of *Exploring Social Psychology*. This website offers students a variety of exercises to enhance their total learning experience, including practice tests, links to relevant internet sites, and more.

Study Guide (ISBN 0-205-42671-9). The *Study Guide* includes chapter outlines, learning objectives, and a series of imaginative and useful exercises that will help students review and understand the material in the text.

Supplements for Instructors

Computerized Test Item File (TestGen). Featuring approximately 110 questions per chapter, Pearson's *TestGen* designed to accompany this text is a computerized version of the *Test Item File* that enables instructors to view and edit existing test questions, add questions, generate tests, and print tests in a variety of formats. Powerful search and sort functions make it easy to locate questions and arrange them in any order desired. *TestGen* also enables instructors to administer tests on a local area network, grade the tests electronically, and prepare the results in electronic or printed reports. Issued on the Instructor's Resource CD-ROM, Pearson's *TestGen* is compatible with IBM and Macintosh systems.

Instructor's Manual. Available via the Instructor's Resource CD-ROM, as well as online through Pearson's protected Instructor Central website (www.pearsoned.ca/instructor), the *Instructor's Manual* includes chapter outlines and learning objectives, discussion questions, suggestions for classroom activities, a film/video list, and a variety of critical thinking and essay questions.

Instructor's Resource CD-ROM (ISBN 0-205-42673-5). This valuable supplement features the *Instructor's Manual*, the Computerized Test Item File, and selected textbook graphics.

Acknowledgments

Some Words of Thanks from the Canadian Author

Preparing this fourth edition has provided plenty of examples of continuity and change. As in previous editions, many people have cooperated and cajoled to complete it; and once again it seemed at times as if the planning fallacy would defeat us. While many of the people I want to acknowledge worked on previous editions of this book, there are also a number of new people to thank.

First, my thanks to Rachel Mines, who once again acted as a researcher for this edition. She contributed many ideas and suggestions for new material and, as always, was unfailingly conscientious.

Second, special thanks to the reviewers of this edition, selected by Pearson Education Canada and listed alphabetically here: Maria Janicki, Douglas College; Ronald F. Kinley, Kwantlen University College; Mary Lou Kneeshaw, Georgian College; Fiona Papps, University of Prince Edward Island; and Sam Parkovnick, Dawson College. The reviewers offered carefully considered comments and really useful suggestions for improvement, many of which have been incorporated into this new edition.

Finally, at Pearson Education Canada, I would like to thank Jessica Mosher, Ky Pruesse, Suzanne Schaan, Richard di Santo, and especially Lise Dupont for their patience and help during the development and production of this text. Also, thanks to Valerie Adams who did a thorough job as copy editor.

ABOUT THE AUTHORS

Robert A. Baron is currently Professor of Psychology and Wellington Professor of Management at Rensselaer Polytechnic Institute. A Fellow of the APA since 1978, he received his Ph.D. from the University of Iowa (1968). Professor Baron has held faculty appointments at the University of South Carolina, Purdue University, the University of Minnesota, University of Texas, University of Washington, and Princeton University. He has received numerous awards for teaching excellence at these institutions. He served as a Program Director at the National Science Foundation from 1979 to 1981. At present, Professor Baron's major research interests focus on applying the principles and findings of social psychology to behaviour in work settings (e.g., the causes and management of organizational conflict; impact of the physical environment on task performance and productivity).

Donn Byrne holds the rank of Distinguished Professor of Psychology and is the Director of the Social-Personality Program at the University at Albany, State University of New York. He received his Ph.D. in 1958 from Stanford University and has held academic positions at the California State University at San Francisco, the University of Texas, and Purdue University as well as visiting professorships at the University of Hawaii and Stanford University. He received the Excellence in Research Award from the University at Albany in 1987 and the Distinguished Scientific Achievement Award from the Society for the Scientific Study of Sex in 1989. His current research interests include interpersonal attraction and the prediction of sexually coercive behaviour.

Gillian Watson immigrated to Canada from Britain in the 1970s, and has been interested in the cross-cultural experience ever since. Maintaining that theme, she received her first degree from McGill University in Quebec (1980), sa doctorate (or D. Phil. as it is called) from Oxford University in England (1985), and spent a postdoctoral year with the Department of Communication in Ottawa. Her research interests include justice, intergroup relations, and cross-cultural psychology. She is a lecturer at the University of British Columbia where she recently won an award for her teaching.

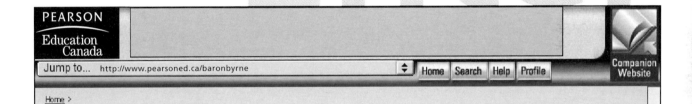

CHAPTER ONE

The Field of Social Psychology:
How We **Think** About and **Interact** with Others

Social Psychology: A Working Definition
Social Psychology Is Scientific in Nature/Social Psychology Focuses on the Behaviour of Individuals/Social Psychology Seeks to Understand the Causes of Social Behaviour and Thought/Social Psychology: Summing Up

Research Methods in Social Psychology
Systematic Observation: Describing the World/Correlation: Predicting Relationships/The Experimental Method: Causation and Explanation/Choosing a Methodology: Description, Prediction or Causation?/Ethics in Research: Consideration of Subject Rights

Social Psychology in the New Millennium: Origins and Trends
Growing Emphasis on Application: Exporting Social Psychology/Influence of the Cognitive Perspective/Adopting a Multicultural Perspective: Taking Account of Diversity/Increasing Influence of the Evolutionary Perspective/Evolution and Culture: An Old Dispute in Modern Form

Using This Book: A Road Map for Readers

SPECIAL SECTIONS

CANADIAN RESEARCH: ON THE CUTTING EDGE
Overcoming the Planning Fallacy: Does Focusing on Pessimism Work?

ON THE APPLIED SIDE
Canadian Culture: Its Impact on Social Behaviour and Social Psychology

■ The Immeasurable Comfort of Social Support in Times of Crisis

FIGURE 1.1 When important events occur, both good and bad, we first turn to those around us for support and companionship and to help us make sense of the world.

The day after the terrorist attack on the World Trade Center in New York, now widely termed "9-11," I (Gillian Watson) taught a large Psychology 100 class at 8:30 a.m. I was still reeling and so were my students. My first words were simply to acknowledge how shocking those relentless TV images were and to ask if anyone had any comments. There was a pause. Then one young woman raised her hand and said, "I feel as if the world's coming to an end." Another two people raised their hands and expressed their fear of Canada being attacked, concern for their own safety and for their whole way of life. Soon there was a forest of hands. People mentioned their shock and disbelief, their anger towards terrorists and politicians, their insecurities and speculations about the future. In fact, the discussion lasted the whole class and, although no psychology was taught that day, this somehow felt right and necessary. In retrospect, what we were doing, and this was probably mirrored in a thousand classrooms and offices all over Canada, was providing each other with the immeasurable comfort of *social support*—the emotional and physical comfort provided by others—see Figure 1.1.

It is a mark of our essentially *social* nature that when important events occur, both good and bad, we first turn to those around us, not only for support and companionship, but to help us make sense of the world. And when other people are not available or have excluded us, then our lives are often more difficult (e.g., Baumeister, 2002; Gottlieb, 1987). The purpose of this book is to explore our social nature and examine how the social world influences an individual's behaviour—this is the fascinating and important topic of *social psychology*.

Because of the importance of the social side of our lives, you may be surprised to learn that the scientific study of social behaviour is relatively new. It was only during the last half of the 20th century that social psychology developed into a really active field. Despite its recent arrival on the scene, however, social psychology has provided some

The Breadth of Social Psychology, about here; note that formatting below needs to be fixed; NOTE that this table should be updated by Gillian at first pass—this table was taken from the last edition, so the description of hot topics should be updated.

TABLE 1.1 The Breadth of Social Psychology

Question	Chapter in Which it is Covered
Why do people commonly underestimate how much time a task will take?	Chapter 1
How can we tell if someone is trying to deceive us?	Chapter 2
What kind of persuasion techniques are used in wartime propaganda?	Chapter 3
Do women and men really differ in their behaviour? If so, why?	Chapter 4
Does Canada's policy of multiculturalism have a positive impact on ethnic relations?	Chapter 5
Why do people fall in love?	Chapter 6
If you try to boost your own image in front of others, does it make them treat you better?	Chapter 7
Why do some people just stand and stare during an emergency? Why don't they offer help?	Chapter 8
How can bullying be reduced in our schools?	Chapter 8
Do people accomplish more when working together or when working alone?	Chapter 9
Does your attractiveness, your gender, or your ethnicity affect how you are treated in the legal system?	Chapter 10

important insights into social behaviour. Perhaps the breadth and potential value of the information it yields are best suggested by a list like the one in Table 1.1. Please note that the questions in the table represent only a small sample of the many topics currently being studied by social psychologists. The field is currently so diverse and so far ranging in scope that no single list could possibly represent all of the topics it considers.

Before getting started, though, it's important that we provide you with some background information about the scope, methods, and nature of social psychology. Why is such information useful? Because research findings in psychology indicate that people have a much better chance of understanding, remembering, and using new information if they are first provided with a framework for organizing it. So that's what this introductory chapter is all about: providing you with a framework for interpreting and understanding social psychology. Specifically, here's what will follow.

First, we'll present a more formal *definition* of social psychology. Every field has its basic assumptions, and understanding these will help you understand why social psychologists study the topics they do and why they approach them in certain ways. Second, we will examine some of the methods used by social psychologists to answer questions about the social side of life. A working knowledge of these basic methods will help you to understand how social psychologists add to our understanding of social thought and social behaviour—how, in short, the knowledge presented in this text was obtained. Third, we'll describe some of the major characteristics of social psychology as it exists right now: where it is and where it seems to be going in this new millennium.

Social Psychology: A Working Definition

Providing a formal definition of almost any field is a complex task. In the case of social psychology, this complexity is increased by two factors: the field's broad scope and its rapid rate of change. Despite this, we can say that for social psychologists there is one central task: understanding how and why individuals behave, think, and feel as they do in social situations—ones involving the actual or imagined presence of other persons. Taking this central focus into account, our working definition of social psychology is as follows: Social psychology *is the scientific field that seeks to understand the nature and causes of individual behaviour and thought in social situations*. Let's now take a closer look at several aspects of this definition.

Social Psychology
The scientific field that seeks to understand the nature and causes of individual behaviour and thought in social situations.

Social Psychology Is Scientific in Nature

What is *science*? Many people seem to believe that this term refers only to fields such as chemistry, physics, and biology. If you share that view, you may find our suggestion that social psychology is a scientific discipline somewhat puzzling. How can a field that seeks to study the nature of love, the causes of aggression, and everything in between be scientific in the same sense as physics, biochemistry, and computer science? The answer is surprisingly simple.

In reality, the term *science* does not refer to a special group of highly advanced fields. Rather, it refers to two things: (1) a set of values, and (2) several methods that can be used to study a wide range of topics. In deciding whether a given field is or is not scientific, therefore, the critical question is: *Does it adopt these values and methods?* To the extent that it does, it is scientific in nature? To the extent that it does not, it falls outside the realm of science. We'll examine the procedures used by social psychologists in their research in detail in the next major section; here, we'll focus on the core values that all fields must adopt to be considered scientific in nature. Four of these are most important:

- *Accuracy*: A commitment to gathering and evaluating information about the world (including social behaviour and thought) in as careful, precise, and error-free a manner as possible.
- *Objectivity*: A commitment to obtaining and evaluating such information in a manner that is as free from bias as humanly possible.
- *Skepticism*: A commitment to accepting findings as accurate only to the extent that they have been verified over and over again.
- *Open-Mindedness*: A commitment to changing one's views—even views that are strongly held—if existing evidence suggests that these views are inaccurate.

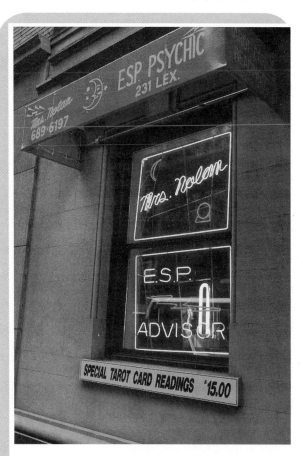

■ Science versus Nonscience: Different Values, Different Methods

FIGURE 1.2 Fields such as the one shown here are definitely *not* scientific; they do not accept the core values of science (accuracy, objectivity, skepticism, open-mindedness) and do not use scientific methods to test specific hypotheses.

Social psychology, as a field, is deeply committed to these values and applies them in its efforts to understand the nature of social behaviour and social thought. For this reason, it makes sense to describe our field as scientific in orientation. In contrast, fields that are not scientific make assertions about the world, and about people, that are not subjected to the careful testing and analysis required by the values listed above. In such fields—ones like astrology and aromatherapy—intuition, faith, and unobservable forces are considered to be sufficient.

"But why adopt the scientific approach? Isn't social psychology just common sense?" Having taught for many years (more than eighty-five between us!), we can almost hear you asking this question. And we understand why you might feel this way; after all, each of us has spent our entire life interacting with other persons. As a result of such experience, we are all amateur social psychologists. So why not rely on our own experience—or even on folklore and "the wisdom of the ages"—in order to understand the social side of life? Our answer is straightforward: Because such sources provide inconsistent and unreliable guides to social behaviour.

For instance, consider the following statement, suggested by common sense: "Absence makes the heart grow fonder." Do you agree? Is it true that when people are separated from those they love, they miss them and so experience increased longing for them? Many people would agree. They would answer "Yes, that's right. Let me tell you about the time I was separated from..." But now consider the following statement: "Out of sight, out of mind." How about this statement? Is it true? When people are separated from those they love, do they quickly forget them or find someone else on whom to focus their affections? As you can see, these two views—both suggested by common sense—are contradictory. The same is true for many other informal observations about human behaviour. We could go on to list others, but by now the main point is clear: Common sense often suggests a confusing and inconsistent picture of human behaviour. This is one important reason why social psychologists put their faith in the scientific method: it yields much more conclusive evidence.

But this is not the only reason why we must be wary of common sense. Another one relates to the fact that unlike Data of *Star Trek* fame, we are *not* perfect information-processing machines. On the contrary, as we'll note many times (e.g., in Chapters 2, 4, and 5), our thinking is subject to several forms of error, or *bias*, that can lead us badly astray. Here's one example. Suppose that while at the shopping mall, you encounter people soliciting donations for a very worthy cause (e.g., donations to help the victims of a recent tragic disaster). What is the probability that you will make a contribution—10 percent? 50 percent? 80 percent? Now, what about other shoppers at the mall—how likely is it that *they* will make a donation? If you are like most people, you probably estimated your own probability of donating as higher than that of other people—something social psychologists describe as the *holier than thou effect* (e.g., Epley & Dunning, 2000). In other words, we tend to believe that we are more likely to engage in kind, generous acts than are other people, and to think that we are better than "average" in many ways (another term for this is the *self-serving bias*; see Chapter 2). Why do we do this? One explanation emphasizes that there are differences in the way we collect and use information about the self or about others. It could be that we tend to focus more often on positive information about the self. In any case, this is just one of the many ways in which we can—and often do—make errors in thinking about other people (and ourselves); we'll consider many others in Chapter 2. Because we are prone to such errors in our informal thinking about the social world, we cannot rely on it—or on common sense—to solve the mysteries of social behaviour. Rather, we need scientific evidence, and that, in essence, is what social psychology is all about.

Social Psychology Focuses on the Behaviour of Individuals

Societies differ greatly in terms of their views of courtship and marriage; yet it is still *individuals* who fall in love. Similarly, societies vary greatly in terms of their overall levels of violence; yet it is still individuals who perform aggressive actions or refrain from doing so. The same argument applies to virtually all other aspects of social behaviour, from prejudice to helping: actions are performed by, and thoughts occur in the minds of, individuals. Because of this basic fact, the focus, in social psychology, is squarely on individuals. Social psychologists realize, of course, that individuals do not exist in isolation from social and cultural influences—far from it. But the field's major interest lies in understanding the factors that shape the actions and thoughts of individual humans in social settings. This contrasts sharply with the field of *sociology*, which you may have studied in other courses. Sociology studies some of the same topics as social psychology, but it is concerned not with the behaviour and thoughts of individuals but with large groups of persons or with society as a whole. For instance, both social psychology and sociology study the topic of violent crime. While social psychologists focus on the factors that cause specific persons to engage in such behaviour, sociologists are interested in comparing rates of violent crime in different segments of the society (e.g., high- and low-income groups), or in examining trends in the rate of violent crime over time.

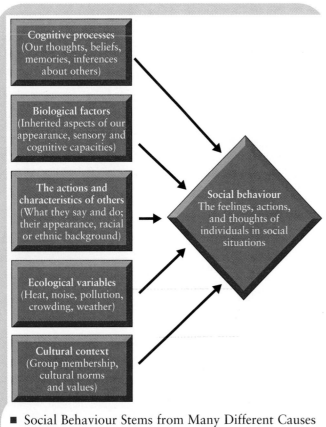

■ Social Behaviour Stems from Many Different Causes

FIGURE 1.3 Among the most important categories are (1) cognitive processes, (2) biological factors; (3) the actions and characteristics of others, (4) ecological (environmental) variables; and (5) cultural context.

Social Psychology Seeks to Understand the Causes of Social Behaviour and Thought

In a key sense, the heading of this section states the most central aspect of our definition, the very core of our field. What it means is that social psychologists are primarily concerned with understanding the wide range of conditions that shape the social behaviour and thought of individuals—their actions, feelings, beliefs, memories, and inferences—with respect to other persons. Obviously, a huge number of factors play a role in this regard ranging from factors within individuals, such as their cognitions and biology, to external factors, such as the presence of others in the immediate social surroundings, the physical environment, and the long-term social context of culture. However, ultimately we can group these factors under the five major headings shown in Figure 1.3, and described below.

Cognitive Processes

Suppose that you have arranged to meet a friend, and this person is late. In fact, after 30 minutes you begin to suspect that your friend will never arrive. Finally, the person does appear and says, "Sorry... I forgot all about meeting you until a few minutes ago." How will you react? Probably with considerable annoyance. Now imagine that instead, your friend says, "I'm so sorry to be late... There was a big accident, and the traffic was tied up for miles." Now how will you react? Probably with less annoyance—but not necessarily. If your friend is often late and has used this excuse before, you may be suspicious about whether this explanation is true. In contrast, if this is the first time your friend has been late, or if your friend has never used such an excuse in the past, you may accept it as true. In other words, your reactions in this situation will depend strongly upon your *memories* of your friend's past behaviour and your *inferences* about whether her or his explanation is really true. Situations like this one call attention to the fact that *cognitive processes* such as memory, reasoning, judgment and interpretation all play a crucial role in social behaviour. Social psychologists are well aware of the importance of such processes and realize that in order to understand people's behaviour in social situations, we must understand their thinking about such situations—*construals,* as they are often termed by social psychologists (e.g., Killeya & Johnson, 1998; Swann & Gill, 1997).

Biological Factors

Is social behaviour influenced by biological processes and by genetic factors? Fifteen years ago most social psychologists would have answered *no*, at least with regard to genetic factors. Now, however, the pendulum of scientific opinion has swung in the other direction, and many believe that our preferences, behaviours, emotional reactions, and even cognitive abilities are affected to some extent by our biological inheritance (Buss, 1998; Pinker, 1997, 2002).

The view that biological factors play an important role in social behaviour comes from the field of **evolutionary psychology** (e.g., Buss, 1995; Cosmides & Tooby, 1987). This new branch of psychology suggests that our species, like all others on the planet, has been subject to the process of biological evolution throughout its history, and that as a result of this process, we now possess a large number of *evolved psychological mechanisms* that help (or once helped) us to deal with important problems relating to survival. How do these become part of our biological inheritance? Through the process of evolution, which, in turn, involves three basic components: *variation, inheritance,* and *adaptation* (Barrett, Dunbar, & Lycett, 2002). *Variation* refers to the fact that the traits of organisms belonging to a given species vary in many different ways; indeed, such variation is a basic part of life on our planet. Human beings, as you already know, come in a wide variety of shapes and sizes, and vary on what sometimes seems to be an almost countless number of dimensions.

Inheritance refers to the fact that some of these trait variations can be passed from one generation to the next through complex mechanisms that we are only now beginning to fully understand. *Adaptation* refers to the fact that some traits make the individuals who possess them better *adapted* to their environment and give them an "edge" in terms of reproduction. They are more likely to survive, find mates, and pass these variations on to succeeding generations. The result is *evolution through natural selection*: over time, more and more members of the species possess these variations until the characteristics of the species as a whole can be considered to have changed. (See Figure 1.4 for a summary of this process.)

Social psychologists who adopt the evolutionary perspective suggest that this process applies to at least some aspects of social behaviour. For instance, consider the question of mate preference. Why do we find some people attractive? According to the evolutionary perspective, it is because the characteristics they show—symmetrical facial features, well-toned and shapely bodies (e.g., a relatively small waist-to-hip ratio in females; Singh, 1993), clear skin, lustrous hair—are associated with

Evolutionary Psychology A new branch of psychology that investigates the evolutionary origins and the potential role of genetic factors in various aspects of human behaviour.

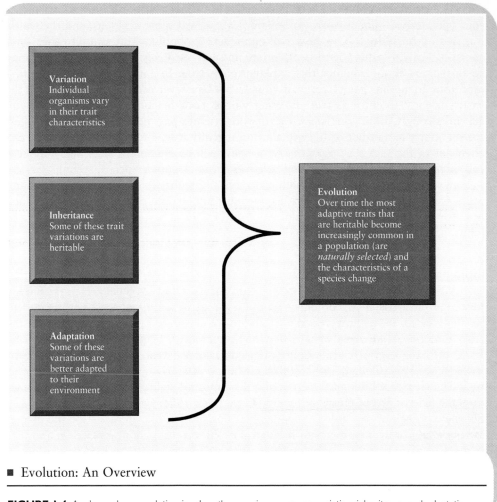

■ Evolution: An Overview

FIGURE 1.4 As shown here, evolution involves three major processes: variation, inheritance, and adaptation.

reproductive capacity. In other words, these are outward signs of inner health and vigour. Thus, a preference for these characteristics in mates among our ancestors increased the chances that they would reproduce successfully; this, in turn, contributed to our preference for these aspects of appearance. (Interestingly, reasonable as these suggestions seem to be, they have not been uniformly confirmed in research findings; e.g., Dion & Dion, 1996; Markus & Kitayama, 1996; Tassinary & Hansen, 1998.)

Because the evolutionary perspective makes many intriguing predictions about social behaviour and thought, it has gained increasing recognition in social psychology. Thus, we'll have reason to refer to it many times in this book. But please don't misunderstand: the evolutionary perspective does *not* suggest that we inherit specific patterns of social behaviour; rather, it contends that we inherit tendencies or predispositions that may or may not be translated into reality, depending on the environments in which we live. For instance, consider an individual who has inherited the tendency to show a very strong sexual drive. Will this person have multiple sexual partners or only one? Clearly, this depends on where he or she lives. If the person lives in a culture where having many multiple partners is considered appropriate, she or he may indeed have many lovers; but if this individual lives in a culture where such behaviour is strongly disapproved, she or he may have only one—or at least a smaller number than would be true in a more permissive cultural setting.

The Actions and Characteristics of Others

Imagine the following events:

- You are standing in line outside a movie theatre; suddenly, another person walks up and cuts in line in front of you.
- The person you've been dating exclusively for six months suddenly says, "I think we should date other people."
- You are playing a computer game when two attractive strangers walk up and begin to watch your performance with great interest.

Will these actions by others have any impact upon your behaviour and thought? Absolutely! So it is clear that often we are strongly affected by the actions of others (See Figure 1.5).

In addition, we are also often affected by the physical appearance of others. Be honest: Have you ever felt uneasy in the presence of a person with a physical disability? Do you ever behave differently toward highly attractive persons than toward less attractive ones? Toward elderly persons than toward young ones? Toward persons belonging to racial and ethnic groups different from your own?

"I don't know why. I just suddenly felt like calling."

■ Others' Behaviour: An Important Factor in Our Social Behaviour and Thought

FIGURE 1.5 As shown here, we are often strongly affected by the actions of other persons, even when we are not aware of this fact.

Your answer to some of these questions is probably *yes*, for we are often strongly affected by others' visible characteristics, such as their appearance (e.g., McCall, 1997; Twenge & Manis, 1998). In fact, findings reported by Hassin and Trope (2000) indicate that we cannot ignore others' appearance, even when we consciously try to do so. These researchers showed participants in their studies photos of people who were supposedly candidates for various jobs (e.g., clerk, optometrist, electrician). Background information about the persons was also provided, and the participants' task was to rate the suitability of these persons for a specific job. Half were told to ignore the photos when making their decisions, while the others were not given such instructions. The photos were chosen to show people who either looked like or did not look like the "typical" holder of the job in question. (Previous research had revealed what the "typical" holder of various jobs looks like.) Results indicated that persons in the photos who looked like the "typical" holder of each job received higher ratings than those who did not. Moreover, this was true even when participants were specifically told to ignore the photos in making their ratings. Findings like these suggest that our reactions to others are indeed strongly affected by their outward appearance.

Ecological Variables: Impact of the Physical Environment

Do we become more irritable and aggressive when the weather is hot and steamy than when it is cool and comfortable (Anderson, Bushman, & Groom, 1997; Rotton & Cohn, 2000)? Does exposure to high levels of noise, particular types of smell (Baron, 1997), or excessive levels of crowding have any impact on whether we are likely to help? Research findings indicate that the physical environment does indeed influence our feelings, thoughts, and behaviour; so ecological variables certainly fall within the realm of modern social psychology.

Cultural Context

Culture The organized system of shared meanings, perceptions, and beliefs held by persons belonging to a particular group. This often includes a particular language or system of communication, social customs and organizations, as well as artifacts and artistic products of that group.

Social behaviour, it is important to note, does *not* occur in a cultural vacuum. On the contrary, it is often strongly affected by *cultural norms* (social rules concerning how people should behave in specific situations), membership in various groups, and shifting societal values. Whom should people marry? How many children should they have? Should they keep their emotional reactions to themselves or demonstrate them openly? How close should they stand to others when talking to them? Is it appropriate to offer gifts to professors or public officials? These are only a small sampling of the aspects of social behaviour that can be—and regularly are—influenced by cultural factors. By culture we mean the organized system of shared meanings, perceptions, and beliefs held by persons belonging to a particular group (Smith & Bond, 1993).

Every day in Canadian cities we encounter people who come from diverse cultural backgrounds. It would be difficult for most Canadians not to be aware of the importance of cultural differences in their interactions with others—and the problems this can sometimes create. Clearly, then, efforts to understand social behaviour must carefully consider cultural factors. If they do not, they stand the very real chance of being what one prominent researcher described as *experiments in a vacuum* (Tajfel, 1982)—studies that tell us little about social behaviour under real-life conditions and in real-life settings. Parallel with the development of *evolutionary psychology*—parallel both in time period and in terms of its impact on psychology—has been the development of **cultural**

Cultural Psychology The comparative study of the way culture and the individual construct each other.

psychology: the comparative study of the way culture and the individual construct each other (Shweder & Sullivan, 1993; Ratner, 1997). Cultural psychologists see the mind of the individual, their thinking and consciousness, as essentially moulded by culture, and, at the same time, see culture as shaped and changed by its members. As one prominent researcher put it, "psychological processes and the cultural system are mutually constitutive" (Kitayama, Matsumoto, Markus, & Norasakkunkit, 1997).

Social Psychology: Summing Up

To conclude: Social psychology focuses mainly on understanding the causes of social behaviour and social thought—on identifying factors that shape our feelings, behaviour, and thought in social situations. It seeks to accomplish this goal through the use of scientific methods, and it takes careful note of the fact that social behaviour and thought are influenced by a wide range of cognitive, biological, social, environmental, and cultural factors.

The remaining chapters of this text are devoted to summarizing some of the key findings of social psychology. This information is naturally interesting to most of us just because we are "social animals," to use Aronson's term (1997). While we're confident you will find much of this material fascinating, we're equally sure it will surprise you. Frequently the findings of social psychology will challenge your current ideas about people and the relationships between them. It is probably safe to predict that after exposure to our field, you'll never think about social relations in quite the same way as before.

KEY POINTS

- *Social psychology* is the scientific field that seeks to understand the nature and causes of individual behaviour and thought in social situations.
- Social psychology is scientific in nature because it adopts the values and methods used in other fields of science.
- Social psychologists adopt the scientific method because "common sense" provides an unreliable guide to social behaviour, and because our thought is influenced by many potential sources of bias.
- Social psychology focuses on the behaviour of individuals and seeks to understand the causes of social behaviour and thought.
- Important causes of social behaviour and thought include cognitive processes, biological and evolutionary factors, other persons, the physical environment, and culture.

Research Methods in Social Psychology

Now that you know what social psychology is, it is appropriate for us to turn to another essential issue: How do social psychologists attempt to answer questions about social behaviour and social thought? How, in short, do they conduct their research? To provide you with a useful overview of this process, we will examine three related issues. First, we will describe *key methods of research* in social psychology. Then we will discuss the criteria used to *choose a methodology*. Finally, we will consider some of the complex *ethical issues* that arise in social psychological research and that, to a degree, are unique to such research.

Systematic Observation: Describing the World

One basic technique for studying social behaviour is *systematic observation*—carefully observing behaviour it as it occurs. Such observation is not the kind of informal observation we all practise from childhood on. Rather, in a scientific field such as social psychology, it is careful observation, maintaining the four core scientific values described above (accuracy, objectivity, skepticism, and open-mindedness). For example, suppose that a social psychologist wanted to find out how frequently people shake hands in different settings. The researcher could study this topic by going to shopping malls, airports, college campuses, and many other settings and observing who shakes hands with whom, how they do this, and with what frequency (see Figure 1.6). Such research (some of which is described in Chapter 2) would be employing what is known as **naturalistic observation**—observation of behaviour in natural settings (Linden, 1992). Note that in such observation, the researcher would simply notice what was happening in various contexts; she or he would make no attempt to change the behaviour of the subjects being observed. In fact, such observation requires that the researcher take great pains to avoid influencing the persons in any way. Thus, the researcher would try to be as inconspicuous as possible, and might even take advantage of any naturally occurring barriers to prevent being noticed.

In recent years, social psychologists have been more frequently involved in *field research*—research conducted outside the laboratory. For example, field research is often used when researchers investigate other cultures (in *cross-cultural psychology*), or attempt to find solutions to real social problems (in *applied social psychology*). In these areas it is particularly important, at least initially, that researchers understand the context and behaviour *as it naturally occurs* with little or no intervention. For example, if, as an outsider, you wanted to understand the significance of the handshake in another culture, you would do well to initially stand back and simply observe this behaviour in that cultural context. Such naturalistic observation usually produces *descriptive data*—data that is more qualitative and less quantitative in nature compared to other methodologies. It can be useful in orienting a researcher to the important social psychological factors that need to be considered and can provide an initial

Naturalistic Observation A method of research in which behaviour is systematically observed in a natural setting, with the minimum amount of impact on the behaviour being observed. This method is more likely to produce descriptive data.

■ Naturalistic Observation in Operation

FIGURE 1.6 How frequently do people shake hands? Who shakes hands with whom, and how? One way to find out would be to perform research employing naturalistic observation.

broad understanding of a new social context. Eventually, however, social psychologists will usually want to go beyond description to *prediction* of the relationships between events and this is where the correlational method comes in.

Correlation: Predicting Relationships

At various times, you have probably noticed that some events appear to be related to each other: as one changes, the other appears to change, too. For example, you might have thought you noticed that high temperatures and irritable driving (or "road rage") seem to coincide, or that your team always wins when you wear your lucky red shirt. If your observations are correct and the two events really are related in this way, we say that they are *correlated* or that a correlation exists between them. The term *correlation* refers to a tendency for one aspect of the world to change as the other changes. Social psychologists refer to such changeable aspects of the world as *variables*, because they can take different values.

From the point of view of science, the existence of a correlation between two variables can be very useful. This is so because when a correlation exists, it is possible to predict one variable from information about one or more other variables. The ability to make such *predictions* is one important goal of all branches of science, including social psychology. For instance, suppose that a correlation was observed between certain patterns of behaviour in married couples (e.g., the tendency to criticize each other harshly) and the likelihood that they would later divorce. This correlation could be very useful in predicting which couples might run into problems in their relationships and, further, it could be helpful in counselling such persons if they were attempting to save their relationship. (See Chapter 6 for a discussion of why long-term relationships sometimes fail.)

How accurately can such predictions be made? The stronger the correlation between the variables in question, the more accurate the predictions. Correlations can range from 0 to -1.00 or +1.00: the greater the departure from 0, the stronger the correlation. Positive numbers (or *positive correlations*) mean that as one variable increases, the other increases too. Negative numbers (or *negative correlations*) indicate that as one variable increases, the other decreases. For instance, there is a negative correlation between age and the amount of hair on the heads of males: the older men grow, the less hair they have.

These basic facts underlie an important method of research sometimes used by social psychologists: the **correlational method**. In this approach, social psychologists attempt to determine whether, and to what extent, different variables are related to each other. This involves making careful observations of each variable, and then performing appropriate statistical tests to determine whether and to what degree the variables are correlated. Perhaps a concrete example will help illustrate the nature of this research method.

Imagine that a social psychologist wants to find out whether one piece of "folk wisdom" is true—the belief that firm handshakes produce better first impressions than weak ones. (This relationship has long been suggested by books on etiquette and gaining success in business, but had never been studied in a scientific manner until one group of social psychologists did so recently; Chaplin et al., 2000.) How could research on this **hypothesis**—an as yet unverified prediction—be conducted? One very basic approach would go something like this. The researcher might arrange for several pairs of strangers to shake hands with each other. They would then rate each other's handshakes (e.g., in terms of strength, vigour, duration, and completeness of grip) and their first impressions of each other (e.g., how much they like the other person, how friendly he or she seemed

Correlational Method A method of research in which a scientist systematically observes two or more variables to determine whether changes in one are accompanied by changes in the other.

Hypothesis An as yet unverified prediction based on a theory.

to be, etc.). If positive correlations are obtained between various aspects of the handshakes (e.g., their strength) and these first impressions, this would provide some evidence for the hypothesis that handshakes do indeed influence our reactions to strangers when we meet them for the first time.

Suppose that the researcher did find such a correlation (e.g., a correlation of +.58 between strength of handshakes and the favourableness of first impression); what could she or he conclude? That firm handshakes lead to (i.e., produce, cause) positive first impressions? Perhaps; but this conclusion, reasonable as it may seem, may be totally false. Here's why: It may well be the case that persons who give firm handshakes are friendlier, more confident, and more outgoing than those who give weak ones. Thus, it may be *these* factors—not the strength of the handshakes themselves—that generate positive first impressions. In other words, if you meet someone who is friendly and confident, she or he is more likely to give you a firm handshake than is someone who is not friendly or confident, and you might like this person because she or he is friendly and confident, *not* because this stranger gave you a firm handshake. There is an important principle in this example, light-hearted as it may be: *The fact that two variables are correlated, even highly correlated, does not guarantee that there is a causal link between them—that changes in one* cause *changes in the other.* The correlation between the variables may be due to chance or random factors, as shown in Figure 1.7. In many other cases, a correlation between variables simply reflects the fact that changes in both are related to a third variable. To use the example above, the correlation between strength of handshake and favourable impression may occur because both are related to a third variable, the *friendliness* of that person. Additional illustrations of the fact that even strong correlations between two variables do not necessarily mean that one causes the other are presented in the Ideas to Take with You feature at the end of this chapter.

This inability to infer *causal* relationships between variables from correlational data is a major drawback for researchers. Despite this, the correlational method of research is often very useful. It can be used in natural settings, where *experimentation* would be difficult, impossible (e.g., studying passionate love), or unethical (e.g., studying the effects of emotional neglect on children's social development). Further, the correlational method is often highly efficient: a large amount of information can be obtained in a relatively short period of time. This is particularly true in the case of one frequently used correlational method—the **questionnaire**. The researcher carefully constructs a series of questions that are usually answered either using a *rating-scale* (where

Questionnaire
Method in which the researcher carefully constructs a series of questions that subjects will answer in an open-ended manner or using a rating scale. Questionnaires are often part of correlational research.

■ Correlation Does Not Equal Causation

FIGURE 1.7 When one event precedes another, it is sometimes tempting to assume that the first event caused the second. As you can see from this cartoon, however, such assumptions are often on shaky ground.

subjects circle a number or a word on the scale to indicate their answers) or in an *open-ended* manner (where subjects give the answer in their own words).

However, the fact that correlation is not conclusive with respect to cause-and-effect relationships is a serious disadvantage-one that often leads social psychologists to prefer a different method. It is to this approach that we turn next.

KEY POINTS

- In systematic observation, behaviour is carefully observed and recorded, providing a description of the world. *Naturalistic observation* involves observation conducted in the settings where the behaviour naturally occurs and with a minimum impact on the setting.
- This method can be useful when researchers are venturing into a new field and do not wish to make too many assumptions about it.
- In the *correlational method*, researchers measure two or more variables to determine if they are related to one another in any way. This enables us to predict one variable from information about the other.
- The existence of even strong correlations between variables does not indicate that they are causally related to each other.

The Experimental Method: Causation and Explanation

As we have just seen, the correlational method of research is very useful from the point of view of one important goal of science: the ability to make accurate predictions. It is less useful, though, from the point of view of reaching yet another goal: *explanation*. Scientists do not merely wish to *describe* the world and *predict* relationships between variables: they want to be able to *explain* these relationships, too. For instance, continuing with the handshaking example used above, if a link between firmness of handshakes and first impressions exists, social psychologists would want to know *why* this is so. Do firm handshakes suggest that the persons who give them are friendly or interested in the recipient? Or, perhaps, do firm handshakes increase activation or arousal among persons who receive them, and so make them more interested in the hand-shaker?

In order to attain the goal of explanation, social psychologists employ a method of research known as **experimentation** or the **experimental method**. This methodology can indicate *causal* relationships between variables and, therefore, can take the researcher one step nearer to explaining social behaviour.

Experimentation (Experimental Method) A method of research in which one or more factors (the independent variables) are systematically changed to determine whether such variations affect one or more other factors (dependent variables).

Experimentation: Its Basic Nature

In its most basic form, the experimental method involves two key steps: (1) *systematic alteration* of the presence or strength of some variable believed to affect an aspect of social behaviour or thought, and (2) *careful measurement* of the effects of such alterations (if any). The factor systematically altered, or varied, by the researcher is termed the **independent variable**, while the aspect of behaviour measured is termed the **dependent variable**. In a simple experiment, then, different groups of participants are exposed to contrasting levels of the independent variable (such as low, moderate, and high). The researcher then carefully measures the participants' behaviour to determine whether it does in fact vary with these changes in the independent variable. If it does—and if two other conditions are also met—the researcher can tentatively conclude that the independent variable does indeed *cause* changes in the aspect of behaviour being studied.

Independent Variable The variable that is systematically varied by the researcher in an experiment.

Dependent Variable The variable that is measured in an experiment. In social psychology, the dependent variable is some aspect of social behaviour or social thought.

To illustrate the basic nature of experimentation in social psychology, let's return again to the handshaking example. How could a social psychologist study this topic through experimentation? One possibility is as follows. The researcher would arrange for participants to come to a laboratory or other setting, where they meet assistants who shake their hands. (The participants would not know that the persons they meet are assistants of the experimenter.) The assistants would have been trained, in advance, to be able to give weak handshakes, moderate handshakes, or firm handshakes, and depending on experimental condition, they would deliver a handshake of the required type to each participant. Then, perhaps, the assistant and the participants would perform some tasks together or have a brief conversation (the assistant's behaviour would be held as constant as possible in these situations). Finally, the participants would rate their first impression of the assistant.

If the results now look like those in Figure 1.8, the researcher could conclude, at least tentatively, that firm handshakes do indeed produce more positive first impressions than do weak ones. It's important to note that in experimentation, such knowledge is obtained through direct intervention: Firmness of handshakes—the independent variable—is systematically changed by the researcher. In the correlational method, in contrast, variables are *not* altered in this manner; rather, naturally occurring changes in them are simply observed and recorded.

Experimentation: Two Requirements for Its Success

Earlier we referred to two conditions that must be met before a researcher can conclude that changes in an independent variable have caused changes in a dependent variable. Let's consider these conditions now. The first involves what is termed

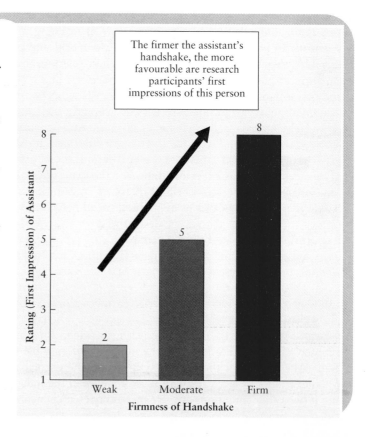

■ Experimentation: An Example

FIGURE 1.8 In the study illustrated here, participants met an assistant who shook their hand. The assistant's handshake was either weak, moderate, or firm in nature. Results indicated that the stronger the handshake, the more favourable were participants' first impressions of the assistant.

The firmer the assistant's handshake, the more favourable are research participants' first impressions of this person

<u>random assignment</u> of participants to experimental conditions. This requirement means that all participants in an experiment must have an equal chance of being exposed to each level of the independent variable. The reason for this rule is simple: If participants are not randomly assigned to each condition, it may later be impossible to determine if differences in their behaviour stem from differences they brought with them to the study, or from the impact of the independent variable, or from both. For instance, imagine that in the study just described, one of the assistants decides to collect all the data for the firm handshake condition on one day, and all the data for the weak handshake condition on the next day. It just so happens that on the first day, all of the participants are students from a music class, while on the second day, all of the participants are members of a weight-lifting club (they volunteered for the experiment together). Results indicate that participants in the firm handshake condition actually give the assistant *lower* ratings than those in the weak handshake condition. Why? One possibility is that the experimenter's hypothesis is wrong: people do not form more positive impressions of strangers who give them firm handshakes; in fact, they like strangers who give them weak handshakes better. But it may also be the case that the findings reflect differences between the two groups of participants: the weightlifters are so strong that they view even the strong handshake as "wimpy," while the musicians like weak handshakes because these mild grips don't harm their delicate fingers. So in fact, we can't tell why the results occurred, because the principle of random assignment of participants to experimental conditions has been violated.

The second condition essential for successful experimentation is as follows: Insofar as is possible, <u>*all extraneous factors must be held constant*</u>. What this means is that any other factors (apart from the independent variable) that might also affect participants' behaviour should be held at a constant level in all experimental conditions. To see why this is so, consider what will happen if, in the study on handshaking, the assistant acts in a friendlier manner when giving the firm handshake than when giving the weak one. Findings indicate that participants who receive a firm handshake report a more favourable impression of the assistant. What is the cause of this result? The firmness of the assistant's handshake (the independent variable), his or her greater friendliness in this condition, or both? Once again, we can't tell; and because we can't, the value of the experiment as a source of new information about human behaviour is greatly reduced. In situations like this, and when subject characteristics have not been randomly assigned to conditions, the independent variable is said to be *confounded* with another variable—one that is not under systematic investigation in the study. When <u>**confounding**</u> occurs, the findings of an experiment may be largely meaningless (see Figure 1.9).

In sum, experimentation is, in several respects, the crown jewel among social psychology's methods. When experimentation is used with skill and care, it can yield results that help us answer complex questions about social behaviour and social thought. So why, you may be wondering, isn't it used all the time? As you will see below, there is no "perfect" methodology.

Choosing a Methodology: Description, Prediction, or Causation?

It is clear that social psychologists are faced with a wide choice of possible methods for exploring social behaviour. How is such a choice made? Unfortunately there is no easy answer—each method has its advantages and limitations. In general, descriptive research such as <u>*naturalistic observation*</u> has the advantage of involving very little intervention in the natural setting—social behaviour is observed as it spontaneously occurs in the real world. As we discussed earlier, this type of method can be useful in

Random Assignment of Participants to Experimental Conditions All participants in an experiment must have an equal chance of being exposed to each level of the independent variable. This ensures that differences subjects bring with them to the study are equally distributed across experimental conditions and so cannot bias results.

Confounding Confusions that occur when factors other than the independent variable in the experiment vary across experimental conditions. When confounding of variables occurs, it is impossible to determine whether results stem from the effects of the independent variable or from the effects of other variables.

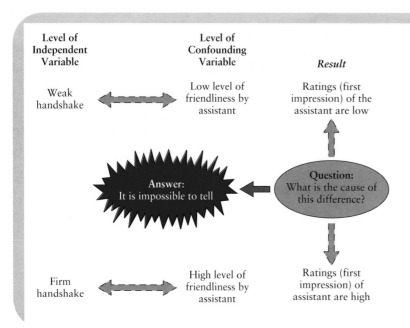

Level of Independent Variable		Level of Confounding Variable		*Result*
Weak handshake	↔	Low level of friendliness by assistant		Ratings (first impression) of the assistant are low
Answer: It is impossible to tell	←	**Question:** What is the cause of this difference?		
Firm handshake	↔	High level of friendliness by assistant		Ratings (first impression) of assistant are high

■ Confounding of Variables: A Fatal Flaw in Experimentation

FIGURE 1.9 In a hypothetical experiment designed to investigate the effects of handshakes on first impressions, firmness of handshake—the independent variable—is confounded with another variable—level of friendliness by the assistant. The assistant acts in a friendlier manner toward participants in the study when giving firm handshakes than when giving weak ones. As a result of this confounding, it is impossible to tell whether any differences between the behaviour of participants in these two conditions stemmed from the independent variable, the confounding variable, or both.

providing an initial overview of a behaviour in a particular social context. The disadvantage of this type of method is that it can be particularly vulnerable to biased interpretation of data. As we will see in later chapters, a common tendency is for people to process incoming information in such a way that it is seen as supporting their expectations or beliefs. This is termed the <u>confirmation bias</u>—and researchers are also subject to it. Data that is descriptive, particularly when it is qualitative rather than quantitative, can more easily be interpreted to support a researcher's theory, even though he or she may be attempting to adhere to scientific principles and values.

Confirmation Bias The tendency to notice and remember mainly information that lends support to our views.

<u>*Correlational research*</u> often shares with descriptive research the advantage of minimal interference with naturally occurring behaviours. Indeed there is much overlap between these two methodologies—the more quantitative type of observational research can produce correlational data. Correlation has the added benefit that if two variables are found to be related then one can be *predicted* from the other. As mentioned previously, correlational methods can produce a large quantity of data efficiently through the use, for example, of questionnaires. However, questionnaire methodology has the limitation that the wording of questions can exert a strong bias on the outcomes obtained. For example, when asked to indicate how satisfied they are with their current jobs, more than 85 percent of persons indicate that they are "satisfied" or "very satisfied." When asked whether they would choose the same job or career again, however, less than 50 percent indicate agreement. So, as experts in constructing questionnaires well know, it's often true that "the way you ask the question determines the answer you get." Finally, one major disadvantage should be very clear to you by now—correlational research cannot provide causal information.

<u>*Experimentation*</u>, on the other hand, has the major advantage of being able to demonstrate that one variable can *cause* changes in another. For researchers, this can provide greater confirmation of hypotheses that are usually expressed in causal terms and greater explanatory power. In the example shown in Figure 1.8, the importance of firmness of handshakes as a *cause* of favourable first impressions is supported by those findings. In addition, researchers usually have greater control of the research context in experimentation, particularly in the laboratory setting. This enables them to have

greater success in avoiding the *confounding* of variables, and greater precision of measurement. The result is that a researcher can then have increased confidence in interpreting his or her data and thus be more certain that errors in the design of research have not been introduced inadvertently. Though experimentation does not, in general, suffer from the problems mentioned in relation to observation and correlation, it isn't perfect. For example, because it is often conducted in laboratory settings that are somewhat artificial and quite different from the locations in which social behaviour actually occurs, the question of <u>external validity</u> often arises—to what extent can the findings of experiments be generalized to real-life social situations and perhaps to persons different from those who participated in the research?

External Validity The extent to which findings from research can be generalized to the real world.

Another possible limitation on use of the experimental method is the ethical restraints that researchers are subject to. Ethical factors may prevent a researcher from conducting a study that is in fact feasible. In other words, the study could be conducted, but doing so would violate ethical standards accepted by scientists or society. Suppose, for example, that a researcher has good reason to believe that certain kinds of cigarette advertisements increase teenagers' tendency to start smoking. Could the researcher ethically conduct an experiment on this topic, exposing some teenagers to many of these ads and others to none and then comparing their rates of smoking? In principle, such research is possible; but no ethical social psychologist would perform it, because of the serious harm to participants that might ensue.

It is partly because of these and related problems that social psychologists often turn from experimentation to systematic observation and the correlational method in their research. So, to underline a point: all research methods offer a mixed bag of advantages and disadvantages, and a social psychologist will choose the method that seems best for studying a particular topic or question at that time. Furthermore, it is advantageous to replicate research using a number of different methodologies and both field and laboratory settings. It is a rule of scientific research that one study is never enough to confirm a hypothesis—there is always the possibility of some error in the research design or simply that results occurred by chance. For this reason, *replication* is always needed and confirmation through different methods can increase confidence in a researcher's conclusions. The section that follows—Canadian Research: On the Cutting Edge—illustrates this point in the context of research on the planning fallacy.

Canadian Research: On the Cutting Edge

Overcoming the Planning Fallacy: Does Focusing on Pessimism Work?

Try to remember the last time you worked on a major project (for instance, a term paper). Did it take more time or less time to complete than you originally estimated? Probably, your answer is "More time...of course!" In predicting how long a given task will take, people tend to be overly optimistic; they predict that they can get the job done much sooner than actually turns out to be the case. Or, turning this around somewhat, they expect to get more done in a

Planning Fallacy The tendency to make optimistic predictions concerning how long a given task will take for completion.

given period of time than they really can. You can probably recognize this tendency in your own thinking. So this tendency to make optimistic predictions about how long a given task will take—a tendency known as the <u>planning fallacy</u>—is both a powerful and a widespread bias. What features of social thought account for this common error?

According to Canadian researcher Roger Buehler and his colleagues (Buehler, Griffin, & MacDonald, 1997), who have studied this tendency in detail, several factors play a role. One is that when individuals make predictions about how long it will take them to complete a given task, they *focus primarily on the future*: planning how they will perform the task. This, in turn, *prevents them from looking backward* in time and remembering how long similar tasks took them in the past. As a result, one important reality check that might help them avoid being overly optimistic is removed. In addition, when individuals do consider past experience in which tasks took longer than expected, such outcomes are attributed to factors *outside their control*. The result: They fail to learn from previous experience, tending to overlook important potential obstacles, and so fall prey to the planning fallacy (Buehler, Griffin, & Ross, 1994).

To make matters worse, further studies, both in the laboratory and in the field, demonstrated that if individuals are *strongly motivated* to complete a task, then they are more likely to suffer from the planning fallacy (Buehler, Griffin, and MacDonald, 1997). This suggests that is it the very time when it is most important to meet a deadline—for example, when you have a number of significant term papers to complete in a limited time period—that you may be more vulnerable to underestimating how much time this will take. In fact, in one of these studies it was when subjects were *most* likely to get a tax refund, that they were most unrealistic about how soon they would file their taxes.

Given the troubling and widespread nature of this bias, it may not surprise you that recent research has turned to prevention of the planning fallacy (e.g., Koole & Spijker, 2000; Newby-Clarke, Ross, Buehler, Koehler, & Griffin, 2000). In particular, Buehler and colleagues (Newby-Clark et al., 2000) examined the impact of asking people to write about *pessimistic* scenarios for deadline completion. For example, their planning scenario would describe a worst-case scenario, in which "everything should go as poorly as possible," when trying to meet a deadline. The researchers' expectation was that this pessimism condition would make subjects more cautious, and perhaps more realistic, in their predictions. However, over a series of three studies in which the context was deadlines for real academic assignments, this hypothesis failed to find support (Buehler, et al., 2000). Writing about pessimistic scenarios did not decrease the planning fallacy—subjects were still overly optimistic in time predictions. Further, subjects consistently saw the *pessimistic* scenario as less plausible or realistic than an *optimistic* scenario—the usual mode of thinking that produces the planning fallacy.

In a final study, Buehler and colleagues (2000) attempted to see if subjects' perception that pessimistic scenarios were implausible could be overcome by specifically manipulating plausibility as an *independent variable*. In fact, there were two independent variables in this study: the *plausibility* and *optimism* of the planning scenarios. Subjects were asked to write a scenario that in their own opinion was "highly likely" to occur (*plausible condition*) or was "highly unlikely" to occur (*implausible condition*). In addition, these scenarios were either *optimistic* ("everything should go as well as possible") or *pessimistic* ("everything should go as badly as possible"). The researchers were hoping that when subjects wrote scenarios that they considered highly likely to occur (plausible) *and* that were pessimistic, this would decrease the planning fallacy. Of course, writing about plausible and *optimistic* scenarios should increase the planning fallacy.

Unfortunately, once again the prediction was not supported for the pessimistic scenario condition. Subjects in all conditions of this study showed the planning fallacy—predicting they would file their taxes on average 3.4 days earlier than they did. As Figure 1.10 shows, optimism in time predictions was not significantly decreased when the pessimistic scenarios were more plausible. That is, when subjects wrote *plausible* and *pessimistic* scenarios, describing realistic difficulties about completing their taxes, the planning fallacy was *not* significantly reduced (compared to those describing *implausible* difficulties). It was only when subjects were writing *optimistic* scenarios that, as predicted, the independent variable of *plausibility* had an impact on the planning fallacy. The planning fallacy was increased for those who wrote a plausible and optimistic scenario.

It appears that subjects were willing to be influenced by the idea that plans for the future would work out well but were unwilling to consider a pessimistic future—even a realistic one. Together, this series of studies demonstrates just how sturdy the planning fallacy is. Subjects were not shaken from their overly optimistic predictions even by considering what they themselves saw as realistic difficulties.

The planning fallacy studies described above provide an example of *replication*. They use of a variety of methods and research contexts—including both field and laboratory studies, and different types of task—to examine the planning fallacy. This serves to strengthen our confidence in their results. The tasks used in some of the earlier laboratory studies (1997, e.g. a word puzzle completion) were somewhat artificial and raise questions about *external validity*. However, the greater control over possible confounding in these laboratory experiments provides greater confidence that the factors investigated *cause* the planning fallacy. In contrast, the field studies described in the later series (2000) had great realism (most readers have come up against academic assignment deadlines or had to complete tax forms before their due date). Therefore, these field studies provide high *external validity*, though in some cases the causal evidence may be less convincing. However, together these studies provide a body of excellent long-term research into an important human phenomenon.

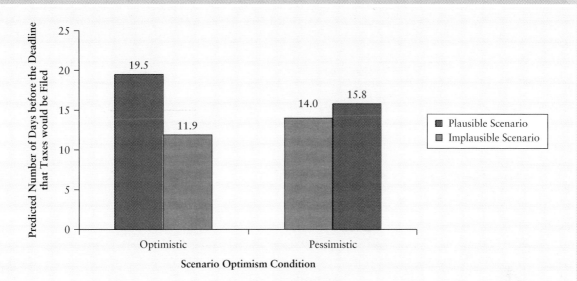

Predicted Number of Days before the Deadline that Taxes would be Filed

Legend: Plausible Scenario / Implausible Scenario

Values: Optimistic — 19.5 (Plausible), 11.9 (Implausible); Pessimistic — 14.0 (Plausible), 15.8 (Implausible)

Scenario Optimism Condition

■ The Impact of Optimism and Plausibility on the Planning Fallacy: Predictions About Filing Taxes

FIGURE 1.10 Subjects created scenarios about filing their taxes with *optimistic* or *pessimistic outcomes*. These scenarios were either *plausible* (realistic) or *implausible* (unrealistic). When subjects wrote about scenarios with *optimistic* outcomes their time predictions were affected by the plausibility of their scenarios—they were less hopeful of beating the tax deadline (the *planning fallacy was reduced*) when their optimistic scenarios were *implausible*. However, when it came to *pessimistic* scenarios (which predicted barriers to completing taxes before the deadline), *plausibility had no impact*. Subjects still showed the planning fallacy, ignoring these potential barriers to completion, whether they were realistic or unrealistic. Unfortunately, this research seems to indicate just how strong and resistant to change the planning fallacy is.

These results indicate that while the planning fallacy can be caused by our biased cognitions, it is also very resistant to attempts to intervene at the cognitive level by changing the focus of our planning. In other words, individuals' estimates of when they will complete a task are influenced by their hopes and desires: they want to finish early, so they ignore possible future problems, and predict that they will do so. Sad to relate, this appears to be one of a number of situations in life where we are resistant to any recognition of our own biases. On a more positive note, there has been some research indicating that helping people to make concrete and specific plans of action to reach their goal will reduce the planning fallacy and the time it takes to complete the task (Koole & Spijker, 2000). As we will see in Chapter 2, the planning fallacy is merely one of the many cognitive biases that have the potential to lead us astray.

KEY POINTS

- *Experimentation* involves systematically altering one or more variables (*independent* variables) in order to determine whether these alterations affect some aspect of behaviour (*dependent* variable).

- Successful use of the experimental method requires *random assignment of participants to experimental conditions*; it also requires that the experimenter *hold constant all other factors* that might also influence behaviour so as to avoid *confounding* of variables.

- Advantages of systematic observation are that it can provide an initial *description* of social behaviour and that it does not interfere with behaviour as it naturally occurs. A disadvantage is that the qualitative data it often produces is vulnerable to the *confirmation bias*—a tendency to bias interpretations of information in the direction of one's expectations or beliefs.

- The correlational method has the advantage of allowing *prediction* of one variable from information about another. It also often allows us to efficiently investigate topics that are not accessible to experimentation. Its major disadvantage is that it does not allow researchers to draw causal conclusions.

- Experimentation does allow causal conclusions to be drawn and aids explanation of behaviour. However, sometimes the context of experiments is artificial, raising questions about their results' *external validity*—the extent to which findings can be generalized to the real world situation.

- Because each method has its limitations, it is recommended that replication of studies should take place using a wide range of methods.

- Using both field and laboratory methods, Buehler and colleagues investigated the *planning fallacy*—our tendency to make optimistic time predictions. It seems to stem from a focus on an optimistic future while ignoring related past events, and any future difficulties. Their studies show that this fallacy persists even when we consider realistic barriers to completion of a task.

Ethics in Research: Consideration of Subject Rights

In their use of experimentation and systematic observation, and in their reliance on comprehensive theories, social psychologists do not differ from researchers in many other fields. One technique, however, does seem to be unique to research in social psychology: <u>deception.</u> Basically, this technique involves efforts by researchers to withhold or conceal information about the purposes of a study from the persons who participate in it. The reason for using this procedure is simple: if participants know the true purposes of an investigation, their behaviour will be changed by that knowledge. The research itself will then have little chance of providing useful information.

Deception A technique whereby researchers withhold information about the purposes or procedures of a study from persons participating in it. Deception is used in situations in which information about such matters might be expected to change subjects' behaviour, thus invalidating the results of the research.

For example, imagine that in a study designed to examine the effects of physical attractiveness on helping behaviour, participants are informed of this purpose. Will they now react differently to a highly attractive stranger than they would have in the absence of this information? Probably so. They will lean over backward to avoid being more helpful to the attractive person, to prove that they are not affected by a stranger's outward appearance.

Because of such considerations, many social psychologists believe that deception—at least on a temporary basis-is essential for their research (Suls & Rosnow, 1988). Adopting this technique is not, however, without its costs. Deceiving research participants or withholding information from them, no matter how justified, raises important ethical issues (Baumrind, 1985).

First, deception, even when temporary, may result in some type of harm to the persons exposed to it. They may experience discomfort, stress, or negative shifts in self-esteem. Second, it is possible that at least some individuals exposed to deception will resent having been led astray. They may then adopt a negative attitude toward social research generally or become suspicious of researchers (Epley & Huff, 1998; Kelman, 1967).

In short, the use of deception does pose something of a dilemma to social psychologists. On the one hand, it seems essential to their research. On the other, its use raises serious problems. How can this issue be resolved? While opinion remains somewhat divided, most social psychologists agree on the following points. First, deception should never be used to persuade people to take part in a study; withholding information or providing misleading information about what will happen in an experiment in order to induce people to take part in it is definitely not acceptable (Sigall, 1997). Second, most social psychologists agree that temporary deception is acceptable provided two basic safeguards are employed. These are **informed consent** and thorough **debriefing**. (Both procedures, by the way, are required by ethical standards published by the Canadian Psychological Association and the American Psychological Association; see Hadjistavropoulos, Malloy, Sharpe, et al., 2002.)

Informed consent involves providing research participants with an as full as possible description of the procedures to be followed *prior* to their decision to participate in the study. By following this principle, researchers ensure that subjects know what they are getting into and what they will be asked to do before making a commitment to participate. In contrast, debriefing *follows* each experimental session. It consists of providing participants with a full explanation of all major aspects of a study, including its true goals and an explanation of the need for temporary deception. The guiding principle is that research participants should leave in at least as favourable or positive a state as when they arrived.

Fortunately, a growing body of evidence indicates that, together, informed consent and thorough debriefing can eliminate—or at least substantially reduce—the potential dangers of deception and any negative effects that might be experienced (Smith & Richardson, 1985). For example, most subjects view temporary deception as acceptable, do not resent its use, and continue to have positive views of research (Rogers, 1980, Sharpe, Adair, & Roese, 1992). Still, it is unwise to take the safety or appropriateness of deception for granted (Rubin, 1985). Rather, it appears that the guiding principles for all researchers planning to use this procedure in their studies should be these: (1) Use deception only when it is absolutely essential to do so—when no other means for conducting a study exist; (2) always proceed with great caution; and (3) make certain that the rights, safety, and well-being of research participants come first, ahead of all other considerations.

Informed Consent A procedure by which subjects are told in advance about the activities they will perform during an experiment. The subjects then take part in the study only if they are willing to engage in such activities.

Debriefing An explanation at the conclusion of a research session in which participants are given full information about the nature of the research and the hypothesis or hypotheses under investigation.

KEY POINTS

- *Deception* involves efforts by social psychologists to withhold or conceal information about the purposes of a study from participants.
- Most social psychologists believe that temporary deception is often necessary in order to obtain valid research results.
- However, they view deception as acceptable only when important safeguards are employed: *informed consent* and thorough *debriefing*.

Social Psychology in the New Millennium: Origins and Trends

In this final section, we will attempt to summarize the state of social psychology today, as well as suggesting some trends for the future. Four themes seem especially worthy of our attention: application, cognition, culture, and evolution. These themes have their origins in the way in which psychology has developed. So it will be useful to place them in the context of psychology's recent history. They also play an important role in shaping the current questions and topics social psychologists study and the methods they choose for their research. Thus, they have guided the work we'll describe in the rest of this book.

Growing Emphasis on Application: Exporting Social Psychology

One major trend in social psychology today is a growing interest in the *application* of social psychological knowledge. This theme is certainly not new in the field—it is really a return to social psychology's beginnings. Kurt Lewin, one of the founders of social psychology, once remarked, "There's nothing as practical as a good theory"—by which he meant that theories of social behaviour and thought developed through systematic research often turn out to be extremely useful in solving practical problems. And Lewin put this into practice by applying his own general theory of social influence, *field theory*, to problems such as community relations and working in groups (Lewin, Lippitt, & White, 1939).

Some 60 years later, the accumulated research findings of social psychologists have proved very useful. Indeed, many of you will find in reading this book that you can apply its principles to your own lives. Similarly, an increasing number of social psychologists have turned their attention to questions concerning *personal health, the legal process, social behaviour in work settings, environmental issues*, and a host of other topics. In other words, there has been growing interest in attempting to apply the findings and principles of social psychology to the solution of practical problems. There seems little doubt that interest in applying the knowledge of social psychology has increased in recent years, with many beneficial results. We'll examine some of this work in Chapter 10 and throughout this book in boxed sections entitled "On the Applied Side." The first of these is near the end of this section; it applies the issue of cultural influence to Canada itself, asking questions about the nature of Canadian culture and its impact and influence on Canadian behaviour.

Influence of the Cognitive Perspective

In recent decades, research on the cognitive side of social psychology has grown dramatically in scope and importance. This particular trend began with what's often called the "cognitive revolution" of the 1960s and '70s. Psychology had, just prior to that time, been focused on the study of overt behaviour to the exclusion, or at least de-emphasis, of internal processes. With the rise of information technology, psychologists became interested in information processing capacities of the human mind. And this renewed interest in internal *cognitive* processes was stimulated by some classic work of social psychologists. One example is the work of Leon Festinger, whose *cognitive dissonance theory* (1957) explains the internal discomfort, or dissonance, we feel when our attitudes clash either with each other or with our behaviour. Just think for a moment about the last time you did something that you think was wrong and you'll feel that discomfort again. This theory continues to have an impact on the study of attitudes, as we'll see in Chapter 3.

Today, two major focuses of this research are perhaps most representative. First, social psychologists attempt to apply basic knowledge about *memory, reasoning, decision-making*, and *interpretation* to a broad range of social behaviours (e.g., Albarracin & Wyer, 2000). Results of such work suggest that our thoughts about other persons and social situations play a key role in virtually *all* forms of social behaviour—from love and sexual attraction on the one hand, to prejudice and conflict on the other. For instance, within this context, researchers have sought to determine whether prejudice stems, at least in part, from our tendency to remember only information consistent with stereotypes of various groups, or tendencies to process information about one's own social group differently from information about other social groups (e.g., Forgas & Fiedler, 1996). In short, biases in memory can be a powerful determinant of behaviour.

Second, there has been growing interest in the question of how we process social information—in a quick-and-dirty manner designed to reduce effort (*heuristically*), or in a more careful, effortful manner (*systematically*; e.g., Eagly & Chaiken, 1998; Killeya & Johnson, 1998). This has been referred to as the *dual-process model* of information processing. As we'll see in several later chapters (e.g., Chapters 2, 3, 5, and 9), these differences in style of processing can strongly influence our inferences, conclusions, decisions, and judgments about others; so they are a key aspect of social cognition.

In conclusion, most social psychologists today believe that how people act in various social situations is strongly determined by their thoughts about these situations. Thus, understanding social thought is, in a real sense, a powerful key for unravelling the complex patterns of our social relations with other persons. But please don't misunderstand: this emphasis on cognitive processes does *not* mean that social psychologists ignore social behaviour. On the contrary, current research often seeks to understand the links between social thought and overt social behaviour.

Adopting a Multicultural Perspective: Taking Account of Diversity

One of the most important trends in social psychology is its increasing recognition of the significance of cultural influences on social behaviour. Cultural diversity has become a fact of life in most Western countries, and Canada's multicultural society is no exception. Canadian 2001 census data provide an *ethnocultural portrait* of this country (Statistics Canada, 2003) that suggests both the continued influence of European cultures and the increasing impact of non-Western cultural groups. When Canadian residents are asked about their own ethnicity, we can see a distinct Canadian ethnicity, as well as a continued identification with European cultures. The top ten ethic identifications are shown in Figure 1.11. Apart from those reporting themselves as "Canadian" (11.7 million), of the remaining nine ethnic identifications, seven were European (totalling 23.8 million reports).

However, patterns of immigration within the last three decades point to increasing ethnic diversity in the long term. Before 1961, 90 percent of immigrants came from Europe but by the end of the twentieth century only 20 percent of those arriving in Canada were European. In contrast, Asian, particularly East Asian, immigration rose from 3 percent before 1961, to 58 percent in the 1990s (Statistics Canada, 2003)—the single largest immigrant group in the last decade. There has also been a gradual increase in immigrants from Africa and the Middle East, South and Central America, and the Caribbean. In the long run, this will mean increasing ethnic diversity in Canada and, as a result, more influence of non-European cultures. Rather than being "Eurocentric," as some have claimed, Canada is becoming truly multicultural.

The existence of such cultural diversity raises an important question for social psychology. Has social psychological research given sufficient weight to the importance of cultural diversity? This issue was raised as far back as the 1970s in the social psychological community. For example, John Berry, an important Canadian researcher in this area, suggested social psychological findings were *culture-biased* because they had been largely produced in one culture—Western culture, particularly that of the United States (Berry, 1978). Can the findings of studies produced in one culture be generalized

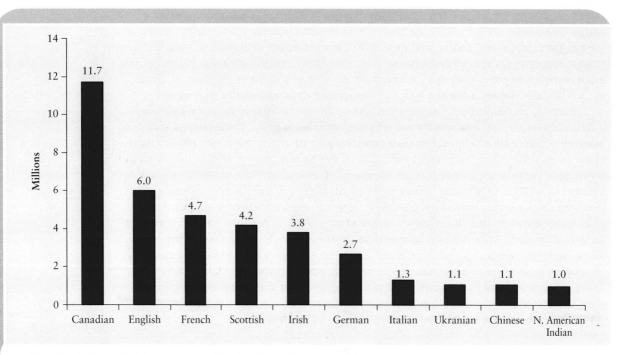

■ Top Ten Ethnic Origins Reported in the Canadian Census, 2001

FIGURE 1.11 The biggest single reported ethnicity in the latest census is "Canadian," claimed by eleven million respondents, but of the remaining ethnic designations, seven are European and together they total more than 20 million individuals.

Source: Adapted from Statistics Canada (2003) *Canada's Ethnocultural Portrait: The Changing Mosaic.*

to other cultures? Until that time, most social psychologists had assumed that the findings of their research could be generalized to other cultures, and that the processes they studied were ones operating among human beings everywhere—universal. However, the expansion since then of cross-cultural research has raised some serious doubts about this assumption in many topic areas of social psychology.

It has become increasingly clear that merely assuming that basic aspects of social behaviour are much the same around the globe is not acceptable. Indeed, cultural research is beginning to reveal that even basic processes may be strongly affected by cultural factors (Smith & Bond, 1998). For example, the sense of self (e.g., Heine, Harihara, & Niiya, 2002), causal interpretations of others' behaviour (e.g., Higgins & Bhatt, 2001), and notions of romantic love (Dion & Dion, 1996) appear to differ fundamentally from one culture to another.

One cultural distinction that has emerged from cross-cultural research (Hofstede, 1980) and has received particular attention is the *individualism-collectivism* dimension. **Individualism** refers to a focus on individual rights and goals, individual self-determination, and the independence of the individual from others. **Collectivism**, in contrast, refers to the importance of group goals (those of the community, work, or family groups) rather than those of the individual; individuals are seen as interdependent with their groups, and importance is given to the need to maintain harmony and balance between people.

Western cultures (e.g., United States, Canada, Western Europe) tend to be more individualistic, and Eastern as well as many other non-Western cultures (e.g., in

Individualism A cultural value emphasizing the importance of individual rights and goals. Individuals are seen as independent from others.

Collectivism A cultural value emphasizing the importance of group goals. Individuals are seen as interdependent with their group.

Africa, South and Central America, and Southern Europe) tend to be more collectivistic. Although distinctions between cultures can be made on many dimensions (e.g., Schwartz, 1992), this particular one has proved useful in research because cultures that vary on this dimension have also been shown to vary in social behaviour and social thought (e.g., Choi & Nisbett, 1998; Crandall et al., 2000). Cross-cultural research presented in every chapter of this book will show this.

A second aspect of social diversity that social psychologists have increasingly recognized is the fact that findings obtained using one gender may not necessarily apply to the other gender. Although differences in the behaviour of females and males have often been exaggerated by gender stereotypes concerning the supposed traits of women and men (e.g., Diekman & Eagly, 2000), some differences in social behaviour do exist (Feingold, 1994; Oliver & Hyde, 1993). For instance, recent results indicate that women show greater appreciation of and insight into their own emotions (and the emotions of others) than do men (e.g., Barrett et al., 2000). They describe their own and others' emotions in richer and more complex terms, are better at remembering emotional events (Davis, 1999), and are also more successful at both "reading" and sending emotional messages (e.g., through facial expressions; Brody & Hall, 1993).

As recognition of the importance of cultural, ethnic, and gender differences has grown, the field of social psychology has adopted an increasingly **multicultural perspective**—an approach that pays careful attention to the role of culture and human diversity. We will highlight this aspect of the field in each chapter of the book with sections emphasizing cultural diversity and its effects. In addition, these sections will be marked, in the margin, by the following special symbol:

Multicultural Perspective Focus on understanding the cultural and ethnic factors that influence social behaviour and that contribute to differences in social behaviour or social thought between various ethnic and cultural groups.

Increasing Influence of the Evolutionary Perspective

Another important trend in modern social psychology—one we mentioned before—is the increasing influence of a biological or *evolutionary perspective* (e.g., Buss, 1999). Growing evidence suggests that biological and genetic factors play at least some role in many forms of social behaviour—everything from physical attraction and mate selection on one side to aggression on the other (see Chapters 6 and 8). As an illustration of such research, consider an intriguing study by Mueller and Mazur (1996). These researchers showed photos of 434 West Point cadets to raters and had these persons assess the extent to which the cadets' faces showed dominance. The evolutionary perspective suggests that, for men, dominance will be a positive attribute—it will give them access to a large number of mates, and in this way, will help increase their potential number of offspring. For women, in contrast, dominance will not be as desirable a characteristic, because no matter how many mates a woman has, she can still produce only a limited number of children. On the basis of such reasoning, Mueller and Mazur (1996) predicted that men who looked dominant (i.e., those who had inherited certain facial characteristics) would attain higher military rank in their careers than would men who did not look dominant (see Figure 1.12). The results of their study offered support for this hypothesis. Of course, we cannot tell from such research precisely *why* looking dominant leads to career success in the military. But this and many other studies conducted from the evolutionary perspective do suggest that biological and genetic factors play some role in many aspects of social behaviour (see, e.g., Buss, 1999).

Throughout the book, we will also highlight research related to this perspective using this symbol:

■ Facial Dominance and Career Success: Evidence for the Role of Genetic Factors in Social Behaviour

FIGURE 1.12 West Point cadets who had dominant-looking faces *(left photo)* rose to higher military rank than did cadets who had non-dominant-looking faces *(right photo)*. Findings such as these indicate that dominance—or even the mere appearance of dominance—is linked to positive outcomes, at least for males. These findings are consistent with predictions from an evolutionary perspective—one whose influence has increased in social psychology in recent years.

Evolution and Culture: An Old Dispute in Modern Form

Finally, it is worth noting that the current parallel expansion of these two approaches to social behaviour (culture and biology) raises the spectre of a traditional dispute in psychology, often termed *the nature-nurture issue.* "Nature" here refers to the influence of evolution and our biology, whereas "nurture" refers to *the influence of our environment* on our behaviour. In modern social psychological terms, it may have occurred to you that the *evolutionary* approach to social psychology does not appear to be compatible with a *multicultural* approach—if a behaviour stems from evolved tendencies, how can culture influence or explain it? Support for one perspective seems to preclude support for the other. From the beginning of psychology, the issue of the extent to which human behaviour is determined by our evolved and genetic predispositions or by the influence of the world around us has been an important one. And theorists have sometimes taken extreme positions—suggesting that one or other of these factors can account entirely for the way in which we behave (Pinker, 2002).

In recent years—and this is definitely the perspective of this book—psychologists acknowledge that *both* factors play a part in human behaviour and, further, that they *interact* in influencing social behaviour (e.g., Simpson & Kenrick, 1997). For example, evolutionary theory suggests that our genetic predispositions develop in the context of a particular culture and this will influence the ways in which they are expressed (Crawford, 1998). In turn, the form that culture takes may be influenced by our behavioural predispositions and, further, innate psychological mechanisms may facilitate the individual's absorption of cultural information (Janicki & Krebs, 1998). Take the issue of aggression—our tendency to find some forms of violent activity exciting may have an evolved and genetic basis and this may have influenced us to develop entertainments like violent sports and films. Being exposed to such violent entertainments can, in turn, increase the likelihood of an individual behaving aggressively, as we will discuss in Chapter 8. Alternatively, the way we construct our environments may also decrease the influence of genetic predispositions. For example, we can create entertainments that foster peaceful interactions. In short, the prevailing view in social psychology today does not support the old opposition of nature *versus* nurture, but rather sees both biology *and* environment, both evolution *and* culture as contributing to behaviour.

Nonetheless, these two approaches do tend to emphasize very different sources or origins of social behaviour. Just one example is their contrastive views of the origins of passionate love, as we will discuss in Chapter 6. At various points in this book, we will juxtapose the evolutionary and cultural approach and compare their explanations.

These sections will be highlighted by the placement of both symbols side-by-side in the following way:

On the **Applied Side**

Canadian Culture: Its Impact on Social Behaviour and Social Psychology

Americans and Canadians are not the same; they are products of two very different histories, two very different situations.

Margaret Atwood, 1982, p. 392

[Canada] began as the part of British North America that did not support the [American] Revolution, and Canadians have continued to define themselves by reference to what they are not—American—rather than in terms of their own national history and tradition.

Seymour Lipset, 1990, p. 3

As these quotations (the first from a Canadian author and the second from an American social scientist) suggest, Canada has struggled to achieve and to maintain a separate sense of identity—one that is different from its British roots and, perhaps more importantly, distinct from its neighbour to the south, the United States. This is a recurring theme in Canadian foreign policy. One recent example was the decision of the Canadian government to withhold active participation in the Iraq war initiated by the United States. The response of politicians and the general public to that decision, both at home and in the United States, demonstrates that this identity struggle is not likely to diminish in the near future.

Social psychologists living and working in Canada have had the same problem in attempting to define a distinctly Canadian social psychology (Earn & Towson, 1986). On the one hand, historically the United States has been the dominant force in the world of psychology (Moghaddam, 1987, 1990), and the bulk of the material in this book reflects that fact. On the other hand, many Canadian social psychologists are aware, as are many of the readers, that Canadian society, and the behaviour of Canadians, is somehow different. But what are these differences? And are they extensive or fundamental enough to define a Canadian character or a distinctly Canadian

social psychology? In ending this first chapter, we want to explore some of these Canadian differences and to suggest the ways in which Canadian culture might influence the social behaviour of Canadians and the development of Canadian social psychology.

Multiculturalism: Canadian Cultural Diversity

One of the most important factors distinguishing Canadian culture from the culture of the United States is its approach towards ethnic diversity. Beyond the fact that the composition of ethnic groups differs in Canada and the United States (Bowman, 2003), cultural diversity is approached in a fundamentally different way. Canada has an official policy of multiculturalism that stresses the value of cultural differences to our society and encourages groups to maintain their cultural identities. The idea behind multiculturalism is that the fabric of Canadian society should represent a *cultural mosaic*: that is, separate cultural groups, secure in their own identities, should come together and form a strong unified whole. The United States, in contrast, has historically emphasized assimilation of immigrant groups. The idea has been that the United States should be a *melting pot* where immigrants, within one or two generations, could assimilate (or "melt") into the American way of life.

Of course, in both countries the ideal and the reality are often quite far apart! In the United States many groups have not "melted." They continue to have separate customs, residential areas, and social relationships. For example, assimilation has not occurred in areas such as Chinatown in San Francisco or in the "ghettos" of many American cities, and this can sometimes lead to ethnic conflict. In Canada, respect for cultural diversity has sometimes been put to the test—see Figure 1.13—and the policy of multiculturalism is not without its critics (e.g., Bisoondath, 1994). We, too, have had our ethnic conflicts, and continuing regional disputes have, at times, threatened to tear holes in Canada's mosaic. Nonetheless, the large majority of Canadians support the policy of multiculturalism (Berry & Kalin, 1995) and Canada has a reputation as one of the most livable and ethnically tolerant of Western societies.

■ Multiculturalism under Threat

FIGURE 1.13 Prime Minister Jean Chrétien attempts to offset the negative response to one ethnic group during the SARS outbreak in 2003.

Does our multiculturalism influence the direction of Canadian social psychology? Awareness of the importance of cultural diversity historically led Canadian researchers and theorists to focus more on cultural issues and relations between groups, as well as studying the effects of multiculturalism itself (e.g., Berry, 1998). However, the importance of cultural diversity is very widely recognized today. Canadian social psychologists were pioneers and remain on the forefront in the areas of cultural psychology (e.g., Berry, Poortinga, & Pandey, 1997; Heine, Lehman, & Peng, 2002), intergroup relations (e.g., Taylor & Moghaddam, 1994), and bilingualism (e.g., Lambert, 1969).

A Kinder, Gentler Society: Stability and Violence in Canada

A second major factor that distinguishes Canadian culture is its relative lack of violence and greater social stability. One indicator is rates of violent crime, which are considerably lower in Canada than in the United States. For example, in 2000 the homicide rate in Canada was 1.8 per 100,000 population, and for the United States it was 5.5—three times greater (Statistics Canada, 2003; U.S. Department of Justice, 2002). Given that we are such close neighbours, the size of this gap suggests a fundamental difference between Canadian and U.S. cultures.

The Canadian self-image is of a peace-loving society, and our values reflect this (as we will discuss further in Chapter 3). Canadians show greater respect for, and confidence in, their legal institutions than those in many other Western cultures (Besserer, 1998; Lipset, 1990a, 2001). In the international arena, Canada's role has traditionally been one of conciliation and peacekeeping. But we cannot become complacent—the current rate of violent crime remains higher than it was 15 years ago (Tremblay, 1999). However, recent crime statistics attest to a continuing decrease in violent crime (Statistic Canada, 2003).

Although we have a less violent society, Canadian social psychologists have still made significant contributions in the areas of aggression (e.g., Rule, 1976, 1986) and in forensic psychology (in which psychology is applied to the legal systems; e.g., Doob, 1976, 1985; Wells, 1984; Dutton, 1992). These topics will be further discussed in Chapters 8 and 10.

Communitarian Values: Canada's Sense of Community

Seymour Lipset has suggested that differences between Canada and the United States can be traced back, in part, to the historical beginnings of both countries:

The concern of Canada's Fathers of Confederation with "Peace, Order, and Good Government" implies control of, and protection for the society. The parallel stress of America's Founding Fathers on "Life, Liberty, and the Pursuit of Happiness" suggests upholding the rights of the individual.

Lipset, 1990, p. 13

As this suggests, the United States has emphasized *individual* rights and freedoms since its beginning, while in Canada relatively greater emphasis has been placed on the maintenance of peace and order in *society as a whole*. The Canadian desire for order is reflected in the relatively lower rates of violence. But further, this historical difference may have led Canadian culture to be more *communitarian*; that is, to focus "upon the cooperation of its citizens and the need to protect their welfare" (Lipset, 1990). Public opinion polls suggest that, relative to Americans, Canadians give greater support to this governmental involvement and give more weight to the importance of equality between groups in society (Lipset, 1990). Broadly, we can say that Canadian society appears to be more *communitarian* (focused on the community) and less *individualistic* (focused on the individual) than the United States. We should emphasize, however, that this is only relative to the United States. According to one researcher, Canada is one of the more individualistic countries in the world (Hofstede, 1983).

In social psychology, the interest of Canadian researchers in group processes, as mentioned above, may be a result of this greater sense of community. Perhaps there has also been more emphasis on the constructive role of group relations in people's lives (Taylor & Moghaddam, 1987; Beaton, Tougas, & Joly, 1996) and the impact of society upon the individual (Berry, Kim, Minde, & Mok, 1987; Taylor & McKirnan, 1984).

In summary, we have suggested that Canadian culture places greater emphasis on multiculturalism, the maintenance of order, and communitarian values relative to the United States. The extent to which these values are reflected in the individual social behaviour of Canadians will vary. However, in general we do see a very marked difference in the levels of violence and support for community intervention by government among Canadians. A word of warning may be necessary here: Do not make the mistake of assuming that every Canadian is more supportive of cultural diversity, less violent, and more community-minded than every American. This is simply not the case. The differences we outlined are average ones and there is considerable overlap in the behaviour and responses of the populations of both countries. Compared to other nations and cultures around the world, these two countries and their citizens have a great deal in common—are perhaps more similar than they are different (Grabb, Curtis, & Baer, 2000; Lipset, 2001).

Similarly, Canadian psychology is not completely distinct from American, as most Canadian social psychologists agree (Rule & Wells, 1981; Earn & Towson, 1986). However, the kind of differences we have discussed can create difficulty in communication between Canadian and American psychologists (see Bowman, 2003). They have also produced an interest in Canadian issues and a particularly Canadian perspective in the areas of language, culture, and group relations. Canadians have also made significant contributions to most of the topic areas of social psychology and we will endeavour to represent this contribution throughout the book.

KEY POINTS

- Current trends in social psychology include: (1) interest in *application* of the knowledge and findings of social psychology to many practical problems; (2) the growing influence of a *cognitive perspective*, which suggests that individuals' interpretations of social situations strongly shape their behaviour; (3) the adoption of a *multicultural perspective*, recognizing the importance of cultural factors; (4) increasing influence of the *evolutionary perspective* focusing on the role of biology and genetics in social behaviour.

- Canadian culture has placed a greater emphasis on cultural diversity, is more communitarian, and tends to be more stable and less violent than the United States. These cultural differences will have an impact on the social behaviour of Canadians and on the development of Canadian social psychology.

Using This Book: A Road Map for Readers

Before concluding this introduction to the field of social psychology, we'd like to comment briefly on several features of this text. First, please note that we've taken several steps to make our text easier and more convenient for you to use. Each chapter begins with an outline of the major topics covered and ends with a summary. Important terms are printed in **boldface type like this** and are followed by a definition. This definition is also placed in the margin nearby. To help you understand and remember what you have read, each major section is followed by a list of Key Points, briefly summarizing major points. Each chapter also ends with a summary and review of these Key Points. Because figures and charts contained in original research reports are often quite complex, every graph and table in this text has been specially created for it. In addition, all graphs contain special labels designed to call your attention to the key findings presented. We think that you'll find all of these illustrations easy to read and—more importantly—that they'll contribute to your understanding of social psychology.

Second, we want to note that we've included several special sections throughout the text. These do not interrupt the flow of text materials; rather, they are presented at natural breaks in content. All are designed to highlight information we feel is especially important and interesting.

The first type of special insert is called "Canadian Research: On the Cutting Edge." These sections describe Canadian research that we believe is on the frontiers of knowledge in social psychology.

The second type of special insert is called "Cornerstones." These sections describe studies that initiated major lines of research in the history of social psychology, exerting a lasting influence on the field.

The third type of special section is entitled "On the Applied Side." These sections highlight the practical implications of social psychology—ways in which its knowledge and principles can contribute to the solution of a wide range of practical problems.

A final type of special section, featured near the end of each chapter, relates to our belief that social psychology can and should be applied to our daily lives. These sections are labelled "Ideas to Take with You." Each is designed to highlight important concepts you should remember—and use—long after this course is over. In our view you may well find these concepts useful in your own life in the years ahead.

As we noted earlier, modern social psychology is distinguished by a growing interest in social diversity and in the potential role of evolutionary influences on human social behaviour. Topics related to these important themes are discussed at numerous points throughout the text.

All of these features are designed to help you get the most out of your first encounter with social psychology. But, in a key sense, only you can transfer the information on the pages of this book into your own memory—and into your own life. So please do use this book. Read the chapter outlines and each set of key points, and review the summary of those points at the end of each chapter. If you are interested in applying this knowledge in your own life, pay special attention to the Ideas to Take with You section. Doing so, we believe, will improve your understanding of social psychology—and your grade, too! Finally, please think of this book as a reference source—a practical guide to social behaviour to which you can refer over and over again. In contrast to some other fields you will study, social psychology really is directly relevant to your daily life—to understanding others and to getting along better with them. Good luck—and may your first encounter with our field be one you'll enjoy and remember for many years to come.

Ideas To Take With You

Why Correlation Doesn't Equal Causation

The fact that two variables are correlated—even strongly correlated—does not necessarily mean that changes in one variable cause changes in the other. This is true because changes in both variables may actually be related to—or caused by—a third variable. Two examples:

OBSERVATION As weight increases, income increases.

POSSIBLE INTERPRETATIONS:

1. Weight gain causes increased income.

   Weight gain $\xrightarrow{\text{Causes}}$ Increased income

2. As people grow older, they tend to gain weight and also to earn higher incomes; both variables are actually related to age.

OBSERVATION The more violent television and movies people watch, the more likely they are to engage in dangerous acts of aggression.

POSSIBLE INTERPRETATIONS:

1. Exposure to media violence is one factor that increases aggression.

   Exposure to media violence $\xrightarrow{\text{Causes}}$ Increased aggression

2. People who prefer a high level of stimulation have little control over their impulses; thus, they choose to watch displays of violence and also act aggressively more often than other people. Both variables are related to a need for certain kinds of stimulation.

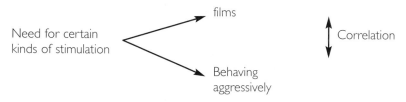

KEY CONCLUSION: EVEN IF TWO VARIABLES ARE STRONGLY CORRELATED, THIS DOES NOT NECESSARILY MEAN THAT CHANGES IN ONE CAUSE CHANGES IN THE OTHER.

Summary

Social Psychology: A Working Definition

- *Social psychology* is the scientific field that seeks to understand the nature and causes of individual behaviour and thought in social situations. (p. 4)
- It is scientific in nature because it adopts the values and methods used in other fields of science. (p. 4)
- Important causes of social behaviour and thought include cognitive processes, biological factors, other persons, the physical environment, and culture. (p. 6)

Research Methods in Social Psychology

- Systematic observation, of which *naturalistic observation* is an example, provides descriptive, more qualitative data. (p. 11)
- *Correlational methods* enable us to predict one variable from information about the other. Even strong correlations between variables, however, do not necessarily indicate causation. (p. 13)
- *Experimentation* involves systematically altering one or more *independent variables* in order to determine their affect on the *dependent variable*. (p. 15)

- The *experimental method* requires *random assignment* of participants to experimental conditions, holding all other factors constant to avoid *confounding* of variables. (p. 15)
- Each method has its advantages and disadvantages: qualitative data is vulnerable to the *confirmation bias*; the correlational method allows prediction, but it does not allow researchers to draw causal conclusions; experimentation allows causal conclusions but laboratory experiments sometimes raise questions about *external validity*. (p. 19)
- Research on the *planning fallacy* and attempts to reduce it provide an example of replication. (p. 19)
- Ethical considerations are involved when *deception* is used. Safeguards are *informed consent* and *debriefing*. (p. 22)

Social Psychology in the New Millennium: Origins and Trends

- Current trends in social psychology include a cognitive perspective, applications of social psychology, a multicultural perspective, and evolutionary influences. (p. 24)
- The culture of Canada differs from the United States and this will impact Canadian social behaviour and social psychology. (p. 26)

For More Information

Jackson, J. M. (1993). *Social psychology, past and present.* Hillsdale, NJ: Erlbaum.

A thoughtful overview of the roots and development of social psychology. Organized around major themes in social psychological research, this book emphasizes the multidisciplinary roots of social psychology. The chapter on current trends is especially valuable.

Buss, D. M. (1999). *Evolutionary psychology: The new science of the mind.* Boston: Allyn and Bacon.

If you'd like to learn more about psychologists' efforts to understand the possible role of genetic and biological factors in our social behaviour, this book is an excellent place to begin. The chapters on mating strategies, kinship, and aggression and warfare are truly fascinating.

Weblinks

www.apa.org/journals/psp.html
Journal of Personality and Social Psychology
www.spssi.org
The Society for the Psychological Study of Social Issues
www.cpa.ca
Canadian Psychological Association

www.apa.org
American Psychological Association
www.uiowa.edu/~grpproc/crisp/crisp.html
Current Research in Social Psychology

CHAPTER TWO

Social **Perception** and Social **Cognition**: Internalizing Our Social World

Nonverbal Communication: The Unspoken Language
Nonverbal Communication: The Basic Channels/Recognizing Deception: The Role of Nonverbal Cues

Attribution: Understanding the Causes of Others' Behaviour
Theories of Attribution: How We Understand the Social World/Attribution: Some Basic Sources of Bias/Culture and Attribution: Holistic versus Analytic Thought

Coping with Information Overload: Schemas, Heuristics, and Automatic Processing
Schemas: Organizing Social Information/Heuristics and Automatic Processing: Cognitive Shortcuts

Errors in Social Cognition: Why We Are Fallible
Negativity Bias: Paying Extra Attention to Negative Information/Optimistic Biases: Looking at the Future through Rose-Coloured Glasses/Counterfactual Thinking: Considering "What Might Have Been"/Social Cognition: A Word of Optimism

Affect and Cognition: The Interplay between Our Feelings and Our Thoughts
The Influences of Affect on Cognition/The Influence of Cognition on Affect

SPECIAL SECTIONS

ON THE APPLIED SIDE
Cultural Differences in Communication: East Asian and North American Contrasts

CORNERSTONES
Evidence for the Self-Confirming Nature of Schemas: The Self-Fulfilling Prophecy

■ Information Overload

FIGURE 2.1 All too often in social situations there is just too much social information to absorb or process. This phenomenon, called *information overload*, influences our social perceptions and social cognitions—how we see and understand the social world.

Think about a typical social situation-the party. You've arrived a little late and, as you stand on the threshold, it's obvious that things are already well underway. There's music, laughter, lights and colour, people dancing, talking, moving. Some of them glance your way, but most don't even notice you. Perhaps someone catches your eye and smiles enticingly. But you hesitate. How can you possibly take in that buzzing mass of people, with different clothing, ways of acting, and facial expressions? Then, what *did* that smile mean? And how are you going to respond? At such moments you are suffering from a common problem when faced with social stimuli—**information overload**—the fact that there is frequently just too much information for you to process it properly, let alone decide how you should respond (See Figure 2.1).

In this chapter we will examine the many ways we *cope with social information*, from the point when we take in that information from the environment around us, then when we use it to understand the social world, to the point when we allow it to influence our social behaviour.

The intake process is generally termed **social perception**-when we seek out social information and register or encode it in our minds. The process through which we use social information is termed **social cognition**-for example, when we recall, interpret, reason, and make judgments about others. Whereas social perception is concerned with the *intake and registering* of social information, social cognition is concerned with the *use and manipulation* of social information.

Although traditionally social perception and social cognition have been seen as distinct processes, they are clearly linked and, at times, inseparable. Our perceptions will influence our cognitions. So, for example, having registered that smile at the party (your *perception*), this perception will then influence your thoughts (or *cognitions*) about the party. Perhaps the party will now seem much more exciting or interesting, or, if you have different priorities, you may see it as a potentially embarrassing social situation. Similarly, our cognitions (i.e., our already existing beliefs and interpretations) can also influence our perceptions. For example, your interpretation of a smile as "enticing" would be based on previous social experience and knowledge, and that social experience will, in part, determine the information that you focus upon at the party. The point here is that social perception and social cognition are *interdependent* processes; that is, they both influence each other. While social perception is concerned with the intake of information, that process is influenced by the way we think about and organize our experiences. Similarly, social cognition is concerned with the use and manipulation of social information, but this information has been filtered through our selective perceptions.

To complicate these processes further, we are not always accurate or objective when faced with other people. Our social perceptions and cognitions are vulnerable to a number of systematic *biases*. Often we see what we expect or want to see, not necessarily what is there. Did that person really smile enticingly or were you just hoping too hard? You can see clearly the importance of misinterpretation here!

You may now have some inkling that social perception and cognition are complex and crucial processes, and so worthy of careful scrutiny by social psychologists. To acquaint you with the key findings of this research, we'll focus on four major topics. First, we'll examine the process of **nonverbal communication**—communication between individuals involving an unspoken language of facial expressions, eye contact, body movements, and postures (e.g., Zebrowitz, 1997). As we'll soon see, information provided by such nonverbal cues can often tell us much about others' current moods or emotions. Next, we'll examine *attribution*, the complex process through which we attempt to understand the reasons behind others' behaviour—why they have acted as they have in a given situation. Third, we'll turn to fundamental ways of coping with information overload—the use of mental shortcuts such as *schemas and heuristics*. Unfortunately, this can sometimes result in *biases* or errors in our social thought. Finally, because our emotional response to the social world is one of the factors that prevent us from being objective, social psychologists are currently attempting to explore the relation between *affect* and *cognitions*.

Nonverbal Communication Communication between individuals that does not involve the content of spoken words. It consists instead of an unspoken language of facial expressions, eye contact, and body language.

Nonverbal Communication: The Unspoken Language

Often, social behaviour is strongly affected by temporary factors or causes. Changing moods, shifting emotions, fatigue, illness, drugs—all can influence the ways in which we think and behave. For example, most people are more willing to do favours for others when in a good mood than when in a bad mood (e.g., Baron, 1997a). Similarly, most people are more likely to lose their tempers and lash out at others in some manner when feeling irritable than when feeling pleasant (Berkowitz, 2003). Because such temporary factors exert important effects on social behaviour and thought, we are often interested in them: we try to find out how others are feeling right now. How do we go about this process?

Our best source of information about others' feelings comes when we pay careful attention to *nonverbal cues*. As noted by DePaulo (1992), such behaviour is relatively *irrepressible*—difficult to control—so that even when others try to conceal their inner feelings from us, these often leak out in many ways through nonverbal cues. In this section, we'll first examine the basic channels through which *nonverbal communication* takes place. Then we'll turn to some interesting findings concerning how we use nonverbal cues to cut through *deception*-efforts by other persons to mislead us about their true feelings or beliefs (e.g., DePaulo, 1994). Before beginning, though, we should make one more point: nonverbal cues emitted by other persons can affect our own feelings even if we are *not* consciously paying attention to these cues or trying to figure out how these persons feel. For instance, Neumann and Strack (2000) found that when individuals listen to another person read a speech, the tone of this person's voice (happy, neutral, or sad) can influence the listeners' moods even though they are concentrating on the content of the speech and not on the reader's emotional state. Neumann and Strack refer to such effects as *emotional contagion*—a mechanism through which feelings are transferred in a seemingly automatic way from one person to another. Now, on to the basic channels of nonverbal communication.

Nonverbal Communication: The Basic Channels

Researchers have identified those channels of nonverbal communication that transmit key information about our inner emotional and affective states. These seem to involve *facial expressions*, *eye contact*, *body movements* and *posture*, and *touching*.

Unmasking the Face: Facial Expressions as Clues to Others' Emotions

More than 2000 years ago, the Roman orator Cicero stated, "The face is the image of the soul." By this he meant that human feelings and emotions are often reflected on the face and can be read there in specific expressions. Modern research suggests that Cicero—and many other observers of human behaviour—were correct: it *is* possible to learn much about others' current moods and feelings from their facial expressions. In fact, it appears that six different basic emotions are represented clearly, and from a very early age, on the human face: anger, fear, sadness, disgust, happiness, and surprise (Izard, 1991; Rozin, Lowrey & Ebert, 1994; see Figure 2.2). Please note: this in no way implies that human beings are capable of demonstrating only six different facial expressions. On the contrary, emotions occur in many combinations (for example, anger along with fear, surprise with happiness). Further, each of these reactions can vary greatly in strength. Thus, while there seem to be only a small number of basic themes in facial expressions, the number of variations on these themes is immense.

■ Facial Expressions: The Range Is Immense

FIGURE 2.2 Although there is general agreement among researchers that only a small number of emotions are represented by distinct facial expressions, emotions can occur in many combinations, so people actually show an enormous number of different expressions.

An important issue that has concerned social psychologists from the beginning is the extent to which facial expressions are universal. Even Charles Darwin, after travelling the world collecting data question support of the theory of evolution, attempted to answer this particular question. Do people living in widely separated geographic areas demonstrate similar facial expressions in similar situations (Darwin, 1872; Ekman, 1989)? Would you expect someone from a remote part of the world to smile in reaction to events that made them happy, or to frown when displeased, as you do? If we found evidence of this type, showing a universal connection between facial expression and emotion, it would suggest that these responses are part of our evolved behaviour patterns. On the other hand, evidence showing cultural variations in facial expression would throw doubt on this conclusion, suggesting that our cultures teach us the acceptable facial expressions of our societies.

Perhaps the most convincing evidence for universality of facial expressions was provided by a series of studies conducted by Ekman and Friesen (1975). These researchers travelled to isolated areas of New Guinea and asked individuals living there to imagine various emotion-provoking events—for example, your friend has come for a visit and you are happy; you find a dead animal that has been lying in the hot sun for several days, and it smells very bad. Then these subjects were asked to show by facial expressions how they would feel in each case. Their expressions were very similar to ones that a North American might show in those situations. Further, when individuals living in widely separated countries were shown photos of strangers from other cultures who were demonstrating anger, fear, happiness, sadness, surprise, and disgust, they were quite accurate in identifying these emotions (e.g., Ekman, 1973). These studies provided strong support for the idea that facial expressions, and the emotions behind them, are universal—that they reflect an evolved and automatic response among humans. And this was the accepted view for some years following their publication (Ekman, 1989).

More recently, however, the accuracy of these conclusions has been called into question by Russell and colleagues (e.g., Russell, 1994; Carroll & Russell, 1996). A re-analysis of the earlier research showed that results were not as universal and consistent as has often been suggested (Russell, 1994). Examining data from many cultures, both Western and Non-western, Russell demonstrated variation as a function of contact with Western culture. That is, recognition of facial expressions was most consistent with Western responses if a cultural group had greater contact with the West and became less consistent as the culture became more remote. This suggests that *cultural socialization* may have a greater impact on our understanding and display of facial expressions than had been acknowledged. Further studies also indicate that while facial expressions may indeed reveal much about others' emotions, our judgments in this respect are also affected by the *social context* in which the facial expressions occur and various situational cues. For instance, if individuals view a photo of a face showing what would normally be judged as *fear* but also read a story suggesting that this person is actually showing *anger*, many describe the face as showing anger, not fear (Carroll & Russell, 1996). Findings such as these suggest that our understanding of facial expressions may be modified by other social cues in a particular context.

Recent findings that support an evolutionary view of facial expressions comes from research on our responses to negative and positive facial expressions. An example is a phenomenon termed the *face-in-the-crowd effect*—a tendency for us to notice negative facial expressions even in a crowd of faces where the majority are not that way (Hansen & Hansen, 1988). A clear illustration of such effects is provided by studies conducted by Ohman, Lundqvist, and Esteves (2001). These researchers asked participants to search for neutral, friendly, or threatening faces present among other faces with discrepant expressions (e.g., the friendly face was shown among neutral or threatening faces; the threatening face was shown among friendly or neutral faces; and so on). Results indicated that regardless of the background faces, participants were faster and more accurate in identifying threatening faces. In an additional study, participants were asked to search for several kinds of faces—threatening, friendly, scheming, or sad—among an array of neutral faces. Again, the threatening faces were identified faster and more accurately than any of the others. Further research shows that we pay less attention to the *content* of a person's speech if he or she smiles while presenting information to us than if this person shows a neutral facial expression or frowns in anger (Ottati, Terkildsen & Hubbard, 1997).

Since threatening persons represent a greater risk to our safety—or survival—than happy ones, these findings are consistent with the view that facial expressions, and our ability to read them, may have evolved because they aid our survival. Those who had a particular sensitivity to negative facial expressions would be better able to avoid danger and, therefore, have an increased chance to pass their genes on to the next generation.

What can we conclude when faced with apparently contradictory evidence—on the one hand for the universality of facial expressions and on the other for sociocultural influences on facial expressions? There is substantial agreement in recognition of some facial expressions (particularly happiness) between those in widely different cultures. However, there is also evidence demonstrating that recognition of facial expressions varies with culture and depends on the social context. Overall, it seems safest to conclude that while facial expressions are not totally universal around the world—cultural and contextual differences do exist with respect to their precise meanings—they generally need much less "translation" than spoken languages. As emphasized in Chapter 1, we can be sure that our facial expressions derive from *both* universal evolutionary tendencies and specific cultural influences. We will further examine cultural variations in other aspects of nonverbal communication in a later section of On the Applied Side entitled, "Showing Your Feelings."

Gazes and Stares: The Language of the Eyes

Have you ever had a conversation with someone who is wearing very dark or mirrored sunglasses? If so, you know that this can be an uncomfortable situation. Since you can't see the other person's eyes, you are uncertain about how she or he is reacting. Taking note of the importance of cues provided by others' eyes, ancient poets often described the eyes as "windows to the soul." In one important sense, they were right: we do often learn much about others' feelings from their eyes. For example, we interpret a high level of gazing from another as a sign of liking or friendliness (Kleinke, 1986). In contrast, if others avoid eye contact with us, we may conclude that they are unfriendly, don't like us, or are simply shy (Zimbardo, 1977).

While a high level of eye contact from others is usually interpreted as a sign of liking or positive feelings, there is one important exception to this general rule. If another person gazes at us continuously and maintains such contact regardless of any actions we perform, she or he can be said to be staring. **Staring** is often interpreted as a sign of anger or hostility—consider the phrase "a cold stare"—and most people find this particular nonverbal cue disturbing (Ellsworth & Carlsmith, 1973). In fact, we may quickly terminate social interaction with someone who stares at us and may even leave the scene (Greenbaum & Rosenfield, 1978). This is one reason why experts on road rage-highly aggressive driving by motorists, sometimes followed by actual assaults—recommend that drivers avoid eye contact with people who are disobeying traffic laws and rules of the road (B. J. Bushman, 1998). Apparently, such persons, who are already in a highly excitable state, interpret anything approaching a stare from another driver as an aggressive act and may react accordingly (see Figure 2.3).

Staring A form of eye contact in which one person continues to gaze steadily at another regardless of what the recipient does.

■ Staring and Road Rage

FIGURE 2.3 If you encounter another driver who is showing signs of road rage—driving in a highly aggressive manner—don't stare at him or her to show your annoyance. If you do, you may cause the person to erupt in unpredictable and dangerous ways.

Body Language: Gestures, Posture, and Movements
Try this simple demonstration:

- First, try to remember some incident that made you angry—the angrier the better. Think about it for about a minute.

- Now try to remember another incident-one that made you feel sad—again, the sadder the better.

Compare your behaviour in the two contexts. Did you change your posture or move your hands, arms, or legs as your thoughts shifted from the first event to the second? The chances are good that you did, for our current moods or emotions are often reflected in the position, posture, and movement of our bodies. Together, such nonverbal behaviours are termed **body language**, and they too can provide us with several useful kinds of information about others.

First, body language often reveals much about others' emotional states. Large numbers of movements—especially ones in which one part of the body does something to another part (e.g., touching, scratching, rubbing)—suggest emotional arousal. The greater the frequency of such behaviour, the higher the level of arousal or nervousness (Harrigan et al., 1991).

Larger patterns of movement, involving the whole body, can also be informative. Such phrases as "he adopted a *threatening posture*" and "she greeted him with *open arms*" suggest that different body orientations or postures can be suggestive of

Body Language Cues provided by the position, posture, and movement of people's bodies or body parts.

contrasting emotional reactions. Aronoff, Woike, and Hyman (1992) supported this possibility by showing that the threatening characters in choreographed ballets (e.g., Macbeth) use angular poses nearly three times as often as the warm characters. In contrast, the warm characters (e.g., Romeo and Juliet) engaged in rounded poses almost four times more often. When combined with additional research (Aronoff et al., 1992), these findings suggest that large-scale body movements or postures can sometimes serve as an important source of information about others' emotions and traits.

Further evidence for the conclusion that body posture and movements can be an important source of information about others is provided by research conducted by Lynn and Mynier (1993). These researchers arranged for servers of both genders either to stand upright or to squat down next to customers when taking drink orders. Lynn and Mynier predicted that squatting servers would receive larger tips because in this position they would make more eye contact with customers and would be physically closer to them (Argyle, 1988) and, therefore, appear friendlier. Results confirmed predictions: Regardless of gender, servers received larger tips when they bent down than when they did not.

Finally, we should add that more specific information about others' feelings is often provided by gestures. Gestures fall into several categories, but perhaps the most important are *emblems*-body movements carrying specific meanings in a given culture. Do you recognize the gestures shown in Figure 2.4? In Canada and other Western countries, these movements have clear and definite meanings. In other cultures, however, they may have no meaning, or even a different meaning. For this reason, it is wise to be careful about using gestures while travelling in cultures different from your own: you may offend the people around you without meaning to do so! Even within one society, communication with those from different cultural backgrounds can be fraught with difficulties, as is discussed below in the On the Applied Side section.

Touching: The Most Intimate Nonverbal Cues

Suppose that during a conversation with another person, she or he touched you briefly. How would you react? What information would this behaviour convey? The answer to both questions is, it depends. And what it depends upon is several factors relating to who does the touching (a friend or a stranger, a member of your own or of the other gender); the nature of this physical contact (brief or prolonged, gentle or rough, what

■ Gesture as a Nonverbal Cue

FIGURE 2.4 Do you recognize the gestures here? Can you tell what they mean? In Canada and other Western cultures, each of these gestures has a specific meaning. However, they may well have no meaning, or entirely different meanings, in other cultures.

part of the body is touched); and the context in which it takes place (a business or social setting, a doctor's office). Depending on such factors, touch can suggest affection, sexual interest, caring, dominance, or even aggression. Despite such complexities, existing evidence indicates that when touching is considered appropriate, it often produces positive reactions in the person being touched (Alagna, Whitcher, & Fisher, 1979; Smith, Gier, & Willis, 1982). This fact is clearly illustrated by a study involving servers in two restaurants who touched customers briefly and innocuously (Crusco & Wetzel, 1984). In this study, both a brief touch on the hand (about one-half second) and a longer touch on the shoulder (one to one-and-a-half seconds) significantly increased tipping over a no-touch control condition. Thus, consistent with previous findings, being touched in an innocuous, nonthreatening way seemed to generate positive rather than negative reactions among recipients. But remember that touching someone when it is considered inappropriate can produce a *very* negative reaction—so be careful!

One acceptable way in which people in many different cultures touch strangers is through handshaking. Pop psychology and even books on etiquette (e.g., Vanderbilt, 1957) suggest that handshakes reveal much about other persons—for instance, their personalities—and that a firm handshake is a good way to make a favourable first impression on others. Are such observations true? Is this form of nonverbal communication actually revealing? Ingenious research by Chaplin and his colleagues (Chaplin et al., 2000) suggests that it is. (As you may recall, we used handshaking as a means of illustrating methods of research in social psychology in Chapter 1.)

To study handshaking as a nonverbal cue to others' personalities, Chaplin and his colleagues (2000) first trained four advanced psychology students to rate handshakes along several basic dimensions (strength, grip, dryness, temperature, vigour, duration, etc.). Then, they had these raters shake hands with undergraduate students (both men and women) twice: when they first came to the laboratory for appointments and again just before they left. In between these two handshakes, the research participants completed questionnaires designed to measure several key aspects of personality (e.g., extroversion, agreeableness, conscientiousness, openness to experience, expressiveness). In addition, the raters indicated their first impressions of each participant.

Several aspects of handshaking (e.g., duration, completeness of grip, strength, vigour) were closely related, so these were combined into a single index of handshakes. Results indicated that this index, in turn, was strongly related to several aspects of participants' personality, as revealed by the questionnaire they completed. Specifically, the higher the participants' handshake index, the more extroverted and open to experience and less shy they were (see Figure 2.5). In addition, for women, but not for men, the higher the participants' handshake index, the more agreeable they were. First impressions, too, were related to handshaking: the higher the participants' handshake index, the more favourable were raters' impressions of them.

In sum, this particular kind of touching was in fact quite revealing about the persons who engaged in it. As the authors of etiquette books and guides to success have long suggested, a firm handshake *is* a valuable asset, at least in cultures where handshakes are used for greetings and departures.

Recognizing Deception: The Role of Nonverbal Cues

A little inaccuracy sometimes saves tons of explanation. (Saki, 1924)

While this quotation may ring true, it is also the case that people often lie for other, less socially desirable reasons—to advance their own interests, to influence others, to conceal their true motives or goals. In short, lying is an all-too-common part of social life. This sad fact raises an important question: How can we tell when others are

■ Handshaking as a Revealing Nonverbal Cue.

FIGURE 2.5 Ratings of individuals' handshakes by trained raters were found to be significantly related to important aspects of the individuals' personalities, as revealed by questionnaires they completed.

Source: Based on data from Chaplin et al., 2000.

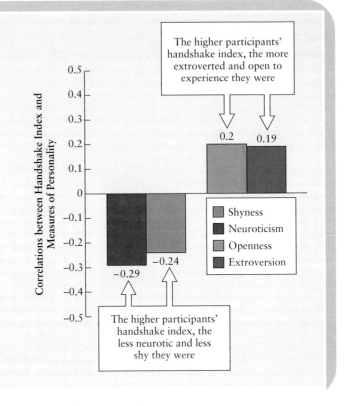

lying? Part of the answer seems to involve nonverbal cues. When people lie, subtle changes often occur in their facial expressions, body posture or movements, and certain nonverbal aspects of speech (aspects that are not related to the meaning of the words they speak—for instance, the tone of their voices). Let's take a look at these and several other facets of our ability to detect deception by other persons.

Nonverbal Cues to Deception

Microexpressions
Fleeting facial expressions lasting only a few tenths of a second.

One useful cue that others are lying is revealed by <u>microexpressions</u>—fleeting facial expressions lasting only a few tenths of a second. Such reactions appear on the face very quickly after an emotion-provoking event and are difficult to suppress (Ekman, 1985). As result, they can be very revealing about others' true feelings or emotions. For instance, if you ask another person whether he or she likes something (you, an idea you have expressed, or anything else), watch that person's faces closely as he or she responds. If you see one expression (e.g., a frown), which is followed very quickly by another (e.g., a smile), this can be a useful sign that that person is lying—he or she is stating one opinion or reaction when, in fact, really having another.

A second nonverbal cue that is revealing of deception is known as *interchannel discrepancies*. These are inconsistencies between nonverbal cues from different basic channels, and they result from the fact that persons who are lying often find it difficult to control all of these channels at once. For instance, they may manage their facial expressions well but may have difficulty looking you in the eye as they tell their lie.

A third nonverbal cue involves *nonverbal* aspects of speech. When people lie, the pitch of their voices often rises and they tend to speak in a more hesitating manner and to make more errors (e.g., DePaulo, Stone, & Lassiter, 1985; Stiff et al., 1989). If you detect these kinds of changes in another person's voice, this, too, can be a sign that he or she is lying.

Fourth, deception is frequently revealed by certain aspects of *eye contact*. Persons who are lying often blink more often and show pupils that are more dilated than do persons who are telling the truth. They may also show an unusually low level of eye contact or—surprisingly—an unusually high one, as they attempt to fake being honest by looking others right in the eye (Kleinke, 1986).

Finally, persons who are lying sometimes show *exaggerated facial expressions*. They may smile more—or more broadly—than usual or may show greater sorrow than is typical in a given situation. A prime example: Someone says "no" to a request you've made and then shows exaggerated regret. This is a good sign that the reasons the person has supplied for saying "no" may not be true.

Through careful attention to these nonverbal cues, we can often tell when others are lying—or merely trying to hide their own feelings from us. Success in detecting deception is far from certain; some persons are very skilful liars. But if you pay careful attention to the cues described above, you will make their task of pulling the wool over your eyes much more difficult.

Cognitive Factors in the Detection of Deception

Our comments so far might seem to suggest that the harder we try to detect deception, the more successful we will be at this task. Surprisingly, though, this is not always the case. Here's why: when others try to deceive us, we can pay careful attention either to their words *or* to their nonverbal cues—because we have limited cognitive capacity, it is difficult to do both at once. Further, it appears that the more strongly motivated we are to detect deception, the more likely we are to pay careful attention to their words—to listen carefully to what they say. In fact, though, the most revealing cues to deception are often nonverbal ones. So, paradoxically, the more motivated we are to detect deception, the less effective we may be at this task.

Direct evidence for this conclusion is provided by research conducted by Forrest and Feldman (2000). These researchers varied the motivation of students who were going to evaluate whether others were lying or not. Half of the subjects (the high-involvement group) were told that they would later be asked questions about the messages on the tape and that success in answering these questions would provide a good measure of their intelligence and social skills. The other half (the low-involvement group) was simply told that they would be asked questions about issues not discussed on the tape.

Forrest and Feldman (2000) predicted that judges in the low-involvement group would actually do better than those in the high-involvement group in determining whether the persons they saw were lying or telling the truth, and as you can see from Figure 2.6, this is precisely what was found. The findings of this study and those of several others suggest that, as is true with respect to many other tasks, trying too hard to detect others' deception can sometimes be counterproductive and actually reduce our success in this respect.

Before concluding this discussion of deception, we should address one final question: Can lies be detected across cultures? Research by Bond and Atoum (2000) indicates that we can indeed tell when people from cultures other than our own are lying. In their research, Bond and Atoum (2000) had persons from widely different cultures (the United States, Jordan, India) view videotapes of persons from their own and other cultures who were either lying or telling the truth. As you might expect, participants were more accurate at recognizing lies by persons in their own culture than by persons from another culture. But they were able to recognize lies with greater than chance success, even when the lies were told by persons from a different culture. Findings such as these suggest that, in contrast to spoken language, the language of nonverbal cues may be universal and require no interpreter.

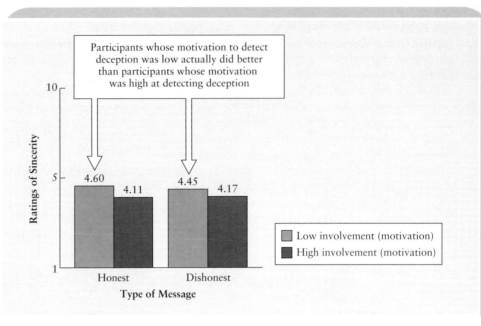

Participants whose motivation to detect deception was low actually did better than participants whose motivation was high at detecting deception

- Motivation to Detect Deception: Evidence That It Can Backfire

FIGURE 2.6 Individuals who were highly motivated to detect others' deception actually did worse at this task than did individuals who were not as highly motivated to detect deception. This may occur because when we are highly motivated to recognize others' deception, we tend to pay close attention to their words—and so overlook important nonverbal cues to deception.

Source: Based on data from Forrest & Feldman, 2000.

On the **Applied Side**

Cultural Differences in Communication: East Asian and North American Contrasts

Cultural differences in styles of communication, both verbal and nonverbal, can be crucial for those of us who daily live and work in a multicultural context such as Canada. You may meet with people of different ethnicities at school, in the office, and in public settings such as restaurants and stores. It is all too easy, particularly if you have been raised in the mainstream culture, to assume that your way of communicating is used and understood by everyone around you, when this isn't so. Further, you may misperceive the behaviour and intentions of people who have a different cultural style of communication from yours. Examining some of the distinctions between communication styles will make the potential for misunderstanding and even conflict more evident. A

major distinction, important to Canadians, has been made between the communication styles of East Asians and North Americans. Yum (2000) for example, has proposed four essential distinctions, summarized in Table 2.1. She suggests that the philosophy of Confucianism, with its focus on social relationships, has fundamentally shaped the communication patterns of East Asians.

First, East Asians will be more focused on the *social processes* of communication—the ways in which it can help them in the development and maintenance of their social relationships. During interaction, individuals strive to interpret the meaning of the other person's communication, continuously adjusting their understanding of the state of their relationship as

TABLE 2.1 A Comparison between North American and East Asian Communication Styles

East Asian Orientation	North American Orientation
1. Process-Oriented	**1. Outcome-Oriented**
Communication is perceived as a process of infinite interpretation.	Communication is perceived as the transference of messages.
2. Indirect Communication Emphasized	**2. Direct Communication Emphasized**
The use of indirect communication is prevalent and seen as normative.	Direct communication is seen as the norm even though indirect communication is also widely used.
3. Socially Differentiated Linguistic Codes	**3. Less Socially Differentiated Linguistic Codes**
Many different forms of address (formal and informal) are used depending upon the social situation and the status or intimacy of interactants.	Fewer differentiations in forms of address, reflecting fewer status distinctions between people.
4. Receiver-Centred	**4. Sender-Centred**
Meaning is in the interpretation.	Meaning is in the messages created by the sender.
Emphasis is on listening, sensitivity, and removal of preconceptions.	Emphasis is on how to formulate the best messages.

Source: Adapted from Yum, 2000, with permission.

they talk. In the same way that a relationship develops and changes, the communication between two people will also be seen as in a continuous state of flux. For North Americans, communication is more likely to be seen as a tool for transmission of information that can aid the individual to achieve personal goals. It is, therefore, the success or failure of that specific *outcome* or goal that is most important.

Second, Yum suggests that East Asians are more likely to emphasize *indirectness* in communication. The use of hidden meaning, hints, innuendos, and irony will be greater than for North Americans. While both indirect and direct communication is used by all cultures, indirectness would be expected to be more widespread as well as more elaborate in East Asian cultures. For example, if an individual were cold and wanted the door closed, an indirect communication in North America might involve saying to the other person "The door is open." This is indirect because it does not directly express the wishes of the speaker for the door to be closed. However, the Japanese are likely to be even more indirect and say, for example, "It is somewhat cold today." Notice that no reference to the door is made at all here (Okabe, 1987).

Thomas Holtgraves (1997) put these suggestions to the test by devising a scale to measure two dimensions of indirectness: (1) *interpretation*—the extent to which individuals interpret others' conversation as having an

underlying rather than an obvious meaning; and (2) *production*—the extent to which they produce such indirect communications when talking to others. For example, those who were high in indirectness would agree with items in the scale such as "I will often look below the surface of a person's remark in order to decide what they really mean" (the *interpretation* dimension) or "My remarks often have more than one meaning" (the *production* dimension). When Holtgraves gave this scale to people from Korea and the United States, systematic differences were found in both interpretation and production of indirectness, as shown in Figure 2.7. Confirming Yum's analysis, Koreans showed greater indirectness in communication than Americans whether the dimension was interpretation or production.

Third, language in East Asian cultures allows many more opportunities for making *social differentiations* between interactants, reflecting the importance of social status distinctions in those cultures. For example, it is common in East Asian languages for the relationship role of the other person (e.g., teacher, aunt, student) to be used instead of the pronoun "you"—a person might say, "How is aunt today?" instead of "How are you today?" This form of address makes the status relationship between communicators more prominent.

Finally, Yum suggests that the focus in communication is on the *receiver* in East Asia (*receiver centred*) and the *sender* or the communicator in North America

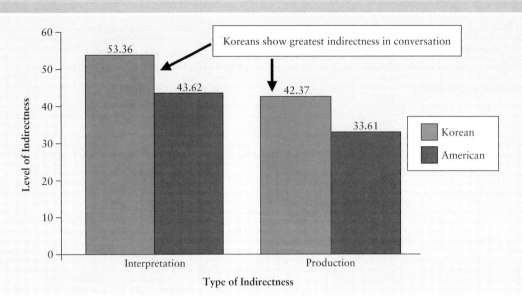

Koreans show greatest indirectness in conversation

■ Cultural Differences in Indirectness

FIGURE 2.7 Koreans reported greater indirectness than Americans, both in terms of their *interpretation* of others' conversation and their own *production* of indirect communications.

Source: Based on Holtgraves, T. (1997).

(*sender centred*). North American communication research has stressed the ways in which a communicator can get his or her message across to the audience. As we'll see when we look at persuasion in Chapter 3, research has traditionally investigated ways in which a communicator can be more effective by looking at characteristics such as the attractiveness and credibility of the sender and the nature of message. In contrast, East Asian communication is premised on the notion that the *receiver* of a communication should be listening, interpreting, and even anticipating the sender's communication and needs. In Japan, for example, the receiver is often expected to guess and anticipate the other person's needs to save him or her the embarrassment of making a request that may not be possible (Lebra, 1976). Apparently, a common social puzzle for East Asian foreign students is the way in which their North American hosts keeps asking them what they want rather than trying to anticipate their needs (Yum, 2000).

Yum's distinction between the East Asian and North American styles of communication should alert us to the importance in everyday communication with people from different cultural backgrounds. A person from a cultural group that uses more direct communication might, for example, completely miss an attempt by someone with a more indirect communication style to be subtle and indirect. And even if the attempt is correctly perceived, it might be seen as somewhat manipu-

lative (Holtgraves, 1997). From the perspective of a person with an indirect style, the directness of someone from another group might appear crass and intrusive, if not distinctly impolite (Holtgraves & Yang, 1990).

Although the potential for miscommunication is very real between those from different cultures, we often manage to avoid real conflict. To some extent this may be because we make allowances for someone when we know that person is from a very different background (e.g., Giles, Mulac, Bradac, & Johnson, 1986). Nonetheless, misunderstandings between cultural groups are not infrequent and can have serious implications for inter-group relations. Those researching nonverbal communication have stressed its importance for educators (Lee, et al., 1992; Wolfgang, 1979), in courts (Blanck & Rosenthal, 1992), for those in the medical profession (Street & Buller, 1987, 1988), and in business (Graham, 1985; Lee, et al., 1992), as well as in social interaction. As one group of researchers has commented,

The success of intercultural interactions depends on the willingness to learn about specific cultural differences in nonverbal behaviours and messages, and on the patience required to attribute cultural transgressions to culture, rather than to the intention of the individual (Lee, et al., 1992, p. 249).

KEY POINTS

- *Social perception* is concerned with the intake of social information and *social cognition* involves the use and manipulation of such information. These two processes interact in determining the way in which we internalize our social world.

- In order to understand others' emotional states, we often rely on *nonverbal communication*—an unspoken language of facial expressions, eye contact, and body movements and postures.

- Although facial expressions may not be as universal as once believed, they do often provide useful information about others' emotional states. Useful information is also provided by eye contact, *body language*, and touching.

- Research findings indicate that handshaking provides useful nonverbal cues about others' personality, and can influence first impressions of strangers.

- If we pay careful attention to certain nonverbal cues, we can recognize efforts at deception by others—even if these persons are from cultures other than our own.

- Cultures vary in their styles of communication. Comparison between North American and East Asian styles show variation on four dimensions including the directness in verbal communication.

Attribution: Understanding the Causes of Others' Behaviour

Nonverbal communication can be useful in beginning to understand others. Yet eventually, we will want to know more, to understand the causes behind other people's behaviour—*why* they acted as they did. The process through which we seek such information is known as *attribution*. More formally, **attribution** refers to our efforts to understand the causes behind others' behaviour and, on some occasions, the causes behind our behaviour, too (see Figure 2.8). Attribution has been a topic of major interest in social psychology for several decades (e.g., Graham & Folkes, 1990; Heider, 1958; Reid & Miller, 1998).

Attribution The process through which we seek to identify the causes of others' behaviour and so gain knowledge of their stable traits and dispositions.

Theories of Attribution: How We Understand the Social World

Because attribution is complex, many theories have been proposed to explain its operation (e.g., Gilbert, Pelham, & Srull, 1988; Trope, 1986). Here we will focus on three that have been especially influential.

The Theory of Correspondent Inferences: When Does Behaviour Correspond to Character?

The first of these theories—Jones and Davis's (1965) *theory of correspondent inference*—asks how we use information about others' behaviour as a basis for inferring that they possess various traits or characteristics. How can we be sure that someone's behaviour reflects his or her character? According to Jones and Davis's theory (Jones & Davis, 1965; Jones & McGillis, 1976), we accomplish this difficult task by focusing our attention on certain types of actions—those most likely to prove informative.

First, we consider only behaviours that seem to have been *freely chosen*. Often, individuals act in certain ways not because doing so reflects their own preferences or traits, but because external factors leave them little choice. So we tend to ignore or at

■ Attribution: Efforts to Understand the Causes behind Others' Behaviour and Our Own

FIGURE 2.8 We often try to understand *why* other people have acted in certain ways, and sometimes (as shown here), we turn this process inward and ask ourselves, "Why did *I* do what I did?"

"It's so silly. Now I can't even remember why I killed him."

Noncommon Effects Effects produced by a particular cause that could not be produced by any other apparent cause.

least discount behaviours that were somehow forced on the person in question. Second, we pay careful attention to actions that produce what Jones and Davis refer to as <u>noncommon effects</u>—effects that can be caused by one specific factor but not by others. (Don't confuse this word with *uncommon*, which simply means infrequent.) Why are actions that produce noncommon effects informative? Because they allow us to zero in on the causes of others' behaviour. Perhaps a concrete example will help.

Imagine that one of your casual friends has just become engaged. Her future spouse is very handsome, has a great personality, is wildly in love with your friend, and is very rich. What can you learn about her from her decision to marry this man? Not much. There are so many good reasons that you can't choose among them. In contrast, imagine that your friend's fiancé is very handsome but that he treats her with indifference and is known to be extremely boring; also, he has no visible means of support and intends to live on your friend's salary. Does the fact that she is marrying him tell you anything about her personal characteristics? Definitely. You can probably conclude that she places more importance on physical attractiveness in a husband than on personality or wealth. As you can see from this example, we can usually learn more about others from actions on their part that show noncommon effects than from ones that do not.

Finally, Jones and Davis suggest that we also pay greater attention to actions by others that are <u>*low in social desirability*</u> than to actions that are high on this dimension. In other words, we learn more about others' traits or characteristics from actions they perform that are somehow out of the ordinary than from actions that are very much like those performed by most other persons.

In sum, according to the theory proposed by Jones and Davis, we are most likely to <u>conclude that others' behaviour reflects their stable traits</u> (i.e., we are likely to reach accurate or *correspondent inferences* about them) when that behaviour (1) occurs by choice; (2) yields distinctive, noncommon effects; and (3) is low in social desirability.

Kelley's Theory of Causal Attributions: How We Answer the Question Why?

Consider the following events:

- You receive a much lower grade on an exam than you were expecting.
- You phone one of your friends repeatedly and leave messages on her answering machine, but she never returns your calls.

What question would arise in your mind in each of these situations? The answer is clear: *Why?* You would want to know *why* your grade was so low and *why* your friend wouldn't return your calls. In countless life situations, this is the central attributional task we face. We want to know why other people have acted as they have, or why events have turned out in a particular way. Such knowledge is crucial, for only if we understand the causes behind others' actions can we adjust our own actions accordingly and hope to make sense out of the social world. Obviously, the number of specific causes behind others' behaviour is large. To make the task more manageable, therefore, we often begin with a preliminary question: Did others' behaviour stem mainly from *internal causes* (their own characteristics, motives, intentions); mainly from *external causes* (some aspect of the social or physical world); or from a combination of the two? For example, did you receive a lower grade than expected because you didn't study enough (an internal cause), because the questions were difficult and tricky (an external cause), or, perhaps, because of both factors? Revealing insights into how we carry out this initial attributional task are provided by a theory proposed by Kelley (Kelley, 1972; Kelley & Michela, 1980).

According to Kelley, in our attempts to answer the question *why* about others' behaviour, we focus on information relating to three major dimensions. First, we consider **consensus**—the extent to which others react to some stimulus or event in the same manner as the person we are considering. The higher the proportion of other people who react in the same way, the higher the consensus. Second, we consider **consistency**—the extent to which the person in question reacts to the stimulus or event in the same way on other occasions. In other words, consistency involves the extent to which the person's behaviour is unvarying over time. And third, we examine **distinctiveness**—the extent to which the person reacts in the same manner to other, different stimuli or events. (Be careful not to confuse consistency and distinctiveness. Consistency refers to similar reactions to a given stimulus or event at *different times*. Distinctiveness refers to similar reactions to *different stimuli* or events.) If an individual reacts in the same way to a wide range of stimuli, distinctiveness is said be low.

Kelley's theory suggests that we are most likely to attribute another's behaviour to *external causes* under conditions in which consensus, consistency, and distinctiveness are all high. In contrast, we are most likely to attribute another's behaviour to *internal causes* under conditions in which consensus and distinctiveness are low, but consistency is high. Finally, we usually attribute behaviour to a combination of internal and external factors when other combinations of information apply. Perhaps a concrete example will help illustrate the reasonable nature of these suggestions.

Imagine that you see a server in a restaurant flirt with a customer. This behaviour might be fun to observe, but it also raises an interesting question: Why does the server act this way? Because of internal causes or external causes? Is he simply someone who likes to flirt (an internal cause)? Or is the customer extremely attractive (an external cause)? According to Kelley's theory, your decision (as an observer of this scene) would depend on information relating to the three factors mentioned above. First, assume that the following conditions prevail: (1) You observe other servers flirting with this customer (consensus is high); (2) you have seen this server flirt with the same customer on other occasions (consistency is high); and (3) you have *not* seen this server flirt with other customers (distinctiveness is high). Under these conditions—high consensus, consistency,

Consensus The extent to which others react to some stimulus or event in the same manner as the person we are considering.

Consistency The extent to which an individual responds to a given stimulus or situation in the same way on different occasions (i.e., across time).

Distinctiveness The extent to which an individual responds in a similar manner to different stimuli or different situations.

■ Kelley's Theory of Causal Attribution: An Example

FIGURE 2.9 Under the conditions shown in the top portion of this figure, we would attribute the server's behaviour to external causes (e.g., the customer is highly attractive). Under the conditions shown in the lower portion, however, we would attribute the behaviour to internal causes (e.g., this server likes to flirt).

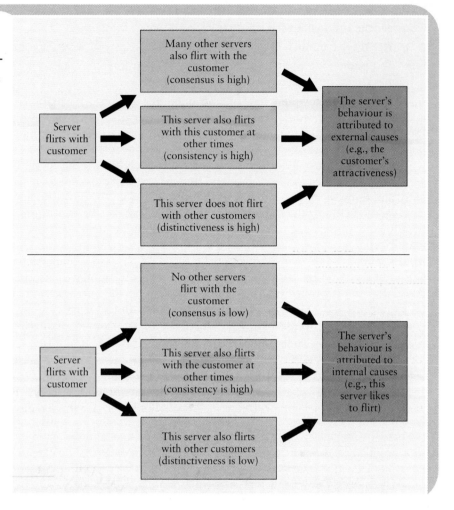

and distinctiveness—you would probably attribute the clerk's behaviour to external causes: this customer is really attractive and that's why the server flirts with her.

Now, in contrast, assume these conditions exist: (1) No other servers flirt with the customer (consensus is low); (2) you have seen this server flirt with the same customer on other occasions (consistency is high); and (3) you have seen this server flirt with many other customers, too (distinctiveness is low). In this case, Kelley's theory suggests that you would attribute the server's behaviour to internal causes: the server is simply a person who likes to flirt (see Figure 2.9).

As we noted earlier, Kelley's theory is reasonable; and it seems applicable to a wide range of social situations. Further, basic aspects of the theory have been confirmed by the results of many different studies (e.g., Harvey & Weary, 1989; McArthur, 1972). We should note, though, that research on the theory also suggests the need for certain extensions. Some of these are described below.

Coping with Multiple Causal Factors: Discounting and Augmenting

Suppose that one day your boss stops by your desk and praises your work, telling you that you are doing a wonderful job and that she is glad to have you working with her. She does this in front of several other employees, who all congratulate you after she leaves. For the rest of the morning you feel great. But then, after lunch, she calls you into her office and asks if you would be willing to take on an extra, difficult work assignment. Now you begin to wonder: Why did she praise your work? Because she really wanted to thank you for doing such a good job *or* because she knew all along that she was going to ask you to take on extra work? There are two possible causes behind her behaviour, and because there are, you may well engage in what social psychologists term **discounting**—you will view the first possible cause (her genuine desire to give you positive feedback) as less important or likely because another possible cause for this action exists, too (i.e., she wanted to "set you up" to agree with her request to do extra work). Many studies indicate that discounting is a common occurrence and exerts a strong impact upon our attributions in many situations (e.g., Gilbert & Malone, 1995; Morris & Larrick, 1995; Trope & Liberman, 1996). However, it is far from universal. Recent research has shown that some individuals are less willing to dismiss any causal factor as important when they consider multiple causes. Discounting is, therefore, much less likely among people who show this cognitive tendency (McClure, 1998).

Now, imagine the same situation with one difference: Your boss has a well-known policy against giving employees feedback publicly, in front of other persons. What will you conclude about her behaviour now? Probably that it was really motivated by a genuine desire to tell you that she is very pleased with your work. After all, she has done so despite the presence of another factor that would be expected to *prevent* her from doing so (her own policy against public feedback). This illustrates what social psychologists describe as **augmenting**—the tendency to assign added weight or importance to a factor that might facilitate a given behaviour when both this factor and another factor that might *inhibit* such behaviour are both present, *yet the behaviour still occurs.* (See Figure 2.10 for an overview of both attributional discounting and

Discounting The tendency to attach less importance to one potential cause of some behaviour when other potential causes are also present.

Augmenting The tendency to attach greater importance to a potential cause of behaviour if the behaviour occurs despite the presence of other, inhibitory causes.

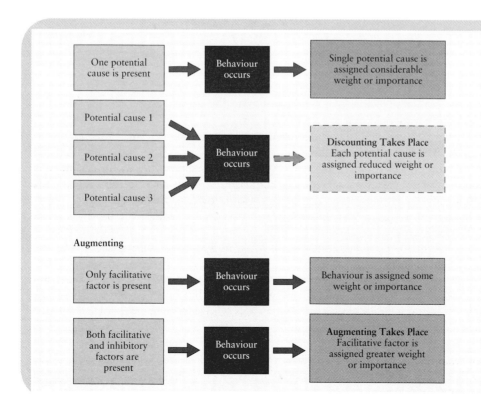

■ Augmenting and Discounting in Causal Attribution.

FIGURE 2.10 According to the *discounting* principle *(upper diagram),* we attach less weight or importance to a given cause of some behaviour when other potential causes of that behaviour are also present. According to the *augmenting* principle *(lower diagram),* we attach greater weight to a potential cause of some behaviour if the behaviour occurs despite the presence of another factor that would tend to inhibit its occurrence.

■ Augmenting in Practice: The Creation of Two Canadian Heroes

FIGURE 2.11 Augmenting has everything to do with how heroes are created. Usually, the people we come to think of as heroes have succeeded *against all odds*. The achievements of Terry Fox and Rick Hansen are two Canadian cases that come to mind, where despite serious disabilities they both had tremendous success athletically and in charity fundraising.

augmenting.) In this case, you conclude that your boss really is very pleased with your behaviour because she praised it publicly despite the presence of a strong inhibitory factor (her policy against public feedback).

Do augmenting and discounting have any practical effects? Absolutely. For instance, augmenting has everything to do with how heroes are created. Usually, the people we come to think of as heroes have succeeded *against all odds*. That is, there have been inhibitory factors present that appear almost insurmountable. When individuals triumph in spite of these barriers, we augment the weight given to their efforts and character to the point that they seem heroic to us. The achievements of Terry Fox and Rick Hansen are two Canadian cases that come to mind, where despite serious disabilities they both had tremendous success athletically and in charity fundraising (see Figure 2.11).

Another example comes from a recent research study by Baron, Markman, and Hirsa (2001). Baron and his colleagues hypothesized that because women face larger obstacles to becoming entrepreneurs (i.e., persons who start their own businesses) than do men, women who actually become entrepreneurs will benefit from attributional augmenting. Specifically, because they have become entrepreneurs despite the presence of major obstacles (inhibitory factors), such women will be perceived more favourably than will women in other fields (e.g., women who are managers). Results confirmed these hypotheses. Ratings on characteristics such as assertiveness, decisiveness, and seriousness about their careers were significantly more favourable for women described as being entrepreneurs than for those described as being managers. For men, however, ratings were not significantly affected by whether they were described as being entrepreneurs or managers because they face smaller obstacles to becoming entrepreneurs. Because positive perceptions of women entrepreneurs may help them to overcome the daunting obstacles they continue to face, even after "taking the plunge" and starting their own businesses (e.g., Cooper, Gimeno-Gascon, & Woo, 1994; Cliff, 1998), these findings appear to have practical-and encouraging-implications.

Weiner's Model of Causal Attribution

While we are often very interested in knowing whether others' behaviour stemmed mainly from internal or external causes, this is not the entire story according to Bernard Weiner (1985, 1995). Particularly when we are looking at the causes for success or failure, we are also concerned with two other questions: (1) Are the causal factors that influence someone's behaviour likely to be *stable* over time or to change? And (2) are these factors *controllable*—can the individual change or influence them if she or he wishes to (Weiner, 1993, 1995)? These dimensions are independent of the internal–external dimension, which is termed *locus* in this theory, referring to the location of the cause—whether internal or external to the actor. For instance, some internal causes of behaviour, such as personality traits and temperament, tend to be quite *stable* over time (e.g., Miles & Carey, 1997). If you did badly on an exam because you were nervous, we could *predict* that this stable trait might influence your academic success in the future. In contrast, other internal causes can and often do change greatly—for instance, motives, health, and fatigue. If these factors were the cause of your exam performance, we would predict this was only a temporary (unstable) effect. Similarly, some internal causes are *controllable*; individuals can, if they wish, learn to hold their tempers in check. Other internal causes, such as chronic illnesses or disabilities, are not. Evidence suggests that the controllable dimension influences our conclusions about whether others are *personally responsible* for their own actions. So criminals whose behaviour is seen as under their own control are held more responsible (and seen as deserving greater punishment) than those whose behaviour is seen as uncontrollable (e.g., Graham, Weiner, & Zucker, 1997). In sum then, a large number of studies have indicated that in trying to understand the causes behind others' failure and success, we do take note of all three of these dimensions—internal–external, stable–unstable, and controllable—uncontrollable (Weiner, 1985, 1995).

KEY POINTS

- In order to obtain information about others' lasting traits, motives, and intentions, we often engage in *attribution*—efforts to understand why others have acted as they have.
- According to Jones and Davis's *theory of correspondent inference*, we attempt to infer others' traits from observing certain aspects of their behaviour—especially behaviour that is freely chosen, produces *noncommon effects,* and is low in social desirability.
- According to Kelley's *theory of causal attribution*, we are interested in the question of whether others' behaviour stemmed from internal or external causes. To answer this question, we focus on information relating to *consensus, consistency,* and *distinctiveness.*

- When two or more potential causes of another person's behaviour exist, we tend to downplay the importance of each—an effect known as the *discounting principle*. When a cause that facilitates a behaviour and a cause that inhibits it both exist but the behaviour still occurs, we assign added weight to the facilitative factor—the *augmenting principle*. Augmenting occurs in many situations. For instance, it can contribute to the perception of heroism and boost perceptions of women who become entrepreneurs.

- Weiner's theory of attribution suggests that in addition to the internal–external dimension of attribution, termed *locus*, we are also interested in the extent to which causal factors are *stable* or changeable over time, and *controllable*, or can be influenced by the individual. These additional dimensions relate to the assignment of personal responsibility.

Attribution: Some Basic Sources of Bias

A basic theme we'll develop throughout this book is that although we generally do a good job in terms of thinking about the social world, we are far from perfect in this respect. In fact, our efforts to understand other persons—and ourselves—are subject to several types of errors that can lead us to false conclusions about why others have acted as they have and how they will behave in the future. Let's take a look at several of these errors now.

The Fundamental Attribution Error: Overestimating the Role of Dispositional Causes

Imagine that you witness the following scene. A man arrives at a meeting 40 minutes late. On entering, he drops his notes all over the floor. While he is trying to pick them up, his glasses fall off and break. Later he spills coffee all over the desk. How would you explain these events? The chances are good that you would reach conclusions such as these: this person is disorganized, clumsy, and generally incompetent. Are such attributions accurate? Perhaps. But it is also possible that the man was late because of unavoidable delays at the airport, dropped his notes because they were printed on very slick paper, and spilled the coffee because the cup was too hot to hold.

The fact that you would be less likely to consider such potential external causes illustrates what Jones (1979) labelled the *correspondence bias*—the tendency to explain others' actions as corresponding to their dispositions. This bias seems to be so general in scope that most social psychologists refer to it as the **fundamental attribution error** overestimating the impact of internal causes on others' behaviour, even in the presence of clear situational causes (e.g., Gilbert & Malone, 1995). In short, we tend to perceive others as acting as they do because they are "that kind of person," rather than because of the many external factors that may influence their behaviour. We should add that while the fundamental attribution error does seem to be very widespread in occurrence, research findings (e.g., Van Overwalle, 1997) indicate that the tendency to attribute others' actions to dispositional (internal) causes seems to occur most strongly in situations in which both consensus and distinctiveness are low, as predicted by Kelley's theory.

The major explanation for the occurrence of this bias has emphasized that when we observe another person's behaviour, we tend to be focused on his or her actions. The person, rather than the situation, has what is termed *perceptual salience* (i.e., is more perceptually prominent to the observer). Further, even if we notice the situation, we tend not to adjust our first impression to allow for the impact of external events or

Fundamental Attribution Error
The tendency to overestimate the impact of dispositional (internal) causes on others' behaviour even in the presence of clear situational causes; also known as the *correspondence bias*.

perhaps we just give them less weight (Gilbert & Malone, 1995). Whatever the basis for the fundamental attribution error, it has important implications. For example, it suggests that even if individuals are made aware of the situational forces that adversely affect disadvantaged groups in a society (e.g., poor diet, shattered family life), they may still perceive these persons as "bad" and responsible for their own plight. In such cases, the fundamental attribution error can have serious social consequences.

However common and inevitable the fundamental attribution error may seem, there is evidence that it is less fundamental than was assumed for many years. As we will discuss in a later section, *culture* appears to have an impact on whether we ignore situational factors.

The Actor–Observer Effect: You Fell; I Was Pushed

Another and closely related type of attributional error involves our tendency to attribute our own behaviour to situational (external) causes, but that of others to dispositional (internal) ones. Thus, when we see another person trip and fall, we tend to attribute this event to his or her clumsiness. If *we* trip, however, we are more likely to attribute this event to situational causes, such as ice on the sidewalk. This bias in our attributions is known as the **actor–observer effect** (Jones & Nisbett, 1971) and has been observed in many different contexts.

Why does the actor–observer effect occur? In part, because we are quite aware of the many external factors affecting our own actions but are less aware of such factors when we turn our attention to the actions of other persons. Thus, we tend to perceive our own behaviour as arising largely from situational causes, but that of others as deriving mainly from their traits or dispositions.

Actor–Observer Effect The tendency to attribute our own behaviour mainly to situational causes but the behaviour of others mainly to internal (dispositional) causes.

The Self-Serving Bias: "I'm Good; You're Lucky"

Suppose that you write a term paper for one of your courses. When you get it back you find the following comment on the first page: "An outstanding paper—one of the best I've read in years. A+." To what will you attribute this success? If you are like most people, you will likely explain your success in terms of internal causes—your high level of talent, the tremendous amount of effort you invested in writing the paper, and so on.

Now, in contrast, imagine that when you get your paper back, this comment is written on it: "Horrible paper—one of the worst I've read in years. D–." How will you interpret this outcome? In all likelihood, you will be sorely tempted to focus mainly on external (situational) factors—the difficulty of the task, your professor's unreasonable standards, and so on.

This tendency to attribute positive outcomes to internal causes but negative ones to external factors is known as the **self-serving bias,** and it can have a powerful effect on social relations (Brown & Rogers, 1991; Miller & Ross, 1975).

Why does this bias in our attributions occur? Several possibilities have been suggested, but most of these can be classified into two categories: cognitive and motivational explanations. The *cognitive* model suggests that the self-serving bias stems primarily from certain tendencies in the way we process social information (Ross, 1977). Specifically, it suggests that we attribute positive outcomes to internal causes but negative ones to external causes because we *expect* to succeed, and we have a stronger tendency to attribute expected outcomes to internal causes than to external causes. In contrast, the *motivational* explanation suggests that the self-serving bias stems from our need to protect and enhance our self-esteem, or the related desire to look good in the eyes of others (Greenberg, Pyszczynski, & Solomon, 1982). While both cognitive and motivational factors may well play a role in this type of attributional error, research evidence seems to offer more support for the motivational view (e.g., Brown & Rogers, 1991).

Self-Serving Bias The tendency to attribute our own positive outcomes to internal causes but our own negative outcomes to external causes.

Some of the most interesting evidence to emerge from cross-cultural psychology has suggested that frequency of these biases may, at least in part, stem from cultural individualism. As we will see in the next section, the self-serving bias as well as the fundamental attribution error may not be the universal tendencies they were assumed to be. In fact, they appear to be much less common in non-Western cultures.

Culture and Attribution: Holistic versus Analytic Thought

One of the most important developments to emerge from cultural psychology has been an increased understanding of the impact of culture on our cognitive processes. And much of this understanding has arisen from cross-cultural research into attribution processes. Over the last two decades, research has clearly demonstrated that culture has an impact on causal reasoning and in particular on the use of attributional biases.

Beginning in the 1980s, research repeatedly found that those in more collectivistic cultures, such as China and Japan, show the *fundamental attribution error* (FAE) to a lesser degree than those in individualistic cultures such as Canada and the United States (see Norenzayan & Nisbett, 2000). In her classic study, Miller asked people in India and the United States to recount real-life instances of other people's behaviour and then to explain why the behaviour occurred. She found that adult Americans showed the FAE as expected. They used many more internal than external attributions, explaining others' behaviour as due to their dispositions (e.g., kindness or dishonesty). For Indians, the reverse was true. They were much more likely to explain other's behaviour as due to external situational factors rather than to internal dispositions. A more recent example comes from Choi and Nisbett (1998). These researchers asked students in the United States and Korea to read essays supposedly written by another person. The essays were either in favour of or against capital punishment, and participants were led to believe that the writer either chose their position freely, or was instructed to write an essay favouring one point of view or the other. When asked questions about the writer's actual attitude toward capital punishment, once again U.S. students showed the FAE quite strongly: they acted as if the essay reflected the writer's true attitudes even if the writer had been *instructed* to write the essay they read. In contrast, Korean students showed this bias to a much weaker degree; indeed, in one condition, when it was made clear that the essay writer had simply repeated arguments given to him by the researchers, they showed no FAE at all!

The impact of culture can also be observed in studies of the *self-serving bias*. For example, Lee and Seligman (1997) found that Americans of European descent showed a larger self-serving bias than either Chinese Americans or mainland Chinese. To date, many studies of both adults and children have shown that the self-serving bias is much less prevalent among those from collectivistic backgrounds (see Smith & Bond, 1998). That is, people from collectivistic cultures tend to make fewer internal attributions when they succeed and more internal attributions when they fail. In some cases, there is a complete reversal of the self-serving bias, and this has been termed a *self-effacement* or *modesty bias*—individuals will make internal attributions for their own failure and external attributions for their own success (e.g., Mizokawa & Ryckman, 1990; Wan & Bond, 1982). Further, Chinese students who used this style of attribution were liked more by their peers than those who did not (Bond, et al., 1982), suggesting that such attributions are an important part of social relations.

Now that these cultural differences have been well documented, researchers have turned to explaining their origin. One starting point is the fact that *both* the FAE and the self-serving bias are reduced among non-Western cultures, suggesting that perhaps a common cognitive process is involved. Nisbett and colleagues (e.g., Nisbett,

Peng, Choi, & Norenzayan, 2001) have suggested that the common cognitive mechanism is a tendency on the part of those from East Asian and other collective cultures to *take greater account of the impact of the social situation* on behaviour. Note, however, that researchers are *not* claiming that dispositional and other internal causes are ignored, but that the social situation is usually *also* considered.

To test the suggestion that the root of these cultural differences lies in a tendency to take greater account of the social situation, Norenzayan and colleagues (Norenzayan, Choi, & Nisbett, 1999) asked Koreans and Americans how much they agreed with three theoretical perspectives: a *strongly dispositional* philosophy (people's behaviour is mostly determined by the their personal characteristics); a *strongly situationist* philosophy suggesting that behaviour is mostly determined by the situation in which people find themselves; and an *interactionist* perspective suggesting that behaviour is always jointly determined by personality and the situation. There were no differences in the level of agreement with the dispositional perspective—Koreans and Americans endorsed this philosophy to the same degree. However, Koreans endorsed both the situationist and the interactionist perspectives significantly more than Americans did. As expected, East Asians were more sensitive to the importance of situational factors, either alone or in interaction with personality dispositions.

How could a tendency to take account of situational factors lead to a reduction in the FAE and the self-serving bias? Imagine, as is the case for many from collective backgrounds, that your culture has primed you to notice the social and physical context in which someone acts. In that case, it would be unlikely that you could completely ignore the situation as a contributing causal factor. So, rather than attributing a person's actions to his or her disposition alone, you would automatically take account of the environment around the person and feel that it must also have had an impact on his or her behaviour. As a result, the FAE would much less likely to occur. Similarly, if the social situation was an ever-present force to be reckoned with, when it came to your own success and failure, you would have a greater tendency to share both the credit for success as well as the blame for failure with others in the social world or with situational forces generally. The self-serving bias in attribution would, therefore, also be less common.

Nisbett and colleagues (2001) have gone further in looking at the origins of this situationist versus dispositional difference and suggested that it has its roots in the philosophical foundations of East Asian and European societies. Specifically, the East Asian philosophy of Confucianism has led to more *holistic thinking*, whereas classical Greek philosophy has led to more *analytic thinking* among Europeans.

Holistic thought is an orientation to the context or "field" *as a whole*. Understanding people means focusing on the *relationships* between them and their social world. People's behaviour will tend to be explained in terms of those relationships and will seldom be seen as independent of their physical and social contexts. More generally, this type of thought involves understanding the world through attempting to encompass as many different perspectives as possible, then finding a "middle way" between apparently contradictory views. Knowledge is based on experience rather than abstract logic.

In contrast, **analytic thought** focuses on individuals as *detached from their context*. The characteristics of individuals are used to explain their internal nature and their behaviour. So from this perspective, to understand people we should analyze their internal characteristics and see their actions as originating from within. Understanding the world generally is seen as rule-bound and logical—objects are classified based on their characteristics, clear rules are used to group them, and formal logic is used to eliminate any contradictions.

Holistic Thought
Thought that is oriented to take account of the field as a whole and the relationships between people and their contexts. It emphasizes experience-based knowledge, encompassing many perspectives and finding a synthesis of these. Explaining the causes of behaviour will tend to take account of both the person and the situation.

Analytic Thought
Thought that is oriented to people and their characteristics, independent of the context. It emphasizes abstract and logical thinking to reach the correct conclusion. Explaining the causes of behaviour will tend to focus more on the person and place greater weight on dispositional causes.

Psychologically, the implications of these insights are profound. Nisbett and colleagues (2001) believe that these differences in thought are based not only on differences between East Asian and Western social behaviour at the current time, but are also based in centuries of historical development leading to distinct practices in social institutions such as education, the legal system, politics, and religion.

KEY POINTS

- Attribution is subject to many potential sources of error. One of the most important of these is the *fundamental attribution error (FAE)*, sometimes called the correspondence bias, which is the tendency to explain others' actions as stemming from internal dispositions even in the presence of situational causes.

- Two other attributional errors are the *actor–observer effect*—the tendency to attribute our own behaviour to external (situational) causes but that of others to internal causes—and the *self-serving bias*—the tendency to attribute our own positive outcomes to internal causes but negative ones to external causes.

- The strength of the fundamental attribution error and the self-serving bias differs across cultures, being stronger in Western, individualistic societies than in Asian, collectivistic cultures. This cultural difference has recently been explained as due to a more fundamental difference between *holistic thought*, developed in East Asian cultures, and *analytic thought*, developed in European cultures.

Coping with Information Overload: Schemas, Heuristics, and Automatic Processing

A few months ago, I (Robert Baron) was driving to my office. On the way, I stopped for a red light at a very busy intersection. The driver of the car in front of me was talking on her cell phone, and I could see from the way she shook her head and waved her arms that it was an important conversation. Then, suddenly, although the light was still red, she began to roll forward, straight into the intersection. I braced for the worst and watched in horror as cars from both directions honked their horns, swerved, and hit their brakes to avoid colliding with her. Fortunately, she made it through without an accident, but I could tell that she was very shaken by the experience; she pulled over and got out of her car. As I drove past her (after the light turned green, of course!), I could see her standing there, still trying to catch her breath.

Why begin with this incident? Because it illustrates several important points about <u>social cognition</u>—how, in essence, our minds work as we try to understand the people around us—that are relevant to this section. First, it often occurs "on automatic." In many situations, we can process information from the world around us (information brought to us by our senses) in a seemingly automatic, effortless, and unintentional manner. This is why we can often do two things at once—drive and listen to the radio, tie our shoelaces while talking to a friend, brush our teeth while thinking about our plans for the weekend (see Figure 2.12). For instance, once we know that someone belongs to a specific social group (e.g., French Canadian, Chinese, Arabic), we tend to assume, often in an automatic and unintentional manner, that they possess certain traits (e.g., see Bargh, Chen, & Burrows, 1996; Greenwald, McGhee, & Schwartz, 1998).

■ Automatic Processes in Cognition

FIGURE 2.12 Because our cognitions *can go on automatic,* we are capable of doing two things at the same time—for example, talk to a friend while driving—but not always without cost. If *information overload* occurs—too many demands are made on our cognitive capacity—our efficiency may suffer and the results can sometimes be dangerous!

Second, and on the other side of the cognitive coin, this traffic incident also illustrates the fact that our *cognitive capacities are definitely limited*. Because of this, in involved social situations it is all too easy for the amount of information we are coping with to exceed our capacity—*information overload* occurs. Yes, the driver in question could sometimes talk on the phone and drive at the same time (although whether she could drive *safely* is an open question currently being debated around the world). On this day, however, the conversation was so absorbing or complex that she "lost it" where driving was concerned and put herself and many other motorists in danger. In an attempt to cope with the amount of social information we face, we often attempt to organize information (into *schemas*) or adopt mental shortcuts (termed *heuristics*) designed to save mental effort and preserve our precious cognitive capacity (e.g., Jonas et al., 2001). While these succeed in reducing such effort, they do so at a cost: sometimes, they lead us into serious errors in our thinking about others.

Finally, this incident also illustrates the important *links between cognition and affect*—how we think and how we feel. After rolling slowly through the intersection, the driver suddenly realized what she had done. As she thought about what might have occurred—a devastating or even fatal accident—she experienced a powerful emotional reaction. As we'll soon see, the link between cognition and affect works both ways: our thinking can influence our emotions and feelings, and our feelings, in turn, can shape our thoughts (e.g., Forgas, 1994).

Our discussion of these cognitive processes will first examine *schemas*. These mental structures or frameworks allow us to organize large amounts of diverse information in an efficient manner (Fiske & Taylor, 1991). Second, we'll turn to *heuristics*, cognitive shortcuts and strategies that help us to make decisions quickly and easily. Third, we'll examine several *biases in social cognition*—tendencies to pay more attention to some kinds of information than to others, sometimes leading to conclusions that are less than accurate. Finally, we will explore the link between *affect*—our current feelings or moods—and social cognition.

Schemas: Organizing Social Information

Schemas Mental frameworks centring around a specific theme that help us to organize social information.

One key finding of research on social cognition is this: Our thoughts about the social world are definitely not a mixture of random ideas and knowledge. On the contrary, information we have acquired through experience is organized into cognitive structures known as <u>schemas</u> (e.g., Fiske & Taylor, 1991; Wyer & Srull, 1994). In essence, schemas can be thought of as "mental scaffolds"—cognitive structures that hold and organize information. Schemas are important because, once formed, they exert powerful effects on the processing of information related to them. For example, they influence which aspects of the social world are selected for attention, what information is entered into memory, what is later retrieved from memory storage, and how it is interpreted (Wyer & Srull, 1994). Schemas can be centred around types of persons (*person schemas*), social roles (*role schemas*), or even common events (*scripts*) such as how to behave in a restaurant. We'll consider another, and very important, type of schema—the self-schema—in Chapter 4.

In these respects schemas play a key role in our understanding of other persons, ourselves, and the social world generally. Their main function is to help us cope with information overload by speeding up the processes of social cognition. However, on the down side, because schemas focus our attention on *particular* aspects of incoming information, some other information about the social world is lost.

As mentioned, schemas have an important influence on basic aspects of social cognition (Wyer & Srull, 1994). With respect to *attention*, schemas often act as a kind of filter: only information consistent with them "registers" and enters our consciousness. Information that does not fit with our schemas is often ignored (Fiske, 1993), unless it is so extreme that we can't help but notice it. And even then, it is often discounted as "the exception that proves the rule." In the *encoding* process—determining which information is entered into memory—the effects of schemas are more complex. It is a basic fact that information that becomes the focus of our attention is much more likely to be stored in long-term memory. So, in general, it is information that is consistent with our schemas that is encoded. However, information that is sharply inconsistent with our schemas—information that does *not* agree with our expectations in a given situation—may sometimes be encoded into a separate memory location and marked with a unique "tag." After all, it is so unexpected that it literally seizes our attention and almost forces us to place it in long-term memory (Stangor & McMillan, 1992). That leads us to the third process: *retrieval from memory*. What information is most readily remembered—information that is consistent with our schemas or information that is inconsistent with these mental frameworks? This is a complex question that has been investigated in many different studies. And there is no simple answer. Rather, this depends on the measure of memory employed. In general, people tend to *report* information consistent with their schemas, but, in fact, research shows that information inconsistent with schemas may also be strongly present in memory (Stangor & McMillan, 1992).

At this point, it's important to note that the effects of schemas on social cognition (e.g., what we remember, how we use this information to make decisions or judgments) are strongly influenced by several other factors. For instance, such effects are stronger when schemas are themselves strong and well developed (e.g., Stangor & McMillan, 1992; Tice, Bratslavky, & Baumeister, 2000), and stronger when *cognitive load*—how much mental effort we are expending at a given time—is high rather than low (e.g., Kunda, 1999). In other words, when we are trying to handle a lot of social information at one time, we fall back upon schemas because these frameworks allow us to process this information with less effort.

Before concluding, we should call attention to the fact that although schemas are based on our past experience (they reflect knowledge we have extracted from our experiences in the social world) and are often helpful to us, they have a serious downside, too. By influencing what we notice, entering into memory, and later remembering, schemas can produce distortions in our understanding of the social world. For example, as we'll see in Chapter 5, schemas play an important role in prejudice, forming one basic component of stereotypes about specific social groups. And, unfortunately, once they are formed, schemas are often very resistant to change—they show a strong **perseverance effect**, remaining unchanged even in the face of contradictory information (e.g., Kunda & Oleson, 1995).

For a discussion of an even more unsettling effect of schemas—the fact that they can often be *self-confirming*-please see the Cornerstones section below.

Perseverance Effect
The tendency for beliefs and schemas to remain unchanged even in the face of contradictory information.

Cornerstones

Evidence for the Self-Confirming Nature of Schemas: The Self-Fulfilling Prophecy

In 1999, Statistics Canada asked teachers and parents of elementary students about their expectations for the children's educational futures. Whereas 60 percent of parents at the lowest income level expected their children to become university graduates, teachers of these same children expected fewer than 20 percent of them to graduate from university. The perceptions of parents in higher income brackets and the teachers of their children did not show as great a disparity. On hearing of these findings, a coordinator of parent programs for the Toronto School Board was quoted as saying, "If someone feels you are not capable, you do not feel capable and you do not perform well" (Galt, 1999). The coordinator is suggesting that if teachers have low expectations of their students, this will be fulfilled in their students' results—see Figure 2.13. But can a teacher's expectations have such a profound effect?

Research suggests that they can. Schemas can influence expectations and produce such effects,

Self-Fulfilling Prophecies
Predictions that, in a sense, make themselves come true.

which are sometimes described as self-fulfilling prophecies—predictions that, in a sense, make themselves come true. The first evidence for such effects was provided by Robert Rosenthal and Lenore Jacobson (1968) during the turbulent 1960s. During that period there was growing concern over the possibility that teachers' beliefs about minority students—their schemas for such youngsters—were causing them to treat such children differently (less favourably) than majority-group students, and that as a result the minority-group students were falling farther and farther behind. No, the teachers weren't overtly prejudiced; rather, their behaviour was shaped by their expectations and beliefs—their schemas for different racial or ethnic groups.

To gather evidence on the possible occurrence of such effects, Rosenthal and Jacobson conducted an

■ The Self-Fulfilling Prophecy

FIGURE 2.13 Research suggests that teachers' expectations about their students can act as *self-fulfilling prophecies*—can influence students' behaviour in the direction expected. In the light of Statistics Canada findings that teachers have much lower expectations of children from low-income families, we can anticipate that such children will in fact achieve less.

ingenious study that exerted a profound effect on subsequent research in social psychology. They went to an elementary school in San Francisco and administered an IQ test to all students. They then told the teachers that some of the students had scored very high and were about to bloom academically. In fact, this was not true: the researchers chose the names of these students randomly. But Rosenthal and Jacobson predicted that this information might change teachers' expectations (and schemas) about these children, and hence their behaviour toward them. Teachers were not given such information about other students, who constituted a control group.

To check on their prediction, Rosenthal and Jacobson returned eight months later and tested both groups of children once again. Results were clear—and dramatic: those who had been described as "bloomers" to their teachers showed significantly larger gains on the IQ test than those in the control group. In short, teachers' beliefs about the students had operated in a self-fulfilling manner: the students teachers believed would bloom academically actually did so.

How did such effects occur? In part, through the impact of schemas on the teachers' behaviour. Further research (Rosenthal, 1994) indicated that teachers gave the bloomers more personal attention, more challenging tasks, more and better feedback, and more opportunities to respond in class. In short, the teachers acted in ways that benefited the students they expected to bloom, and as a result, these youngsters really did.

As a result of this early research, social psychologists began to search for other self-confirming effects of schemas in many settings—in education, therapy, and business, to name just a few. They soon uncovered much evidence that schemas do often shape behaviour in ways that lead to their confirmation. For example, they soon found that teachers' lower expectations for minority students or females often undermined the confidence of these groups and actually contributed to poorer performance by them (e.g., Sadker & Sadker, 1994). So the research conducted by Rosenthal and Jacobson has had far-reaching effects and can be viewed as one important cornerstone of research in our field.

KEY POINTS

- Social cognitive processes have limited capacity and can suffer from *information overload*. We cope through the use of automatic thinking, by being selective, and by using shortcuts to reduce mental effort.

- *Schemas*—mental frameworks centring around a specific theme—help us to organize social information. They can relate to persons or events.

- Once formed, schemas exert powerful effects on what we notice (attention), enter into memory (encoding), and later remember (retrieval). Even in the face of disconfirming information, schemas tend to persist, showing the *perseverance effect*.

- Schemas can also exert self-confirming effects—the *self-fulfilling prophecy*—causing us to behave in ways that confirm them.

Heuristics and Automatic Processing: Cognitive Shortcuts

While schemas help us to *organize* information, our next topics—heuristics and automatic processing—help us to take *shortcuts* in decision-making or coming to conclusions about the social world. Together these two processes are the backbone of our means of dealing with information overload. To be successful, such cognitive shortcuts must have two properties. First, they must provide a quick and simple way of dealing with large amounts of social information. Second, they must work—they must be reasonably accurate most of the time, but notice this isn't *all* the time.

<u>Heuristics</u> are simple decision-making rules we often use to make inferences or draw conclusions quickly and easily. To understand how heuristics work, consider an analogy. Suppose you want to estimate the dimensions of a room but don't have a tape measure. What will you do? One possibility is to pace off the length and width of the room by placing one foot almost exactly in front of the other. Since the distance from the heel to the toe of an adult's foot is approximately 12 inches, you will be able to get rough estimates of the room's dimensions through this "quick-and-dirty" method.

Heuristics Simple rules for making complex decisions or drawing inferences in a rapid and seemingly effortless manner.

Another means of dealing with the fact that the social world is complex yet our information-processing capacity is limited is to put many activities—including some aspects of social thought and social behaviour—on *automatic* (or *automatic processing*, as psychologists term it; e.g., Ohman, Lundqvist, & Esteves, 2001). After discussing several heuristics, therefore, we'll consider this process and its effects.

In a similar manner, we make use of many different mental heuristics in our efforts to think about and use social information. Two of these that are used frequently in everyday life are known as *representativeness* and *availability*. These heuristics can also lead to a number of biases or fallacies (false reasoning or conclusions).

Representativeness: Judging by Resemblance

Imagine that you have just met your neighbour for the first time. On the basis of a brief conversation with her, you determine that she is very neat in her habits, has a good vocabulary, reads many books, is somewhat shy, and dresses conservatively. Later you realize that she did not mention what she does for a living. Is she a business executive, a librarian, a server, a lawyer, or a dancer? One quick way of making a guess is to compare her with other members of each of these occupations; simply ask yourself how well she resembles persons you have met in each of these fields. If you proceed in this fashion, you may well conclude that she is a librarian. After all, her traits seem to

Representativeness Heuristic A strategy for making judgments based on the extent to which current stimuli or events resemble ones we view as being typical.

resemble the traits many people associate with librarians more closely than the traits of dancers, lawyers, or servers. In this instance, you would be using the <u>representativeness heuristic</u>. In other words, you would make your judgment on the basis of a relatively simple rule: *The more similar an individual is to "typical" members of a given group, the more likely he or she is to also belong to that group.*

Are such judgments accurate? Often they are, because belonging to certain groups does affect the behaviour and style of persons in them, and because people with certain traits are attracted to particular groups in the first place. But sometimes, judgments based on representativeness are wrong, mainly for the following reason: Decisions or judgments made on the basis of this rule tend to ignore *base rates*—the frequency with which given events or patterns (e.g., occupations) occur in the total population (Tversky & Kahneman, 1973; Koehler, 1993). In fact, there are many more business managers than librarians—perhaps 50 times as many! Thus, even though your neighbour seemed more similar to librarians than to managers in her personal traits, the chances are actually higher that she is in business than that she is a librarian. In this and related ways, the representativeness heuristic can lead to errors in our thinking about other persons.

Availability: What Comes to Mind First?

Which is more common—words that start with the letter k (e.g., *king*) or words with k as the third letter (e.g., *awkward*)? Tversky and Kahneman (1982) put this question to more than 100 people. Their findings were revealing. In English there are more than twice as many words with k in third place as there are with k in first place. Yet despite this fact, most of the subjects guessed incorrectly. Why? In part, because of their use of another heuristic—the **availability heuristic**. According to this heuristic, the easier it is to bring instances of some group or category to mind, the more prevalent or important these are judged to be. This heuristic, too, makes good sense: after all, events or objects that are common are usually easier to think of than ones that are less common, because we have had more experience with them. But relying on availability in making social judgments can also lead to errors. For instance, it can lead us to overestimate the likelihood of events that are dramatic but rare, because they are easy to bring to mind. Consistent with this principle, many people fear travel in airplanes more than travel in automobiles, even though the chance of dying in an auto accident is hundreds of times higher (see Figure 2.14). In this and many other situations, the fact that information is easy to remember does not guarantee that it is important or common. Yet our subjective feeling that something is easy to remember may lead us to assume that it is important (Schwartz, et al., 1991). To the extent that this assumption is correct then the availability heuristic can be useful.

Availability Heuristic A strategy for making judgments on the basis of how easily specific kinds of information can be brought to mind.

Interestingly, research suggests that there is more to the availability heuristic than merely the subjective *ease* with which relevant information comes to mind. In addition, the *amount* of information we can bring to mind seems to matter, too (e.g., Schwarz et al., 1991b). The more information we can think of, the greater its impact on our judgments. Which of these two factors is more important? The answer appears to involve the kind of judgment we are making. If it is one involving emotions or feelings, we tend to rely on the "ease" rule, while if it is one involving facts or information, we tend to rely more on the "amount" rule (e.g., Rothman and Hardin, 1997).

Priming: Some Effects of Increased Availability

The availability heuristic has been found to play a role in many aspects of social thought, including the self-serving bias and also in several topics we'll examine in later chapters (e.g., stereotyping; see Chapter 5). In addition, it is related to another especially

■ The Availability Heuristic: Sometimes, It Leads to Errors

FIGURE 2.14 Many people express stronger fears about being hurt or killed in airplane crashes than they do about being hurt or killed in automobile accidents. Yet, in fact, the odds of injury or death are much higher for automobiles. This difference may stem from the fact that airplane crashes are much more dramatic and receive much more attention from the media than do automobile accidents. As a result, airplane crashes are brought to mind more easily and so have a stronger impact on individuals' judgments and thoughts.

important process: <u>priming</u>—increased availability of information resulting from exposure to specific stimuli or events.

Here's a good example of such priming. During the first year of medical school, many students experience the "medical student syndrome": they begin to suspect that they or others have many serious illnesses. An ordinary headache may lead them to wonder if they have a brain tumour, while a mild sore throat may lead to anxiety over the possibility of some rare but fatal type of infection. What accounts for such effects? The explanation favoured by social psychologists is as follows. The students are exposed to descriptions of diseases day after day in their classes and assigned readings. As a result, such information increases in availability and is used more often to interpret physical symptoms.

Priming effects occur in so many contexts that they can be considered an important aspect of social thought (e.g., Higgins & King, 1981; Higgins, Rohles, & Jones, 1977). In fact, research evidence indicates that priming may occur even when individuals are unaware of the priming stimuli—an effect known as *automatic priming* (e.g., Bargh & Pietromonaco, 1982). In other words, the availability of certain kinds of information can be increased by priming stimuli even though we are not aware of having been exposed to these stimuli. This can occur with advertising. You may be talking to friends during a break in your favourite television program and don't notice the commercial break much. Nonetheless, shortly after an advertisement for pizza delivery, you find yourself feeling incredibly hungry—and it must be pizza!

In sum, it appears that priming is a basic fact of social thought. External events and conditions—or even our own thoughts—can increase the availability of specific types of information. And increased availability, in turn, influences our judgments with respect to such information. "If I can think of it," we seem to reason, "then it must be important, frequent, or true," and we often reach such conclusions even if they are not supported by social reality.

Priming Increased availability of information in memory or consciousness, resulting from exposure to specific stimuli or events.

Automatic Processing in Social Thought: Doing Two Things at Once

As we've noted repeatedly, a central dilemma we face with respect to social cognition is this: Our capacity to process information (including social information) is limited, yet daily life floods us with large amounts of information and requires us to deal with it both effectively and efficiently. As we've already seen, heuristics is one means of solving this problem. Another involves **automatic processing**. This occurs when, after extensive experience with a task or type of information, we reach the stage where we can perform the task or process the information in a seemingly effortless, automatic, and nonconscious manner. Do you remember your efforts to learn to ride a bicycle? At first, you had to devote a lot of attention to this task; if you didn't, you would fall down! But as you mastered it, riding required less and less attention until, finally, you could do it while thinking of entirely different topics, or even while engaging in other tasks, such as talking to a friend. So, in many cases, the shift from *controlled processing* (which is effortful and conscious) to *automatic processing* is something we *want* to happen: it saves us a great deal of effort.

To an extent, this is true with respect to social thought as well. For instance, once we have a well-developed schema for a social group (e.g., for doctors or any other profession), we can think in short-hand ways about members of that group. We can, for instance, assume that all doctors will be busy, so it's necessary to get right to the point with them; that they are intelligent but not always very considerate; and so on. But as is usually the case, these gains in efficiency or ease are offset by potential losses in accuracy. For instance, growing evidence indicates that one type of schema—stereotypes— can be activated in an automatic and nonconscious manner by the physical features associated with the stereotyped group (e.g., Pratto & Bargh, 1991). Similarly, attitudes (beliefs and evaluations of some aspect of the social world) may be automatically triggered by the mere presence of the attitude object (e.g., Wegner & Bargh, 1998). Such automatic processing of social information can, of course, lead to serious errors.

Perhaps even more surprising, research findings indicate that schemas, once activated, may even exert seemingly automatic effects on behaviour. In others words, people may act in ways consistent with these schemas, even though they do not intend to do so, and are unaware that they are acting in this manner. A clear illustration of such effects is provided by research conducted by Bargh, Chen, and Burrows (1996).

In one study, these researchers first activated either the schema for the trait of *rudeness* or the schema for the trait of *politeness* through priming. Participants worked on unscrambling scrambled sentences containing words related either to rudeness (e.g., *bold, rude, impolitely, bluntly*) or words related to politeness (*cordially, patiently, polite, courteous, discreetly*). Exposure to words related to schemas has been found, in past research, to prime or activate these mental frameworks. Persons in a third (control) group unscrambled sentences containing words unrelated to either trait (e.g., *exercising, flawlessly, occasionally, rapidly, normally*). After completing these tasks, participants in the study were asked to report back to the experimenter, who would give them additional tasks. When they approached the experimenter, he or she was engaged in a conversation with another person (an accomplice). The experimenter continued this conversation, ignoring the participant. The major dependent measure was whether the participant interrupted the conversation in order to receive further instructions. The researchers predicted that persons for whom the trait *rudeness* had been primed would be more likely to interrupt than would those for whom the trait *politeness* had been primed. As you can see from Figure 2.15, this is precisely what happened.

In another study (Bargh, Chen, & Burrows 1996), subjects who were primed with the stereotype for *elderly* (again through exposure to words related to this schema) actually walked slower! Together, the results of these studies indicate that activating

Automatic Processing This occurs when, after extensive experience with a task or type of information, we reach the stage where we can perform the task or process the information in a seemingly effortless, automatic, and nonconscious manner.

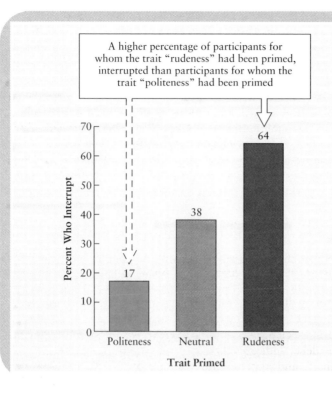

A higher percentage of participants for whom the trait "rudeness" had been primed, interrupted than participants for whom the trait "politeness" had been primed

Percent Who Interrupt (y-axis): 0, 10, 20, 30, 40, 50, 60, 70

Trait Primed (x-axis): Politeness (17), Neutral (38), Rudeness (64)

■ Automatic Processing and Social Behaviour

FIGURE 2.15 Individuals for whom the schema for "rudeness" had been primed were much more likely to interrupt an experimenter's conversation than were individuals for whom the schema for "politeness" had been primed. This was true despite the fact that both groups rated the experimenter the same in terms of politeness.

Source: Based on data from Bargh, Chen, & Burrows, 1996.

stereotypes or schemas can exert seemingly automatic effects on behaviour—effects that occur in the absence of intention or conscious awareness. These findings have important implications. For instance, they suggest that once stereotypes are activated, individuals not only *think* in terms of these mental frameworks—they may actually *behave* in ways consistent with them as well. Thus, negative stereotypes of minority groups may lead the persons possessing them to act in hostile ways toward members of these groups, even if they do not intend to do so. Clearly, then, automatic processing is an important aspect of social thought—one that may often become visible in outward, overt behaviour.

KEY POINTS

- *Heuristics* help us cope with information overload by making decisions in a quick and relatively effortless manner.
- The *representativeness* heuristic, in which we make judgments about others based on how typical they are, can lead to ignoring of base rates.
- The *availability* heuristic is used to make judgments based on the ease and amount of information we can bring to mind.
- *Priming* refers to increased availability of information resulting from exposure to specific stimuli or events.
- Another means of reducing mental effort involves *automatic processing* of social information—processing that occurs in a seemingly automatic, effortless, and nonconscious manner. Research findings indicate that, once activated, schemas and other mental frameworks may influence not only social thought, but social behaviour as well.

Errors in Social Cognition: Why We Are Fallible

Human beings are definitely not computers. Although we can *imagine* being able to reason in a perfectly logical way, we know from our own experience that we often fall short of this goal. We have already seen that in our attempts to cope with information overload through the use of schemas and heuristics, we sometimes jump to inaccurate or biased conclusions. In this section we will extend this exploration of our inaccuracies by looking at a number of systematic biases in social cognition. You will notice that while these biases can lead us to erroneous conclusions, they can also sometimes be adaptive and useful, helping us to interpret and respond to the social world. There are numerous instances of cognitive biases (e.g., Rozin & Nemeroff, 1990; Wilson & Schooler, 1991; Zusne & Jones, 1989): we will focus on some notable recent examples.

Negativity Bias: Paying Extra Attention to Negative Information

Imagine that in describing someone you haven't met, one of your friends mentions many positive things about this person—he or she is pleasant, intelligent, good-looking, friendly, and so on. Then, your friend mentions one negative piece of information: this person is also somewhat conceited. What are you likely to remember? Research findings indicate that, probably, the negative information will stand out in your memory (e.g., Kunda, 1999). Moreover, because of this, the negative information will have a stronger influence on your desire to meet this person than will any one equivalent piece of positive information. Such findings suggest that we show a strong **negativity bias**—greater sensitivity to negative information than to positive information. This is also true of both social information and information about other aspects of the world (see Figure 2.16).

Negativity Bias The fact that we show greater sensitivity to negative information than to positive information.

Why do we have this tendency? From an evolutionary perspective, it makes a great deal of sense. Negative information reflects features of the external world that may be threatening to our safety or well-being. For this reason, it is especially important that we be sensitive to such stimuli and thus able to respond to them quickly.

■ The Negativity Bias in Operation

FIGURE 2.16 As suggested by this cartoon, we tend to be more sensitive to negative information than positive information.

Several research findings offer support for this reasoning. For instance, consider our ability to recognize facial expressions in others. The results of many studies indicate that we are faster and more accurate in detecting negative facial expressions than positive facial expressions as we saw earlier. Further, recent studies of electrical activity in the brain activity indicate that negative stimuli produce larger neural responses than either positive or neutral stimuli (Cacioppo, Gardner, & Berntson, 1999; Crites, 1995). Such findings suggest that the negativity bias operates during very early stages of social cognition—the stage at which we are first evaluating a stimulus on a simple positive—negative dimension. This finding is consistent with the evolutionary perspective, which suggests that quick responses to negative stimuli are often important for survival.

Optimistic Biases: Looking at the Future through Rose-Coloured Glasses

Although the tendency to notice negative information is a strong one, don't despair: despite its existence, we also have a seemingly opposite tendency known as the optimistic bias—a predisposition to expect things to turn out well overall. When we look toward the future, particularly our own, we sometimes tend to be more optimistic than is warranted.

A robust example of such a tendency is termed **unrealistic optimism**—the tendency to believe that you are more likely to experience positive events, and less likely to experience negative events, when compared to similar others. This bias is a common one, particularly where negative life events (e.g., losing your job, becoming alcoholic, getting AIDS) are concerned (Perloff, 1983; Perloff & Fetzer, 1986; Weinstein, 1982, 1984). One review estimated that at least 121 studies had demonstrated this phenomenon (Taylor & Brown, 1994). You may be thinking that in your case optimism about the future is not unrealistic. After all, perhaps you are doing very well in your education; perhaps your character and behaviour are such that you feel you can avoid many of life's pitfalls. Indeed, you may have a rosy future ahead of you. However, before you feel too complacent, be aware that research shows that this is how most students feel. That is, the average student believes that his or her future will be better than the average student of the same age and gender—and statistically it is not possible for the average to be greater than average! For this reason, this kind of optimism can be considered truly unrealistic. The unrealistic optimism bias has been explained as part of a broader inclination to be _self-enhancing_: to see our lives and ourselves somewhat more positively than reality might dictate. We should note here that recent research has raised questions about the universality of this effect. Cross-cultural research is beginning to suggest that, as with other self-enhancing biases, unrealistic optimism may not be as common in other cultures as it is in North America (Heine & Lehman, 1995).

A second optimistic bias can be seen in public as well as private life. The _planning fallacy_, described in Chapter 1, is our tendency to make optimistic predictions about the completion of a task. In public life examples abound, from the completion (or incompletion) of the Olympic Stadium in Montreal in 1976 to the federal government's gun registry. All too often, public officials and professionals seem to underestimate the time (and cost) of building projects, government programs, and government inquiries—to name a few. Perhaps this is understandable when we consider the complexities of such plans. But as we saw, many people in their private lives make the same error, in situations where more detailed knowledge of past performance and current temporal limitations is available. Further, this bias seems resistant to change. Even reminding people of realistic difficulties has little impact on the strength of the planning fallacy (Newby-Clarke et al., 2000).

Optimistic Bias Our predisposition to expect things to turn out well overall.

Unrealistic Optimism The tendency to believe that we are more likely to experience positive life events and less likely to experience negative life events, than similar others.

Counterfactual Thinking: Considering "What Might Have Been"

Counterfactual Thinking The tendency to imagine outcomes in a situation other than those that actually occurred—to think about "what might have been."

Have you ever had the experience of almost winning in a competition or a lottery? Perhaps you had most, but not enough, of the winning numbers on a lottery ticket. How did you react to this situation? If you are like most people, you may have spent some time imagining "what might have been"—what it would have been like to be a millionaire, to be able to buy whatever you wanted, to have all those possibilities. Such thoughts about what might have been—known in social psychology as **counterfactual thinking**—occur in a wide range of situations, not just ones in which we experience disappointments. Remember the driver who drifted across a busy intersection while talking on her cell phone? She imagined what might have happened if she hadn't been so lucky. She imagined *worse* outcomes than she experienced, not better ones. So, counterfactual thinking can involve imagining either better outcomes (*upward* counterfactuals) or worse ones (*downward* counterfactuals) than we actually experience.

Engaging in counterfactual thought can strongly influence affective states (Medvec & Savitsky, 1997). So, for example, *downward counterfactual thinking*—when individuals compare their current outcomes with less favourable ones—they may experience positive feelings of satisfaction. Such reactions have been found among Olympic athletes who win bronze medals, and who therefore imagine what it would be like to have won no medal whatsoever (e.g., Gleicher et al., 1995).

Alternatively, *upward counterfactual* thinking (imagining better outcomes than those that occurred) is closely related to the experience of regret. If we contemplate alternatives to *someone else's* misfortune, it can produce a sympathetic response (Macrae, 1992; Miller & McFarland, 1986). However, if it is our *own* misfortune, then such regrets will be more intense when they involve things we *did not do* but wish we had, rather than things we did do that turned out poorly (Gilovich & Medvec, 1994). If we persist in thinking about those missed opportunities, we gradually downplay or lose sight of the factors that prevented us from acting at the time—these seem less and less important. Even worse, we tend to imagine in vivid detail the wonderful benefits that would have resulted if we *had* acted. The result: our regrets intensify over time and can haunt us for an entire lifetime (Medvec, Madey, & Gilovich, 1995). The feelings of dissatisfaction or envy that result from upward counterfactual thinking can be especially strong if the person does not feel capable of obtaining better outcomes in the future (Sanna, 1997). Olympic athletes, for example, who win a silver medal but imagine winning a gold one experience such reactions (see Figure 2.17; e.g., Medvec, Madey, & Gilovich, 1995).

In sum, imagining what might have been in a given situation can yield many effects, ranging from despair and intense regret on the one hand, through satisfaction and hopefulness on the other. Our tendency to

■ Counterfactual Thinking at the Olympics

FIGURE 2.17 Research findings indicate that Olympic athletes who win bronze medals are actually happier than those who win silver medals. Why? Because they imagine not winning any medal at all (downward counterfactuals) and so are glad to have received any medal at all. In contrast, those who win a silver medal imagine winning a gold medal (upward counterfactuals) and so are relatively dissatisfied with the medal they actually received.

think not only about what is but also about what *might* be, therefore, can have far-reaching effects on many aspects of our social thought and social behaviour.

Social Cognition: A Word of Optimism

Having discussed these sources of error in social thought—the negativity bias, the optimistic bias, the planning fallacy, and counterfactual thinking—you may be ready to despair: can we ever get it right? The answer, we believe, is *absolutely*. No, we're not perfect information-processing machines. We have limited cognitive capacities and we can't increase these by buying pop-in memory chips. And yes, we are somewhat lazy: we generally do the least amount of cognitive work possible in any situation. Despite these limitations, though, we frequently do an impressive job in thinking about others. Despite being flooded by truly enormous amounts of social information, we manage to sort, store, remember, and use a large portion of this input in an intelligent and highly efficient manner. Our thinking is indeed subject to many potential sources of bias, and we do make errors. But by and large, we do a very good job of processing social information and making sense out of the social worlds in which we live. So, while we can imagine being even better at these tasks than we actually are, there's no reason to be discouraged. On the contrary, we can take pride in the fact that we accomplish so much with the limited tools at our disposal.

Affect and Cognition: The Interplay Between Our Feelings and Our Thoughts

In our earlier discussion of the optimistic bias, we used the phrase "seeing the world through rose-coloured glasses" to reflect our tendency to expect positive outcomes in many situations. But there's another way in which these words apply to social cognition: they also illustrate the effects that being in a good mood has on our thoughts and

KEY POINTS

- Systematic biases in our social cognitions can result in erroneous conclusions about the social world, but they can also be adaptive at times.
- We show a strong *negativity bias*—a tendency to be highly sensitive to negative stimuli or information. This tendency appears to be very basic and may be built into the functioning of our brains. Thus, it may be the result of evolutionary factors.
- We also show a strong *optimistic bias,* expecting positive events and outcomes in many contexts. Examples are *unrealistic optimism,* seeing one's own future as more optimistic than those of comparable others, and the *planning fallacy,* making overly optimistic predictions about how long it will take to complete a given task.
- In many situations, individuals imagine "what might have been"—they engage in *counterfactual thinking.* Such thinking can affect our sympathy for persons who have experienced negative outcomes and can cause us to experience strong regret over missed opportunities.

perceptions. Think of a time in your own life when you were in a very good mood; didn't the world seem to be a happier place? And didn't you see everything and everyone with whom you came into contact more favourably than you would when in a less pleasant mood? Experiences such as this illustrate the fact that there is often a complex interplay between *affect*—our current moods—and *cognition*—the ways in which we process, store, remember, and use social information (Forgas, 1995a; Isen & Baron, 1991). We say *interplay* because research on this topic indicates that, in fact, the relationship is very much a two-way street: our feelings and moods strongly influence several aspects of cognition, and cognition, in turn, exerts strong effects on our feelings and moods (e.g., McDonald & Hirt, 1997; Seta, Hayes, & Seta, 1994). What are these effects like? Let's see what research findings tell us.

The Influence of Affect on Cognition

Impact of Affect on Perception: The Influence of Good Moods

We have already mentioned the impact of moods on our perceptions of the world around us. Such effects apply to people as well as objects. Imagine, for instance, that you have just received some very good news—you did much better on an important exam than you expected. As a result, you are feeling great. Now, you run into one of your friends and she introduces you to someone you don't know. You chat with this person for a while and then leave for another class. Will your first impression of the stranger be influenced by the fact that you are feeling so good? The findings of many different studies suggest strongly that it will (Bower, 1991; Mayer & Hanson, 1995; Clore, Schwarz, & Conway, 1993). Being in a good mood, for example, can influence us to be more helpful to others (e.g., Isen & Levin, 1972), to make more positive judgments of others in an interview (e.g., Robbins & DeNisi, 1994) and increase our creativity in solving problems (Estrada, Isen, & Young, 1995). In other words, a good mood can strongly affect our reactions to others and to new stimuli we encounter for the first time, causing us to perceive them more favourably than would otherwise be the case.

There is, however, another side to the impact of positive affect. Evidence indicates that while positive emotions or feelings are certainly enjoyable, they may reduce our tendency to think carefully or systematically, unless we are specifically (and highly) motivated to do so (e.g., Bodenhausen, Kramer, & Susser, 1994; Mackie & Worth, 1989). One way in which this can have a harmful effect is illustrated by a recent study (Park & Banaji, 2000). Based on previous research, Park and Banaji predicted that being in a good mood would lead individuals to rely more heavily on stereotypes, because this reduces systematic thinking and mental effort. To test this idea, these researchers asked participants to indicate whether various names—some African American and some European American in nature—belonged to the category "criminal" or to the category "politician." Half of the participants were placed in a good mood by watching a funny segment of a TV show and half were placed in a more neutral mood by viewing scenes of mountains, rivers, and so on. As they had predicted, Park and Banaji found that being in a good mood increased the use of stereotypes—participants in a good mood showed an enhanced tendency to place African-American names in the "criminal" category and an increased tendency to place European-American names in the "politician" category. So, an unfortunate side effect of this kind of cognitive "laziness" can be that a person responds in a more prejudiced way to others.

Why do such effects occur? One explanation is provided by a theory known as the cognitive tuning model (Schwarz, 1990). This theory suggests that positive affective states inform us that the current situation is safe and therefore doesn't require careful attention or processing of information. In contrast, negative affective states, such as those induced by seeing another person frown, signal us that the situation is potentially dangerous and that we had better pay careful attention to what's happening. This reasoning is an extension of the evolutionary explanation for the *negativity bias* in the previous section: there the emphasis was on the way in which *external* negative stimuli are more likely to be noticed. Here, we see that *internal* negative affect states can also places us on alert.

Impact of Affect on Memory: Mood Dependence and Mood Congruence

Another way in which affect influences cognition involves its impact on *memory*. Here, two different, but related, kinds of effects seem to occur. One is known as mood-dependent memory. This refers to the fact that what we remember while in a given mood may be determined, in part, by what we learned when previously in that mood. For instance, if you stored some information into long-term memory when in a good mood, you are more likely to remember this information when in a similar mood. A second kind of effect is known as mood congruence effects. This refers to the fact that we are more likely to store or remember positive information when in a positive mood and negative information when in a negative mood; in other words, we notice or remember information that is congruent with our current moods (Blaney, 1986). A simple way to think about the difference between mood-dependent memory and mood congruence effects is this: in mood-dependent memory, the nature of the information doesn't matter—only your mood at the time you learned it and your mood when you try to recall it are relevant. In mood congruence effects, in contrast, the affective nature of the information—whether it is positive or negative—is crucial. When we are in a positive mood, we tend to remember positive information, and when in a negative mood, we tend to remember negative information (see Figure 2.18).

Research confirms the existence of mood-dependent memory (Eich, 1995) and also suggests that such effects may be quite important. For instance, mood-dependent memory helps explain why depressed persons have difficulty in remembering times when they felt better (Schachter & Kihlstrom, 1989): being in a very negative mood now, they tend to remember information they entered into memory when in the same mood—and this information relates to feeling depressed. This is important because being able to remember what it felt like to *not* be depressed can play an important part in successful treatment of this problem. (We'll discuss other aspects of personal health in Chapter 10.)

Finally, findings indicate that information that evokes affective reactions may be processed differently from other kinds of information, and that, as a result, this information may be almost impossible to ignore or disregard (e.g., Edwards, Heindel, & Louis-Dreyfus, 1996; Wegner & Gold, 1995). Clear evidence pointing to such conclusions has been reported by Edwards and Bryan (1997).

The Influence of Cognition on Affect

Most research on the relationship between affect and cognition has focused on how feelings influence thought. However, there is also strong evidence for the reverse—the

Cognitive Tuning Model Theory suggesting that positive affective states inform us that the current situation is safe and doesn't require careful thought. In contrast, negative affective states signal that the situation is potentially dangerous and requires careful processing.

Mood-Dependent Memory The fact that what we remember while in a given mood may be determined, in part, by what we learned when previously in that mood.

Mood Congruence Effects Our tendency to store or remember positive information when in a positive mood and negative information when in a negative mood.

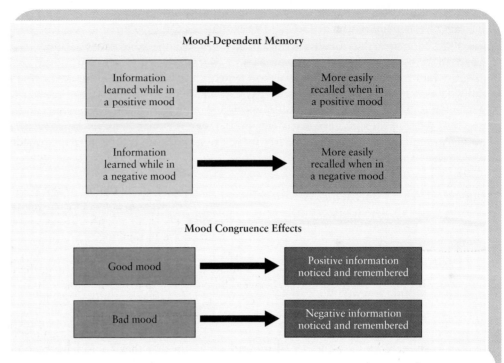

Mood-Dependent Memory

| Information learned while in a positive mood | → | More easily recalled when in a positive mood |
| Information learned while in a negative mood | → | More easily recalled when in a negative mood |

Mood Congruence Effects

| Good mood | → | Positive information noticed and remembered |
| Bad mood | → | Negative information noticed and remembered |

■ The Effects of Mood on Memory

FIGURE 2.18 Our moods influence what we remember through two mechanisms: *mood-dependent memory,* which refers to the fact that what we remember while in a given mood is determined, in part, by what we learned when previously in that mood; and *mood congruence effects,* which refer to the fact that we are more likely to store or remember positive information consistent with our current mood.

impact of cognition on affect. One aspect of this relationship is described in what is known as the *two-factor theory* of emotion (Schachter, 1964). This theory suggests that, often, we don't know our own feelings or attitudes directly. Rather, because these internal reactions are often somewhat ambiguous, we infer their nature from the external world—from the kinds of situations in which we experience these reactions. For example, if we experience increased arousal in the presence of an attractive person, we may conclude that we are in love. In contrast, if we experience increased arousal after being cut off in traffic by another driver, we may conclude that what we feel is anger.

A second way in which cognition can influence emotions is through the activation of schemas containing a strong affective component. For example, if we label an individual as belonging to some group, the schema for this social category may suggest what traits he or she probably possesses. In addition, it may tell us how we *feel* about such persons. Thus, activation of a strong racial, ethnic, or religious schema or stereotype may exert powerful effects upon our current feelings or mood. (We'll return to this topic in Chapter 6.)

A third way in which our thoughts can influence our affective states involves our efforts to regulate our emotions and feelings. This topic is so important and is receiving so much attention at present; we'll examine it more closely.

Cognition and the Regulation of Affective States

Learning to regulate our emotions is an important task; negative events and outcomes are an unavoidable part of life, so learning to cope with the negative feelings these events generate is crucial for effective personal adjustment—and for good social relations with others. For example, individuals who often lose their tempers usually find it difficult to get along with others and may, in fact, be avoided by others. Among the most important techniques we use for regulating our moods and emotions are ones involving cognitive mechanisms. In other words, we use our thoughts to regulate our feelings. Many techniques for accomplishing this goal exist, but here, we'll consider two that are especially interesting: a tactic that could be termed the "It was inevitable" effect and another involving yielding to temptation.

Research by Tykocinski and colleagues (e.g., Tykocinski & Pittman, 1998) related to counterfactual thinking shows that we can regulate our reactions to disappointment, or even severe loss, by thinking of them as inevitable. For example, after tragic events such as the death of a loved one, people often find solace in thinking, "Nothing more could be done; the death was inevitable." In other words, they adjust their view concerning the inevitability of the death so as to make it seem more unavoidable and, therefore, more bearable. In contrast, if they have different counterfactual thoughts—"If only the illness had been diagnosed sooner…" or "If only we had gotten him to the hospital quicker…"—their suffering may be increased. For example, Tykocinski (2001) found that people who failed to get to a store before it closed and missed out on a bargain subsequently decreased their estimates of the probability of that they could have been on time—making the loss seem inevitable. These findings indicate that we do indeed sometimes use counterfactual thinking to reduce the bitterness of disappointments: by mentally reducing the odds of success-that is, by convincing ourselves that "we never had a chance"—we reduce our disappointment, and so regulate our affective states.

Another cognitive mechanism we use to regulate our affective states—and especially to reduce or eliminate negative feelings—involves giving in to temptation. When they are feeling "down" or distressed, many persons engage in activities that they know are bad for them but which make them feel better, at least temporarily (e.g., eating fattening snacks, wasting time by watching television). These actions make them feel better, but only temporarily. Recently, Tice, Bratslavky, and Baumeister (2000) have provided evidence that cognitive factors play a role in such behaviour. Their studies provide support for the idea that people consciously choose to yield to temptations at times when they experience strong negative affect. In other words, this is not an automatic behaviour or a sign of weakness; rather, it is a *strategic choice*. People yield to temptation because, in the face of intense negative affect, they shift their priorities. Reducing their negative affect becomes their primary goal, so they do whatever it takes to achieve this objective. It is important to note, however, that while this technique may succeed, it may involve high costs—the actions we take to counter our negative feelings may be damaging to our health or well-being. Clearly, then, this is one tactic we should use with care!

KEY POINTS

- Affect influences cognition in several ways. A positive mood can cause us to react constructively in many ways, including being more helpful to others and judging them more positively, as well as increasing our creativity in problem solving.

- On the down side, a positive mood can also cause us to process information about others more superficially, relying on stereotypes. According to the *cognitive tuning model*, positive affective states act as a signal that careful processing is unnecessary.

- Affect can also influence memory through *mood-dependent memory* and *mood congruence effects.*
- Cognition influences affect through our interpretation of emotion-provoking events and through the activation of schemas containing a strong affective component.
- We employ several cognitive techniques to regulate our emotions or feelings; through counterfactual thinking, we can make negative outcomes seem inevitable and so less distressing. Also when distressed, we can consciously choose to give into temptation and engage in activities that, while damaging in the long run, make us feel better in the short run.

Ideas To Take With You

Minimizing the Impact of Errors in Social Cognition

Attribution and social cognition are subject to many errors, and these can prove quite costly both to you and to the people with whom you interact. Thus, it's well worth the effort to avoid such pitfalls. Here are our suggestions for recognizing—and minimizing—several important cognitive errors.

The Fundamental Attribution Error.
We have a strong tendency to attribute others' behaviour to internal (dispositional) causes even when strong external (situational) factors that might have influenced their behaviour are present. To reduce this error, always try to put yourself in the shoes of the person whose behaviour you are trying to explain. In other words, try to see the world through his or her eyes. If you do, you will often realize that from that person's perspective there are many external factors that played a role in his or her behaviour.

The Self-Serving Bias: "I'm good; you're lucky."
Perhaps the strongest attributional error we make is that of attributing our own positive outcomes to internal causes such as our own abilities or effort but our negative outcomes to external factors such as luck or forces beyond our control. This can lead us to overestimate our own contributions to group projects, thus producing unnecessary friction with others. It can also reduce the chances that we will learn something valuable from negative outcomes—for instance, how we might do better the next time. You can help minimize this error simply by being aware of it; once you know it exists, you may realize that not all your positive outcomes stem from internal causes, and that you may have played a role in producing negative ones. In addition, try to remember that other people are subject to the same bias; they, too, instinctively want to take credit for positive outcomes but to shift the blame for negative ones to external causes—such as you!

The Planning Fallacy.
Often, we underestimate the amount of time it will take us to complete a task. The stronger our motivation to be done with the task, the stronger this effect. Next time you have a deadline, allow what seems like too much time for it to be completed and you will probably finish it on time.

Summary

- *Social perception* and *social cognition* defined. (p. 36)

Nonverbal Communication: The Unspoken Language

- *Nonverbal communication*—facial expressions, eye contact, body movements, and postures and touch. (p. 37)
- Cultures vary in their styles of communication. (p. 45)
- We can recognize efforts at deception by others—even in persons are from other cultures. (p. 46)

Attribution: Understanding the Causes of Others' Behaviour

- Jones and Davis's theory of *correspondent inference*: allows *dispositional attribution*. (p. 49)
- Kelley's theory of *causal attribution* suggests three types of information are used: consensus, consistency, and distinctiveness. (p. 51)
- Coping with multiple causal factors: *discounting* principle and *augmenting principle*. (p. 52)
- Weiner's *theory of attribution* suggests three causal dimensions: locus, stability, and control. (p. 55)
- Attributional errors: the *fundamental attribution error* (or correspondence bias), the *actor–observer effect*, and the *self-serving bias*. (p. 56)
- Culture affects the strength of attributional biases: This is influenced by *holistic thought* in East Asian cultures and *analytic thought* in European cultures. (p. 58)

Coping with Information Overload: Schemas, Heuristics, and Automatic Processing

- Coping with information overload by the use of automatic thinking, by being selective, and by using shortcuts to reduce mental effort. (p. 61)

- *Schemas* organize social information, exert powerful effects on attention, encoding, and retrieval, and show the *perseverance effect*. (p. 62)
- Schemas can also exert self-confirming effects—e.g., the *self-fulfilling prophecy*. (p. 63)
- *Heuristics* help us to make decisions in a quick and effortless manner. Examples: the *representativeness heuristic* and the *availability heuristic*, which can involve *priming*. (p. 65)
- *Automatic processing* of social information may influence social thought and behaviour. (p. 68)

Errors in Social Cognition: Why We Are Fallible

- A strong *negativity bias* may be built into the functioning of our brains and be the result of evolutionary factors. (p. 70)
- *Optimistic bias* examples: *unrealistic optimism* and the *planning fallacy*. (p. 71)
- *Counterfactual thinking* can affect our sympathy for others and can cause regret over missed opportunities. (p. 72)

Affect and Cognition: The Interplay between Our Feelings and Our Thoughts

- Positive moods can cause us to react constructively in many ways but also to process information more superficially. The *cognitive tuning model* suggests positive affective states act as a signal that careful processing is unnecessary. (p. 75)
- Affect can influence memory through *mood-dependent memory* and *mood congruence effects*. (p. 75)
- Cognition influences affect through our interpretation of emotion-provoking events, and can be used to regulate our emotions through counterfactual thinking and giving into temptation. (p. 76)

For More Information

Malandro, L. A., Barker, L., & Barker, D. A. (1994). Nonverbal communication (3rd ed). New York: Random House.

A basic and very readable text that examines all aspects of nonverbal communication. Body movements and gestures, facial expression, eye contact, touching, smell, and voice characteristics are among the topics considered.

Kunda, Z. (1999). Social cognition: Making sense of people. Cambridge, MA: MIT Press.

This text describes our current knowledge about many aspects of social cognition. It is well written and discusses many of the topics covered in this chapter (e.g., schemas, errors in social cognition) in detail.

Wyer, R. S., Jr., & Bargh, J. A. (Eds.). (1997). The automaticity of everyday life. Advances in Social Cognition, 10.

To what extent is our social thought and social behaviour "automatic"—occurring without conscious thought? The papers in this excellent volume present data suggesting that, in fact, our thoughts and behaviours are often triggered in an automatic manner by external conditions.

Weblinks

nonverbal.ucsc.edu
Exploring Nonverbal Communication, a site by Dana Archer, University of California at Santa Cruz

www.ai.univie.ac.at/archives/Psycoloquy/1998.V9/0068.html
"The Bet on Bias: A Foregone Conclusion?" by Joachim Krueger, Brown University

Attitudes:

Evaluating the Social World

SPECIAL SECTIONS

CORNERSTONES
The Attitude–Behaviour Link: A Classic Study Throws Doubt on Its Existence

ON THE APPLIED SIDE
Psychological Warfare: Persuasion and Propaganda during the Iraq War

CANADIAN RESEARCH: ON THE CUTTING EDGE
Can Subliminal Priming Influence Our Behaviour?

When the decision was made to send troops into Iraq, how did you feel about that? Were you one of the people opposed? Perhaps you were among the many demonstrators in Canada. Or were you in support of the decision? Did you believe that the Canadian military should also have been involved? At that time in Canada it would have been difficult to avoid some discussion of these issues, and impossible to avoid awareness that there were *strong* differences of opinion. Did you find yourself wondering why people oppose each other so vehemently over such important issues? How can people, often with the same level of ability and knowledge, reach such differing conclusions? And how can they be persuaded to change their views to something more sensible? (Your perspective, of course!) Social psychologists would suggest that in order to answer these questions—and truly understand why people hold the views they do—it is necessary to consider the topic of *attitudes*.

Attitudes have been a central concept in social psychology since its earliest days (e.g., Allport & Hartman, 1924) and for good reason: they shape both our social perceptions and our social behaviour (Pratkanis, Breckler, & Greenwald, 1989). But what, precisely, are they? **Attitudes** refer to *our evaluations of virtually any aspect of the social world* (e.g., Fazio & Roskos-Ewoldsen, 1994; Tesser & Martin, 1996), the extent to which we have favourable or unfavourable reactions to issues, ideas, persons, social groups, objects—any and every element of the social world. They are more enduring than passing preferences—once formed they tend to persist and are often strongly resistant to change, especially if they are long-term and are strongly related to the interests of the persons who hold them (e.g., Crano, 1997). However, not all attitudes are uniformly favourable or unfavourable—on occasions we are "of two minds" about something. For example, many people who were strongly opposed to the decision to begin the Iraq war were also pleased that Saddam Hussein's regime was overthrown. Similarly, people who had supported the decision to go to war might also have hated the suffering involved (see Figure 3.1). This is termed **attitude ambivalence** and refers to the fact that our evaluations are often mixed, consisting of *both* positive and negative reactions (e.g., Priester & Petty, 2001; Thompson, Zanna, & Griffin, 1995).

The importance of attitudes to social psychology stems from their two major features. First, attitudes strongly influence our social thought, even if they are not always reflected in our overt behaviour. In fact, growing evidence suggests that attitudes, as evaluations of the world around us, represent a very basic aspect of social cognition. As we saw in Chapter 2, the tendency to evaluate stimuli as positive or negative—something we like or dislike—appears to be an initial step in our efforts to make sense out of the social world. In fact, it occurs almost immediately, and certainly before we attempt to understand the meaning of stimuli or integrate them with our previous experience (Ito et al., 1998). So, in a sense, attitudes truly reflect an essential, and early, building block of social thought (e.g., Eagly & Chaiken, 1998).

Second, it has been widely assumed, attitudes strongly affect behaviour. For example, do you hold a negative attitude toward the current prime minister or the premier of your province? Then you may not vote for those persons or their parties in the next election. If attitudes influence behaviour, then knowing something about them can help us predict people's behaviour in a wide range of contexts. As we'll see in Chapter 6, we also hold attitudes toward specific persons—for example, we like them or dislike them. Clearly, such attitudes can play a crucial role in our relations with these persons.

In this chapter we'll provide you with an overview of what social psychologists have discovered about attitudes, proceeding as follows. First, we'll examine the process through which attitudes are *formed* or *developed*. Next, we'll consider the relationship between *attitudes and behaviour*. This link is more complex than you might expect, so be prepared for some surprises. Third, we'll examine how attitudes are sometimes

Attitudes Evaluations of various aspects of the social world.

Attitude Ambivalence Refers to the fact that we often have positive and negative evaluations of the same attitude object; thus, our attitude towards it is ambivalent.

■ Attitudes
Ambivalence

FIGURE 3.1 Our attitudes are often ambivalent: we evaluate various issues, people, groups, or objects both positively *and* negatively. Individual responses to the 2003 Iraq war were often mixed—there were supporters of the decision to enter Iraq who also felt terrible about the suffering involved and antiwar protesters who felt glad that the Saddam Hussein regime was overthrown.

changed through *persuasion* and related processes. The word *sometimes* should be emphasized, for as we'll note in another section, changing attitudes that are important to those who hold them is far from easy. Finally, we'll consider *cognitive dissonance*— an internal state with far-reaching implications for social behaviour and social thought that, surprisingly, sometimes leads individuals to change their own attitudes in the absence of external pressure to do so.

Attitude Formation: How—and Why—Attitudes Develop

What are your views about the legalizing marijuana? What about gun control? Aboriginal hunting and fishing rights? Sexual harassment? Pizza? Almost certainly, you have views—attitudes—about all of these. But where, precisely, did these attitudes come from? Were you born with them? Or did you acquire them as a result of various life experiences? Most people—and most social psychologists—accept the view that attitudes are *learned*, and most of our discussion of this issue will focus on the processes through which attitudes are acquired. But please take note: we would be remiss if we did not mention that a small but growing body of evidence suggests that attitudes may be influenced by genetic factors, too. We'll describe some of the evidence for this surprising idea below.

Turning to the first question—*why* do we form attitudes (i.e., what functions do they serve?)—we'll soon see that, in fact, attitudes serve several different functions and are useful to us in many different respects.

Social Learning: Acquiring Attitudes from Others

Social Learning The process through which we acquire new information, forms of behaviour, or attitudes from other persons.

One important source of our attitudes is obvious: we acquire them from other persons through the process of **social learning**. In other words, many of our views are acquired in situations where we interact with others or merely observe their behaviour. Social learning occurs through several processes.

Classical Conditioning: Learning Based on Association

Classical Conditioning A basic form of learning in which one stimulus, initially neutral, acquires the capacity to evoke reactions through repeated pairing with another stimulus. In a sense, one stimulus becomes a signal for the presentation or occurrence of the other.

It is a basic principle of psychology that when one stimulus regularly precedes another, the one that occurs first may soon become a signal for the one that occurs second. In other words, when the first stimulus occurs, individuals expect that the second will soon follow. As a result, they gradually acquire the same kind of reactions to the first stimulus as they show to the second stimulus, especially if the second is one that induces fairly strong and automatic reactions. For instance, consider a woman whose shower emits a low hum just before the hot water runs out and turns into an icy stream. At first, she may show little reaction to the hum. After the hum is followed by freezing water on several occasions, though, she may well experience strong emotional arousal (fear!) when it occurs. After all, it is a signal for what will soon follow—icy cold water.

What does this process, which is known as **classical conditioning**, have to do with attitude formation? Potentially, quite a lot. To see how this process might influence attitudes under real-life conditions, imagine the following scene. A young child sees her mother frown and show other signs of displeasure each time the mother encounters a member of a particular ethnic group. At first, the child is neutral toward members of this group and their visible characteristics (e.g., skin colour, style of dress, accent). After these cues are paired with the mother's negative emotional reactions many times, however, classical conditioning occurs; the child comes to react negatively to these stimuli, and to members of this ethnic group (see Figure 3.2). The result: The child acquires a negative attitude toward such persons—an attitude that may form the core of a full-blown ethnic prejudice. (We'll examine prejudice in detail in Chapter 5.)

Interestingly, studies indicate that classical conditioning can occur below the level of conscious awareness—even when people are not aware of the stimuli that serve as the basis for this kind of conditioning. For instance, in one experiment on this topic (Krosnick et al., 1992), students saw photos of a stranger engaged in routine daily activities such as shopping in a grocery store or walking into her apartment. While these photos were shown, other photos known to induce either positive or negative feelings were presented very briefly—so briefly that participants were not aware of their presence (i.e., they were *subliminal*). One group of research participants was exposed to photos that induced positive feelings (e.g., a bridal couple, people playing cards and laughing); another group was exposed to photos that induced negative feelings (e.g., open-heart surgery, a werewolf). Later, both groups expressed their attitudes toward the stranger. Results indicated that even though participants were unaware of the second group of photos (the ones presented very briefly), these stimuli significantly influenced their attitudes toward the stranger. Those exposed to the positive photos reported more favourable attitudes toward this person than those exposed to the negative photos. These findings suggest that attitudes can be influenced by **subliminal conditioning**—classical conditioning that occurs in the absence of conscious awareness of the stimuli involved. A closely related process termed *subliminal priming* occurs when stimuli presented below the level of awareness stimulate our cognitive processes. This is the topic of the Canadian Research: On the Cutting Edge section.

Subliminal Conditioning Classical conditioning that occurs through exposure to stimuli that are below individuals' threshold of conscious awareness.

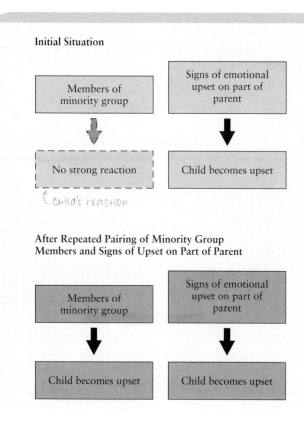

Initial Situation

Members of minority group → No strong reaction ↑ child's reaction

Signs of emotional upset on part of parent → Child becomes upset

After Repeated Pairing of Minority Group Members and Signs of Upset on Part of Parent

Members of minority group → Child becomes upset

Signs of emotional upset on part of parent → Child becomes upset

■ Classical Conditioning of Attitudes

FIGURE 3.2 Initially, a young child has little or no emotional reaction to the visible characteristics of members of some minority group. If she sees her mother showing signs of negative reactions when in the presence of these persons, however, she too may gradually acquire negative reactions to them, through the process of classical conditioning.

Canadian Research: On the Cutting Edge

Can Subliminal Priming Influence Our Behaviour?

The issue of whether subliminally presented stimuli can have an impact on our behaviour has been debated since the 1950s. An advertising executive, James Vicary, claimed to have increase Coke sales by 18 percent and popcorn sales by almost 58 percent by secretly flashing the words "Drink Coke!" and "Eat Popcorn" on the cinema screen for one 3000th of a second. The idea that we could be manipulated into changing our behaviour by images that we couldn't even see was a scary prospect. And, even though it turned out that James Vicary was lying to give his advertising agency a boost, psychologists have spent considerable amounts of time since then researching this issue (e.g., Key, 1973; Greenwald, Spangenberg, Pratkanis, & Eskenazi, 1991)—with mixed results.

On the one hand, there has been evidence in a number of recent studies, like the one described in the previous section (Krosnick, et al., 1992), indicating that subliminal stimuli can influence our impressions of another person or an object (Murphy & Zajonc, 1993) and even change our behavioural response (Dijksterhuis & Bargh, 2001). In contrast, research on the impact of subliminal self-help tapes (ones that provide subliminal messages designed to help people improve their self-esteem or to lose weight) finds that they are totally ineffective in changing people's behaviour (Greenwald, et al., 1991). Further, a review of 200 academic papers on the subject found no clear evidence of the impact of subliminal messages on behaviour (Pratkanis & Aronson, 1991).

Canadian researchers Erin Strahan, Steven Spencer, and Mark Zanna (2002) at the University of Waterloo believe the solution to these contradictory findings lies in consideration of the whether the subliminal stimuli are *relevant to a person's motivation*. They reason that in the absence of relevance to

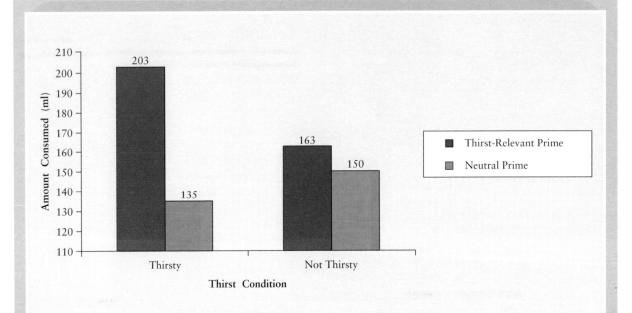

■ The Amount of Liquid Consumed after Priming with a Relevant and a Neutral Prime

FIGURE 3.3 Subliminal priming can have an impact on behaviour, but only if it is relevant to a person's current motivational state. Thirsty subjects exposed to a *subliminal prime* relevant to thirst (e.g., "dry" or "thirst") were significantly more likely to drink an overly sweet drink than thirsty subjects who were exposed to a neutral prime (e.g., "won" or "pirate"). However, when subjects were not thirsty, exposure to the thirst-relevant subliminal prime had little impact on the amount they drank.

Source: Based on information in Strahan, Spencer, & Zanna, 2002.

a person's real needs and motives in a current situation, priming with subliminal stimuli will have little impact. In much the same way, supraliminal stimuli (ones that you are consciously aware of) will have little influence on your behaviour unless they are relevant at that time. For example, when you are completely full to the point of bursting from a large meal, the sight of a rich cream cake will not induce you to eat. On the other hand, when you are very hungry that cake can tempt you to break your strict diet—it is all too relevant to you.

To test these ideas Strahan and colleagues (2002) used a *subliminal priming* technique—a concept or idea is presented to a subject subliminally (for 16 milliseconds) in the form of a word flashed on a television monitor. Subjects were students at the University of Waterloo and they were told that they would be involved in a marketing study in which they would evaluate different food and drink products. For the purposes of this study they would be required not to eat or drink for three hours before the experimental session. This intervention meant that subjects were likely to be thirsty when they came to the lab. Their first task on arrival was a "taste test" rating some cookies. Two different thirst conditions were then created by allowing half of the subjects to drink as much water as they wanted, ostensibly "to cleanse your palate" (*not thirsty condition*), while the other half of the subjects were provided with no water (*thirsty condition*). Subjects were next required to take part in a visual perception task measuring the speed with which they could recognize a group of letters on a monitor as a word or a non-word. While this task was being completed, subliminal priming occurred. Additional words were flashed on the monitor subliminally, that were either relevant to thirst (e.g., "thirst" and "dry") in the *thirst-relevant prime condition*, or the words were neutral (e.g., "pirate" and "won") in the *neutral prime condition*. Following the perception task, subjects were again asked to do a "taste test"—this time with two different kinds of beverages. These consisted of Kool-Aid drinks with extra sugar added to make them not particularly refreshing unless subjects were very thirsty.

The researchers predicted that thirsty subjects who had been exposed to the relevant prime would consume the greatest amount of this beverage and, as you can see in Figure 3.3, this is exactly what happened. These results provide clear evidence in support of the idea that subliminal priming can have an impact on behaviour. Notice that the thirst-relevant prime had little impact on subjects who were *not* thirsty—it wasn't relevant to them. Also thirst alone was not enough to make subjects drink—thirsty subjects who hadn't been primed with a relevant stimulus were no more likely to drink than people who weren't thirsty.

This research demonstrates that the influence of subliminal stimuli on our behaviour isn't quite as wholesale or mechanistic as was first implied. Yes, subliminal stimuli can have an impact but *only* if they are relevant to our goals in the current situation—if they are not, then our behaviour will not be changed. Nonetheless, there is one side of such processes that can still cause us concern. When the process of persuasion takes place at this unconscious level, we have very little opportunity to resist its influence. We will discuss this issue further in a later section on persuasion.

Instrumental Conditioning: Learning to Hold the "Right" Views

Have you ever heard a three-year-old state, with great conviction, that he is a Liberal? Or that Fords (or Hondas) are better than Chevrolets (or Toyotas)? Children of this age have little understanding of what these statements mean. Yet they make them all the same. Why? The answer is obvious: They have been praised or rewarded in various ways by their parents for stating such views. As we're sure you know, behaviours that are followed by positive outcomes are strengthened and tend to be repeated. In contrast, behaviours that are followed by negative outcomes are weakened, or at least suppressed. Thus, another way in which attitudes are acquired from others is through the process of **instrumental conditioning**. By rewarding children with smiles, approval, or hugs for stating the "right" views—the ones they themselves favour—parents and other adults play an active role in shaping youngsters' attitudes. It is for this reason that until they reach their teen years, most children express political, religious, and social views highly similar to those of their families. Given the powerful effect of reinforcement on behaviour, it would be surprising if they did not.

Instrumental Conditioning A basic form of learning in which responses that lead to positive outcomes or permit avoidance of negative outcomes are strengthened. Also known as operant conditioning.

Observational Learning: Learning by Example

A third process through which attitudes are formed can operate even when parents have no desire to transmit specific views to their children. This process is **observational learning**, and it occurs when individuals acquire new forms of behaviour or thought simply by observing the actions of others (Bandura, 1997). Where attitude formation is concerned, observational learning appears to play an important role. In many cases, children hear their parents say things not intended for their ears, or observe their parents engaging in actions the parents tell them not to perform. For example, parents who smoke often warn their children against this habit, even as they light up (see Figure 3.4). What message do children acquire from such instances? The evidence is clear: They often learn to do as their parents do, not as they say.

Observational Learning A basic form of learning in which individuals acquire new forms of behaviour or thought through observing and imitating others. Also known as modelling.

In addition, of course, both children and adults often acquire attitudes from exposure to the mass media—television, magazines, films, and so on. For instance, the characters in many films today make liberal use of swear words that in the past were considered unacceptable. The result: Many persons under the age of 30, who have grown up watching such films, don't find these words as objectionable as older persons sometimes do.

■ Observational Learning in Action

FIGURE 3.4 Children learn many things through observation, including attitudes their parents may not want the children to acquire, such as a positive view of smoking.

Cultural Factors: The Role of Cultural Values

Cultural background can also influence attitude formation (Davidson & Thompson, 1980). In Chapter 2 we saw that culture can have a fundamental influence on our cognitions (Nisbett, Peng, Choi, & Norenzayan, 2001). When considering cultural differences in the area of attitudes, researchers have often examined broader *cultural values* rather than specific attitudes.

Values Broad and abstract principles of life. They contain our moral beliefs and our standards of conduct.

Values are broad and abstract principles of life. They contain our moral beliefs and our standards of conduct. Where they differ from attitudes is in their generality or abstractness (Schwartz, 1992). For example, *equality*, a well-known value suggesting that all people should have the same rights or status, does not relate to one particular type of event or object as an attitude does. Rather, it guides our thinking over a broad range of situations. A value such as equality may guide your attitudes to issues as diverse as how we should distribute health services and whether professors should be called by their first names. So, compared to attitudes, values then are broader in application and more abstract because they are less attached to one particular object. Further, there is evidence that values are translated into action via our attitudes. That is, values may determine attitudes, which in turn may determine behaviour (Homer & Kahle, 1988).

Values can also be culturally transmitted through processes of social learning and shaped by social comparison at home, in school, and among our friends. Major studies comparing values of over 50 nations have found measurable differences between the values of those from different cultures (Hofstede, 1980; Schwartz, 1992). Findings of Hofstede's study (1980), for example, showed that Canadians and Americans had very similar rankings in three out of four values—see Table 3.1. They were similar in showing high *individualism* (focus on individual choice rather than group goals), low *power distance* (little value on hierarchical relationships), and low *uncertainty avoidance* (placed little value on stability and order). A difference did occur for one value related to achievement orientation (termed *masculinity* by Hofstede)—Americans showed a higher ranking for this value than Canadians. However, citizens of both countries'

Four dimensions of cultural values emerged from Hofstede's original research in 40 countries (1980). These dimensions are described below.

TABLE 3.1 Four Dimensions of Cultural Values

Individualism/Collectivism

Description: Valuing loosely knit social relations in which individuals are expected to care only for themselves and their immediate families versus tightly knit relations in which they can expect their wider in-group (e.g., extended family, clan) to look after them in exchange for unquestioning loyalty.

Power Distance

Description: Accepting an unequal distribution of power in institutions as legitimate versus illegitimate (from the viewpoint of the less powerful person).

Uncertainty Avoidance

Description: Feeling uncomfortable with uncertainty and ambiguity and therefore valuing beliefs and institutions that provide certainty and conformity.

Masculinity/Femininity (Now Usually Termed Agency/Communion)

Description: Valuing achievement, heroism, assertiveness, and material success versus valuing relationships, modesty, caring for the weak, and interpersonal harmony.

Source: Adapted from Hofstede, 1980; Smith & Bond, 1998; Smith & Schwartz, 1997.

responses differed markedly from those of a number of other cultures, particularly the more collectivistic cultures of South America, Africa, and Asia. The cultural value dimension of individualism/collectivism has emerged as an important one in social psychological research (Triandis, 1995), and Hofstede also points out that this dimension correlates negatively with the power distance dimension. Western cultures tended to be high on individualism and low on power distance, whereas Latin American and Asian cultures show the reverse pattern: low on individualism and high on power distance (Smith & Bond, 1998).

Those who monitor recent trends in Canadian social values agree that there have been important changes in values among Canadians, particularly those aged roughly 18–30 years (Adams, 1997; Armstrong, 1996; Bibby, 1995; Foote, 1996; Sauve, 1994). One commentator has even suggested that this shift in values amounts to a "social revolution" (Adams, 1997). There appear to be three major trends: *greater individualism*, a *devaluing of institutions* in Canada, and *greater diversity of values.* First, Canadians seem to be becoming somewhat less communitarian, or group-oriented, and more individualistic. Adams (1997) suggests that the emerging values of the current generation reveal this individualism: placing greater importance on personal autonomy, hedonism (the valuing of pleasure), and a quest for personal meaning or spiritual fulfillment. There has also been a general decline in membership of many community and organized religious groups (e.g., a 27 percent decrease in membership in religious organizations since 1975; Bibby, 1995). Second, accompanying this decreasing group-orientation in Canada is a devaluing of institutions and their leaders. For example, only 16 percent of Canadians express "a great deal" or "quite a lot" of confidence in the House of Commons (Gallup, 1993, cited in Sauve, 1994). In addition, there has been a drop over the last ten years in the proportion of Canadians expressing confidence in the leaders of institutions such as the federal government, the court system, and the police (Bibby, 1995). Finally, a trend toward diversity is mentioned by researchers—a greater diversity in values (Adams, 1997), and an acceptance of greater variety in attitudes, lifestyles, and forms of family life (Bibby, 1995).

Despite claims of a "social revolution," most of the trends described here are gradual and many of the more traditional Canadian values persist in the population as a whole. For example, over 70 percent of Canadians continue to place a high value on kindness, concern for others, and politeness, and Canadians maintain a belief that the underprivileged in society have a right to health care (96 percent) and an adequate income (84 percent; Bibby, 1995).

One final note: when discussing these very general trends we are not reflecting the diversity of values among the many subcultural groups in Canada. This is an issue that will be pursued further in Chapter 4 when we look at issues in *cross-cultural psychology*.

Genetic Factors: Some Surprising Recent Findings

Can we inherit our attitudes—or, at least, a propensity to develop certain attitudes about various topics or issues? At first glance, most people would answer with an emphatic *no*. While we readily believe that genetic factors can shape our height, eye colour, and other physical characteristics, the idea that such factors might also influence our thinking—including our preferences and our views—seems strange to say the least. Yet if we remember that thought occurs within the brain and that brain structure, like every other part of our physical being, is certainly influenced by genetic factors, the idea of genetic influences on attitudes becomes, perhaps, a little easier to imagine. And in fact, a small but growing body of empirical evidence indicates that genetic factors may play some small role in attitudes (e.g., Arvey et al., 1989; Keller et al., 1992; Hershberger, Lichtenstein, & Knox, 1994).

Most of this evidence involves comparisons between identical (monozygotic) and nonidentical (dizygotic) twins. Since identical twins share the same genetic inheritance, while nonidentical twins do not, higher correlations between the attitudes of the identical twins would suggest that genetic factors play a role in shaping such attitudes. This is precisely what has been found: the attitudes of identical twins do correlate more highly than those of nonidentical twins (e.g., Waller et al., 1990). Moreover, this is the case even if the twins have been separated early in life and raised in sharply contrasting environments from then on (see Figure 3.5; Bouchard et al., 1992; Hershberger,

■ Identical Twins Separated Very Early in Life: Often, Their Attitudes are Very Similar

FIGURE 3.5 The attitudes of identical twins separated very early in life correlate more highly than those of nonidentical twins or unrelated persons. This finding provides support for the view that attitudes are influenced by genetic factors, at least to some extent.

Lichtenstein, & Knox, 1994). Under these conditions, greater similarity in the attitudes of identical twins than in the attitudes of other persons cannot be attributed to similarity in environmental factors.

Additional results suggest, not surprisingly, that genetic factors play a stronger role in shaping some attitudes than others—in other words, that some attitudes are more *heritable* than others. While it is too early to reach definite conclusions, some findings seem to suggest that attitudes involving gut-level preferences (e.g., a preference for certain kinds of music) may be more strongly influenced by genetic factors than attitudes that are more "cognitive" in nature (e.g., attitudes about abstract principles or about situations and objects with which individuals have had little direct experience; Tesser, 1993). In addition, it appears that attitudes that are highly heritable may be more difficult to change than ones that are not, and that highly heritable attitudes may exert stronger effects on behaviour (e.g., Crealia & Tesser, 1998). For instance, we seem to like strangers who express attitudes similar to ours more when these attitudes are highly heritable than when they are less heritable (Tesser, 1993). We'll return to these points in a later discussion of the effects of attitudes on behaviour.

But how, we can almost hear you asking, can such effects occur—how can genetic factors influence attitudes? One possibility is that genetic factors influence more general dispositions, such as the tendency to experience mainly positive or negative affect—to be in a positive or negative mood most of the time (George, 1990). Such tendencies, in turn, could then influence evaluations of many aspects of the social world. Only time, and further research, will allow us to determine whether, and how, genetic factors influence attitudes. But given that such factors appear to influence many other aspects of social behaviour and social thought, ranging from our choice of romantic partners through aggression (e.g., Buss, 1999), the idea that attitudes, too, may be subject to such influences is accepted by many social psychologists.

Attitude Functions: Why We Form Attitudes in the First Place

That we hold many attitudes is obvious; in fact, it is safe to say that we are rarely completely neutral on almost *any* aspect of the world around us. But why do we bother to form the many attitudes each of us has? One answer is that attitudes serve a number of useful functions for us.

First, they have a *knowledge function.* Attitudes are useful in organizing and interpreting social information—operating as a kind of evaluative *schema*. And as such, they strongly colour our perceptions and thoughts about the issues, persons, objects, or groups to which they refer. For instance, research findings indicate that we view information that offers support for our attitudes as more convincing and accurate than information that refutes them (e.g., Munro & Ditto, 1997), although, surprisingly, we do *not* remember information that supports our views better than information that does not (Eagly et al., 2000). Similarly, we view sources that provide evidence contrary to our views as highly suspect—biased and unreliable (e.g., Giner-Sorolla & Chaiken, 1994, 1997). In sum, attitudes are useful in terms of our efforts to make sense out of the social world—although, like other cognitive frameworks and shortcuts, they can sometimes lead us astray.

Second, attitudes permit us to express our central values or beliefs—a *self-expression* or *self-identity function*. For instance, if being politically liberal is crucial to your self-identity, you may find it important to hold pro-environmental attitudes, because these allow you to express your central beliefs.

Third, attitudes also sometimes serve an *ego-defensive function* (Katz, 1960), helping people to protect themselves from unwanted information about themselves.

For instance, many persons who are quite bigoted express the view that they are against prejudice and discrimination. By stating such attitudes, they protect themselves from seeing that, in fact, they *are* actually highly prejudiced against others.

Finally, attitudes may also often serve an *impression motivation function*. We often wish to make a good impression on others, and expressing the "right" views is one way of doing so (e.g., Chaiken, Giner-Sorolla, & Chen, 1996). Interestingly, recent findings indicate that the extent to which attitudes serve this function can strongly affect their impact on the processing of social information. Such effects are clearly demonstrated in a study by Nienhuis, Manstead, and Spears (2001).

These researchers reasoned that when attitudes serve an impression motivation function, individuals will tend to generate arguments that support them, and that the stronger this function of the attitudes, the more arguments they will generate. To test this prediction, they asked participants to read a message arguing in favour of legalizing hard drugs. Then, participants were told that they would be asked to defend this view later to another person. To vary the level of participants' impression motivation, some were told that their performance in this role would not be evaluated (low motivation), others were told that it would be evaluated by one other person (the person they tried to convince; this was the moderate motivation condition), and still others were informed that it would be evaluated by the recipient plus two other people (high motivation). After receiving this information and reading the message, participants reported their attitudes and also indicated to what extent they had generated new arguments in favour of this position. As predicted, those in the high-motivation condition generated more new arguments and also reported that they would be more likely to use them in convincing the other person (see Figure 3.6).

The findings of this study indicate that the greater the extent to which attitudes serve an impression motivation function, the more they lead individuals to formulate

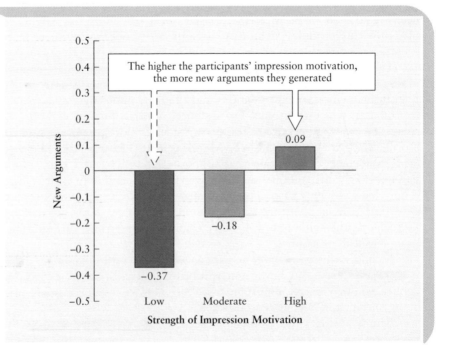

■ Attitudes: Their Impression Motivation Function

FIGURE 3.6 We sometimes use attitudes to make a good impression on others. In the study presented here, participants whose impression motivation was high generated more new arguments in support of their attitudes than did participants whose impression motivation was moderate or low.

Source: Based on data from Nienhuis, Manstead, & Spears, 2001.

The higher the participants' impression motivation, the more new arguments they generated arguments favouring these views. As we'll see in a later section, this, in turn, may make it more difficult to change such attitudes; after all, the persons who hold them can offer many arguments for doing so! In short, our attitudes serve many functions for us, and these functions, in turn, can strongly shape the impact of our attitudes' influence on our processing of social information.

KEY POINTS

- *Attitudes* are evaluations of any aspects of the social world.
- Attitudes are often acquired from other persons through *social learning*. Such learning can involve *classical conditioning, instrumental conditioning,* or *observational learning*. Subliminal stimuli can influence these processes.
- Culture can play a part in the transmission of *values*—broad and abstract principles of life. The cultural value dimension of individualism–collectivism has emerged as an important distinction.
- Studies conducted with identical twins suggest that attitudes may also be influenced by genetic factors, although the strength of such effects varies greatly for different attitudes.
- Attitudes serve a number of useful functions: a knowledge function, helping us to organize information; a self-expression function, expressing our beliefs; an ego defensive function, defending us from negative aspects of ourselves; and an impression motivation function, managing the impression we make on others.

The Attitude–Behaviour Link: When—and How— Attitudes Influence Behaviour

Do our attitudes influence our behaviour? Your first answer is likely to be "of course." After all, you can remember many incidents in which your own actions were strongly shaped by your opinions. You may be surprised to learn, therefore, that until quite recently, evidence concerning the strength of the link between attitudes and behaviour was far from conclusive. Many studies seemed to suggest that this relationship was sometimes more apparent than real. The classic study by LaPiere that triggered interest in this issue is featured in the Cornerstones section below.

Cornerstones

The Attitude–Behaviour Link: A Classic Study Throws Doubt on Its Existence

The classic study to be described here was conducted by LaPiere (1934) during the great economic depression of the 1930s. It was one of the first to bring the attitude–behaviour connection into question and had an unusual methodology—measuring the behaviour *before* the attitude.

At the time, social psychologists generally defined attitudes largely in terms of behaviour—as a set of tendencies or predispositions to behave in certain ways in social situations (Allport, 1924). Thus, they assumed that attitudes were generally reflected in overt behaviour. LaPiere, however, was not so certain.

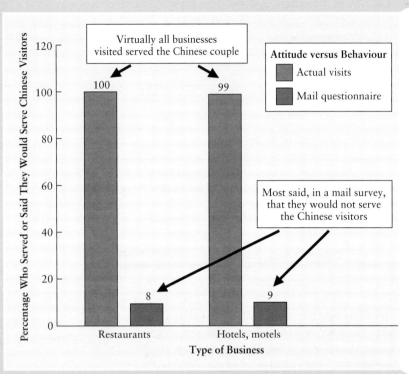

Virtually all businesses visited served the Chinese couple

Attitude versus Behaviour
Actual visits
Mail questionnaire

Most said, in a mail survey, that they would not serve the Chinese visitors

Percentage Who Served or Said They Would Serve Chinese Visitors

Restaurants — 100 / 8
Hotels, motels — 99 / 9

Type of Business

■ Evidence That Attitudes Don't Always Influence Behaviour

FIGURE 3.7 Virtually all restaurants, hotels, and motels visited by LaPiere and a young Chinese couple offered courteous service. When asked through the mail whether they would serve Chinese visitors, however, more than 90 percent said no. These findings suggest that there is sometimes a sizable gap between attitudes and behaviour.

Source: Based on data from LaPiere, 1934.

In particular, he wondered whether persons holding various prejudices—such as negative attitudes toward the members of various social groups (see Chapter 5)—would demonstrate these actions in their overt behaviour. To find out, he adopted a novel technique to discover how people would actually behave. For more than two years LaPiere travelled around the United States with a young Chinese couple. During these travels, they stopped at 184 restaurants and 66 hotels and "tourist camps" (predecessors of the modern motel). In the overwhelming majority of the cases, they were treated with courtesy and consideration. In fact, they were refused service only once; and in most cases they received what LaPiere (1934) described as an average to above-average level of treatment.

Now, however, the study gets really interesting. After the travels were complete, LaPiere measured people's attitudes by writing to all the businesses where he and the Chinese couple had stayed or dined, and asking whether they would offer service to Chinese visitors. The results were nothing short of astonishing: Out of the 128 establishments that responded, 92 percent of the restaurants and 91 percent of the hotels said no. In short, there was a tremendous gap between the attitudes expressed by these businesses (generally, by their owners or managers), and what they had done when confronted with live, in-the-flesh Chinese guests (see Figure 3.7). Similar attitudes were expressed by hotels and restaurants

LaPiere did not visit, so the sample appears to have been a representative one.

With the benefit of hindsight, we can see that this study had some design flaws. For example, the behaviour and attitude measures may have used different subjects—mangers may have been the ones writing back to LaPiere, reporting the establishment's policy (attitude measure), while their staff were the ones who actually served the couple (behaviour measure). Further, the attitude and behaviour measures covered somewhat different circumstances. The Chinese couple was not alone when served (they were accompanied by LaPiere, who was part of the mainstream society), but the attitude measure just asked about willingness to serve Chinese visitors.

Despite these problems, the study is considered a classic because of its place in social psychology—it stimulated debate and research into an important issue. LaPiere himself (1934) interpreted the results as indicating that there is often a sizable gap between attitudes and behaviour—between what people say and what they actually do. And related findings reported in later decades provided additional evidence that this can be the case (e.g., Wicker, 1969). Social psychologists began to focus a great deal of attention on the questions of *when* and *how* attitudes predict behaviour. In this respect, LaPiere's study, conducted so long ago and with methods so different from the rigorous ones used in modern research, exerted a strong and lasting impact on our field.

When Do Attitudes Influence Behaviour? Situational and Attitudinal Factors

Research on the question of *when* attitudes influence behaviour has uncovered several different factors that serve as what social psychologists term *moderators*—factors that influence the extent to which attitudes affect behaviour. We'll now consider two of the most important of these moderators: aspects of the situation and aspects of attitudes themselves.

Aspects of the Situation: Factors That Prevent Us from Expressing Our Attitudes

Have you ever been in the following situation? You are in a restaurant eating with a group of friends, and when the food arrives, there's something wrong—for instance, it's not what you ordered or it's cold. Yet when the server asks, "How is everything?" you and your friends all answer, "Fine." Why don't you express your true reactions? In other words, why doesn't your behaviour in this situation reflect your underlying attitudes? In this and many other contexts, *situational constraints* moderate the relationship between attitudes and behaviour: they prevent attitudes from being expressed in overt behaviour (e.g., Ajzen & Fishbein, 1980; Fazio & Roskos-Ewoldsen, 1994).

Situational factors can influence the link between attitudes and behaviour in one additional way worth noting. In general, we tend to prefer situations that allow us to express our attitudes in our behaviour. In other words, we often choose to enter and spend time in situations in which what we say and what we do can coincide (Snyder & Ickes, 1985). Indeed, because individuals tend to choose situations where they can engage in behaviours consistent with their attitudes, the attitudes themselves may be strengthened by this overt expression and so become even better predictors of behaviour (DeBono & Snyder, 1995). In sum, the relationship between attitudes and situations may be a two-way street. Situational pressures shape the extent to which attitudes can be expressed in overt actions; but in addition, attitudes determine whether individuals enter various situations. In order to understand the link between attitudes and behaviour, then, we must carefully consider both sets of factors.

Aspects of Attitudes Themselves

While the situation may limit our action, attitudes themselves also differ in ways that can affect the attitude–behaviour link. For example, considerable evidence indicates that attitudes formed on the basis of *direct experience* often exert stronger effects on behaviour than ones formed indirectly, through hearsay. Apparently, attitudes formed on the basis of direct experience tend to be stronger. You know yourself that if a particular attitude or value is very close to your heart—perhaps related to important political or religious views—it would be very difficult to ignore it in a relevant situation. So some types of attitude are more likely to influence behaviour than others.

Attitude Strength

Clearly, one of the most important factors in determining when attitudes predict behaviour is typically termed the *strength* of the attitudes. The stronger attitudes are, the greater their impact on behaviour (Petkova, Ajzen, & Driver, 1995). The term strength, however, includes several components: (1) the extremity or *intensity* of an attitude (how strong the emotional reaction provoked by the attitude object is); (2) *knowledge* (how much an individual knows about the attitude object); and (3) its *importance* (the extent to which an individual cares deeply about and is personally affected by the attitudinal object). Examining attitude importance, results of many studies indicate that the greater the personal relevance, the stronger the impact of the attitude on a person's behaviour (e.g., Crano, 1995, 1997; Crano & Prislin, 1995). For instance, in one famous study on this issue, Sivacek and Crano (1982) telephoned students at a large university and asked them if they would participate in a campaign against raising the legal age for drinking alcohol from 18 to 21. As you might have guessed, responses depended on age. Forty-seven percent of the students who were under 21, and therefore had a vested interest, agreed to take part in the campaign, whereas only 12 percent of those in older age groups did so. In sum, research findings indicate that all three components (intensity, knowledge, and importance) play a role in attitude (Krosnick et al., 1993; Kraus, 1995).

Attitude Specificity

A second aspect of attitudes themselves that influences their relationship to behaviour is *attitude specificity*—the extent to which attitudes are focused on specific objects or situations rather than on general ones. For example, you may have a general attitude toward religion (e.g., you believe that it is important for everyone to have religious convictions as opposed to not having them); in addition, you may have several specific attitudes about various aspects of religion—for instance, about the importance of attending services every week (this is important or unimportant) or about wearing a religious symbol (it's something I like to do—or don't like to do). Research findings indicate that the attitude–behaviour link is stronger when attitudes and behaviours are *measured at the same level of specificity*. For instance, we'd probably be more accurate in predicting whether you'll go to services this week from your attitude about the importance of attending services than from your attitude about religion generally. On the other hand, we'd probably be more accurate in predicting your willingness to take action to protect religious freedoms from your general attitude toward religion than from your attitude about wearing religious jewellery (Fazio & Roskos-Ewoldsen, 1994). So attitude specificity, too, is an important moderator of the attitude–behaviour link.

Attitude Ambivalence

We mentioned earlier that some attitudes can be more ambivalent than others—that is, they can involve mixed emotions, both positive and negative. It may not surprise you to hear that this characteristic can influence the extent to which an attitude influences the way we behave. For example, let's consider a recent study by Armitage and Conner (2000), which was concerned with the role of attitudinal ambivalence in the attitude–behaviour link. They hypothesized that ambivalent attitudes are weaker predictors of behaviour than attitudes that are not ambivalent. To find out, they asked more than 500 hospital employees to express their attitudes toward eating a low-fat diet (both positive and negative feelings about this action) and their intentions to do so. Five months later, these persons completed the same measures and also indicated whether they had actually eaten a low-fat diet during the intervening months. Finally, three months after the second session, participants once again reported their attitudes, intentions, and behaviour. On the basis of their reported attitudes toward a low-fat diet, participants were divided into those with ambivalent and nonambivalent attitudes (i.e., those who had both positive and negative feelings about such a diet, and those who had only positive or only negative feelings about it). The researchers predicted that ambivalent attitudes would be a weaker predictor of actual behaviour (following or not following such a diet) than nonambivalent attitudes, and this is precisely what happened. Those who had ambivalent attitudes were more weak-willed in their behaviour. Here the result is unfortunate, but this is not always the case—there is also evidence that ambivalence in prejudiced attitudes makes them more amenable to change (Son Hing, Li, & Zanna, 2002), as we will discuss in Chapter 5.

In sum, as we noted earlier, existing evidence suggests that attitudes really can and often do affect behaviour (e.g., Petty & Krosnick, 1995). However, the strength of this link is strongly determined by many different factors—situational constraints that permit or do not permit us to give overt expression to our attitudes, as well as several aspects of attitudes themselves (e.g., their strength, specificity, and ambivalence).

How Do Attitudes Influence Behaviour? Intentions, Willingness, and Action

Understanding *when* attitudes influence behaviour is an important topic. But, as we noted in Chapter 1, social psychologists are interested not only in the *when* of social thought and behaviour but in the *why* and *how* as well. So it should come as no surprise that researchers have also tried to understand how attitudes influence behaviour. Work on this issue points to the conclusion that in fact there are several basic mechanisms through which attitudes shape behaviour.

Attitudes, Reasoned Thought, and Behaviour

The first of these mechanisms operates in situations where we give careful, deliberate thought to our attitudes and their implications for our behaviour. Insights into the nature of this process are provided by the **theory of planned behaviour** (based on an earlier version of this framework known as the *theory of reasoned action*), proposed by Ajzen and Fishbein (1980; Ajzen, 1991). This theory suggests that the decision to engage in a particular behaviour is the result of a rational process that is goal-oriented and that follows a logical sequence. In this process we consider our behavioural options, evaluate the consequences or outcomes of each, and reach a decision to act or not to act. That decision is then reflected in our *behavioural intentions*, which, according to Fishbein, Ajzen, and many other researchers, are often strong predictors of how we will act in a given situation (Ajzen, 1987). Perhaps a specific example will help illustrate the very reasonable nature of this idea.

Suppose a student is considering body piercing—for instance, wearing a nose ornament. Will she actually take this action? According to Ajzen and Fishbein, the answer depends on her behavioural intentions, and these, in turn, are strongly influenced by three key factors. The first factor is the person's *attitudes toward the behaviour* in question. If the student really dislikes pain and the idea of someone sticking a needle through her nose, her intention to engage in such behaviour may be weak. The second factor is the person's beliefs about how others will evaluate this action (this factor is known as *subjective norms*). If the student thinks that others will approve of body piercing, her intention to perform it may be strengthened. If she believes that others will disapprove of it, her intentions may be weakened. Finally, intentions are also influenced by *perceived behavioural control*—the extent to which a person perceives a behaviour as hard or easy to accomplish. If it is viewed as difficult, intentions are weaker than if it is viewed as easy to perform. Together, these factors influence intentions, and intentions are the best single predictor of an individual's behaviour, as shown in Figure 3.8.

Recent surveys of research related to this model confirm its usefulness (e.g., Armitage & Conner, 2001). For instance, it has been used to predict people's intentions to use various drugs, such as marijuana, alcohol, and tobacco (e.g., Morojele & Stephenson, 1994; Conner & McMillan, 1999). And more recent work suggests that these theories are useful for predicting whether individuals will use *ecstasy,* a highly dangerous drug that is now used by a growing number of young persons between the ages of fifteen and twenty-five.

Theory of Planned Behaviour A theory of how attitudes guide behaviour suggesting that individuals consider the implications of their actions before deciding to perform various behaviours. An earlier version was known as the *theory of reasoned action*.

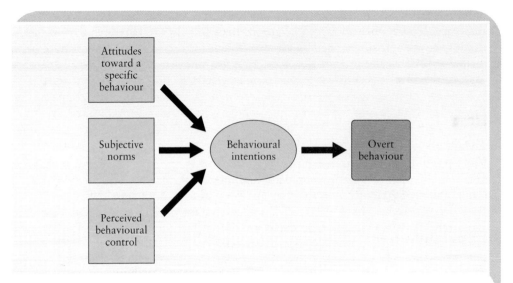

■ The Theory of Planned Behaviour

FIGURE 3.8 The theory of planned behaviour suggests that several factors (attitudes toward a given behaviour, subjective norms concerning that behaviour, and perceived ability to perform it) determine behavioural intentions concerning the behaviour. Such intentions, in turn, are a strong determinant of whether the behaviour is actually performed.

Source: Based on suggestions by Ajzen & Fishbein, 1980; Ajzen, 1991.

For instance, consider a study by Orbell and her colleagues (2001). They approached young people in various locations and asked them to complete a questionnaire designed to measure (1) their attitude toward ecstasy (e.g., is this drug enjoyable or not enjoyable, pleasant or unpleasant, beneficial or harmful, etc.), (2) their intention to use it in the next two months, (3) subjective norms (whether their friends would approve of their using it), and (4) two aspects of perceived control over using this drug—whether they could obtain it and whether they could resist taking it if they had some. Two months later, the same persons were contacted and asked whether they had actually used ecstasy ("How many pills of ecstasy have you taken in the last two months?"). Results indicated that attitudes toward ecstasy, subjective norms, and control over using it were all significant predictors of intention to use this drug. Further, attitudes, subjective norms, and intentions were significant predictors of actual use of ecstasy. Thus, overall, results were consistent with the theories of reasoned action and planned behaviour and indicated that the variables identified by these theories are very useful in predicting whether specific persons will or will not use this dangerous drug.

Attitudes and Immediate Behavioural Reactions

The model described above seems to be quite accurate in situations where we have the time and opportunity to reflect carefully on various actions. But what about situations in which we have to act quickly or when our actions are impulsive rather than reasoned? According to one theory—Fazio's **attitude-to-behaviour process model**—when we don't have time for careful thought, attitudes influence behaviour in a more direct and seemingly automatic manner (Fazio, 1989; Fazio & Roskos-Ewoldsen, 1994). The process is initiated when an event activates (primes) an attitude, making your attitude more accessible to you. The attitude then directly influences your perceptions of the

Attitude-to-Behaviour Process Model A model of how attitudes guide behaviour that emphasizes the influence of both attitudes and stored knowledge of what is appropriate (social norms) in a given situation on an individual's definition of the present situation. This definition, in turn, influences overt behaviour.

attitude object and your understanding or "definition" of the current situation. At the same time, *social norms* (stored social knowledge) will also contribute to your definition of the current situation. So both the attitude and the social norm together shape your definition of the situation; and it is this definition of the situation that influences your behaviour. Let's consider a concrete example.

Imagine that a panhandler approaches you on the street. What happens? This event triggers your attitude toward panhandlers and also your understanding of how people are expected to behave on public streets (the social norm). Together, these factors influence your definition of the situation, which might be "Oh no, another one of those worthless bums!" or "Gee, these homeless people have it rough!" Your definition of the event then shapes your behaviour. Several studies provide support for this model, so it seems to offer a useful explanation of how attitudes influence behaviour in some situations (e.g., Bargh, 1997; Dovidio et al., 1996).

In sum, it appears that attitudes affect our behaviour through at least two mechanisms, and that these operate under somewhat contrasting conditions. When we have time to engage in careful, reasoned thought, we can weigh all the alternatives and decide, quite deliberately, how to act. Under the hectic conditions of everyday life, however, we often don't have time for this kind of deliberate weighing of alternatives; in such cases, our attitudes seem to shape our perceptions of the situation and thus our immediate behavioural reactions to them.

KEY POINTS

- Several factors serve as moderators of the link between attitudes and behaviour, affecting the strength of this relationship. *Situational constraints* may prevent us from expressing our attitudes overtly. In addition, we tend to prefer situations that allow us to express our *attitudes*, and this may further strengthen these views.

- Several aspects of attitudes themselves also moderate the attitude—behaviour link. These include *attitude strength* (which includes attitude knowledge, intensity and importance), *attitude specificity* and *attitude ambivalence*

- Attitudes seem to influence behaviour through several mechanisms. The *theory of planned behaviour* suggests that when we can give careful thought to our attitudes, intentions derived from our attitudes strongly predict behaviour.

- In situations where we can't engage in such deliberate thought, the *attitude-to-behaviour process model* suggests that attitudes influence behaviour by shaping our perceptions of the situation.

Persuasion: The Art of Changing Attitudes

How many times during the past 24 hours has someone, or some organization, tried to change your attitudes? If you stop and think for a moment you may be surprised at the result, for it is clear that every day we are bombarded with countless efforts of this type—see Figure 3.9. Newspaper and magazine ads, radio and television commercials, political speeches, appeals from charitable organizations—the list seems almost endless. To what extent are such attempts at **persuasion**—efforts to change our attitudes through the use of various kinds of messages—successful? And what factors determine whether they succeed or fail? It is to these issues that we turn next.

Persuasion The process through which one or more persons attempt to alter the attitudes of one or more others.

Persuasion: A Part of Daily Life

FIGURE 3.9 Each day we are literally bombarded with dozens of messages designed to change our attitudes and behaviour.

Persuasion: The Early Approach

In most cases, efforts at persuasion involve the following elements: some source (a communicator) directs some type of message (the communication) to a person or group (the audience). Taking note of this fact, much early research on persuasion from Yale University (Hovland, Janis, & Kelley, 1953) focused on these key elements of the process of communication. This approach yielded many interesting findings, and among the most consistent—having stood the test of time—are those summarized in Table 3.2.

When Hovland and colleagues investigated factors that increased persuasion, they focused on (1) the *communicator*—the source of the communication; (2) the *message*—the content of the persuasive communication; and (3) the *audience*—the recipients of the communication. In other words, they investigated "*who* said *what* to *whom*."

TABLE 3.2 Persuasion: The Early Approach

Factors that increase effectiveness of a persuasive communication:

Communicator

Credibility
Includes expertise, trustworthiness, and sincerity
(e.g., Hovland & Weiss, 1951)

Attractiveness
Includes good looks, popularity, and likeability
(e.g., Hovland et al., 1953)

Speaks rapidly
Rapid speech seems to suggest expertise
(e.g., Miller et al., 1976)

Message

Non-obvious persuasion
Messages that do not seem too obvious in their attempt to influence
(e.g., Walster & Festinger, 1962)

Both sides of the issue
Presenting both sides of an issue is more effective, especially if the audience is knowledgeable about the issues and you can refute an opponent's perspective
(e.g., Lumsdaine & Janis, 1953)

Arousing emotion
Strong emotion can enhance persuasion; use of fear is effective if the level is moderate and ways to avoid the feared situation are included
(e.g., Leventhal, Stinger & Jones, 1965; Rodgers, 1984)

Audience

Low or moderate self-esteem
Early research suggested that people with low self-esteem are more persuadable, but recent research suggests it is those with moderate self-esteem
(e.g., Janis, 1954; Rhodes & Wood, 1992)

Younger age groups
Younger individuals are more persuadable compared to adults over 25
(e.g., Sears, 1981)

Advertisers today are still using the principles of persuasive communication that the Yale University researchers discovered.

The Cognitive Approach to Persuasion: Systematic versus Heuristic Processing

The early approach to understanding persuasion has certainly been useful; it provided a wealth of insights into factors that influence persuasion. It did not, however, offer a coherent account of *how* people (the audience) change their attitudes in response to persuasive messages and under what conditions this will occur. This issue has been brought into sharp focus in a more modern approach to understanding the nature of persuasion known as the *cognitive perspective* (Petty, Cacioppo, Strathman, & Priester, 1994, 1986; Eagly & Chaiken, 1998). This approach rests firmly on social psychology's increasingly sophisticated understanding of the nature of social thought—in this case how we process (absorb, interpret, and evaluate) the information contained in persuasive messages. What happens when individuals receive a persuasive message? According to the cognitive approach, that depends upon whether the individual subjects the message to *systematic processing*, thinking carefully about it, or uses more simple *heuristic processing*.

The Elaboration Likelihood Model: Two Routes to Persuasion

The most influential theory from this perspective, the **elaboration likelihood model** (ELM), suggests that two different cognitive routes to persuasion are possible, reflecting whether the recipient elaborates upon—thinks carefully about—a persuasive message. The first of these is known as the **central route**, and it involves *systematic processing*—careful consideration of message content, the ideas it contains, and so on. Such processing is quite effortful and absorbs much of our information-processing capacity. The second approach, known as the **peripheral route**, involves *heuristic processing*—the use of simple rules of thumb or mental shortcuts—such as the belief that "experts can be trusted" or the idea that "if it makes me feel good, I'm in favour of it." This kind of processing is much less effortful and allows us to react to persuasive messages in an automatic manner. It occurs in response to **persuasion cues** in the message—cues that evoke various mental shortcuts (e.g., beautiful models who evoke the "What's beautiful is good and worth listening to" heuristic). This model is summarized in Figure 3.10.

When do we engage in each of these two distinct modes of thought? The answer, in part, is that it depends upon our capacity and our motivation to process the persuasive message. Briefly, we use the systematic processing (or the central route) when our capacity to process information relating to the persuasive message is high (e.g., when we have lots of knowledge about the subject or lots of time to engage in such thought) or when we are motivated to do so—when the issue is important to us, when we believe it is important to form an accurate view, and so on (e.g., Maheswaran & Chaiken, 1991; Petty & Cacioppo, 1990). In contrast, we use heuristic processing (or the peripheral route) when we lack the ability or capacity to process more carefully (we must make up our minds very quickly, we have little knowledge about the issue, and so on) or when our motivation to perform such cognitive work is low (the issue is unimportant to us or has little potential effect on us, and so on). Advertisers, politicians, salespersons, and others wishing to change our attitudes often prefer to push us into the heuristic mode of processing because, for reasons we'll describe below, it is often easier to change our attitudes when we think in this mode than when we engage in more careful and systematic processing.

Elaboration Likelihood Model (of persuasion) A theory suggesting that persuasion can occur in either of two distinct ways, differing in the amount of cognitive effort or elaboration they require.

Central Route (to persuasion) Attitude change resulting from systematic processing of information presented in persuasive messages.

Peripheral Route (to persuasion) Attitude change that occurs in response to heuristic processing or persuasion cues.

Persuasion Cues Simple cues in a persuasive communication, involving superficial characteristics of the communicator or the message, that often evoke the use of mental shortcuts or heuristic processing.

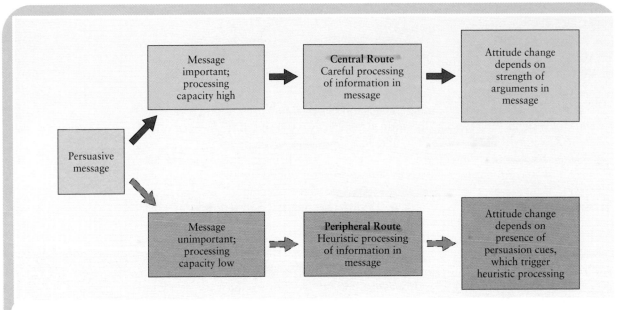

■ The ELM: One Cognitive Theory of Persuasion

FIGURE 3.10 According to the *elaboration likelihood model* (ELM), persuasion can occur in either of two distinct ways: through careful, systematic processing of the information contained in the persuasive messages (the *central route*) or through less systematic processing based on heuristics or mental shortcuts (the *peripheral route*). We engage in *systematic processing* when the message is important to us and we have the cognitive resources (and time) to think about it carefully. We engage in *heuristic processing* when the message is not important to us or we do not have the cognitive resources (or time) to engage in careful thought.

Source: © Based on suggestions by Petty & Cacioppo, 1986.

Earlier, we noted that the discovery of these two contrasting modes of processing provided an important key to understanding the process of persuasion. The existence of these two modes of thought has helped us solve many intriguing puzzles. For instance, it has been found that when persuasive messages are not interesting or relevant to individuals, the amount of persuasion they produce is *not* strongly influenced by the quality of the arguments they contain. But when such messages are highly relevant to individuals, they are much more successful in inducing persuasion if the arguments they contain are strong and convincing. Can you see why this so? According to modern theories such as the ELM, when relevance is low, individuals tend to process messages through the heuristic mode, by means of cognitive shortcuts. Thus, argument quality has little impact on them. In contrast, when relevance is high, they process persuasive messages through the systematic (central) route, and in this mode, argument quality is important (e.g., Petty & Cacioppo, 1990).

Similarly, the systematic-versus-heuristic distinction helps explain why people are more easily persuaded when they are somehow distracted—in a sense, asked to do two things at once—than when they are not. Under these conditions, the capacity to process the information in a persuasive message is limited, so people adopt the heuristic mode of thought. If the message contains the "right" persuasion cues (e.g., communicators who are attractive or seemingly expert), persuasion may occur because distracted people respond to these cues and not to the arguments being presented. In sum, this modern cognitive approach really does seem to provide a crucial key to understanding many aspects of persuasion.

Finally it should be noted that research investigating cultural differences in the effectiveness of persuasion cues, points to the importance of cultural values in a persuasive communication. Han and Shavitt (1994) found that advertisements in Korea used slogans that reflected collectivistic values (e.g., "Sharing is beautiful"; "We have a way of bringing people together"), while advertisements in the United States reflected individualistic values (e.g., "The art of being unique"; " You only get better"). Further, these slogans were more effective with those from the appropriate culture. Given that we live in a multicultural society, persuaders of all kinds should increase their knowledge of different cultural values.

In the following On the Applied Side section, we once again examine a context in which persuaders make use of heuristic processing—the use of propaganda in times of war.

On the **Applied Side**

Psychological Warfare:
Persuasion and Propaganda during the Iraq War

There's a well-known saying—*the first casualty of war is the truth*—referring to the fact that communication from both sides during conflict is likely to be biased. But more than just biased, this communication has a *persuasive* purpose—one that is usually multifaceted. For example, persuasion may attempt to turn public opinion towards supporting the war, or give the impression that the war is going well; alternatively, it may try to demoralize the opposition or persuade its citizens to cooperate with the invaders; or perhaps attempt to do all these things at once.

During the Iraq war in 2003, many of us were glued to our televisions or radios, keeping track of developments, listening to news broadcasts. We were, therefore, recipients of this special kind of persuasive communication. Did you feel that this media coverage had an impact on you? In retrospect, were you influenced to think and feel in ways that the communicators intended? If so, then you were the victim of what is termed propaganda—a type of persuasion used to influence a large population, usually through mass communication, towards ideology, beliefs, and behaviours that will benefit the propagandist (Jowett & O'Donnell, 1999; Pratkanis & Aronson, 1991). The term *psychological warfare* is used when propaganda attempts to influence the

Propaganda
A type of persuasion, usually using methods of mass communication, that attempts to influence large numbers of people towards ideological beliefs and behaviours that will benefit the propagandist.

enemy (Taylor, 1995). Compared to most forms of persuasion, propaganda is often seen by researchers as less benevolent and *more self-interested* in its purpose and *more indirect* in its manipulations (Jowett & O'Donnell, 1999).

Propaganda is seen as more self-interested in purpose than persuasion because there is less attempt to be interactive or cooperative with the needs of recipients (Jowett & O'Donnell, 1999). As one communication researcher put it, "...what distinguishes propaganda from all other processes of persuasion is the question of *intent*. Propaganda uses communication to convey a message, an idea, or an ideology that is designed primarily to serve the self-interest of the person or people doing the communicating" (Taylor, 1995, p. 7). Similarly, psychologists Pratkanis and Turner (1996) see *persuasion* generally as based in "debate, discussion and careful consideration of options" between communicator and recipient in order to find "better solutions for complex problems." Propaganda, on the other hand is less cooperative and "results in the manipulation of the mob by the elite."

Propaganda is also seen as more indirect because it has its impact through the use of heuristic processing and *persuasion cues* rather than though reasoned arguments. It appeals to the emotions and relates itself to culturally important values—it "creates resonance with the target audience," as one researcher put it (Jowett & O'Donnell, 1999). It uses "simple images and slogans that truncate thought by playing on prejudices and emotions" (Pratkanis & Turner, 1996). One example is the naming of military operations. In

FIGURE 3.11 This photo is one of the enduring symbols of the overthrow of Saddam Hussein and has now been shown thousands of times around the world. At the point that this occurred, it provided an important propaganda image for the U.S.–British coalition, symbolizing not only the defeat of Saddam Hussein but the endorsement of this by Iraqi people who were seen to be helping in the toppling of this statue.

the case of the Iraq war it was "Operation Iraqi Freedom." Freedom is perhaps the central American value and would certainly resonate with the American public and many in the West. Here, by implication, the invasion of Iraq is being presented as a mission of liberation. The simple and truncated communication of propaganda is full of symbolism (see Figure 3.11) and metaphor. In one example, Saddam Hussein threatened that "Americans will swim in their own blood," referring to their eventual defeat.

When talking of the actions of your own side, euphemisms (mild and pleasant ways of describing harsh realities) abound in wartime propaganda. Using the term "collateral damage" to refer to civilian casualties is one well-known example. In his address to the United States at the start of the war in March 2003, George W. Bush referred to the actions of coalition forces as "military operations to disarm Iraq" and "a campaign...helping Iraqis to achieve a united, stable and free country..."—no mention was made of the destruction and suffering this might involve and certainly no use of the word "war." The images shown can be equally euphemistic. For example, Iraqi casualties were seldom shown in Western media. Pictures of Iraqi citizens greeting troops and waving emphasized how much the coalition was welcomed by the ordinary Iraqi. In contrast, when propaganda describes the enemy, its language and images become harsher. For example, Saddam Hussein referred to the first President Bush at various times as "Oppressor Bush," "Loathsome Criminal," "Evil Butcher," and "America's Satan" (Jowett & O'Donnell, 1999). George W. Bush referred to "Saddam and his corrupt gang."

The effectiveness of propaganda in war has recently led to the formation of military units dedicated to *psychological warfare*—persuasive communication directed towards the enemy's military and citizens. These units are termed "psyops"—short for psychological operations—and one example in the Iraqi war was a unit of 42 Commando Royal Marines who distributed 50 different types of leaflets to Iraqi military and civilian targets as well as setting up propaganda radio stations (Edwards, Guardian Newspapers, March, 2003). Their role was to encourage the Iraqi military to surrender, to reassure civilians they would not be harmed if they cooperate, and to counter the negative propaganda about the invading forces coming from the Hussein regime. In the last weeks of the Iraq conflict, a television station called *Towards Freedom Television* was set up in a Hercules aircraft to broadcast statements from President Bush and Prime Minister Blair, as well as American news programs, to the Iraqi people. When propaganda is directed at the opposition, ensuring that it is culturally appropriate can be crucial. References to "freedom" in the naming of this station may not have had the same resonance in Iraq as they would in the West. Similarly, the elaborate language used in Arab rhetoric often seems overblown and, therefore, less convincing to Western ears.

The impact of wartime propaganda is weakened if the enemy also has access to the same population that the propagandist is trying to shape. This is because the simplified and emotional language of propaganda is responded to with superficial heuristic processing and the attitudes formed this way tend to be vulnerable to counter-persuasion. They can be swayed in the other direction by new images as easily as they were initially formed. In contrast, attitudes formed through systematic thinking tend to be much stronger and more resistant to counter-persuasion (Petty et al., 1994). Because they are aware of the vulnerability of their persuasive attempts, propagandists will often attempt to control the media—censorship is an integral part of wartime propaganda (Taylor, 1995). Military briefings for the media and the new practice of "embedding" journalists during the Iraq war (individual journalists travelled with a military units) may have enabled greater control of their broadcasts and decreased journalistic independence.

However, with the advent of the modern media technologies—the Internet and flexible broadcasting techniques—control of the media is much more difficult to achieve. For example, Al-Jazeera, the Qatar-based Arab network, provided very different images and information from CNN broadcasts, both on television and the Internet. It showed pictures of U.S. prisoners of war and dead British soldiers, as well as many images of injured Iraqi civilians, both adults and children. Interviews with

Colin Powell (the U.S. Secretary of State) were inter-cut with critical commentary or photos of dead civilians. American commentators accused the station of bias (Jimenez, *National Post*, April, 2003). Al-Jareera saw itself as telling the real truth about the war and countered by accusing the Western media of bias, as well as sabotage of the Al-Jazeera Web site (Bodi, *The Guardian Newspaper*, March 28, 2003).

Finally, when considering the issue of propaganda, particularly as it applies to such a difficult time, two things should be kept in mind: (1) because something is propaganda doesn't necessarily mean it is untrue (though biased presentation and selection of material are at the heart of propaganda); and (2) propaganda can be used for positive as well as negative purposes. What defines something as propaganda is not the content of its message, but its *method* and that its purpose is to further the ends of the *propagandist*. Of course, your view of the truth or necessity of Iraq war propaganda, from either side, will depend on your view of the necessity of that war—and, as you know, opinions differ.

KEY POINTS

- Early research on *persuasion*-efforts to change attitudes through the use of messages-focused primarily on characteristics of the communicator (e.g., expertise, attractiveness), the message (e.g., one-sidedness versus two-sidedness), and the audience.

- More recent research has focused on the cognitive processes that play a role in persuasion. Research related to the elaboration *likelihood model* (ELM) suggests that we process persuasive messages in two distinct ways: through systematic processing with the *central route*, which involves careful attention to message content, or through heuristic processing, with the *peripheral route*, which involves the use of mental shortcuts (e.g., "experts are usually right").

- We will utilize the central route, using systematic processing, when our cognitive capacity is high and when the message is important or relevant to us. In this mode, quality of the arguments is crucial.

- We will use the peripheral route and heuristic processing when message relevance and cognitive capacity are low. Persuasion cues, rather than argument quality, will influence persuasion. Cultural values reflected in persuasion cues may play a part in the effectiveness of peripheral route persuasion.

- Propaganda is a special type of persuasion that influences attitudes through heuristic processing, and is used during wartime to influence public opinion.

When Attitude Change Fails: Resistance to Persuasion

In view of the frequency with which we are exposed to persuasive messages, one point is clear: We are highly resistant to them. If we were not, our attitudes on a wide range of issues would be in a constant state of change. This raises an intriguing question:

Why are we such a "tough sell" where efforts to change our attitudes are concerned? The answer involves several factors that, together, enhance our ability to resist even highly skilled efforts at persuasion.

Reactance: Protecting Our Personal Freedom

Have you ever found yourself becoming irritated at one of the "motivational" speakers on television or a salesperson who tries too hard? You begin to feel "brow-beaten" and feel that you want to find holes in their every argument. You may, in fact, turn off your television or escape from the salesperson. This is an example of what social psychologists term <u>reactance</u>—the negative reactions we experience when we conclude that someone is trying to limit our personal freedom by getting us to do what he or she wants us to do. Research findings suggest that in such situations we often change our attitudes (or behaviour) in a direction exactly opposite to that being urged on us—an effect known as *negative attitude change* (Brehm, 1966; Rhodewalt & Davison, 1983). Indeed, so strong is the desire to resist excessive influence that in some cases individuals shift away from a view someone is advocating even if it is one they would otherwise normally accept!

The existence of reactance is one main reason why hard-sell attempts at persuasion often fail. When individuals perceive such appeals as direct threats to their personal freedom (or to their image of being a free and independent human being), they are strongly motivated to resist. And such resistance, in turn, virtually guarantees that many would-be persuaders are doomed to fail.

Forewarning: Prior Knowledge of Persuasive Intent

On many occasions when we receive a persuasive message, we know full well that it is designed to change our views. Indeed, situations in which a communicator manages to catch us completely unprepared are quite rare. Does such advance knowledge or <u>forewarning</u> of persuasive intent help us to resist? Research evidence suggests that it does (e.g., Cialdini & Petty, 1979; Johnson, 1994). When we know that a speech, taped message, or written appeal is designed to alter our views, we are often less likely to be affected by it than if we do not possess such knowledge. The basis for such beneficial effects seems to lie in the impact that forewarning has on key cognitive processes. Forewarning provides more opportunity to formulate *counterarguments* and the time in which to recall relevant facts and information from memory (Wood, 1982). Such effects are more likely to occur with respect to attitudes we consider to be important (Krosnick, 1989), but they occur to a smaller degree even for attitudes we view as fairly trivial.

Further, if a communicator provides not only forewarning but also provides the counterarguments against the persuasive attempt, an individual's ability to withstand persuasion is increased. This process is referred to as "inoculation" because it helps the recipient to "build resistance" to that specific type of persuasion by building up effective arguments. Several early studies demonstrated the effectiveness of this process (McGuire, 1961; McGuire & Papageorgis, 1961). They show that, truly, to be forewarned is to be forearmed where persuasion is concerned.

Selective Avoidance and Biased Assimilation: Protecting Existing Attitudes

We mentioned in Chapter 2 that schemas tend to be self-perpetuating. Attitudes, which can act as schemas, are much the same: our cognitive and emotional responses to a

Reactance Negative reactions to perceived threats to one's personal freedom. Reactance often increases resistance to persuasion.

Forewarning Advance knowledge that one is about to become the target of an attempt at persuasion. Forewarning often increases resistance to the persuasion that follows.

Passive (① & ②) Defence.

persuasive message sometimes help to preserve existing attitudes. Two ways in which this happens are through selective avoidance and biased assimilation. **Selective avoid-ance** is a tendency to direct our attention away from information that challenges our existing attitudes. For example, consider the act of television viewing. Often people do not simply sit in front of the tube and absorb whatever the media decide to dish out. Instead, they channel surf, push the mute button, or cognitively tune out when confronted with information contrary to their existing views. The opposite effect occurs as well: When we encounter information that supports our views, we tend to give it increased attention. We stop changing channels and listen carefully. Together, these tendencies to ignore or avoid information that contradicts our attitudes while actively seeking information consistent with them constitute the two sides of *selective exposure*—deliberate efforts to obtain information that supports our views.

When we cannot avoid information that contradicts our attitudes, our attitudes can still be protected through **biased assimilation**—evaluating information that dis-confirms our existing views as less convincing and less reliable than information that confirms our existing views (e.g., Lord, Ross, & Lepper, 1979; Miller et al., 1993). Through this mechanism, we often protect our current attitudes against persuasion and assure that they remain largely intact for long periods.

As a result of these two processes, our attitudes really do seem to be beyond the reach of many efforts to change them, and they tend to persist even when we are confronted with new information that strongly challenges them (e.g., Munro & Ditto, 1997).

Selective Avoidance
A tendency to direct one's attention away from information that challenges existing atti-tudes. Such avoidance increases resistance to persuasion.

Biased Assimilation
The tendency to evalu-ate information that disconfirms our existing views as less convincing or reliable than infor-mation that confirms these views.

Active Defence of Our Existing Attitudes: Counterarguing against Competing Views

Active Defence

Ignoring or misperceiving information incongruent with our current views is certainly one way of resisting persuasion. But growing evidence suggests that, in addition to this kind of passive defence of our attitudes, we also use a more active strategy: We actively counterargue against views contrary to our own (e.g., Eagly et al., 1999). Doing so makes these opposing views more memorable but reduces their impact on our attitudes. Clear evidence for such effects has been reported recently by Eagly and her colleagues (2000).

These researchers exposed students previously identified as either for or against abortion on demand to persuasive messages delivered by a female communicator; these messages were either consistent with their attitudes or contrary to their views. After hearing the messages, participants reported their attitudes toward abortion, how sure they were of their views (a measure of attitude strength), and all of the arguments in the message they could recall (a measure of memory). In addition, they listed the thoughts they had while listening to the message; this provided information on the extent to which they counterargued internally against the message that was contrary to their own views.

Results indicated that, as expected, the counterattitudinal message and the proat-titudinal message were equally memorable. However, participants reported thinking more systematically about the counterattitudinal message, and reported having more oppositional thoughts about it—a clear sign that they were indeed counterarguing against this message. In contrast, they reported more supportive thoughts in response to the proattitudinal message (see Figure 3.12).

So it appears that one reason we are so good at resisting persuasion is that we not only ignore information inconsistent with our current views—we also carefully process such counterattitudinal input and argue actively against it. In a sense, we pro-vide our own strong defence against efforts to change our attitudes.

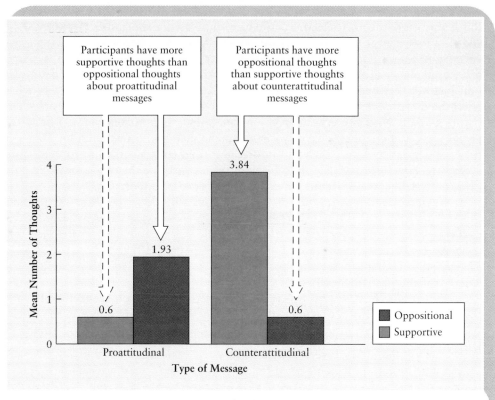

Participants have more supportive thoughts than oppositional thoughts about proattitudinal messages

Participants have more oppositional thoughts than supportive thoughts about counterattitudinal messages

- Counterarguing against Counterattitudinal Messages

FIGURE 3.12 Participants reported having more oppositional thoughts about a counterattitudinal message than about a proattitudinal message. In contrast, they reported having more supportive thoughts about a proattitudinal message than about a counterattitudinal message. These findings are consistent with the view that one reason we are so good at resisting persuasion is that we actively defend our attitudes against opposing views by counterarguing against them.

Source: Based on data from Eagly et al., 2000.

KEY POINTS

- Our attitudes tend to remain quite stable despite many efforts to change them. Several factors contribute to such resistance to persuasion. One such factor is *reactance*—negative reactions to efforts by others to reduce or limit our personal freedom. When we interpret efforts at persuasion as producing such effects, we reject them and may even adopt views opposite to these being urged upon us.

- Resistance to persuasion is often increased by *forewarning*, the knowledge that someone is trying to change our attitudes and by providing counterarguments in an inoculation process. Protection of existing attitudes is achieved through *selective avoidance* (avoiding exposure to information that contradicts our views) and by *biased assimilation* (when contradictory information is judged as less convincing than information confirming our views).

- In addition, when we are exposed to persuasive messages contrary to our existing views, we actively counterargue against the information they contain. This too increases our resistance to persuasion.

Cognitive Dissonance: How Our Behaviour Can Influence Our Attitudes

Suppose that you have very strong feelings about the need to protect the environment and have always tried to behave in environmentally sound ways: recycling, getting involved in the environmental movement, and refusing to drive a car even though this is inconvenient—you live a long way from school and work. Now, however, a family member is offering you his old car at virtually no cost. Of course, you should refuse. But it's the middle of winter and you have just taken on extra hours at work, which makes your schedule very tight. A car would make life so much simpler and those long, cold waits at the bus stop would be a thing of the past! You accept this generous offer, telling yourself this is just a temporary state of affairs. However, six months later, in the middle of summer, you still have the car. One day you meet a friend who is involved in the environmental movement and is shocked that you own a car after your previously strong stand on this issue. You find yourself explaining at length that this is only a temporary situation, it's an absolute necessity with your very busy lifestyle, and it doesn't imply that your beliefs about the environment have changed. But afterward, you find yourself feeling very uncomfortable—somehow these justifications rang hollow, even in your own ears. What accounts for this discomfort? You have just become aware that your behaviour is clearly inconsistent with your attitudes—now you are also questioning your own commitment to the environment. Social psychologists term this kind of discomfort __cognitive dissonance__ (Festinger, 1957).

This is the feeling, usually unpleasant (e.g., Harmon-Jones, 2000), that arises when we discover inconsistency between two of our attitudes or between our attitudes and our behaviour (see Figure 3.13). There are many causes of dissonance. It can occur when individuals must choose between two attractive alternatives, such as rejecting one job, school, or lover in favour of another. This rejection is inconsistent with the positive features of the rejected option. Most relevant to our present discussion, though, is the fact that dissonance is generated whenever individuals say things they don't mean or behave in ways that are inconsistent with their underlying attitudes or values. In such cases, the dissonance produced can sometimes have a startling effect: It can lead the people involved to change their attitudes so that these more closely reflect their words and deeds. In other words, saying or doing things that are inconsistent with their own attitudes sometimes causes people to *change the attitudes themselves*. How can this be so? Read on.

Cognitive Dissonance An unpleasant internal state that results when individuals notice inconsistency between two or more of their attitudes or between their attitudes and their behaviour.

Dissonance and Attitude Change: The Effects of Induced Compliance

There are many occasions in everyday life when we must say or do things inconsistent with our real attitudes. For example, your friend has a new haircut and asks you how you like it. You really hate it but know your friend has to walk around with it for at least a few weeks. What do you say? Probably something like "Nice, really nice."

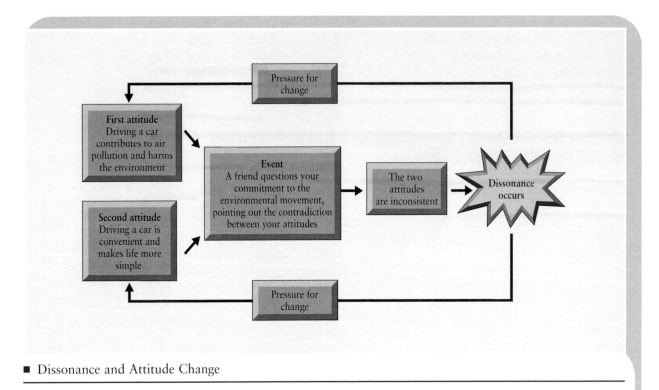

■ Dissonance and Attitude Change

FIGURE 3.13 When individuals notice that two attitudes they hold are somehow inconsistent, cognitive dissonance occurs. This process generates pressure to change one or both of the attitudes involved.

Induced Compliance Situations in which individuals are somehow induced to say or do things inconsistent with their true attitudes; also known as *forced compliance*.

Methods to reduce dissonance caused by induced compliance (direct tactics)

Trivialization The conclusion that the attitudes or behaviours in question are not important, so the inconsistency itself is trivial.

Similarly, imagine that at an important meeting your boss turns to you and asks your opinion of her new plan. Since you value your relationship with her (and your job!) you praise the plan, even though you realize it has serious problems. In these and countless other situations, our actions and our attitudes are inconsistent. What happens in these situations, which social psychologists describe as involving **induced compliance** (or *forced compliance*)? This term derives from the fact that in such incidents we are induced or forced by circumstances to say or do things contrary to our real views. Since dissonance is an unpleasant state (Elliot & Devine, 1994), people who experience it are motivated to reduce it. So something has to give (change). The theory focuses on three basic mechanisms.

First, individuals can use *actual change* of their attitudes or their behaviour so that they are now consistent with each other. For example, you may convince yourself that your boss's plan is actually better than you thought or, in the first example, you might decide to sell your car to bring your behaviour in line with your environmental attitudes. Second, dissonance can be reduced by acquiring *new information*—information that is consistent with the attitudes or actions that, at first blush, seem inconsistent. For example, you might eagerly read a news report claiming that cars contribute relatively little to air pollution compared to industrial chemicals (ignoring the fact that this report was sponsored by a major car manufacturer). Finally, dissonance can be reduced by *minimizing the importance* of the inconsistency. This is termed **trivialization**—when we conclude that the attitudes or behaviours in question are not important, so the inconsistency itself is trivial (Simon, Greenberg, & Brehm, 1995).

All of these strategies can be viewed as *direct* approaches to dissonance reduction: they focus on the attitude—behaviour discrepancies that are causing the dissonance. Research by Steele and his colleagues (e.g., Steele, 1988; Steele & Lui, 1983), however, indicates that dissonance can also be reduced through *indirect* tactics—ones that leave the basic discrepancy between attitudes and behaviour intact but reduce the unpleasant negative feelings generated by dissonance. According to Steele (1988), adoption of such indirect routes to dissonance reduction is most likely to occur when an attitude—behaviour discrepancy involves important attitudes or self-beliefs. Under these conditions, individuals may focus not so much on reducing the gap between their attitudes and their behaviour as on *self-affirmation*—restoring positive self-evaluations that are threatened by the dissonance (e.g., Elliot & Devine, 1994; Tesser, Martin, & Cornell, 1996). How can they accomplish this goal? By focusing on their positive self-attributes—good things about themselves (e.g., Steele, 1988). For instance, in the original example, you might focus on what a caring person you are in general. You have given many hours to helping your friends as well as regularly volunteering to help the elderly. Contemplating these positive actions would help reduce the discomfort produced by your failure to act in a way consistent with your pro-environmental attitudes.

Other research suggests that almost anything we do that reduces our discomfort and negative affect can sometimes succeed in reducing cognitive dissonance—everything from consuming alcohol (e.g., Steele, Southwick, & Critchlow, 1981) to engaging in distracting activities that take one's mind off the dissonance (e.g., Zanna & Aziza, 1976) to simple expressions of positive affect (Cooper, Fazio, & Rhodewalt, 1978).

Thus, dissonance can be reduced in many different ways—through indirect tactics as well as through direct ones focused on reducing the attitude–behaviour discrepancy. In general, the principle behind our choice of these dissonance-reduction techniques is "Whenever possible, take the path of least resistance." Our choice may also be a function of what's available and the specific context in which dissonance occurs (e.g., Fried & Aronson, 1995). So we will seek to reduce dissonance by changing whatever it is easiest and possible to change and sometimes that is our attitude itself.

Dissonance and the Less-Leads-to-More Effect

Social psychologists generally agree that the *induced compliance effect* occurs: When individuals say or do things they don't believe, they often experience a need to bring their attitudes into line with these actions. There is one complication in this process we have not yet considered, however: How strong are the reasons for engaging in counterattitudinal actions? If these reasons are quite strong, little or no dissonance will be generated. After all, if the last person to disagree with your boss publicly was fired on the spot, you would have strong grounds for praising her plan even if you don't like it. But what if good, convincing reasons for engaging in such actions are lacking? Under these conditions, dissonance will be stronger, for you must confront the fact that you said or did something you didn't believe *even though you had no strong or clear basis for doing so*. In short, dissonance theory points to the unexpected prediction that the weaker the reasons for engaging in counterattitudinal behaviour, the stronger the dissonance generated, and hence the greater the pressure to change one's attitudes, as shown in Figure 3.14. Social psychologists often refer to this paradoxical prediction as the <u>less-leads-to-more effect:</u> The more inducements there are for engaging in attitude-discrepant behaviour, the weaker the pressures toward attitude change.

Less-Leads-to-More Effect The fact that offering individuals small rewards for engaging in counterattitudinal behaviour often produces more dissonance, and so more attitude change, than offering them larger rewards.

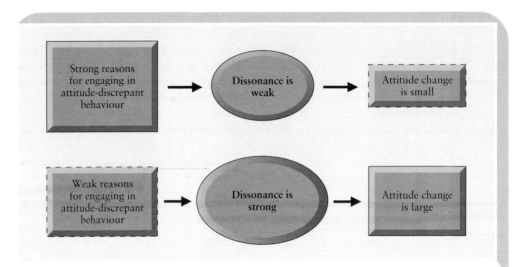

Strong reasons for engaging in attitude-discrepant behaviour → Dissonance is weak → Attitude change is small

Weak reasons for engaging in attitude-discrepant behaviour → Dissonance is strong → Attitude change is large

■ Why Less (Smaller Inducements) Often Leads to More (Greater Attitude Change) after Attitude-Discrepant Behaviour

FIGURE 3.14 When individuals have strong reasons for engaging in attitude-discrepant behaviour, they experience relatively small amounts of dissonance and relatively weak pressure to change their attitudes. However, when individuals have weak reasons for engaging in attitude-discrepant behaviour, they experience larger amounts of dissonance and stronger pressure to change their attitudes. The result: Less (smaller rewards) leads to more (greater amount of attitude change).

Surprising as it may seem, this effect has been confirmed in many different studies (e.g., Riess & Schlenker, 1977). For example, in the first and most famous of these experiments (Festinger & Carlsmith, 1959), subjects were offered either a small reward (one dollar) or a large one (20 dollars) for telling another person that some dull tasks they had just performed were very interesting. (One of the tasks consisted of placing spools on a tray, dumping them out, and repeating the process several times.) After engaging in this attitude–discrepant behaviour (telling another subject the tasks were interesting when they knew full well that they were not), participants were asked to indicate their own liking for the tasks. As predicted by the less-leads-to-more effect, subjects actually reported greater liking for the dull tasks when they had received the small reward than when they had received the large one.

ie. attitude changed as a result of lower reward

While the less-leads-to-more effect has been confirmed many times, we should note that it does not occur under all conditions. Rather, it seems to happen only when several conditions exist (Cooper & Scher, 1994). First, this effect occurs only in situations in which people believe that they have a choice as to whether or not to perform the attitude–discrepant behaviour. Second, small rewards lead to greater attitude change only when people believe that they are personally responsible for both the chosen course of action and any negative effects it produces. And third, the less-leads-to-more effect occurs only when people view the reward they receive as a well-deserved payment for services rendered, not as a bribe. Since these conditions do often exist, however, the strategy of offering others just barely enough to induce them to say or do things contrary to their true attitudes can often be an effective technique for inducing attitude change.

Dissonance as a Tool for Beneficial Changes in Behaviour

At the beginning of the twenty-first century, public health campaigns have been successful at increasing awareness of many of the most immediate dangers in our everyday environment (e.g., Carey, Morrison-Beedy, & Johnson, 1997); so most people have generally favourable attitudes toward using seat belts, quitting smoking, losing weight, and engaging in safe sex. Yet, as you well know, these attitudes are often not translated into overt actions: people continue to drive without seat belts, to smoke, and so on. What's needed, in other words, is not so much changes in attitudes as shifts in overt behaviour. Can dissonance be useful in promoting such beneficial changes? A growing body of evidence suggests that it can (e.g., Gibbons, Eggleston, & Benthin, 1997; Stone et al., 1994b), especially when it is used to generate feelings of <u>hypocrisy</u>—awareness that one is publicly advocating some attitude or behaviour but then acting in a way that is inconsistent with these attitudes or behaviour. Under these conditions, several researchers have reasoned (e.g., Aronson, Fried, & Stone, 1991), an individual should experience strong feeling of dissonance. Moreover, these feelings should be so intense that adopting indirect modes of dissonance reduction (e.g., distracting oneself or bolstering one's ego by thinking about or engaging in other positively evaluated behaviours) would not do the trick: only actions that reduce dissonance directly, removing the discrepancy between one's words and deeds, would be effective.

Hypocrisy Publicly advocating some attitude or behaviour and then acting in a way that is inconsistent with this espoused attitude or behaviour.

These predictions have been tested and confirmed in several studies where the behaviour in question was using safe sex methods to prevent transmission of HIV—a particularly important topic for young people today (Stone et al., 1994b, 1997). Such findings suggest that using dissonance to generate awareness of hypocrisy can indeed be a powerful tool for changing people's behaviour in desirable ways—ones that protect their health and safety. To be maximally effective, however, such procedures must involve several elements: the persons in question must publicly advocate the desired behaviours (e.g., using condoms, wearing safety belts), must be induced to think about their own failures to show these behaviours in the past, and must be given access to direct means for reducing their dissonance. When these conditions are met, beneficial changes in behaviour can definitely follow.

Does Culture Influence Dissonance?
Evidence from a Cross-National Study

Human beings, dissonance theory contends, dislike cognitive conflict and inconsistency. The discomfort they feel, then, often leads them to engage in active efforts to reduce it. As we have already seen, a large body of evidence offers support for these ideas, so dissonance theory has long been seen as providing important insights into several aspects of social thought. There is one major fly in this ointment, however: the vast majority of studies on dissonance have been conducted in North America and Western Europe. Does cognitive dissonance exist and operate in the same manner in other countries? A few studies have examined this question (e.g., Takata & Hashimoto, 1973; Yoshida, 1977), but the findings of this work have been inconsistent; some studies have suggested that dissonance operates in the same way everywhere, while others have called this generality into question.

Fortunately, important new insights into the effects of cultural factors on dissonance have recently been provided by <u>Steve Heine and Darrin Lehman</u> of the University of British Columbia (1997). These researchers reasoned that some types of dissonance (in particular *post-decision dissonance*) might actually be less likely to occur in collective cultures. It has been shown that after making a choice between closely ranked alternatives, persons from individualistic cultures such as Canada would

■ Cultural Factors in the Occurrence of Dissonance

FIGURE 3.15 In Western cultures, the self is linked closely to individual actions or choices. In many Asian cultures, however, the self is more strongly tied to roles and status—to an individual's place in society and the obligations this involves. For these reasons, post-decision dissonance may be stronger for persons from Western cultures than for persons from several Asian cultures. This prediction has recently been confirmed (Heine & Lehman, 1997).

be more likely to experience what is termed *post-decision dissonance* caused by having to reject a perfectly viable option. This occurs because in Western cultures the self is linked to individual actions, such as making correct decisions. Thus, after making a difficult choice, individuals in Western cultures may experience a potential threat to the self posed by the possibility of making a wrong decision. In many Asian cultures, in contrast, the self is not as closely linked to individual actions or choices. Rather, it is more strongly tied to roles and status—to an individual's place in society and the obligations this involves (see Figure 3.15). Thus, persons in Asian cultures should be less likely to perceive the possibility of making an incorrect decision as a threat to their self, and so also less likely to experience dissonance.

To test this reasoning, Heine and Lehman (1997) had both Canadian students and Japanese students temporarily living in Canada rank and evaluate a list of CDs. They were then asked to choose one of two CDs that were ranked next to each other, that they would be able to keep. After making their choices, participants evaluated the two CDs once again. Previous research on *post-decision dissonance* suggests that in order to reduce dissonance, individuals who make decisions between closely ranked alternatives often down-rate the item they didn't choose while raising their rating of the item they did choose—an effect known as *spreading of alternatives* (e.g., Steele et al., 1993). The researchers predicted that such effects would be stronger for Canadians than for Japanese participants, and this is precisely what happened. The Canadian students showed the spreading of alternatives effect that results from dissonance reduction to a significant degree; the Japanese students did not.

These findings suggest that cultural factors do indeed influence the operation of dissonance. While all human beings are made somewhat uneasy by inconsistencies between their attitudes or inconsistencies between their attitudes and their behaviour, the intensity of such reactions, the precise conditions under which they occur, and the strategies used to reduce them may all be influenced by cultural factors. Even with respect to very basic aspects of social thought, then, it is essential to take careful account of cultural diversity.

KEY POINTS

- *Cognitive dissonance* is an unpleasant state that occurs when we notice discrepancies between our attitudes or between our attitudes and behaviour.

- Dissonance often occurs in situations involving *induced compliance*—ones in which we are induced by external factors to say or do things that are inconsistent with our true attitudes.

- In such situations, attitude change is maximum when we have reasons that are barely sufficient to get us to engage in attitude-discrepant behaviour. Stronger reasons (or larger rewards) produce less attitude change—the *less-leads-to-more effect*.

- Inducing individuals to advocate certain attitudes or behaviours and then reminding them of their *hypocrisy*—the fact that they haven't always behaved in ways consistent with these views—can be a powerful tool for inducing dissonance and thus promoting beneficial changes in behaviour.

- Dissonance appears to be a universal aspect of social thought, but the conditions under which it occurs and the tactics individuals choose to reduce it appear to be influenced by cultural factors.

Ideas to Take with You

Resisting Persuasion: Some Useful Steps

Each day we are exposed to many attempts to change our attitudes. Advertisers, politicians, and charities all seek to exert this kind of influence upon us. How can you resist such efforts, which are often highly skilled? Here are some suggestions, based on the research findings of social psychology.

View Attempts at Persuasion as Assaults on Your Personal Freedom.
No one likes being told what to do, but in a sense this is precisely what would-be persuaders are trying to do when they attempt to change your attitudes. So when you are on the receiving end of such appeals, remind yourself that you are in charge of your own life and that there's no reason to listen to or accept what advertisers, politicians, and the like tell you.

Recognize Attempts at Persuasion When You See Them.
Knowing that someone is trying to persuade you—being *forewarned*—is often useful from the point of view of resisting efforts at persuasion. So whenever you encounter someone or some organization that seeks to influence your views, remind yourself that no matter how charming or friendly they are, persuasion is their goal. This will help you resist.

Remind Yourself of Your Own Views and of How These Differ from the Ones Being Urged upon You.
While *biased assimilation*—the tendency to perceive views different from our own as unconvincing and unreliable—can prevent us from absorbing potentially useful information, it is also a useful means for resisting persuasion. Similarly, developing *counterarguments* can be useful when others present views different from your own. Focus on how different these ideas are from those you hold and the rest will often take care of itself!

Summary

Attitude Formation: How—and Why—Attitudes Develop

- *Attitudes* are evaluations of any aspects of the social world. (p. 82)
- Attitudes are often acquired through social learning, including *classical conditioning, instrumental conditioning*, or observational learning. (p. 84)
- Culture can play a part in the transmission of values. (p. 88)
- Attitudes may also be influenced by genetic factors. (p. 90)
- Attitude functions include a knowledge function, a self-expression function, an ego defensive function, and an impression motivation function. (p. 91)

The Attitude—Behaviour Link: When—and How—Attitudes Influence Behaviour

- Moderators of the link between attitudes and behaviour include situational constraints (p. 95) and aspects of attitudes, such as *attitude strength, attitude specificity*, and *attitude ambivalence*. (p. 96)
- Two theories explaining how attitudes influence behaviour are the *theory of planned behaviour* (p. 97) and the *attitude-to-behaviour process model*. (p. 98)

Persuasion: The Art of Changing Attitudes

- Early research on persuasion focused on characteristics of the communicator, the message, and the audience. (p. 100)
- Recent research has focused on cognitive processes, such as the *elaboration likelihood model (ELM)*, which contrasts systematic processing by the *central route* with heuristic processing by the *peripheral route* and the use of *persuasion cues*. (p. 101)
- Research suggests that cognitive capacity, relevance, and cultural values influence effectiveness of these processes. (p. 102)
- Propaganda is used during wartime to influence public opinion. (p. 103)

When Attitude Change Fails: Resistance to Persuasion

- Factors contributing to resistance to persuasion include reactance (p. 106), forewarning, and the inoculation process. (p. 106)
- Protection of existing attitudes is achieved through selective avoidance and by biased assimilation. (p. 106)
- In addition, we can actively counterargue. (p. 107)

Cognitive Dissonance: How Our Behaviour Can Influence Our Attitudes

- *Cognitive dissonance* occurs when there are discrepancies between our attitudes or between our attitudes and behaviour. (p. 109)
- In situations involving *induced compliance*, we are induced to say or do things that are inconsistent with our true attitudes. (p. 110)
- The *less-leads-to-more effect* suggests stronger justification (or larger rewards) produce less attitude change. (p. 111)
- Inducing feelings of *hypocrisy* can be a powerful tool for promoting beneficial changes in behaviour. (p. 112)
- Cultural factors influence the conditions under which post-decision dissonance occurs. (p. 113)

For More Information

Shavitt, S., & Brock, T. C. (1994). *Persuasion: Psychological insights and perspectives.* Boston: Allyn and Bacon.

Explores all aspects of persuasion. The chapters on when and how attitudes influence behaviour, on cognitive dissonance, and on the cognitive perspective on persuasion are all excellent.

Taylor, P.M. (1995). *Munitions of the mind: A history of propaganda from the ancient world to the present era.* Manchester, U.K.: Manchester University Press.

Insightful history of the use of wartime propaganda, from ancient to modern times, including a discussion of the impact of information technologies.

Weblinks

www.colorado.edu/communication/meta-discourses/Theory/dissonance
Professor Robert Craig describes the cognitive dissonance theory
www.freeminds.org/psych/propfail.htm
"When Prophecies Fail: A Sociological Perspective on Failed Expectation in the Watchtower Society" by Randall Watters

spartan.ac.brocku.ca/~lward/
George Herbert Mead page
www.calvin.edu/academic/cas/gpa
Archive of Nazi and East German Propaganda collected by Randall Bytwerk at Calvin College

CHAPTER FOUR

The Social Self:

Personal and Social Identities

Evolutionary and Cultural Origins of the Self
Evolutionary Origins of the Self/Cultural Construction of the Self/Evolution and Culture Combine

Personal Identity: Aspects of the Individual Self
The Cognitive Organization of the Self-Concept/Self-Esteem: Attitudes about Oneself/Self-Focusing: Awareness of the Self

Social Identity: The Self in a Social Context
Social Identity Theory: The Importance of a Collective Sense of Self/Gender as a Crucial Aspect of Social Identity/Cultural Influences on Identity: Ethnicity and Interdependence

SPECIAL SECTIONS

CANADIAN RESEARCH: ON THE CUTTING EDGE
Paradoxical Self-Esteem: When Self-Liking and Competence Diverge

CORNERSTONES
Bem's Concept of Psychological Androgyny as an Alternative to Masculinity versus Femininity

ON THE APPLIED SIDE
Self-Enhancement: A Universal or Cultural Phenomenon?

■ William James

FIGURE 4.1 William James was to become a major figure in psychology and fundamentally shape our understanding of the self. However, at the time of this self-portrait, age 24, he was ill and struggling with "neurasthenia" a vague condition characterized by fatigue, headaches, and irritability, usually ascribed to emotional breakdown. There was little sign at that point of the great figure he was to become, but his personal struggles would later inform his understanding of the self.

In 1869, a young man named William James (see Figure 4.1) had recently graduated from Harvard with a degree in medicine. However, his health was poor and he never took the next step of setting up a medical practice. His younger brother Henry was already beginning to be recognized and would soon publish the novels that would make him famous. But William, or W.J. as he called himself, was confined in his father's house, a semi-invalid undergoing a profound mental crisis—questioning the direction of his life, its meaning and his own worth—he even thought of suicide (Pajares, 2002). He had, by the age of 27, already dabbled in many possible selves: he'd studied painting with William Hunt; he'd traveled to the Amazon with a famous naturalist, Louis Agassiz; he'd studied physiology and the new psychology in Germany. Yet despite these wide interests and his education, he was directionless and despairing. At that point, neither he nor his family would have believed that William James was to become a major figure in the development of psychology and particularly in our understanding of the self. Within two years, he was offered a teaching position at Harvard and there he found his niche for the next 30 years (Goodman, 2003). William James went on to teach physiology and psychology, to set up one of the first laboratories in North America to study psychological processes, and to produce a seminal and beautifully written book, *The Principles of Psychology* (1890)—one whose influence is reflected in many of the topics in this chapter on the self.

Perhaps because of his personal difficulties, the nature of the self and self-understanding were central to James's psychology. He suggested that the sense of self has both internal and external components, including a *spiritual* component (our values and feelings or "inner sensibilities"), a *social* component (our relationships and social position), and a *material* component (our physical bodies and our possessions). He discussed self-evaluation and multiple selves, topics that are still researched today. He suggested the self and processes that maintain it may have evolved because they provide human beings with an advantage in the struggle for survival and reproduction—again an idea that has been revived by today's evolutionary social psychologists. Throughout this chapter, many of the issues that are being hotly debated today refer directly or indirectly to James's work.

Today we can agree with James that the sense of self combines both the internal private person and the external, more social, person who identifies with their family and with various social groups. This idea is summarized in Figure 4.2, showing Brewer's (2001) conception of the individual, relational, and collective self. The individual, or private, self provides us with a sense of *personal identity*, while the more social self provides us with a sense of *social* or *collective identity* (Tajfel & Turner, 1979; Sedikides & Brewer, 2001). In this chapter, we will discuss these two major aspects of the self. First, we will contrast the ways in which evolutionary psychology and cultural psychology view the origins of the self. Next, we will describe some of the crucial elements of the *personal* self, including self-concept, self-esteem, self-focusing, and self-monitoring. And finally, we will turn to the more *social* aspects of the self, concentrating on gender and the sense of cultural or ethnic identity, which is so important within a Canadian context.

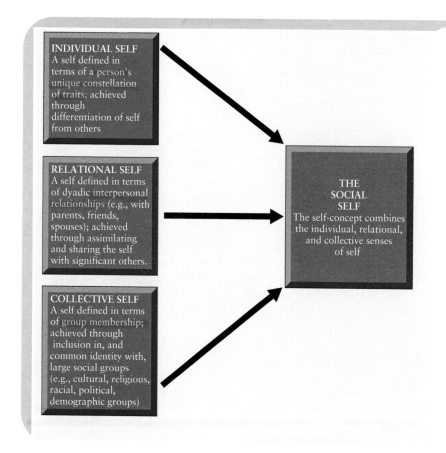

■ The Individual Self, Relational Self, and Collective Self

FIGURE 4.2 According to Sedikides and Brewer (2001), the self-concept consists of three components: the individual self, the relational self, and the collective self. These represent different ways in which people attempt to achieve self-definition and self-interpretation. All three are essentially social because other individuals and groups play a part in their formation and in their evaluation.

INDIVIDUAL SELF
A self defined in terms of a person's unique constellation of traits; achieved through differentiation of self from others

RELATIONAL SELF
A self defined in terms of dyadic interpersonal relationships (e.g., with parents, friends, spouses); achieved through assimilating and sharing the self with significant others.

COLLECTIVE SELF
A self defined in terms of group membership; achieved through inclusion in, and common identity with, large social groups (e.g., cultural, religious, racial, political, demographic groups)

THE SOCIAL SELF
The self-concept combines the individual, relational, and collective senses of self

Evolutionary and Cultural Origins of the Self

Evolutionary Origins of the Self

Evolutionary psychologists have suggested that the human sense of self is one that is unique among animal species (Sedikides & Skowronski, 1997). In pondering the origins of the self, the first question that an evolutionary psychologist asks about this characteristic is its evolutionary purpose: that is, how that particular feature helped to solve problems of survival and reproduction for our ancestors (Kenrick, Sadalla, & Keefe, 1998). How can the development of the *human self* have contributed to our success as a species? This question arises because it is only when a particular characteristic enhances the *reproductive success* of an individual that it is likely to be passed on to subsequent generations. If the feature provides a consistent advantage for its owner, then, through the process of natural selection, it will eventually become part of a species' characteristics. Sedikides and Skowronski (1997) propose that the human sense of self evolved in just this way because it was an adaptive characteristic. They identify three types of self-knowledge that appeared in evolutionary history.

The first aspect to evolve was *subjective self-awareness*; this involves the ability of the organism to differentiate itself to some degree from its physical and social

■ Objective Self-Awareness: Recognizing Oneself

FIGURE 4.3 Only among primates, such as the chimp shown here and humans, does there appear to be *objective self-awareness*—including the capacity to be aware of oneself. When a red spot is placed on the forehead of a chimpanzee, it can't be seen by the animal except in a mirror. The fact that seeing this image in the mirror leads a chimp to touch its own forehead is powerful evidence that there is some recognition that the reflected image is itself.

environment. Most animals share this characteristic, which makes it possible to survive (Damasio, 1994; Lewis, 1992). Over time, *objective self-awareness* developed among primates; this term refers to the organism's capacity to be the object of its own attention (Gallup, 1994), to be aware of its own state of mind (Cheney & Seyfarth, 1992), and "to know it knows, to remember it remembers" (Lewis, 1992, p. 124). See Figure 4.3 for an example from research on objective self-awareness in chimpanzees. Only humans seem to have developed the third level of self-functioning—*symbolic self-awareness*—which permits adults of our species to form an abstract cognitive representation of the self through language. Because the self can be represented in the human mind in abstract form, we can, for example, imagine ourselves in different situations and make plans to bring these about. Further, we can communicate our plans and the understanding of the self to other people. So this abstract or symbolic representation of the self enhances our ability to communicate, form relationships, set goals, evaluate outcomes, develop self-related attitudes, and defend ourselves against threatening communications.

In sum, the evolutionary advantage of symbolic self-awareness is that it has enabled the complex communication and development of long-term plans that are necessary to build human communities. In a word, it is *adaptive*.

Essentially, the evolutionary perspective attempts to identify basic aspects of human experience that have been shaped by evolutionary forces. And to the extent that any particular characteristic, such as symbolic self-awareness, is *pancultural* (shown across all cultures), this provides evidence of its evolved nature (Buss & Kenrick, 1998). The evolutionary perspective has also suggested that other aspects of the self are universal. As we will see at the end of this chapter, a vigorous debate is being waged between evolutionary psychologists and cultural psychologists over whether a tendency towards *self-enhancement* is universal (Heine, 2003; Brown & Kobayashi, 2003).

KEY POINTS

- The sense of self has both a personal and a social side and includes individual, relational, and collective components.

- Evolutionary approaches to the self have suggested that the human sense of self has evolved to have subjective, objective, and symbolic states of self-awareness. Symbolic self-awareness is exclusive to humans.

Cultural Construction of the Self

Cultural psychologists believe that the influence of culture is much more profound than that of evolution. Human beings' reliance on prewired (instinctive) behaviours is minimal and, in fact, we are open to, and dependent on, culture to provide the form and meaning of our behaviours (Heine, 2001). Indeed, from the perspective of cultural psychology we have *evolved to be responsive to culture.*

How this occurs is best described in the **collective constructionist model** (Kitayama, Matsumoto, Markus, & Norasakkunkit, 1997; Markus, Mullally & Kitayama, 1997), as shown in Figure 4.4. According to this model, the self develops within a culture, and the beliefs and practices of the culture are absorbed into the individual's psychology. Markus and Kitayama use the term **selfways** to describe the various cultural structures and situations that have an impact on the individual's development. That is, a culture will provide social situations and social institutions that represent and foster the culture's ideas of what it means to be a person and the way its members should behave (Markus, Mullally, & Kitayama, 1997). These cultural structures and situations allow the developing child to practise culturally appropriate behaviours, and they shape the child's mind.

As individuals' psychology is built through the *selfways* of their culture, their behaviour and thinking allow them to live comfortably within the culture and to communicate more easily with others. Above all, this way of being feels as if it is the "natural" way for human beings to think and act. However, this is not just a one-way process: culture constructs the person, but the person then reciprocates. As shown in Figure 4.4, when people are raised in a particular culture, their internal processes and overt behaviours support and reproduce that culture. Parents and educators raised in a given culture provide situations that allow the children in their care to practise culturally appropriate ways of being. So, for example, children in Canadian schools are given the opportunity to express themselves and come up with their own ideas, while school children in Japan are given the opportunity to cooperate and to think about self-improvement (Tweed & Lehman, 2000). Individuals who have constructed themselves around a particular culture then go on to perpetuate it.

Collective Constructionist Model A model that suggests that the culture and the individual are inextricably linked and mutually constitutive.

Selfways A culture's ideas and practices related to personhood: that is, what it means to become a person and how to act as a member of that particular cultural community, as well as the social situations, norms, and institutions of a culture that represent and foster these ideas.

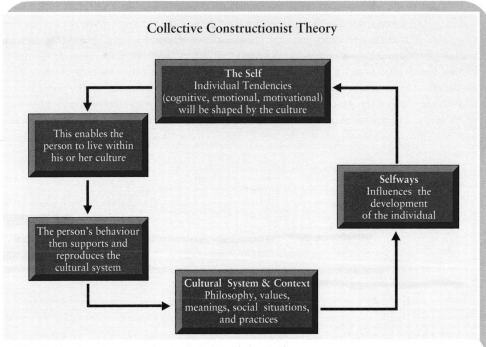

Collective Constructionist Theory

The Self
Individual Tendencies
(cognitive, emotional, motivational)
will be shaped by the culture

This enables the person to live within his or her culture

Selfways
Influences the development of the individual

The person's behaviour then supports and reproduces the cultural system

Cultural System & Context
Philosophy, values, meanings, social situations, and practices

■ The Collective Constructionist Model of the Self

FIGURE 4.4 Kitayama and colleagues suggest that the cultural system and the individual's psychological system are "mutually constitutive." That is, the culture shapes the self, and the individual then goes on to behave in ways that shape and support the culture.

Source: Based on Kitayama, Matsumoto, Markus, & Norasakkunkit, 1997; Markus, Mullally, & Kitayama, 1997.

Cross-Cultural Psychology The branch of psychology concerned with the discovery of cultural differences, cultural influences, and cultural changes in behaviour.

The groundwork for the cultural perspective has been developing since the 1980s. At that time, the topic of culture was investigated by <u>cross-cultural psychology</u>, which was chiefly concerned with discovering *differences* between cultures, and exploring cultural influence on behaviour. Where *cultural psychology* suggests that culture and the self construct each other and are therefore inextricably linked, *cross-cultural psychology* has tended to see culture as one of many sources of influence on the individual, though a profound one (e.g., Berry, Poortinga, & Pandey, 1997), and has been more prepared to look for underlying universalities (Heine, 2001). One of the major contributions of early cross-cultural psychology was to alert us to the importance of culture bias in our outlook on the world (e.g., Berry, 1978; Triandis, 1980). A few of the ideas that arose from this perspective will be useful to consider as you read this book.

Culture Bias in Our Daily Lives

Ethnocentrism Evaluating other cultures from the perspective of your own. Your own group standards are used as the norm and other groups are then seen as "abnormal" or "wrong."

If you have travelled to a foreign country or spent time with people from another cultural group, you may have found yourself thinking that their customs were strange or, perhaps, that their food was odd and their accents funny. If so, you were displaying <u>ethnocentrism.</u> This term was first used in 1906 by William Sumner and was defined by him as: "the view of things in which one's own group is the centre of everything and all others are scaled and rated with reference to it" (in Brewer, 1986, p. 88). That is, the culture in which you were raised tends to be seen as the "centre of everything," the norm, and, by comparison, other cultural groups are seen as "abnormal" or "wrong"-they don't quite do things in the right way. Beyond this, ethnocentrism can often make us deride other groups' customs as ridiculous, or make us feel morally superior.

You may not be strongly ethnocentric, but there are few people who have not at times seen things from their culture's perspective, taken pride in their group's superiorities, or ridiculed the ways of other groups. Many Canadians believe that they live in the best country in the world—by comparison, other countries just don't match up. Social psychology itself may have been guilty of ethnocentrism (or "Eurocentrism") when it overgeneralized its theories and findings based on a largely European-American population to other non-Western subcultures within that society or to other nations.

Culture Bias in Social Psychology: Etic versus Emic Research

A distinction made by Canadian John Berry (1969) has proved very useful for examining ethnocentric biases in social psychology. He suggested that social psychological research and findings can be approached in two different ways. An **etic analysis** of social behaviour focuses on universal factors—ones that apply across all cultures. For example, all cultures have family relations or a set of cultural norms. An **emic analysis** focuses upon factors that are culturally specific—that vary between cultures and have specific meaning within a particular culture. For example, the concept of "the self" may have different meanings in different cultures.

The importance of this distinction is in its implications for social-psychological research. An etic analysis has often led researchers to assume that their measures, or the distinctions they made between variables, were of equal significance in another culture. It was assumed that the psychological concepts and findings from Western research would hold in other cultures (Smith & Bond, 1998). Berry terms this approach to research an **imposed etic.** That is, such research *imposed* Western values and concepts as if they were universal.

Increasing awareness of this danger has led to a call for indigenous psychologies by Canadian psychologists (e.g., Adair, 1992, 1996; Berry, 1989; Segall, Dasen, Berry, & Poortinga, 1999), non-Western psychologists (e.g., Moghaddam, 1990; Sinha, 1988, 1996), and those in cultural psychology (e.g., Shweder, 1990; Shweder & Sullivan, 1993). An **indigenous psychology** would be one arising from within a particular culture and that adequately represents that culture (Adair, 1996). It would examine psychological issues that naturally arise in a culture and would make culturally relevant distinctions. A comparison of indigenous findings from many different cultures could then identify universal or etic factors: ones that were common to all cultures. John Berry has termed this approach a *derived etic*: the discovery of universal characteristics is derived from culturally valid indigenous research, rather than being assumed or imposed by Western researchers.

Later in this chapter and throughout the book we will showcase research related to cultural issues. This research reflects the tremendous expansion of interest in cross-cultural psychology, and its findings are fascinating for those of us who live in a multicultural society.

Evolution and Culture Combine

We have talked about the differences between evolutionary and cultural approaches to the self. It might be instructive to also look at their points of consensus. Both perspectives agree on three points: (1) that evolution has an impact on our behaviour and that human beings have something in common fundamentally at the biological level; (2) that culture has an impact on our behaviour and that culture can create significant differences in human beings' behaviour and cognition; and (3) that evolution and culture

Etic Analysis Research that attempts to discover universal aspects of behaviour that appear to be consistent across cultures.

Emic Analysis A research approach that attempts to discover aspects of behaviour that differ between cultures; that are culturally specific.

Imposed Etic Assuming a universality that does not exist, or imposing your culture's values as if they were universal. Most commonly, this occurs in social psychology when Western findings and concepts are assumed to apply to non-Western cultures.

Indigenous Psychology A psychological discipline that arises from within a particular culture, adequately representing naturally occurring psychological processes and distinctions of that culture.

interact. That is, evolved fundamental tendencies will provide the basis, and possibly the limitations, for cultural impact. Culture works with and upon the essential biological responses forged by evolution.

Where they differ is in the degree and level of influence they attribute to culture or evolution (Heine, 2003). To what extent can observed human behaviour be explained as directly influenced by evolved tendencies? To what extent do cultural influences determine the fundamental form and patterns of our behaviour? Evolutionary psychology suggests that many human behaviours rest on a basis of prewired, built-in tendencies, which have evolved because they helped us to survive or reproduce. A typical example is the evolutionary approach to relationships, which assumes that male-female differences in sexual behaviour directly reflect our evolved tendencies, as we will discuss in Chapter 6.

Cultural psychology and cross-cultural psychology, on the other hand, put a much greater weight on the importance of culture in shaping the individual. Cultural psychologists suggest that the influence of evolved tendencies in the patterns of human behaviour is minimal. We, more than any other species, are shaped by our experience, and culture is essential to understanding the individual.

KEY POINTS

- A major cultural theory of the construction of the self, the *collective constructionist model*, suggests that culture and the individual are mutually constitutive: they form each other. The sense of self is constructed through a culture's provision of *selfways*—beliefs and social situations that guide the development of the self.

- *Cross-cultural psychology* investigates the influence of culture, cultural differences, and cultural change. If we are raised in one culture, we can suffer from *ethnocentrism* and evaluate other cultural groups from the perspective of our own.

- Social psychology has tended to have a somewhat *ethnocentric* perspective in understanding social behaviour. It has tended to assume that it is studying *etic* factors (universal factors), when in fact it is studying factors that are specific to Western culture—that is, they are *emic* or culturally specific factors.

- Increased awareness of the possibility of an *imposed etic* in Western research has led to a call for the development of *indigenous psychologies* in non-Western cultures.

Personal Identity: Aspects of the Individual Self

In this second part of the chapter we are focusing on the *individual self* (see Figure 4.2), based on our unique differences from others. Notice as you read this section, however, that inevitably the *relational self* has to be considered as well. This is because, in defining the individual sense of self, other people influence us at many levels, from the long-term impact of our parents, to the daily interactions and comparisons with others. Much of the material described in this section comes from work on social cognition (see Chapter 2). This perspective has focused on the self as a *schema*, an organizational framework that influences our processing of information, as well as influencing our motivations, emotional states, and feelings of well-being (Klein, Loftus, & Burton, 1989; Van Hook & Higgins, 1988).

The Cognitive Organization of the Self-Concept

Who are you? Before you read further, try to give 20 different answers to that question.

Investigating the content of a person's self-concept, questions such as "Who are you?" and "Who am I?" have been asked for more than a century as psychologists, beginning with William James (1890), have endeavoured to determine the specific content of the individual self-concept (Ziller, 1990).

Rentsch and Heffner (1994) utilized this technique when they asked more than 200 college students to give repeated answers to the question "Who are you?" The basic content of the self, as perceived by these students, consisted of eight categories. Some of these refer to aspects of social identity (nationality, race, etc.) and others refer to personal attributes (relationships, hobbies, etc.).

The Self-Schema

The cognitive perspective emphasizes the way in which information related to the self is handled, suggesting that each of us has a self-schema in which our self-knowledge is organized (Markus & Nurius, 1986). That is, the **self-schema** is a cognitive framework that guides the way we process information about ourselves. Self-schemas are probably much more complex and detailed than can be determined by questions about who you are. Consider some of the possibilities. Beyond an overall framework, a self-schema would include your past experiences, your detailed knowledge about what you are like now as opposed to in the past, and your expectancies about the changes you will undergo in the future. In other words, a self-schema is the sum of everything a person remembers, knows, and can imagine about herself or himself. A self-schema also plays a role in guiding behaviour (Kendzierski & Whitaker, 1997). For example, the intention to lose weight is quite common, but the ability to link that intention to mildly unpleasant behaviours (dieting, exercising on a very hot day) requires a consistent guiding force. It helps to have a clear conceptualization of who you are now and who you want to be in the future. Otherwise, it is much easier simply to eat and drink whatever you want and avoid working up a sweat.

Self-Schema A framework for organizing information, beliefs, and feelings relevant to the self.

Because the self is the centre of each person's social universe and our self-schemas tend to be well developed, it follows that we should do a better job of processing information that is relevant to ourselves than any other kind of information. Self-relevant information should be more likely to capture our attention, to be entered into memory, and to be recalled (Higgins & Bargh, 1987). These hypotheses have been confirmed in studies of memory in which words deliberately made relevant to self ("Does this word describe you?") were later recalled more easily than words not made relevant ("Is this word printed in big letters?"). This tendency for information related to the self to be most readily processed and remembered is known as the **self-reference effect**.

Self-Reference Effect The tendency for information related to the self to be processed more efficiently (in several respects) than other forms of information.

This effect occurs because you are likely to spend more time thinking about words or events that are relevant to yourself than about any other words or events (*elaborative processing)* and because self-relevant material is more likely to be well organized or categorized in your memory (*categorical processing*) (Klein & Loftus, 1988). There is even evidence from studies of brain activation that while memory encoding processes involve the left frontal regions of the brain, self-related information is encoded there *and* in the right frontal lobe (Craik et al., 1999). Thus, the self-reference effect appears to have a neurological as well as a psychological basis. The self-reference effect seems to be so fundamental to our information processing that it goes beyond important information about the self. For example, we tend to remember and have a positive bias towards those letters of the alphabet that are in our names and the numbers that make up our birth dates (Koole, Dijksterhuis, & van Knippenberg, 2001).

Sexual Self-Schema
Cognitive representations of the sexual aspects of the self.

Schemas related to the self can also be content specific. For example, Anderson and colleagues have studied the **sexual self-schema**—the cognitive representations of the sexual aspects of self (Andersen & Cyranowski, 1994; Andersen, Cyranowski, & Espindle, 1999). In research, they found different types of schema for both men and women. Both males and females revealed a dimension involving passion and romance (e.g., describing the self as warm, loving, sympathetic, and sensitive) and both also described themselves on dimensions that involve such concepts as open-minded and direct or inhibited and cautious (e.g., frank, outspoken, uninhibited). However, major gender differences were also found. First, many women had a quite negative schema related to their sexuality of embarrassed/conservative that suggests anxiety and guilt in response to sex—men did not ordinarily respond in this way. Men had a schema based on behavioural traits involving aggression and power—this was not characteristic of women. As you can imagine, these sexual self-schemas were related to sexual activity. For example, those who had positive schemas (e.g., passionate/romantic) were more likely to be sexually active and form long-term relationships, whereas negative or cautious schemas predicted less activity. Also the powerful/aggressive schema for males is associated with more one-night stands, a greater number of sexual partners, sexual coercion, and less commitment. These findings can be summarized as suggesting that a major source of conflict in female sexuality centres on positive and negative reactions to sexuality. For males, the conflict is between being passionate and loving on the one hand and aggressive and domineering on the other.

The Changing Self-Concept

When people speak about themselves, they often assume stability and the absence of change. Despite this, most of us realize that we can and do change. You are not the same person you were 10 years ago, and you can safely assume that 10 years from now you will not be exactly the same person you are today. In fact, comparing oneself now with oneself in the past is often gratifying because it is possible to see improvement over time (Wilson & Ross, 2000, 2001). So, along with our current self-concept, we are also aware of other **possible selves**.

Possible Selves
Mental representations of what we might become, or should become, in the future.

Markus and Nurius (1986) suggest that a self-concept at any given time is actually just a *working self-concept*, one that is open to change in response to new experiences, new feedback, and new self-relevant information. The existence of alternative possible selves affects us in several ways. The image of a future self may have an effect on one's *motivation*; you may be able to study harder or to give up cigarettes if you imagine the new and improved you that will result. The custom of making New Year's resolutions seems to be based on such images. Nevertheless, the failure to keep such resolutions is a common experience. Polivy and Herman (2000) suggest that embarking on self-change induces feelings of control and optimism. Such confidence is good, but overconfidence in one's ability to change leads to false hope, unrealistic expectations of success, and, eventually, the unhappy realization of failure. Research shows that those who are characteristically optimistic have higher expectations about actually attaining a positive possible self than do those who are pessimistic (Carver, Reynolds, & Scheier, 1994).

People differ with respect to the *number of possible selves* they can imagine. Research by Niedenthal, Setterlund, and Wherry (1992) indicated that people who have a very limited number of possible future selves are emotionally vulnerable to relevant feedback. For example, if you are considering 20 possible future careers, information that you don't have the necessary ability for one of them is of relatively limited importance—there are 19 other possibilities. If you have only one career goal, however, information indicating a lack of ability may be devastating. In a similar way, the more strongly and the more exclusively a person identifies with the role of athlete, the more emotionally upsetting is an athletic injury (Brewer, 1993). More broadly, it appears that those who can envision many different selves adjust better to setbacks (Morgan & Janoff-Bulman, 1994). It seems that having a complex view of one's possible selves (assuming that they are realistically grounded) is more emotionally beneficial than having a very simple view.

A change in occupational status can lead to a radical altering of the self-concept. One example is the negative effects on a person's self-concept when he or she loses a job and suddenly has a new social identity—unemployed (Sheeran & Abraham, 1994). The opposite experience—entering a new occupation—also leads to changes in the self-concept; for example, new police officers are found to develop new views of themselves (Stradling, Crowe, & Tuohy, 1993). Even greater changes occur when an individual joins the armed forces and is thrust into combat. We have seen much television footage in recent years showing Canadian military personnel leaving their families to become involved in conflicts in other parts of the world (see Figure 4.5). Research shows that such experiences can lead to many self-relevant problems, including confusion about "Who am I?" ("Am I a civilian or a military person?"), confusion about time perspective ("I was too young to feel so old"), interpersonal and work-related problems, and the development of a negative self-identity (Silverstein, 1994). Changing social relationship contexts can also affect the self-concept. For example, just thinking about a significant other leads research participants to shift their self-descriptions to reflect the way they are when they're with this other person (Hinkley & Andersen, 1996). The self-perceptions and interpersonal perceptions of same-sex college roommates change as they interact over time. Each roommate's self-concept influences how the other sees them and in turn their self-concepts change when others perceive them differently (McNulty & Swann, 1994). Given the fact that mutual influences occur in pairs of roommates, it seems very likely that this process is even stronger in close relationships such as friendship and marriage. A close partner's support and affirmation can cause an individual to move closer to his or her ideal self. Drigotas and his colleagues (1999) describe such a partner as a *sculptor*, and the resulting change in the other individual as the *Michelangelo phenomenon*.

■ Self-Concepts Change as Situations Change

FIGURE 4.5 Research shows that changes involved in a new occupation, especially one as all-encompassing as joining the military and being sent into combat, can have a disruptive effect on a person's sense of self (Silverstein, 1994).

Self-Esteem: Attitudes about Oneself

Self-Esteem The self-evaluation made by each individual; one's attitude toward oneself along a positive–negative dimension.

One of the most important attitudes each person holds is his or her attitude about self, an evaluation that we label <u>self-esteem</u> (James, 1890). If you were asked right now to evaluate yourself on a scale of 1 to 10 (with 1 indicating an extremely negative evaluation and 10 an extremely positive one), what number do you think would best describe your attitude toward yourself? Figure 4.6 depicts someone at the negative end of this dimension. Keep your own answer in mind as you read the following section.

There can be various motives for evaluation of our selves. Sedikides (1993) suggests three of these: People may seek *self-assessment* (to obtain accurate knowledge about themselves), *self-enhancement* (to provide positive information about themselves), or *self-verification* (to confirm what they already know about themselves). Which motive is most likely to be activated is a matter of one's culture and personality as well as the situation (Bosson & Swann, 1999; Heine, 2003; Rudich & Vallacher,

■ Self-Esteem: Evaluating Oneself

FIGURE 4.6 Self-esteem refers to the attitude one has about oneself, ranging from very negative to very positive. The individual shown here presumably holds a negative attitude about himself.

1999). The cultural basis of self-evaluation will be discussed in the section entitled "Social Identity: The Self in Social Context." The self-assessment motive tends to occur when accuracy is very important, such as wanting to have a really accurate idea of how good a driver you are before you try to take the test. A search for self-verification is common among those with negative self-views who don't want to change. To maintain their negative self-evaluation, they seek partners who view them negatively, behave so as to elicit negative perceptions, and perceive the reactions of others as negative whether they are or not (Swann, 1997).

Self-Esteem and Social Comparison

The *relational self* (see Figure 4.2) often comes into play when we are seeking a basis for self-evaluation. We use the people we know as a major source of information relevant to the self. This is termed <u>social comparison</u>—comparing ourselves with other people in order to establish our own standing (Festinger, 1954; Browne, 1992; Wayment & Taylor, 1995). If we are comparing ourselves with someone worse off than ourselves on a particular dimension (e.g., others in the line-up didn't manage to get tickets to the show when you did), the term **downward social comparison** is used. However, if we are comparing ourselves with someone better off (e.g., your classmate did better than you on the test), this is termed **upward social comparison**. What do you think would be the impact on your self-esteem of each of these types of comparison? You might assume that upward social comparison (e.g., "I don't speak French as well as my friends") would make you feel bad (lower your self-esteem), and, in contrast, that downward social comparison (e.g., "No one in the club plays pool as well as I do") would make you feel good (raise your self-esteem). That seems sensible, doesn't it? Unfortunately, things are more complicated. Crucially, it depends upon your *comparison group* and how the comparison process *affects your mood*. The general underlying principle is that any experience that creates a positive mood raises self-esteem, whereas a negative mood lowers self-esteem (Esses, 1989). Consider three possible comparison groups: strangers, in-group peers, and people who are very close to you (intimates).

A downward comparison with a stranger has a positive effect on your mood and raises your self-esteem (Crocker, 1993): "She's fatter than I am, so I feel better about myself." This is termed a <u>*contrast effect*</u> because you have emphasized the *difference* between yourself and another person. However, contrast effects do not always result in a rise in self-esteem, as we will explain below (Reis, Gerrard, & Gibbons, 1993). A downward comparison with a member of your in-group also results in a positive contrast effect: "I can draw better than any of my classmates." This is the kind of boost to self-esteem experienced by a big frog in a little pond (McFarland & Buehler, 1995). But when someone very close to you exhibits inferior qualities, this has a negative effect on your self-esteem; because this kind of downward comparison means that you are associated with the inadequacy: "My best friend is emotionally disturbed (so maybe I'm a little off myself)." This is termed an <u>*assimilation effect*</u> because you have emphasized the *similarity* between yourself and another person.

Analogous differences occur when you observe others better off than yourself. An *upward comparison* can be a matter of indifference if the comparison is with distant strangers: "I could never play chess as well as the Russian champion, but who cares?" If, however, the upward comparison is with your usual comparison in-group such as your classmates, their superiority makes you feel depressed and lowers your self-esteem (Major, Sciacchitano, & Crocker, 1993). The *contrast effect* here is a negative one: "I'm the worst tennis player in the tenth grade." Finally, social comparison with someone with qualities superior to your own can enhance your self-esteem, if that person is someone to whom you feel close—this time an assimilation effect has a positive impact

Social Comparison
The process through which we compare ourselves to others in order to determine our own standing.

Downward Social Comparison
Comparing yourself to someone who is worse off than you with respect to a particular attribute.

Upward Social Comparison
Comparing yourself to someone who is better off than you with respect to a particular attribute.

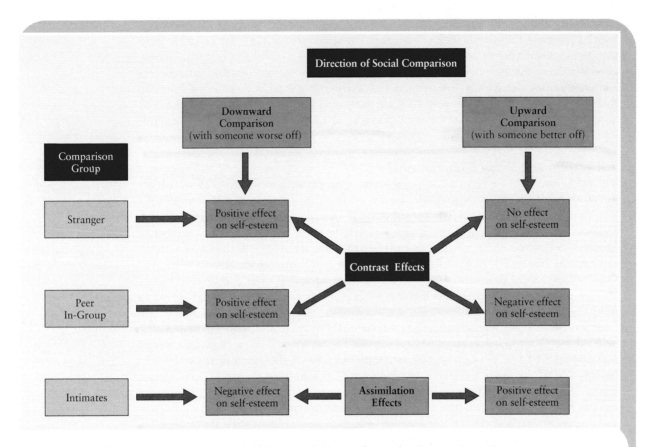

■ The Effects of Social Comparison on Self-Esteem: It Depends on the Comparison Group

FIGURE 4.7 When you compare yourself with others, the effects on your self-esteem depend upon the particular comparison group you are using—whether it's a stranger, your peer in-group, or someone close to you (an intimate). We will tend to emphasize the similarity between ourselves and those close to us (an *assimilation effect*), which can have a positive impact on self-esteem if that person is superior to you, but a negative impact if that person is not. If we are emphasizing the difference (a *contrast effect*) between ourselves and our peer group, or between ourselves and a stranger, then *upward comparison* tends to result in lowered self-esteem (or indifference to a distant stranger). However, when we see ourselves as superior to those persons (a *downward comparison*), this raises our self-esteem.

on self-esteem (Pelham & Wachsmuth, 1995): "My brother won the tennis tournament, and that makes me look good." These effects of social comparison are summarized in Figure 4.7.

The Effects of High versus Low Self-Esteem

In most instances, high self-esteem has positive consequences, while low self-esteem has the opposite effect (Leary, Schreindorfer, & Haupt, 1995). For example, negative self-evaluations are associated with inadequate social skills (Olmstead et al., 1991), loneliness (McWhirter, 1997), and depression (Jex, Cvetanovski, & Allen, 1994). It also appears that self-esteem relates to our biology. For example, low self-esteem can weaken the body's immune system, while high self-esteem helps ward off infections and illness (Strauman, Lemieux, & Coe, 1993). There is evidence that *serotonin* levels in the blood are associated with self-esteem—lower esteem and lower serotonin levels are associated with impulsivity and aggressiveness (Wright, 1995). However, a note of caution should be sounded. Decades of research provides evidence that we should not assume that high self-esteem is always good and low self-esteem is always bad, the effects are much more complicated than either alternative and not yet fully understood (Dubois & Tevendale, 1999). One area where the importance of high and low self-esteem has been disputed is in cultural research—see the On the Applied Side section towards the end of this chapter.

While depression is associated with low self-esteem, it is even more strongly associated with *variable self-esteem*. That is, people whose self-evaluations fluctuate up and down in response to changes in the situation are the ones most likely to become depressed (Butler, Hokanson, & Flynn, 1994). The reason seems to be that anyone whose self-esteem is strongly affected by minor occurrences has a less stable base of self-worth than people whose self-esteem remains relatively constant (Kernis et al., 1998). High, stable self-esteem acts as a buffer when negative events occur (Wiener, Muczyk, & Martin, 1992). Unstable self-esteem is also associated with low self-determination, a less clear self-concept, and tenseness about reaching one's goal (Kernis et al., 2000; Nezlek & Plesko, 2001). In contrast, high, stable self-esteem acts as a buffer when negative events occur (Wiener, Muczyk, & Martin, 1992).

Self-Esteem and Performance

Levels of self-esteem can be related to our behaviour. For example, lowered self-esteem can result in decreased effort on a task following failure (Tafarodi & Vu, 1997). Research has even suggested that the performance of medical doctors can be influenced in part by their self-esteem. Investigating resident physicians at a large teaching hospital in southern Taiwan, Huang (1998) found that the higher the self-esteem of these doctors, the better their medical practices. Another important perspective suggests that self-evaluation is also directed at our *performance* on particular tasks. Bandura has suggested we make evaluations of **self-efficacy**—evaluation of one's ability to perform a task in a particular domainIand that this type of evaluation directly influences whether we attempt a task. Self-efficacy can vary greatly across different tasks (Cervone, 1997). You might, for example, feel very capable when it comes to taking French tests but hopeless when it comes to math.

Self-Efficacy A person's evaluation of his or her ability or competency to perform a task, reach a goal, or overcome an obstacle.

Performance in coping with both physical and psychological problems (Cheung & Sun, 2000; Courneya & McAuley, 1993; Gould & Weiss, 1981; Ng et al., 1999), with academic tasks (Sanna & Pusecker, 1994), and job performance (Huang, 1998) is enhanced by strong feelings of self-efficacy. Unless people believe that they are able to achieve a goal (such as giving up drugs) as the result of what they do, they have little or no incentive to act (Bandura, 1999). People high in such self-confidence also tend to stop working on unsolvable tasks more quickly than those who are low in self-confidence—instead, they prefer to allocate their time and effort to tasks that *can* be solved (Aspinwall & Richter, 1999).

Taking the idea of personal self-efficacy a step further, Bandura (2000) has recently proposed *collective self-efficacy*—the shared belief by members of a group that collective action will produce the desired effects. Among basketball players, a shared belief in the collective efficacy of the team (measured at the beginning of the season) is found to be associated with the team's overall success by the end of the season (Watson, Chemers, & Preiser, 2001). In general, those who don't believe in such collective-efficacy assume that they can't change things, so they give up and become apathetic about political issues. If the governing system is perceived as trustworthy, collective self-efficacy leads to positive political activism, such as persuading people to vote. If the system is perceived as untrustworthy, the collective behaviour leads to confrontational and coercive activism, such as protests and riots.

Changes in Self-Esteem

Short-term changes in self-esteem can be brought about fairly easily. In the laboratory, when participants are given false feedback about how well they did on a personality test, self-esteem goes up (Greenberg et al., 1992). Similarly, in real life interpersonal feedback indicating acceptance or rejection by others can raise or lower one's self-evaluation (Leary et al., 1998). For example, when problems arise in school, at work, within the family, or among friends, self-esteem decreases, anxiety increases, and the beleaguered individual often seeks reassurance in a variety of ways (Joiner, Katz, & Lew, 1999). A familiar, but important, effect is based on clothing: self-esteem increases when people like the clothes they are wearing (Kwon, 1994). It is even possible to bring about such changes by directing your thoughts toward positive or negative content. For example, simply thinking about desirable versus undesirable aspects of oneself can, respectively, raise or lower self-esteem (McGuire & McGuire, 1996).

Self-Ideal Discrepancies Discrepancies between the perception of the actual self (the way you see yourself) and the ideal self (the way you feel you should be).

Because of the negative associations with low self-esteem, many forms of psychotherapy have aimed at improving self-esteem, such as that of Carl Rogers (1951). For Rogers (Rogers & Dymond, 1954), a major way to raise self-esteem was to decrease the discrepancy between a person's actual and ideal self, termed the <u>self-ideal discrepancy</u> (i.e., discrepancy between the perception of the *actual self*—the way you see yourself— and the *ideal self*—the way you feel you should be). The greater the discrepancy, the lower the self-esteem and the greater the depression an individual shows (Higgins, 1987, 1989); and this discrepancy tends to remain stable over time, even though the specific content may change (Strauman, 1996). It is a positive experience to receive feedback indicating that some aspects of our ideal self are functioning well, and a negative one to receive evidence that we are not living up to our ideal (Eisenstadt & Leppe, 1994). An interesting kind of discrepancy in a person's self-concept, *paradoxical self-esteem*, is described in Canadian Research: On the Cutting Edge.

Canadian Research: On the Cutting Edge

Paradoxical Self-Esteem: When Self-Liking and Competence Diverge

Occasionally, individuals have a discrepant self-concept of a particularly puzzling kind. This occurs when perceptions of your own competence and your own self-worth are very much at odds with each other. The term used by the University of Toronto's <u>Romin Tafarodi</u> (1998; Tafarodi, Tam & Milne, 2001) for this phenomenon is <u>para-doxical self-esteem</u>, which occurs when perceptions of *self-competence* and *self-lik-ing* are strongly discrepant. Paradoxical self-esteem can occur for someone who has low self-worth (termed *para-doxical low self-esteem*) or for someone who has high self-worth (termed *paradoxical high self-esteem*). For example, a person might be admired by others because

Paradoxical Self-Esteem When perceptions of self-competence and self-liking are discrepant.

of her achievements, and even acknowledge that she is very capable (be high in self-competence), and yet really dislike herself (have paradoxical low self-esteem). In contrast, someone might be seen by those around him as incompetent, and might see himself in the same way, and yet feel strong self-liking (paradoxical high self-esteem). Most people are *nonparadoxical*: That is, usually peoples' senses of competence and self-worth are in accord. So nonparadoxical persons who have low self-esteem also see themselves as incompetent, and nonparadoxical persons who have high self-esteem see themselves as competent.

The real puzzle with this phenomenon is how it is maintained, and research indicates that it is not just a passing state for some people (Bednar, Wells, & Peterson, 1989). We mentioned earlier that self-esteem usually varies with feedback from others—if others rate us positively we feel better about ourselves; if they rate us negatively our self-esteem goes down. However, this does not seem to occur for those with long-term paradoxical self-esteem. Individuals with paradoxical self-esteem will continually receive social feedback that is discrepant with their self-liking: those with paradoxical high self-esteem will receive feedback that they are incompetent, while those with paradoxical low self-esteem will receive feedback that they are competent. Yet their self-liking does not respond to this feedback. How can this occur?

Tafarodi and colleagues (1998, 2001) suggest that *biased processing of self-relevant information* is at the root of the maintenance of paradoxical self-esteem. Further, that the focus for such biased processing is *negative information about self worth*. How would this work? A person with *paradoxical low self-esteem* (low self-liking/high self-competence) might selectively notice, remember, and recall negative information relevant to self-worth. Giving greater weight to negative information would maintain that person's sense of low

self-worth. However, the person with *paradoxical high self-esteem* (high self-liking/low self-competence) might selectively *ignore* negative information relevant to the self. By giving less weight to negative information about self-worth, the high paradoxical individual avoids feeling bad about him- or herself. This reasoning is in line with the *negativity bias* mentioned in Chapter 2—that is, we have greater sensitivity for negative information than for positive information. So both low and high paradoxicals will bias their processing in relation to negative information about the self. And the bias would have to be particularly strong for paradoxicals (compared to nonparadoxicals) in order to minimize the impact of feedback from others that constantly contradicts their self-view.

Tafarodi and colleagues put these ideas to the test in study of selective memory bias (2001). Undergraduates at the University of Toronto were screened for paradoxical or nonparadoxical self-esteem, making four groups in all: *paradoxical low self-esteem* (low self-liking/high self-competence), *nonparadoxical low*

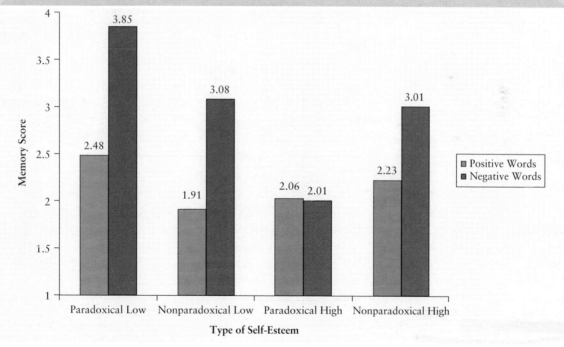

■ Paradoxical Self-Esteem and Memory

FIGURE 4.8 Those who had paradoxical self-esteem showed a stronger selectivity memory bias than nonparadoxicals, particularly for words related to negative self-worth. Subjects who had paradoxical low self-esteem (disliked themselves, despite being competent) remembered many more negative words than nonparadoxicals. Those who had paradoxical high self-esteem (liked themselves, despite being incompetent) remembered fewer negative words than nonparadoxicals.

self-esteem (low self-liking/low self-competence), *paradoxical high self-esteem* (high self-liking/low self-competence) and *nonparadoxical high self-esteem* (high self-liking/high self-competence). Subjects were shown a list of trait words related to self-worth. Some of the words were related to *negative self-worth* (e.g., inferior, despised, rejected) and some of the words were related to positive self-worth (e.g., attractive, worthy, likeable). Subjects were told that they should read the words and "consider how descriptive each word is of your personality." A surprise test of memory for these trait words was later administered. If Tafarodi's ideas were to receive support, then we would expect that subjects with paradoxical self-esteem would show a stronger memory bias compared to nonparadoxicals and that the memory bias would be particularly evident with words related to negative self-worth.

The results confirmed these expectations. As you can see by looking at Figure 4.8, the biggest differences between groups are for memory of *negative words*. Those with paradoxical low self-esteem have much higher memory scores for negative words than those with nonparadoxical low self-esteem. In contrast, those with paradoxical high self-esteem have much *lower* memory scores for negative words than those with

nonparadoxical high self-esteem. The fact that the memory bias of paradoxicals is focused on negative information is shown by the much smaller differences between groups for memory of positive words.

In summary, this study demonstrates that those with paradoxical self-esteem bias their cognitions more strongly than normal in a way that enables them to maintain their discrepant self-view. Paradoxicals do this not by being passively immune to others' evaluations of them, but through actively either enhancing their recall, or reducing their memory, for negative information about self-worth.

One question that remains, however, is the source of such stubborn self-liking or self-loathing in the face of others' constant contradictions. Tafarodi suggests that this may reflect a particularly strong early experience with primary caregivers such as parents. Perhaps, for example, a vivid sense of self-liking—if formed early enough because of loving treatment from our parents—so strongly colours our emotions and cognitions that it is resistant to later external influence or even our own perceptions of ourselves as incompetent. This speculation relates to research we will discuss in Chapter 6, showing that early parent—child *attachment patterns* can have a lasting effect on a person's social interactions.

KEY POINTS

- *Self-esteem* consists of self-evaluation, or the attitudes we hold about ourselves in general and in specific domains. It is based in part on *social comparison* processes, both *upward comparison* and *downward comparison*.

- There are many positive benefits associated with high as opposed to low self-esteem. However, variable self-esteem has even more negative consequences than low self-esteem.

- Self-esteem can influence performance through our sense of *self-efficacy*.

- Changes in self-esteem are possible particularly if we reduce the discrepancy between the actual and ideal self—termed a *self-ideal* discrepancy.

- However, individuals who have *paradoxical self-esteem*—where self-liking and perceptions of self-competence are discrepant—show strongly biased cognitive processing, which allows them to be impervious to outside opinions.

Self-Focusing: Awareness of the Self

Self-Focusing The act of directing attention toward some aspect of oneself as opposed to outward toward the environment.

So far we have examined several aspects of the self, including the origins of the self, the way knowledge about the self is organized, and the way self-esteem varies. We will now turn to self-awareness in general—when we are conscious of the self. This is termed **self-focusing** and refers to the centrality at a given moment of an individual's sense of self—the extent to which your attention is directed inward toward yourself as opposed to outward toward the environment (Fiske & Taylor, 1991).

Situational factors have a strong effect on self-focusing, and even simple instructions can determine where one focuses. For example, right now, please think about the ceiling in your room. If you did so, your focus was away from yourself. Now, please think about the most positive aspects of yourself. If you did, you just engaged in self-focusing. Self-focusing also occurs when such environmental cues as a mirror or a video camera are present (Fenigstein & Abrams, 1993). The tendency to focus on oneself increases between childhood and adolescence (Ullman, 1987), and some adults consistently self-focus more than others (Dana, Lalwani, & Duvall, 1997).

The ability to change one's focus can be seen as part of the more general process of _self-regulation_ of one's thoughts (Macrae, Bodenhausen, & Milne, 1998). Darwin (1871) recognized the importance of such mental activity when he said, "the highest possible stage in moral culture is when we recognize that we ought to control our thoughts" (p. 123). A brief period of self-focusing can improve insight. After deliberately spending a few minutes thinking about themselves, research participants show increased accuracy in judging social feedback (Hixon & Swann, 1993). Sometimes continual and consistent self-focusing can create difficulties. For example, in response to an unpleasant social interaction, individuals with a self-focusing style experience more negative feelings, and this reaction is stronger for women than for men (Flory et al., 2000). However, self-focusing can also be a useful way of coping with a stressful situation if it involves taking control of one's affective state and thinking of ways to solve the problem (Taylor et al., 1998). For example, external focusing is helpful in improving the affective state of someone who is depressed (Lyubomirsky & Nolen-Hoeksema, 1995). So the key is not simply to self-focus but to control and regulate the content of the thought processes. Those who do so are said to take a *reflective orientation* to their moods (McFarland & Buehler, 1998; Trapnell & Campbell, 1999). When a negative mood was induced in a laboratory setting, participants who were characteristically successful at mood regulation were better able to retrieve positive memories, and thus reverse the negative mood, than were participants who were low in the ability to regulate moods (Rusting & DeHart, 2000).

The way in which information about the self is organized can also influence self-focusing. Some people file positive and negative aspects of their experiences separately in memory—to engage in *compartmentalized self-organization* (Showers, 1992a; Showers & Kling, 1996). When that is done, one's mood can be controlled by deciding whether to focus on the positive or the negative elements. However, some people store positive and negative experiences together in memory (Showers, 1992b). This pattern is called *evaluatively integrated self-organization*, and the result is that self-focusing can never involve purely negative elements because positive elements are also present as part of the same memories. As a result, these individuals experience less severe negative affect and have higher self-esteem. That sounds good, but there are some drawbacks. If you experience severe stress, it is helpful to focus on purely positive self-content. The presence of separate, positive elements of the self makes it easier to protect yourself against depression and anxiety (Showers & Ryff, 1996).

Monitoring Your Behaviour by Using Internal or External Cues

A specialized form of self-focusing termed **self-monitoring** has been the subject of much research. Self-monitoring refers to the tendency to regulate one's behaviour on the basis of external cues such as how other people react (high self-monitoring) or on the basis of internal cues such as one's own beliefs and attitudes (low self-monitoring) (Gangestad & Snyder, 1985; Snyder & Ickes, 1985). Low self-monitors tend to behave in a consistent way regardless of the situation, whereas high self-monitors tend to change as the situation changes (Koestner, Bernieri, & Zuckerman, 1992). Scale items such as "I can

Self-Monitoring The degree to which an individual regulates his or her behaviour on the basis of the external situation and the reactions of others (high self-monitors) or on the basis of internal factors such as beliefs, attitudes, and values (low self-monitors).

■ High Self-Monitoring: Behaviour in Response to the Reactions of Others

FIGURE 4.9 In interpersonal situations, a person who is a high self-monitor (such as former Prime Minister Jean Chrétien) responds to the reactions of others and then attempts to behave so as to meet their expectations. A low self-monitor, in contrast, responds to his or her own personal standards and then attempts to behave in a way that matches those standards. High self-monitoring is associated with success in politics, acting, and sales.

only argue for ideas that I already believe" are answered as *true* by low self-monitors and *false* by high self-monitors. High self-monitors engage in role-playing in order to obtain positive evaluations from other people (Lippa & Donaldson, 1990). This is a useful characteristic for politicians, salespeople, and actors (see Figure 4.9).

Self-monitoring tendencies are revealed in many aspects of social behaviour. For example, high self-monitors tend to use the third person (he, she, them, etc.) when they verbalize; low self-monitors use the first person (I, me, my, etc.) (Ickes, Reidhead, & Patterson, 1986). More positive self-esteem is characteristic of high self-monitors (Leary et al., 1995), and low self-monitors tend to have fewer and longer-lasting romantic relationships than do high self-monitors (Snyder & Simpson, 1984).

Interestingly, those who are either extremely high or extremely low in self-monitoring are more neurotic and less well adjusted than those who fall in the middle of this dimension (Miller & Thayer, 1989). For high self-monitors, depression and anxiety result from a discrepancy between self-characteristics and what *other people* think those characteristics should be; for low self-monitors, depression and anxiety result from a discrepancy between self-characteristics and what *the individual* thinks they should be (Gonnerman et al., 2000).

There is evidence that self-monitoring is genetic (Gangestad & Simpson, 1993). On some of the questionnaire items used to measure this dispositional variable, identical twins responded in the same way more often than did fraternal twins. Examples are greater similarity in having the ability to imitate others, wanting to impress or entertain people, liking to play charades, and being able to lie. All four of these behaviours are characteristic of high self-monitors, and responses to all four are more similar in identical than in fraternal twins.

KEY POINTS

- *Self-focusing* refers to the extent to which an individual is directing attention toward the self or toward the external world. This can be part of a process of self-regulation involving focus on positive or negative information about the self.

- *Self-monitoring* refers to a dispositional tendency to regulate behaviour on the basis of external factors (high self-monitoring) or on the basis of internal beliefs and values (low self-monitoring).
- Differences in self-monitoring tendencies influence speech patterns, response to advertising content, and interpersonal behaviour. Individual levels of self-monitoring are based in part on genetic factors.

Social Identity: The Self in a Social Context

As we mentioned earlier in this chapter, William James (1890) saw the social world as part of the self—other people, friends, family, and ancestors were seen by as an important part of the self. This theme was picked up in the first part of the twentieth century by *symbolic interactionists*, theorists who suggested that the development of a sense of self occurred through interaction with others and with society (Cooley, 1902/1964; Mead, 1934). Today those who take a *cultural perspective* see the self as "property of the culture" (Sampson, 1991, p. 212). It is this social side of our identity on which we will focus in this section of the chapter, specifically, our *gender identity* and our *cultural identity*.

Social Identity Theory: The Importance of a Collective Sense of Self

One of the most influential theories to emerge from European social psychology is **social identity theory** (Tajfel, 1978, 1982; Tajfel & Turner, 1979). Social identity theorists have stressed that group belonging is a major contributor to the individual's self-concept. Your **social identity** is that part of your self-concept derived from membership in, and identification with, social groups. This is often now termed a person's **collective identity,** (as we saw in Figure 4.2) because this term more clearly denotes the group-based nature of this component of the self (Sedikides & Brewer, 2001; Taylor 2002). Social identity theory distinguishes *social* or *collective identity* from **personal identity**, which is the unique and individual aspects of your self-concept. In other words, social identity is the part of your sense of self that comes from the knowledge that you are part of particular groups in society. Some of these groups are chosen by you, such as when you decide to become a student at one particular college or decide to join a club. But membership in other groups is involuntary or ascribed: you are born into them or assigned them by your society. For example, we do not choose our gender group, age group, or cultural background. By an accident of birth you may be a young, male, Italian-Canadian or a middle-aged, female, English-Canadian. Notice that the group-title (e.g., Italian-Canadian) is one that is defined by the society in which you live. You may or may not identify yourself in that way. However, it is almost impossible not to be aware that such designations are of social significance in Canada-whether you like it or not, others often identify you in that way.

Often our sense of self-worth is tied to our group-membership or group-identification (Crocker et al., 1994; Tajfel, 1982). For example, sports-fans' self-esteem will rise and fall with the success or failure of their team (Hirt, Zillman, Erickson, & Kennedy, 1992). In line with this, a fundamental assumption of social identity theory is that we *strive to maintain or achieve a positive and distinctive social identity*. First, we are concerned that our group can be distinguished from other groups—this is what gives us an identity. So, for example, when the North American Free Trade Agreement (NAFTA) was signed in 1993, there were fears expressed that Canada would suffer the loss of its distinctive identity through economic and cultural domination by the United States.

Social Identity Theory The theoretical approach that stresses the importance of a person's group-membership and identification to the self-concept. Individuals are motivated to achieve or maintain a positive and distinctive social identity.

Social Identity/Collective Identity The group-based aspects of an individual's self-definition, derived from membership in and identification with social groups.

Personal Identity The unique aspects of the individual's internal and private self-definition.

Second, as well as being distinctive, we are also concerned that our groups are positively evaluated, relative to other groups in society. In order to establish whether our group has a positive or a negative social identity, we use *intergroup social comparison*. We compare the status and respect of our group with other groups in society.

If you want a measure of how important group status can be to the individual, think how strongly many people react when Canada is denigrated by someone from another country. The importance of social identity becomes evident here, and you can see some of its ramifications. If someone runs down your country, you often feel the urge to defend it by describing its positive qualities. Further, you might want to point out that the speaker's own country has a few problems, too. This is just what social identity theory suggests: an individual who has been assigned a negative social identity is motivated to improve it and this often involves a clash of competing identities with other groups. Further, it can lead to prejudice and conflict (Taylor & Moghaddam, 1987), as will be discussed in Chapter 5.

More recently, Jackson and Smith (1999) have extended Tajfel's original conceptualization by describing social identity as varying on four dimensions: perception of the intergroup context, in-group attraction, interdependency of beliefs, and depersonalization, as outlined in Figure 4.10. They suggest that the role that social identity plays in intergroup relationships depends on which dimensions are operating. Jackson and Smith (1999) suggest that underlying the four dimensions are two basic types of social identity: *secure* and *insecure*. When there is a high degree of *secure identity*, the individual tends to evaluate out-groups more favourably, to be less biased in comparing the in-group with the out-group, and to be less likely to believe in the homogeneity of the in-group. In contrast, a high degree of *insecure identity* is associated with a very positive evaluation of the in-group, greater bias in comparing in-groups and out-groups, and the perception of greater in-group homogeneity.

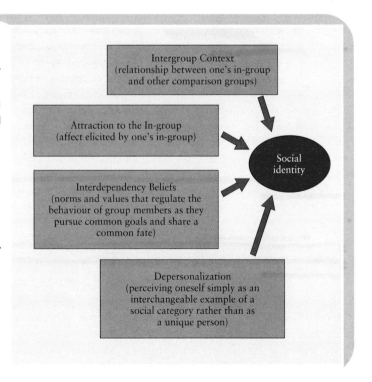

■ Four Dimensions of Social Identity

FIGURE 4.10 Jackson and Smith (1999) proposed a conceptualization of social identity involving four dimensions: perception of the intergroup context, in-group attraction, interdependency of beliefs, and depersonalization, as shown here.

Source: Based on information in Jackson and Smith, 1999.

Gender as a Crucial Aspect of Social Identity

It seems the most pervasive aspect of social identity derives from categorizing ourselves as either female or male. That is, you may or may not pay much attention to your ethnic identity or your social class but it would be extremely rare to find someone who was unaware and unconcerned about being a male versus being a female. In hundreds and hundreds of ways, we are reminded each day of our gender by how we dress, how we act, and how others respond to us.

The terms *sex* and *gender* are often used to mean the same thing. In our discussion, however, we follow the terminology of those in the field (e.g., Beckwith, 1994) who distinguish them in the following way. **Sex** is defined in *biological* terms as the anatomical and physiological differences between males and females that are genetically determined. **Gender** refers to everything else associated with one's sex, including the roles, behaviours, preferences, and other attributes that define what it means to be a male or a female in a given *culture*. Please note that the specific definitions used here are not universally accepted by those actively working in this field (e.g., Deaux, 1993b; Gentile, 1993; Unger & Crawford, 1993).

Gender Identity

Each of us has a **gender identity** in that a key part of our self-perception involves the label "male" or "female." For the vast majority of people, biological sex and gender identity correspond, though there is a small proportion of the population in which gender identity differs from sex. What is the origin of our gender identity?

Explanations of sex differences in psychological attributes usually emphasize biological factors based on evolution (Archer, 1996), cultural factors (Mischel, 1967), or some combination of the two (Costa, Terracciano, & McCrae, 2001; Wright, 1994). Though this topic can lead to arguments that are political as well as scientific (Eagly, 1995; Hyde & Plant, 1995), university and college students are found to accept the idea that both social and biological variables are operating, but that learning outweighs genetics (Martin & Parker, 1995).

Evolutionary and Biological Perspectives

From the evolutionary perspective, universal gender differences in interpersonal and sexual behaviour are often assumed to stem from differences in *parental investment* in reproduction (Trivers, 1972). Biologically, reproduction demands a larger minimum commitment on the part of women in terms of physical effort (pregnancy, birth, breast-feeding) as well as behavioural and temporal limitations (restrictions during pregnancy, birth, and child-care)—and these investments would have been more difficult as well as dangerous among early humans. In contrast, for males the minimum physical investment in reproduction is much less: it can be as small as a few minutes of time and a

Sex Maleness or femaleness as determined by genetic factors present at conception that result in anatomical and physiological differences.

Gender The attributes, behaviours, personality characteristics, and expectancies associated with a person's biological sex in a given culture.

Gender Identity That part of the self-concept involving a person's identification as a male or a female. Consciousness of gender identity usually develops at about the age of two.

teaspoon of sperm (Miller, 1998). Males' reproductive priorities and behaviours related to reproduction would, therefore, differ from those of females. Evolutionary theorists have suggested that these differences in reproductive priorities are at the basis of evolved male-female differences in behaviour. This perspective will be further discussed as it applies to interpersonal relationships (see Chapter 6) and aggression (see Chapter 8).

At the biological level, researchers have examined the role of the male hormone **testosterone**. Testosterone is consistently found to be associated with dominant behaviour; men have higher levels of testosterone than do women, and men therefore behave in a more dominant way than women. As a plausible evolutionary background, it is proposed that the prehistoric males whose bodies produced the most testosterone were the most combative and dominant, thus being the individuals best able to subdue rival males, obtain mates, and reproduce. Their male descendents have the same biological characteristics. Females also produce testosterone, but high levels provide no special advantages in attracting a mate or reproducing. As a result, today's men are more aggressive and dominant, more strongly motivated to engage in sexual activity, and more willing to take risks than are today's women (Anderson & Aymami, 1993; Baumeister, Catanese, & Vohs, 2001; Berman, Gladue, & Taylor, 1993; Moskowitz, 1993; Wilson et al., 1996). Analogous research on the behavioural effects of the female hormone **estrogen** is lacking.

What are some of the other behavioural correlates of testosterone level? Males with the highest hormone levels tend to choose dominant and controlling occupations; they become trial lawyers, actors, politicians, and criminals (Dabbs, 1992). Even female trial lawyers have higher testosterone levels than other female lawyers. In competitive sports such as basketball, just before the game begins, the team members *and* their male fans show a rise in testosterone level, and these levels go even higher when a team wins (Dabbs, 1993).

Sex differences in other interpersonal behaviours can also be explained in terms of evolutionary differences. For example, women are more likely than men to be aware of their emotions (Barrett et al., 2000), to share rewards (Major & Deaux, 1982), and to be concerned with maintaining relationships rather than controlling them (Timmers, Fischer, & Manstead, 1998). Evolutionary theorists would suggest that such differences have evolved because the most successful prehistoric mothers were those who shared with their offspring and formed positive relationships. It seems equally possible that such behaviour reflects learned gender roles (Major & Adams, 1983). That is, women are subjected to social pressures that induce them to strive for cooperation and generosity rather than competition and selfishness (Nadkarni, Lundgren, & Burlew, 1991). In a similar way, women may have better social skills than men because they *have* to (Margalit & Eysenck, 1990).

Social Cognitive Perspective

The social cognitive perspective suggests that, while the tendency to create schemas related to gender may be prewired in us, the actual content of those schemas, our understanding of being male and female, comes from cultural socialization. Sandra Bem's *Gender schema theory* (1981, 1983) suggests that children have a "generalized readiness" to organize information about the self in a way that is based on cultural definitions of appropriate male and female attributes. Once a young child learns to apply the label "girl" or "boy" to herself or himself, the stage is set for the child to learn the "appropriate" roles that accompany these labels. As childhood progresses, **sex typing** occurs when children learn in detail the stereotypes associated with maleness or femaleness in their culture. We learn such stereotypes from our parents, our media, and our peers, and they affect our judgments of each other from an early age. In one study,

Testosterone The male "sex hormone."

Estrogen The female "sex hormone."

Sex Typing Acquisition of the attributes associated with being a male or female in a given culture.

children and adolescents both agreed that nine-month-old infants given the name "Mary" and "Karen" (whether the infants were actually female or not) were smaller, more beautiful, nicer, and softer than when the same infants were given the names "Stephen" and "Matthew" (Vogel, Lake, Evans, & Karraker, 1991). It seems clear that the stereotypes associated with each gender determine our perceptions of them even when they are still infants!

The influence of gender stereotypes may not be deliberate or obvious, as a recent field study has shown. Video recordings were made of several hundred parents and their offspring (ages one to eight) at the science exhibits in a children's museum (Crowley et al., 2001). Parents were found to be three times more likely to explain scientific information to boys than to girls, even though they were equally likely to talk to their sons and daughters about other topics. This difference was true of both fathers and mothers, and it held true for children regardless of age, as shown in Figure 4.11. Presumably, an interest in science is thought to be more appropriate for boys than for girls. Such findings suggest at least one reason for sex differences in scientific interest in later years.

Generally, children are rewarded for engaging in gender-appropriate behaviour and discouraged (or ridiculed) when they engage in gender-inappropriate behaviour. Consider, for example, the probable response to a little girl who requests a doll for Christmas versus the response to a little boy who makes the same request. On the basis of how adults, older siblings, and others respond, a little girl learns that wanting a doll is acceptable but wanting boxing gloves is not, while a little boy learns that for him

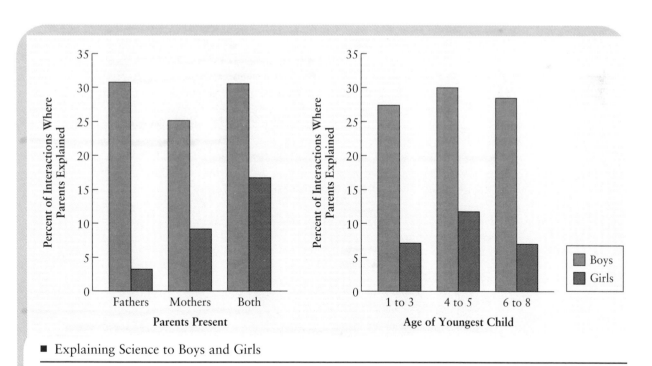

■ Explaining Science to Boys and Girls

FIGURE 4.11 Parent-child interactions were videotaped at science exhibits in a museum. It was found that parents (both fathers and mothers) spent much more time explaining the exhibits to their sons than to their daughters, whether the children very young (one to three) or older (four to eight). This kind of gender-specific parental behaviour is just one example of the ways that gender stereotypes (e.g., science is for boys, not girls) are passed between generations.

Source: Based on material in Crowley et al., 2001.

boxing gloves are cute but a doll is unacceptable. As the years pass, the lessons are well learned, and by the time they reach the sixth grade, the overwhelming majority of children have learned the prevailing gender stereotypes (Carter & McCloskey, 1984). Even people who disagree with the stereotypes know what is considered suitable for each gender and what constitutes out-of-role behaviour. This developmental progression is outlined in Figure 4.12. The specific content of these stereotypes about masculinity and femininity in our culture and the possibility of nonstereotyped behaviour are presented in the Cornerstones box.

■ The Developmental Aspects of Gender

FIGURE 4.12 Beginning with the genetic determination of sex at conception, each of us progresses through developmental stages in which we learn to label self and others as male or female, internalize gender identity as part of our self-concepts, learn our culture's gender stereotypes, and eventually adopt gender roles that may or may not match these stereotypes.

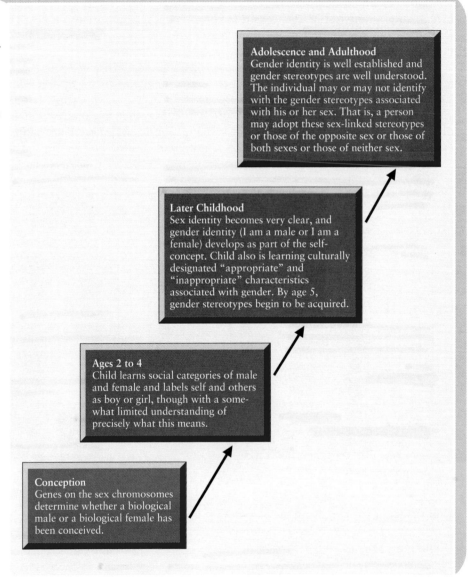

Adolescence and Adulthood
Gender identity is well established and gender stereotypes are well understood. The individual may or may not identify with the gender stereotypes associated with his or her sex. That is, a person may adopt these sex-linked stereotypes or those of the opposite sex or those of both sexes or those of neither sex.

Later Childhood
Sex identity becomes very clear, and gender identity (I am a male or I am a female) develops as part of the self-concept. Child also is learning culturally designated "appropriate" and "inappropriate" characteristics associated with gender. By age 5, gender stereotypes begin to be acquired.

Ages 2 to 4
Child learns social categories of male and female and labels self and others as boy or girl, though with a somewhat limited understanding of precisely what this means.

Conception
Genes on the sex chromosomes determine whether a biological male or a biological female has been conceived.

Cornerstones

Bem's Concept of Psychological Androgyny as an Alternative to Masculinity versus Femininity

Nearly three decades ago, Sandra Bem (1974, 1975) produced a new theoretical formulation and a measuring device that revolutionized how gender is conceptualized and studied. At the time she began this work, most people (including psychologists) assumed that masculinity and femininity represented the opposite ends of a single dimension. Thus, each person was relatively masculine and therefore not feminine or relatively feminine and therefore not masculine. Of course, many people actually do fit into just one of these two categories (Kagan, 1964; Kohlberg, 1966). And a person who fits a masculine or feminine stereotype is motivated to behave in ways consistent with the gender role he or she has learned: small children are not the only ones encouraged to conform to stereotypes, and "inappropriate" gender behaviour is strongly discouraged.

Bem rejected the idea of a single dimension and suggested that various personal characteristics associated with masculinity and femininity lie on two separate dimensions: one ranging from low to high masculinity and the other ranging from low to high femininity. In this conceptualization, many individuals may actually be high on characteristics associated with both genders. For example a person could be competitive (supposedly masculine) and also sensitive to the needs of others (supposedly feminine). A person who combines traditional masculine characteristics with traditional feminine ones is considered to be androgynous.

To identify masculine, feminine, and androgynous individuals, the **Bem Sex-Role Inventory (BSRI)** was developed. Note that in the terminology used in this chapter, this measure would be labelled the "Bem *Gender*-Role Inventory." Research participants identified more than 400 positive characteristics as being socially desirable for men and/or for women. The final measure contains 20 items desirable for males but not for females, 20 items desirable for females but not desirable for males, and 20 that are equally desirable for males and females. The male and female items are

> **Androgynous**
> Characterized by the possession of both traditional masculine characteristics and traditional feminine ones.

> **Bem Sex-Role Inventory (BSRI)**
> Bem's measure of the extent to which an individual's self-description is characterized by traditional masculinity, traditional femininity, a mixture of the two (androgyny), or neither (undifferentiated).

shown in Table 4.1. Note that additional studies have indicated very little change in these gender stereotypes over time (Martin, 1987; Raty & Snellman, 1992).

A person taking the BSRI indicates, for all 60 items, how accurate each one is as a description of herself or himself. The results provide a person's **gender-role identification**, or the extent to which an individual does or does not identify with the culture's gender stereotypes. The four possibilities are a *sex-typed* masculine male or feminine female, a *reverse-typed* individual (a masculine female or feminine male), an *androgynous* individual of either gender, or an *undifferentiated type* who has few characteristics of either gender. Research indicates that about a third of males fit the masculine gender type, and about the same proportion of females fit the feminine gender type. About one out of three males is androgynous, as are a third of females. The undifferentiated and cross-gender categories make up the rest. This classification indicates *gender-role identification*, or the extent to which an individual does or does not identify with the culture's gender stereotypes.

> **Gender-Role Identification**
> The degree to which an individual identifies with the gender stereotypes of his or her culture.

Research has been consistent with the implication that "androgyny is good." For example, compared to gender-typed individuals, androgynous men and women were found to be better liked (Major, Carnevale, & Deaux, 1981); better adjusted (Orlofsky & O'Heron, 1987; Williams & D'Alessandro, 1994); more adaptable to situational demands (Prager & Bailey, 1985); more flexible in coping with stress (McCall & Struthers, 1994); more comfortable with their sexuality (Garcia, 1982); more satisfied interpersonally (Rosenzweig & Daley, 1989); and, in an elderly sample, more satisfied with their lives (Dean-Church & Gilroy, 1993). Spouses report happier marriages when both partners are androgynous than with any other combination of roles (Zammichieli, Gilroy, & Sherman, 1988). Further, sexual satisfaction is greater if one or both partners are androgynous than if both are sex-typed (Safir et al., 1982).

Further, extreme adherence to traditional gender roles is often found to be associated with relationship problems. For example, men who identify with the extreme masculine role behave more violently and aggressively than men who perceive themselves as having some feminine characteristics (Finn, 1986).

A person taking the Bem Sex-Role Inventory rates a series of characteristics in terms of how well they describe him or her. Those items shown here are the ones that are perceived as more characteristic of males than of females or vice versa. That is, they represent pervasive gender stereotypes in our culture.

TABLE 4.1 Gender Stereotypes Identified by Bem

Characteristics of the Male Stereotype	Characteristics of the Female Stereotype
acts as a leader	affectionate
aggressive	cheerful
ambitious	childlike
analytical	compassionate
assertive	does not use harsh language
athletic	eager to soothe hurt feelings
competitive	feminine
defends own beliefs	flatterable
dominant	gentle
forceful	gullible
has leadership abilities	loves children
independent	loyal
individualistic	sensitive to the needs of others
makes decisions easily	shy
masculine	soft-spoken
self-reliant	sympathetic
self-sufficient	tender
strong personality	understanding
willing to take a stand	warm
willing to take risks	yielding

Source: Based on information in Bem, 1974.

Among adolescent males, high masculinity is associated with having multiple sexual partners, the view that men and women are adversaries, low condom use, and the belief that getting a partner pregnant is a positive indication of one's masculinity (Pleck, Sonenstein, & Ku, 1993). Both men and women who endorse a purely feminine role are lower in self-esteem than either masculine or androgynous individuals (Lau, 1989).

Currently there is increasing recognition of the multifaceted nature of sexuality and sexual- or gender-identity. In the 1990s, Bem (1995, p. 334) borrowed an analogy from anthropologist Kathryn March to make a more general point: "Sex is to gender as light is to colour." That is, sex and light are physical phenomena, whereas gender and colour are culturally based categories that arbitrarily divide sex and light into designated groups. With colour, some cultures have only two categories, others three, while in North America there are Crayola boxes with 256 different hues, each with its own assigned name. With respect to gender, the reverse is true. We have traditionally emphasized only two genders, whereas other cultures have had Crayola boxes of possibilities ranging from bisexuality to an array of heterosexual and homosexual roles and lifestyles.

Gender and Self-Perception

Gender differences in self-perception are commonly found. Compared to men, women are much more likely to be concerned about their body image (Pliner, Chaiken, & Flett, 1990), to express dissatisfaction about their bodies (Heinberg & Thompson, 1992) and physical appearance in general (Hagborg, 1993), to develop eating disorders (Forston & Stanton, 1992; Hamilton, Falconer, & Greenberg, 1992), and to become depressed (Strickland, 1992). They are much more likely to suffer from *appearance anxiety*—to worry about how they look to others (Dion, Dion, & Keelan, 1990). Obesity is a special issue for women. When an overweight woman is viewed as an unacceptable date by a male, instead of being mad at him and attributing the problem to his prejudice, she is more likely to blame herself (Crocker, Cornwell, & Major, 1993). Even though obese women tend to attribute rejection in the workplace as caused by unfair biases, romantic rejection is perceived to be justified (Crocker & Major, 1993).

Why is appearance a major problem for women? Possibly because from infancy on, others respond to appearance differently on the basis of gender. Even parents discriminate against overweight daughters (but not overweight sons) with respect to providing financial support for university or college (Crandall, 1995). To the extent that young men express any appearance anxiety, it is a relatively mild dissatisfaction about not measuring up to the body-builder muscular ideal of male attractiveness (Davis, Brewer, & Weinstein, 1993).

Consider for a moment the day-to-day negative effects of the special emphasis our society places on the physical attractiveness of women in general and on specific anatomical details such as breast size (Thompson & Tantleff, 1992). One consequence is that women often are vulnerable and easily upset when their appearance becomes an issue (Mori & Morey, 1991). For example, after looking at magazine pictures showing ultra-thin models, undergraduate women respond with feeling of depression, stress, guilt, shame, insecurity, and dissatisfaction with their own bodies (Stice & Shaw, 1994). As they age, women are perceived as increasingly less feminine, though men are not viewed as becoming less masculine with age (Deutsch, Zalenski, & Clark, 1986).

The cultural basis of this dramatic difference in self-perceptions between men and women is strongly suggested by the fact that such problems are much more common in Western industrialized nations than in developing countries. Even within the United States, Canada, and the United Kingdom, women of Asian and African descent have fewer eating disorders than Caucasian women. Caucasian females are also more likely to view themselves as overweight and to evaluate their bodies negatively. White women denigrate overweight women much more than black women do (Hebl & Heatherton, 1998). One possible explanation is that men of Asian and African descent are less concerned about the weight of their romantic partners. Whatever the reason, white women have more weight concerns than their nonwhite counterparts. Comparing white and Asian female students aged 14 to 22 in London schools, Wardle and colleagues (1993) found that both groups had the same ideals about appearance (thin is good). Nevertheless, white females differed from Asian females in wanting to lose weight, being actively involved in trying to lose weight, and weighing themselves more frequently-even when their current size and weight did not differ from those of their Asian classmates. Among the thinnest participants, more white than Asian females said that they felt "fat."

Beyond appearance, other self-perceptions also differ for men and women. On self-report measures, women describe themselves as more anxious, gregarious, trusting, and nurturing than men, while men describe themselves as more assertive than women (Feingold, 1994). Compared to men, women respond with greater emotional intensity, as indicated by self-reports and by physiological assessment (Grossman & Wood, 1993). Some evidence suggests that the explanation for such gender differences rests on differences in the specific areas of the brain used by men and women in thinking and responding to emotional cues (Gur, 1995; Kolata, 1995; Shaywitz & Shaywitz, 1995).

We have focused on the contribution of gender to a sense of self. While our biology (our sex) certainly contributes to our sense of femaleness or maleness, it is the social side of this aspect of our self-concept that has been the concern here. In short, we can say that the society in which we are raised, along with its beliefs and stereotypes, plays a large part in determining our gender identity: one of the earliest and most fundamental aspects of our social identity. We will now turn to the contribution of cultural and ethnic background to social identity.

KEY POINTS

- One important aspect of social identity is *gender*-the societal expectations associated with a person's *biological sex*. Children develop a sense *of gender identity*, a sense of maleness or femaleness, as part of the self-concept. This usually includes some sex typing of behaviour as children learn the culturally appropriate forms of behaviour for their gender.

- Research on *androgyny*, using the *Bem Sex-Role Inventory (or BSRI)*, has provided evidence that those who are androgynous (have both traditionally masculine and feminine traits) tend to be more adaptable than those who adhere strongly to traditional gender roles.

- Gender differences in self-perception are common, particularly differences in perception of *body image*. Typically, females tend to be more concerned about many aspects of physical appearance than males. One possible reason is the greater emphasis society places on physical attractiveness in women.

Cultural Influences on Identity: Ethnicity and Interdependence

One of the most important aspects of a person's social identity is his or her cultural background. *Culture* was defined in Chapter 1 as the organized system of shared meanings, perceptions, and beliefs held by persons belonging to a particular group. The shared understanding of a culture is often communicated among members by a shared language. For example, French-Canadian culture has its own system of communication, which has evolved with marked differences from the language spoken in France, and it is an essential component of the Quebecois identity.

Ethnic Identity

Ethnic Identity The part of an individual's social identity that is derived from membership in, or identification with, a particular cultural or racial group.

A person's identification with a particular cultural or racial group is often termed **ethnic identity**—that part of someone's social identity that is derived from membership in, or identification with, a particular ethnic group. When individuals are from a minority cultural group, developing a sense of ethnic identity can be problematic. Adolescents sometimes find that reconciliation of their own cultural group with that of the larger society is difficult (Ethier & Deaux, 1994; Spencer & Markstrom-Adams, 1990). Phinney (1990) has described four styles of resolving the dilemma of whether to identify with one's own cultural group or the mainstream culture: These are shown in Figure 4.13.

Canadian research has demonstrated that these identifications have important consequences. For example, John Berry (1976) examined *acculturative stress* (a reduction in health status related to contact between cultural groups) among members of ten native samples across Canada. In eight of these groups it was found that those who believed in *integration* or in *assimilation* showed less acculturative stress than those who had *separatist* beliefs. It is not surprising that a person who has separatist beliefs,

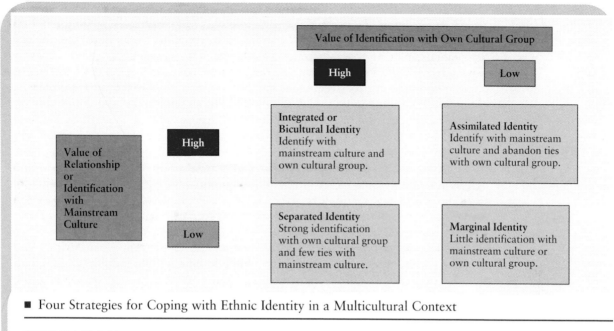

Value of Identification with Own Cultural Group

High | Low

Value of Relationship or Identification with Mainstream Culture

High:
Integrated or Bicultural Identity Identify with mainstream culture and own cultural group.

Assimilated Identity Identify with mainstream culture and abandon ties with own cultural group.

Low:
Separated Identity Strong identification with own cultural group and few ties with mainstream culture.

Marginal Identity Little identification with mainstream culture or own cultural group.

■ Four Strategies for Coping with Ethnic Identity in a Multicultural Context

FIGURE 4.13 Building on the work of Canada's John Berry, Phinney (1990) has proposed a model of *ethnic identity* based on the extent to which individuals identify with their own cultural group or with mainstream culture. This model applies specifically to those, such as immigrants, who have a cultural background that differs from the mainstream.

or a *separated identity*, might find contact with the mainstream culture unwelcome and, therefore, stressful. In contrast, for an integrated or assimilated individual, contact would be more welcome and less stressful. More recent research has suggested that those who have a strong ethnic identity with their own cultural group tend to have higher self-esteem and cope better in a multicultural context but only if they also have a positive attitude to the mainstream culture (LaFromboise, Coleman, & Gerton, 1993; Phinney, 1991; Sanchez & Fernandez, 1993).

Another Canadian study demonstrated that these identifications are also related to cross-cultural contact. Dona (1991; Dona & Berry, 1994) found that refugees from Central America who had an integrated identity had greater contact with Canadian society than those who had a separated identity. In fact, John Berry (2001) has recently made a case for the benefits of integration as an optimal strategy for immigrants striving to achieve a place in their new society. Further, he suggests that a policy of multiculturalism in a host society can encourage such integration.

Cultural Influences on the Self: The Effects of Individualism or Collectivism

Though it is commonly assumed that one's self-concept is formed in the context of social interactions, the implications of this proposal are difficult to appreciate within a single culture. When we look across cultures or subcultures, however, aspects of the self that are based on social factors become much more obvious. This impact goes beyond identification with a particular ethnic group, to fundamental differences in perception of how self is related to the social world and others.

Two researchers who have written extensively about the importance of culture to the self are Markus and Kitayama (1991a, 1991b). Reviewing a considerable body of research conducted in Asian countries, they have concluded that there are fundamental differences

Independent Conception of the Self The self is viewed as separate and distinct from other individuals and from the environment. The individual will tend to be seen as autonomous and unique. This construal of the self is typical of Western cultures.

Interdependent Conception of the Self The self is viewed as fundamentally connected to others and to the environment: the self is integrated into the social context. Such individuals will strive for acceptance and to maintain harmonious relations with others. This construal of the self is more typical of non-Western cultures.

in Eastern and Western conceptions of the self. The **independent conception of the self** is of an individual who is separate and distinct from other individuals and from the social and physical environment. Those who have an independent sense of self will see themselves as autonomous and tend to strive to achieve individuality and uniqueness. Their behaviour will tend to be influenced by reference to their own thoughts, feelings, and beliefs. This has been characterized as a construal of the self that is common in *individualistic* cultures such as Canada, the United States, and Britain. Independence tends to be seen as the right, and even the healthy, way to be in Western culture. We believe someone should "stand on your own two feet," "think for yourself," and "don't follow the crowd," "be true to yourself," but this may not be how most non-Western cultures conceptualize the self (Geertz, 1974).

In contrast, the **interdependent conception of the self** views it as fundamentally connected to others and to the environment: the self is integrated into the social context. Those who have an interdependent sense of self will strive for acceptance, attempt to fit in with others, and maintain harmonious relations. Their behaviour will be more likely to be influenced by the thoughts, feelings, and actions of significant others. This construal of the self is more typical of *collectivistic* cultures in Asia, Africa, South America, and Southern Europe (see also, Smith & Bond, 1998; Triandis, 1989).

Research has begun to confirm these cultural distinctions in fundamental self-concept. Cousins (1989) found greater context-dependence in the self-concepts of students from Japan (a collectivistic culture) compared to those from the United States (an individualistic culture). American self-concept was more independent of social context. Once again, the focus has been on the differences between the self in North America and the East Asian self (e.g., in Japan, China, Korea) and a number of dimensions of difference have been emphasized (see Table 4.2). One cultural difference shown in this table has received particular attention—differences in the tendency to be *self-enhancing*. A debate has arisen recently over the extent to which this is a universal, or a culturally specific, phenomenon. This issue explored in the following On the Applied Side section.

Recent research exploring the cultural difference between North American and East Asian senses of the self has found a number of dimensions of contrast shown in the table below. Together, these contrasts suggest that there are profound differences in the ways in which individuals from each culture relate to the self and to the world around them.

TABLE 4.2 Some Cultural Differences in the North American and East Asian Self

North American Self	East Asian Self
1. Independent self-concept.	1. Interdependent self-concept.
2. More self-enhancing.	2. More self-critical.
3. Strive to become individuated.	3. Individuation is less positive and more complex.
4. Strive to influence others.	4. Strive to adjust to others.
5. Emphasize consistency of self.	5. Emphasize flexibility of self.
6. The self is invariant; the world is malleable.	6. The self is malleable; the world is invariant.
7. Seek internal information to understand the self.	7. Seek social-situational information to understand the self.
8. Relationships provide for one's needs.	8. Relationships define the self.

Source: Based on information in Heine, 2001; Kwan, Bond, Boucher, Maslach, & Gan, 2002; Morling, Kitayama, & Miyamoto, 2002.

On the **Applied Side**

Self-Enhancement: A Universal or Cultural Phenomenon?

Is the motive to self-enhance *pancultural* (shown across all cultures)? We have seen in Chapter 2 and in this chapter that the use of self-enhancing biases, which help to bolster the self-esteem of individuals, is common and often seen as beneficial, at least in moderation (e.g., Fiske & Taylor, 1991). This tendency has also been viewed as an evolved and universal one (Brown & Kobayashi, 2002, 2003; Sedikides, Gaetner, & Toguchi, 2003). Evolutionary explanations for the self-enhancing bias rest on the idea that it may function to increase social acceptance. Among early humans, maintaining one's place in the social group may have been crucial—solitary individuals would have found it difficult to survive and reproduce. Therefore, developing a mechanism to monitor social inclusion or exclusion would have been adaptive. Leary and colleagues claim that self-evaluation generally provides a measure of the degree of social acceptance by others—it is a "sociometer" of the quality of a person's relationships (Leary, Tambor, Terdal, & Downs, 1995). The person who is rejected by others feels bad and is motivated to improve his or her social situation. Biasing the way we present ourselves to others in a self-enhancing direction can help to make us more acceptable to our social group and to potential mates. So Leary and colleagues suggest that the function of a self-enhancement mechanism is to avoid social exclusion. Not all explanations have pointed to it as an evolved mechanism (e.g., Taylor & Brown, 1988), but, nonetheless, there was for many years widespread acceptance of self-enhancement as a general human tendency.

Recently, cultural psychologists have been critical of the universal perspective, suggesting it is a case of an *imposed etic*—a Western phenomenon being assumed to be universal (Heine, 2001; 2003; Heine, Lehman, Markus, & Kitayama, 1999). Would self-enhancement be relevant to those with an interdependent self-concept? After all, their priority may not be maintenance of a positive self-concept but maintenance of the group and its needs. To stand out, even in a positive self-enhancing way, implies alienation from the group for the interdependent individual, with a consequent loss of a sense of self.

Self-Enhancing Biases Any cognitive bias that serves to enhance the positive self-view of the person using it. Examples are the self-serving bias and unrealistic optimism.

In line with their *collective constructionist model*, Kitayama and his colleagues (1997) have proposed that people raised in Western, individualistic cultures learn that everyday life presents repeated opportunities for *self-enhancement*. In contrast, for those in Eastern, collectivistic cultures, everyday life is believed to present opportunities for *self-criticism*, which facilitates striving towards self-improvement.

In comparing the behaviour of college students in Japan and the United States, these investigators first had people from each culture describe success situations (e.g., getting an A+ on a paper) and failure situations (e.g., being rejected by your friends). They then took these descriptions and asked another sample of students from each culture to rate the situations in terms of how *relevant* each one was to their self-esteem—whether they expected the situation to have an impact. As shown in Figure 4.14, the Japanese students found failure situations far more relevant to their self-esteem than success situations, but the reverse was true for Americans. Notice that Japanese students in the United States were in between these two extremes, suggesting there had been some acculturation to a Western perspective. They also found that, when asked to rate the positive or negative impact of these situations on self-esteem, the accumulated impact was positive for Americans (the total impact of all situations was self-enhancing) and negative for the Japanese (the total impact was self-criticizing).

Evidence has accumulated showing that self-enhancement may be prevalent in Western cultures but is rare in Eastern cultures. Across many studies, North Americans are found to express unrealistically optimistic self-evaluations (Regan, Snyder, & Kassin, 1995) and to show self-serving attributional biases (see Chapter 2), while Japanese people seldom do either (see Heine et al., 1999). In a similar way, Chinese college students in Hong Kong are much less self-enhancing than comparable students in Canada (Yik, Bond, & Paulhus, 1998). The bulk of research demonstrates that compared to Western subjects, non-Western subjects show either a decreased level of self-enhancement, no self-enhancement or sometimes *self-effacement*—showing the opposite of these biases (e.g., blaming the self for negative outcomes or seeing oneself as less likely than others to experience a positive future).

It is worth noting, however, that self-enhancement sometimes occurs even within a collectivist culture,

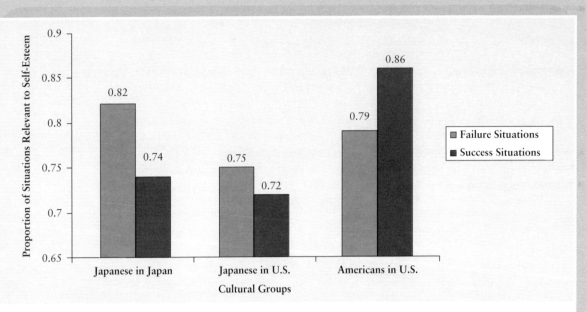

■ Is Success or Failure More Relevant to Your Self-Esteem?

FIGURE 4.14 Students were asked whether situations describing successes and situations describing failures were relevant to their self-esteem. Japanese students found a higher proportion of failure situations as relevant to their self-esteem than success situations. Americans found success situations more relevant and Japanese students in the U.S. were in between.

but frequently in a modest and non-obvious way. For example, Japanese students prefer the letters in their own names and the numbers corresponding to the month and day of their birth over other letters and other numbers (Kitayama & Karasawa, 1997). Also, researchers from the universal perspective have recently provided evidence of self-enhancement by Japanese people and those with interdependent self-concepts. This is particularly likely to occur when they are asked to compare the self with similar others on *culturally important dimensions* (Brown & Kobayashi, 2002; Sedikides, et al., 2003). For example, Japanese students rated themselves as more likely to perform behaviours that reflected collectivistic values (e.g., conform to your group's decision) than the typical member of their own group. They also rated collectivistic traits (e.g., compromising, cooperative, respectful) as more descriptive of themselves than typical members of their group. The researchers suggest that the self-enhancing motive is present among collectivistic/interdependent individuals, but expresses itself along culturally important dimensions only—if modesty is important, then the individual will see the self as more modest than most.

As research stands at this moment there is an impasse. Evolutionary researchers, as well as others who see self-enhancement as universal, suggest that previous research did not take sufficient account of culturally important contexts (Brown & Kobayashi, 2003; Sedikides et al., 2003). Cultural psychologists, on the other hand, insist that cultural differences are real and profound—that fundamental motives among East Asians differ from North Americans. Their desire is not to self-enhance but to strive for improvement (through self-criticism) particularly in relation to the group. In other words, in cultures like Japan, people "concern themselves more with the *process of becoming better,* than with *being good*" (Heine, et al, 1999, p. 771, my emphasis).

As mentioned at the beginning of this chapter, evolutionary and cultural researchers disagree about the degree and level of cultural influence—and that is reflected in the current dispute. However, the researchers involved in this dispute all agree with William James that we have a need to *evaluate our self-worth.* Where the disagreement remains is whether that is synonymous with a self-enhancement—exaggerating our own positive qualities—and whether that particular motive is universal.

KEY POINTS

- *Cultural groups* are an important source of social identity and can determine our understanding of the self. We gain our ethnic identity from the cultural or racial group to which we belong. Contact with other cultural groups in a multicultural society can create problems for the development of an individual's *ethnic identity*.

- Cultures can vary in terms of whether they have an *independent* or *interdependent* conception of the self and this has implications for the extent to which individuals show self-enhancing or self-improvement tendencies.

- Research on cultural differences in the self has focused on whether the tendency to be self-enhancing is universal.

Ideas To Take With You

Dealing with Negative Self-Perceptions

A very consistent and pervasive difference between men and women in Western societies involves the way they perceive and evaluate their appearance. Beginning in adolescence, women are much more concerned about body image than men. Changing this isn't easy but you can start with yourself.

Be Realistic about the Importance of Appearance.
"Be realistic" is obviously easier to say than to accept. By definition, most of us lie outside of the top one-tenth of one percent of the population who are represented in professional sports, modelling, or movie stardom. If you decide you are imperfect because you are not in such a category, you will spend many unhappy hours brooding about not reaching an impossible goal. Also, as you will discover in Chapter 6, the adage that "you can't judge a book by its cover" is true. The most attractive individuals in the world do not differ from the rest of us in intelligence, creativity, character, kindness, or anything else that matters—except in the fact that they are liked on the basis of their looks. Think of the most unkind, dishonest, and totally detestable human being you know. Would you find that person more acceptable if he or she suddenly acquired a very attractive face and body? If you meet an attractive person for the first time, try to remember that appearance gives you no information at all about this individual.

Ask Yourself How Important Your Weight Is to Others.
Women in Canada and other Western nations are often obsessed with their weight. Do you know how much you should weigh on the basis of height—weight charts? If you fit within those norms, are you satisfied? Or do you want to weigh less? Why? Do other people perceive you as underweight, average, or overweight? How much do you think you would have to lose or to gain for anyone to notice? Some of us know that you can work hard to lose a few kilograms, only to find that no one has a clue unless you tell them. You may think about your weight a lot and about fatness/thinness as you observe others, but other people are not obsessed with your weight! They don't care nearly as much as you do.

Recognizing and Countering Your Own Ethnocentrism

Next time you find yourself critical of the way other cultural groups respond to the social world—perhaps they seem to display too much emotion, or too little; perhaps their practices or clothing seem ridiculous—stop and realize that you are being ethnocentric, assuming that your group's customs are the normal and the right ones.

Learn about Other Cultures.
One way to counter such tendencies is through education about cultural differences and you are already doing that! Learning to understand about different cultural views of the world is interesting as well as enlightening. It can help you to become aware that there are many different ways of being human and each culture's solution, including your own, has its advantages and disadvantages.

Try to See Things from Other Cultures' Perspectives.
Another way to counter ethnocentrism is to visualize things from the perspective of other cultural groups. This is being empathic and of course must be based in real understanding of their culture. One way to achieve this is to mix with and make friends with people from other cultural groups. This is always an experience that broadens your mind. You can then begin to appreciate the richness of your multicultural society.

Summary

Evolutionary and Cultural Origins of the Self

- The sense of self includes individual, relational, and collective components. (p. 119)
- Evolutionary approaches to the self suggest that the human sense of self has evolved. (p. 119)
- The *collective constructionist model*, suggests that culture and the individual are mutually constitutive. The self is formed through a culture's *selfways*. (p. 121)
- *Cross-cultural psychology* investigates the influence of culture in social behaviour. (p. 122)
- *Ethnocentrism* can be a source of bias in everyday life and in social psychology. (p. 122)
- Increased awareness of this has led to a call for *indigenous psychologies* in non-Western cultures. (p. 123)

Personal Identity: Aspects of the Individual Self

- Cognitive information related to the self is organized into *self-schemas* and is processed more efficiently—*the self-reference effect*. (p. 125)
- The self-concept changes when we envision possible future selves and when there are changes in our environment or occupational status. (p. 126)

- *Self-esteem* consists of self-evaluation, and can be based on both *upward* and *downward social comparison processes*. (p. 128)
- There are positive benefits associated with high as opposed to low self-esteem, and self-esteem can influence performance through evaluation of *self-efficacy*. (p. 131)
- Improvements in self-esteem can occur through a reduction in *self-ideal discrepancy*. (p. 132)
- Individuals with *paradoxical self-esteem* show biased cognitive processing, allowing them to remain impervious to outside opinions. (p. 133)
- *Self-focusing* refers to the extent to which an individual is directing attention towards the self or toward the external world. (p. 134)
- *Self-monitoring* is a type of self-focusing in which behaviour is regulated on the basis of external or internal factors. (p. 135)

Social Identity: The Self in a Social Context

- *Social identity theory* suggests that the groups to which we belong form an important part of our identity. We are motivated to achieve a positive and distinctive social identity. (p. 137)
- Gender is an important aspect of social identity associated with a person's *biological sex*. Children develop a sense of *gender identity* as part of their self-concept. (p. 139)

- Research on *androgyny* has used the Bem *Sex-Role Inventory (or BSRI)* to investigate *gender-role identification*. (p. 143)
- *Gender* differences in self-perception are common, particularly differences in perception of *body image*. (p. 145)
- *Cultural groups* are an important source of social identity and provide our *ethnic identity*. (p. 146)

- Culture can influence the self-concept to be *independent* or *interdependent*. (p.148)
- Research on cultural differences in the self has focused on whether a tendency to be self-enhancing is universal. (p. 149)

For More Information

Sedikides, C. & Brewer, M.B. (2001). Individual self, relational self, collective self. Philadelphia: Taylor & Francis.

A collection of articles by many of the leading researchers of social identity. The theme of the collection is the interrelationship between the individual, relational, and collective selves. Included are chapters from a cognitive, interpersonal, and cultural perspective.

Worell, J. (Ed.). (2001). Encyclopedia of women and gender. Orlando, FL: Academic Press.

A comprehensive collection of articles in a two-volume set written by leaders in the research field, concentrating on issues involving women and gender. Included among the many topics are discussions of individualism and collectivism, media stereotypes, parenting, prejudice, self-esteem, sex differences, sexuality, social identity, and working environments.

Weblinks

www.spsp.org
Society for Personality and Social Psychology
www.sil.org/sil/roster/headland-t/ee-intro.htm
"Etics and Emics: The Insider/Outsider Debate" by Thomas Headland

www.emory.edu/education/mfp/james.html
Well illustrated and comprehensive information about William James
www. webster.edu/~woolflm/sandrabem.html
A biographical essay about Sandra Bem by Nicolle Bettis

CHAPTER FIVE

Prejudice and Discrimination:
Understanding Their Nature, Countering Their Effects

Prejudice and Discrimination: Their Nature and Forms
Prejudice: Choosing Whom to Hate/Discrimination: Prejudice in Action/Prejudice and Discrimination Go Underground

The Origins of Prejudice: Contrasting Perspectives
Intergroup Conflict: Competition and Categorization as Sources of Prejudice/Early Experience: The Role of Social Learning/Social Cognition: Its Role in Maintaining Prejudice/The Authoritarian Personality/The Evolution of Prejudice

Responses of the Victims of Prejudice
Types of Possible Responses to Prejudice and Discrimination/Research on Victim Responses to Prejudice

Challenging Prejudice: Why It Is Not Always Inevitable
Institutional Interventions: Putting Multiculturalism to the Test/Changing Relations between Groups/Breaking the Cycle of Prejudice: On Learning Not to Hate/Cognitive Interventions: When Stereotypes Become Less Compelling

SPECIAL SECTIONS

ON THE APPLIED SIDE
Women in the Workplace: Does Neosexism Have an Impact?

CORNERSTONES
The Economics of Racial Violence: Do Bad Times Fan the Flames of Prejudice?

CANADIAN RESEARCH: ON THE CUTTING EDGE
Challenging Implicit Racism by Inducing Feelings of Hypocrisy

Virtually everyone reading this chapter has experience with prejudice or discrimination. You may have been the victim of spiteful remarks about your race, gender, or physical attributes, or perhaps you were systematically excluded by a group on the same basis. If so, you know about prejudice and discrimination from the receiving end. And, if you are like many victims, this has left a lasting and painful memory.

On the other hand, you may have been the perpetrator of prejudice or discrimination. You may have made a negative assumption about someone based on their gender, ethnicity, age, or appearance and excluded them for that reason. Perhaps you have repeated a joke that contains racist or sexist stereotypes, or laughed at one. If so, then you know about prejudice and discrimination from the other side—as a perpetrator. In contrast to the experiences of victims, being the perpetrator does not lead to emotional scars—at least for you. In fact, you have probably dismissed any suggestion that you could be a "bigot"—it is almost certainly inconsistent with your self-concept. You were "just having a little fun," and you probably "didn't mean anything by it." The point here is that none of us is immune from the experience of prejudice and discrimination as either victim or perpetrator, or, often, both. Even if you are the (very rare) person who has been neither victim nor perpetrator, you have certainly observed its destructive effects in society as a whole.

A quick review of the past millennium indicates that prejudice and discrimination have often, alas, been part of human society. Despite Canada's positive reputation as a tolerant society (Dion, 2002), at the beginning of the new millennium we too continue to have distressing examples of the extremes to which prejudice can lead. For example, in 1999, five young men between 19 and 26 years old, who had been in the Canadian military, were convicted of beating and killing a 65-year-old man, Nirmal Singh Gill. They belonged to white racist groups and this man was a Sikh who was about to open his temple. In 2001, Aaron Webster was killed by a group of youths who attacked him as he was walking with a friend in a gay area of Vancouver (See Figure 5.1). By

■ The Extreme Effects of Prejudice and Discrimination

FIGURE 5.1 Prejudice and discrimination are some of the most destructive forces in our diverse society. This photograph shows a memorial to Aaron Webster, attacked and killed in Vancouver because of his sexual orientation.

January 2004, only two of the group, both of whom were under 18 years at the time of the killing, had been charged. In the international arena, religious and ethnic hatred continues to fuel murder, terrorism, and genocide in Africa, the Middle East, and the United States.

But what, precisely, is *prejudice*, and how does it differ from another term with which we are also, unfortunately, too familiar—*discrimination*? What factors contribute to the existence of prejudice and discrimination? And perhaps even more important, how can these negative forces in human society be reduced? Given the great diversity of the human species, plus the fact that contact among people of different racial, ethnic, and national backgrounds is increasing, these are vital questions and ones with which we surely must grapple. In fact, it does not seem too extreme to suggest that combating prejudice and discrimination is one of the most crucial tasks confronting humanity today. The alternative—permitting them to exist unchecked—seems to condemn us to an ever-rising tide of hatred and violence. If nothing else, then, social psychology's commitment to understanding, and combating, prejudice and discrimination seems more timely than ever.

First, we'll examine the nature of both prejudice and discrimination, indicating what these concepts are and how they differ. Second, we will consider the causes of prejudice and discrimination—why they occur and what makes them so intense and so persistent. Third, we will look at the responses of victims of prejudice and discrimination. Finally, we will explore various strategies for reducing prejudice and discrimination.

Prejudice and Discrimination: Their Nature and Forms

In everyday speech, the terms *prejudice* and *discrimination* are used interchangeably. Are they really the same? Most social psychologists draw a clear distinction between them. **Prejudice** refers to a special type of attitude—generally, a negative one—toward the members of some social group. In contrast, **discrimination** refers to negative actions toward those individuals. Since this is an important difference, let's consider it more closely.

Prejudice
Negative attitudes toward the members of specific social groups.

Discrimination
Negative behaviours directed toward members of social groups who are the object of prejudice.

Prejudice: Choosing Whom to Hate

We'll begin with a more precise definition: *Prejudice* is an attitude (usually negative) toward the members of some group, based solely on their membership in that group. In other words, a person who is prejudiced toward some social group tends to evaluate its members in a specific manner (usually negatively) merely because they belong to that group. Their individual traits or behaviour play little role; they are disliked (or, in a few cases, liked) simply because they belong to a specific social group.

When prejudice is defined as a special type of attitude, two important implications follow. First, our *cognitions* are involved. As we noted in Chapter 3, attitudes often function as *schemas*—cognitive frameworks for organizing, interpreting, and recalling information (Wyer & Srull, 1994). Thus, individuals who are prejudiced toward particular groups tend to process information about these groups differently from the way they process information about other groups. For example, prejudiced individuals take longer or pay closer attention to material related to their prejudice (Blascovich et al., 1997). Similarly, information consistent with their prejudiced views is rehearsed more frequently, and, as a result, tends to be remembered more accurately than information that is not consistent with these views (Bodenhausen, 1988; Judd, Ryan, & Park, 1991). To the extent that this happens, prejudice becomes a kind of closed cognitive loop, and tends to grow stronger over time.

Second, if prejudice is a negative attitude, then negative feelings or *emotions* are shown by prejudiced persons when they are in the presence of, or merely thinking about, members of the groups they dislike (Bodenhausen, Kramer, & Susser, 1994; Vanman et al., 1997). And as we'll soon see, prejudice can also be *implicit*—it can be triggered in a seemingly automatic manner by exposure to members of the disliked group, and can influence overt behaviour even when the persons involved are largely unaware their feelings and might deny vigorously that they hold them (e.g., Fazio et al., 1995; Fazio & Hilden, 2001). Like other attitudes, prejudice also includes beliefs and expectations about members of various groups—for instance, beliefs that all members of these groups show certain traits. We'll discuss such beliefs, known as *stereotypes*, later in this chapter (e.g., Jussim, 1991). Finally, prejudice may involve tendencies to act in negative ways toward those who are the object of prejudice; several of these are examined in the next section, which explores the various forms that discrimination can take.

[handwritten margin note: implicit vs. explicit prejudice.]

KEY POINTS

- *Prejudice* is an attitude (usually negative) toward members of some social group based solely on their membership in that group.
- Prejudice, like other attitudes, influences our processing of social information and our beliefs and feelings about others. Prejudice can also be *implicit*—triggered automatically even when we are unaware of it.

Discrimination: Prejudice in Action

Attitudes, as we noted in Chapter 3, are not always reflected in overt actions and prejudice is definitely no exception to this rule. In many cases, persons holding negative attitudes toward the members of various groups cannot express these views directly. Laws, social pressure, fear of retaliation—all serve to deter them from putting their prejudiced views into open practice. Further, those who are prejudiced may restrain themselves from overt actions that might violate their own standards and cause guilt (Devine & Monteith, 1993; Monteith, 1996). In fact, the incidence of blatant *discrimination* may have decreased in recent years in North America (e.g., Swim, Aikin, Hall, & Hunter, 1995; Tougas, Brown, Beaton, & Joly, 1995). However, such restraining forces are sometimes absent. Then the negative beliefs and feelings referred to above may find expression in overt actions. Such discriminatory behaviour can take many forms and is often quite subtle. At relatively mild levels it involves simple avoidance— prejudiced persons simply avoid or minimize contact with the objects of their dislike (Henry, 1995). While such discrimination may seem relatively benign, it can sometimes have serious consequences for its victims. For example, studies indicate that sizable proportions of health-care professionals (physicians, nurses, hospital workers) report spending less time with AIDS patients than with people suffering from other illnesses (Gordin et al., 1987, Hunter & Ross, 1991). Clearly, such discrimination can add to the pain and suffering of the victims. At stronger levels, discrimination can produce exclusion from jobs, educational opportunities, or neighbourhoods. Finally, in the most extreme cases, prejudice leads to overt forms of aggression against its targets such as *hate crimes*—ones that are based in whole or in part upon the victim's race, religion, nationality, ethnic origin, gender, disability, or sexual orientation—and genocide, the destruction of whole groups in a society.

Prejudice and Discrimination Go Underground

As public disapproval of overt prejudice and discrimination increases and, further, is enforced in our legal system, the prejudiced person goes underground. They may be reluctant to express their feelings and beliefs, except among the like-minded. Yet there is evidence that their negative attitudes still manage to influence their behaviour. How is this achieved? One answer involves the use of subtle forms of discrimination—ones that permit their users to conceal the underlying negative views from which they stem. We'll focus on two major examples that have been studied in recent years: *modern racism* and *neosexism*.

The New Racism

At one time, many people felt no qualms about expressing openly racist beliefs. They would state they viewed members of minority groups as inferior in various ways, and that they would consider moving away if persons belonging to these groups took up residence in their neighbourhoods (Sears, 1988). Now, of course, very few persons would openly state such views. Does this mean that racism, a particularly virulent form of prejudice and discrimination, has disappeared? While many social psychologists would argue that this is the case (e.g., Martin & Parker, 1995), others would contend that, in fact, all that has happened is that "old-fashioned" racism (read "blatant" for "old-fashioned") has been replaced by more subtle forms, which these researchers term <u>modern racism.</u> What is such racism like? According to Swim and her colleagues (Swim, et al., 1995), modern racism has three essential components: (1) denial that there is continuing discrimination against minorities; (2) antagonism to the demands of minorities for equal treatment; and (3) resentment about special favours for minority groups. This form of racism may not be as blatant as the old-fashioned kind, but it can still be very damaging to the victims. For example, as noted by Swim and colleagues (1995), modern racism may influence the likelihood of voting for a minority. So—and we want to emphasize this point strongly—despite the fact that blatant forms of racism have diminished sharply in this and many other countries, this repulsive and damaging form of prejudice is still very much alive and represents a serious problem in many societies.

Modern Racism
Subtle forms of prejudice and discrimination against other (usually minority) ethnic groups. This involves apparent support for egalitarian principles while also denying continued discrimination against minorities, and showing antagonism towards minority demands and resentment against any preferential treatment designed to redress past imbalances.

Measuring Modern Racism

Most persons who show this type of racism will tend to conceal it from others and even from themselves (i.e., their prejudiced attitude is *implicit*). In fact, in some cases, these persons would vigorously deny that they have such views, especially when they relate to such "loaded" issues as racial prejudice (e.g., Dovidio & Fazio, 1991; Dovidio et al., 1997; Greenwald & Banaji, 1995). Because of this, social psychologists have developed unobtrusive means for studying such attitudes.

Implicit prejudices may be elicited automatically by members of the groups toward whom the prejudice is directed or by stimuli associated with such persons. How can we measure such subtle forms of prejudice? Several different methods have been developed (Kawakami & Dovidio, 2001), but most are based on *priming* or *subliminal priming* (concepts we discussed in Chapters 2 and 3) and the measurement of response times to positive or negative trait words associated with the stereotype. The idea is that if a person has an implicit prejudice he or she will have well-formed (but unacknowledged) associations between negative traits (e.g., inferior) and their disliked group. Researchers can take advantage of this and anticipate a faster response time when subjects are asked to identify a negative adjective *if the subjects have been primed beforehand with a stimulus related to a disliked group* (e.g., shown the face of a visible minority person). For people with no prejudice, response times would not change with the prime. Notice that such techniques do not rely on asking persons directly for their prejudiced opinions or feelings and are, therefore, much less vulnerable to the effect of subjects' self-presentation concerns. Research indicates that these techniques can provide a reliable indication of a person's true underlying prejudices (e.g., Fazio & Hilden, 2001; Towles-Schwen & Fazio, 2001).

We'll have more to say about such effects in later sections. For now, the important point to note is this: Despite the fact that blatant forms of racism have decreased in public life in Canada and many other countries, this damaging type of prejudice is still very much alive and, through more subtle kinds of reactions, continues to represent a very serious problem in many societies.

Covert Institutional Racism

Historians of racism in Canada suggest that it has an *institutional* origin; historically, it was a part of the "institutional framework" of this society—built into its system of social stratification and legitimized by regulations, laws, and established customs (Barrett, 1987; Kinsella, 1994; Sher, 1983). As Stanley Barrett concluded from his analysis of racism and racist groups in Canada:

> *My argument is that racism—quite apart from the formally organized [racist] groups—has been institutionalized into Canadian society since the country's beginning. The right wing, including the most extreme racists and anti-semites, simply represent a more crystallized and overt form of a broader phenomenon (Barrett, 1987, p. 4).*

Evelyn Kallen (1995) has described institutional racism in Canada as having occurred through restriction or denial of (1) immigration, (2) educational opportunities, (3) property or land ownership and use, (4) employment opportunities, (5) the franchise (i.e. the right to vote), and (6) housing. Some examples of these types of institutional racism from Canadian history are shown in Table 5.1. The examples shown can be thought of as _overt institutional racism_—discrimination that is explicit in the laws and regulations of a society. However, not all institutional racism is as obvious as this kind. **Covert institutional racism** exists when ethnic discrimination is not openly approved in an institution, but nonetheless is present. This latter type of racism can perhaps be thought of as the institutional form of *modern racism*. It is often difficult to detect or to prove and tends to become evident when certain ethnic groups are systematically (though unofficially) excluded from certain areas of social, economic, or political life in a country.

Covert Institutional Racism Racism that exists when ethnic discrimination is not openly approved in an institution, but nonetheless is present.

In Canada today, *overt* institutional racism is rare. Human rights legislation specifically prohibits discrimination against individuals or groups on the basis of race and ethnicity, sex, religion, age, and disability. However, we should not make the mistake of thinking that this has eliminated problems of racial discrimination in this country. Covert institutional racism does occur. In March 1997, the Human Rights Commission rendered a landmark decision against a government department, Health Canada, stating that it had discriminated against visible minority employees. That is, members of visible minority groups systematically failed to achieve promotion, despite suitable qualifications and work records. Health Canada was ordered to promote more minority employees to senior management positions within the following six months. Such cases of covert institutional racism tend to occur not because of any deliberate policy on the part of an organization, but because those in management positions use their power to exclude or otherwise discriminate against people from other ethnic groups. The institution itself turns a blind eye or is unaware that discrimination is occurring.

Some examples of institutional racism from Canada's history.

TABLE 5.1 Institutional Racism in Canadian History

Restriction or Denial of Immigration. At the end of the nineteenth century, Chinese men were encouraged to emigrate to Canada to help build the great railway that links this country. With the railway completed, in 1886 a head tax of $50 was imposed on all Chinese immigrants. When this tax did not stem the tide of immigrants, it was increased to $500 by 1903—effectively preventing many families from being united. Finally, in 1923 the Chinese Immigration Act was passed prohibiting all Chinese immigration.

Restriction of Educational Opportunities. From 1920 to the 1950s and 60s, it was mandatory for Native children to be sent away from their often remote homes to special residential schools. There they were discouraged from maintaining their own cultural heritage. If they spoke their own language or practised their own customs they were punished. Laws had also been passed banning important Native ceremonies such as the *potlatch*. The effect of this program was to severely disrupt the Native culture and way of life. Family relationships were destroyed by enforced separation for two or three generations, and today communities are still recovering.

Control of Property Ownership/Restriction of Movement. Subsequent to the Japanese attack on Pearl Harbor in December 1941, 23,000 Canadian residents of Japanese descent were placed in internment camps. Their property was placed in the hands

of the "Custodian of Enemy Alien Property" and later sold at well below market prices. Approximately 75 percent of these people were Canadian citizens. Again, this government action was clearly discriminatory. People of German descent did not receive this harsh treatment, although Germany was also an enemy of Canada during World War II.

Denial of Franchise and Employment Opportunities. Canadians of Chinese descent did not receive the vote until 1947. Canadians of Japanese descent did not receive the vote until 1949. Note that for both groups immigration had begun as early as the 1880s. The Inuit first received the federal vote in 1962 and Status Indians first received the vote in 1960. A person who could not vote could not hold public office, could not be in the public service, and was prevented from entering many professions such as law and pharmacy.

Restriction of Education and Housing Facilities. Until 1942, McGill University entrance requirements were a 65 percent average for Jews, but a 50 percent average for non-Jews. The law authorizing segregated schools was not repealed until 1965. As late as 1973, residential property deeds in Vancouver's affluent "British Properties" stipulated that no person of Asiatic or African ancestry could stay on the premises overnight unless he or she was a servant.

Source: Based on Barrett, 1987; Kallen, 1994.

Two field studies in Toronto indicate that governmental organizations are not the only places in which covert institutional racism can occur. Henry and her colleagues (Henry, 1999; Henry & Ginzberg, 1985) had researchers pose as job applicants for positions advertised in newspapers. The approach was either on the telephone or in person. Applicants on the telephone had a standard Canadian accent, a European-origin foreign accent, a West Indian accent, or an Indo-Pakistani accent. Those who applied in person were either black or white. In the first study, there was considerable discrimination against nonwhite subjects whether they applied by phone or in person. For example, when applying in person, the jobs offered to white applicants outnumbered those offered to black applicants by a ratio of 3 to 1, although their résumés were exactly the same. Although in the second study, carried out about five years later (Henry, 1999), discrimination against the in-person applicants was not found, applicants on the telephone were still discriminated against and to the same extent as in the first study. That is, the nonwhite applicants were about twice as likely to be told that the job was no longer available than the white applicants.

In sum, although great progress has been made in Canada in terms of overt institutional racism, we cannot be complacent. It appears that the covert form of institutional racism is still common.

Sexism and Neosexism

Sexism (prejudice and discrimination based on gender) has been widely investigated since the 1970s (Bem, 1995; Cameron, 1977; Eagley, 1995). It should be emphasized that *both* sexes have been negatively affected by *sexism*—the personal and professional limitations that traditional sex roles impose. Both males and females have felt the pressure to conform to the social definition of their gender behaviour and have found it difficult to step beyond the traditional occupational roles open to each sex. However, usually these limitations have been much greater for women: They have been excluded from economic and political power; they have been the subject of stronger negative stereotypes; and they have faced overt discrimination in many areas of life, such as work, education, and government (Fisher, 1992; Heilman, Block, & Lucas, 1992). For this reason, most research has focused upon the effects of sexism on women.

But not all sexism is appears to be completely negative. In the same way that other forms of prejudice sometimes include positive as well as negative stereotypes, sexism can also show two different faces. One is known as hostile sexism—the view that women have many negative traits (e.g., they seek special favours, are overly sensitive, or manipulate to seize power from men). The other is what Glick and his colleagues (2000) describe as benevolent sexism—views suggesting that women deserve protection, are superior to men in various ways (e.g., they are more pure, have better taste, are more naturally nurturing), and are truly necessary for men's happiness (e.g., no man is truly fulfilled unless he has a woman he adores in his life). According to Glick and his colleagues (2000), both forms of sexism reflect the fact that men have long held a dominant position in most human societies. As a result of this power, they have come to see women as inferior in various ways. At the same time, however, men are dependent on women for the domestic roles they play and for the intimacy and love they provide. These facts, in turn, have contributed to the development of benevolent sexism.

Evidence of the existence of both aspects of sexism exist was provided by Glick and his associates (2000) in a massive study involving more than 15,000 participants in 19 different countries. Researchers measured both types of sexism with a questionnaire. Results indicated that both hostile and benevolent sexism seem to exist in every country studied. As found in previous research, men generally express higher hostile sexism than women in all countries studied. However, this difference disappears for benevolent sexism (see Figure 5.2). Women actually subscribe to such views even more than men in several countries (e.g., Colombia, Turkey, Germany, and Belgium).

Further, countries that had higher levels of both types of sexism, were also the ones that United Nations data indicated had lower the levels of gender equality (in terms of women's presence in high-status jobs, education, and standard of living). Overall, then, it seems clear that sexism does *not* imply uniformly negative views of women or hostility toward them. It involves what at first might seem to be a kinder, gentler face as well. As noted by Glick and his colleagues (2000), however, benevolent

Sexism Prejudice or discrimination based upon gender.

Hostile Sexism The view that women, if not inferior to men, have many negative traits (e.g., they seek special favours, are overly sensitive, or manipulate to seize power from men).

Benevolent Sexism Views suggesting that women deserve protection, are superior to men in various ways (e.g., they are more pure, have better taste), and are truly necessary for men's happiness (e.g., no man is truly fulfilled unless he has a woman he adores in his life).

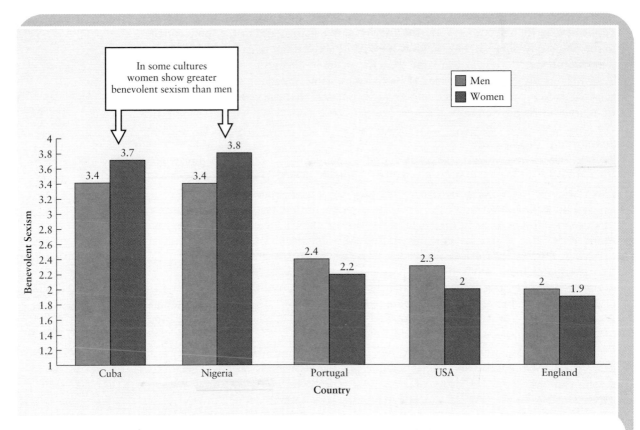

In some cultures women show greater benevolent sexism than men

Legend: ▪ Men ▪ Women

Y-axis: Benevolent Sexism (1 to 4)

- Cuba: Men 3.4, Women 3.7
- Nigeria: Men 3.4, Women 3.8
- Portugal: Men 2.4, Women 2.2
- USA: Men 2.3, Women 2
- England: Men 2, Women 1.9

X-axis: Country

■ Benevolent Sexism around the Globe

FIGURE 5.2 Two forms of sexism seem to exist—hostile and benevolent. Research typically shows that men express *hostile sexism* much more strongly than do women. However, Glick and colleagues' research found that gender differences decrease or are even reversed with respect to *benevolent sexism*, as shown here.

Source: Based on data from Glick et al., 2000.

sexism, too, is a form of prejudice: it also serves to keep women in a subordinate role. So benevolent sexism also runs counter to the goal of full equality.

Parallel to the findings of the work on *modern racism*, research has noted a decrease in overt forms of sexism towards women (e.g., Kahn & Crosby, 1985; Sutton & Moore, 1985) and a new form of sexism has been investigated termed **neosexism**— subtle forms of prejudice and discrimination against women, defined by its major researchers as a "manifestation of a conflict between egalitarian values and residual negative feelings towards women" (Tougas, Brown, Beaton, & Joly, 1995, p. 843). According to their analysis the "old-fashioned" form of sexism, based on the presumed inferiority of women to men (Cameron, 1977), has been supplanted by this new form. They suggest that because social norms in our society are largely egalitarian and changes in the law have made overt discrimination more difficult, the expression of sexist attitudes has become more covert. As we will see in the On the Applied Side section, there is evidence that neosexism may contribute to *maintaining* inequalities in the workplace.

Neosexism Subtle forms of prejudice and discrimination against women produced by a conflict between egalitarian values and residual negative feelings towards women.

On the Applied Side

Women in the Workplace: Does Neosexism Have an Impact?

During the past 20 years, human rights legislation made occupational discrimination on the basis of gender illegal (in the Human Rights Act, 1985). However, given the evidence of covert institutional racism mentioned above, we might expect that *sexism* or *neosexism* will continue to have an impact in the workforce. Is there any evidence to support this suggestion?

First the good news: the world of work has certainly improved for women in Canada. For example, in 1951 only 24 percent of women in Canada were in the labour force, whereas by 2002 this had risen to 56 percent (Creese & Beagan, 1999; Statistics Canada, 2003). Within the past 20 years, women's average education and earnings have increased. In 1981 only 10.8 percent of adult women (16.5 percent of men) had a degree, but in 2001 the figure was 22.6 percent for both men and women—and in that same time

period when salaries tended to make little progress, women's average salary rose by 6.3 percent (adjusted for inflation) (MacKinnon, 1999). At the psychological level, research has shown that attitudes to women in the workplace have improved (Kahn & Crosby, 1985). For example, there are more positive stereotypes of women in the workplace (Eagly & Mladinic, 1994) and in one study, the proportion of men expressing negative attitudes towards female executives declined from 41 percent in 1965 to 5 percent in 1985 (Sutton & Moore, 1985).

Despite real gains in women's position in the workforce, change often comes slowly. For example, female government workers had to wait over a decade before the Canadian government put its own legislation regarding equal pay for work of equal value (part of the Human Rights Act of 1985) into practice in the late 1990s. Further, inequalities still abound. By 2001

The gender wage gap for Canadians in full-time work, 1997.

TABLE 5.2 The Gender Wage Gap in Canada

	Average Hourly Wages		
	Women	Men	Women's Wages as % of Men's
Educational Level			
Some high school	$10.71	$15.49	69.1%
High school graduates	$13.04	$16.64	78.4%
University graduates	$20.57	$24.34	84.5%
Occupation			
Clerical	$13.36	$15.41	86.7%
Sales	$11.86	$17.85	66.4%
Service	$10.03	$14.74	68.0%
Professional/managers	$18.89	$23.94	78.9%
Natural or social sciences	$19.70	$23.72	83.1%
Total workforce	**$15.12**	**$18.84**	**80.3%**

Source: Drolet, M. (2001)."The Persistent Gap: New Evidence on the Canadian Gender Wage Gap." Statistics Canada. Catalogue No. 11F0019MPE No. 157.

in Canada, the same proportion of men and women were achieving an undergraduate degree, but the incomes they achieved were not parallel, as shown in Table 5.2. Overall, the average *hourly* wage of women in full-time work was 80 percent of the average male hourly rate. Even when we compare those with the same level of education or within the same occupation, men earn considerably more than women (Drolet, 2001). Research attempting to explain the gap takes into account important productivity-related differences between men and women, particularly the fact that many women have interruptions in their careers due to family responsibilities. This will have the effect of limiting promotions and career opportunities generally. Although these kinds of factors do have an impact, they can explain at most 50 percent of the reason for the gender gap according to one Canadian study (Drolet, 2001). Even in traditionally female occupations—sometimes called "pink collar" occupations (e.g., clerical work or nursing)—men earn more than women (Creese & Beagan, 1999). Also, note that gaps tend to be smaller for those with higher educational levels—the hourly wage of female university graduates is 84.5 percent of men's. If we look at *total yearly earnings*, the gap is even wider (overall, women's annual salary is only 68 percent of men's), because women on average do not work as many hours as their male counterparts. In summary, despite real gains for Canadian women in the workplace and in education, a puzzling wage gap remains that is usually attributed to a lingering bias against women in the workforce (Drolet, 2001).

Women in High-Status Occupations

There has also been an increasing proportion of working women in Canada who attain high-status positions such as managerial and professional occupations: for example, only 23 percent of women in the workforce were in such positions in 1971, whereas there were 34.5 percent in 1991 (Baer, 1999). But women tend to be underrepresented in the upper ranks of management: in 1995 they made up only 12.3 percent of upper management and 44.3 percent of middle and lower management positions; in 1997 only 10 of the top 500 companies in Canada were run by women (Wells, 1997). These facts have led many authors to suggest the existence of a *glass ceiling*—a final barrier that prevents females, as a group, from reaching the top positions in many companies (e.g., Glass Ceiling Commission, 1995). More formally, the **glass ceiling** has been defined as "those artificial barriers based on attitudinal or organizational bias that prevent qualified individuals from advancing upward in their organization" (U.S. Department of Labor, 1992). Is this barrier real? And if so, why does it exist? Research evidence on these issues is beginning to accumulate, and some tentative answers can be suggested.

Glass Ceiling Subtle barriers based on attitudinal or institutional bias that prevent qualified females from advancing to top-level positions. The glass ceiling can be seen as one form of neosexism.

First, a glass ceiling does not appear to be the result of blatant and overt efforts to keep women out of male domains (Powell & Butterfield, 1994). Rather, as the concept of *neosexism* suggests, more subtle factors seem to produce this effect. For example, females may receive fewer opportunities to develop their skills and competency than males—opportunities that prepare them for top-level jobs (Ohlott, Ruderman, & McCauley, 1994). For instance, females report fewer chances than males to take part in projects that increase their visibility or widen the scope of their responsibilities. In addition, females report encountering more obstacles in their jobs: they note that it is harder to find personal support, that they are often left out of important networks, and that they have to fight hard to be recognized for excellent work (Ohlott et al., 1994).

Second, neosexism in the attitudes of those in the workplace also has an impact. Research in Canada has shown that when male managers in a federal agency felt *threatened* by an increased representation of women in management, this increased the likelihood that they endorsed neosexist views. Further, the greater their neosexism, the more likely managers were to downgrade women's qualifications and competence in comparison to men's and the less willing they were to personally mentor or support women in management (Beaton, Tougas, & Joly, 1996).

Both supervisors and subordinates make distinctions in evaluation of female and male leaders. Although subordinates often say much the same things to female and male leaders, research findings indicate that they actually demonstrate more negative nonverbal behaviours toward female leaders (Butler & Geis, 1990). In their **role congruity theory** of prejudice against female leaders, Eagly & Karau (2002) suggest that such biases are based on perceptions of an incongruity between the traditional characteristics of women and the requirements of leadership roles. Women were traditionally seen as gentle, caring, and nurturing (termed *communal* characteristics), whereas the role of a leader is seen as a more forceful and assertive one (having *agentic* characteristics).

Role Congruity Theory A theory of prejudice against female leaders that suggests that biases are based on perceptions of incongruity between traditional female characteristics and the characteristics required for leadership.

This perception of incongruity surrounding female leaders has two major impacts. First, women are less likely to be seen as having leadership potential; second, when they are in leadership positions, agentic behaviours on their part are more likely to be evaluated negatively. The result is less access to leadership roles for women and more obstacles to be overcome when women are leaders.

A third source of barriers to women's occupational achievement may be unintentional limits that women place upon themselves. For example, Pratto and her colleagues (1997) provide evidence that one factor contributing to continued inequalities is gender differences in *self-selection for various occupations*. That is, women themselves are more likely to select "pink collar" occupations even when no barriers exist. Tannen (1994) stresses the additional importance of gender differences in communication styles. For example, women are not as likely as men to brag about their accomplishments; as a result, they often fail to receive the appropriate credit when their work is exceptionally good (Tannen, 1995). Further, research has found that a woman is more likely than a man to expect (Jackson, Gardner, & Sullivan, 1992) or believe that she deserves (Janoff-Bulman & Wade, 1996) a lower salary. Even in carrying out a laboratory task, women suggest lower pay for themselves than men do (Desmarais & Curtis, 1997).

Taken together, these findings suggest that the glass ceiling is indeed real, and that it stems from factors suggestive of neosexism—lingering forms of prejudice and discrimination towards females. While the glass ceiling may be breaking down in some organizations, its presence in many work settings appears to be an additional subtle barrier to female achievement.

In sum, major gains have occurred in many work settings in recent years, and at least some of these changes appear to be ones that have lessened, if not eliminated, barriers to females' success. However, covert forms of discrimination still exist and appear to have very real impacts in women's lives at the economic and psychological level.

KEY POINTS

- *Discrimination* involves negative actions, based on prejudice, toward members of various social groups.
- While *blatant* discrimination has clearly decreased in Western societies, more subtle forms such as *modern racism, covert institutional racism, benevolent sexism* and *neosexism* persist.
- There have been improvements for women in the workplace with increases in their qualification, pay, and promotion to higher-status positions.
- Nonetheless, subtle barriers, often termed the *glass ceiling*, are still evident in the continuing wage gap and the few women in upper management.
- *Role congruity theory* suggests that prejudice against female leaders is based in perceptions of an incongruity between the traditional role of women and the role of leaders.

The Origins of Prejudice: Contrasting Perspectives

That prejudice exists is all too obvious. The question of why it occurs, however, is more complex. Why do so many people hold negative views about members of particular social groups? What factors or conditions foster such attitudes and lead to their persistence? The answers to these questions are not simple. As with many complex forms of social behaviour, a simple explanation for the existence of prejudice will not suffice. Prejudice exists and is maintained at many different social levels: from the societal to the individual. And the theoretical views of prejudice reflect this fact. We will begin at the societal level, examining institutional origins of prejudice. Next we will explore prejudice in intergroup relations. This level of explanation looks to conflict between social groups in society as the source of prejudice. A third level of explanation points to socialization processes or social learning of prejudice from many sources in an individual's life, from parents and peers, to education and the media. Finally, at the individual level, we can point to limitations in our own cognitive processes as, at the least, maintaining existing prejudices. Further, individual personality characteristics have also been suggested to incline some people toward prejudice. In particular, one of the earliest approaches was to study the authoritarian personality (Adorno, et al., 1950).

At this point, we should note that these different approaches should not be regarded as competing or conflicting explanations. Rather, they view the same phenomenon from different perspectives. Each of these perspectives is necessary to fully understand the complexities of prejudice and, as we will see in the section entitled "Challenging Prejudice," each of them is necessary in order to combat prejudice in society.

Intergroup Conflict: Competition and Categorization as Sources of Prejudice

Competition as a Source of Prejudice

It is sad but true that the things people value most—good jobs, nice homes, high status—are always in short supply. There's never quite enough to go around. This fact serves as the foundation for what is perhaps the oldest explanation of prejudice—__realistic conflict theory__ (e.g., Bobo, 1983). According to this view, prejudice stems from competition among social groups over valued commodities or opportunities. In short, prejudice develops out of the struggle over jobs, adequate housing, good schools, and other desirable outcomes. The theory further suggests that as such competition continues, the members of the groups involved come to view each other in increasingly negative terms (White, 1977). They label one another as "enemies," view their own group as morally superior, and draw the boundaries between themselves and their opponents ever more firmly. The result, of course, is that what starts out as simple competition relatively free from hatred gradually develops into full-scale emotion-laden prejudice. All over the world, when there is dispute between groups about territory or trade, antagonism and prejudice can grow to horrific levels. See Figure 5.3 for one example.

Realistic Conflict Theory The view that prejudice sometimes stems from direct competition among social groups over scarce and valued resources.

■ Realistic Conflict Theory: When Intergroup Conflict Leads to Prejudice

FIGURE 5.3 When groups compete with each other for valued resources (e.g., land, jobs, housing), they may come to view each other in increasingly negative terms. The result may be the development of full-scale ethnic prejudice. And that, unfortunately, often finds expression in overt, harmful actions directed toward the perceived enemy (i.e., the out-group).

Evidence from several different studies seems to confirm the occurrence of this process: as competition persists, the individuals or groups involved come to perceive each other in increasingly negative ways. Even worse, such competition often leads to direct and open conflict. A very dramatic demonstration of this principle in operation is provided by a well-known field study conducted by Sherif and his colleagues (Sherif et al., 1961).

For this unusual study, the researchers sent 11-year-old boys to a special summer camp in a remote area where, free from external influences, the nature of conflict and its role in prejudice could be carefully studied. When the boys arrived at the camp (named The Robber's Cave in honour of a nearby cave that was once, supposedly, used by robbers), they were divided into two separate groups and assigned to cabins located quite far apart. There they chose names for their groups (Rattlers and Eagles), made up flags with their symbols, and began to develop a group identity.

After one week, the second phase of the study began. The boys in both groups were told that they would now engage in a series of competitions to receive a trophy and prizes. Since these were prizes the boys strongly desired, the stage was set for intense competition. Would such conflict generate prejudice? The answer was quick in coming. As the boys competed, the tension between the groups rose. At first it was limited to verbal taunts and name-calling, but soon it escalated into more direct acts—for example, the Eagles burned the Rattlers' flag. The next day the Rattlers struck back by attacking the rival group's cabin, overturning beds, tearing out mosquito netting, and seizing personal property. Such actions continued until the researchers intervened to prevent serious trouble. At the same time, the two groups voiced increasingly negative views of each other. They labelled their opponents "bums" and "cowards," while heaping praise on their own group at every turn. In short, after only two weeks of conflict, the groups showed all the key components of strong prejudice toward each other.

Fortunately, the story had a happy ending. In the study's final phase, Sherif and his colleagues attempted to reduce the negative reactions described above. Merely increasing the amount of contact between the groups failed to accomplish this goal; indeed, it seemed to fan the flames of anger. But when conditions were altered so that the groups found it necessary to work together to reach *superordinate goals*—ones they both desired—dramatic changes occurred. After the boys worked together to restore their water supply (previously sabotaged by the researchers), pooled their funds to rent a movie, and jointly repaired a broken-down truck, tensions between the groups largely vanished. In fact, after six days of such experiences the boundaries between the groups virtually dissolved, and many cross-group friendships were established.

The research reported by Sherif and his colleagues is viewed as a classic in the study of prejudice. Yet it was not the first, nor the most dramatic, study of the relationship between conflict and prejudice conducted by social psychologists. That honour goes to a much earlier, and much more disturbing, investigation conducted by Hovland and Sears (1940)—a study described in detail in the Cornerstones section.

Cornerstones

The Economics of Racial Violence: Do Bad Times Fan the Flames of Prejudice?

In 1939, several psychologists published an influential book entitled *Frustration and Aggression* (Dollard et al., 1939). In this book they suggested that aggression often stems from frustration—interference with goal-directed behaviour. In other words, aggression often occurs in situations where people are prevented from getting what they want. As we'll see in Chapter 8, this hypothesis is only partially correct. Frustration can sometimes lead to aggression, but it is definitely not the only, or the most important, cause of such behaviour.

In any case, the *frustration–aggression hypothesis* stimulated a great deal of research in psychology, and some of this work was concerned with prejudice. The basic reasoning was as follows: when groups are competing for scarce resources, they come to view one another as potential or actual sources of frustration. After all, if "they" get the jobs, the housing, and other benefits, then "we" don't. The result, it was reasoned, is not simply negative attitudes toward opposing groups; in addition, strong tendencies to aggress against them may also be generated.

Although this possible link between conflict, prejudice, and aggression was studied in several different ways, the most chilling findings were reported by Carl I. Hovland and Robert R. Sears (1940)—two psychologists who made important contributions to social psychology in several different areas (e.g., in the study of attitudes and persuasion; see Chapter 3). These researchers hypothesized that economic conditions provide a measure of frustration, with

"bad times" being high in frustration for many people and "good times" somewhat lower. They reasoned that if this is so, then racially motivated acts of violence such as lynchings should be higher when economic conditions are poor than when they are good. To test this unsettling hypothesis, Hovland and Sears obtained data on the number of lynchings in the United States in each year between 1882 and 1930. Most of these lynchings (a total of 4,761) occurred in 14 southern states, and most (though not all) of the victims were African-Americans. Next, Hovland and Sears (1940) related the number of lynchings in each year to two economic indexes: the farm value of cotton (the total value of cotton produced that year) and the per-acre value of cotton. Because cotton played a major role in the economies of the states where most lynchings occurred, Hovland and Sears assumed that these measures would provide a good overview of economic conditions in those states.

As you can see from Figure 5.4, results were dramatic: The number of lynchings rose when economic conditions declined, and fell when economic conditions improved. Hovland and Sears (1940, p. 307) interpreted these findings as reflecting *displaced aggression*:

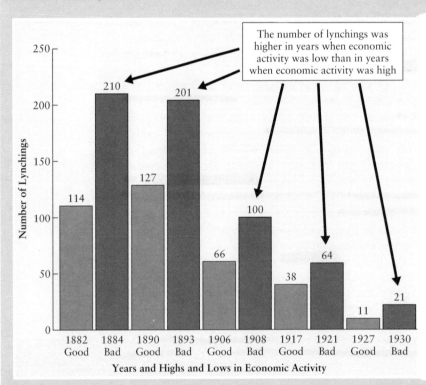

The number of lynchings was higher in years when economic activity was low than in years when economic activity was high

■ Racial Violence and Economic Conditions

FIGURE 5.4 As shown here, the number of lynchings in the United States—primarily of African-Americans and mainly in southern states—varied with economic conditions. Lynchings increased when times were bad, but decreased when economic conditions improved. These findings provide indirect support for both the realistic conflict model and the scapegoating perspective.

Source: Based on data from Hovland & Sears, 1940.

since farmers could not aggress against the factors that were causing their frustration (e.g., a lack of rainfall), they aggressed against African-Americans—a group they disliked and that was, at that time, relatively defenceless. This process has also been termed *scapegoating*—taking one's frustrations out on the easiest,

though not legitimate, target (Allport, 1954). Today most social psychologists prefer a somewhat different interpretation—one suggesting that competition for scarce economic resources increases when times are bad, and that this increased competition intensifies racial prejudice. Lynchings and other violence then result from increased prejudice rather than from displaced aggression.

Dramatic though these findings are, researchers since that time have questioned the methodology and the validity of this classic study (Green, Glaser, & Rich, 1998; Hepworth & West, 1988). In one recent example, Green and colleagues (1998) obtained records of all *hate crimes* perpetrated in New York City during a nine-year period, and then related the incidence of these crimes to the unemployment rate as a measure of economic conditions. Green, Glaser, and Rich (1998) conducted these analyses using the most modern statistical techniques available; for instance, they related unemployment rates at a given time to the incidence of hate crimes at 12 later times (e.g., one month later, several months later, etc.). Yet, despite these sophisticated techniques of data analysis, results were generally negative: no strong or stable relationship between unemployment and hate crimes was uncovered.

So where does this leave us? Why did Hovland and Sears find evidence of a strong relationship between economic hardship and racially motivated violence, while

the modern research did not? A number of possibilities arise. For example, the two studies took place in very different times. Hovland and Sears's data was from an unsettled and difficult period for the southern United States and one when antagonism towards minorities would have been much more acceptable than in the period when Green and colleagues collected their data. Perhaps the general state of minorities and ethnic relations is a crucial factor in determining whether antagonism occurs. Further, the two studies used very different measures of economic conditions—these may not be comparable and the validity of the earlier measure has been questioned (Green et al., 1998). Finally, it is possible that the more unsophisticated statistical methods used by Hovland and Sears (the best available at the time) simply produced questionable findings. In short, we cannot at this juncture be sure why these studies produced such different findings. However, what we can conclude is that the link between economic hardship and violence against minority groups is probably far more complex in nature, and much harder to discern, than the frustration–aggression theory suggests.

Social Identity and Social Categorization as a Source of Prejudice

A second perspective that points to conflict between groups as the source of prejudice is based on Tajfel's *social identity theory* (Tajfel & Turner, 1979; Tajfel, 1970). This time the conflict is not over material concerns such as housing or jobs. Rather, as you will recall from our discussion of this theory in Chapter 4, Tajfel suggests that groups compete for a *distinctive and positive social identity*. This is essentially a desire for one's own group to be seen as both *different from*, and *better than*, other groups. Obviously, not all groups can achieve this desirable position in society. However, when they attempt this, the conflict in social perceptions that arises, termed *social competition*, results in prejudice.

Initiating this process is the cognitive mechanism of **social categorization**. In order to cope with the overload of social information, we classify the social world into groups along socially important dimensions. Such distinctions are based on many dimensions, including ethnicity, religion, gender, age, occupation, and income, to name a few. But we go beyond mere categorization and identify *us* and *them*. We identify the groups to which we belong (usually termed the **in-group**) and the groups to which we do not belong (the **out-group**).

If the process of dividing the social world into "us" and "them" stopped there, it would have little bearing on prejudice. Unfortunately, however, it does not. Our desire for a positive social identity leads to sharply contrasting feelings and beliefs about members of one's in-group and members of various out-groups. Persons in the former ("us") category are viewed in favourable terms, while those in the latter ("them") category are perceived more negatively. This tendency even extends to extraneous attributes of the in-group and out-group. For example, individuals tend to perceive their own country's products as being of higher quality and more reliable than another country's, even when they are of the same standard—this tendency is termed the *country-of-origin effect* (Peterson & Jolibert, 1995). Out-group members are assumed to possess more undesirable traits, are perceived as being more alike (i.e., more homogeneous) than members of the in-group, and are often strongly disliked (Judd, Ryan, & Park, 1991; Lambert, 1995; Linville & Fischer, 1993). In total, this process of in-group-out-group bias has been called the **us-versus-them effect**.

Social Categorization Our tendency to divide the social world into two separate categories: our in-group ("us") and various out-groups ("them").

In-group The social group to which an individual perceives herself or himself as belonging ("us").

Out-group Any group other than the one to which individuals perceive themselves as belonging ("them").

The Us-versus-Them Effect The tendency to show bias towards the in-group and against the out-group. It is suggested that this is an inevitable outcome of social categorization and identification of in-groups and out-groups.

The in-group-out-group distinction also affects *attribution*—the ways in which we explain the actions of persons belonging to these two categories. Specifically, we tend to attribute desirable behaviours by members of our in-group to stable, internal causes (e.g., their admirable traits), but attribute desirable behaviours by members of out-groups to transitory factors or to external causes—we "explain away" positive attributes and outcomes of out-groups (Hewstone, 1990). This tendency to make more favourable and flattering attributions about members of one's own group than about members of other groups is sometimes described as the **ultimate attribution error**, since it carries the self-serving bias we described in Chapter 2 into the area of intergroup relations—with potentially devastating effects.

That strong tendencies exist to divide the social world into these contrasting groups has been demonstrated in many studies (e.g., Stephan, 1985; Tajfel, 1982; Turner et al., 1987). In these investigations, participants generally expressed more negative attitudes toward members of out-groups and treated them less favourably than members of their own group. Further, these patterns held true even when these categories were purely arbitrary and had no existence beyond the experiment, and when the persons involved never met face to face.

But why, precisely, does the us-versus-them effect occur? Why does the definition of others as out-group members lead us to view them in biased and mainly negative ways? Tajfel and his colleagues (e.g., Tajfel, 1982) suggest that *social identity* processes are the key. Individuals seek to enhance their self-esteem by becoming identified with specific social groups. This tactic can succeed, however, only to the extent that the persons involved perceive their groups as somehow distinctive and superior to other competing groups. Since all individuals are subject to the same forces, the final result is inevitable: each group seeks to view itself as somehow better than its rivals, and prejudice arises out of this clash of social perceptions, termed *social competition* (see Figure 5.5).

Convincing evidence of such group biases has been provided by numerous studies (e.g., Hewstone, 1990; Mullen, Brown, & Smith, 1992). For example, subjects who had received (bogus) information that they had scored badly on an IQ test, were more likely to derogate a job candidate they were evaluating, particularly if she was from a minority ethnic group (Fein & Spencer 1997). Further, this was shown to help have the effect of maintaining subjects' self-esteem, as the theory suggests.

In a second study investigating the *distinctiveness* component of social identity theory, Hornsey and Hogg (2000) reasoned that it is only when individuals feel secure in their own group or cultural identity that can they be generous and tolerant toward other groups or cultures. Under conditions in which individuals feel that the distinctiveness of their own group or culture is somehow threatened, they will react negatively to other groups, and, moreover, these reactions will be intensified by perceived similarity between their own group and the other groups. Why? Because such similarity brings even greater threat to the distinctiveness of their group's identity. In contrast, when individuals do not feel that the distinctiveness of their own group is being threatened or challenged, similarity to other groups has opposite effects: the greater the similarity perceived between their own group and these other groups, the more positive their reaction to these groups.

To test these predictions, Hornsey and Hogg (2000) had students at a large university in Australia read short passages indicating either that math–science students and humanities students are very different in their ideas and attitudes (the *low-similarity* condition) or that they are actually very similar (the *high-similarity* condition). Participants belonged to one group or the other. After reading these passages, half of the participants were induced to think about the fact that they are students at the same university (a procedure designed to threaten the distinctiveness of their own

Ultimate Attribution Error
The tendency to make more favourable and flattering attributions about members of one's own group than about members of other groups.

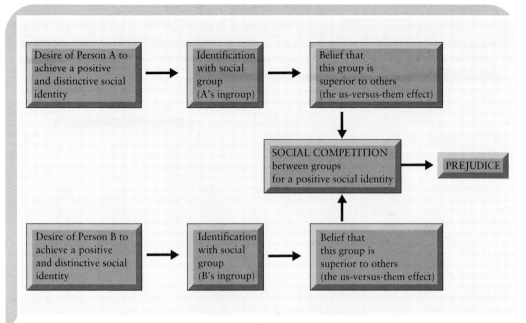

■ Why Social Identity and Social Categorization Processes Sometimes Lead to Prejudice

FIGURE 5.5 According to Tajfel's social identity theory (1982), prejudice sometimes arises out of social competition. This process reflects the desire of individuals to achieve a positive and distinctive social identity by identifying with groups they view as desirable or superior. Since the members of many groups have the same desire, conflict between them occurs. Prejudice then follows from this clash of social perceptions.

Source: Based on suggestions by Tajfel, 1982.

group—either humanities or math–science); this was the *superordinate* condition. The remaining participants were induced to think both about being students at the same university and about their identity as either a math–science or a humanities student; this was the *simultaneous* condition.

After these procedures were completed, students rated the extent to which they thought they would enjoy working with a group of humanities or math–science students, and how difficult working with such students would be. Participants rated both their own group and the other group in this manner. It was predicted that in the simultaneous condition, in which the distinctiveness of their own group was not threatened, participants would express less bias toward the other group when it had been described as similar rather than dissimilar to their own. In contrast, in the superordinate condition, in which the distinctiveness of their own group had been threatened, the opposite would be true: participants would actually express more bias toward an out-group described as similar to their own, because this would pose an even bigger threat to their group's distinctiveness or superiority. As you can see from Figure 5.6, both predictions were confirmed.

These findings suggest that efforts to reduce prejudice between groups by breaking down the distinction between "us" and "them" can succeed, but only if doing so does not threaten each group's unique identity. In other words, our tendency to divide

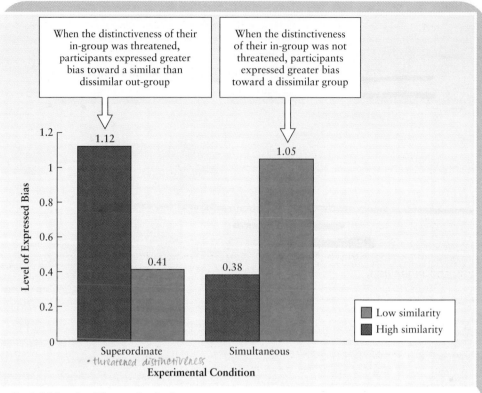

When the distinctiveness of their in-group was threatened, participants expressed greater bias toward a similar than dissimilar out-group

When the distinctiveness of their in-group was not threatened, participants expressed greater bias toward a dissimilar group

■ Social Identity Theory in Action

FIGURE 5.6 When the distinctiveness of their own group was not threatened, individuals reported less bias toward an out-group when it was similar to their own group than when it was dissimilar. However, when the distinctiveness of their own group had been threatened, the participants actually expressed more bias toward an out-group described as similar to their own. These findings are predicted by *social identity theory*.

Source: Hornsey & Hogg, 2000.

the social world into these two opposing categories seems to serve important esteem-boosting and distinctiveness functions for us; if these are overlooked, efforts to reduce prejudice by urging distinct cultural or ethnic groups to view themselves as "one" or as highly similar may well backfire. We'll have more to say about this later, in our discussion of techniques for reducing prejudice.

KEY POINTS

- Prejudice stems from several different sources. *Realistic conflict theory* suggests that one of these is direct intergroup conflict—situations in which social groups compete for the same scarce resources.
- Classic studies examining competition in boys' camps and the correlation between hate crimes and economic indices provide data that are mostly supportive of this perspective.

- *Social identity theory* suggests that the desire of social groups for a positive and a distinctive group-based identity provides the motive to divide the social world into two camps—"us" and "them" (the *us-versus-them* effect)—and to show biases in the form of the *ultimate attribution error.*

- Research confirms that decreases in self-esteem and loss of secure distinctive identity can exacerbate prejudice.

Early Experience: The Role of Social Learning

A third explanation for prejudice is one you will not find surprising: it suggests that prejudice is *learned* and that it develops in much the same manner, and through the same basic processes, as other attitudes (refer to our discussion in Chapter 3). According to this **social learning view**, children acquire negative attitudes toward various social groups through processes of *classical conditioning, instrumental conditioning*, and *modelling.*

Often *classical conditioning* occurs when we come to associate particular groups with negative characteristics through exposure to the media. For example, until quite recently members of some ethnic minority groups were shown infrequently in movies or television and when they did appear, they were usually cast in low-status, comic, or victim roles. Given repeated exposure to such material over the years, it is not surprising that many children came to believe that members of these groups were inferior, powerless, or merely to be pitied rather than respected (Weigel, Loomis, & Soja, 1980; Weigel, Kim, & Frost, 1995). In classical conditioning terms, the originally neutral stimulus of that group has been repeatedly paired with negative emotion-provoking stimuli and we have learned to respond to the group with similar negative responses. Such processes are often very subtle. We may not even be aware that learning has taken place until we experience surprise on first meeting an individual from the group who does not fulfill our expectations.

The processes of *modelling* and *instrumental conditioning* of prejudice attitudes often occur together for children. We may hear influential people in our lives, such as parents, peers, or a media hero, express prejudiced views. These individuals are likely to be seen as role models and, if that is the case, we are likely to imitate their behaviour by adopting such attitudes ourselves. Subsequently, the social reinforcement we are given (direct praise, approval, or acceptance by others) for expression of such prejudices, will entrench them in our cognitive repertoire. As we will see in the section on social cognition, once such attitudes are formed, they may be difficult to overcome because they tend to be self-confirming.

Direct experience during childhood with persons belonging to other groups also shapes prejudiced attitudes and related behaviours (Fazio & Towles-Schwen, 1999). Caucasian college students completed a survey in which they were asked to report childhood encounters with minorities, their parents' degree of prejudice toward minority groups, motivation to avoid acting in a prejudiced manner, and restraint (social awkwardness) when interacting with minority persons (Towles-Schwen & Fazio, 2001). In a separate session, an unobtrusive measure of their implicit racial attitudes was obtained.

Overall, the study showed that racial attitudes are indeed related to direct social experience and reflect our parents' attitudes and the frequency and nature of our childhood experiences with minority group members. The less prejudiced our parents are and the more positive our contact with minority group members when we were children, the

Social Learning View
The view that prejudice is learned—acquired through direct and vicarious experiences—in much the same manner as other attitudes.

■ Effects of Childhood Experiences and Parents' Attitudes on Aspects of Racial Prejudice

FIGURE 5.7 Individuals' racial attitudes as adults reflect influences from their parents' attitudes and also from their childhood experiences with minority group members. The less prejudiced peoples' parents and the more positive individuals' interactions with minorities, the more favourable their racial attitudes, the greater their motivation to avoid acting in a prejudiced manner, and the less restraint they experience when interacting with minority persons.

Source: Based on suggestions from Towles-Schwen & Fazio, 2001.

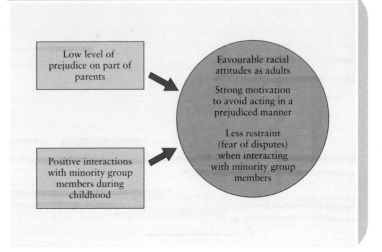

less prejudiced we are as adults, the greater our concern over acting in a prejudiced manner, and the less restraint we experience when interacting with minority group members (see Figure 5.7).

To this point, we have talked as if social learning only occurs in childhood. This is, of course, a crucially important period for the development of prejudices. However, we should emphasize that social learning occurs throughout our lives. Although as adults we may be less malleable, nonetheless we are still open to the influence of social norms around us (Pettigrew, 1969). And if those norms allow prejudice to be expressed, it often takes courage to challenge them and put up with immediate social disapproval. As we will see in Chapter 7, most people choose to conform to the *social norms* of groups to which they belong, even when they disagree.

Social Cognition: Its Role in Maintaining Prejudice

This source of prejudice is in some ways the most unsettling of all. It involves the possibility that prejudice stems, at least in part, from basic aspects of each individual's social cognition—how we think about other persons. We will now consider several forms of evidence pointing to this conclusion.

Stereotypes: What They Are and How They Operate

Consider the following groups: Chinese-Canadians, French-Canadians, homosexuals, and Jews. Suppose you were asked to list the traits that are most characteristic of each. Would you experience much difficulty? Probably you would not. You would be able to construct quite easily a list of traits for each group. Moreover, you could do this *even for groups with which you have had limited personal contact*. Why? The reason involves the existence and operation of stereotypes. As we saw earlier, these are cognitive frameworks that suggest that all members of a social group demonstrate certain characteristics and behave in certain ways. As noted by Judd, Ryan, and Park (1991), stereotypes involve generalizations about the typical or "modal" characteristics of members of various social groups. That is, they suggest that all members of such groups possess certain traits, at least to a degree. Once a stereotype is activated, these traits come readily to mind; hence the ease with which you could construct the lists described above (Higgins & Bargh, 1987).

Stereotypes Beliefs to the effect that all members of specific social groups share certain traits or characteristics. Stereotypes are cognitive frameworks that strongly influence the processing of incoming social information.

Like other cognitive frameworks or *schemas*, stereotypes exert strong effects on the ways in which we process social information. For example, information relevant to a particular stereotype is processed more quickly than information unrelated to it (Dovidio, Evans, & Tyler, 1986). Similarly, stereotypes lead the persons holding them to pay attention to specific types of information—usually, information consistent with the stereotypes. And, if information inconsistent with a stereotype does manage to enter consciousness, we may actively refute it, perhaps by recalling facts and information that are consistent with the stereotype (O'Sullivan & Durso, 1984). For instance, research findings indicate that when we encounter information inconsistent with our stereotype, we draw *tacit inferences* (conclusions and ideas not contained in the information) that change the meaning of this information to make it consistent with the stereotype (e.g., Kunda & Sherman-Williams, 1993; Dunning & Sherman, 1997). Alternatively, we may simply place such counter-stereotypic persons into a special category or *subtype* consisting of persons who do not confirm the schema or stereotype (e.g., Richards & Hewstone, 2001), leaving our original stereotype intact.

In view of such effects—which appear to be both strong and general in scope—two social psychologists, Dunning and Sherman (1997), have described stereotypes as *inferential prisons*: once they are formed, they shape our perceptions of other persons so that new information about these persons is interpreted in order to confirm our stereotypes, even if this is not justified (see Figure 5.8).

Implicit Stereotypes: When Beliefs We Don't Recognize Influence Our Behaviour
Earlier, we noted that prejudiced attitudes could be *implicit*: they exist and can influence many forms of behaviour, even when the persons holding them are unaware of

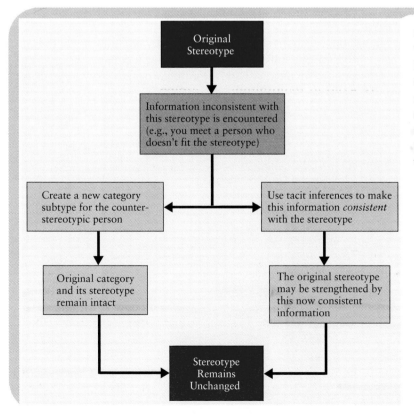

■ Stereotypes: Inferential Prisons?

FIGURE 5.8 Once stereotypes exist, they strongly influence the way we process information relating to them. When we encounter information inconsistent with a stereotype, rather than changing it, we formulate tacit inferences or create new subtypes that leave the stereotype intact.

their existence or of their impact on behaviour. The same seems to hold true for stereotypes and this has been shown in recent research (see Greenwald & Banaji, 1995). To demonstrate the existence of implicit stereotypes, Kawakami and Dovidio (2001) used a technique based on *subliminal priming*—stimuli are presented for such a short period of time that participants can't recognize or identify them. In this case, the primes were schematic faces of blacks or whites. After the primes were shown for a very short period (15 to 30 milliseconds), a specific kind of word category was cued by a letter or symbol—in this study, one letter stood for "houses" and the other for "persons." Finally, words related to racial stereotypes for blacks and whites, or to the neutral category *houses*, were presented. For instance, one target word related to the racial stereotype for whites was *conventional*, while one target word related to the racial stereotype for blacks was *musical*. An example of the words related to houses was *drafty*. For each target word, participants were asked to indicate whether these words could ever describe a member of the cued word category (i.e., a person or a house).

If implicit racial stereotypes are activated by the priming stimuli (faces of black and white persons), then response times to the target words should vary as a function of these primes. Specifically, participants should respond more quickly to words related to the racial stereotype for whites after seeing a white prime than a black prime, and faster to words related to the racial stereotype for blacks after seeing a black prime than a white prime. As you can see from Figure 5.9, this is precisely what was found. Similar results have been reported in many other studies, which, together, indicate that implicit stereotypes can be automatically activated toward blacks (e.g., Devine, 1989; Kawakami, Dion, & Dovidio, 1998), women and men (e.g., Banaji & Hardin, 1996), elderly people (e.g., Hense, Penner, & Nelson, 1995), Asians (e.g., Macrae, Bodenhausen, & Milne, 1995), and many other groups (e.g., soccer hooligans, child abusers, skinheads) (e.g., Kawakami et al., 2000)—even professors (Dijksterhuis & van Knippenberg, 1996).

The important thing about such stereotypes is this: We may not be aware of the fact that they are operating, but they can still strongly influence our judgments or decisions about other people, or even how we interact with them. In particular, growing evidence

Measuring Implicit Racial Stereotypes

FIGURE 5.9 Participants responded more quickly to words related to the racial stereotype for blacks after seeing a black prime (a schematic black face) than after seeing a white prime (a schematic white face). Similarly, they responded faster to words related to the racial stereotype for whites after seeing a white prime than a black prime. These findings provide evidence for the existence of automatically activated, implicit stereotypes.

Source: Based on data from Kawakami & Dovidio, 2001.

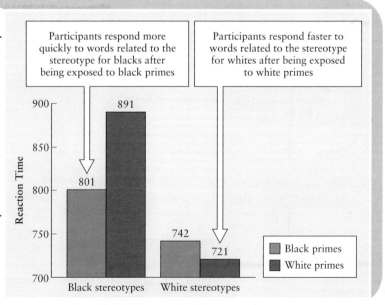

suggests that such *implicit stereotypes* may be better predictors of subtle or spontaneous expressions of bias than *explicit* measures obtained through attitude questionnaires or other kinds of self-report (e.g., Dovidio et al., 1997). Clearly, then, implicit stereotypes are something we should definitely not overlook in our efforts to understand the basic nature of prejudice and discrimination.

Other Cognitive Mechanisms in Prejudice: Illusory Correlations and Out-Group Homogeneity

Illusory Correlation: Perceiving Relationships That Aren't There

Consider the following information: (1) There are 1000 members of Group A, but only 100 members of Group B; (2) 100 members of Group A were arrested by the police last year, and 10 members of Group B were arrested. Suppose you were asked to evaluate the criminal tendencies of these two groups. Would your ratings of them differ? Your first answer is probably "Of course not—why should they?" The rate of criminal behaviour is 10 percent in both groups, so why rate them differently? Surprisingly, though, a large body of evidence suggests that you might actually assign a less favourable rating to Group B (Johnson & Mullen, 1994; McConnell, Sherman, & Hamilton, 1994). Social psychologists refer to this tendency to overestimate the rate of negative behaviours in relatively small groups as **illusory correlations.** This term makes a great deal of sense, because such effects involve perceiving links between variables that aren't really there—in this case, links between being a member of Group B and the tendency to engage in criminal behaviour.

Illusory Correlations The perception of a stronger association between two variables than actually exists because each is a distinctive event and the co-occurrence of such events is readily entered into and retrieved from memory.

As you can readily see, illusory correlations, to the extent they occur, have important implications for prejudice. In particular, they help explain why negative behaviours and tendencies are often attributed by majority group members to the members of various minority groups. For example, some social psychologists have suggested that illusory correlation effects help explain why people might overestimate crime rates among visible minorities (Hamilton & Sherman, 1989).

Why do such effects occur? One explanation is based on the distinctiveness of infrequent events or stimuli. According to this view, infrequent events are distinctive—readily noticed. As such, they are encoded more extensively than are other items when they are encountered, and so become more accessible in memory. When judgments about the groups involved are made at later times, therefore, the distinctive events come readily to mind, and this leads to overinterpretation of their importance. For example, in Canada visible minorities represent only 10 percent of the population (Esses & Gardner, 1996). So in most social contexts they would be distinctive. Violent crime is also a relatively rare occurrence for most people. Thus, when majority-group individuals read or hear about a violent crime committed by someone from a visible minority group, two relatively infrequent stimuli are connected because both are distinctive. This leads the information to be processed extensively and it becomes highly accessible in memory. Thus, it is readily available at later times and may lead to the tendency to overestimate crime rates among visible minorities—an instance of illusory correlation. Further, illusory correlations also lead people to ignore the many factors that may be responsible for such relationships and that have nothing whatsoever to do with race or ethnic background (e.g., poverty, discrimination, growing up in a highly violent environment, and so on). A large number of studies offer support for this *distinctiveness-based interpretation* of illusory correlation (Stroessner, Hamilton, & Mackie, 1992), so it appears to be quite useful in understanding the roots of this kind of cognitive error.

In-Group Differentiation, Out-Group Homogeneity: "They're All the Same"—Or Are They?

Persons who hold strong prejudice toward some social group often make remarks like these: "You know what they're like; they're all the same." What such comments imply is that the members of an out-group are much more similar to one another (more homogeneous) than are the members of one's own group. This tendency to perceive persons belonging to groups other than one's own as all alike is known as the <u>illusion of out-group homogeneity</u> (Linville, Fischer, & Salovey, 1989). The mirror image of this is <u>in-group differentiation</u>—the tendency to perceive members of our own group as showing much larger differences from one another (as being more heterogeneous) than do those of other groups.

Existence of the illusion of out-group homogeneity has been demonstrated in many different contexts. For example, individuals tend to perceive persons older or younger than themselves as more similar to one another in terms of personal traits than are persons in their own age group—an intriguing type of generation gap (Linville, Fischer, & Salovey, 1989); they even perceive students from another university as more homogeneous than students at their own university—especially when these persons appear to be biased against *them* (Rothgerber, 1997).

What accounts for the tendency to perceive members of other groups as more homogeneous than members of our own group? One explanation involves the fact that we have a great deal of experience with members of our own group, and so are exposed to a wider range of individual variation within that group. In contrast, we generally have much less experience with members of other groups, and hence less exposure to their individual variations (e.g., Linville, Fischer, & Salovey, 1989). Whatever the precise basis for its existence (see Lee and Ottati, 1993), the tendency to perceive other groups as more homogeneous than our own can play an important role in prejudice and in the persistence of negative stereotypes.

The Authoritarian Personality

Can your personality make you more vulnerable to prejudice? One of the earliest efforts to explain prejudice took this approach. In the 1950s, Adorno and colleagues developed the concept of the *authoritarian personality*. This type of individual is highly conventional, submissive to strong leaders, and is threatened by those in society who are different or unconventional. High authoritarians were found particularly likely to be racially prejudiced and homophobic (prejudiced against homosexuals).

Current research in this area is dominated by the work of Bob Altemeyer (1981, 1988) in Manitoba. He has carried out a thorough revision and validation of the original scales, which are now much more reliable and measure what is termed <u>right-wing authoritarianism</u> (RWA). The right-wing authoritarianism scale measures three basic attitudinal clusters. Those who are high in right-wing authoritarianism will show: (1) *authoritarian submission*, a high degree of submissiveness to figures of authority who are perceived as legitimate and established; (2) *authoritarian aggression*, a general aggressiveness toward various people (often minorities, the unconventional and socially deviant) when it appears that such aggression is sanctioned by established authority; and (3) *conventionalism*, a high degree of adherence to social values and customs that are perceived as endorsed by society and established authorities.

Extensive studies have found that high scores in right-wing authoritarianism correlate with ethnic and racial prejudice, acceptance of government high-handedness or illegality (e.g., illegal wire-taps and intimidation of opponents), endorsement of severe punishment for law-breakers, and religious orthodoxy and fundamentalism (e.g., Altemeyer, 1988). So while all of us may be able to acquire prejudices through exposure to intergroup conflict

---

Illusion of Out-Group Homogeneity The tendency to perceive members of out-groups as more similar to one another (less variable) than the members of one's own in-group.

In-Group Differentiation The tendency to perceive members of our own group as showing much larger differences from one another (as being more heterogeneous) than do those of other groups.

Right-Wing Authoritarianism (RWA) The tendency to be particularly vulnerable to prejudice and show submissiveness to figures of authority and aggression towards nonconformists or those who are different and who hold unconventional values.

and to various types of social learning, there will be some individuals who are particularly likely to adopt prejudices—those high in authoritarianism.

The Evolution of Prejudice

Evolutionary ideas about the origins of prejudice rest on notions of *kin selection* (Hamilton, 1964). This theory, which was a major and influential extension of Darwin's theory of natural selection, suggests that the natural selection process can apply to characteristics that enhance the reproductive success of those who are genetically related to us—our *kin*. We can increase the probability of passing our genes on to the next generation if we help those who share our genes (e.g., siblings, cousins, as well as children). You can already see that this idea predicts that we will be especially helpful to our relatives, a notion we will discuss further in Chapter 8.

Evolutionary perspectives on prejudice turn this idea around somewhat and suggest that the preference for one's kin is matched by an evolved suspicion towards non-kin. For example, *genetic similarity theory* (Rushton, 1989) suggests that there is a "biological basis for ethnocentrism"—we have evolved to recognize and show preference towards those who are genetically similar and we will exclude or reject those who are dissimilar. Shaw and Wong (1989) suggest that evolution has provided "central tendencies"—general predispositions to show in-group amity and out-group enmity—and that these tendencies will supply the basis for **xenophobia,** the fear and intolerance of strangers. Such suspicion may have been necessary for the survival of our evolutionary ancestors living in small hunter-gatherer groups, but it is often seen as a destructive force in today's world—a "sad legacy" of our evolution (Gould, 1996). On the positive side, Shaw and Wong propose that, because this is only a tendency, it can be inhibited by cultural norms and structures that encourage acceptance of others and emphasize our common humanity.

Xenophobia A fear and intolerance of strangers or outsiders generally.

KEY POINTS

- The *social learning* perspective suggests that *early experience*, can lead children to acquire prejudices. Findings indicate that parents' level of prejudice and direct experience with minorities can play an important role.

- Prejudice sometimes stems from basic aspects of social cognition—the ways in which we process social information.

- *Stereotypes* are cognitive frameworks suggesting that all persons belonging to a social group show similar characteristics. Stereotypes can act as inferential prisons: they lead us to draw *tacit inferences* about others and change our categories so that stereotypes remain unchanged even in the face of contradictory information.

- Recent findings indicate that priming can evoke implicit stereotypes, which can influence our judgments and responses to others.

- Other cognitive sources of prejudice include *illusory correlations* (overestimations of the strength of relationships between social categories and negative behaviours) and the *illusion of out-group homogeneity* (the tendency to perceive out-groups as more homogeneous than our own in-group).

- Individuals who have personalities high in *right-wing authoritarianism* show a propensity towards prejudice against minority groups in society.

- Evolutionary theory suggests that we may have evolved to show ethnocentrism and *xenophobia*—a fear and suspicion of strangers.

Responses of the Victims Of Prejudice

As well as understanding the sources of prejudice and discrimination, we must also attempt to understand its impact. How do the targets of prejudice cope with such treatment? What impact does it have on their self-concepts, self-esteem, and identification with their own group? These are the kinds of questions that have been raised with increasing frequency in recent years. However, it is to early writings on this topic that we can turn for an overview.

Types of Possible Responses to Prejudice and Discrimination

An early and influential theoretical approach to prejudice was presented in Gordon Allport's book, *The Nature of Prejudice* (1954). Among the topics considered were responses of the victims of prejudice. Allport described a broad range of possible responses from passivity to aggression against the source of prejudice. These responses could be classified into two fundamental types based on whether the victim attributed blame for prejudice and discrimination internally or externally. An **intropunitive response** turns the blame for victimization inward, on the self or on the victim's group. Thus, intropunitive defences against others' prejudice include self-hatred, aggression against or denial of one's own group, sympathy for other victims, clowning (a form of self-ridicule), or neuroticism and passive withdrawal. In contrast, an **extrapunitive response** turns the blame for victimization outward, upon other individuals or groups. Examples are aggression and obsessive suspicion towards out-groups, fighting back or militancy, strengthening of in-group ties, and increased striving for self-improvement.

A second early perspective comes from *social identity theory* (Tajfel, 1982; Tajfel & Turner, 1979) and suggests that there are two major types of response to a negative social identity: *personal strategies* or *group-based strategies*. Examples of personal strategies are attempting personal upward mobility (termed a *social mobility* strategy) or perhaps leaving one's own group. Group-based strategies for improvement of social identity will be used when individuals are able to anticipate the possibility of change in the structural relations between groups in society (termed *social change* strategies). Perhaps this perspective is also chosen when *collective efficacy* is high—the group itself is seen as able to bring change about (see Chapter 4). Use of such strategies improves an individual's social identity through improvement of the whole group's position in society. For example, when Aboriginal people in Canada demand recognition of Aboriginal rights or work to settle land claims, this will benefit their whole tribe or nation (see Figure 5.10).

These broad categories are evident in the research described below and provide a useful way of organizing and understanding the varied responses of victims of prejudice.

Research on Victim Responses to Prejudice

Responding to Discrimination
The work of Kenneth Dion at the University of Toronto was some of the earliest research that used laboratory experimentation to investigate the responses of victims of prejudice (Dion, 1975; Dion & Earn, 1975). Members of minority groups were given the impression that they had failed because of discrimination by members of the majority group. Their emotional responses and endorsement of in-group stereotypes were measured. Emotional and self-esteem measures were more frequently *extrapunitive than intropunitive*. For example, victims of discrimination showed greater aggression and less social affection toward majority-group members, as well as an increase

Intropunitive Response A response of the victim of prejudice and discrimination that turns the blame inward towards the self or the victim's group.

Extrapunitive Response A response of the victim of prejudice and discrimination that turns the blame outward, towards other individuals or groups.

■ Group-Based Responses to Prejudice and Discrimination

FIGURE 5.10 These Native Canadians fighting for Aboriginal fishing rights are using *group-based strategies* for improvement of social identity. If such strategies are successful, they benefit the whole group by changing its position in society.

in egotism. In addition, these studies found very few negative effects on self-esteem among subjects. Subsequent work has also shown that when individuals fail at a task, the perception of oneself as the victim of prejudice can sometimes act as a "buffer" to self-esteem (Crocker & Major, 1989; Dion, 2002). This is because the presence of discrimination by others enables the victims to make an external attribution for their own failures (see also Major, Kaiser, & McCoy, 2003). However, the experience of being the victim of discrimination is seldom a pleasant one, even if on occasion it allows you to avoid responsibility for failure.

Dion (2002) suggested recently in his *stress model* that the perception of oneself as the target of discrimination is likely to produce a stress response among victims. Further, this stress response can lead to increased identification with the in-group. Indeed, in his early studies a number of *intropunitive* responses indicative of stress were shown by those who believed they were the target of discrimination, including greater sadness and anxiety (Dion, 1975; Dion & Earn, 1975), as well as decreased satisfaction and sense of control (Birt & Dion, 1987). Chinese students at the University of Toronto who reported more experience of racial discrimination also had higher symptoms of psychological stress (Pak, Dion, & Dion, 1991). As suggested in the stress model, subjects also increased their group identifications. In the earlier experiments, Jews and women who perceived themselves as victims of discrimination responded by increasing identification with positive aspects of their stereotype. Similarly, Chinese students who experienced the most discrimination were also most positive towards the Chinese community (Pak et al., 1991).

The responses of those experiencing discrimination don't stop there, however. Dion and colleagues were also concerned with the *behavioural* responses of victims, in particular with their militancy (Birt & Dion, 1987; Dion, 2002). A number of studies with racial minorities, gays, and lesbians found that perception of discrimination towards one's own group predicted subjects' willingness to be involved in social or political activism (see Figure 5.11). Thus, Dion's work demonstrates that victims of discrimination show a mixture of intropunitive and extrapunitive responses, though the latter appear to be more prominent. His research also indicates that discrimination can influence both the group identifications and the activism of its victims.

Responding to a Negative Stereotype

Recent research shows that those who are the victims of prejudice can be particularly sensitive to the possibility of being negatively stereotyped. This is known as **stereotype threat**—the threat, perceived by persons who are the target of stereotypes, that they will be evaluated in terms of these stereotypes (Steele, 1997). Concerns about stereotype threat may disrupt task performance in many contexts. For example, in one recent study on this

Stereotype Threat The threat perceived by persons who are the target of stereotypes that they will be evaluated in terms of these stereotypes.

■ Discrimination Can Lead to Activism

FIGURE 5.11 Research has shown that people who perceive themselves and others in their group as the victims of discrimination are more willing to become involved in social activism in order to change their situation.

possibility, Croizet and Claire (1998) had persons from high or low socioeconomic backgrounds work on a test that was described either as a measure of their intellectual ability or as a measure of the role of attention in memory. The researchers predicted that when the test was described as one of intellectual ability, this would induce anxiety about stereotype threat among persons from low a socioeconomic background, who would fear that they would be evaluated in terms of a negative stereotype. Thus, individuals from the low socioeconomic background would actually perform worse on the test than those from the high socioeconomic background. When the test was described as a measure of attention, however, such differences would not occur. Results offered clear support for these predictions. Findings such as these suggest that the existence of stereotypes can indeed have harmful effects on the persons to whom they apply—effects that are quite distinct from those generated by discrimination against such persons.

Interestingly, it is not only those who suffer persistent prejudice who anticipate the possibility of being negatively stereotyped. Jacquie Vorauer and colleagues at the University of Manitoba (Vorauer, Main, & O'Connell, 1998) found that white Canadians anticipated negative views of themselves from Aboriginal Canadians. Further, such *meta-stereotypes* (perceptions of negative stereotyping from another group) had an impact on anticipated interaction with Aboriginal individuals. White students who had more extensive meta-stereotypes expected to enjoy interaction less and to experience greater negative emotion. Indeed when simulated interaction did occur with an Aboriginal person, high-prejudice white students were more likely than low-prejudice white students to believe that they had been negatively stereotyped by their Aboriginal interactant.

By taking place in an artificial laboratory setting and involving simulation rather than real interaction with out-group members, the laboratory studies described above may be somewhat lacking in *external validity*. Real-life long-term discrimination can have the effect of gradually eroding its victim's self-esteem (Clark & Clark, 1947). For examination of the victims of prejudice in their social context, we can turn to field studies.

Focusing on One's Group, Not Oneself, as the Target of Prejudice and Discrimination

An intriguing finding from research in the area of victim responses is that members of minority groups often perceive higher levels of discrimination as directed at their group as a whole than at themselves personally (Crosby, 1982, 1984; Guimond & Dubé-Simard, 1983; Taylor, Wright, Moghaddam, & Lalonde, 1990). It is as if individuals are saying, "My group as a whole has been treated badly, but personally I've been lucky enough to avoid such treatment." While it is possible that an occasional individual from a targeted minority group may be lucky enough to avoid this treatment, it is not possible that this is the typical experience of its members. The question then arises: Why do group members typically perceive themselves (or present themselves) in this way?

Crosby (1982), for example, found that when asked about their working life, women expressed some resentment and bitterness about "women's employment situation." However, they did not generally feel discriminated against personally at work. This **personal/group discrimination discrepancy** (PGDD) has been documented among a wide range of groups including Canadian cultural groups such as francophone *Québécois* (Guimond & Dubé-Simard, 1983), anglophone *Québécois* (Taylor, Wong-Rieger, McKirnan, & Bercusson, 1982), and among Haitian and Indian women immigrants to Quebec (Taylor et al., 1990). In the latter study, despite the fact that fairly high levels of personal discrimination were reported, particularly by the Haitian subjects, both groups of subjects saw greater racial and cultural discrimination directed at their group in general than at themselves personally.

Personal/Group Discrimination Discrepancy (PGDD) A common tendency on the part of minority individuals to deny or minimize the personal experience of discrimination, while confirming that it occurs to their group as a whole.

A number of explanations have been put forward for this discrepancy (Crosby, 1982; Taylor et al., 1990). One is that individuals may be *motivated to deny the discrimination* that they have experienced, presumably because this protects them from perceived threat, shame in front of others, or lowered self-esteem (Taylor et al., 1990; Hodson & Esses, 2002). Or, similarly, they may see it as less appropriate to complain about their own personal situation than about that of the group as a whole (Crosby, 1982).

A second perspective points to *limitations in our cognitive* processes as the source of the PGDD. For example, it is suggested that social comparison processes differ when someone is asked about discrimination towards the self or towards the group as a whole (e.g., Quinn, Roese, Pennington, & Olson, 1999). When a person is asked about discriminatory treatment of his or her group, this may lead to comparisons of the whole group with other groups in society (a process of <u>*intergroup social comparison*</u>). For example, when asked about women as a group, the obvious source of comparison is men as a group. However, when asked about discrimination against the self, evaluation may involve comparison of the self with other individuals within one's group (a process of <u>*intragroup social comparison*</u>). For example, when a woman is asked about her own experience of discrimination, the source of comparison is more likely to be other women. Such differences in the direction of social comparison will lead to differing estimates of levels of discrimination for the self and the group. A complementary finding is that the PGDD decreases when the individual is focusing on the *collective self* rather than the personal self. If the individual is thinking about the self as a group member, estimates of discrimination towards the self and the group become more similar (Foster & Matheson, 1999).

KEY POINTS

- Theorists have distinguished between *intropunitive* responses of victims, which involve self-blame, and *extrapunitive* responses, which involve other-blame. Further, responses can be classified as responses aimed at *personal* improvement or at *group-based* improvement. *– Social Identity Theory*

- The perception of oneself as the target of discrimination can produce a stress response and lead to increased identification with the in-group, as well as greater militancy.

- Research has demonstrated that the victims of prejudice respond to *stereotype threat*—the threat of being stereotyped—in a variety of ways. They can perform more badly on a task, anticipate less enjoyment from interaction, or change self-presentations and affect.

- Minority individuals frequently show the *personal/group discrimination discrepancy*—they perceive higher levels of discrimination towards their group than towards themselves personally.

Challenging Prejudice: Why It Is Not Always Inevitable

Whatever the specific origins of prejudice, there can be no doubt about the following point: Prejudice is a brutal, negative force in human society. Wherever and whenever it occurs, it is a drain on precious human resources. So reducing prejudice and countering its effects are important tasks—and especially crucial at a time when the world population exceeds 6 billion and the potential harm stemming from irrational hatred is greater than ever before. Do any effective strategies for accomplishing these goals—for lessening the impact of prejudice—exist? Fortunately, they do; and while they cannot totally eliminate prejudice or discrimination, these strategies can make a substantial dent in the problem. Several of these tactics will now be reviewed, ranging from intervention at the group and societal level to attempts to change our individual cognitions. We begin with societal or institutional intervention.

Institutional Interventions: Putting Multiculturalism to the Test

Canada's *policy of multiculturalism* represents an ambitious attempt to combat prejudice and discrimination at the institutional level. Canada is one of the only countries in the world that has an official multiculturalism policy, encouraging ethnic groups to maintain their own cultural heritage while participating fully in the larger society. When introduced in 1971, the policy statement suggested that

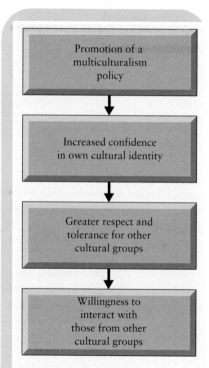

■ The Multiculturalism Hypothesis

FIGURE 5.12 The multiculturalism hypothesis suggests that promotion of a policy of multiculturalism, which encourages the maintenance of ethnic identity while participating in the larger society, will lead to increased confidence in an individual's sense of identity. From this will stem an increased respect and tolerance for other ethnic groups and, in turn, a willingness to interact and communicate with them.

National unity, if it is to mean anything in the deeply personal sense must be found in the confidence in one's own individual identity; out of this can grow respect for that of others and a willingness to share ideas, attitudes and assumptions (quoted in Kalin & Berry, 1994).

This statement is expressed in social psychological terms, assuming that the promotion of multiculturalism would increase the confidence of individuals in their own cultural identity. In turn, this greater confidence would lead to increased respect for the identity of other cultural groups and a willingness to interact and communicate. This suggestion has been termed the "multiculturalism assumption" (Kalin & Berry, 1994) or the **multiculturalism hypothesis**—see Figure 5.12 (Lambert, Mermigis, & Taylor, 1986).

More than three decades after its introduction, is Canada's multiculturalism policy fulfilling its promise? The answer to that question is still being debated. There are those who suggest that this policy merely maintains divisions between people rather than bringing unity (e.g., Bissoondath, 1995). Further, sociologist Reginald Bibby suggests that the Canadian public is losing confidence in multiculturalism and moving toward a preference for the American "melting pot" over the Canadian "mosaic" (Bibby, 1990).

On the other hand, social psychological research conducted by John Berry and his colleagues comes to a more positive conclusion (see Berry, 1999). Two national surveys of attitudes

Multiculturalism Hypothesis The assumption that the promotion of multiculturalism will increase the confidence of individuals in their own cultural identity, which in turn will lead to increased respect for the identity of other cultural groups and increased interaction with them.

to multiculturalism and Canadian ethnic groups have been carried out, one in 1974 (Berry, Kallin, & Taylor, 1977) and one in 1991 (Berry & Kalin, 1995). In the most recent survey, over 90 percent of Canadians were supportive of multiculturalism and committed to Canada. Further, support for multicultural programs and ideology had increased since 1974.

Testing the Multiculturalism Hypothesis

The second of the national surveys (Kalin & Berry, 1995) put the multiculturalism hypothesis to the test by investigating the relationship between cultural identity, tolerance for other groups, and willingness to interact or communicate. While it is not possible to establish a causal relationship between these variables from a survey, correlational support can be provided. In terms of cultural identity, the 1991 survey found that most respondents (64 percent) felt a strong sense of identity as "Canadian." Compared to the 1974 survey, the 1991 results showed an increase in self-identity as "Canadian" and a decrease in ethnic identity (e.g., Italian-Canadian or Italian) or provincial identity (e.g., Québécois or Manitoban). Further, those with a Canadian or an ethnic identity tended to be somewhat more tolerant of other cultural groups than were those with a provincial identity. Tolerance was also positively correlated with levels of comfort when interacting with those from other groups (Berry & Kalin, 1995). That is, those who scored higher on measures of tolerance also reported feeling more "comfortable being around" people from other ethnic groups. In total, the results of the 1991 survey suggest considerable support not only for Canada's policy of multiculturalism, but also for the multiculturalism hypothesis itself. However, we should re-emphasize that the *causal* role of multiculturalism in combating prejudice cannot be definitively established by such survey results.

Areas of Concern in Canadian Intergroup Relations

While the bulk of findings from this survey were encouraging, it also revealed some areas of concern for Canadian intergroup relations. First, all groups, with the exception of South Asians, showed some in-group favouritism: They had more positive attitudes towards their own group than other groups and were most comfortable interacting with the in-group. Second, not all groups were equally accepted. There was generally a higher level of tolerance and comfort with those of European origin (British, French, and Italian ethnic groups were rated highest) than with those of non-European origin (e.g., Arabs, Muslims, Indo-Pakistanis, and Sikhs were given lowest ratings). Finally, on a number of measures, those of French origin (especially in Quebec) showed differences from the rest of the sample. They displayed greatest preference for the in-group, least self-identity as Canadian (only 32 percent), and greatest provincial identity (i.e., Québécois). In addition, those of French origin in Quebec had the lowest ratings of commitment and attachment to Canada. Results in these three areas indicate potential and ongoing problems for intergroup relations in Canada.

In 1998 John Berry won the Donald O. Hebb Award for Distinguished Contribution to Psychology as a Science. In his address when receiving this award, he emphasized that while public policy can have an impact on the psychological processes of prejudice and intercultural relations, this influence can be reciprocal. That is, psychological research, such as the work described above, can contribute to public policymaking by increasing our understanding of the complex psychological mechanisms that inform ethnic relations in a multicultural society (Berry, 1999).

Changing Relations between Groups

Direct Intergroup Contact

We often have little contact with other cultural groups or minorities, particularly if we hold strong prejudices against them. For example, a study carried out in Toronto found that only 18 percent of those who described themselves as "very prejudiced" had experienced close contact with minority groups, whereas over 56 percent of those who were "very tolerant" had experienced close contact (Henry, 1978). This state of affairs raises an important question: Can prejudice be reduced by somehow increasing the degree of contact between antagonistic groups? The idea that it can is known as the **contact hypothesis,** and there are several good reasons for predicting that such a strategy might prove effective (Pettigrew, 1981). First, increased contact between persons from different groups can lead to growing recognition of similarities between them. As we will see in Chapter 6, perceived similarity can generate enhanced mutual attraction. Second, while stereotypes are resistant to change, they can be altered when sufficient information inconsistent with them is encountered or when individuals meet a sufficient number of "exceptions" to their stereotypes (Kunda & Oleson, 1995). Third, increased contact may help to counter the illusion of out-group homogeneity described earlier. For these reasons it seems possible that direct intergroup contact may be one effective means of combating prejudice. Is it?

A large number of studies, both in the laboratory and in the field, have investigated the contact hypothesis (Cook, 1985; Kalin & Berry, 1982; Stephan, 1985). This accumulated evidence has confirmed that intergroup contact can reduce prejudice, but only under certain conditions.

First, the groups interacting must be roughly equal in social, economic, or task-related status. If they differ sharply in such respects, communication may be difficult and prejudice can actually be increased by contact. Second, the contact situation must involve cooperation and interdependence so that the groups work toward shared goals (as in the famous Robber's Cave experiment described earlier in the chapter). Third, contact between the groups must be informal so that they can get to know one another as individuals. Fourth, contact must occur in a setting in which existing norms favour group equality. Fifth, the groups must interact in ways that permit disconfirmation of negative stereotyped beliefs about one another. And sixth, the persons involved must view one another as typical of their respective groups; only then will they generalize their pleasant contacts to other persons or situations (Wilder, 1984).

When contact between initially hostile groups occurs under these conditions, prejudice between them does seem to decrease (Cook, 1985; Riordan, 1978). Such effects have been observed in the United States, where increased contact between African-Americans and whites has been found to reduce prejudice between them (Aronson, Bridgeman, & Geffner, 1978), and in many other nations as well. For example, increased school contact between Jews of Middle Eastern origin and Jews of European or American origin tends to reduce in-group bias among Israeli soldiers (Schwarzwald, Amir, & Crain, 1992).

On the basis of these findings, it seems reasonable to suggest that, when used with care, direct group contact can be an effective tool for combating cross-group hostility and prejudice. When people get to know one another, it seems, many of the anxieties, stereotypes, and false perceptions that have previously kept them apart seem to melt in the warmth of new friendships.

Recently, however, a modified version of the contact hypothesis, known as the *extended contact hypothesis*, has been developed that examines the impact of indirect contact.

The **extended contact hypothesis** suggests that direct contact between persons from different groups is not essential for reducing prejudice between them. In fact, such beneficial effects can be produced if the persons in question merely *know* that persons in their own group have formed close friendships with persons from the other group (e.g., Pettigrew, 1997; Wright et al., 1997). How can knowledge of such cross-group

Contact Hypothesis The view that increased contact between members of various social groups can be effective in reducing prejudice between them. Such efforts seem to succeed only when contact takes place under specific, favourable conditions.

Extended Contact Hypothesis A view suggesting that simply knowing that members of one's own group have formed close friendships with members of an out-group can reduce prejudice against this group.

friendship help to reduce prejudice? In several different ways. For instance, knowledge of such friendship can indicate that contact with out-group members is acceptable—that the norms of the group are not so anti–out-group as individuals might initially have believed. Similarly, knowing that members of one's own group enjoy close friendships with members of an out-group can help to reduce anxiety about interacting with them: If someone we know enjoys such contact, why shouldn't we? Third, the existence of such cross-group friendships suggests that members of an out-group don't necessarily dislike members of our own in-group. Finally, such friendships can generate increased empathy and understanding between groups; in other words, we don't necessarily have to experience close contact with persons from an out-group to feel more positively toward them—learning that members of our own in-group have had such experiences can be sufficient.

A growing body of research evidence provides support for the accuracy of this reasoning, and for the extended contact hypothesis. For instance, in one investigation of this hypothesis (Pettigrew, 1997), almost 4,000 people living in several European countries completed a questionnaire that measured the extent to which they had friendships with people outside their own cultural group, their level of prejudice toward out-groups generally, their beliefs about immigration, and their feelings toward a very wide range of ethnic and cultural groups (e.g., people from various European countries, North Africans, Turks, black Africans, Asians, West Indians, and Jews). Results offered striking support for the benefits of intergroup friendships. The greater the number of cross-group friendships participants reported, the lower their prejudice toward various out-groups and the more favourable their beliefs about immigration into their country. In addition, the greater their experience with intergroup friendships, the more positive their feelings toward many other groups—including ones with which they had experienced little or no contact. This latter finding is very important, for it suggests that reductions in prejudice produced by friendships with persons from one out-group may generalize to other out-groups as well.

Additional support for the value of intergroup friendships has been provided by laboratory as well as survey research (e.g., Wright et al., 1997), so it appears that contact between persons who belong to different groups can be a highly effective means for reducing prejudice between them, especially if these contacts develop into close friendships. Moreover, the beneficial effects of such friendships can readily spread to other persons who have not themselves experienced such contacts: simply knowing about them can be enough. In other words, merely learning that some people in one's own group get along well with persons belonging to other groups can be a highly effective means for countering the detestable effects of prejudice.

Recategorization: Redrawing the Group Boundaries

In many countries there are rivalries between major cities or regions and these often centre on their sports teams—think of the historical opposition between the Toronto Maple Leafs and Montreal Canadiens. Given the long-term histories of such antagonisms, it is astonishing to see fans of each side suddenly united in cheering for the same team—as happens if one of the teams is in the play-offs against an American team. When the Toronto Blue Jays won the World Series, young baseball fans in Vancouver paraded up and down Robson Street shouting "We're number one!" And we can expect a similar unity from all sides of the country when the Olympics come to Vancouver in 2010 (see Figure 5.13).

What happens when rival fans are suddenly united in situations like these? In terms of the principles discussed in this chapter, sports fans shift the location of the boundary between "us" and "them." When the normal situation is in effect, the

■ Recategorization: From Them to Us

FIGURE 5.13 When Canada hosts the Olympics, we can be certain that regional rivalries will be forgotten as Canadians recategorize former regional rivals into the "us" category.

boundary is between cities or regions. However, when a single Canadian team or athlete is left competing against another country, then the boundary is between Canada and the other country.

Situations like this, in which we shift the boundary between "us" and "them," are quite common in everyday life, and they raise an interesting question: Can such shifts—or **recategorizations,** as they are termed by social psychologists—be used to reduce prejudice? A theory proposed by Gaertner and his colleagues (1989, 1993a) suggests that it can. This theory, known as the **common in-group identity model,** suggests that when individuals belonging to different social groups come to view themselves as members of a *single social entity*, their attitudes toward each other become more positive. These favourable attitudes then promote increased positive contacts between members of the previously separate groups, and this, in turn, reduces intergroup bias still further. In short, weakening or eliminating initial us–them boundaries starts a process that carries the persons involved toward major reductions in prejudice and hostility.

How can we induce people belonging to different groups to perceive each other as members of a single group? Gaertner and his colleagues (1990) suggest that one crucial factor is the experience of working together cooperatively. When individuals belonging to initially distinct groups work together toward shared goals, they come to perceive themselves as a single social entity. Then, feelings of bias or hostility toward the former outgroup—toward "them"—seem to fade away, taking prejudice with them. Such effects have been demonstrated in several studies (e.g., Brewer et al., 1987; Gaertner et al., 1989, 1990, 1993a), both in the laboratory and the field, so it appears that *recategorization* can be another useful technique for reducing many kinds of prejudice.

Recategorization Shifts in the boundary between an individual's in-group ("us") and some out-group ("them"), causing persons formerly viewed as out-group members now to be viewed as belonging to the in-group.

Common In-group Identity Model A theory suggesting that to the extent individuals in different groups view themselves as members of a single social entity, positive contacts between groups will increase and intergroup bias will be reduced.

KEY POINTS

- Social psychologists believe that prejudice is not inevitable; it can be reduced by several techniques.
- Canada's major institutional intervention is its policy of multiculturalism. The *multiculturalism hypothesis*, which assumes that confidence in cultural identification will lead to improved relations with other ethnic groups, has received considerable support in research.
- As the *contact hypothesis* suggests, direct intergroup contact also seems to be helpful, provided that the contact occurs under appropriate conditions. Research on the *extended contact hypothesis* suggests that improvements in group relations can be shown even when the contact is more indirect.
- Another useful technique, *recategorization*, involves somehow inducing individuals to shift the boundary between "us" and "them" so that former out-group members are included in the in-group, providing a *common in-group identity*.

Breaking the Cycle of Prejudice: On Learning Not to Hate

Few persons would suggest that children are born with prejudices firmly in place. Rather, most would contend that bigots are made, not born. Social psychologists share this view: they believe that children acquire prejudice from their parents, other adults, their peers, and—as we noted earlier—the mass media. Given this fact, one useful technique for reducing prejudice follows logically: somehow, we must discourage parents and other adults from training children in bigotry.

Having stated this principle, we must now admit that putting it into practice is far from simple. How can we induce parents who are themselves highly prejudiced to encourage unbiased views among their children? One possibility involves calling parents' attention to their own prejudiced views. Few persons are willing to describe themselves as prejudiced; instead, they view their own negative attitudes toward various groups as entirely justified. A key initial step, therefore, would be to convince parents that the problem exists. Once people come face to face with their own prejudices, many do seem willing to modify their words and behaviour so as to encourage lower levels of prejudice among their children. True, some extreme fanatics actually want to turn their children into hate-filled copies of themselves. Most people, however, recognize that we live in a world of increasing diversity and that this environment calls for a higher degree of tolerance than ever before.

Another argument that can be used to shift parents in the direction of teaching their children tolerance rather than prejudice lies in the fact that prejudice harms not only those who are its victims but those who hold such views as well (Dovidio & Gaertner, 1993; Jussim, 1991). Persons who are prejudiced, it appears, live in a world filled with needless fears, anxieties, and anger. They fear attack from presumably dangerous social groups; they worry about the health risks stemming from contact with such groups; and they experience anger and emotional turmoil over what they view as unjustified incursions by these groups into their neighbourhoods, schools, or offices. In other words, their enjoyment of everyday activities and life itself is reduced by their own prejudice (Harris et al., 1992). Of course, as we discussed earlier, offsetting such costs is the boost in self-esteem prejudiced persons sometimes feel when they derogate or scapegoat out-group members (Branscombe & Wann, 1994; Fein & Spenser, 1997).

Overall, though, it is clear that persons holding intense racial and ethnic prejudices suffer many harmful effects from these views. Most parents want to do everything in their power to further their children's well-being, so calling these costs to parents' attention may help discourage them from transmitting prejudiced views to their offspring.

Cognitive Interventions: When Stereotypes Become Less Compelling

It is generally assumed that the effects of stereotyping on social relations are negative and, indeed, much research has supported this view. However, Don Taylor at McGill University has suggested that, in the context of intergroup relations, stereotyping is not always destructive (1981; Taylor & Moghaddam, 1987). His _intergroup stereotyping model_ explores both negative and positive forms of stereotyping and suggests that when groups are not in conflict, intergroup stereotyping can have a constructive effect on intergroup relations. How can this occur? First, Taylor points out that the content of stereotypes is not necessarily negative. For example, groups with high status are often viewed positively by other groups in society (e.g., Berry, Kalin, & Taylor, 1977; Berry & Kalin, 1995; Kalin & Berry, 1996). Frequently, groups will also characterize themselves positively. Kirby and Gardner (1973), for instance, found that English-Canadians stereotyped themselves as "clean, intelligent, good, and modern." Second, he suggests that such positive stereotypes help to create a distinct identity for a group. Building on notions of social identity theory, Taylor's model then suggests that if groups wish to maintain a distinctive and positive social identity, they will welcome stereotyping to the extent that it has two qualities: (1) it is perceived as accurate by the group itself; and (2) it is positively evaluated by others. Thus, in the context of intergroup relations we have to consider the positivity and accuracy of each group's stereotypes of other groups and of themselves.

The implications of this model for intergroup relations in Canada are that stereotyping need not be a destructive force. When groups are in conflict, then this is reflected in their negative stereotyping of each other. However, if groups understand and respect each other, stereotyping can, at times, provide the positive and distinctive identity for which groups strive (Tajfel, 1982).

Throughout this chapter, we have noted that stereotypes play an important role in prejudice. The tendency to think about others in terms of their membership in various groups or categories (known as _category-driven processing_) appears to be a key factor in the occurrence and persistence of several forms of prejudice. If this is so, then interventions designed to reduce the impact of stereotypes may prove highly effective in reducing prejudice and discrimination. How can this goal be attained? Several techniques seem to be effective.

The impact of stereotypes can be reduced if individuals are encouraged to think carefully about others—to pay attention to their unique characteristics rather than to their membership in various groups. Research findings indicate that such _attribute-driven processing_ can be encouraged even by such simple procedures as informing individuals that their own outcomes or rewards in a situation will be affected by another's performance, or telling them that it is very important to be accurate in forming an impression of another person. Under these conditions, individuals are motivated to be accurate, and this reduces their tendency to rely on stereotypes (Neuberg, 1989).

Attribute-driven processing requires some conscious acknowledgement of a need to change one's response to an out-group. But what if the individual is not aware that there is any need for change—that is, if he or she is a modern racist and the prejudice is implicit? The following Canadian Research: On the Cutting Edge section describes research on the forefront of social psychology's attempts to combat implicit racism.

Canadian Research: On the Cutting Edge

Challenging Implicit Racism by Inducing Feelings of Hypocrisy

As prejudice becomes more socially unacceptable, it doesn't disappear completely, it becomes less overt and often takes new, more subtle forms—as in neosexism and modern racism. Further, it is less likely to be acknowledged both publicly and to oneself. We have seen that psychologists have developed more indirect ways of measuring these *implicit prejudices* (prejudices of which the persons holding them are unaware). The next logical step has recently been taken, as researchers have begun to explore ways of decreasing implicit prejudice. The fundamental problem here is how to change someone's prejudice when that person is unaware of its existence.

Researchers at the University of Waterloo (Son Hing, Li, & Zanna, 2002) recently suggested that hypocrisy procedures (see Chapter 3) are particularly suitable for challenging implicit prejudice—or in this case *implicit racism*. You may recall that hypocrisy procedures involve reminding someone of that person's failure to behave in accord with his or her own attitudes. It is this person's awareness that he or she has been hypocritical, and the discomfort that results, which ensures that behaviour is changed to be more in line with attitudes.

So why should implicit racists be particularly likely to respond to such procedures? The researchers reasoned as follows: Given that those with implicit prejudice claim to be not racist, and also given that because of their underlying prejudice they have probably discriminated in the past, if researchers can point out this dissonance between attitude and behaviour, feelings of hypocrisy might be induced. The result: implicit racists may be moved to decrease their discriminatory behaviour.

Son Hing and colleagues selected two groups of subjects through pre-screening: *low prejudice* subjects (low on measures of explicit racism and low on measures of implicit racism) and *implicit racist* subjects (low on measures of explicit racism but high on measures of implicit racism). The racism in this case focused on Asians, as this group represented the largest visible minority on campus. Notice that none of these subjects was blatantly racist. Such subjects had been screened out by use of the Asian Modern Racism Scale, which asks subjects to agree or disagree with statements such as, "There are too many Asian students being allowed to attend university in Canada."

In the first phase of the experimental procedure, subjects were induced to make a public declaration of anti-racism. The two groups of subjects were asked to write persuasive essays on why they believed it is important to treat minority students on campus fairly. Further, they were told that excerpts of their essays might be featured in a pamphlet to promote racial equality on campus.

In the second phase, for half of the subjects hypocrisy was induced by having them describe two situations in which "you reacted more negatively to an Asian person than you thought you should or treated an Asian person in a prejudiced manner." The other half of the subjects were in a control group and did not complete this second phase.

Finally, after filling out a number of questionnaires measuring their affect, all subjects were told that the experiment was over. In fact, the experimenter then went on to measure the major dependent variable—discrimination against Asians. Subjects were asked if they could fill out a supposedly anonymous ballot for the Federation of Students on campus. The ballot asked for their opinion on how a 20 percent cut in funding for student groups could be implemented. Subjects could indicate which groups in a list of ten (including the Asian Students Association) they thought deserved the most and least percentage cutbacks. It was the recommended cuts to the Asian Students Association that were of interest.

Researchers hypothesized the hypocrisy induction procedure would produce most negative affect (discomfort) in subjects high in implicit racism because the conflict between their non-racist attitude (expressed in the essay) and the discriminatory behaviour they had subsequently described would be greatest. Low prejudiced subjects would, on the other hand, have less inner conflict because their behaviour would generally be less discriminatory and their attitudes more clearly non-racist. The greater discomfort should lead implicit racists in the hypocrisy condition to bend over backwards to demonstrate a *lack* of discrimination.

This is exactly what was found. Measures of negative affect were highest for implicit racists in the hypocrisy condition and, compared to controls, these subjects were much less likely to recommend cutbacks in funding to the Asian Students Association, as shown in Figure 5.14. The results of this study are indeed encouraging. Prejudice may have gone underground but its purveyors are more likely to be affected if they can be induced to see the hypocrisy in their behaviour. It appears that implicit prejudice is more open to change than the old-fashioned kind.

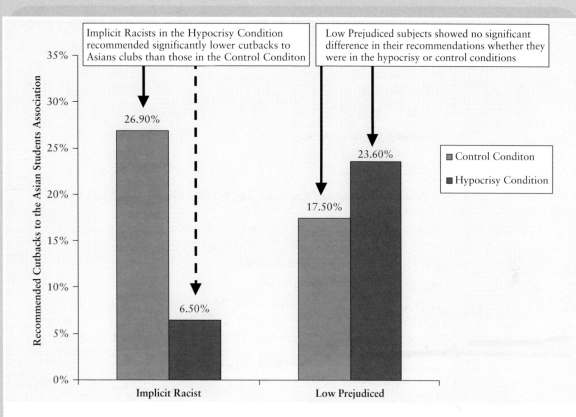

Implicit Racists in the Hypocrisy Condition recommended significantly lower cutbacks to Asians clubs than those in the Control Conditon

Low Prejudiced subjects showed no significant difference in their recommendations whether they were in the hypocrisy or control conditions

- Control Conditon
- Hypocrisy Condition

26.90%
6.50%
17.50%
23.60%

Implicit Racist   Low Prejudiced

(y-axis: Recommended Cutbacks to the Asian Students Association, 0%–35%)

- **Hypocrisy Induction and Implicit Racism**

FIGURE 5.14 When implicit racists (low on measures of *explicit* racism but high on measures of *implicit* racism) were induced to see their own hypocrisy, they reacted with strong negative affect and bent over backwards to demonstrate a lack of discrimination. This is shown above by the fact that implicit racists in the hypocrisy condition recommended the lowest cutbacks to the Asian Students' Association, compared both to controls and to those low in racism.

KEY POINTS

- One way to reduce prejudice is to change children's early experiences by encouraging parents and others to transmit to them accepting rather than prejudiced attitudes.
- Cognitive interventions, such as inducing individuals to focus on others' specific attributes rather than on their group membership, helps reduce the impact of stereotyping.
- Research shows that implicit racism can be reduced if individuals are induced to face their own hypocrisy.

Ideas To Take With You

Techniques for Reducing Prejudice

Prejudice is an all-too-common part of social life, but most social psychologists believe that it can be reduced—it is not inevitable. Here are some techniques that seem to work.

Teaching Children Acceptance Instead of Bigotry.
If children are taught from an early age to respect all groups—including ones very different from their own—prejudice can be nipped in the bud, so to speak.

Increased Intergroup Contact—or Merely Knowledge That It Occurs.
Recent findings indicate that if people merely know that friendly contacts occur between members of their own group and members of various outgroups, their prejudice toward these groups can be sharply reduced.

Recategorization.
Once individuals mentally include people they once excluded from their in-group within it, prejudice toward them may disappear. Reminding people that they are part of larger groups—for instance, that they are all Canadians, Americans, or even human beings—can help accomplish this kind of recategorization.

Undermining Stereotypes.
Stereotypes suggest that all persons belonging to specific social groups are alike—that they share the same characteristics. Such beliefs can be weakened if people are encouraged to think about others as individuals, not simply as members of social groups. Also, some evidence suggests that affirmative action programs may actually encourage positive perceptions of the persons who benefit from them, and so serve to counter prejudice by undermining stereotypes.

Summary

Prejudice and Discrimination: Their Nature and Forms

- *Prejudice* is an attitude toward members of some social group. (p. 156)
- Prejudice influences our processing of social information and can also be implicit. (p. 156)
- *Discrimination* involves negative actions toward members of social groups. (p. 156)
- Discrimination becomes less overt and is shown in subtle forms. (p. 156)
- Women's position in the workplace has improved but *neosexism* and the *glass ceiling* provide subtle barriers. (p. 161)

The Origins of Prejudice: Contrasting Perspectives

- *Realistic conflict* theory suggests prejudice arises from intergroup conflict over scarce resources. (p. 166)
- Classic studies of boys' camps and hate crimes and economic conditions provide support. (p. 167)
- *Social identity theory* suggests prejudice stems from the desire for a positive and a distinctive group-based identity. (p. 169)
- The *social learning* perspective suggests that early *experience*, both direct and indirect, leads to prejudice. (p. 173)
- Social cognitive processes such as stereotyping and implicit stereotypes can play a part in forming prejudices. (p. 174)

- *Stereotypes* tend to remain unchanged even in the face of contradictory information and can be evoked automatically through priming. (p. 174)
- Other cognitive sources of prejudice include *illusory correlations* and the *illusion of out-group homogeneity*. (p. 178)
- Personalities high in *right-wing authoritarianism* show a propensity towards prejudice. (p. 178)
- Evolutionary theory suggests that ethnocentrism and *xenophobia* may have evolved. (p. 179)

Responses of the Victims of Prejudice

- Victim responses can be *intropunitive* or *extrapunitive*; aimed at *personal* improvement or *group-based* improvement. (p. 180)
- The perception of oneself as the target of discrimination can produce a stress response. (p. 180)
- Victims respond to *stereotype threat*. (p. 182)

- Minority individuals frequently show the *personal/group discrimination discrepancy*. (p. 183)

Challenging Prejudice: Why It Is Not Always Inevitable

- A major institutional challenge to prejudice is the policy of multiculturalism. (p. 186)
- The *contact hypothesis* suggests that direct and indirect intergroup contact seems to be helpful. (p. 187)
- *Recategorization* shifts the boundary between "us" and "them," providing a *common in-group identity*. (p. 188)
- Children can learn not to hate through parental influence. (p. 190)
- One cognitive intervention is encouraging an attribute-driven rather than category-driven focus. (p. 191)
- Implicit racism can be reduced through hypocrisy induction. (p. 192)

For More Information

Zanna, M. P., & Olson, J. M. (1994). *The psychology of prejudice: The Ontario symposium on personality and social psychology* (Vol. 7). Mahwah, NJ: Erlbaum.

Thought-provoking chapters by Canadian experts in the fields of stereotypes, intergroup conflict, and attitudes. Together, the authors present a very comprehensive view of what social psychologists have discovered about the origins and effects of prejudice.

Henry, F., Tator, C., Mattis, W., & Rees, T. (1995). *The colour of democracy: Racism in Canadian society.* Toronto: Harcourt Brace.

An assessment of racism in Canada today from a long-time researcher in the field of social anthropology. This book examines racism in each of Canada's major institutions and is full of striking examples and research.

Weblinks

www.cpa.ca/cjbsnew/1996/ful_kalin2.html
"Interethnic Attitudes in Canada: Ethnocentrism, Consensual Hierarchy and Reciprocity" by Kalin, Berry, Queen's University
www.ceifo.su.se/icsey/icsey.html
International Comparative Studies of Ethnocultural Youth Page from the Centre for Migration and Ethnic Relations, Stockholm, Sweden

www.Trinity.Edu/~mkearl/race.html
Race and Ethnicity Web resources
www.acusd.edu/ethics/race.html
Literature and Web resources on race, ethnicity, and multiculturalism

CHAPTER SIX

Relationships:

From Attraction to Parting

Interpersonal Attraction: Becoming Acquainted
Physical Proximity/Responding to Observable Characteristics: External Cues to Attraction/Affect and Cognition in Attraction/The Need for Affiliation: The Motive to Relate to Others

Building a Relationship: Self-Disclosure, Similarity, and Reciprocity
Self-Disclosure: Growing Intimacy/Similarity: We Like Those Most like Ourselves/Reciprocity in Attraction: Mutual Liking

From Liking to Loving: Moving beyond Casual Friendships
Passionate Love: The Basis of Romantic Relationships/What's Love Got to Do with It? Cultural and Evolutionary Explanations/Cultural Differences in Passionate Love/The Many Forms of Love: Beyond Passion

Long-Term Close Relationships
Adult Attachment Patterns/Long-Term Spousal and Family Relationships

Troubled Relationships: From Dissatisfaction to Dissolution
Problems in Relationships, and Possible Solutions/Breaking Up Is Hard to Do

SPECIAL SECTIONS

CORNERSTONES
The Capilano Bridge Experiment: Cognition and Emotion in Attraction

ON THE APPLIED SIDE
Relating on the Net: Positive or Negative Social Impacts?

■ Relationships Are an Essential Part of Our Lives

FIGURE 6.1 The importance of relationships in our lives reflects our essentially social nature. They can provide us with some of the most wonderful experiences of our lives, as shown here. However, the importance of relationships has a further implication—when things go wrong, the pain can be severe.

It is a testament to our essentially *social* nature that relationships provide us with some of the most wonderful experiences of our lives, as well as some of the most painful. In all societies throughout history, relationships have typically been seen as crucial for an individual—including family and close friends, as well as the pivotal experience of falling in love. And despite changes in values and attitudes about relationships, most people, whatever their culture, expect to go through the processes of making friends, meeting a mate, establishing long-term relationships and perhaps becoming a parent (see Figure 6.1).

However, we are all aware, after exposure to films and novels as well as to real-life experiences, that this isn't always easy—often families feud, friendships fade, and love can turn to hate—sometimes "love hurts." Still, despite negative examples, other people are important to us and we tend to maintain our hopes about what relationships can and should be.

Levinger (1980) described relationships as passing through five possible stages: (1) *initial attraction*; (2) *building a relationship*; (3) *continuation*; and—for some— (4) *deterioration*; and (5) *ending*. This chapter will follow this outline, beginning with the initial attraction and building stages of the relationship. The majority of the research on relationships, until recent years, had concentrated on these first two stages, under the heading of **interpersonal attraction**. This area is concerned with the initial steps involved in establishing relationships.

We will first describe the initial factors involved in becoming acquainted. This process is often only indirectly related to the personality characteristics of the people involved. Rather, chance and external factors seem more likely to play a role at the initial stage of relationships: such as close *physical proximity* and *observable characteristics* of the other person (physical attractiveness, skin colour, height, and

Interpersonal Attraction The degree to which we like other individuals. Interpersonal attraction varies along a dimension ranging from strong liking on one extreme to strong dislike on the other.

so forth). Internal processes also contribute, such as cognitive processes that occur while we are *forming an impression* of someone else, the emotions or *affect* we feel, and our own *need for affiliation*.

Once interaction begins, interpersonal attraction is strongly determined by the extent to which the two people discover that they are *similar* in various attitudes, beliefs, values, and interests. And attraction can become stronger still if it is mutual. This is the power of *reciprocity*: we tend to like those like us.

If relationships are to progress to *continuation*, the third stage, then *love* often provides the emotional underpinning in the long term. Research has tended to focus on romantic or *passionate love* but we will also consider the many different forms that love can take.

Contrary to the impression from fairy tales—remember the line "and they all lived happily ever after"—maintenance of long-term intimate relationships is not easy. As the final two stages of relationship in the Levinger model (1980) suggest, *deterioration* and *ending* can occur. This is not to suggest that relationships inevitably reach this point. However, few relationships are entirely trouble-free, and it is often our response to problems that determines whether the relationship continues or ends. Therefore, we'll also consider troubled relationships, how problems arise, and the effects of dissolution.

Interpersonal Attraction: Becoming Acquainted

There are over 30 million people in Canada today, and you could possibly like several thousand of them well enough to consider them as your friends. That is exceedingly unlikely to happen, however. Any one of us is likely to become aware of, interact with, and get to know only a tiny percentage of these individuals. Of those in this relatively small subgroup, only a few will become acquaintances, fewer still will become friends, and most will remain strangers. What determines awareness, interaction, and differential attraction?

An obvious, but often overlooked, determinant is controlled by our physical surroundings. Many seemingly unimportant details of where we live, work, and go to school represent important influences on our relationships. Simply stated, two people tend to become acquainted if external factors (e.g., the location of dormitory rooms, classroom seats, office desks, etc.) bring them into repeated contact. Such contact is the result of physical **proximity**—or closeness.

Proximity In attraction research, the physical closeness between two individuals in their daily lives. The closer the physical distance, the greater the probability of the individuals' coming into regular contact and thus experiencing repeated exposure.

Physical Proximity

Friendships often begin because of a series of unplanned encounters that are controlled by the physical details of the immediate environment. On the basis of these casual, accidental contacts, each person begins to recognize the other. At this point it is common for people to exchange greetings when they see one another and to exchange remarks about the weather or whatever. This positive response to a familiar face can be observed even among infants. They are, for example, more likely to smile when exposed to a photograph of someone they have seen before than in response to a stranger's picture (Brooks-Gunn & Lewis, 1981).

The first empirical data suggesting a *proximity effect* were provided by sociological studies in the 1930s, which demonstrated that prior to marriage most couples had lived within the same neighbourhood (Bossard, 1932; Davie & Reeves, 1939). Later studies in student residences, where individuals or couples had been randomly assigned to units, showed similar effects of proximity. Most friendships occurred among those who were on the same or adjacent floors in dormitories, or within seven metres of each other in apartments (e.g., Evans & Wilson, 1949; Festinger, Schachter, & Back, 1950).

In the classroom, those sitting side by side are most likely to become acquainted. The total number of friends you make in a class depends in part on where you sit. If you have someone sitting on your right and someone on your left, you have the possibility of making two friends, whereas a seat on the end of a row yields the likelihood of only one (Byrne & Buehler, 1955). Among other implications, those in a corner seat or a seat on the end of a row make fewer friends (Maisonneuve, Palmade, & Fourment, 1952). It also follows that those who want to maintain privacy can select a seat accordingly. The back of the room as far from others as possible is most likely to deter acquaintances being formed (Pedersen, 1994).

The important point here is that it is in those ordinary daily encounters, in the proximity of our home, school, or neighbourhood, that we are most likely to meet our future friends and romantic partners.

Why Does Proximity Lead to Attraction?

To some extent, we are affected by proximity because we tend to avoid strangers unless we are forced to come in contact because of where we live, where we are seated in a classroom, and so forth. But there is another, more basic, reason. As Zajonc (1968) and his colleagues have reported, repeated exposure to a new stimulus (frequent contact with that stimulus) leads to a more and more positive evaluation of the stimulus—as long as the initial reaction is not an extremely negative one. Whether the stimulus is a drawing, a word in an unknown foreign language, a new product being advertised, a political candidate, or a stranger, the greater the exposure, the more positive the response (Moreland & Zajonc, 1982). Something familiar is preferable to something new and strange. The general idea is that we respond with at least mild discomfort to anything or anyone new. With repeated exposure we become desensitized, anxiety decreases, and that which was new becomes *familiar*.

In one study of the *repeated exposure effect* in a college classroom, Moreland and Beach (1992) arranged for three experimental assistants to attend the class as if they were students. One of these women attended four times, one ten times, and one 15 times. To control for other variables that might influence attraction, the experimenters selected assistants who were similar in appearance, and they instructed the assistants not to interact with any of the actual students, in or out of class. At the end of the class students were asked to evaluate these three women. Their attraction toward the three strangers simply increased as the number of classroom exposures increased; thus, the effect of repeated exposure was clearly evident.

As you might expect from the discussion of subliminal conditioning in Chapter 3, repeated exposure to a stimulus influences a person's evaluation of that stimulus even when he or she is unaware that exposure has taken place. In fact, the effect is stronger under these conditions. Bornstein and D'Agostino (1992) presented stimuli to some research participants at a normal speed and to others at a speed so rapid that they were not aware of having seen them (a speed considered to be *subliminal* or *below threshold*). The repeated exposure effect was found in both conditions, but the effect was greater when the stimuli were presented subliminally rather than at a normal speed.

The subliminal repeated exposure effect can *generalize* to other similar stimuli (Monahan, Murphy, & Zajonc, 2000). In other words, the positive affect generated by exposure to a specific set of stimuli will also be felt towards other stimuli that are similar. In an interesting experiment, undergraduate research participants were subliminally exposed to stimuli that consisted of either Chinese ideographs or drawings of polygons for either a single exposure or repeated exposures. In a second stage of the study, they were exposed to 15 more stimuli for one second each, and then asked to indicate how

Repeated Exposure
Frequent contact with a stimulus. According to Zajonc's theory of repeated exposure, as the number of contacts with any neutral or mildly positive stimulus increases, the evaluation of that stimulus becomes increasingly positive.

much they liked each one. Some were shown the same stimuli to which they had originally been exposed (*Old-Same* Condition)—the *same* Chinese ideographs or the *same* polygons. Some were shown new but similar stimuli (*Novel-Similar* Condition)—*different* Chinese ideographs if they had originally been exposed to Chinese ideographs, or *different* polygons if they had been exposed to polygons. Still other participants rated new but different stimuli (*Novel-Different* Condition)—polygons if they had been exposed to Chinese ideographs or Chinese ideographs if they had been exposed to polygons.

As depicted in Figure 6.2, those in the *Old-Same* condition (Chinese ideographs both times or polygons both times) showed the usual repeated exposure effect. The

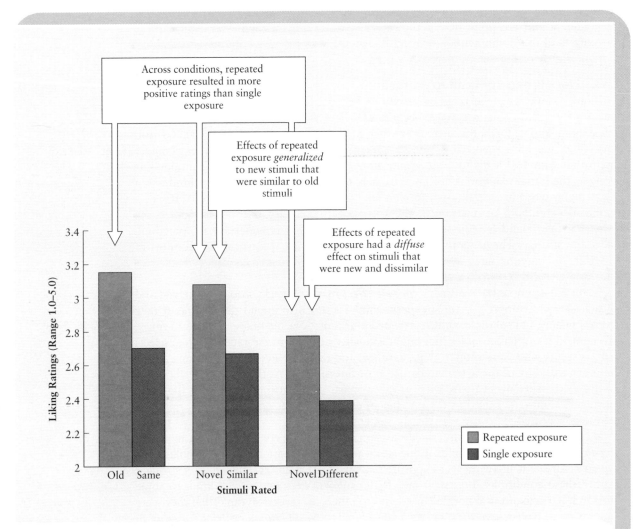

■ Repeated Exposure: Specific and Generalized Effects

FIGURE 6.2 In the first part of an experiment, research participants were subliminally exposed to a given type of stimulus once or repeatedly. In the second part of the experiment, the participants were asked to rate either the same stimuli they had seen in the first part, novel stimuli similar to those seen in the first part, or stimuli different from those seen earlier. The usual *repeated exposure effect* was found in the group rating the same stimuli they had seen before, a *generalized effect* was found in the group rating new stimuli that were similar to those seen before, and a milder repeated effect was found in the group rating new, different stimuli.

Source: Based on data from Monahan, Murphy, & Zajonc, 2000.

Novel-Similar group (e.g., Chinese ideographs the first time and different ideographs the second time) was also more positive toward novel but similar stimuli *if* they had been repeatedly exposed to those similar stimuli. The *Novel-Different* group (ideographs the first time and polygons the second, or vice versa) also showed a mild repeated exposure effect even though they had been repeatedly exposed to quite different stimuli. Presumably, the positive affect aroused by repeated exposure lingers on and has a positive effect on subsequent evaluations of other stimuli.

Note that although repeated proximity generally produces a positive response, it is not 100 percent effective in fostering attraction. Repeated exposure to a stranger who behaves in an unpleasant fashion leads to more and more dislike (Swap, 1977). Also, there is some individual variation. The strength of the repeated exposure effect depends on a person's *need for structure*—how much organization a person prefers in his or her world (Neuberg & Newsom, 1993). People who have a high need for structure in their world have a more positive reaction to the familiar (as well as a more negative reaction to the unfamiliar) and show a stronger repeated exposure effect (Hansen & Bartsch, 2001).

Physical proximity may have brought us close to a stranger and increased the odds that we might form a relationship, but our initial response to others is also strongly influenced by their *observable characteristics*, such as race, sex, age, height, physique, accent, and so forth. Among the most influential of these characteristics is physical attractiveness.

KEY POINTS

- Relationships can be seen as passing through five possible stages: (1) *initial attraction*, (2) *building a relationship*, (3) *continuation*, (4) *deterioration*, and (5) *ending*.

- The term *interpersonal attraction* refers to the attitudes we form about other people, expressed along a dimension ranging from like to dislike, based on feelings ranging from extremely positive to extremely negative.

- One's initial contact with others is very often based on *proximity* resulting from such physical aspects of the environment as classroom seating assignments, the location of residences, and how a workplace is arranged.

- Proximity allows for *repeated exposure* to some individuals in one's environment; repeated exposure tends to result in positive affect, and positive affect results in attraction. This can be generalized to other similar stimuli.

Responding to Observable Characteristics: External Cues to Attraction

When we like—or dislike—someone at first sight, it is an indication that we have observed something about that person that appears to provide information about him or her. You may tend to like a stranger simply on the basis of a superficial resemblance to someone else you know and like (Andreoletti, Zebrowitz, & Lachman, 2001). In other instances, the cue may not be related to a specific person in your past but to a subgroup of people to whom you respond positively—the stranger has a Newfoundland accent, for example, and you have a fondness for Newfoundlanders. As discussed in Chapter 5, stereotypes are poor predictors of behaviour, but we nevertheless find ourselves reacting to other people on the basis of them and we make incorrect assumptions based on superficial characteristics. Among the numerous examples of the response to superficial characteristics is our reaction to appearance—the pervasive effects of **physical attractiveness**—the facial and bodily characteristics that people generally regard as visually appealing (or unappealing). Both sexes respond strongly to the physical attractiveness of those they meet (Collins & Zebrowitz, 1995; Hatfield & Sprecher, 1986), though males are more responsive to female attractiveness than females are to male attractiveness (Feingold, 1990, 1992b; Pierce, 1992). Also, individuals differ in the importance they attach to physical appearance (Cash & Jacobi, 1992).

Evaluation of Others on the Basis of Physical Attractiveness

We may say that "beauty is only skin deep," but people are very likely to respond positively to those who are attractive and negatively to those who are unattractive (Collins & Zebrowitz, 1995). There are some individual differences, however. For example, people who are high in the need for cognition (the tendency to engage in and enjoy cognitive activity) are less affected by the attractiveness of a stranger than are those with low cognitive needs (Perlini & Hansen, 2001).

Physical appearance influences many types of interpersonal evaluations, including liking, judgments of guilt or innocence in a courtroom (see Chapter 10), and even the grade that is assigned to an essay (Cash & Trimer, 1984). And people respond more positively to attractive infants than to unattractive ones (Karraker & Stern, 1990). Attractiveness is *especially* crucial, however, with respect to evaluating a potential romantic partner (Sprecher & Duck, 1994). Handsome men are believed to be more masculine, and beautiful women to be more feminine (Dion & Dion, 1987; Hatfield & Sprecher, 1986a). Though both men and women are responsive to the attractiveness of a possible date, lover, or spouse, female attractiveness is more important to men than male attractiveness is to women (Feingold, 1990; Pierce, 1992). Overall, though, an appealing appearance is perceived as a positive characteristic that influences interpersonal attraction and interpersonal preferences. Altogether, as social psychologists discovered three decades ago, most people assume that "what is beautiful is good" (Dion, Berscheid, & Hatfield, 1972).

Despite the powerful effects of attractiveness, people are not very accurate in estimating how others rate their appearance. Men, especially, overestimate how attractive they are to others (Gabriel, Critelli, & Ee, 1994). **Appearance anxiety**—an undue concern with how one looks—is generally a more acute problem for women than for men, but is found in members of both sexes. Those with the greatest anxiety agree with test items such as "I feel that most of my friends are more physically attractive than myself" and disagree with items such as "I enjoy looking at myself in the mirror" (Dion, Dion, & Keelan, 1990).

Although cross-cultural research suggests that positive stereotypes about attractiveness are universal, the *specific content* of the stereotypes depends on which characteristics are valued by a particular culture (Dion, Pak, & Dion, 1990). For example, in a collectivist culture such as Korea, attractiveness is assumed to be associated with integrity and concern for others, but these attributes do not appear among the attractiveness stereotypes common among individualistic North Americans (Wheeler & Kim, 1997). There is general agreement across cultures that attractiveness indicates social competence, adjustment, intelligence, and sexual warmth. Nevertheless, a Canadian study reported that women did *not* attribute socially desirable traits to men based on either the man's attractiveness or his age (Perlini, Marcello, & Hansen et al., 2001).

Despite widespread acceptance of the belief that attractiveness is an important cue to personality and character, most of the stereotypes based on appearance are *incorrect* (Feingold, 1992; Kenealy et al., 1991). Among the few that are correct, research finds, for example, that compared with less beautiful and handsome individuals, those who are most attractive are believed to be more popular (they are) and to have better interpersonal skills and feel better about themselves (they do) (Diener, Wolsic, & Fujita, 1995; Johnstone, Frame, & Bouman, 1992). The more attractive a person is, the more he or she self-discloses to members of the opposite sex, thus facilitating the establishment of a relationship (Stiles et al., 1996). Presumably, the popularity, social skills, high self-esteem, and tendency to self-disclose among those who are attractive occur primarily because such individuals have spent their lives being liked and treated nicely by others who respond positively to their good looks (Zebrowitz, Collins, & Dutta, 1998). In other words, appearance is not directly linked to these attributes; instead, the way other people react to appearance is the causative factor.

It should be added that a few *negative* attributes are also associated with physical attractiveness. For example, beautiful women are sometimes perceived as vain and materialistic (Cash & Duncan, 1984). Also, though handsome male politicians are more likely to be elected than relatively unattractive ones, an attractive woman running for elective office is not helped by her appearance (Sigelman et al., 1986).

Explanations for the Importance of Physical Appearance

If appearance is a poor predictor of other attributes, why in the world should people place great emphasis on it? Is it possible that this is a built-in response based on biological determinants? Note that attractive people arouse positive affect (Johnston & Oliver-Rodriguez, 1997; Kenrick et al., 1993), and we know that positive affect leads to attraction. But, why should physical attractiveness arouse positive affect? The two basic explanations are (1) we are born with this kind of preference—it is an evolved response or (2) we learn this preference from various sources in our culture.

The general evolutionary point, based on extensions of Darwin's original theory, is that if men are attracted to and mate with young, healthy, fertile women, this enhances their odds of reproductive success (Buss, 1999). As a result, over hundreds of thousands of years, males with a preference for youthful beauty were more likely to pass on their genes to the next generation than were males for whom youth and beauty were irrelevant (Fink & Penton-Voak, 2002). The fact that females are less concerned about male youth and attractiveness is explained by the fact that women have a relatively limited age span in which reproduction is possible, whereas men are usually able to reproduce from puberty well into old age. For prehistoric females, the selection of a fertile male was a matter of less importance because young and old were both fertile. Instead, the choice of a man with the ability to provide resources and to protect her and their offspring was crucial (Kenrick et al., 1994), although she might also be concerned with the quality of genes represented by the male (Buss, 1999).

From the perspective of evolutionary determinants, female beauty is believed to be sexually attractive to men because beauty is associated with youth, health, and fertility. Research supports this relationship, but the association is not a very strong one (Kalick et al., 1998; Shackelford & Larsen, 1999). One side effect of this emphasis on beauty is that women—more than men—seek cosmetic surgery in order to "look as young as they feel" (Grant, 2001).

This evolutionary perspective has been received with some controversy (e.g., Eagly & Wood, 1999; Kasser & Sharma, 1999) and research continues into various aspects of this approach, as we will see later in the chapter. The basic tendency is well established, but the ultimate explanation is more difficult to validate.

One source of evidence for gender difference in line with evolutionary predictions comes from personal ads looking for a romantic partner. Consistent with evolutionary theory, women stress their appearance and men stress their material resources (Deaux & Hanna, 1984; Harrison & Saeed, 1977). In a more recent study, Baize and Schroeder (1995) went a step farther by looking at the number of replies each ad received. In other words, do some factors in the ads attract more potential mates than others? Gender differences were found that are consistent with predictions based on evolutionary theory. For example, a personal ad placed by a man was most effective if it indicated a mature, rich, educated individual. In ads placed by a woman, the only ad content related to its effectiveness was *age*—the younger the more replies.

A potential problem for the biological theory is the finding that ads placed by gay men indicate a preference for younger male partners in the same way that heterosexual men prefer younger female partners (Kenrick et al., 1995). Such findings could be interpreted to mean that both straight and gay men have been subjected to the same cultural influences stressing the importance of youth and good looks. A biological explanation obviously cannot be based on reproductive success. It may be, however, that the preferences that developed among heterosexual men operate just as strongly among homosexual men despite the fact that such preferences are only relevant to genetic survival for heterosexuals.

Evidence with respect to the content of personal ads could also be interpreted as consistent with cultural psychology—preferences across cultures and across sexual

■ Personal Ads: One Source of Evidence for Gender Differences

FIGURE 6.3 Research has shown that certain qualities in personal ad descriptions—wealth and education in males and youth in females—are more likely to receive replies.

orientation simply reflect what most of us have been taught by the media about the importance of females being young and beautiful versus the importance of males being older and richer. Such themes are familiar in ancient fairy tales such as *Beauty and the Beast* and in modern movies (Gallo & Byrne, 2001). However, some evidence is very difficult to explain in cultural terms. For example, year-old infants prefer attractive adults, and they spend more time playing with attractive dolls than with unattractive ones (Langlois et al., 1991; Langlois & Roggman, 1990). It is not reasonable to argue that the preferences of these infants have been moulded by cultural influences. Perhaps the most sensible conclusion at this point is that humans quite possibly are genetically programmed to respond positively to attractiveness and that such preferences are strongly encouraged and supported by cultural factors. We will examine some of the many cultural differences in relationships later in this chapter.

The Physical Constituents of Attractiveness

A number of different lines of research have attempted to discover the essential factors that make someone appear more physically attractive. As discussed in Chapter 4, evaluations of attractiveness have generally focused more on women than men. Research has reflected this bias by generally attempting to discover the basis for female attractiveness before turning to the constituents of male attractiveness. Two aspects of physical attractiveness have been emphasized: the *face*, its features, and its symmetry, or the *body* and its proportions.

The Face: Features, Averaging, and Symmetry

In relation to the face, the facial features found to be most attractive in women show either *neoteny* (having childlike features in adulthood) or maturity (more well-defined features)—see Figure 6.4. These same two general facial types are found among fashion models, and they apply equally to white, black, and Asian women (Ashmore, Solomon, & Longo, 1996). Men perceived as most attractive are those who have big eyes, prominent cheekbones, and more rugged chins compared to women (Hatfield & Rapson, 1996). Though comparing different types of male features, women show a preference for the more feminized male faces (slender noses, cupid lips, and finer chins) compared to masculinized faces (larger nose and jaw, square face, heavier brow) (Little & Hancock, 2002)—think Brad Pitt rather than Russell Crowe (see Figure 6.4). However, this preference has also been shown to depend upon the stage of a woman's menstrual cycle or on the type of relationship she desires (Penton-Voak, Perrett, et al., 1999). Specifically, the more masculinized male face was preferred for short-term relationships and when women were ovulating. Research generally shows that people tend to agree extremely well about who is or is not attractive, even across racial and ethnic lines (Cunningham et al., 1995).

Langlois and Roggman (1990) took a very different approach to determine what is meant by attractiveness. They began with photographs of faces, and then produced computer-generated pictures that combined several faces into one. That is, the image in each photo was transformed into a series of numbers representing shades of grey, the numbers were averaged across the group of pictures, and the result was translated back into a photo. The male faces in Figure 6.4 are computer averaged from 12 different males. For both male and female faces, a composite face was rated as more attractive than most of the individual faces that went into making it (e.g., Little & Hancock, 2002). Further, the more faces that were used to make the composite, the more attractive the result. These investigators concluded that, for most people, an attractive face is simply one whose components represent the arithmetic mean of the details of many faces (Langlois, Roggman, & Musselman, 1994).

■ Attractive Facial Features

FIGURE 6.4 *Women.* Research shows that two types of facial feature are rated as most attractive in women: (1) faces that show *neoteny*—retain childlike features in adulthood—with large, widely spaced eyes and a small nose and chin; and (2) mature faces with more defined features—prominent cheekbones, narrow cheeks, high eyebrows, large pupils, and a big smile. Canadian figure skater Jamie Sale (left) is an example of the first type, and actress Wendy Crewson exemplifies the second.

Men. Research shows that large eyes, a more rugged jaw-line, and a heavier brow than women's are preferred in males. However, when comparing a more masculinized or feminized male face, both male and female subjects rate the more feminized face with finer features as more attractive. The images here are from a computer composite face that was manipulated to be 30 percent more masculinized on the left and 30 percent more feminized on the right (Little & Hancock, 2002).

Cognitive Perspective:

Why should composite faces be especially attractive? One possibility, from a cognitive perspective, is that the average is closer to each person's schema of women and men (see Chapter 2). That is, we form such schemas on the basis of our experiences with many different images, so a composite face is closer to one's schema than is any specific face. This might be a kind of *generalized repeated exposure* effect in operation. As we saw at the beginning of this chapter, if a stimulus is *similar* to one we have seen many times before (as the computer composite might be similar to our schemas of women and men), we rate it more positively.

Evolutionary Perspective

An alternative explanation suggests that we are born with a preference for symmetry, and a face based on the average of many faces is more symmetrical than individual faces. Further, studies indicate that people find symmetrical faces more attractive than asymmetrical ones (Cowley, 1996). Why do we like symmetry? Evolutionary psychologists once again propose that we respond positively to symmetry because it is an indicator of health and hence reproductive fitness (Mealey, Bridgstock, & Townsend, 1999). Though this idea is plausible, experiments have shown that an average face is preferred even when symmetry is held constant (Rhodes, Sumich, & Byatt, 1999). We can conclude that the attractiveness of a composite face is well established, but explanations of these findings based on simply a preference for familiar schemas or on a preference for symmetry do not seem to be totally convincing. We realize that it would be more satisfactory to provide a final answer to such questions, but science is based on generating ideas and testing them empirically. Sometimes we simply have to wait a bit before a correct solution is offered and tested. In other words, stay tuned.

The Body: Weight and Proportion

Considerable research has established that weight is a crucial factor is whether someone is perceived as attractive. As we saw in Chapter 4, females' appearance anxiety in relation to their weight is paralleled by other people's negative evaluations of those who are overweight. However, there is also evidence of cultural variation between cultures and across time in what has been considered attractive in terms of weight (e.g., Randall, 1995). Within Western society we need only go back over the past 100 years to see the variation in whether a rounded or a waif-like female shape is considered most desirable (see Figure 6.5) (Banner, 1983; Hatfield & Rapson, 1996; Randall, 1995).

Current interest has turned to body proportion rather than weight per se. Singh (1993) found that men are sensitive to a woman's **waist-to-hip ratio** (WHR)—waist measurement divided by hip measurement. His research using mostly outline drawings, found that a WHR of .7 in women was most preferred by men and rated by them as attractive, healthy, and well built to bear children. Singh (1995) also found that the WHR women find most attractive in men is .9. Women of quite varied ages, educational backgrounds, and income levels rated line drawings of men most favourably when they were in the normal range rather than being underweight or overweight. Results for female WHR were further confirmed among Chinese-Indonesian subjects in U.S. (Singh & Luis, 1995) and the assumption was made that this was a universal and evolved response.

Waist-to-Hip Ratio (WHR) Measurement of circumference of the waist relative to the hips. Calculated by dividing waist measurement by hip measurement. Hypothesized to be particularly important to evaluation of female attractiveness.

■ Cultural Change in Perception of an Attractive Body Weight for Women

FIGURE 6.5 Culture has an impact on the body weight that is seen as most attractive in a woman. As shown here, the ideal weight for a woman changed radically in the twentieth century.

Body Mass Index (BMI) Measurement of body weight relative to height. Calculated by dividing weight in kilograms by height in metres squared: BMI = weight (kg)/height (m)^2

However, subsequent research has thrown doubt on the significance of WHR in attraction. There is evidence that *weight* as measured by the **body-mass index** (BMI) is more important than WHR as an indicator of attractiveness in the West (e.g., Puhl & Boland, 2001; Tovee, & Cornelissen, 2001). Research has also found cultural variation in the importance of WHR in women as a function of contact with the West. WHR was found to have less impact on attractiveness rating, and BMI to have more, if cultures were more remote (Yu & Shepherd, 1998; Wetsman & Marlow, 1999). In all, research seems to be indicating that weight (as measured by the BMI) has greater impact on evaluation of women's attractiveness. Recent research has further suggested that the WHR may be inappropriate as an indicator of male health or reproductive fitness. Hughes and Gallup (2003) found that *shoulder-to-hip ratio* (SHR) is a better predictor of male sexual behaviour than WHR—specifically, the larger the shoulder circumference relative to the hips, the earlier and more numerous a man's sexual involvements.

Explanations for the importance of body type follow the lines above. As before, evolutionary explanations point to the association between body type and health or fecundity (the ability to be reproductive) in women. The suggestion is that preference for particular body types in a mate may have evolved because those who chose the body type most associated with health were more likely to pass their genes on to the next generation. For example, a slim waist (providing a lower WHR) can be an indication of health and youth, and also that a woman is not pregnant.

Research showing considerable cultural variation in perceptions of body proportion supports the cultural perspective, which emphasizes the influence of cultural norms about desirable body shape and would predict such variation. However, cultural differences can be accounted for in evolutionary theories if they take account of ecological factors and social structure (Anderson, et al., 1992). Increasingly, researchers investigating the relationship between body structure and attractiveness suggest an interaction of evolved tendencies and food scarcity in a culture—cultures with greater variation in food supply appear to have a preference for larger size in the female body (Furnham, Moutafi, & Baguma, 2002). In sum, body evaluations appear to depend upon the culture of the evaluator, the gender of both the evaluator and the target, and to take account of multiple factors such as weight, height, and the relative size of hips, waist, and shoulders.

Research overwhelmingly indicates that *external* factors such as proximity and appearance have a strong impact on evaluations of attractiveness. But research has also been interested in the *internal* cognitive and emotional processes that underlie attraction to another person. As emphasized in Chapter 2, affect and cognition can influence each other and this will be evident in the following section.

KEY POINTS

- Interpersonal attraction and interpersonal judgments are strongly influenced by various observable characteristics of those we meet, including *physical attractiveness*.
- People are found to like and to make positive attributions about attractive men and women of all ages, despite the fact that assumptions based on appearance are usually inaccurate.

- In general, evolutionary theory suggests that the features we find attractive in others are those associated with their health and *reproductive success*. Other research suggests that cultural beliefs have a strong impact on our stereotypes of attractiveness.

- Research has begun to identify some of the constituents of attractiveness, although there is also cultural variation. Among these characteristics are average and symmetrical facial features, body proportions related to the *waist-to-hip ratio*, and *body-mass index*.

Affect and Cognition in Attraction

A theme in this chapter is the idea that attraction is based on affective responses. This general concept, known as the **affect-centred model of attraction** (Byrne, 1992), combines the role of both cognitive and affective processes in attraction. Affective responses toward another person can result *indirectly* from association of the person with environmental events (such as pleasant or unpleasant music) or *directly* from the person themselves. For example, you may find pleasure in looking at someone you find beautiful, or the person might say something you like. The emphasis on affect does not mean, however, that cognitive processes are irrelevant. Cognitive processing of all available information also takes place. Because this information (including impressions, stereotypes, beliefs, and factual knowledge) can be affectively arousing, it contributes to the affect and in turn to the final evaluative response—liking or disliking the other person. We automatically form and store such evaluations in memory (Betsch et al., 2001).

> **Affect-Centred Model of Attraction** A conceptual framework in which attraction is assumed to be based on positive and negative emotions. These emotions can be aroused directly by another person, or indirectly through association with that person, and/or mediated by cognitive processes.

A great many quite varied experiments have consistently found that positive affect leads to positive evaluations of other people—liking—while negative affect leads to negative evaluations—disliking (Dovidio et al., 1995). As the affect-centred model of attraction suggests, affect influences attraction in two different ways. A *direct effect* occurs when another person says or does something that makes you feel good or bad. It is not surprising that you like someone who makes you feel good and dislike one who makes you feel bad (Downey & Damhave, 1991; Shapiro, Baumeister, & Kessler, 1991).

The other way in which affect influences us is less obvious. An *associated effect* occurs when another person is simply present at the moment your emotional state is positive or negative—for reasons that have nothing to do with the person to whom you are responding. Though he or she was not the cause of how you feel, you nevertheless tend to evaluate the other person on the basis of your own affective state. For example, if you meet a stranger on your way to a dental appointment, you are less inclined to like him or her than if you meet on your way to a long-anticipated new movie. We will now take a look at research dealing with both direct and associated effects of emotions.

Direct Effect of Emotions on Attraction

We have already described how the positive affect aroused by repeated exposure can determine liking. Attraction can also be based on affective reactions directly to a person's appearance, attitudes, and other attributes.

Even more direct and obvious effects are represented by studies showing that a student in an experiment likes the experimenter better if that person has administered rewards as opposed to punishments (McDonald, 1962). In addition, both males and females tend to dislike strangers who invade their personal space by choosing to sit inappropriately close in a library setting (Fisher & Byrne, 1975), and females dislike males who try to impress them with annoying opening lines such as

"Bet I can out-drink you" rather than a neutral opening such as "Hi" (Cunningham, 1989; Kleinke & Dean, 1990).

You can be sure that a stranger will like you better if you do or say something pleasant (e.g., "That's a beautiful dog you've got.") as opposed to something unpleasant (e.g., "Where did you find such an ugly mutt?").

Indirect Effects of Emotions on Attraction

Very often, our positive and negative feelings aren't based on what the individual with whom we are interacting has said or done. Instead, other sources of emotion, such as some recent experience, your physical state, or your current mood, influence not only

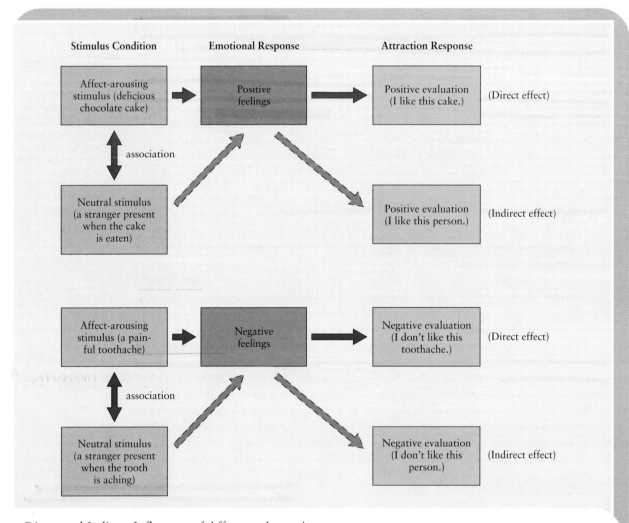

■ Direct and Indirect Influences of Affect on Attraction

FIGURE 6.6 When any stimulus (including a person) arouses positive affect, that stimulus is liked. If it arouses negative affect, it is disliked. This is a direct effect. An indirect effect occurs when any neutral stimulus (including a person) is present at the same time that affect is aroused by some unrelated source. The neutral stimulus becomes associated with the affect and is therefore liked or disliked. Such indirect effects represent a type of classical conditioning.

Source: Based on material in Byrne & Clore, 1970.

your feelings, but also your immediate evaluations of others. If another person just happens to be there when your feelings are positive, you tend to like that individual. If the person is present when your feelings are negative, your reaction tends to be one of dislike. The general idea is based on classical conditioning, as outlined in Figure 6.6 on the previous page.

Such indirect influences of affective state on attraction have been demonstrated in many experiments in which emotional states were manipulated in a wide variety of ways. Examples include subliminal presentation of pleasant versus unpleasant pictures (Krosnick et al., 1992), background music (May & Hamilton, 1980), radio news (Kaplan, 1981), and room lighting (Baron, Rea, & Daniels, 1992). In a similar way, existing positive versus negative mood states (not brought on by anything the experimenter did or by anything the other person did) also lead to positive versus negative evaluations of the other person (Berry & Hansen, 1996). In these and numerous other experiments, it has consistently been shown that positive affect results in positive evaluations (liking), while negative affect results in negative evaluations (disliking).

Taking this model a step further, the affect aroused by one person can become associated with a second person. If the affect is negative, such as when we have a prejudice against a particular type of person, anyone associating with this person can also be evaluated negatively—this is sometimes called _stigma by association_. Stigma refers to any characteristic of a person that at least some people don't like. Stigmas can include race, age, accent, physical disability or disease, unattractiveness, obesity, or sexual orientation (Frable, 1993; Neuberg et al., 1994; Rodin & Price, 1995). When an individual interacts with a stigmatized person, the experience is perceived as threatening, blood pressure increases, and performance is poorer (Blascovich et al., 2001). With continuing contact, however, the threat is diminished. As with any other type of prejudice (see Chapter 5), stigmatization is most often based on irrational assumptions. Nevertheless, the emotions that are aroused may be quite strong and easily transferred to someone else even though the second person does not share the stigma.

As we saw in previous chapters, cognitive processes often influence our emotions. An early study exploring this interplay is described in the following Cornerstones section.

Cornerstones

The Capilano Bridge Experiment:
Cognition and Emotion in Attraction

In the early 1970s, Don Dutton and Arthur Aron (1974), working at the University of British Columbia, were interested in a fundamental mechanism of attraction—the fact that it is often associated with intense emotional arousal. Further, in line with the expansion of interest in cognition at that time, they were interested in the possibility that our cognitions might lead us to misinterpret or mislabel our emotions. In fact, their _mislabelling hypothesis_ suggested that if you were in a state of emotional arousal when you met an attractive potential partner, this

arousal might be attributed to the attractive person— you would misinterpret your arousal as due to the person in front of you and conclude that you were strongly attracted.

They were able to take advantage of a field setting nearby where arousal was naturally varied (see Figure 6.7). The Capilano Canyon near Vancouver is a popular tourist attraction. It contains two types of bridge: one a suspension bridge, 1.5 metres wide and swaying 80 metres above a rocky canyon, and the other a broader bridge only 3 metres above a calm and shallow stream.

The researchers could be assured that people crossing the Capilano suspension bridge would feel considerably more arousal (fear) than those on the lower bridge. If the mislabelling hypothesis were correct, Dutton and Aron predicted that those crossing the suspension bridge (high arousal group) would be more likely to experience attraction if they encountered a potential partner, than those crossing the low bridge (low arousal group).

An attractive female interviewer asked males coming off both bridges if they would fill out a questionnaire, supposedly for her class psychology project concerned with the effects of scenic beauty on creativity. They were asked to write a small passage about an ambiguous picture presented to them, and then the interviewer offered each subject her telephone number in case they wanted more information about the study. We should also mention that the experiment was repeated with a male interviewer questioning male subjects.

Results supported the hypothesis: Men in the high arousal (suspension bridge) group showed greater sexual imagery in their written passages and were more than three times as likely to call the female interviewer than men in the low arousal (low bridge) group. Results for the male interviewer showed no significant difference between the high and low arousal conditions: the presence of a potential partner was necessary before arousal was interpreted as sexual attraction.

This study, now a classic in the attraction literature, demonstrated the importance of emotional arousal to the process of attraction, and the interplay of affect and cognition in our understanding of a social situation.

Since this study, research into the subtleties of affect in interpersonal attraction have continued. Over 20 years after the Capilano Bridge experiment, a meta-analysis summarizing the results of 33 studies on this topic confirmed that emotional arousal does intensify attraction (Foster et al., 1998). They also found that the mislabelling hypothesis could explain results but through an automatic cognitive process rather than through deliberate rational thought—evidently cognitive *mislabelling* of our emotions can occur instantly, and sometimes irrationally, in the highly charged field of sexual attraction.

■ Attraction on the Capilano Bridge

FIGURE 6.7 Dutton and Aron's classic research might suggest that people crossing this bridge have an increased likelihood of being attracted to others because of the increased emotional arousal that its great height induces.

To summarize, if two people are brought into repeated contact by proximity and experience relatively positive affect, they may both have formed positive impressions of each other. They are now at a transition point. They may simply remain superficial acquaintances who nod and perhaps say hello when they happen to see one another. Another possibility is that they may begin to converse from time to time, learn each other's names, and begin to exchange information about themselves, thus becoming close acquaintances. Which alternative is chosen may depend on the underlying *need for affiliation* of each individual.

The Need for Affiliation: The Motive to Relate to Others

A good part of our lives is spent interacting with other people, and this tendency to affiliate seems to have a neurobiological basis (Rowe, 1996). Human infants are apparently born with the motivation and the ability to make social relationships (Baldwin, 2000), and even newborns are predisposed to look toward faces in preference to other stimuli (Mondloch et al., 1999). The need to affiliate with others and to be accepted by them is hypothesized to be as basic to our psychological makeup as hunger and thirst are to our physical makeup (Baumeister & Leary, 1995). Presumably, it was a distinct advantage to our distant ancestors to interact socially in order to procure food, ward off danger, and reproduce.

People differ, of course, in the strength of this **need for affiliation,** and such differences constitute a relatively stable *trait* (or *disposition*). People seem to seek the amount of social contact that is optimal for them, preferring to be alone part of the time and in social situations part of the time (O'Connor & Rosenblood, 1996). Further, external events can at times arouse this motive in most of us, particularly collective events, such as sports games, festivals, and community disasters (Humphriss, 1989). In situations like this, total strangers begin to talk to one another and often come together to offer practical as well as emotional support.

Need for Affiliation
The motive to seek interpersonal relationships.

Beginning with the early work of Murray (1938), psychologists have investigated behavioural differences in those high and low in the need to affiliate. Some of these findings are summarized in Table 6.1.

Affiliation and Social Comparison

One underlying reason for responding to a stressful situation with affiliative behaviour was first recognized in the 1950s in the work of Asch (1954) and Schachter (1959)—affiliation provides an opportunity for us to compare our fears with other people's. In that decade, Leon Festinger developed his influential **theory of social comparison** (1954). He hypothesized that each human being has a drive to evaluate his or her opinions and abilities. While we will turn to objective criteria whenever possible, there are types of opinion or ability for which there are no objective standards. In this case, we use our social world as the basis for evaluation by comparing ourselves to others. That is, we make a *social comparison*. Further, we generally prefer to make such comparisons with others who are similar to ourselves. You cannot evaluate yourself very accurately if you compare yourself with someone who is too different from you.

Theory of Social Comparison
Festinger's influential theory of our tendency to evaluate our opinions and abilities based on comparison with other people and our preference for making comparisons with others similar to ourselves

Over the years, investigators have found differences in interpersonal behaviour that are associated with measures of affiliation need. Consistent with Murray's (1938) original definition of this disposition, an individual's need for affiliation is related to the tendency to form friendships and to socialize, to interact closely with others, to cooperate and communicate with others in a friendly way, and to fall in love.

TABLE 6.1 The Effect of Need for Affiliation on Social Behaviour

Individuals Who Are Comparatively High in the Need for Affiliation:

Write more letters and make more local telephone calls (Lansing & Heyns, 1959).

Laugh more and remain physically close to others (McAdams, 1979).

Avoid making negative comments to fellow workers (Exline, 1962).

Desire more dates per week and are more likely to be emotionally involved in a relationship (Morrison, 1954).

Are more likely to express a desire to marry right after college (Bickman, 1975).

Engage in fewer antisocial or negative acts with fellow workers. Spend less time alone (Constantian, 1981).

Are more likely to be described by other people as likable, natural, and enthusiastic (McAdams, 1979).

The first clear demonstration of the part played by social comparison in affiliation was provided by Schachter's classic (1959) study. Participants were told they would receive painful electric shocks, while others expected to receive only mild, tickling electrical stimulation. As they waited anxiously for this (nonexistent) procedure to begin, the participants were asked to indicate whether they preferred to remain alone or to spend the time with others. Many of those expecting pain preferred to wait with other participants, while those not expecting pain wanted to wait alone or expressed no preference. And Schachter concluded that the affiliative motive of his fearful participants was based on a need for social comparison: We want to compare our own anxieties with others who are in the same position. As he said, "misery doesn't love just any kind of company, it loves only miserable company" (Schachter, 1959, p. 24).

Evidence for the positive effects of such social comparison-based affiliation is provided by a study of patients before and after coronary bypass surgery (Kulik, Mahler, & Moore, 1996). Patients showed greatest affiliative behaviour (talking and asking for information) if their roommate was also a cardiac patient and if the individual was postoperative (rather than preoperative), because this type of roommate would give more opportunity for social comparison. In addition, patients having this opportunity experienced beneficial effects during recovery.

We should remember that social comparison is just one of a number of motives for affiliation. According to Hill (1987), we are also motivated to affiliate by our need for social support, as well as for attention and positive stimulation. Often we are drawn to other people not because we seek comfort and support but just because they are enjoyable—they can provide positive stimulation and attention.

KEY POINTS

- Individuals high, as opposed to low, in *need for affiliation* are more likely to engage in establishing and maintaining interpersonal relationships and are more interpersonally skilled.

- People can be differentiated with respect to their reasons for wanting to affiliate, and these reasons lead to different types of affiliative behaviour oriented toward different goals.

- Research related to the *theory of social comparison* suggests that we affiliate when anxious in order to compare our reactions with those of others; often this results in positive effects.

Building a Relationship: Self-Disclosure, Similarity and Reciprocity

What have we learned about attraction so far? Briefly, we know that once two people are brought together by physical proximity, the probability that they will like each other and establish some kind of relationship is increased if each (1) evaluates the appearance of the other favourably, (2) forms a positive first impression, (3) is in a positive emotional state, and (4) is motivated by affiliative needs. The next steps toward interpersonal intimacy involve communication. Three crucial aspects of this communication are the degree to which the acquaintances reveal information about themselves (show *self-disclosure*), discover areas of *similarity*, and the extent to which they show *reciprocity* in positive evaluations of one another.

Self-Disclosure: Growing Intimacy

One of the most important parts of building a relationship is conversation. As individuals begin to interact, they communicate information about themselves that is increasingly personal. This process of **self-disclosure** usually proceeds from communication of relatively superficial information about their occupation, background, and preferences, to progressively more intimate details of their lives, such as their relationships, their opinions and beliefs, their feelings, and perhaps their personal problems (Altman & Taylor, 1973; Jourard, 1968). In developing friendships, the progression towards greater intimacy tends to occur through reciprocal exchanges. One individual will disclose something at a more intimate level about himself or herself and the other person will reciprocate with greater intimacy. Many studies have confirmed that self-disclosure generally increases liking (Collins & Miller, 1994). When strangers are asked to engage in relationship-building activities such as self-disclosure in a laboratory interaction, they later express greater feelings of closeness (Aron et al., 1997). But this is only true if it is appropriate within the relationship (Miller, 1990). When one individual discloses too much, too soon, he or she is not liked to the same extent and is sometimes seen as maladjusted (Chaiken & Derlega, 1974).

Research shows gender and culture differences in self-disclosure as you might expect. A meta-analysis reviewing more that 200 studies of self-disclosure (Dindia & Allen, 1992) confirms the stereotype that females are more emotionally expressive—women are more willing to self-disclose than men, though the difference is not as great as the stereotype would suggest and depends on the type of relationship. In same-sex friendships, women friends do disclose more to each other than male friends. Women

Self-Disclosure The revelation of personal information about the self to another person. Seen as an integral part of the growing intimacy between two people who are becoming friends.

view talking and sharing personal confidences as an important and enjoyable part of the relationship, whereas men place greater emphasis on shared activities (Caldwell & Peplau, 1982). With opposite-sex relationships, particularly those of romantic partners or spouses, the self-disclosure differences between men and women are smaller. Both sexes expect some disclosure in such intimate relationships and there tend to be quite high and equal levels of disclosure among university couples (Rands & Levinger, 1979; Rubin, Hill, Peplau, & Dunkel Schetter, 1980).

Investigation of culture differences has shown that self-disclosure depends on cultural norms about *whom* it is appropriate to disclose to. In most Western cultures it is the norm for men to direct most of their self-disclosures towards the women in their lives rather than to same-sex friends. In many collective cultures, in contrast, where the roles of men and women are more separated, the norm for males is to confide in same-sex friends rather than the opposite sex, particularly before marriage. For example, in one study male students from Hong Kong and Jordan were compared with American students. Results showed that indeed the male students from collective cultures were more disclosing to other males than were American males (Reis & Wheeler, 1991).

Further, norms about the appropriateness of self-disclosure between members of an in-group and an out-group vary. The work of Gudykunst has shown that students from Japan, Hong Kong, and Taiwan showed more intimate disclosing communications with in-group members than with out-group individuals (Gudykunst, Gao, Schmidt, et al., 1992). However, Americans showed the same degree of disclosure to in-groups and out-groups. With so-called "confessional" television becoming commonplace in North America, this particular cultural difference is probably increasing.

KEY POINTS

- Relationship building involves increasingly close communication between individuals. One essential part of this process is *self-disclosure* as interactants reveal increasingly personal information about themselves.

- Research shows that women disclose somewhat more than men, particularly to same-sex friends. Cultural variation depends upon cultural norms about the appropriateness of disclosure to same- or opposite-sex interactants and to in-group or out-group members.

Similarity: We Like Those Most like Ourselves

Over 20 centuries ago, Aristotle described the nature of friendship and hypothesized that people who agree with one another become friends, while those with dissimilar attitudes do not. In books and movies opposites may attract, but in real life birds of a feather flock together. As tennis pro Bjorn Borg said of his new wife, "She's a great woman. She's just like me" (Milestones, 1989).

Attitude Similarity and Attraction

When people interact, their conversation often involves the expression of their attitudes about whatever topics come up—school, music, television shows, politics, religion, and so on. As people talk, each person indicates his or her likes and dislikes (Hatfield & Rapson, 1992; Kent, Davis, & Shapiro, 1981). Often people discover as they talk that they share the same attitudes about a range of topics. Research has specifically shown that each individual in the interaction responds to the other on the basis of the **proportion of similar attitudes** that are expressed. For example, we are equally attracted to someone

Proportion of Similar Attitudes
The number of topics on which two individuals hold the same views in relation to the total number of topics on which they compare their views. Expressed as a percentage or proportion: the number of topics on which there is agreement divided by the total number of topics discussed.

who has views like our own on two of the four topics we discuss or on 50 of the 100 topics we discuss; the proportion is 0.50 in each instance. The higher the proportion of similar attitudes, the greater the liking (Byrne & Nelson, 1965).

Critics have questioned one or more aspects of the concept of similarity-attraction (Bochner, 1991; Rosenbaum, 1986; Sunnafrank, 1992). One of the most challenging criticisms was offered by Rosenbaum (1986) with his **repulsion hypothesis**. Simply stated, he proposed that dissimilar attitudes decrease attraction but that similar attitudes have no effect (see Figure 6.8).

Research did not support the repulsion hypothesis in total. In fact, both similar and dissimilar attitudes have an impact on attraction (Smeaton, Byrne, & Murnen, 1989), though a slightly greater effect for dissimilar attitudes is found, particularly if we initially assume a stranger will hold similar attitudes (Chapman, 1992; Hoyle, 1993; Krueger & Clement, 1994). Because agreement is expected, we find disagreement surprising and it, therefore, has more impact on our evaluation of another person (Singh & Tan, 1992; Smeaton et al., 1995).

The wide-ranging generality of the similarity-attraction relationship holds for romantic college and university students and high school dropouts; for children and senior citizens; and for students representing a variety of cultures, including India, Japan, and Mexico, as well as the United States (Byrne et al., 1971). The tendency of people to form relationships on the basis of similarity has been termed the **matching hypothesis** and a mountain of research confirms its importance. Even on the Internet, people using e-mail exchange lists are likely to seek out others who share their views and to exclude those with dissimilar views (Schwartz, 1994). Others are better liked if they are similar to oneself in sociability (Joiner, 1994), marijuana smoking (Eisenman, 1985), religious affiliation (Kandel, 1978), personality traits and affective traits (Watson, Hubbard, & Wiese, 2000), self-concept (LaPrelle et al., 1990), traditional versus nontraditional gender roles (Smith, Byrne, & Fielding, 1995), being a "morning person" versus an "evening person" (Watts, 1982), and laughing at the same jokes (Cann, Calhoun, & Banks, 1995). Given the importance of similarity, theorists have questioned why this should be so.

Repulsion Hypothesis Rosenbaum's proposal that attraction is not enhanced by similar attitudes; instead, people initially respond positively to others but are repulsed by the discovery of dissimilar attitudes.

Matching Hypothesis The proposal that individuals are attracted to one another as friends, romantic partners, or spouses on the basis of similar attributes—physical attractiveness, age, race, personality characteristics, or social assets such as wealth, education, or power.

"Let's face it: you and this organization have never been a good fit."

■ Attraction to Similar Others and Rejection of Dissimilar Others

FIGURE 6.8 As unpleasant as the consequences often are, there seems to be a basic tendency to like those who are similar to oneself and to dislike those who are dissimilar.

Why Do We Care about Similarity?

Three possible explanations have been offered as to why people respond emotionally to the similar and dissimilar attitudes expressed by others.

The oldest formulation, **balance theory** (Heider, 1958), rests on the assumption that humans organize their likes and dislikes in a symmetrical way. *Balance* exists when two people like each other and agree about some topic (Newcomb, 1961). When they like each other and disagree, however, a state of *imbalance* is created, which is emotionally unpleasant (Orive, 1988). Each person attempts to restore balance through such means as changing attitudes, convincing the other person to change attitudes, or reducing liking (Monsour, Betty, & Kurzweil, 1993). When two people dislike each other, they are in a state of *nonbalance* and each is indifferent about the other's attitudes.

While balance theory leads to a number of interesting predictions about how people will respond to agreement and disagreement, it really doesn't explain why such information is important. A convincing answer is provided by Festinger's (1954) *social comparison theory*, which we discussed earlier. In effect, you compare your attitudes with those of other people because that is the only way to evaluate what you believe to be true. You turn to others to obtain **consensual validation** of your views about the world. According to this theory, as described earlier, when someone agrees with you, the agreement validates your views—provides "evidence" that you are correct. Not surprisingly, you like the person who makes you feel good about yourself. Disagreement has just the opposite effect and suggests that perhaps you have faulty judgment, are not too bright, and have poor taste. Such information makes you feel bad about yourself, and you dislike the other person. As discussed in Chapter 4, this idea fits with the evidence of a tendency to seek self-enhancement.

In a broader sense, however, the positive response to similarity of all kinds could be a very general one. According to *genetic similarity theory* (see Chapter 5), it may be based on an evolved tendency to respond most positively to those who are genetically similar to ourselves and most negatively to those who are genetically different (Rushton, 1989, 1990). From this and other similar perspectives (e.g., Porter, 1987), we act so as to maximize the survival of our own genes as well as the survival of the genes of whoever is most like us. We will explore some of the consequences of the positive response to similarity in the following section.

Reciprocity in Attraction: Mutual Liking

Having discovered similarities, a final confirmation is needed for a relationship to be established—the discovery that your liking is *reciprocated* by the other person (Condon & Crano, 1988). Sociologist Alvin Gouldner (1960) suggested that reciprocity is a fundamental and universal rule of all social relations—behaving to others as they have behaved to you. Whether this is true, reciprocity certainly intensifies attraction for human beings.

Most of us are pleased to receive positive feedback and displeased to receive negative evaluations (Gordon, 1996). Even relatively gentle or well-intentioned negative remarks (as suggested in Figure 6.9) are unlikely to be well received. The first signs of mutual liking are often nonverbal (see the discussion of nonverbal cues in Chapter 2). For example, when a woman converses with a man while maintaining eye contact and leaning toward him, he often interprets her behaviour (sometimes incorrectly) as an indication that she likes him, and so he may be attracted to her (Gold, Ryckman, & Mosley, 1984). As we saw above, reciprocal exchange of *self-disclosure* increases intimacy, in part because it increases the feeling of being liked and trusted (Derlega & Grzelak, 1979).

Balance Theory Theory that specifies the relationships among (1) an individual's liking for another person, (2) his or her attitude about a given topic, and (3) the other person's perceived attitude about the same topic.

Consensual Validation The perceived validation of one's views that is provided when someone else expresses identical views.

■ Positive Evaluations from Others Are Much Better than Even Well-Intended Negative Evaluations

FIGURE 6.9 We like to be liked and evaluated positively, and we hate to be disliked and evaluated negatively. When two people interact, even a mild, potentially helpful, and well-meant criticism can have a negative effect on emotions and hence on attraction.

"Theresa, what I am about to say should not be construed as criticism."

It seems very clear that we like those who like us, or who we believe like us. You may find it useful to consider several techniques that should lead people to like you, as outlined in the Ideas to Take with You feature at the end of the chapter. In the following chapter we will see that knowledge that liking tends to be reciprocated can be used as a technique of social influence—through flattery and ingratiation.

KEY POINTS

- One of the factors determining attraction is *similarity* of attitudes, beliefs, values, and interests. Though dissimilarity has a greater impact on attraction than similarity, we respond to both. The higher the *proportion of similar attitudes* (including beliefs, values, etc.), the greater the attraction.

- As the *matching hypothesis* suggests, people are most attracted to others who resemble them on a wide variety of dimensions. That is, we like, become friends with, date, and marry those who are similar to us.

- Explanations of the similarity effect include *balance theory*, the need for *consensual validation*, and the importance of genetic similarity.

- We also like other people who *reciprocate* our positive evaluations of them, either in what they say or in what they do; and we tend to dislike others who evaluate us negatively. In a great many situations, flattery will get you everywhere.

From Liking to Loving: Moving beyond Casual Friendships

Moving from acquaintance to romantic relationships, social psychological research in recent years has provided considerable information about what is involved in romance, love, and sexual intimacy. Note that as a relationship develops, each of these three components may or may not be involved; and they may take place simultaneously or in any sequence. Also, it is generally true that people who are successful in making friends and establishing close friendships are likely to be successful in forming romantic relationships (Connolly & Johnson, 1996).

Most of the following discussion will be based on research with heterosexual relationships, because most psychological research has dealt with such relationships. However, within the last two decades, as relationship research has become more diverse generally, focusing on a wider range of types of relationship, it has also begun to take account of sexual orientation. Where research has compared sexual orientations, the major differences found are not between gay and straight relationships but between the responses of males and females, regardless of their sexual orientation (Duffy & Rusbult, 1986; Kurdek, 1996, 1998; Peplau, 2003). For example, both homosexual and heterosexual men have the same expectations with respect to a romantic relationship, and these expectancies include having similar attitudes and values, providing mutual support, being honest and loyal, spending time together, sharing resources, and having something special together—"something magic" (Baccman, Folkesson, & Norlander, 1999). Although research continues, at this stage it is probably safe to say that the commonalities between gay and straight relationships are greater than the differences—the ecstasies and agonies of love are ones to which we can all relate.

Commonly, the beginning of romance is often the focus for more social anxiety than in friendship formation (Snell, 1998). University and college undergraduates say that they hesitate to "make the first move" because they fear rejection. Their judgments are often unrealistic, because each individual is searching for uncomplicated, totally positive feedback from the partner (Simpson, Ickes, & Blackstone, 1995). Another way to describe romance, then, is to say that such relationships are built in part on fantasy and positive illusions and that such illusions actually help to create better relationships (Martz et al., 1998; Murray & Holmes, 1997; Murray, Holmes, & Griffin, 1996). Perceptions of one's partner tend to be biased; the other person is perceived as being more like one's ideal self (see Chapter 4) than is actually the case (Klohnen & Mendelsohn, 1998). One consequence of these tendencies is that, as documented in the United States, Canada, and the Netherlands, as well as among Asian Canadians, couples judge their own relationships to be better than the relationships other people have (Buunk & van der Eijnden, 1997; Endo, Heine, & Lehman, 2000; Van Lange & Rusbult, 1995), especially when they are induced to think about the possible failure of their relationships (Rusbult et al., 2000). This emphasis on the positive makes it difficult for partners to imagine the relationship ever ending; as a result, their ability to predict how long the relationship will last is less accurate than predictions made by their roommates or their parents (MacDonald & Ross, 1999)—see Figure 6.10.

Passionate Love: The Basis of Romantic Relationships

Love can take many forms, but it is passionate love that is the focus of popular songs and has been the topic of most research (Hendricks & Hendricks, 1986). As we saw, proximity and similarity are major determinants of friendship. Love, in contrast, is

■ Predicting How Long a Relationship Will Last

FIGURE 6.10 The positive illusions that accompany falling in love make it difficult for the couple to see the possibility of failure. Research finds that roommates and parents are more accurate in their ability to predict how long a relationship will last.

much more likely to be precipitated by desirable aspects of the other person, such as an attractive appearance, pleasing personality, and reciprocal liking (Lamm, Wiesmann, & Keller, 1998). It is even possible to love someone who does not love you. This one-way flow of affection is known as *unrequited love*. In one large survey about 60 percent of respondents said that they had had such an experience within the past two years (Bringle & Winnick, 1992). Men in late adolescence and early adulthood report more instances of unrequited love than women do, and more instances of unrequited than of mutual love (Hill, Blakemore, & Drumm, 1997). The incidence of love that is not reciprocated is greatest among those whose attachment style is *preoccupied*—the individual feels ambivalent and insecure about relationships (Aron, Aron, & Allen, 1998). When unrequited love develops, the one who loves in vain feels rejected and loses self-esteem, while the one who fails to respond to the other's love feels guilty (Baumeister, Wotman, & Stillwell, 1993).

In any event, romance often begins as a sudden, intense, all-consuming response to another person. Phrases such as *falling head over heels in love* imply that love is an accident—something like slipping on a banana peel (Solomon, 1981). This kind of interpersonal response is labelled **passionate love** (Hatfield, 1988), one of several varieties of love that have been identified. A person experiencing passionate love tends to be preoccupied with his or her partner—and to perceive the love object as being perfect. Responses include sexual attraction, physiological arousal, the desire to be in constant contact, despair at the thought of the relationship ending, and the intense need to be loved in return. Hatfield and Sprecher (1986) developed the Passionate Love Scale to measure this emotion, with items such as "I would feel deep despair if _____ left me" and "For me, _____ is the perfect romantic partner."

Passionate Love An intense and often unrealistic emotional response to another person. When two individuals respond to one another in this way, they interpret their feelings as "true love," while observers often label their response as "infatuation."

Under the "right" conditions, passionate love can arise suddenly and without warning. Even a brief contact with a stranger can sometimes lead to love at first sight (Averill & Boothroyd, 1977). When two opposite-sex strangers in a laboratory experiment are simply asked to gaze into each other's eyes for two minutes, they are likely to report feelings of passionate love for each other (Kellerman, Lewis, & Laird, 1989). What is the explanation for this seemingly irrational response?

What's Love Got to Do with It? Cultural and Evolutionary Explanations

Why do we fall in love? Is it because our culture has taught us to expect it to happen or is it an inbuilt and instinctive response? This is essentially the distinction between the cultural approach to passionate relationships and the evolutionary approach. How much do our cultures and biology contribute to the experience of passionate love?

Culture's Contribution to Passionate Love

Three-Factor Theory of Passionate Love This theory suggests that for passionate love to develop, an individual must (1) come from a cultural background that teaches about love, (2) be in the presence of another person considered an appropriate love object by the culture, and (3) be physiologically aroused.

In an explanation that focuses on the cultural contribution to passionate love, Hatfield and Walster's (1981) **three-factor theory of passionate love** suggests that three conditions are necessary (see Figure 6.11). First, you must learn what love is and develop the expectation that it will happen to you (Dion & Dion, 1993). Beginning in early childhood, most of us are exposed to the idea that people fall in love and get married. Remember *Snow White* and *Cinderella*? If you were raised on such stories, how much did they shape your own expectations about love? The second condition required for the occurrence of passionate love is the presence of a culturally appropriate target person with whom one can fall in love. Cultural theorists propose that we have been taught by parents, movies, books, songs, and peers to seek an attractive partner of the

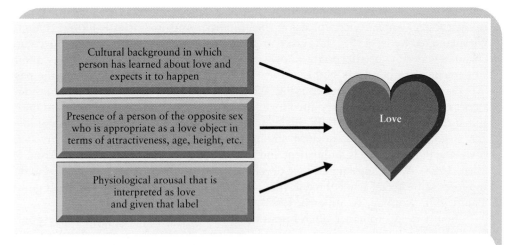

■ Love-Oriented Culture + Love Object + Arousal = Love

FIGURE 6.11 According to the three-factor theory of passionate love, love is likely to occur when three conditions are met. If you live in a culture that teaches you what love is, meet someone who is an appropriate love object, and are physiologically aroused, you may very well interpret your aroused state as indicating love. This process underlies the behaviour that has led to such familiar phrases as "love at first sight," "love is blind," and "head over heels in love." Sadly enough, passionate love is not likely to last, and enduring love requires a more realistic foundation.

opposite sex—someone similar to ourselves in most respects. Thus, we base our romantic choices on culturally prescribed criteria and problems often arise with our friends and relatives if we stray from that prescription.

The third requirement for passionate love is that a state of emotional arousal occur while the love object is present. If arousal occurs in the presence of an attractive person of the opposite sex, attraction, romantic feelings, and sexual desire often result (Foster et al., 1998). The Capilano Bridge experiment (Dutton & Aron, 1974) described earlier demonstrated that this arousal can involve the states as fear, and in other research it has been frustration and anger (Driscoll, Davis, & Lipetz, 1972). In such cases the term "passionate love" is simply a misattribution. When the arousal involves sexual excitement (Istvan, Griffitt, & Weidner, 1983), being "in love" may be a more accurate label for one's aroused state. Though it was long assumed that romantic love was invented in medieval Europe, today psychologists, historians, and anthropologists have become convinced that it is a universal phenomenon (Gray, 1993; Hatfield & Rapson, 1996).

Evolution's Contribution to Passionate Love

A second explanation of passionate love's apparently universal presence is based on *evolutionary theory* (Buss & Schmitt, 1993; Fisher, 1992). In evolutionary terms, survival of our species depended on reproductive success (Buss, 1999). That is, men and women had to be sexually attracted and also willing to invest time and effort in feeding and protecting their offspring. These two different but equally crucial aspects of reproductive success—sexuality and commitment—were enhanced among those humans whose physiology led them to seek and enjoy not only sexual satisfaction but also bonding between male and female and between parent and child. Note that animal research provides evidence of the effect of brain chemistry on pair bonding (Rensberger, 1993). With emotional attachments motivated by physiological underpinnings, early human male–female pairs became more than simply sex partners—they also liked and trusted one another and divided up the necessary tasks into hunting and gathering food versus caring for the children. Thus, according to this scenario, love enhances *reproductive success*. As a consequence, today's humans are genetically primed to seek sex, fall in love, and care for their children. Brain chemistry may underlie monogamy (Insel & Carter, 1995), and most young married adults expect their relationship to be a monogamous one (Wiederman & Allgeier, 1996).

Sexual Strategies: Gender Differences in Mate Choice

The evolutionary perspective above can explain why men and women have a similar tendency to fall in love; however, it does not explain why the genders differ in their romantic or sexual behaviours. For that we must turn to Buss's **sexual strategies theory** (Buss & Schmitt, 1993; Buss, 1999), the dominant evolutionary explanation for gender differences in behaviour (Miller, 1998). As mentioned in Chapter 4, this perspective suggests that differences in gender behaviour have evolved because the biology of reproduction requires differences in *parental investment* from the two sexes (Trivers, 1972). Females by necessity have the greater physical investment—they gestate and birth the child as well as provide food for the first months directly from their own bodies. They also have a greater restriction on the number of offspring they can produce. Males can be reproductive most of their adult life, while a female's reproductive years are limited, as are the number of offspring she can produce during that time—perhaps one a year at maximum. Trivers (1972) suggested that in animal species where there is a large inequality in parental investment, there would be divergent strategies for reproductive success. Specifically, the sex with the greater investment (usually, but not always, the

Sexual Strategies Theory An evolutionary theory suggesting that the two sexes will have evolved different reproductive strategies, due to differences in their physical investment in the process of reproduction.

female) will tend to be more careful and discriminating in mate choice, whereas the sex with the lesser investment (usually the male) will be more sexually indiscriminate and more competitive with its own sex for available members of the opposite sex.

From this basic idea, Buss (1994) developed a number of specific hypotheses about the differences we should find between men and women in their romantic and sexual choices or strategies. In general, he predicts that males will be more interested than females in short-term sexual relationships and will be attracted on the basis of characteristics that signal health and fecundity (e.g., youth and beauty, as discussed earlier in the chapter). Males can also seek a long-term relationship, as there are reproductive benefits that accrue with such a strategy. For example, if a male is willing to invest long term in a relationship, there is a greater likelihood of attracting a high-quality mate and more certainty that his offspring will survive. In such a case a male's criteria for a mate expand to include, for example, good quality genes, good parenting skills, and paternity confidence (confidence that the children he raises are in fact his own). Females, on the other hand, will be more likely to seek a long-term mate to help her in the arduous process of child-bearing and child-rearing and will be attracted to characteristics in a male that signal a capacity to provide long-term support—for example, his resources and status in the group. The cartoon in Figure 6.12 suggests how this female preference might be expressed today. Although it should be noted that *sexual strategies theory* also suggests that she would be looking for good genetic material to contribute to her offspring.

Evolutionary researchers have found a wide range of support for predictions derived from sexual strategies theory (Buss, 1999). For example, studies of undergraduate and graduate students indicate, as predicted by evolutionary theory, that men assess the sexual attractiveness of women on the basis of physical attributes, while women's ratings of male sexual attractiveness is based on social status (Townsend & Wasserman, 1997). Research also supports the observation that a male's income is positively associated with his desirability, especially as a marriage partner (Kenrick et al., 2001). A massive study of mate choice comparing 37 cultures around the world, found a pervasive male preference for young, healthy females and that females were more likely than males to desire mates with good financial prospects (Buss, 1994, 1998), and this is consistent with a biological explanation.

■ Mr. Right—Looks or Money?

FIGURE 6.12 From the evolutionary perspective, it makes reproductive sense for males to be programmed to emphasize the youth, health, and hence the attractiveness of potential mates. For women, reproductive success is better served by an emphasis on resources.

However, these same data found some cultural variation in the extent to which females placed importance on resource-rich mates, with the greatest importance found in cultures where women are less well educated and have less control over conception and family size (Kasser & Sharma, 1999). There was also variation in the extent to which chastity in a female is ranked as desirable (predicted on the basis of males' desire for paternity confidence). Both results are inconsistent with Buss's predictions and consistent with cultural theory.

Critics of sexual strategies theory have claimed that it underestimates human males' investment in reproduction. Males can also be considered to contribute physically through protection and hunting for the social group, activities that in early times would have put them at considerable risk. When this is taken into account, estimates of male and female investments are more equal. If this proved to be the case, we might expect greater similarity in the mating behaviours of males and females than sexual strategies theory has suggested and this is indeed what some critics claim (Gangestad & Simpson, 2000; Miller, Putcha-Bhagavatula, & Pendersen, 2002). One interesting development has been the recent acknowledgement that females are not as monogamous as had previously been thought (Greiling & Buss, 2000). In North America, for example, between 20 and 50 percent of married women report having affairs (e.g., Glass & Wright, 1992), and they will tend to do so when they are most fertile (Baker & Bellis, 1994). It appears that females as well as males engage in short-term mating strategies, though the evolutionary benefit for females is, as yet, unclear (Greiling & Buss, 2000).

Keep in mind that although we do not have a complete answer to the theoretical issues raised here, we can be sure that both evolution and culture contribute to passionate love (Hatfield & Rapson, 1996). What is being sorted out in the vigorous discussions between evolutionary and other researchers is the degree and level of influence of evolution and culture, and in exactly what way these factors influence our mating behaviours. Stay tuned for more developments.

KEY POINTS

- Romantic relationships differ from friendships in a number of ways. They tend to involve a number of illusions about the partner and the relationship.

- The basis for romantic relationships is often *passionate love*, an intense, overpowering emotional experience. The *three-factor theory* emphasizes the role of cultural socialization in passionate love, while evolutionary theory stresses its biological or genetic basis.

- *Sexual strategies theory* suggests that males and females will have evolved different reproductive strategies, due to differences in their physical investment in the process of reproduction. There is still dispute about the validity of this perspective.

Cultural Differences in Passionate Love

Canadian researchers Karen and Ken Dion at the University of Toronto are major figures in the field of relationships, particularly in the area of cultural differences. They suggest that different value orientations on the individualism–collectivism dimension will affect how people conceptualize love and intimacy (Dion & Dion, 1993). The idea of romantic or passionate love as the most important basis for marital relationships is seen as a particularly individualistic one, emphasizing the personal satisfaction and excitement to be gained from the relationship. However, in collectivistic societies where group benefits take precedence over individual, the personal satisfactions of romantic love will be viewed as less important. Here we find that family involvement in the choice of a partner is more likely, with a focus on how marital partners will benefit the extended family.

Their review of the literature (Dion and Dion, 1996) suggests that the younger generation in many of the developed Asian countries (e.g., Japan and Taiwan) is turning to more individualistic conceptions of romantic love. Further, we can expect that within a predominantly individualistic but multicultural society, such as Canada, there will be variations between subgroups in the extent to which they endorse the predominant values. In addition, there will be intergenerational differences as a function of exposure to Canadian society—that is, the extent of acculturation. Research is beginning to accumulate in support of these suggestions.

Typically, research shows that those in collectivistic countries are less likely to endorse romantic or passionate love styles than those in individualistic countries. For example, a study of college students in Japan, Germany, and the United States found that Japanese students placed much less value on romantic love than students in the two Western countries and they also saw being in love as a state of having primarily negative connotations—being in a dazed state and feeling jealous (Simmons, Von Kolke, & Shimizu, 1986). Within Canada, Dion and Dion (1993) found greater endorsement of friendship love among Chinese-Canadians than among European-Canadians. Chinese residents of Hong Kong place greater stress on the importance of *yuan*, the idea that love is predestined and a matter of fate. Belief in yuan is associated with logical and selfless love styles, which are fairly uncommon among Westerners (Goodwin & Findlay, 1997).

Those from Western cultures also tend to see romantic love as the basis for marriage (Hatfield & Rapson, 1996). Research has used the question "If a man (woman) had all the other qualities you desired, would you marry this person if you were not in love with him (her)?" to examine the importance of passionate love in marriage to those in different cultures. In one study of 11 cultures (Levine, Sato, Hashimoto, & Verna, 1994), those from the United States and England overwhelmingly answered "No" to this question, as would be expected from those in an individualistic society. In contrast, in India, Thailand, and Pakistan, traditionally collectivistic societies, the majority answered "Yes." Interestingly, around 60 percent of subjects from Japan and the Philippines answered "No." Dion and Dion suggest that this endorsement of love as the basis for marriage in Japan and the Philippines reflects an intergenerational difference in these cultures. The subjects for this study were largely students in their early 20s and appear to be becoming Westernized in their values. Yang (1986) has suggested a similar trend among the young Chinese of Hong Kong and Taiwan. He describes this generation as turning away from a "social orientation" and toward the "individual orientation" of the West—putting greater emphasis on personal gratification and self-expression.

The Many Forms of Love: Beyond Passion

Passionate love may be a common experience, but it is too intense to be maintained indefinitely. Love that is totally based on emotion is sufficiently fragile that simply being asked to think about a relationship and answer questions about it can interfere with one's feelings of love (Wilson & Kraft, 1993). Passionate love seems to thrive best when our fantasies are not interrupted by detailed, rational examination.

Other kinds of love can, however, be long lasting and able to survive rational inspection. Hatfield (1988, p. 205) describes companionate love as the "affection we feel for those with whom our lives are deeply entwined." Unlike passionate love, **companionate love** is based on a very close friendship in which two people are attracted, have a great deal in common, care about each other's well-being, and express mutual liking and respect (Caspi & Herbener, 1990). This is a kind of love that can sustain a relationship over time—even though it does not lend itself to many songs and movies.

Hendrick and Hendrick (1986) extended the conception of love by adding four additional "love styles" to passionate and companionate love, as shown in Table 6.2. Among the research findings involving the six love styles are indications that men endorse both passionate love and game-playing love more than women, while the reverse gender difference is found for companionate love, logical love, and possessive love (Hendrick et al., 1984). Women high in possessive love report high levels of verbal and physical aggression in their dating relationships (Bookwala, Frieze, & Grote, 1994). Game-playing love is most characteristic of those who are concerned with themselves and their own independence (Dion & Dion, 1991); this is considered the least satisfactory style, because it is associated with multiple sexual partners, unhappy relationships, loneliness, and coercive sexual behaviour (Hensley, 1996; Kalichman et al., 1993; Rotenberg & Korol, 1995). Very religious individuals are likely to be highest in friendship, logical, and selfless love (Hendrick & Hendrick, 1987). And in general, romantic partners tend to have similar love styles (Hendrick, Hendrick, & Adler, 1988; Morrow, Clark, & Brock, 1995).

Still another major conceptualization of love is Sternberg's (1986, 1988a, 1988b) **triangular model of love**. This formulation suggests that each love relationship contains three basic components (intimacy, passion, and commitment) that are present in varying degrees for different couples (Aron & Westbay, 1996). **Intimacy** is the closeness two people feel and the strength of the bond that holds them together. Partners high in intimacy are concerned with each other's welfare and happiness, and they value, like, count on, and understand one another. The second component,

Companionate Love Feelings of love that are based on friendship, mutual attraction, common interests, mutual respect, and concern for each other's happiness and welfare.

Triangular Model of Love Sternberg's formulation that conceptualizes love relationships in terms of the relative emphasis placed on intimacy, passion, and decision/commitment.

Intimacy In Sternberg's triangular model of love, the closeness or bondedness of two partners.

Hendrick and Hendrick (1986) have proposed six distinct styles of love. These include passionate and companionate (friendship) love, but they add four other possibilities. This table indicates the six "love styles" and presents sample items from a scale designed to measure each of them. People differ in the kind of love they feel, so the question of love style is a crucial issue for a couple attempting to work out a relationship that is satisfying to both.

TABLE 6.2 How Do I Love Thee? Six Styles of Love

Basic Love Styles	Sample Test Item
Eros: Passionate love	My lover and I were attracted to each other immediately after we first met.
Storge: Friendship love	Love is really a deep friendship, not a mysterious, mystical emotion.
Ludus: Game-playing love	I have sometimes had to keep two of my lovers from finding out about each other.
Mania: Possessive love	I cannot relax if I suspect that my lover is with someone else.
Pragma: Logical love	It is best to love someone with a similar background.
Agape: Selfless love	I would rather suffer myself than let my lover suffer.

Passion In Sternberg's triangular model of love, the sexual drives and sexual arousal associated with an interpersonal relationship.

Decision/Commitment In Sternberg's triangular model of love, the cognitive elements involved in deciding to form a relationship and in being committed to it.

passion, is based on romance, physical attraction, and sexuality. **Decision/commitment** is the third component, representing cognitive factors such as the decision that you love the other person and the commitment to maintain the relationship. Actual lovers subjectively experience these three components as overlapping and related aspects of love. When all three components are present for a couple, the relationship is likely to be a long-lasting one (Whitley, 1993); and when all three components are strong and equally balanced, the result is *consummate love.*

Now that we have discussed the many varieties of love, you may find it useful to think about some of the love-related issues that are raised in the Ideas to Take with You feature near the end of the chapter.

KEY POINTS

- There are cultural differences in attitudes to passionate love. Those from individualistic cultures tend to value passionate love and see it as the basis for marriage to a greater extent.

- Love can take many forms. A close, caring friendship is labelled *companionate love*—a less intense and more lasting state than passionate love. Hendrick and Hendrick describe six love styles: Passionate, friendship, game-playing, possessive, logical and selfless.

- Sternberg's *triangular model of love* describes love as a blend of three possible components: *intimacy, passion,* and *decision/commitment.*

Long-Term Close Relationships

When university and college students are asked to identify the one person in the world to whom they feel most close, they describe one of three types of relationship (Berscheid, Snyder, & Omoto, 1989). Some (14 percent) specify a family member, 36 percent identify a friend, and almost half (47 percent) name a romantic partner. Canadian undergraduates reported close attachment relationships with an average of about five individuals, including family members, romantic partners, and friends (Trinke & Bartholomew, 1997). At the basis of any close relationship are the individuals' *attachment styles,* the enduring patterns of relating that individuals show.

Four-Category Model of Adult Attachment Bartholomew's theory of adult attachment styles, in which a person's pattern of relationships with others stems from the individual's model of the self (positive or negative) and model of others (positive or negative). These two dimensions produce four categories of attachment style: secure, preoccupied, dismissing, and fearful-avoidant.

Adult Attachment Patterns

Observations of different infant–mother attachment styles led Hazan and Shaver (1990) to propose that adults follow similar attachment patterns in forming relationships with their peers in romantic or friendship relationships. A recent model developed by Kim Bartholomew of Simon Fraser University is the **four-category model of adult attachment** (Bartholomew, 1990, 1993; Bartholomew & Horowitz, 1991). Basing her model on the original writings of John Bowlby on attachment in children (1973), Bartholomew proposes that adult attachment patterns can be conceptualized as derived from two related dimensions: (1) the positivity of the individual's model of the self (the extent to which the individual's self-concept is characterized by anxiety related to the self); and (2) the positivity of the individual's model of others in general (the extent to which the orientation to others is avoidant). Table 6.3 shows the four categories of adult attachment that result from these two dimensions: *secure, preoccupied,*

The pattern that adults demonstrate depends on the positivity of their model of the self and the positivity of their model of others.

TABLE 6.3 The Four-Category Theory of Adult Attachment

	Model of Self	
	Positive (Low Anxiety)	**Negative (High Anxiety)**
Positive (Model of Others)	**Secure Pattern** "It's easy for me to become emotionally close to others. I am comfortable depending on them and having them depend on me. I don't worry about being alone or having others not accept me."	**Preoccupied Pattern** "I want to be completely emotionally intimate with others, but I often find that others are reluctant to get as close as I would like. I am uncomfortable being without close relationships, but I sometimes worry that others don't value me as much as I value them."
Negative (Model of Others)	**Dismissing Pattern** "I am comfortable without close emotional relationships. It is very important to me to feel independent and self-sufficient, and I prefer not to depend on others or have others depend on me."	**Fearful-Avoidant Pattern** "I am uncomfortable getting close to others. I want emotionally close relationships, but I find it difficult to trust others completely, or to depend on them. I worry that I will be hurt if I allow myself to become too close to others

Source: Based on Bartholomew & Horowitz, 1991.

dismissing, and fearful-avoidant. Beneath each one is the description used in research to define that particular type of attachment to others in general (Griffin & Bartholomew, 1994). Most people, rather than showing a single type of response pattern, display elements of two or more (Bartholomew & Horowitz, 1991). Of these attachment styles, only the secure style is likely to enable individuals to form long-lasting, committed, satisfying relationships (Shaver & Brennan, 1992). Research indicates that self-reports of cold or inconsistent relationships with one's parents are associated with later avoidant and/or preoccupied romantic attachments, whereas parental relationships described as warm are associated with secure romantic attachments (Bringle & Bagby, 1992).

Attachment Style and Relating

It is generally true that attachment style is most likely to influence social interaction when such interaction is with those who are close or potentially close to you (Pietromonaco & Barrett, 1997). Research shows that *secure* individuals express trust in their partners (Mikulincer, 1998b) and are able to engage in collaborative problem solving with their partners (Lopez et al., 1997). It has been argued that a secure attachment style is roughly equivalent to the concept of androgyny that was described in Chapter 4—an ideal combination of masculine and feminine characteristics (Shaver et al., 1996). A person with a secure style tends not only to have a warm relationship with parents (Bringle & Bagby, 1992) but (in adulthood) to describe both his or her original and new families in positive and nonpunitive terms (Diehl et al., 1998; Levy, Blatt, & Shaver, 1998) and to provide warmth and security for his or her own offspring (Scher & Mayseless, 1994). Compared to the people with other attachment styles, secure individuals are less prone to becoming angry, attribute less hostile intent to others, and expect more positive and constructive outcomes when an angry interaction occurs (Mikulincer, 1998a). Altogether, such individuals get along well with people, feel close to their parents, and express positive feelings about relationships (McGowan et al., 1999b). Compared to people with other attachment styles, secure individuals have a more balanced, complex, and coherent self-concept (Mikulincer, 1995). As you might guess from the descriptions of the four attachment styles, people prefer a secure romantic partner over any of the other three, regardless of their own attachment style (Chappell & Davis, 1998; Latty-Mann & Davis, 1996).

University and college students who are *fearful-avoidant* describe their parents as punitive and malicious (Levy et al., 1998). Among the characteristics of these individuals are a high level of hostility and a failure to realize when they are becoming angry (Mikulincer, 1998a). Fearful-avoidant people also explain interpersonal events in a negative way and defend themselves from emotional distress by failing to recall emotional experiences (Fraley, Garner, & Shaver, 2000). Perhaps as a result, they report less intimacy and enjoyment in interacting with the opposite sex (Tidwell, Reis, & Shaver, 1996), more jealousy, and a greater likelihood of using alcohol to reduce anxiety in social situations (McGowan et al., 1999b).

Preoccupied persons, along with those who are fearful-avoidant, are prone to feelings of shame in their relationships (Lopez et al., 1997). In responding to events in a relationship, preoccupied individuals interpret what is going on in more negative ways than do secure individuals, report more emotional distress, and expect more conflict (Collins, 1996). Both *dismissing* and fearful-avoidant individuals evaluate relationships in negative terms, tend to avoid face-to-face interactions in favour of impersonal contacts such as e-mail, and are more likely to drink alone (McGowan et al., 1999b).

Though there is considerable consistency across the life span (Klohnen & Bera, 1998) and between different generations in the same family (Benoit & Parker, 2000), there is also evidence that the security of one's attachment varies depending upon the particular relationship considered (La Guardia et al., 2000). Our attachment styles can be changed by good and bad relationship experiences (Brennan & Bosson, 1998; Shaver & Hazan, 1994). For example, dating couples were studied on two occasions over a five-month period. Among those who experienced a breakup during that time period, secure attachment *decreased;* secure attachment increased when the couple remained in a relationship (Ruvolo, Fabin, & Ruvolo, 2001).

Recently, interest has turned to how the Internet will impact the pattern of our social lives. One question raised is whether the proliferation of Internet relationships will enrich our social lives or reduce our connections with those around us. The following On the Applied Side section discusses this issue.

On the **Applied Side**

Relating on the Net: Positive or Negative Social Impacts?

In 2001, 60 percent of Canadian households had at least one member who uses the Internet, and this figure rises each year. These users are most likely to have higher than average income and education, and to be below 55 years of age (Statistics Canada, 2003). While the Internet enables us to have wider access to people we could not possibly meet through face-to-

face contact, it is also a new form of interacting. For social psychologists this provides an intriguing context for studying a new type of relationship formation. Research beginning in the mid-1990s investigated one central question—whether the effect of the Internet on our social lives is positive (enriching our connections to others) or negative (leading to impoverishment of our social lives and greater isolation) (Parks & Floyd, 1996).

Those who suggested a positive social impact of the Internet pointed to the fact that not only can it broaden a person's social contacts, but that many common barriers to communication have less impact on the Net—barriers such as social anxiety, being stigmatized due to a disability, social class and convention, and stereotyping. From this perspective the context of Internet communication is seen as a great liberalizer and equalizer of interpersonal relations (e.g., Berry, 1993; Rheingold, 1993).

Those who took a more negative view saw many of these social benefits as illusory (e.g., Civin, 1999). They claimed that the individual may have a wider circle of contacts, but that the relationships formed on the Net will tend to be more shallow and less developed. Further, extensive Internet use might detract from the investment of time and effort into local relationships with family, friends, and community, and those relationships may suffer (Kraut, Patterson, Lundmark, Kiesler, Mukhopadhyay, & Scherlis, 1998).

Initial research, using subjects who were introduced to the Internet and then followed over two years, seemed to indicate a widespread, but mild, negative effect such that those who spent more time on the Net became somewhat more depressed and lonely (Kraut et al., 1998). However, in a follow-up for a further year, that negative effect had disappeared—except for a remaining higher level of stress with greater Internet use (Kraut et al., 2002).

Now it is generally accepted that the Internet is not in itself a negative force in peoples' social lives (Tyler, 2002). Its effects depend on the way in which it is used and the type of individuals who are using it (McKenna & Bargh, 2000). Among the qualities of Internet communication that McKenna and colleagues (McKenna, Green & Gleason, 2002) suggest facilitate social relationships is its relative *anonymity*, which can enhance self-disclosure. As we saw earlier, *self-disclosure* (revealing personal information about yourself) increases the intimacy in a relationship and the suggestion is that this can occur faster with online acquaintances because anonymity removes many of the usual barriers.

But does faster self-disclosure bring faster liking and closer relationships? In one study by McKenna and colleagues, male and female undergraduates who did not know each other were randomly paired for two 20-minute meetings. Meetings were either face-to-face both times (*face-to-face condition*) or Internet initiated in the first meeting, then face-to-face for the second (*Internet condition*). All participants were instructed to get acquainted with one another. They assessed their partner and the interaction after each meeting using a 14-point scale to

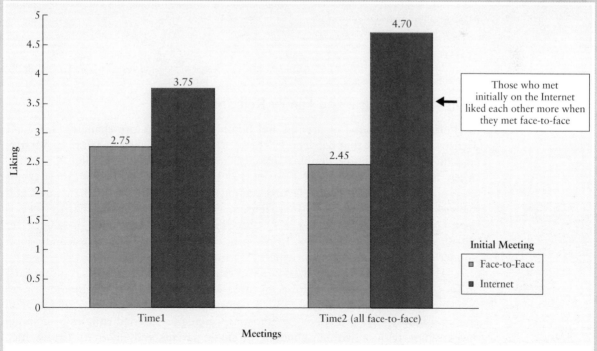

■ Relating on the Net versus Relating Face-to-Face

FIGURE 6.13 Those who first (Time 1) became acquainted on the Internet liked each other more when meeting face-to-face (Time 2), compared to those who had met twice (both Time 1 and 2) face-to-face.

measure liking (ranging from strong dislike at –7 to strong liking at +7) and a similar scale to assess perceptions of the intimacy level established.

Results, shown in Figure 6.13, indicated greater liking for the partner in the Internet condition. When the relationship was initiated on the Internet, subjects liked their partner more than if the initial contact was face-to-face. Further, at the second meeting (Time 2), which was face-to-face for all subjects, those in the Internet condition showed a significant increase in liking for their partner, whereas those in the face-to-face condition showed no increase in liking. The quality of the interactions also differed as a function of whether the Internet was involved. Those who interacted on the Net reported that they had been more intimate in their communications—they felt they knew their partner better and were more likely to have told their partners what they liked about them. These findings support the researchers suggestion that communication via the Internet facilitates more self-disclosure and the formation of relationships.

However, interaction was for a total of 40 minutes in this study. Would real-life spontaneous contacts made on the Net develop into close relationships or remain superficial? In order to examine this issue, the same researchers followed 568 subjects who were taking part in common-interest newsgroups over two years. Most subjects reported that their online relationships had gone beyond casual acquaintances—the largest groups being close friends or romantic partners—and these relationships were reported to have developed faster, compared to face-to-face. For example, 63 percent had spoken on the telephone to someone they met online, and 54 percent had met face-to-face for an average of eight times. In addition, these online relationships remained fairly stable over the two years of the study. Of the people the researchers managed to contact again two years later (only 214 of the original sample), 75 percent of them had maintained their relationship and for 54 percent it had become closer. In particular 71 percent of all romantic relationships were intact after two years. In sum, results showed that the formation of relationships was facilitated by initial Internet communication and these relationships frequently moved into long-term real-life contact.

Before you assume that the Internet is purely beneficial, one major concern is that people are more willing to misrepresent themselves online than in face-to-face relationships (Cornwell & Lundgren, 2001). Further, adolescents who are troubled or lonely have a greater tendency to form their closest relationships with strangers on the Net, putting them at risk from predators (Gross, Juvonen, & Gable, 2002; Wolak, Mitchell, & Finkelhor, 2003).

Nonetheless, if used with caution, the absence of social barriers and the anonymity of communication on the Internet can help people to express themselves and make real connections with others. Ultimately, as McKenna and Bargh (2000) point out, like all past technological advances, the Internet can be used for good or evil—it's up to the users.

Long-Term Spousal and Family Relationships

It is clear that patterns of marital and family relationships are changing in Canada. Census figures show that between 1971 and 1996 the marriage rate fell from 8.9 to 5.3 and divorce rates almost doubled from 1.3 to 2.5 per 1000 population (Che-Alford, Allen, & Butlin, 1994; Statistics Canada, 1999). In addition, the proportion of couples choosing not to marry in their first conjugal relationships more than quadrupled between the 1970s and 2001—see Figure 6.14. Incidentally, the proportion of common-law relationships is higher in Quebec: for example, 70 percent of women aged 30–39 years chose common-law. Apparently, common-law was accepted and adopted sooner in Quebec than other provinces (Statistics Canada, 2002).

However, this definitely doesn't mean that marriage or family life is disappearing in Canada. First of all, the majority of those who choose to live in common-law relationships will eventually marry (73–78 percent). Second, the majority of Canadians live in a family setting (defined by Statistics Canada as married couples or common-law couples, with or without children, or single parents and children). Family life in Canada has slowly evolved from the extended family, common at the beginning of the twentieth century, to the two-parent "nuclear" family of the mid-twentieth century that remains the dominant form at the beginning of the twenty-first century. What has changed is the number of divorces and the number of second marriages (legal or common law), both of which are increasing steadily. This has the effect of increasing the

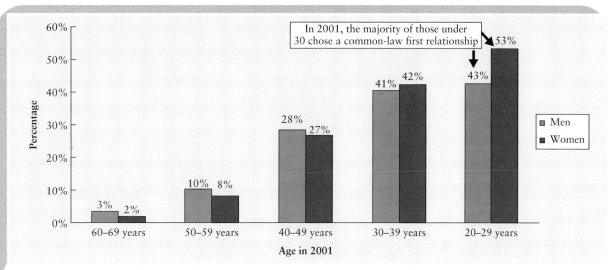

In 2001, the majority of those under 30 chose a common-law first relationship

■ Men
■ Women

Age in 2001

■ Common-Law First Relationships Become More Common in Canada

FIGURE 6.14 For the first time in 2001, the General Social Survey found that the majority of 20- to 29-year-olds in a relationship chose common-law as their first union. This compares with less than 5 percent of those aged 60–69 years in 2001 who had chosen common-law as their first union. However, the vast majority (73–78 percent) of couples living common-law will marry at some point in their conjugal life.

Source: The General Social Survey, 2001: *The Daily*, July 11, 2002, Statistics Canada.

number of step- and blended families (where children live with one of their own parents and with a stepparent, or with the stepparent and his or her children). For example, stepfamilies increased from 10 percent of all couples in 1995 to 12 percent in 2001 (Statistics Canada, 2002). Though taking different forms, we can say that the family is alive and well in Canada.

Whatever the composition of the family, one of life's greatest challenges continues to be finding happiness in such relationships and discovering how to avoid dispute or breakup.

Similarity and Assumed Similarity in Long-Term Relationships

Not surprisingly, a century of research has indicated consistently that spouses are similar in their attitudes, values, interests, and other attributes (Pearson & Lee, 1903; Terman & Buttenwieser, 1935a, 1935b; Smith et al., 1993). Further, a longitudinal study of couples from the time they became engaged through 20 years of marriage indicated very little change in the degree of similarity over time (Caspi, Herbener, & Ozer, 1992). In other words, similar people marry, and the similarity neither increases nor decreases as the years pass. Because greater similarity is associated with a positive relationship (Acitelli, Kenny, & Weiner, 2001; Nemechek & Olson, 1999), a couple contemplating marriage might do well to think beyond physical attractiveness and sex in order to look closely at their similarities and dissimilarities.

Not only do similar people marry, but a positive relationship is also characterized by **assumed similarity**. Spouses tend to assume greater similarity than is actually the case (Byrne & Blaylock, 1963; Schul & Vinokur, 2000), and marital satisfaction is positively related to both similarity and assumed similarity.

Assumed Similarity
The extent to which two people believe they are similar in certain respects, as opposed to the extent to which they are actually similar.

Are similarity and assumed similarity equally strong in other kinds of relationships? Watson, Hubbard, and Wiese (2000) answered this question by comparing married couples, dating couples, and friendship pairs with respect to the Big Five Personality Dispositions and for measures of positive and negative affect. The pairs of individuals in each type of relationship were more similar than chance, but the spouses were more similar than were the dating couples or friends. Assumed similarity, however, was highest in the dating couples, perhaps reflecting the romantic illusions we discussed earlier. Friends and spouses were slightly more realistic. If married couples indicate more actual similarity and less assumed similarity than is true for dating couples, this suggests that many couples are making relatively wise and realistic decisions before deciding on marriage. It has also been shown that close and well-adjusted couples are more likely to make momentary changes in their expressed attitudes so that they become more similar to their partners, particularly if the issue is one that is important to the partner (Davis & Rusbult, 2001).

Relationship Patterns among Long-Term Couples

A common question for long-term couples and for those studying them is the degree to which the partners are content with their relationship. Do people ever live happily ever after? Or are they often disappointed by the realities of spending a lifetime with a given spouse? Let's look at a few of the factors that influence marital satisfaction.

Surveys consistently indicate that for long-term couples sexual interactions become less frequent over time, and the most rapid decline occurs during the first four years of marriage (Udry, 1980). Nevertheless, 41 percent of all couples have sex twice a week or more often, whereas only 23 percent of single individuals have sex that frequently. Cohabiting, rather than legally married, couples are the most sexually active category, however, in that 56 percent have sex at least twice a week (Laumann et al., 1994; Michael et al., 1994). One reason, of course, is that unmarried couples who live together are usually within the early years of their sexual relationship. With respect to the relationship in general and to sexuality specifically, parenthood can create problems (Alexander & Higgins, 1993; Hackel & Ruble, 1992), although the majority of parents also report they enjoy the experience (Feldman & Nash, 1984). With multiple children, women report less and men report more marital satisfaction (Grote, Frieze, & Stone, 1996). Becoming a parent is also accompanied by a decrease in feelings of passionate love (Tucker & Aron, 1993).

It is not surprising that passionate love tends to decrease over the years (Tucker & Aron, 1993), but Aron and Henkemeyer (1995) found that women who still felt passionate love after the passage of several years were more satisfied with their marriages than women who no longer had these feelings. Male satisfaction with the marriage was unrelated to feelings of passionate love. For both men and women, satisfaction is related to behaviour that suggests companionate love—sharing activities, exchanging ideas, laughing together, and working together on projects (Lauer & Lauer, 1985).

A major task for both spouses is discovering how best to adjust to the demands of a two-career family (Gilbert, 1993; Helson & Roberts, 1992). Any married individual who is employed faces a potential conflict between the motivation to do a good job at work and the motivation to engage in family activities (Senecal, Vallerand, & Guay, 2001). One major issue in many households is housework. As shown in Figure 6.15, when Canadian couples have no children, women do over 60 percent more housework than men, and the gap is even wider when children enter the picture. Even when the number of hours of outside employment is controlled for,

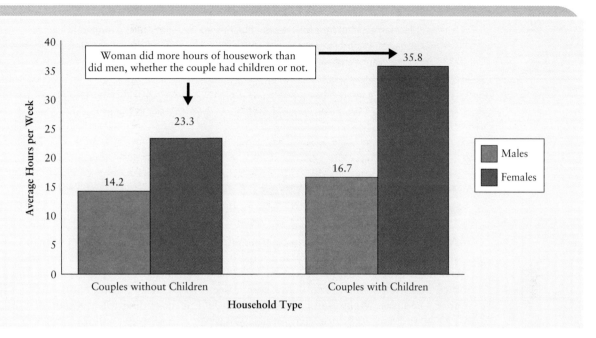

Woman did more hours of housework than did men, whether the couple had children or not.

■ Hours of Housework among Canadian Couples

FIGURE 6.15 As more and more Canadian households contain dual-career families, the issue of who does what in the house becomes increasingly relevant. The *General Social Survey* of Statistics Canada (1992) found that women do considerably more housework than men. Of course, overall more women stay home and have fewer hours of paid external employment relative to men. But even when these factors are controlled statistically, women's hours of housework are still much greater than men's.

Source: Adapted from McQuillan & Belle, 1999; Statistics Canada, *General Social Survey*, 1992.

women still contributed over 50 percent more hours of housework than men (McQuillan & Belle, 1999). In fact, compared to heterosexual and gay couples, only lesbian pairs seem able to share household labour in a fair manner (Kurdek, 1993). Perceived unfairness in the division of chores is associated with marital conflict and dissatisfaction (Grote & Clark, 2001), and many general stressors concerned with maintaining a household can add to that (Fincham, 2003).

KEY POINTS

- Adults' *attachment styles* reflects their positive and negative feelings about the self and others. This conceptualization yields four attachment styles that are labelled *secure, dismissing, fearful-avoidant,* and *preoccupied.* Individuals who are secure are best able to form long-lasting, committed, satisfying relationships.

- Research on the effects of Internet relationships suggests this medium may enhance self-disclosure and speed up friendship formation. However, there will be individual differences.

- Despite an increase in the divorce rate and common-law relationships, most people marry or form a long-term relationship. Similarity and *assumed similarity* between partners is greater than would be expected by chance, and the greater the similarity the more satisfying the relationship.

- Relationship patterns among married people change over time in terms of the frequency of marital sex and the predominance of passionate love. Couples must often cope with the demands of a two-career family and with the pressures of child-rearing.

Troubled Relationships: From Dissatisfaction to Dissolution

People usually enter long-term relationships with high hopes. So, each year in Canada about 160,000 couples marry and most of them are convinced that their marriage will last. However, in each year another 75,000 couples divorce. People can change after they become partners, and many people seem to be nicer during courtship than they are as spouses. Maintaining a relationship is a never-ending job (Harvey & Omarzu, 1997), and success is not guaranteed. Whatever the problem, solutions may be possible, but couples differ in how well they deal with them. In this section, we will explore some major sources of conflict, possible ways to prevent or resolve problems, and some of the consequences of a broken relationship.

Problems in Relationships, and Possible Solutions

What happens to transform a loving romantic relationship into one characterized by unhappiness, dissatisfaction, and—sometimes—hate? People who believe they are ideally suited for one another can discover that there are negative as well as positive elements in the relationship. Studies of married couples indicate that most report having disagreements regularly (from more than once a week to monthly), while only 1.2 percent say they *never* have disagreements (McGonagle, Kessler, & Schilling, 1992).

Discovering Dissimilarities
The genders tend to have different sources of dissatisfaction in the relationship. While some behaviours are equally upsetting to both sexes (e.g., unfaithfulness), others are more annoying to one sex than to the other. Buss (1989a) asked several hundred men and women to describe the source of their conflicts with a romantic partner. Generally, women become upset if their partners are not loving and gently protective, while men become upset if their partners reject them sexually or ignore them.

Because no partner (including oneself) is perfect, spouses who once believed that they were ideally suited for each other almost inevitably come to realize that there are negative as well as positive elements in the relationship. Spouses greatly overestimate how much they are in agreement about most matters (Byrne & Blaylock, 1963), and they are then disappointed when they discover that their views actually differ (Sillars et al., 1994). *Secure* individuals are most accurate in perceiving how similar they are to another individual, while those who are *fearful-avoidant* underestimate and those who are *preoccupied* overestimate similarity (Mikulincer, Orbach, & Iavnieli, 1998).

Even personal characteristics that once seemed to be especially positive attributes of the future spouse can become a primary reason for disliking him or her as time passes (Felmlee, 1995; Pines, 1997). For example, dissimilarity from oneself may seem interesting and intriguing in a romantic partner, but this can eventually become a source of distress and dislike. Early in the relationship, some things the other person says or does may seem cute. Later on, what was once cute becomes annoying. Felmlee's (1998) research suggests that if you are drawn to someone because that person is very different from yourself or even unique, chances are good that disenchantment will set in over time. One obvious solution is for two individuals to know as much as possible about one another early in the relationship (Byrne & Murnen, 1988).

Destructive Forms of Behaviour and Communication

Problems in a relationship are often accompanied by increases in abusive or destructive communications and behaviours. Even in the healthiest relationships conflicts arise. When people take the time to consider the long-term consequences for the relationship, a constructive response is more likely to follow (Yovetich & Rusbult, 1994). For example, when one partner makes the effort to apologize for something that was said or done and the other makes the effort to indicate forgiveness, they have engaged in constructive behaviour (Azar, 1997; McCullough, Worthington, & Rachal, 1997). Less obviously, those who learn simply to give in are more likely to have happy, stable marriages (Maugh, 1998). Marital disagreement is not a sport in which you need to score points or win every time. Couples interact in a more favourable way if each individual responds to the other person's need to maintain a positive self-evaluation (Mendolia, Beach, & Tesser, 1996) and works to understand the partner's perspective when problems arise (Arriaga & Rusbult, 1998). The most general characteristic of people who deal well with interpersonal conflict is agreeableness (Graziano, Jensen-Campbell, & Hair, 1996).

Destructive patterns of communication can arise over time when partners shift from providing one another with positive evaluations to words and deeds that indicate negative evaluations. Dating couples and newlyweds frequently express their positive feelings about one another. Gradually, however, quite different expressions of feeling occur. It is easy enough to think (or say), "I don't have to tell you I love you; I married you, didn't I?" Other indications of love can also fade away, as in "You don't bring me flowers anymore." Miller (1991) suggests that we become rude and impolite to intimate partners for three reasons. (1) In an intimate relationship there is more opportunity to discover a mate's many trivial imperfections than in other relationships, in part because each person feels confident of being accepted by the partner, feels less need for impression management, and so relaxes and becomes "himself" or "herself." (2) When the other person's flaws become apparent, misplaced expectations lead each spouse naïvely to assume that the other will change for the better; it is frustrating and annoying when change doesn't occur—and it usually doesn't. (3) It is easy enough to stop complimenting and rewarding a partner because of *lack of motivation*. It requires less effort and less thought to be selfish and impolite than to be socially skilful and thoughtful. We save that for others. This kind of shift is characteristic of unsuccessful relationships.

A person's attachment style (see Table 6.3 on page 229) has been found to relate to the occurrence of destructive and even abusive behaviour in a relationship. For example, individuals with negative self models (*preoccupied* and *fearful-avoidant* styles), compared to those with positive self models (*secure* and *dismissing*), find themselves in less satisfying relationships because they underestimate how much they are loved by their partners (Murray et al., 2001). Thus, insecurity leads to misperception, and, based on the misperception, there is a less positive evaluation of the partner and of the relationship, as well as less optimism about the future. Over time, the vulnerability of those with low self-esteem gets worse rather than better (Murray, Holmes,

& Griffin, 2000). Dutton, Bartholomew and colleagues (1994) explored the relationship between adult attachment patterns and abusive behaviour between couples. Verbal and physical abuse were most likely for those with a *fearful-avoidant* style and least likely with a *secure* or a *dismissing* style. Once again, research indicates that attachment patterns are related to success in adult relationships (Carnelley, Pietromonaco, & Jaffe, 1996; Radecki-Bush, Farrell, & Bush, 1993).

Jealousy: A Special Threat

Jealousy The thoughts, feelings, and actions that arise when a relationship is threatened by a real or imagined rival for a partner's affection.

Jealousy is a person's reaction to a perceived threat to the continuity or quality of a relationship (DeSteno & Salovey, 1994). The possibility of attraction toward someone new is a common problem in relationships, and jealousy is the usual response of one's partner (White & Mullen, 1990). Among the negative emotions aroused by jealousy are suspicion, rejection, hostility, and anger (Smith, Kim, & Parrott, 1988). Jealousy endangers a relationship. An individual who is dependent on a relationship, cares deeply about it, or is low in self-esteem is most likely to become jealous (Salovey & Rodin, 1991; White & Mullen, 1989). Jealousy also precipitates a decrease in self-esteem (Mathes, Adams, & Davies, 1985). Much like passionate love in reverse, jealousy elicits a flood of all-consuming negative thoughts, feelings, and behaviours (Pines & Aronson, 1983). Men and women also differ: Men become more jealous in response to sexual infidelity, while women's jealousy is stronger in response to indications of a partner's emotional commitment to someone else.

Taking an evolutionary perspective, Buss (1989) has proposed that such responses occur because of differences in the sexual strategies of men and women, as mentioned earlier. According to this view, women seek a mate who will be able to provide resources and protection, and women become especially upset by any indication that a partner is not eager to continue with such support—signs of emotional commitment to another are, therefore, most threatening. It is suggested that men, however, are more threatened by sexual infidelity because this throws doubt on the paternity of their children. Consequently, although jealousy is a common problem in relationships (Buunk, 1995; Sharpsteen, 1995), the reason for jealousy differs as a function of gender. The evolutionary perspective also suggests that a rival's potential threat is based on these gender differences. Males are most troubled by a male rival who is dominant and powerful (signalling a capability to acquire resources), while females are most threatened by a female rival who is young and physically attractive (Dijkstra & Buunk, 1998). Support for the evolutionary explanation of these differences is strengthened by the finding that the same gender differences are found cross-culturally, in the Netherlands, Germany, and the United States (Buunk, 1995). Research has also shown that while women experience more jealousy than men if a rival has a low *waist-to-hip ratio*, the reverse is true (men experience more jealousy) if the rival has a relatively high *shoulder-to-hip ratio* (Dijkstra & Buunk, 2001). Throwing some doubt on the evolutionary explanation for jealousy, recent research, using a more sophisticated range of research methods (DeSteno, 2002; Harris, 2002), has found greater gender similarity in response to jealousy. That is, both genders are upset by sexual infidelity *and* by emotional commitment to another on the part of their partners.

Jealousy has also been studied from the perspective of *attachment effects* (Sharpsteen & Kirkpatrick, 1997). Securely attached individuals tend to express anger toward the partner but to maintain the relationship. Those with a fearful-avoidant style tend to express anger and blame toward the outsider rather than the partner, while preoccupied individuals resist expressing any anger based on jealousy. In response to feeling jealous, preoccupied individuals express the most negative affect, whereas dismissing individuals report the least fear and unhappiness (Guerrero, 1998).

Though a lot of marital research focuses on problems, it should be remembered that still more marriages succeed than fail. A successful long-term relationship seems to involve an emphasis on friendship, commitment, similarity, and efforts to create positive affect (Adams & Jones, 1997; Lauer & Lauer, 1985). Older couples who remain together express more positive affect than younger and middle-aged couples (Levenson, Cartensen, & Gottman, 1994), perhaps because people get smarter and more mellow about relationships as they grow older (Locke, 1995).

KEY POINTS

- Problems and conflicts arise in long-term relationships. Among the common difficulties are dissimilarities between the partners.
- Destructive forms of interaction, particularly during conflict, can increase when partners introduce more negative evaluations into the relationship.
- *Jealousy* endangers relationships and is most common in dependent, low self-esteem individuals. Evolutionary theory suggests male-female differences relate to sexual strategies.

Breaking Up Is Hard to Do

Social psychologists have become increasingly interested in understanding the last two stages in the relationship process: *deterioration* and *ending*. Friendships often fade away quietly when friends move to new locations or develop new interests (Rose, 1984). When love is involved, however, it is very difficult to drift apart peacefully. Instead, painful emotions are aroused, feelings are hurt, and anger can become intense.

Romantic relationships don't end easily because they involve the investment of one's time, the exchange of powerful rewards, and commitment (Simpson, 1987). If an acceptable substitute is readily available, the loss of a partner is less traumatic than when one is simply cast adrift (Jemmott, Ashby, & Lindenfeld, 1989).

Responding to Relationship Problems

Men and women differ in how they cope with a failed relationship. Women confide in their friends, whereas men tend to start a new relationship as quickly as possible (Sorenson et al., 1993). Divorce is, of course, a stressful experience for almost anyone; but, compared to persons with insecure attachment styles, an individual with a secure style experiences less distress and has a greater ability to cope (Birnbaum et al., 1997).

Rusbult and Zembrodt (1983) have pointed out that people respond either *actively* or *passively* to an unhappy partnership. To summarize the alternatives they suggest, an active response can involve ending the relationship (*exit*—"Here's the name of my lawyer; I'm filing for divorce") or working to improve it (*voice*—"I believe we should give marital counselling a try"). Passively, one can simply wait for improvement (*loyalty*—"I'll stand by my partner until things get better") or wait for the inevitable breakup (*neglect*—"I just won't do anything until the situation gets totally impossible"). These alternatives are diagrammed in Figure 6.16. If the goal is to maintain a relationship, exit and neglect are clearly the least constructive and voice the most constructive choice. Compared to secure individuals, those who are insecure are more likely to react with exit and neglect and less likely to react with voice. Loyalty tends to go unnoticed or to be misinterpreted: often, when people say that they have responded with loyalty, their partners perceive them as being uninterested or unaware (Drigotas, Whitney, & Rusbult, 1995). Among quite divergent types of couples (university and college students, older spouses, gays, lesbians), men and women with high self-esteem tend to respond to relationship failure by exiting, while low self-esteem is often associated with passive neglect (Rusbult, Morrow, & Johnson, 1990).

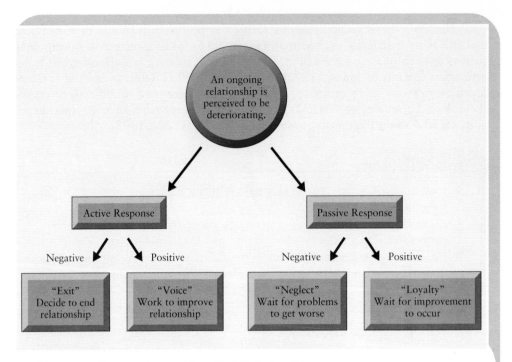

■ Alternative Responses to a Troubled Relationship

FIGURE 6.16 When a relationship is beginning to fail, the partners can respond in either an active or a passive way. Either way, a partner can take a positive or a negative approach. Assuming the best, a partner can work actively to improve the situation or wait passively in the hope that improvement will simply occur. Assuming the worst, a partner can actively end the relationship or passively wait for it to fall apart. If the relationship is not hopeless, the adaptive response is an active, positive one.

Source: Based on suggestions by Rusbult & Zembrodt, 1983.

Characteristics that spouses bring to the relationship can be a source of problems. For example, anxiety, negative affect, and neuroticism (measured when the spouses were newlyweds), have been found to be associated with interpersonal negativity in a marriage and a partner's subsequent dissatisfaction at various points in the marriage (Huston et al., 2001) (see Figure 6.17). Data indicate that the negative characteristics present when the marriage began predicted marital happiness and difficulty over the subsequent 13 years of marriage (Caughlin, Huston, & Houts, 2000).

The Importance of Commitment

Commitment A tendency to feel attached to, and to behave in such a way as to maintain, a long-term relationship.

Although it is very difficult to reverse a deteriorating relationship, couples can sometimes remain together despite their difficulties, particularly if they show **commitment**—the tendency to feel attached to a relationship and behave in ways that maintain it. As researchers began to study relationships over the long term, this concept emerged as central. We saw commitment as one element in the *triangular model of love* and Sternberg (1988) has suggested that the long-term marital relationship will be maintained by feelings of intimacy and commitment (or *companionate love*) rather than intimacy and passion (or *romantic love*). Caryl Rusbult's *investment model of commitment* (1981, 1983) describes the components of commitment. It suggest that commitment will be high and relationships more likely to last: (1) if the partnership provides satisfaction and comes up

| Beginning of Marriage | | During Marriage | | End of Marriage |
| One or both partners often express anxiety, negative affect, and neurotic tendencies | → | Negative affect in marital interactions | → | Marital dissatisfaction |

■ Negative Affectivity and Marital Dissatisfaction

FIGURE 6.17 Some factors present at the time of a wedding predict later negative interactions and marital dissatisfaction. For example, when one or both spouses are disposed to behave in ways that indicate anxiety, negative affect, and neurotic behaviour, the result is repeated negative marital interactions. Over time, the continued negative affect leads to dissatisfaction with the marriage.

Source: Based on information in Caughlin, Huston, & Houts, 2000; Huston et al., 2001.

to each person's standards of expectation; (2) if alternative lovers are not available; and (3) if both partners have invested a great deal of themselves and their life in the relationship (Arriaga & Agnew, 2001; Rusbult, Martz, & Agnew, 1998). The greater such investments, the greater the costs for the individual if the relationship ends. And the degree of a person's dependency can increase those costs. For example, a dependent spouse is often reluctant to give up the relationship even when she is the victim of physical abuse (Drigotas & Rusbult, 1992; Holtzworth-Munroe, 2000; Rusbult & Martz, 1995). One positive note comes from research showing that highly committed individuals will avoid threats to their relationship by seeing an available individual as less attractive than he or she really is (Lydon, et al., 1999). However, the cartoon in Figure 6.18 implies that many people today don't take their commitments seriously.

Breakup and Divorce

Although about 84 percent of Canadians have been married by the age of 34 years (Kerr & Ram, 1994), almost 40 percent of those marriages will end in divorce, with the average duration of the marriage being 11 years (Che-Alford et al., 1994; *Canadian Social Trends*, 1994).

Longitudinal research on the dissolution of long-term relationships can indicate how important each of the problems discussed above is in determining whether couples break up. Kurdek (1993) obtained data from 222 newlywed couples each year for five years. Over that period, 64 of the couples dissolved their marriages. Several psychological factors were found to predict marital outcome. Associated with marital failure were dissimilarities in spouses' need for independence, in the value they placed on attachment, and in their motives for marriage. Further, breakup was associated with decreased positivity and problematic handling of conflict. These and other factors (each present at the time of the marriage) permitted a fairly accurate prediction of which couples would and would not remain married. A very similar pattern was shown in a five-year study of gay and lesbian relationships (Kurdek, 1996). Such findings suggest the possibility that couples planning a long-term relationship might find it valuable to be interviewed, tested, and counselled about the likelihood that their relationship will have problems.

■ Commitment in Long-Term Relationships: In Short Supply?

FIGURE 6.18 Researchers have studied the constituents of commitment. According to Caryl Rusbult's investment model, commitment will be higher if a relationship provides satisfaction and comes up to expectations, if partners have invested a great deal of themselves and their lives, and when they do not have alternative relationships available. However, these factors don't seem to be a part of marriage for the couple here!

Social psychologists, as well as other behavioural scientists, are focusing more and more attention on the study of long-term close relationships (Duck & Barnes, 1992; Morgan & White, 1993; Werner, Altman, & Brown, 1992) and from increasingly diverse perspectives (Hatfield & Rapson, 1996; Kurdek, 1996). Given the importance of family, love, and marriage to most people, social psychology's continuing attempt to discover what makes close relationships thrive, and how problems arise, is one of its most significant tasks. It is to be hoped that research on relationships can help people make better decisions about entering romantic partnerships and provide needed information about how to maintain such relationships. The Ideas to Take with You section below also has some useful suggestions.

KEY POINTS

- When dissatisfaction becomes great, the individuals involved generally respond either actively or passively in moving toward restoring or ending the relationship.
- When partners exhibit neurotic behaviours and express negative affect, this can lead to dissatisfaction.
- *Commitment*—the tendency to feel attached to and maintain a relationship—emerges as an important factor that can help people avoid breakup.
- Problems that partners bring to a relationship often appear to be the cause of breakup, including increases in negativity and poor problem coping skills.

Ideas to Take with You

How to Encourage Others to Like You

Most of us would much rather be liked than disliked, and yet many of us have trouble getting to know other people and establishing friendly relationships. The suggestions outlined here are based on social psychological research, and you may find them helpful. If, of course, you don't want to be liked and prefer to be left alone, just do the opposite.

Control Proximity Factors.
Whenever possible, play an active role in arranging the ordinarily accidental contacts that control who becomes acquainted with whom. In the classroom, for example, sit beside others and avoid seats on the end of rows or in the corners. After a while, if you haven't become acquainted with those sitting near you, move to a new location and start over.

Create Positive Affect.
In situations where you hope to make friends, do whatever you can to create a pleasant mood. Depending on the situation, this could involve playing pleasant music, finding upbeat conversational topics, providing something good to eat and drink, as well as being nice yourself. It's as easy to be nice as to be obnoxious, and "nice" includes saying sincerely positive things to others. Compliments, praise, congratulations, and positive evaluations are almost always guaranteed to create a favourable impression; insults, criticisms, derogatory remarks, and negative evaluations are almost always guaranteed to cause discomfort.

Make the Most of Your Appearance and Look beyond Appearances.
Because observable characteristics play an important role in how others react to you, anything you can do to improve your physical appearance and outward manner can be helpful. Without becoming obsessed about it, there are multiple ways to improve how you look and (much more easily) to improve whatever you say or do that pleases or offends others. On the other hand, try very hard to overcome inaccurate stereotypes based on superficial characteristics that may influence your response to others.

Stress Similarities and Minimize Differences.
Remember that people respond well to agreement and similarity. You don't need to deceive anyone about your own views or beliefs or interests, but there is absolutely no need to emphasize and dwell on areas of dissimilarity when you can find areas of similarity instead. No one likes to have their beliefs and values continually challenged (and potentially threatened), so approach disagreements in an open-minded and nondogmatic way. At the same time, try to make sense of the views of others without becoming threatened and defensive yourself. Keep in mind that agreement need not mean you are correct, and disagreement need not mean you are wrong.

Summary

Interpersonal Attraction: Becoming Acquainted

- Relationships can be seen as passing through five possible stages. (p. 197)
- *Interpersonal attraction* refers to the attitudes we form about other people. (p. 198)
- One's initial contact with others is very often based on physical *proximity*. (p. 198)
- Proximity can lead to *repeated exposure*, which normally results in positive affect. (p. 198)
- Interpersonal attraction is in part determined by physical attractiveness. (p. 201)
- We make positive attributions about those who are attractive. (p. 202)
- Evolutionary theory suggests that the features we find attractive are those associated with reproductive success. (p. 204)
- Cultural theory suggests socialization has an impact on our stereotypes of attractiveness. (p. 205)
- Physical constituents of attractiveness relate to facial features and body proportions. (p. 205)
- The *affect-centred model* of attraction: attraction is determined by direct and indirect sources of affect. (p. 206)
- Cognitive mislabelling of arousal as attraction was shown in the Capilano Bridge experiment. (p. 211)
- *Need for affiliation* will determine the motive to relate. (p. 213)
- We affiliate for a number of reasons, including a desire for *social comparison* when anxious. (p. 213)

Building a Relationship: Self-Disclosure, Similarity, and Reciprocity

- Relationship building involves *self-disclosure*. (p. 215)
- Research shows gender and culture differences in self-disclosure. (p. 216)
- Similarity and dissimilarity have a great impact on attraction. (p. 216)
- Explanations for this include *balance theory*, *consensual validation*, and genetic similarity. (p. 218)
- The *matching hypothesis* suggests that we form relationships with those who are similar to us. (p. 218)

- We also like other people who *reciprocate* our positive evaluations of them. (p. 218)

From Liking to Loving: Moving beyond Casual Friendships

- Romantic love tends to involve a number of illusions about the partner and the relationship. (p. 220)
- *Passionate love* is explained as due to cultural socialization or evolutionary tendencies. (p. 220)
- *Sexual strategies theory* suggests there are sex differences in reproductive strategies. (p. 223)
- Cultures differ in their attitudes toward love. (p. 225)
- Love can take many forms, as shown in the *love styles theory* and the *triangular model of love*. (p. 226)

Long-Term Close Relationships

- *Adults' attachment styles* determine orientation to long-term relationships. (p. 228)
- Relating on the Internet may enhance self-disclosure and speed friendship formation. (p. 230)
- Despite an increased divorce rate, most people form long-term relationships. (p. 231)
- Similarity, or *assumed similarity*, enhances satisfaction. (p. 233)
- Relationship patterns among married people change over time. (p. 234)

Troubled Relationships: From Dissatisfaction to Dissolution

- Problems often arise in long-term relationships because of dissimilarities (p. 236), destructive forms of interaction (p. 238) and jealousy (p. 239).
- Responses to dissatisfaction can vary from active to passive. (p. 237)
- Neurotic behaviours can lead to dissatisfaction. (p. 238)
- *Commitment* can be important in helping to avoid breakup. (p. 240)
- Problems partners bring to a relationship often appear to be the cause of breakup. (p. 242)

For More Information

Duck, S. (1994). Meaningful relationships: Talking, sense, and relating. Thousand Oaks, CA: Sage.

A leading investigator and theorist in the field of interpersonal behaviour, Steve Duck describes how relationships are a constant challenge, requiring continued effort and maintenance.

Hatfield, E., & Rapson, R. L. (1996). Love and sex: Cross-cultural perspectives. New York: Allyn & Bacon.

This very readable book was co-authored by a social psychologist and her historian husband. It examines love, sexuality, and relationships with particular emphasis on cultural and historical differences.

Harvey, J. H., & Wenzel, A. (Eds.). (2001). Close romantic relationships: Maintenance and enhancement. Hillsdale, NJ: Erlbaum.

This book comprises a collection of chapters by some of the leading investigators and theorists in the field of relationships and deals with theoretical approaches and applied issues.

Booth, A., Crouter, A. C, & Clements, M. (2001). Couples in conflict. Hillsdale, NJ: Erlbaum.

Based on presentations at a national symposium on couples in conflict, this collection of chapters focuses on many family issues. The content addresses four major issues: the societal and evolutionary underpinnings of couple conflict, the interpersonal roots of couple conflict and its consequences, the effects on children, and policies and programs dealing with couple conflict.

Weblinks

www.apa.org/journals/amp/amp5391017.html
"Internet Paradox: A Social Technology That Reduces Social Involvement and Psychological Well-Being?" by Kraut, Lundmark, Carnegie Mellon University

www.neoteny.org/a/femalesexualselection.html
Female Sexual Selection
www2.hawaii.edu/~elaineh/
Speeches and essays from a long-term researcher of passionate love, Elaine Hatfield

CHAPTER SEVEN

Social Influence:
Changing Others' Behaviour

Conformity: Group Influence in Action
Factors Affecting Conformity: Determinants of Whether We "Go Along"/The Basis of Conformity: Why We Often "Go Along"/Resisting Conformity: Individuality and Control/Minority Influence: Why the Majority Doesn't Always Rule

Compliance: To Ask—Sometimes—Is to Receive
Compliance: The Underlying Principles/Tactics Based on Liking: Using Impression Management/Tactics Based on Commitment or Consistency/Tactics Based on Reciprocity/ Putting Others in a Good Mood: The Basis of Many Compliance Techniques

Extreme Forms of Social Influence: Obedience and Intense Indoctrination
Destructive Obedience: Some Basic Findings/Cultural Differences in Obedience/Destructive Obedience: Its Social Psychological Basis/Destructive Obedience: Resisting Its Effects/Intense Indoctrination: Social Influence Carried to the Extreme

SPECIAL SECTIONS

CORNERSTONES
Conformity Pressure: The Irresistible Social Force?

CANADIAN RESEARCH: ON THE CUTTING EDGE
Conforming in Response to "Jeer Pressure"

"Sometimes I wish they'd never perfected setless television."

- Social Influence: What the Future Has in Store?

FIGURE 7.1 While efforts to change our attitudes and behaviour haven't yet reached this stage, they are becoming increasingly sophisticated— and perhaps effective.

Where course grades are concerned, I (Robert Baron) have a simple policy: Once they are assigned, I never change them—and I mean *never*—unless, of course, there has been some error in addition. I announce this policy to my classes at the start of the semester and repeat it before and after every exam. I urge my students to come to see me during the semester if they want to discuss their grades, but remind them over and over again that once the semester is done, I will stick firmly to my "no change" policy. Despite these efforts, though, there are always several students in my class who make appointments to see me after final grades have been posted. And when they come to my office, they use every tactic of __social influence__—techniques designed to change my attitudes, beliefs, perceptions, or behaviour (Cialdini, 1994)—under the sun.

They offer excuses for poor exam scores, tell me how disappointed their parents will be, describe the health or personal problems that interfered with their performance, plead, and even, in some cases, threaten ("If you won't help me, I'll go to the Dean"). None of these tactics works because I decided long ago that it was simply not fair to change grades; after all, if I did so, I would be assigning grades on the basis of students' ability to exert social influence—not on their performance in the course. But believe me, I am frequently tempted because some of the students put on a great performance!

Clearly, this is far from the only time I am exposed to efforts by other persons to exert social influence—to change my attitudes or behaviour. Every time I see a TV commercial, drive by an advertising sign, or look through a magazine, I am exposed to efforts to change my attitudes and behaviour. So I am definitely on the receiving end of such attempts all through the day—though not yet at the level shown in Figure 7.1.

Where social influence is concerned, however, we don't merely receive it—we "dish it out" as well. How many times each day do *you* try to influence others—friends, roommates, family members, romantic partners? If you are like most people, you practise many forms of social influence each day.

Because social psychologists have long recognized the importance of social influence in our daily lives, this topic has long been a central focus of our field. We have

Social Influence Efforts on the part of one person to alter the behaviour or attitudes of one or more others.

already considered some of this work in Chapter 4, where we examined the process of *persuasion*. Here, we'll expand on that earlier discussion by examining many other aspects of social influence. First, we'll focus on the topic of <u>*conformity*</u>—behaving in ways that are viewed as acceptable or appropriate in our group or society. As we'll soon see, such pressure to conform can be very hard to resist. Next, we'll turn to *compliance*—efforts to get others to say yes to various requests. Finally, we'll examine two extreme forms of social influence: *obedience*—a form of social influence in which one person simply orders one or more others to do what that person wants—and *intense indoctrination*—efforts by extremist groups to recruit new members and induce them to accept the group's beliefs in an unquestioning manner (R. S. Baron, 2000).

Conformity: Group Influence in Action

Have you ever found yourself in a situation in which you felt that you stuck out like the proverbial sore thumb? If so, you have already had direct experience with pressures toward **conformity**. In such situations, you probably experienced a strong desire to "get back into line"—to fit in with the other people around you. Such pressures toward conformity stem from the fact that in many contexts, there are spoken or unspoken rules indicating how we should or ought to behave. These rules are known as <u>social norms</u>. In some instances, norms can be both detailed and precise. For instance, governments generally function through constitutions and written laws and athletic contests are usually regulated by written rules. Signs in many public places (e.g., along highways, in parks, and at airports) frequently describe expected behaviour in considerable detail—see Figure 7.2.

In contrast, other norms are unspoken or implicit. Most of us obey such unwritten rules as "Don't stand too close to strangers on elevators if you can help it" and "Don't arrive at parties or other social gatherings exactly on time." Similarly, we are often strongly influenced by current and rapidly changing standards of dress, speech, and personal grooming. Regardless of whether social norms are explicit or implicit, one fact is clear: *Most people obey them most of the time.* For example, few persons

Conformity A type of social influence in which individuals change their attitudes or behaviour in order to adhere to existing social norms.

Social Norms Rules indicating how individuals are expected to behave in specific social situations.

■ Social Norms: Regulators of Everyday Life

FIGURE 7.2 Social norms tell us what we should do (or not do) in a given situation. They are often stated explicitly in signs like these.

visit restaurants without leaving a tip for their server. And virtually everyone, regardless of personal political beliefs, stands when the national anthem of their country is played at sports events or other public gatherings.

Although social norms restrict individuals' options—prevent people from "doing their own thing"—there is a strong basis for the existence of so much conformity. Without conformity we would quickly find ourselves facing social chaos. Imagine what would happen outside movie theatres or voting booths or at supermarket checkout counters if people did not follow the simple rule, "Form a line and wait your turn." Given that strong pressures toward conformity do exist in many settings, it is surprising to learn that conformity, as a social process, was not the subject of systematic investigation by social psychologists until the 1950s. At that time Solomon Asch (1951) carried out a series of experiments that yielded dramatic results. In fact, the results obtained by Asch were so strong and so surprising that they quickly captured the attention of both social psychologists and the general public. This research is described in the Cornerstones section below.

Cornerstones

Conformity Pressure: The Irresistible Social Force?

Imagine that just before an important math exam, you discover that your answer to a homework problem—a problem of the type that will be on the test—is different from that obtained by one of your friends. How do you react? Probably with mild concern. Now imagine that you learn that a second person's answer, too, is different from yours. To make matters worse, it agrees with the answer reported by the first person. How do you feel now? The chances are good that your anxiety will be considerable. Next, you discover that a third person agrees with the other two. At this point, you know that you are in big trouble. Which answer should you accept? Yours or the one obtained by your three friends? The exam is about to start, so you have to decide quickly.

Life is filled with such dilemmas—instances in which we discover that our own judgments, actions, or conclusions are different from those reached by other persons. What do we do in such situations? Important insight into our behaviour in such cases was provided by a series of studies conducted by Solomon Asch (1951, 1955)—studies that are considered to be true classics in social psychology. In his research, Asch asked participants to respond to a series of simple perceptual problems such as the one in Figure 7.3. On each problem they indicated which of three comparison lines matched a standard line in length. Several other persons (usually six to eight) were also present during the session; but, unknown to the real participant, all were accomplices of the experimenter. On certain occasions known as critical trials (12 out of the 18 problems) the accomplices offered answers that were clearly wrong: they unanimously chose the wrong line as a match for the standard line. Moreover, they stated their answers before the participant responded. Thus, on these critical trials, the participants faced the type of dilemma described above. Should they go along with the other persons present or stick to their own judgments? A large majority of the participants in Asch's research opted for conformity. Indeed, in several different studies, fully 76 percent of those tested went along with the group's false answers at least once; in fact, they voiced their agreement with these errors about 37 percent of the time. In contrast, only 5 percent of the subjects in a control group, who responded to the same problems in the absence of any accomplices, made such errors.

Of course, there were large individual differences in this respect. Almost 25 percent of the participants never yielded to the group pressure. At the other extreme were persons who went along with the majority nearly all the time. When Asch questioned them, some of these persons stated, "I am wrong, they are right"—they had little confidence in their own judgment. Others, however, said they felt that the other persons present were the victims of some sort of optical illusion, or were merely sheep following the responses of the first person. Nevertheless, when it was their turn to speak, these participants still went along with the group.

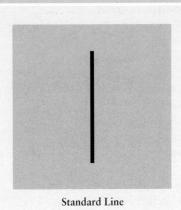

■ Asch's Line Judgment Task: An Example

FIGURE 7.3 Participants in Asch's research were asked to report their judgments on problems such as this one. On each problem, they indicated which of the comparison lines (1, 2, or 3) best matched the standard line in length.

Standard Line

Comparison Lines

In further studies, Asch (1951, 1956) investigated the effects of shattering the group's unanimity by having one of the accomplices break with the others. In one study, this person gave the correct answer, becoming an "ally" of the real participant; in another, he chose an answer in between the one given by the group and the correct one; and in a third, he chose an answer that was even more incorrect than that chosen by the majority. In the latter two conditions, in other words, he broke from the group but still disagreed with the real participant. Results indicated that conformity was reduced under all three conditions. However, somewhat surprisingly, this reduction was greatest when the dissenting accomplice expressed views even more extreme (and wrong) than the majority. Together, these findings suggest that it is the unanimity of the group that is crucial: once that unanimity is broken, no matter how, resisting group pressure becomes much easier.

One more aspect of Asch's research is important to mention. In later studies, he repeated his basic procedure, but with one important change: Instead of stating their answers out loud, participants wrote them on a piece of paper. As you might guess, conformity dropped sharply. This finding points to the importance of distinguishing between public conformity—doing or saying what others around us say or do—and private acceptance—actually coming to feel or think as others do. Often, it appears, we follow social norms overtly, but don't actually change our private views (Maas & Clark, 1984). This distinction between public conformity and private acceptance is an important one, and we'll have reason to comment on it at several points in this book.

Asch's research was the catalyst for much activity in social psychology, as many other researchers rushed to investigate the nature of conformity, to identify factors that influence it, and to establish its limits (e.g., Crutchfield, 1955; Deutsch & Gerard, 1955). Indeed, such research is continuing today and is still adding to our understanding of this crucial form of social influence (e.g., Baron, Vandello, & Brunsman, 1996; Bond & Smith, 1996; Buehler & Griffin, 1994).

KEY POINTS

- *Social influence*—efforts by one or more persons to change the attitudes or behaviour of one or more others—is a common part of life.

- Most people behave in accordance with *social norms* most of the time; in other words, they show strong tendencies towards *conformity*.

- Conformity was first systematically studied by Solomon Asch, whose classic research indicated that many persons will yield to social pressure from a *unanimous* group.

Factors Affecting Conformity: Determinants of Whether We "Go Along"

Asch's research demonstrated the existence of powerful pressures toward conformity, but even a moment's reflection suggests that conformity does not occur to the same degree in all settings. Fashion is one example. We see fads sweep the country—tattoos, piercing, bare midriffs, bell-bottoms. Suddenly you look around and every other person is now sporting a particular fashion. But what about those who aren't? Why do some people conform to a particular fashion while others don't? (See Figure 7.4.) Many variables seem to play a role in conformity; however, we will focus on five that have been considered important: (1) _cohesiveness_—degree of attraction to the group or persons exerting influence; (2) _group size and unanimity_—how many persons are exerting influence; (3) the _type of social norm_ involved in the influence attempt; (4) the effect of _cultural background_.

Cohesiveness and Conformity: Accepting Influence from Those We Like

Let's return to fashion and consider hair-length. For some years now short hair for men has been in—even shaved heads have been fashionable—as sported by action film star Vin Diesel. Suppose that this fashion suddenly begins to change (and this does seem to be the case at the moment). Now imagine (or perhaps remember) the first time you saw longer hair on a guy in your own neighbourhood. If this was an individual who was really popular with the group of people you know, how would this influence your view of longer hair on guys? Would you start to see this as attractive, as a possible look for you or your friends?

■ Conformity to the Latest Fashion?

FIGURE 7.4 When any fashion or fad occurs, there are strong conformity pressures on group members. Yet there are many who don't go along at all. Why? What factors determine the extent to which individuals will yield to conformity pressure or resist it?

Quite likely. Now supposing the individual you saw was definitely not considered popular, then what would be the impact? Almost certainly, your opinion of longer hair would not be improved—after all, who would want to be like that person?

This example illustrates one factor that plays an important role where conformity is concerned: **cohesiveness**, which can be defined as the degree of attraction felt by individuals toward some group. When cohesiveness is high—when we like and admire some group of persons—pressures toward conformity are magnified. After all, we know that one way of gaining the acceptance of such persons is to be like them in various ways, even if this involves alterations in our own anatomy. When cohesiveness is low, on the other hand, pressures toward conformity are also low—why should we change our behaviour to be like other people we don't especially like or admire? Research findings indicate that cohesiveness exerts strong effects on conformity (Crandall, 1988; Latané & L'Herrou, 1996), so it is definitely one important determinant of the extent to which we yield to this type of social pressure.

Cohesiveness With respect to conformity, the degree of attraction felt by an individual toward an influencing group.

Group Size and Unanimity

A second factor that exerts important effects on the tendency to conform is the _size_ of the influencing group. Asch (1956) and other early researchers (e.g., Gerard, Wilhelmy, & Conolley, 1968) found that conformity increased with group size, but only up to about <u>three</u> members; beyond that point, it appeared to level off or even decrease. More recent research, however, has failed to confirm these early findings (e.g., Bond &

Smith, 1996). Instead, these later studies have found that conformity tends to increase with group size up to eight group members and beyond. So it appears that the larger the group, the greater our tendency to go along with it, even if this means behaving in ways different from the ones we'd really prefer.

However, it is also important that the group members agree. In Asch's early research, and in many later studies of conformity, subjects were exposed to social pressure from a *unanimous* group. Under those conditions, most subjects yielded to social pressure. But, as we saw above, when another person present broke with the majority, conformity was reduced considerably, even if their dissent was inaccurate (Asch, 1951, 1956). These and other findings suggest that almost any form of *social support* can help a person resist social pressure.

Descriptive and Injunctive Social Norms: When Norms Affect Behaviour

Social norms, we have already seen, can be formal or informal in nature. This is not the only way in which norms differ, however. Another important distinction is that between **descriptive norms** and **injunctive norms** (e.g., Cialdini, Kallgren, & Reno, 1991; Reno, Cialdini, & Kallgren, 1993). Descriptive norms are ones that simply describe what most people do in a given situation. They influence behaviour by informing us about what is generally seen as effective or adaptive in that situation. In contrast, injunctive norms specify what *ought* to be done—what is approved or disapproved behaviour in a given situation. Both norms can exert strong effects upon behaviour (e.g., Brown, 1998). However, injunctive norms may exert somewhat stronger effects when antisocial behaviour (not approved by society) is involved (Reno, Cialdini, & Kallgren, 1993).

But when, precisely, do injunctive norms influence behaviour? It is clear that they don't always produce such effects. For instance, although there is an injunctive norm stating "Clean up after your dog," and despite the fact that most cities have laws requiring this, you may observe your neighbours looking the other way while their dog "does its thing" on someone else's property. Why do people sometimes disobey or ignore even strong injunctive norms? One answer is provided by **normative focus theory** (e.g., Cialdini et al., 1990). This theory suggests that norms will influence behaviour only to the extent that they are focal for the persons involved at the time the behaviour occurs. In other words, people will obey injunctive norms only when they think about them and see them as related to their own actions. Cialdini and his colleagues have conducted several studies that provide support for this view (e.g., Cialdini, Reno, and Kallgren, 1990), but perhaps the clearest evidence is that reported by Kallgren, Reno, and Cialdini (2000).

This study tested normative focus theory by manipulating two independent variables: the *relevance of an injunctive norm* and level of *physiological arousal*. Prior research had shown that arousal intensifies the likelihood of automatic or strong responses (Zajonc, 1965). The study, which took place not in the laboratory but in an enclosed stairwell, first exposed participants to brief written passages relating to the injunctive norm against littering in public places. These passages varied in how closely linked they were to this norm: some participants read passages that were closely related to littering (e.g., the passages discussed graffiti and water pollution), others read passages moderately related to littering (they discussed the issue of containers and turning down stereo sets at night), and still other participants read passages that were only distantly related to littering (voting, returning library books on time). A final group read passages that did not focus on any injunctive norms. All of the written passages used had previously been rated by a large group of raters for closeness to the norm against littering.

Descriptive Norms
Norms that simply indicate what most people do in a given situation.

Injunctive Norms
Norms specifying what ought to be done—what is approved or disapproved behaviour in a given situation.

Normative Focus Theory A theory suggesting that norms will influence behaviour only to the extent that they are focal for the persons involved at the time the behaviour occurs.

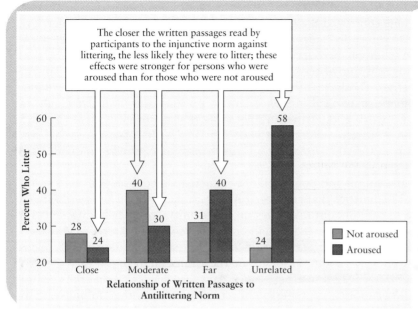

The closer the written passages read by participants to the injunctive norm against littering, the less likely they were to litter; these effects were stronger for persons who were aroused than for those who were not aroused

Percent Who Litter

Relationship of Written Passages to Antilittering Norm

Close: 28 (Not aroused), 24 (Aroused)
Moderate: 40 (Not aroused), 30 (Aroused)
Far: 31 (Not aroused), 40 (Aroused)
Unrelated: 24 (Not aroused), 58 (Aroused)

■ When Injunctive Norms Do, and Do Not, Affect Behaviour

FIGURE 7.5 Research participants who read passages closely related to the injunctive norm against littering were less likely to engage in littering than were those who read passages less closely related to this norm. Moreover, this effect was much stronger among persons who had exercised, and so were experiencing high arousal. These findings provide support for _normative focus theory_—the view that norms affect overt behaviour only to the extent that they are focal (i.e., salient) to the persons involved.

Source: Based on data from Kallgren, Reno, & Cialdini, 2000.

After reading these passages, participants were told that to test a new physiological measure, some would exercise while others would not (varying arousal levels). Those in the exercise group walked up and down the stairs for three minutes, while the others simply sat and rested. Heart rate was measured for both groups before and after exercising or sitting quietly, and as part of these procedures, the experimenter placed a sticky ointment on participants' hands. At the end of the study, participants were given a paper towel to remove this ointment. They were then observed as they left the study to determine whether they threw the towel on the ground—that is, engaged in littering.

The major prediction was that the more closely related the passages were to the anti-littering norm, the less likely participants would be to litter and that this effect would be stronger for those in the high-arousal group because their automatic response would be intensified. As shown in Figure 7.5, this is precisely what happened.

Overall, then, it seems clear that norms influence our actions primarily when they seem relevant to us at the time when we can choose either to obey or to ignore them.

Culture and Conformity

Beyond factors such as cohesiveness, group size, and norms, another more enduring feature of group influence is _culture_. That is, some cultures may encourage greater conformity in their members than others and such socialization differences could be expected to have lasting influence upon individuals.

One of the earliest cross-cultural studies of conformity was carried out by John Berry (1967) of Queen's University. He reasoned that the extent of conformity expected in a culture would be related to its means of subsistence. Specifically, individuals in agricultural communities tend to be very interdependent because the cooperation of all members is needed in order to achieve successful food production. Therefore, these cultures would emphasize conformity to group needs. In contrast, where subsistence involves hunting, food is usually available throughout the year and the hunter can be more independent of others in the community.

Adapting Asch's (1950) line-judgment task, Berry compared the responses of two traditional cultural groups: the Temne (farmers) and the Inuit (hunters). He had hypothesized that greater conformity would be shown by Temne subjects than by Inuit subjects, and results confirmed the hypothesis. Later studies confirmed the high level of independence in perceptual judgments among other hunting cultures—for example, among Canadian Aboriginal groups (Berry & Annis, 1974).

Berry's study was one of the earliest in social psychology to compare individualist and collectivistic cultures (though these terms were not widely used at that time) and to suggest that social influence and conformity vary along this cultural dimension. But his work goes further in suggesting that the origins of such cultural differences are in a society's major means of subsistence. If subsistence requires a high level of cooperation, then greater conformity may be required of individuals in that culture. (ex. agricultural cultures)

More recently, Smith and Bond (1996) conducted a meta-analysis of 133 studies drawn from 17 countries that replicated Asch's classic study. They found strong evidence for the impact of cultural values on conformity, specifically differences in individualism and collectivism. Individuals from collectivistic cultures (e.g., China, Japan, Zimbabwe) tend to conform more than individuals from individualistic cultures (e.g., the United Kingdom, Holland, or the United States) and this was true regardless of the size of the influencing group. They also suggested that the need for conformity would be more acceptable in collectivistic cultures than in individualistic cultures where individuals will often feel uneasy about the lack of independence when they conform. Indeed, research shows that North Americans often feel a need to justify their conformity after the fact (e.g., Buehler & Griffin, 1994). Another way of conceptualizing this cultural distinction in social influence is to say that while people in North America value their capacity to *directly influence* the context and other people, East Asians value *adjusting* to the context and influencing their situation in that way (Morling, Kitayama, & Miyamoto, 2002). Both types of response can be conceived as different ways to control one's position in relation to *individualistic* the environment: they have been termed *primary control* (attempting to influence the environment) and *secondary control* (adjusting oneself to circumstances) (Rothbaum, Weisz & Snyder, 1982). *collectivistic*

In summary, an accumulation of studies (e.g., Hamilton & Sanders, 1995) suggest that conformity may be better understood when we consider the interdependence of individuals in a culture, or even within a subculture of a larger society. The more one's fate is interdependent with that of others, the greater the likelihood of conformity occurring (Smith & Bond, 1998).

KEY POINTS

- Many factors determine whether, and to what extent, conformity occurs. These include *cohesiveness*, or the degree of attraction felt by an individual toward some group; *group size* and *unanimity*; type of social norm—*descriptive* or *injunctive*—operating in that situation; and cultural background.

- *Normative focus theory* suggests that norms affect overt behaviour only to the extent that they are focal (i.e., salient) to the persons present.

- Some cultures place greater emphasis on the need for conformity among members and this appears to derive from the need for cooperation in order to survive. Generally, there is more pressure to conform in collectivistic cultures than in individualistic ones.

The Basis of Conformity: Why We Often "Go Along"

As we have just seen, several factors determine whether and to what extent conformity occurs. Yet this does not alter the essential point: Conformity is a basic fact of social life. Most people conform to the norms of their groups or societies most of the time. Why? Why do people so often choose to go along with these social rules or expectations instead of combating them? The answer seems to centre primarily on two powerful needs possessed by all human beings: the desire to be liked or accepted by others and the desire to be right (Insko, 1985).

Normative Social Influence: The Desire to Be Liked and the Fear of Rejection

How can we get others to like us? This is one of the eternal puzzles of social life. As we will discuss later in this chapter, there are many tactics that are effective in this regard. One of the most successful of these is to appear to be as similar to others as possible. From our earliest days, we learn that agreeing with the persons around us, and behaving as they do, causes them to like us. Parents, teachers, friends, and others often heap praise and approval on us for showing such similarity (see our discussion of attitude formation in Chapter 3). One important reason we conform, therefore, is this: we have learned that doing so can help us win the approval and acceptance we crave. This source of conformity is known as normative social influence, because it involves altering our behaviour to meet others' expectations.

If our tendency to conform to social norms stems, at least in part, from our desire to be liked and accepted by others, then it stands to reason that anything that threatens our acceptance or increases our fear of rejection will increase our conformity. And one thing that might trigger fears of rejection is witnessing another person being held up to ridicule. Can the threat of ridicule increase our conformity? This question was investigated by researchers Janes and Olson at the University of Western Ontario, who coined the phrase *jeer pressure* to describe such effects. Their study is described in the following Canadian Research: On the Cutting Edge section.

Normative Social Influence Social influence based on the individual's desire to be liked or accepted by other persons.

Canadian Research: On the Cutting Edge

Conforming in Response to "Jeer Pressure"

Think back to your distant grade school days. Can you remember what it was like to witness another child being teased and made fun of? This is a phenomenon that is all too common in schools (Shapiro, Baumeister, & Kessler, 1991). Most of us witnessed this kind of ridicule in school and most of us, to our shame, didn't intervene. A study by Janes and Olson can perhaps help us to understand why intervention might be difficult. Their focus was on

the effect of ridicule—humour that derogates some aspect of an individual's behaviour or appearance—on conformity and fear of failure. They reasoned that those who witnessed someone else being mocked would react by attempting to conform to the majority—to avoid standing out and, therefore,

ie, to avoid the same rejection.

Ridicule Humour that derogates some aspect of an individual's behaviour or appearance.

to avoid a similar rejection. They would also exhibit an increased fear of failure, as public failure might provide an excuse for others to ridicule them.

Subjects were told that the study was an exploration of the relationship between humour and hand/eye coordination. In the first phase of the study, they viewed an eight-minute videotape of a stand-up comedian telling one of three types of jokes. In the *other ridicule* condition, jokes mocked a friend of his who was off camera (e.g., "His acne was so bad as a teenager we used to call him 'pizza face'" or "He tried to join a lonely hearts club but they said, 'Hey, we're not that desperate!'"). In the *self-ridicule* condition, he mocked himself (e.g., "My acne was so bad as a teenager they used to call me 'pizza face'"). In the *no-target humour* condition, jokes did not ridicule a particular individual (e.g., "What has two gills, scales, and warns us about the dangers of smoking? The Sturgeon General!").

Next, subjects were asked to rate four cartoons for funniness. Beneath each cartoon were other rating scales that had already been used, supposedly by previous subjects. Researchers explained that, to prevent unnecessary paper usage, they were having all participants use the same page for their ratings. In fact, these were bogus ratings and provided a social norm that might influence subjects. Thus, the main measure of conformity was the number of times subjects' own ratings matched this social norm.

Finally, subjects' fear of failure was measured by using a ring-toss task (supposedly a test of hand/eye coordination) in which subjects had to throw a rope ring onto a peg. Subjects were told that they could stand at the distance from the peg where they would feel most comfortable. Previous research (e.g., Sorrentino, et al., 1992) had shown that those with a high fear of failure would either choose to position themselves closer than average to the peg (to make the task easier) or further away than average (to make the task impossible and avoid the shame of failure). Thus the dependent variable was the absolute amount of deviation (in feet) from the average position (whether further away from the peg or nearer to it)—so the higher the deviation from the average position, the higher the fear of failure. Results are shown in Figure 7.6.

Subjects responded to the sight of someone else being ridiculed with increased conformity and greater fear of failure compared to those in the other humour conditions. Janes and Olson coined the term *jeer pressure* (after the term peer pressure) to describe this effect, and its power is clearly demonstrated in this study given that the pressure was so indirect. In contrast to a real-life situation, subjects in this study witnessed the ridicule on videotape, not in person, the target was not visible to them, and there was no possibility that the derision might turn on them. Yet they "kept their heads down" by conforming and their fear of failure seemed to indicate fear of ridicule as well. Perhaps this apparent overreaction is a testament to past experience at school or elsewhere with the embarrassment of being the victim of ridicule.

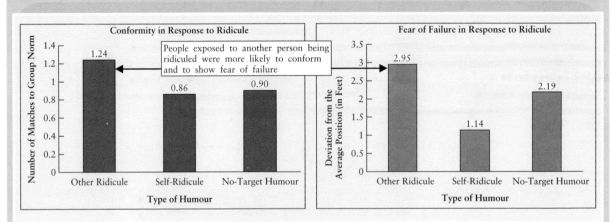

■ Jeer Pressure: The Effects of Ridicule on Conformity and Fear of Failure

FIGURE 7.6 Subjects exposed to someone else being ridiculed (Other Ridicule Condition) were more likely to conform to a social norm and to show fear of failure than both other humour conditions (Self-Ridicule and No Target Humour) combined. Even though subjects only viewed the ridicule on video and did not see or know its recipient, they still responded to this *jeer pressure* by keeping their heads down and avoiding failure.

Some theorists have proposed that, in settings such as the schoolyard, the social function of ridicule is to punish nonconformity (Wilson, 1979). If that is so, then it works. Now perhaps we can begin to understand why so often onlookers to teasing don't intervene—they are attempting to avoid that same punishment. Indeed, when a survey asked high school students to name their principle fears, the fear of being ridiculed was number one (Shapiro, Baumeister, & Kessler, 1991). So when we witness such scenes, we wish to avoid rejection ourselves, and one way of doing this is to stick more closely to what is viewed as "acceptable" or "appropriate" in our group—in other words, to conform even more with existing social norms. These findings provide additional support for the view that one reason we conform is to be liked by others—or, at least, to avoid rejection by them.

The Desire to Be Right: Informational Social Influence

If you want to know your weight, you can step on to a scale. Similarly, if you want to know the dimensions of a room, you can measure them directly. But how can you establish the "accuracy" of your own political or social views or decide which hairstyle suits you best? There are no simple physical tests or measuring devices for answering these questions. Yet most of us have just as strong a desire to be correct about such matters as about questions relating to the physical world. The solution is obvious: to answer these questions, or at least to obtain information about them, we must turn to other people. We use their opinions and their actions as guides for our own. Obviously, such reliance on others can be another source of conformity, for in an important sense, other people's actions and opinions define social reality for us. This source of social influence is known as **informational social influence**, since it is based on our tendency to depend on others as a source of information about many aspects of the social world.

> **Informational Social Influence** Social influence based on the desire to be correct (i.e., to possess accurate perceptions of the social world).

Because our motivation to be correct or accurate is very strong, informational social influence is a very powerful source of conformity. However, as you might expect, this is most likely to be true in situations in which the motivation to be accurate is high (the outcome is *important* to us) yet we are highly *uncertain* about what is "correct" or "accurate." That this is so was clearly illustrated in a study conducted by Robert S. Baron, Vandello, & Brunsman (1996). (Robert S. Baron is not the Robert Baron who is a co-author of this text.) These researchers found that when the motivation to be accurate was high (the task was described as important), research participants showed a greater tendency to conform to the judgments of others when they were uncertain about the correct answer (the task they were given was difficult) than when they had confidence in their own judgments (the task was easy). However, when motivation to be accurate was low (the task was described as unimportant), no such differences occurred.

Together, normative and informational social influence provide a strong basis for our tendency to conform—to act in accordance with existing social norms. In short, there is nothing mysterious about the compelling and pervasive occurrence of conformity; it stems directly from basic needs and motives that can be fulfilled only when we do indeed decide to "go along" with others.

KEY POINTS

- *Normative social influence*, the desire to be liked by those we like or respect, is one motive that seems to underlie conformity
- A desire to avoid the punishment of "jeer pressure"—the social pressure we feel when subject to *ridicule*—may be one basis for normative social influence.
- A second major motive for conformity is *informational social influence*—the desire to be right or accurate.

Resisting Conformity: Individuality and Control

Having read this discussion of normative and informational social influence, you may now have the distinct impression that pressures toward conformity are all but impossible to resist. If that's so, take heart. While such pressures are indeed powerful, they are definitely not irresistible. In many cases, individuals—or groups of individuals—decide to dig in their heels and say *no*. This was certainly true in Asch's research, where, as you may recall, most of the subjects yielded to social pressure, but only part of the time. What accounts for this ability to resist even powerful pressures toward conformity? Research findings point to two key factors.

First, as you probably already realize, many people have a strong desire to maintain their uniqueness or *individuality*. People want to be like others, but not to the extent that they lose their personal identity. In other words, along with the needs to be right and to be liked, many of us possess a desire for **individuation**—for being distinguished in some respects from others (e.g., Maslach, Santee, & Wade, 1987; Snyder & Fromkin, 1980). It is partly because of this motive that individuals sometimes choose to disagree with others or to act in unusual or even bizarre ways. They realize that such behaviour may be costly in terms of gaining the approval or acceptance of others, but their desire to maintain a unique identity is simply stronger than various inducements to conformity.

Individuation
Differentiation of oneself from others by emphasis on one's uniqueness or individuality.

Another reason why individuals often choose to resist group pressure involves their desire to maintain *control* over the events in their lives (e.g., Burger, 1992; Daubman, 1993). Most persons want to believe that they can determine what happens to them, and yielding to social pressure sometimes runs counter to this desire. After all, going along with a group implies behaving in ways one might not ordinarily choose; and this, in turn, can be viewed as a restriction of personal freedom and control. The results of many studies suggest that the stronger an individual's need for personal control, the less likely he or she is to yield to social pressure; so this factor, too, appears to be an important one where resisting conformity is concerned.

In sum, two motives, the desire to retain our individuality and the desire to keep control over our own lives, serve to counter the motives that tend to increase conformity—our desires to be liked and to be accurate. Whether we conform in a given situation, then, depends on the relative strength of these various motives and the interplay between them.

People Who Cannot Conform

So far in this discussion, we have been focusing on people who can conform but choose not to do so. There are also many persons who cannot conform for physical, legal, or psychological reasons. For instance, consider persons who are physically challenged. While they can certainly lead rich, full lives and participate in many activities that other persons enjoy, they cannot adhere to some social norms because of their physical limitations. For instance, some cannot stand when the national anthem is played, and others cannot adhere to accepted styles of dress for similar reasons.

Homosexuals, too, face difficulties in adhering to social norms. Many persons in this group participate in stable, long-term relationships with a partner and would like to conform to the social norm stating that those who love each other may get married. Until, recently, however, this was not possible in most countries. Even now, marriage between homosexuals is fully legal in only one—the Netherlands— though it is progressing (with some dissent) towards legality in Canada as we write in 2003 (see Figure 7.7). While this is a complex issue relating to moral, religious, and ethical concerns, and is outside the realm of science, it is important to note that

■ Some People Cannot Conform

FIGURE 7.7 Some persons who would like to conform to existing social norms cannot do so because of physical, psychological, or legal barriers. For instance, in most countries, homosexual couples cannot marry, even if they are in a long-term stable relationship and wish to do so. Only in one country—the Netherlands—have such marriages been legal for some time. Here in Canada, at the time of writing, gay marriage is legal in Ontario and British Columbia and legislation is about to be tabled in Parliament.

many people find it difficult or impossible to adhere to existing social norms even when they wish to, and that, as a result, they face difficulties and conflicts unfamiliar to others.

Minority Influence: Why the Majority Doesn't Always Rule

As we have just noted, individuals can—and often do—resist group pressure (Wolfe, 1985). Lone dissenters or small minorities can dig in their heels and refuse to go along. Yet even this is not the total story; in addition, there are cases in which such persons or groups can turn the tables on the majority and *exert* rather than merely *receive* social influence. History provides numerous examples of such events. Such giants of the scientific world as Galileo, Pasteur, and Freud faced virtually unanimous majorities who rejected their views in harsh terms. Yet over time they won growing numbers of colleagues to their side until, ultimately, their opinions prevailed. More recent examples of minorities influencing majorities are provided by the success of environmentalists. Initially such persons were viewed as wild-eyed radicals operating at the fringes of society. Over time, however, they have succeeded in changing strongly held attitudes and laws, with the result that society itself has been altered through their efforts.

When do minorities succeed in exerting social influence on majorities? Research findings suggest that they are most likely to be successful under certain conditions (Kruglanski & Mackie, 1991; Moscovici, 1985).

First, the members of such groups must be *consistent* in their opposition to majority opinions. If they waffle or show signs of yielding to the majority view, their impact is reduced. Second, in order for a minority to affect a larger majority, its members must avoid appearing rigid and dogmatic (Mugny, 1975). A minority that merely repeats the same position over and over again is less persuasive than one that demonstrates a degree of *flexibility* in its stance. Third, the general social context in which a minority operates is important. If a minority argues for a position that is consistent *with current social trends* (e.g., conservative views at a time of growing conservatism), its chances of influencing a majority are greater than if it argues for a position that is out of step with such trends.

Of course, even when these conditions are met, minorities face a tough uphill fight. The power of majorities is great, especially in ambiguous or complex social situations; in such situations majorities are viewed as more reliable sources of information about what is true than are minorities. In other words, majorities function as an important source of both informational and normative social influence (Wood et al., 1996). Why then, are minorities sometimes able to get their message across? One possibility is that their new ideas stimulate *systematic processing* in members of the majority (e.g., Smith, Tindale, & Dugoni, 1996; Wood et al., 1996). They are puzzled and exert cognitive effort to understand why these people hold their views and why they are willing to take a strong stand against the majority (Nemeth, 1995; Vonk & van Knippenberg, 1995). Eventually, these new ideas may come to seem more reasonable and acceptable.

While minorities may eventually have an impact on the majority, minority members themselves continue to cope with influences from the majority group. According to Tafarodi and colleagues at the University of Toronto (Tafarodi, Kang, & Milne, 2002), this can create a dilemma that is particularly relevant for minority individuals who have an *integrated* or *bicultural identity*—who identify both with their own minority culture and with the mainstream culture (see our discussion of ethnic identity in Chapter 4). The dilemma arises because, more than other types of ethnic identification, their bicultural identity will leave them open to two different, and sometimes competing, sources of influence—the mainstream majority norms and their own minority group norms. How can they maintain the balance of influences needed for a bicultural identity?

To investigate this issue, researchers chose as subjects first- and second-generation Chinese-Canadian female university students, who had lived in Canada at least five years and for whom *integration* was the dominant identification (Zheng & Berry, 1991). Because this group was part of a visible minority, yet was well integrated into mainstream Canadian culture, Tafarodi and colleagues (2002) predicted that they would show a **compensatory conformity** if faced with a reminder of their visible difference from the majority. Specifically, making subjects' visible-minority status salient would remind them of past experiences of social exclusion, and they would automatically respond by emphasizing their identification with mainstream norms and attitudes. Further, they were also expected to de-emphasize their minority identification by increased opposition to own-group's cultural norms.

To put these ideas to the test, subjects were asked to indicate their liking for a series of very similar abstract paintings. After evaluating one series of paintings, a second set was introduced together with some normative anchors. Participants were shown the average rating of each painting either by "Canadians of European descent"

Compensatory Conformity
Compensating for awareness of minority status by emphasizing one's agreement with majority group norms and attitudes.

(*Euro-Canadian norm*) or, in another condition, by "Canadians of Chinese descent" (*Chinese-Canadian norm*). There was also a *control* condition in which subjects were given no normative information.

As well as varying exposure to different cultural norms, the researchers also varied whether the subjects' visible minority status was made salient. This was achieved very simply by having subjects sit where they could see themselves in a mirror as they completed the study. Previous research has demonstrated that observing yourself in a mirror increases self-awareness.

Researchers were predicting *compensatory conformity* (lower opposition to the norm) in the Euro-Canadian norm condition but only when subjects were reminded of their visible-minority status. This prediction was confirmed—see Figure 7.8. Chinese-Canadian subjects showed the lowest percentage of opposing responses, when they could see themselves in the mirror and were presented with the majority-group norm. But researchers' predictions were not confirmed when subjects were presented with the Chinese-Canadian norm. The percentages of opposing responses in the mirror and no-mirror conditions were not significantly different— subjects showed no significant increase in opposition to own-group norms.

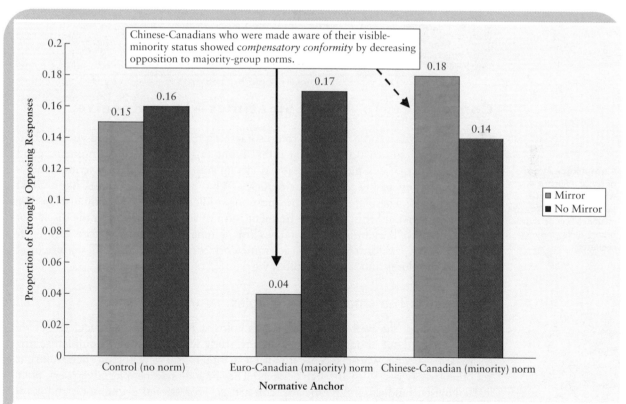

■ Moderating Majority Influence: The Bicultural Identity and Balancing Social Norms

FIGURE 7.8 When Chinese-Canadian students were made aware of their minority status by seeing themselves in a mirror, they showed *compensatory conformity*—they made fewer opposing responses to the majority norm. This did not occur in response to Chinese-Canadian (minority) norms: in fact, there was no significant increase or decrease in opposition to these norms compared to the control group. Thus, subjects maintained allegiance to both majority and minority cultural perspectives, confirming their bicultural identity.

Source: Based on data from Tafarodi, Kang, & Milne, 2002.

If this study is replicated, it can provide real insight into the process of social influence for integrated visible minorities. When made aware of their minority status, these Chinese-Canadian university students did indeed show compensatory conformity by staying close to mainstream norms. However, they also did *not* reject the norms of their own group. Perhaps that is the essence of what it means to be integrated—to accept both cultural perspectives. Though, as this study implies, if you are a member of a visible minority group, you may need to assert your right to be part of the mainstream again and again.

KEY POINTS

- Although pressures toward conformity are strong, many persons resist them, at least part of the time. This resistance seems to stem from two strong motives: the desire to retain one's individuality, or *individuation*, and the desire to exert *control* over one's own life.

- Under some conditions, minorities can induce even large majorities to change their attitudes or behaviour. Recent evidence suggests that this may occur, in part, because minorities induce majorities to think more systematically about the issues they raise.

- Minorities with a bicultural or integrated ethnic identity cope with increased awareness of their minority status by showing *compensatory conformity*—showing less opposition to majority norms.

Compliance: To Ask—Sometimes—Is to Receive

Suppose that you wanted someone to do something for you, how would you go about getting that person to do it? If you think about this question for a moment, you'll quickly realize that you have quite a few tricks up your sleeve for gaining **compliance**—for getting others to say yes to your requests. What are these techniques like? Which ones work best? These are among the questions studied by social psychologists in their efforts to understand this, the most frequent form of social influence. In the discussion that follows, we'll examine many tactics for gaining compliance. Before turning to these, however, we'll introduce a basic framework for understanding the nature of all of these procedures and why they often work.

Compliance A form of social influence in which one or more persons attempt to influence one or more others through direct requests.

Compliance: The Underlying Principles

Some years ago, the well-known social psychologist Robert Cialdini decided that the best way to find out about compliance was to study what he termed "compliance professionals"—people whose success (financial or otherwise) depends on their ability to get others to say yes. Who are such persons? They include salespeople, advertisers, political lobbyists, fund-raisers, politicians, con artists, professional negotiators, and many others. Cialdini's technique for learning from these people was simple: he temporarily concealed his true identity and took jobs in various settings where gaining compliance is a way of life. In other words, he worked in advertising, direct (door-to-door) sales, fund-raising, and other compliance-focused fields. On the basis of these firsthand experiences, he concluded that although techniques for gaining compliance take many different forms, they all rest to some degree on six basic principles (Cialdini, 1994):

1. *Liking/friendship*: In general, we are more willing to comply with requests from people we like or from friends than with requests from strangers or people we don't like.

2. *Commitment/consistency*: Once we have committed ourselves to a position or action, we are more willing to comply with requests for behaviours that are consistent with this position or action than to accede to requests that are inconsistent with it.

3. *Reciprocity*: We are generally more willing to comply with a request from someone who has previously provided a favour or concession to us than to oblige someone who has not. In other words, we feel impelled to pay people back in some way for what they have done for us.

4. *Scarcity*: In general, we value, and try to secure, outcomes or objects that are scarce or decreasing in their availability. As a result, we are more likely to comply with requests that focus on scarcity than with ones that make no reference to this issue.

5. *Social validation*: We are generally more willing to comply with a request for some action if this action is consistent with what we believe persons similar to ourselves are doing (or thinking). We want to be correct, and one way to be so is to act and think like others.

6. *Authority*: In general, we are more willing to comply with requests from someone who holds legitimate authority—or who simply appears to do so.

According to Cialdini (1994), these six basic principles underlie many techniques that professionals—and we ourselves—use for gaining compliance from others. Below we shall focus on three of the most researched topics from this list: liking, commitment/consistency, and reciprocity.

Tactics Based on Liking: Using Impression Management

The desire to make a favourable impression on others is strong. Most of us engage in active efforts to regulate how we appear to others in order to appear in the best or most favourable light possible. This process is known as **impression management** (or **self-presentation**), and considerable evidence indicates that persons who can perform it successfully gain important advantages in many social settings (e.g., Schlenker, 1980; Wayne & Liden, 1995). Our aim when we do this is to achieve **ingratiation**—make others like us in order that we can influence them (Liden & Mitchell, 1988; Wortman & Linsenmeier, 1977). But what tactics do individuals use to create favourable impressions on others and appear likeable? And which of these are most successful? These are the issues we'll consider next.

As your own experience probably suggests, impression management takes many different forms and involves a wide range of specific tactics. Most of these, however, seem to fall into two major categories: *other-enhancement* (efforts to make a target person feel good in our presence) and *self-enhancement* (efforts to boost our own image).

Other-Enhancement: Aren't You Wonderful?

The first type of impression management tactics involves what are sometimes described as **other-enhancement techniques**—efforts to induce favourable reactions in target persons by specific actions toward them. A review of existing studies on this topic (Gordon, 1996) suggests that *flattery*—praising others in some manner—is one of the best. As the cartoon in Figure 7.9 suggests, flattery doesn't have to focus on the recipient to succeed; it can also heap praise on someone close to this individual (e.g., his or her children). Other techniques that seem to work are emitting many positive nonverbal cues, expressing agreement, and doing small favours for the target persons (Gordon, 1996; Wayne & Liden, 1995).

Impression Management (Self-Presentation) Efforts by individuals to produce favourable first impressions on others.

Ingratiation A technique for gaining compliance in which requesters first induce target persons to like them, then attempt to change their behaviour in some desired manner.

Other-Enhancement Techniques of impression management in which the individual attempts to make the target person feel good about him- or herself.

■ Flattery: A Powerful Tool for Gaining Compliance

FIGURE 7.9 Flattery is one highly effective technique for gaining compliance. As shown here, it doesn't have to focus on the recipient to be effective; compliments for persons close to the recipient (e.g., his or her children) can also succeed.

Close to Home

Having narrowed the field of applicants to three, sales director Mark Sutton runs them through the critical brownnosing portion of the interview.

Self-Enhancement: Aren't I Wonderful?

Self-Enhancement Techniques of impression management in which the individual attempts to increase his or her own appeal to others.

Among **self-enhancement techniques**, perhaps the most obvious is altering our own appearance in specific ways. For example, we dress in ways that we believe will be evaluated favourably by others. Such tactics appear to succeed. It has been found, for example, that when women dress in a professional manner (business suit or dress, subdued jewellery), they are evaluated more favourably for management positions than when they dress in a more traditionally feminine manner (dresses with patterns, large jewellery; Forsythe, Drake, & Cox, 1985). Many other aspects of personal appearance, too, are involved in efforts at impression management, including hairstyles, cosmetics, and even eyeglasses (e.g., Baron, 1989; Terry & Krantz, 1993). Additional tactics include *self-deprecation* (providing negative information about oneself as a means of promoting the image of modesty) and *self-disclosure*, or offering personal information about oneself even if it is not requested. This tactic fosters the belief that the ingratiator is honest and likes the target person (Tedeschi & Melburg, 1984).

That individuals often employ such tactics is obvious: you can probably recall many instances in which you either used or were the target of such strategies. A key question, however, is this: Do impression management tactics work? In part, this depends on a person's *cognitive load*—how much of their cognitive capacity is absorbed by other tasks. Often cognitive overload leads people to put down their guards and reveal their true selves, usually with a negative effect. However, relaxing one's guard can have a positive effect for the shy or introverted, who tend to reveal too little (Pontari & Schlenker, 2000). In general, research findings from a growing body of literature indicate that all of the tactics mentioned can be successful and increase the likelihood of *ingratiation*—that target persons will be influenced and agree to various requests (e.g., Kacmar, Delery, & Ferris, 1992; Paulhus, Bruce, & Trapnell, 1995; Wayne & Liden, 1995). However, recent research also suggests that there may be limitations on their effects.

When Impression Management Fails

First of all, if *other-enhancement* is overused, or used ineffectively, it can backfire and produce negative rather than positive reactions from others. For instance, in a thought-provoking study, Vonk (1998) found strong evidence for what he terms the **slime effect**—a tendency to form very negative impressions of others who "lick upward but kick downward"—that is, persons in a work setting who play up to their superiors but treat subordinates with disdain and contempt. The moral of these findings is clear: while tactics of impression management often succeed, this is not always the case; sometimes they can boomerang, adversely affecting reactions to the persons who use them.

A second line of research suggests that constant use of *self-enhancement* techniques can also backfire in the long run. Paulhus and colleagues at the University of British Columbia have examined **trait self-enhancers**—individuals who show an enduring tendency to exaggerate their achievements, abilities, and knowledge (Paulhus, Harms, Bruce, & Lysy, 2003). In contrast to people who use self-enhancement as a deliberate part of ingratiation attempts, trait self-enhancers are not consciously attempting to mislead their audience—they honestly believe in their own superiority (Paulhus, 1998). Thus as well as being extremely self-important, or *narcissistic*, such individuals are also strongly *self-deceiving* in their lack of insight and their inability to respond to feedback about themselves.

Slime Effect A tendency to form very negative impressions of others who "lick upward but kick downward"—that is, persons in a work setting who play up to their superiors but treat subordinates with disdain and contempt.

Trait Self-Enhancers Those who show an enduring tendency to exaggerate their own achievements, abilities, and knowledge. The underlying trait involves narcissistic self-importance and a self-deceptive lack of insight.

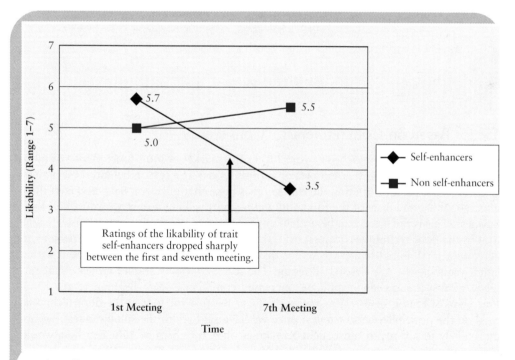

■ The Effectiveness of Self-Enhancement in the Long Run

FIGURE 7.10 At a first meeting, those who showed trait self-enhancement were liked more by others in their group than were non self-enhancers. However, this positive social effect was short-lived—by the seventh meeting, liking had dropped sharply. In contrast, liking of non self-enhancers did not drop and showed a tendency to increase as other group members became more familiar with them.

Source: Based on Paulhus, 1998, and personal communication, 2000.

Subjects were students in an undergraduate class who were randomly assigned to discussion groups as part of their class attendance. Before their first meeting, each group member completed a series of questionnaires designed to measure *trait self-enhancement*. Discussion groups met seven times and evaluated each other after the first and after the seventh meeting.

Results showed that self-enhancement had a positive social impact at the first meeting: Trait self-enhancers were liked by other group members more than non-self-enhancers. However, as shown in Figure 7.10, this positive impact was short-lived. By the seventh meeting, liking for trait self-enhancers had deteriorated drastically, whereas non-self-enhancers had maintained their position and even made some inroads. These findings indicate that, over the long term, the continued self-promotion shown by trait self-enhancers is not socially effective. But as Paulhus put it, trait self-enhancement appears to be a "mixed blessing." Although this type of self-enhancement was ineffective with others in the long run, it certainly seems to work for the enhancers themselves—compared to non-self-enhancers, the trait self-enhancers showed much higher self-esteem.

KEY POINTS

- Individuals use many different tactics for gaining *compliance*—getting others to say *yes* to various requests. Many of these tactics rest on basic principles well known to social psychologists.
- The use of *impression management* techniques—techniques to regulate how we appear to others—such as *other-enhancement* and *self-enhancement* can help to achieve *ingratiation*, or compliance through increased liking.
- Sometimes such techniques fail if applied ineffectively (as in the *slime effect*) or if over-used (as occurs with *trait self-enhancers*).

Tactics Based on Commitment or Consistency

Have you ever been approached at your local supermarket or food court by one or more persons who offered you free samples of various foods? The reason behind these actions is obvious: the persons offering the free samples hope that once you have accepted these gifts, you'll like the taste of the food and will be more willing to buy your lunch at their business. This is the basic idea behind an approach for gaining compliance known as the **foot-in-the-door technique**. In operation, this tactic involves inducing target persons to agree to a small initial request ("Accept this free sample") and then hitting them with a larger request—the one desired all along. The results of many studies indicate that this tactic works: it succeeds in inducing increased compliance (e.g., Beaman et al., 1983; Freedman & Fraser, 1966). Why is this the case? Because the foot-in-the-door technique rests on the principle of *consistency*: once we have said yes to the small request, we are more likely to say yes to subsequent and larger ones, too, because refusing these would be inconsistent with our previous behaviour (e.g., DeJong & Musilli, 1982).

The foot-in-the-door technique is not the only tactic based on the consistency/commitment principle, however. Another is the **lowball** procedure. In this technique, which is often used by automobile salespersons, a very good deal is offered to a customer. After the customer accepts, however, something happens that makes it necessary for the salesperson to change the deal and make it less advantageous for the customer—for example, the sales manager rejects the deal. The totally rational reaction for customers, of course, would be to walk away. Yet often, they agree to the changes and accept the less desirable arrangement (see Figure 7.11).

Foot-in-the-Door Technique A procedure for gaining compliance in which requesters begin with a small request and then, when this is granted, escalate to a larger one (the one they actually desired all along).

Lowball A technique for gaining compliance in which an offer or deal is changed (made less attractive) after the target person has accepted it.

■ The Lowball Technique: A Procedure for Gaining Compliance Based on the Principle of Commitment

FIGURE 7.11 Many automobile salespersons use the *lowball technique*. In this procedure for gaining compliance, customers are offered a very attractive deal, which they accept. The deal is then rejected by the sales manager, who raises the price or makes some other change unfavourable to the customer. Rationally, people should walk away from such deals, but because of prior commitment, they often accept them.

These informal observations have been confirmed by careful research. In one investigation of the lowball procedure, for example, students first agreed to participate in a psychology experiment. Only after making this commitment did they learn that it started at 7:00 a.m. (Cialdini et al., 1978). Despite the inconvenience of this early hour, however, almost all students in this lowball condition appeared for their appointments. In contrast, a much smaller proportion of students who learned about the 7:00 a.m. starting time *before* deciding whether to participate agreed to take part in the study. In instances such as this, an initial commitment seems to make it more difficult for individuals to say no, even though the conditions under which they said yes are now changed.

Tactics Based on Reciprocity

Reciprocity is a basic rule of social life: we usually do unto others as they have done unto us. If they have done a favour for us, therefore, we feel that we should be willing to do one for them in return. While most people view this convention as fair and just, the principle of reciprocity also serves as the basis for several techniques for gaining compliance. One of these is, on the face of it, the opposite of the foot-in-the-door technique. Instead of beginning with a small request and then escalating to a larger one, persons seeking compliance sometimes start with a very large request and then, after this is rejected, shift to a smaller request—the one they wanted all along. This tactic is known as the **door-in-the-face technique** (because the first refusal seems to slam the door in the face of the requester), and several studies indicate that it can be quite effective. For example, in one well-known experiment, Cialdini and his colleagues (1975) stopped college students on the street and presented a huge request: Would the students serve as unpaid counsellors for juvenile delinquents two hours a week for the next *two years*? As you can guess, none agreed. When the experimenters then scaled down their request to a much smaller one—would the same students take a group of delinquents on a two-hour trip to the zoo—fully 50 percent agreed. In contrast, fewer than 17 percent of those in a control group agreed to this smaller request when it was presented cold rather than after the larger request.

Door-in-the-Face Technique A procedure for gaining compliance in which requesters begin with a large request and then, when this is refused, retreat to a smaller one (the one they actually desired all along).

The same tactic is often used by negotiators, who may begin with a position that is extremely advantageous to themselves but then retreat to a position much closer to the one they really hope to obtain. Similarly, sellers often begin with a price they know buyers will reject, and then lower the price to a more reasonable one—but one that is still quite favourable to themselves, and close to what they wanted all along.

Another procedure based on reciprocity is known as the **"that's-not-all" technique**. Here, an initial request is followed, *before the target person can say yes or no*, by something that sweetens the deal—a small extra incentive from the persons using this tactic (e.g., a reduction in price, "throwing in" something additional for the same price). For example, television commercials for various products frequently offer something extra to induce viewers to pick up the phone and place an order. Several studies confirm informal observations suggesting that the "that's-not-all" technique really works (Burger, 1986). These studies also suggest that it is based on the principle of reciprocity: persons on the receiving end of this technique view the "extra" thrown in by the other side as an added concession, and so feel obligated to make a concession themselves. The result: the probability that they will say yes is increased.

Another possible explanation is that compliance in this case is based on the use of heuristics or simple *mindless* processing of information (e.g., Langer, 1989). You may not be thinking deeply about the influencer's tactics, particularly if an item is not going to stretch your budget. All that you are aware of is "This is a bargain," and in accordance with this heuristic thinking, you become more likely to say yes than if you were thinking more systematically. Evidence for this suggestion has recently been reported by Pollock and colleagues (1998). They found that a small price reduction produced the "that's-not-all" effect for a low-cost item (a $1.25 box of chocolates reduced to $1.00), but did not produce this effect for a more expensive item (a $6.25 box reduced to $5.00). Apparently, individuals thought more carefully about spending $5.00, and this countered their tendency to respond automatically. Whatever its precise basis, the "that's-not-all" technique can often be an effective means for increasing the likelihood that others will say yes to various requests.

A more subtle use of the notion of reciprocity underlies what social psychologists term the **foot-in-the-mouth technique** (e.g., Howard, 1990). Briefly, this involves a requester establishing some kind of relationship, no matter how trivial, with the target person, and so increasing the target's feelings of an obligation to comply with reasonable requests. By admitting the existence of this relationship (e.g., "We're all human beings, right?")—which may be a very tenuous one—the target person gives the requester an important edge. In a sense, then, the target person "puts his or her foot in his or her mouth" by agreeing that the relationship exists. A clear demonstration of the power of this tactic is provided by research conducted by Aune and Basil (1994).

These researchers had female accomplices stop students on a university campus and ask them to contribute to a well-known charitable organization. In the foot-in-the-mouth condition, they asked passers-by if they were students, and then commented, "Oh, that's great, so am I." Then they made their request for funds. Results indicated that a much larger percentage of the persons approached made a donation in the foot-in-the-mouth condition (25.5 percent) than in a control condition where no relationship was established (9.8 percent). These findings, and those of a follow-up study by the same authors, suggest that the reciprocity principle can be stretched even to such tenuous relationships as "We're both students, right? And students help students, right? So how about a donation?"

"That's-Not-All" Technique A technique for gaining in which requesters offer additional benefits to target persons before the target persons have decided whether to comply with or reject specific requests.

Foot-in-the-Mouth Technique A procedure for gaining compliance in which the requester establishes some kind of relationship, no matter how trivial, with the target person, thereby increasing this person's feeling of obligation to comply.

Putting Others in a Good Mood: The Basis of Many Compliance Techniques

Many of the tactics for gaining compliance involve putting others in a good mood. Flattery and other tactics of ingratiation, as we noted earlier, are often used for this purpose and can be quite successful if not overdone (Gordon, 1996). As mentioned in Chapter 6, we tend to like people who put us in a good mood and, as a result, we are more willing to allow them to influence us. People also feel happy about snagging a real bargain or being the one lucky enough to get the last one left. But many other techniques can—and apparently do—accomplish the same end (e.g., Rind, 1996). For example, Rind and Bordia (1996) found that female servers who put smiley faces on their bills had tips almost 19 percent greater than when there was no smiling face. This effect was not observed for male servers, probably because drawing smiley faces is not considered gender appropriate. These results, and those of many other studies conducted both in the lab and in the field (e.g., Baron, 1997; Rind, 1996), suggest that almost anything that puts people in a better mood (i.e., that induces positive affect) can increase their tendency to say *yes* to various requests.

For an overview of various tactics for gaining compliance, please see the Ideas to Take with You feature at the end of the chapter.

KEY POINTS

- Two widely used tactics, the *foot-in-the-door technique* and the *lowball* procedure, rest on the principle of commitment/consistency.

- In contrast, the *door-in-the-face*, the *"that's-not-all,"* and the *foot-in-the-mouth* techniques all rest on the principle of reciprocity.

- Putting others in a good mood before making a request is a common feature of many compliance techniques.

Extreme Forms of Social Influence: Obedience and Intense Indoctrination

What is the most direct technique one person can use to change the behaviour of another? In one sense, the answer is as follows: he or she can order the target to do something. This approach is less common than either conformity pressure or tactics for gaining compliance, but it is far from rare. Business executives issue orders to their subordinates; military officers bark commands that they expect to be followed at once; and parents, police officers, and sports coaches, to name just a few, seek to influence others in the same manner. **Obedience** to the commands of sources of authority is far from surprising; such sources usually possess some means of enforcing their directives (e.g., they can reward obedience and punish resistance). More surprising, though, is the fact that even persons lacking in such power can sometimes induce high levels of submission from others. The clearest and most dramatic evidence for the occurrence of such effects has been reported by Stanley Milgram in a series of famous—and controversial—investigations (Milgram, 1963, 1974).

Obedience A form of social influence in which one person simply orders one or more others to perform some action(s).

Destructive Obedience: Some Basic Findings

In his research Milgram wished to learn whether individuals would obey commands from a relatively powerless stranger requiring them to inflict what appeared to be considerable pain on another person—a totally innocent stranger. Milgram's interest in this topic derived from the occurrence of tragic real-life events in which seemingly normal, law-abiding persons actually obeyed such directives. For example, during World War II, troops in the German army obeyed commands to torture and murder unarmed civilians—millions of them—in infamous death camps set up specifically for this grisly purpose. Similar appalling events have occurred in many other cases and at many other points in history (e.g., the My Lai massacre during the Vietnam war; or the murder of unarmed civilians in Kosovo). To try to gain insights into the nature of such events, Milgram designed an ingenious, if disturbing, laboratory simulation. The experimenter informed participants in his studies (all males) that they were participating in an investigation of the effects of punishment on learning. Their task was to deliver electric shocks to another person (actually an accomplice) each time he made an error in a simple learning task. These shocks were to be delivered by means of 30 switches on the equipment shown in Figure 7.12. Participants were told to move to the next higher switch each time the learner made an error. Since the first switch supposedly delivered a shock of 15 volts, it was clear that if the learner made many errors, he would soon be receiving powerful jolts. Indeed, according to the labels on the equipment, the final shock would be 450 volts! In reality, of course, the accomplice (the learner) *never received any shocks during the experiment*. The only real shock ever used was a mild demonstration pulse from one button (number three) to convince subjects that the equipment was real.

During the session, the "learner" (following prearranged instructions) made many errors. Thus, subjects soon found themselves facing a dilemma: Should they continue punishing this person with what seemed to be increasingly painful shocks? Or should they refuse to go on? The experimenter pressured them to continue; whenever they hesitated or protested, he made one of a series of graded remarks.

■ Studying Obedience in the Laboratory

FIGURE 7.12 Left: The apparatus Stanley Milgram used in his famous experiments on obedience. (It has recently been displayed in a special exhibit at the Smithsonian Institution in Washington, D.C.) Right: The experimenter (right front) and a participant (rear) attaching electrodes to the learner's (accomplice's) wrists.

These began with "Please go on," escalated to "It is absolutely essential that you continue," and finally shifted to "You have no other choice; you *must* go on."

Since subjects were all volunteers and were paid in advance, you might predict that they would quickly refuse the experimenter's orders. Yet, in reality, fully *65 percent showed total obedience* to the experimenter's commands, proceeding through the entire series to the final 450-volt level (see Figure 7.13). In contrast, subjects in a control group who were not given such commands generally used only very mild shocks during the session. Many persons, of course, protested and asked that the session be ended. When ordered to proceed, however, a majority yielded to the experimenter's social influence and continued to obey. Indeed, they continued to do so even when the victim pounded on the wall as if in protest against the painful treatment he was receiving.

In further experiments (1965a, 1974), female subjects showed the same degree of obedience as males and Milgram also found that similar results could be obtained even under conditions that might be expected to reduce such obedience. When the study was moved from its original location on the campus of Yale University to a rundown office building in a nearby city, subjects' level of obedience remained remarkably high. Similarly, a large proportion continued to obey even when the accomplice complained about the painfulness of the shocks and begged to be released. Most surprising of all, many (about 30 percent) continued to obey even when they were required to grasp the victim's hand and force it down upon the "shock" plate! That these chilling results were

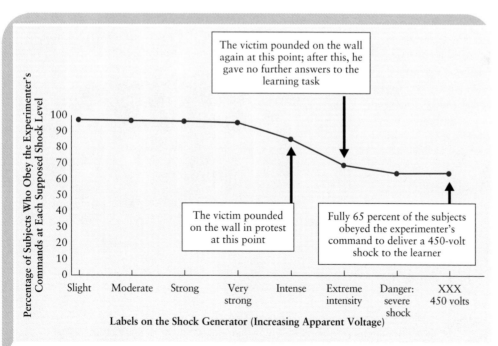

■ Obedience to the Commands of a Powerless Authority

FIGURE 7.13 A surprisingly large proportion of the male participants in Milgram's research obeyed the experimenter's orders to deliver electric shocks of increasing strength to an innocent victim. Fully 65 percent demonstrated total obedience to these commands.

Source: Based on data from Milgram, 1963.

not due to special conditions present in Milgram's laboratory is indicated by the fact that similar findings were soon reported in studies conducted in other countries.

Cultural Differences in Obedience

Researchers in at least eight other countries have attempted to replicate Milgram's studies. Generally, the findings indicate that levels of obedience were similar to those found with American subjects (Smith & Bond, 1993). The Australian and the British subjects were slightly less obedient than the Americans, whereas the Jordanians were comparable to U.S. levels, and the Spanish, Austrians, Germans, and Italians were slightly higher (see Figure 7.14). Although the exact procedures of the non-American studies may have differed slightly from Milgram's original studies, the general pattern of consistent results suggests that substantial numbers of people in a variety of countries (though mostly industrialized Western countries) will carry out orders from authority, even when this compliance will harm others. However, it is important to remember that obedience to authority is not absolute and certain strategies can be utilized to reduce this tendency to obey. These will be discussed later in the chapter.

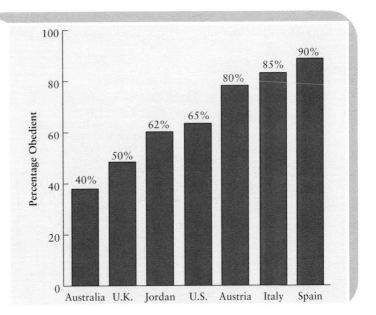

■ Cultural Differences in Destructive Obedience

FIGURE 7.14 Destructive obedience to authority figures is a common response among people all over the world. However, some cultural variation is evident—notably, studies from Australia and the United Kingdom show lowest levels, while those from Italy and Spain show the highest.

Source: Based on data from Smith and Bond, 1993.

KEY POINTS

- *Obedience* is a form of social influence in which one or more persons are ordered to do something, and they do it. It is, in a sense, the most direct form of social influence.
- Research by Stanley Milgram indicates that many persons readily obey commands from a relatively powerless source of authority, even if these commands require them to harm an innocent stranger.
- When cultures are compared some variation is found, although considerable levels of destructive obedience are found in all cultures studied.

Destructive Obedience: Its Social Psychological Basis

As we noted earlier, one reason why Milgram's results are so disturbing is that they seem to parallel many real-life events involving atrocities against innocent victims. Why does such *destructive obedience* occur? Why were participants in these experiments—and in tragic situations outside the laboratory—so willing to yield to this powerful form of social influence? Several factors seem to play a role.

First, persons in authority relieve those who obey of the responsibility for their own actions. "I was only carrying out orders," is the defence many offer after obeying harsh or cruel directives. In life situations, this transfer of responsibility may be implicit. In Milgram's experiments, in contrast, it was quite explicit. Subjects were told at the start that the experimenter (the authority figure), not they, would be responsible for the victim's well-being. Given this fact, it is not surprising that many tended to obey.

Second, persons in authority often wear visible signs of their status and power, such as special uniforms or insignia (see Figure 7.15). Faced with such obvious reminders of who is in charge, most people find it difficult to resist. For example, a female researcher who ordered pedestrians to give a nickel to a young man for parking, was more likely to be obeyed if she was wearing a uniform than if she was dressed as a business executive or a panhandler (Bushman 1984, 1988). Further, in the famous Stanford *prison experiment*, normal college students who were given the uniform and role of "guards" soon showed cruel behaviour towards other students in the role of "prisoners," despite the fact that they had not been instructed to behave in that way (Zimbardo, et al., 1982).

These and related studies (Darley, 1995), suggest that the possession of outward signs of authority impresses both wearer and observer and can play an important role in the ability of authority figures to induce high levels of obedience to their commands.

■ Symbols of Authority: Often They Are Hard to Resist

FIGURE 7.15 Few of us would choose to ignore someone in an official uniform. Uniforms are outward signs of authority that are designed, in many cases, to tell us who is in charge; we disobey people who wear them at our own risk.

A third reason for obedience in many situations in which the targets of such influence might otherwise resist involves the gradual escalation of the authority figure's orders. Initial commands may call for relatively mild actions, such as merely arresting people. Only later do orders come to require behaviour that is dangerous or objectionable. For example, police or military personnel may at first be ordered only to question or threaten potential victims. Gradually, demands are increased to the point where these personnel are commanded to beat, torture, or even murder unarmed civilians. In a sense, persons in authority use the foot-in-the-door technique, asking for small actions first but ever-larger ones later. In a similar manner, participants in Milgram's research were first required to deliver only mild and harmless shocks to the victim. Only as the sessions continued did the intensity of these "punishments" rise to potentially harmful levels.

Finally, events in many situations involving destructive obedience move very quickly: demonstrations quite suddenly turn into riots, arrests into mass beatings or mass murder. The fast pace of such events gives participants little time for reflection or systematic processing: people are ordered to obey and—almost automatically—they do so. Such conditions prevailed in Milgram's research; within a few minutes of entering the laboratory, participants found themselves faced with commands to deliver strong electric shocks to the learner. This fast pace, too, may tend to increase obedience.

In sum, several factors contribute to the high levels of obedience witnessed in laboratory studies and in a wide range of real-life contexts. Together these merge into a powerful force—one that most persons find difficult to resist. Unfortunately, the consequences of this compelling form of social influence can be disastrous for many innocent and largely defenceless victims.

Destructive Obedience: Resisting Its Effects

Now that we have considered some of the factors responsible for the strong tendency to obey sources of authority, we will turn to a related question: How can this type of social influence be resisted? Several strategies seem to be effective in helping to reduce the tendency to obey.

First, individuals exposed to commands from authority figures can be reminded that they—not the authorities—are responsible for any harm produced. Under these conditions, sharp reductions in the tendency to obey have been observed in American, Australian, German, and Dutch subjects (e.g., Hamilton, 1978; Kilham & Mann, 1974; Mantell, 1971; Meeus & Raaijmakers, 1986).

Second, individuals can be provided with an indication that, beyond some point, unquestioning submission to destructive commands is inappropriate. For example, they can be exposed to the actions of *disobedient models*—people who refuse to obey an authority figure's commands. Research findings suggest that this strategy, too, is quite effective in reducing obedience (Milgram, 1965b; e.g., Rochat & Modigliani, 1995). Again, this strategy was also effective in reducing obedience in Dutch and German participants.

Third, individuals may find it easier to resist influence from authority figures if they question the expertise and motives of the authority figures. Are such persons really in a better position to judge what is appropriate and what is inappropriate? What motives lie behind their commands—socially beneficial goals or selfish gain? By asking such questions, persons who might otherwise obey may find support for independence rather than submission.

Finally, simply knowing about the power of authority figures to command blind obedience may be helpful in itself. Some research findings (e.g., Sherman, 1980) suggest that when individuals learn about the results of social psychological research, they often recognize these as important (Richard, Bond, & Stokes-Zoota, 2001) and sometimes change their behaviour in light of this new knowledge. With respect to destructive obedience, there is some hope that knowing about this process can enhance individuals' ability to resist. To the extent this is so, then, even exposure to findings as disturbing as those reported by Milgram can have positive social value.

To conclude: The power of authority figures to command obedience is certainly great, but it is definitely *not* irresistible. Under appropriate conditions it can be countered and reduced. As in many other spheres of life, there is a choice. Deciding to resist the dictates of authority can, of course, be dangerous. Those holding power wield tremendous advantages in terms of weapons and technology. Yet, as events in Eastern Europe, the former Soviet Union, and elsewhere have demonstrated, the outcome is by no means certain when committed groups of citizens choose to resist. In short, the human spirit is not so easily controlled or extinguished as many dictators would like to believe.

KEY POINTS

- Destructive obedience, which plays a role in many real-life atrocities, stems from several factors. These include shifting of responsibility to the authority figure, outward signs of authority on the part of this person, a gradual escalation of the scope of the commands given (related to the foot-in-the-door technique), and the rapid pace with which such situations proceed.

- Several strategies can help reduce the occurrence of destructive obedience. These include reminding individuals that they share in the responsibility for any harm produced, reminding them that beyond some point obedience is inappropriate, calling into question the motives of authority figures, and informing people of the findings of social psychological research on this topic.

Intense Indoctrination: Social Influence Carried to the Extreme

In 1978, 914 members of the People's Temple committed suicide when ordered to do so by their leader. In 1993, members of the Branch Davidian cult engaged in what amounted to suicidal resistance to the demands of government agents—resistance that resulted in the deaths of many members of the group. These tragic events have focused much public attention on extreme religious groups, and have revealed some truly shocking things about conditions in them. In many of these groups, new members must give all of their possessions to the group on joining, and they must agree to live by rules and regulations that most of us would find completely incomprehensible. For example, among the Branch Davidians, all members, except the leader, were forbidden to engage in sexual relations; he reserved this right strictly for himself.

The extreme and often bizarre conditions of life in these groups raise an intriguing question: How do they manage to exert such total control over the lives of their members? In other words, how do these groups succeed in exercising profound levels of social influence over the persons who join them? At first glance, it might seem as though they achieve this goal by means of mysterious forces and processes outside the realm of science. A recent analysis of conditions in these groups by one social psychologist, though, suggests that, actually, the powerful influence of extreme groups over their members can be fully understood in terms of the principles and processes considered in this chapter (R. S. Baron, 2000). Let's see how this can be so.

In his analysis of *intense indoctrination*—a process through which individuals become members of extreme groups and come to accept the beliefs and rules of the group in a totally unquestioning and highly committed way—Baron (2000) suggests that such indoctrination involves four distinct stages, and that at each stage, factors well known to social psychologists play an important role. We'll first describe these stages and then indicate what aspects of social influence shape them.

Stages of Intense Indoctrination

In the first, or *softening-up*, stage, new recruits are isolated from friends and family, and efforts are made to keep them confused, tired, disoriented, and emotionally aroused. The main goal here is to cut new recruits off from their former lives and to put them in a state in which they are receptive to the group's message (see Figure 7.16).

This stage is followed by a second one, known as *compliance*. During this stage, recruits are asked to pay lip service to the demands and beliefs of the group and actively "try out" the role of member. A third stage, *internalization*, quickly follows. Now, recruits begin to accept the views of the group as correct and to actually believe these views. In other words, public compliance is replaced by inner acceptance.

Finally, in the *consolidation* stage, recruits solidify their membership by engaging in costly acts that make it difficult, if not impossible, to go back: they donate all their personal possessions to the group, cut off all ties with former friends and family, begin

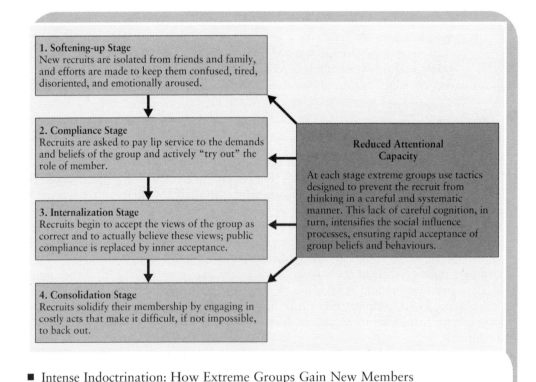

■ Intense Indoctrination: How Extreme Groups Gain New Members

FIGURE 7.16 Extreme groups expose new recruits to conditions designed to reduce their attentional capacity. This, in turn, increases the susceptibility of new recruits to various tactics of social influence, and it makes it more and more difficult for them to withdraw before becoming fully committed members.

to actively recruit new members, and so on. The result is that the new members now accept the beliefs and philosophy of the group in an unquestioning manner, and come to hold negative views about "outsiders."

Social Psychological Processes: Why Intense Indoctrination Succeeds

Now for *the* central question: Why do individuals continue through these phases? Why do they gradually surrender almost total control over their own lives to the groups they join? According to R. S. Baron (2000), a key part of the answer involves the fact that, in these groups, vigorous efforts are made to place members in a state that maximizes the impact of tactics of social influence upon them at each of the stages described above. This key state is *reduced attentional capacity*. In other words, extreme groups use various tactics to ensure that new recruits are rendered incapable of thinking carefully or systematically. This, in turn, increases their susceptibility to the group's efforts to reshape their attitudes and behaviour. How do extreme groups do this? As noted above, by keeping new recruits exhausted (e.g., through lack of sleep or poor nutrition), emotionally aroused, and isolated from their former lives.

The resulting state of reduced attentional capacity, in turn, plays a key role in each of the stages described above. For example, consider internalization, the stage at which members begin to accept the group's extreme views. Here, reduced attentional capacity lowers the recruits' ability to think carefully and systematically about the information they are receiving. It also increases their tendency to conform, because conformity is often enhanced when people are confused, uncertain about how to act, and are experiencing reduced confidence (e.g., Baron, Vandello, & Brunsman, 1996). At the same time, reduced attentional capacity increases the tendency of new recruits to think stereotypically—for instance, to develop negative views about nonmembers (e.g., Paulhus, Martin, & Murphy, 1992).

Other social psychological factors are at work during the consolidation stage. Here, individuals who have made public statements supporting the group's views or who have engaged in actions such as donating all their possessions to the group may experience strong dissonance (see Chapter 3), accompanied by powerful motives to justify these past actions. Previous research indicates that reduced attentional capacity (or emotional arousal) can intensify such effects (e.g., Stalder & Baron, 1998). The result? Their commitment to the group's extreme views is increased.

In sum, by placing new recruits in a state that lessens their attentional capacity (i.e., their capacity to think carefully and systematically), extreme groups increase the susceptibility of these persons to various influence tactics. These tactics (e.g., intense peer pressure, inducing recruits to make public statements supporting the group's views) are then applied to potential members forcefully and consistently over prolonged periods of time, until recruits reach a point where they accept the group's views in a totally unquestioning manner. In short, while the level of influence exerted by extreme groups over their members is indeed unsettling, it is by no means mysterious. Rather, it can be fully understood in terms of principles and processes of social influence—factors and events very familiar to social psychologists.

KEY POINTS

- Extreme groups subject new recruits to a process of *intense indoctrination* directed toward the goal of inducing recruits to accept the beliefs and rules of the group in a totally unquestioning and highly committed way.

- New members pass through four stages in this process: softening up, compliance, internalization, and consolidation.
- At each of these stages, reduced attentional capacity increases recruits' susceptibility to various tactics of social influence. Thus, their powerful commitment to the group can be understood in terms of processes and principles well known to social psychologists.

Ideas To Take With You

Tactics for Gaining Compliance

How can we get other persons to say yes to our requests? This is an eternal puzzle of social life. Research by social psychologists indicates that all of the techniques described here can be useful—and that they are widely used. So, whether or not you use these approaches yourself, you are likely to be on the receiving end of many of them during your lifetime. Here are tactics that are especially common.

Ingratiation.
Getting others to like us so that they will be more willing to agree to our requests. We can ingratiate ourselves through flattery, by making ourselves attractive, and by showing liking for and interest in the target person. But be careful not to go too far.

The Foot-in-the-Door Technique.
Starting with a small request and, after it is accepted, escalating to a larger one.

The Door-in-the-Face Technique.
Starting with a large request and then, when this is refused, backing down to a smaller one.

Putting Others in a Good Mood.
Using any of countless tactics to make other people feel more cheerful—and thus more likely to say yes to our requests.

Summary

Conformity: Group Influence in Action

- *Social influence* defined. (p. 247)
- *Conformity*, a form of social influence in which people behave in line with *social norms*. (p. 248)
- Asch's classic conformity research shows we yield to pressure from a unanimous group. (p. 249)
- Factors that determine conformity include *cohesiveness*, group size, unanimity, and type of social norm. (p. 251)
- Conformity is higher in collective cultures and relates to

the means of subsistence. (p. 253)
- *Normative social influence*, a motive for conformity, may be influenced by fear of ridicule. (p. 255)
- A second motive for conformity is *informational social influence*. (p. 256)
- Resistance to conformity seems to stem from the desire for *individuation* and control. (p. 258)
- Minority influence occurs under certain conditions. (p. 259)
- *Compensatory conformity* may be shown by minorities made aware of their status. (p. 260)

Compliance: To Ask—Sometimes—Is to Receive

- Tactics for gaining *compliance* rest on basic social psychological principles. (p. 262)
- *Impression management* techniques include *other-* and *self-enhancement* and can achieve *ingratiation*. (p. 263)
- The *slime effect* and *behaviour or trait self-enhancers* show *ineffective use of impression management*. (p. 265)
- The *foot-in-the-door technique* and *lowball procedure* rest on commitment/consistency. (p. 266)
- The *door-in-the-face*, *"that's-not-all,"* and *foot-in-the-mouth* techniques rest on reciprocity. (p. 267)
- Putting others in a good mood is a common feature of compliance techniques. (p. 269)

Obedience: Social Influence by Demand

- *Obedience* defined. (p. 269)
- Milgram's classic studies of destructive obedience. (p. 270)
- Cultural variation in destructive obedience is found. (p. 272)
- Factors that determine destructive obedience include signs of authority, responsibility shifts, gradual escalation, and the rapid pace of proceedings. (p. 273)
- Reduced destructive obedience can occur when individuals take responsibility, question the motives of authority, and know about research. (p. 274)
- Intense indoctrination involves four stages of influence and reduced attentional capacity. (p. 276)

For More Information

Cialdini, R. B. (1994). *Influence: Science and practice* (3rd ed.). New York: HarperCollins.

An insightful account of the major techniques people use to influence others. The book draws both on the findings of systematic research and on informal observations made by the author in a wide range of practical settings (e.g., sales, public relations, fund-raising agencies, organizations). This is the most readable and informative account of knowledge about influence currently available.

Milgram, S. (1974). *Obedience to authority.* New York: Harper & Row.

Almost 30 years after it was written, this book remains the definitive work on obedience as a social psychological process. The untimely death of its author at age 51 only adds to its value as a lasting contribution to our field.

Weblinks

www.csj.org
Resources about psychological manipulation, cult groups, sects, and new religious movements
www.stanleymilgram.com
Comprehensive information about the life and work of Stanley Milgram prepared by Professor Thomas Blass

sun.science.wayne.edu/~wpoff/cor/grp/influenc.html
Part of a web-based course on social influence processes

CHAPTER EIGHT

Helping and Harming:
Prosocial Behaviour and Aggression

Bystander Response to an Emergency
Providing Help: Five Essential Cognitive Steps
Prosocial Motivation: Why Do People Help?
Empathy–Altruism: Concern for Others as Basis for Helping/Negative-State Relief: Helping Can Reduce Your Own Negative Affect/Empathic Joy: Helping Can Lead to the "Helper's High"/Evolutionary Origins of Prosocial Behaviour: Genetic Determinism
Further Determinants of Helping Behaviour: Internal and External Influences
Attributions of Responsibility: Assessing the Victim/Dispositional Differences in Prosocial Behaviour: The Altruistic Personality/Role Models: Providing Helpful Cues/Who Needs Help? Characteristics of the Victim/Cultural Context: Regional and Societal Differences in Prosocial Behaviour.
Sources of Aggression: Theories about Its Nature and Causes
The Evolution of Aggression: A Part of Human Nature?/Drive Theories: The Motive to Harm Others/Modern Theories of Aggression: Taking Account of Learning, Cognition, Mood, and Arousal
Further Determinants of Aggression: Internal and External Influences
Heightened Arousal: Emotion, Cognition, and Aggression/Dispositional Influences on Aggression: Aggressive Personality Factors/Evaluating Others' Behaviour: Provocation and Attribution/Gender and Aggression: Are There Real Differences?/Situational Determinants of Aggression: Alcohol Consumption and Exposure to Violent Media/Culture and Aggression: The Social Context of Violence
The Prevention and Control of Aggression: Some Useful Techniques
Punishment: An Effective Deterrent to Violence?/Catharsis: Does Getting It Out of Your System Really Help?/Cognitive Interventions: Apologies and Overcoming Cognitive Deficits

SPECIAL SECTIONS

CORNERSTONES
The Bystander Effect: Explaining Why Bystanders Don't Respond

CANADIAN RESEARCH: ON THE CUTTING EDGE
Alcohol and Aggression: The Effects Depend on Sex and Predisposition

ON THE APPLIED SIDE
Bullying: Singling Out Others for Repeated Abuse

"Before we set out, there's this little matter of a waiver."

■ Prosocial Behaviour Sometimes Involves Risk

FIGURE 8.1 Prosocial acts do not provide direct benefits to the person who performs them, and they may involve a degree of risk. This Boy Scout doesn't want his helpfulness to lead to future legal problems.

Even if you live a sheltered life, there are few of us who aren't aware that human behaviour can vary tremendously. Just a brief exposure to any newspaper can bring that clearly to consciousness. One page may feature a story of domestic violence or the report of atrocities inflicted by one national group on another. Yet an adjacent column may give details of heroism—an incident where someone took considerable risks to rescue a stranger. Social psychologists have focused a great deal of attention on both topics—the factors that influence whether we *help* or *harm* others.

In the first part of this chapter we will examine issues related to prosocial behaviour. By **prosocial behaviour**, we mean actions that provide benefit to others rather than the person who carries them out. A related term, **altruistic behaviour**, refers to acts that involve an unselfish concern for the welfare of others, and can be costly for the actor or even involve real risks—see Figure 8.1. We will begin with classic research on the *bystander effect*. Back in 1964, a real-life case generated an important program of research investigating why people fail to help in an emergency. We then turn to the other side of this issue, the source of our *prosocial motivation*—when we help, and we often do, what is the source of our motivation? Is it fundamentally selfish (we are helping ourselves by helping others) or is it altruistic (we really care about others suffering)? Finally, we will look at some additional variables, both internal and external to the helper, which increase or decrease the likelihood of prosocial behaviour.

The second part of this chapter examines **aggression**—the intentional infliction of some form of harm on others. In view of its destructive impact on society and its prevalence (Geen, 1990), it is hardly surprising that aggression has been an important topic of research in social psychology for half a century (Baron & Richardson, 1994). First,

Prosocial Behaviour Acts that benefit others rather than the person who carries them out.

Altruistic Behaviour Acts that suggest an unselfish concern for the welfare of others, are costly for the individual who behaves altruistically, and sometimes involve risk.

Aggression Behaviour directed toward the goal of harming or injuring another living being who is motivated to avoid such treatment.

we'll describe several different theoretical perspectives on aggression—contrasting views about the nature and origins of such behaviour. Next, we'll review important determinants of aggression—aspects of others' behaviour (or our interpretations of their actions) and of the situations that play a role in the initiation of aggressive outbursts. Finally, we'll end on an optimistic note by examining various techniques for the prevention and control of human aggression. As will soon become apparent, a degree of optimism really is justified in this respect, for several effective techniques for reducing overt aggression do indeed exist.

Bystander Response to an Emergency

Research in social psychology is often stimulated by observation of real-life events and perhaps the classic case of this subject occurred in 1964. In this incident the need for help was unambiguous and many bystanders were present, but not one of them responded. As a result, a young woman was murdered. This instance of what newspapers at the time called "bystander apathy" motivated two social psychologists to try to understand why no one had helped, as described in the following Cornerstones section.

Cornerstones

The Bystander Effect: Explaining Why Bystanders Don't Respond

The event involving the absence of prosocial behaviour became a matter of widespread concern. It took place in the early morning hours of March 13, 1964. In New York City, Catherine (Kitty) Genovese was returning home from her job as manager of a bar. As she crossed the street from her car to the apartment building where she lived, a man armed with a knife approached her. She began running in an effort to avoid him, but he ran in pursuit, caught up to her, and then stabbed her. She screamed for help, and numerous people apparently heard her, because lights quickly came on in several of the apartment windows that overlooked the street. The attacker retreated briefly, but when no one came to help his bleeding victim, he returned to finish the job. She screamed again, but he stabbed her repeatedly until she lay dead. It was later determined that this horrifying 45-minute interaction was seen and heard by 38 witnesses, but no one took direct action or even bothered to call the police (Rosenthal, 1964).

On the basis of the many news stories about this incident, the general response was one of shock and disappointment about the failure of the bystanders to come to the victim's aid. Why didn't they help?

Possibly people in general had become apathetic, cold, and indifferent to the problems of others. Perhaps living in a big city made people callous. Perhaps violence on TV and in the movies had desensitized viewers to the horror of real violence and real suffering. Maybe modern American society, which had recently experienced the assassination of a president, was no longer able to empathize with the plight of a stranger in need of help.

As we now know, there are psychological explanations for the failure of those bystanders to respond—explanations that do not involve apathy, indifference, callousness, or a general absence of empathy. A novel idea began to take shape shortly after the murder as Professors John Darley and Bibb Latané ate lunch and discussed what had happened in their city. They believed that the problem was not that the bystanders didn't care about the crime victim, but that something about the situation must have made them hesitate to act. As these psychologists speculated, they began to outline proposed experiments on their tablecloth (Krupat, 1975).

The initial hypothesis (Darley & Latané, 1968) was that the inaction of the bystanders in the Genovese murder resulted from the fact that many people were present at the scene and that no one person felt responsible for taking action. Thus, there was **diffusion of responsibility**. Darley and Latané tested the hypothesis that as the number of bystanders increases, the diffused responsibility results in a decrease in prosocial behaviour. Each subject in their initial experiment was exposed to a bogus medical emergency and believed himself or herself to be either the only one who knew about the problem, one of two bystanders, or one of five bystanders. The basic question was whether helpfulness would decrease as the number of bystanders increased.

Diffusion of Responsibility The presence of multiple bystanders at the scene of an emergency, resulting in the responsibility for taking action being shared among all members of the group. As a result of diffusion of responsibility, each individual feels less responsible and is less likely to act than if he or she were alone.

When undergraduate subjects arrived at the laboratory to participate in a psychological experiment, the instructions indicated that they would discuss with fellow students some of the problems involved in attending college in a high-pressure urban setting. The participants were told that each of them would be assigned to a separate room and could communicate only by an intercom system; they could hear each other, but the experimenter would not be listening. This arrangement was supposedly designed to avoid any embarrassment about discussing personal matters.

Some subjects were told that they were one of two discussants, others that they were part of a group of three, and still others that six students were participating. Each participant was supposed to talk for two minutes, after which the listener or listeners would comment on what the others had said. In reality, only one subject took part in each session, and the other participant or participants were simply tape recordings. Thus, the stage was set for a controlled emergency apparently overheard by varying numbers of bystanders.

In each session the first person to speak was the tape-recorded individual who was to be the "victim." He said, sounding embarrassed, that he sometimes had seizures, especially when facing a stressful situation such as exams. After the participant (and, in two of the conditions, other "participants") had given a two-minute talk about college problems, the victim spoke again:

> I er I think I need er if if could er er somebody er er help because I er I'm er h-h-having a a a real problem er right now and I er if somebody could help me out it would er er s-s-sure be good because er there er er a thing's coming on and and I could really er

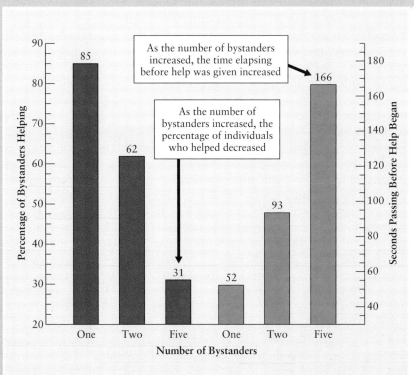

■ The Bystander Effect: More Bystanders = Less Help

FIGURE 8.2 In the initial experiment designed to explore the bystander effect, students heard what seemed to be a fellow student having a seizure. The research participant was supposedly either the only bystander to this emergency, one of two bystanders, or one of five. As the number of bystanders increased, the percentage of individuals who tried to help the "victim" decreased. In addition, among those who did help, as the number of bystanders increased, the more time passed before help began. This effect was initially explained on the basis of diffusion of responsibility.

Source: Based on data from Darley & Latané, 1968.

use some help so if somebody here er help er uh uh uh (choking sounds) I'm gonna die er er I'm gonna die er help er er seizure (chokes, then is quiet). (Darley & Latané, 1968, p. 379.)

Two aspects of bystander responsiveness were measured, and the results are shown in Figure 8.2 on the previous page. A helpful response consisted of leaving the experimental room to look for the imaginary victim. As the number of apparent bystanders increased, the percentage of subjects attempting to help decreased. Further, among those who did respond, an increase in the number of bystanders led to increased delay in taking action. Such findings are consistent with Darley and Latané's hypothesis that the presence of others leads to diffused responsibility and makes helpfulness less probable.

It is well worth noting that the student bystanders who hesitated or failed to respond were not apathetic or uncaring. Compared to the 85 percent of lone bystanders who helped in the first 60 seconds, far fewer participants tried to help in the conditions in which fellow bystanders were believed to be present; but even the totally unhelpful individuals appeared to be concerned, upset, and confused

The conclusion is that the prosocial tendencies of a single witness to an emergency are inhibited by the presence of additional witnesses, a phenomenon that became known as the **bystander effect**. Darley (1991) has indicated that neither he nor his colleague could have foreseen the flood of research that their experiment initiated. As you will see in the remainder of this section, this one experiment was just the first of a great many investigations that have made prosocial behaviour much more understandable and predictable. The initial insight about diffusion of responsibility was only the beginning.

Bystander Effect
The finding that as the number of bystanders witnessing an emergency increases, the likelihood of each bystander's responding, and the speed of responding, decrease.

Providing Help: Five Essential Cognitive Steps

Following the initial experiment on diffusion of responsibility, Latané and Darley (1970)—as well as others—carried out numerous interrelated experiments, and they eventually formulated a theoretical model (see Figure 8.3) to explain why bystanders sometimes do and sometimes do not help a victim. They described a helping response as the end point of a series of cognitive decisions. Help is provided only if the appropriate decision is made at each step. What are these crucial choice points?

Step 1: Noticing the Emergency Event

The first decision is whether to shift one's attention from whatever one is doing to the unexpected emergency—to notice that something is wrong. Many factors can prevent this. You may not be facing the emergency situation, so seeing or hearing it may be impaired. Other people or sounds in your immediate vicinity may distract you. Or you may be so involved in your present activity that you notice very little else.

The role of such preoccupation was studied by Darley and Batson (1973). Seminary students served as experimental subjects, and their task was to go to a nearby building to present a talk. In an attempt to prime a helping response, the researchers specified that the talk was to be either about providing help to a stranger in need (Luke's parable of the Good Samaritan) or about jobs. To manipulate preoccupation, the investigators told the subjects that they were (1) ahead of schedule, with plenty of time; (2) right on schedule; or (3) late for the speaking engagement. It was assumed that the third group would be the least attentive to an emergency situation.

On their way to give the talk, the subjects each encountered an experimental assistant who was slumped in a doorway, coughing and groaning. Would they notice this individual and offer help? The topic of the upcoming speech had no effect on their response, but the time pressure did. As shown in Figure 8.4, help was offered by 63 percent of those who believed they had time to spare, 45 percent of those who were on

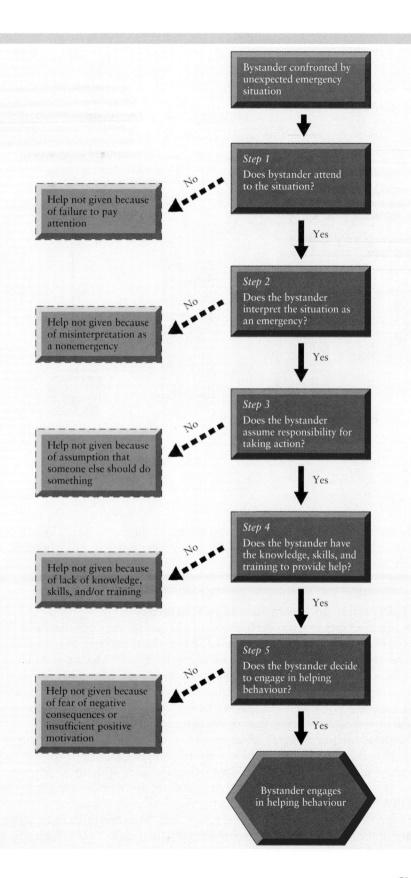

■ Five Steps: Prosocial Action or Failure to Help?

FIGURE 8.3 Latané and Darley conceptualized prosocial behaviour as the end point of a series of five cognitive steps, representing choice points. At each step in the process, the choices (whether conscious or unconscious) result in either (1) no help being given or (2) movement to the following step in a progression toward possible helping.

Bystander confronted by unexpected emergency situation

Step 1
Does bystander attend to the situation?

No → Help not given because of failure to pay attention

Yes

Step 2
Does the bystander interpret the situation as an emergency?

No → Help not given because of misinterpretation as a nonemergency

Yes

Step 3
Does the bystander assume responsibility for taking action?

No → Help not given because of assumption that someone else should do something

Yes

Step 4
Does the bystander have the knowledge, skills, and training to provide help?

No → Help not given because of lack of knowledge, skills, and/or training

Yes

Step 5
Does the bystander decide to engage in helping behaviour?

No → Help not given because of fear of negative consequences or insufficient positive motivation

Yes

Bystander engages in helping behaviour

■ Preoccupation with Time Pressure Interferes with Perception of Emergency

FIGURE 8.4 When potential helpers are preoccupied with other concerns, they are much less likely to help a person in need. Among other factors, they are too busy to pay attention to the victim. Research participants who believed they had plenty of time to reach the room in which they were giving a talk were most likely to stop and help a stranger who was slumped, coughing and groaning, in a doorway. Those who believed they were running behind schedule were least likely to help.

Source: Based on data from Darley & Batson, 1973.

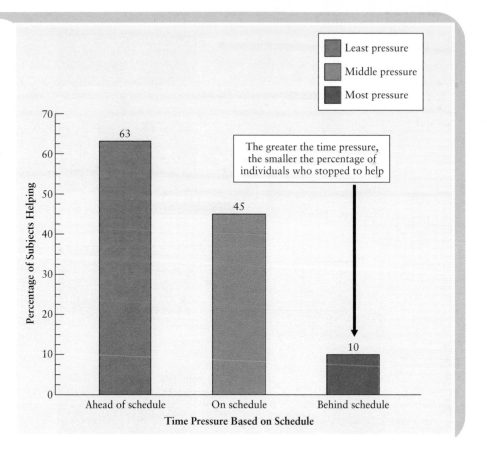

schedule, and only 10 percent of those who were told they were late. The preoccupied subjects were in such a hurry that even when they were going to talk about the Good Samaritan, some simply stepped over the victim and rushed along to keep the speaking appointment.

Step 2: Interpreting an Emergency as an Emergency

Once the situation gets a bystander's attention, the second step is to interpret the situation correctly. What is going on? In general, it is easier to imagine a routine, everyday explanation of events than a highly unusual and unlikely one (Macrae & Milne, 1992). And a problem with interpreting an everyday situation as an emergency is that you can end up looking foolish. To avoid being embarrassed about being incorrect and behaving in an inappropriate way, most people fail to engage in any drastic action until the evidence is clear and convincing that an emergency is actually occurring.

Often there is some degree of ambiguity in emergency situations, so potential helpers hold back and wait for additional information in order to be sure about what is going on. Ambiguity sometimes includes indecision as to whether a victim wants to be helped (Shotland & Strau, 1976). That is one reason why people are hesitant to respond to a domestic quarrel; sometimes the victim of domestic aggression resents an outsider's interference as much as the aggressor does. In general, the more ambiguous the situation, the less likely people are to offer help (Bickman, 1972). With ambiguous information as to whether one is witnessing a serious problem or something inconsequential, most people are inclined to accept a comforting and nonstressful interpretation that indicates no need to do anything (Wilson & Petruska, 1984).

When more than one bystander witnesses an emergency, each interprets the event in part on the basis of what the others do or say—each relies on social comparison (see Chapter 2). If fellow witnesses fail to react, helping behaviour is strongly inhibited. A special problem is that in our culture we are taught to remain calm in an emergency; it isn't socially acceptable to begin screaming when we see a stranger slip on an icy path, for example. As a result, most bystanders pretend to be calm, and this cool response is perceived by other bystanders as evidence that nothing serious is occurring. In an actual emergency, therefore, multiple bystanders can inadvertently and incorrectly inform one another that everything is all right.

This phenomenon is known as **pluralistic ignorance,** and an experiment by Latané and Darley (1968) demonstrates how it operates. The investigators asked subjects to fill out questionnaires in a room either alone or in groups of three. Shortly after they began, smoke was pumped into the room through a vent. The experimenters waited for the subjects to respond (but terminated the experimental session after six minutes if the subjects remained in their seats and failed to act). When subjects were in the room alone, 75 percent went out to report the smoke, and half of those who responded did so within two minutes. When three people were in the room, only one person reacted in the first four minutes—the majority (62 percent) did nothing for the entire six minutes even though the smoke became thick enough to make it difficult to see.

Step 3: Assuming That Helpfulness Is Your Responsibility

Once an individual pays attention to some external event and interprets it correctly as an emergency, a prosocial act will follow only if the person takes responsibility for providing help. In many instances the responsibility is clear. Firefighters are the ones to do something about a burning house; police officers are the ones to do something about a crime; medical personnel deal with injuries and illnesses. When responsibility is not as clear as in those examples, people tend to assume that anyone in a leadership role must be responsible (Baumeister et al., 1988). For example, professors should be responsible for dealing with classroom emergencies and bus drivers for emergencies involving their vehicles. When there is one adult and several children, the adult is expected to take charge.

One of the reasons that a lone bystander is more likely to act than a bystander in a group is that there is no one else present who could take responsibility. With a group, as we have discussed, the responsibility is diffuse and much less clear.

Step 4: Knowing What to Do

Even if a bystander reaches the point of assumed responsibility, nothing useful can be done unless that person knows how to be helpful. Some emergencies are sufficiently simple that almost everyone has the necessary skills. If you see someone slip on an icy sidewalk, you help that person up. If you see two suspicious strangers trying to break into a parked car, you find a phone and dial 911. Even in the latter instance, though, a child or a recent immigrant might not possess the necessary information.

Some emergencies require special knowledge and skills that are not possessed by most bystanders. For example, you can help someone who is drowning only if you know how to swim and how to handle a drowning person. With bystanders at an accident, a registered nurse is more likely to assume responsibility and more likely to help than someone not employed in a medical profession (Cramer et al., 1988).

Pluralistic Ignorance A phenomenon that can occur when multiple bystanders witness an emergency: Each interprets the event in part on the basis of what the others do or say, but when none of them is sure about what is happening, all hold back and pretend that everything is all right. Each then uses this "information" to justify not responding.

Step 5: Deciding to Help

Even if a bystander's response at each of the first four steps is yes, help will not occur unless he or she makes the final decision to act. Helping at this point can be inhibited by fears (often realistic) about potential negative consequences. In effect, people seem to engage in "cognitive algebra" as they weigh the positive versus the negative aspects of helping (Fritzsche, Finkelstein, & Penner, 2000). And the potential costs are many. For example, if you try to help a person who slipped on the ice, you might fall yourself. A sick person who has collapsed in a doorway may throw up on your shoes when you try to provide assistance. The person who seems to be in need may be a crook who is only pretending.

An especially unpleasant consequence may arise when there is family violence: The well-meaning outsider often arouses only anger. For this reason, bystanders rarely offer help when they believe that a woman is being attacked by her husband or boyfriend (Shotland & Strau, 1976) or that a child is being physically abused by a parent (Christy & Voigt, 1994). And police have learned that even when they have been called to an angry domestic scene by someone involved in the situation, intervention in this kind of family violence is more dangerous than interference in a hostile interaction between two strangers.

For some very good reasons, then, bystanders may decide to hold back and avoid the risks that are sometimes associated with performing prosocial acts. While the five steps are still fresh in your mind, you might want to review them by taking a close look at the Ideas to Take with You section at the end of the chapter.

KEY POINTS

- The purest form of *prosocial behaviour* is *altruism*—selfless actions that benefit another and are costly to the actor. Such behaviour contrasts with *aggression*—behaviour that intends harm to others.

- In part because of *diffusion of responsibility*, the more bystanders present as witnesses to an emergency, the less likely is help to be given and the greater the delay before the help occurs: this is termed the *bystander effect*.

- When faced with an emergency, a bystander must go through five crucial steps involving decisions that either inhibit or enhance the likelihood of a prosocial response. First, he or she must notice the emergency; second, correctly interpret what is occurring, and this process can be blocked by *pluralistic ignorance*; third, assume responsibility for providing help; fourth, have the necessary skills and knowledge to help; and fifth, actually decide to provide assistance.

Prosocial Motivation: Why Do People Help?

Research on the *bystander effect* has focused on explaining why we fail to help—and the answers it has provided have been invaluable to emergency workers. But in beginning with this classic research, we do not want to give you the impression that generally we are an unhelpful species. The fact is that human beings help each other all the time—from the mild assistance of picking up an object that someone else has dropped, to the extreme situation in which people risk their lives to save a stranger. In this section we want to turn the bystander question around and ask why people do help? That is, given that we help each other out, what are our fundamental motives? In attempting to answer this question, social psychologists are investigating basic aspects of

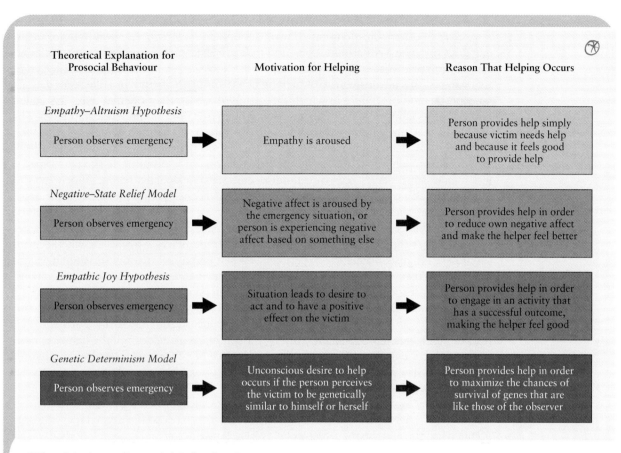

Theoretical Explanation for Prosocial Behaviour	Motivation for Helping	Reason That Helping Occurs
Empathy–Altruism Hypothesis Person observes emergency	Empathy is aroused	Person provides help simply because victim needs help and because it feels good to provide help
Negative–State Relief Model Person observes emergency	Negative affect is aroused by the emergency situation, or person is experiencing negative affect based on something else	Person provides help in order to reduce own negative affect and make the helper feel better
Empathic Joy Hypothesis Person observes emergency	Situation leads to desire to act and to have a positive effect on the victim	Person provides help in order to engage in an activity that has a successful outcome, making the helper feel good
Genetic Determinism Model Person observes emergency	Unconscious desire to help occurs if the person perceives the victim to be genetically similar to himself or herself	Person provides help in order to maximize the chances of survival of genes that are like those of the observer

■ What Motivates Prosocial Behaviour?

FIGURE 8.5 Four major explanations of the motivation underlying prosocial behaviour are outlined here: *empathy–altruism hypothesis, negative-state relief model, empathic joy hypothesis,* and *genetic determinism model.* The first three formulations stress the importance of increasing positive affect or decreasing negative affect. The fourth formulation rests on the assumption that prosocial behaviour is genetically determined and that such behaviour evolved because it enhanced reproductive success.

human nature—attempting to answer the question of whether we are fundamentally selfish or unselfish. Accordingly, theories tend to stress either relatively selfish, *egoistic motives* or relatively unselfish, *altruistic motives* for behaving in a prosocial manner (Campbell & Sprecht, 1985). There are four major theories that attempt to explain prosocial motivation. These formulations are summarized in Figure 8.5.

Empathy–Altruism: Concern for Others as Basis for Helping

Perhaps the least selfish explanation of prosocial behaviour is that empathetic people help others because they desire to reduce another person's suffering. On this underlying assumption, Batson and his colleagues (1981) proposed the empathy–altruism hypothesis. They suggest that at least some prosocial acts are motivated solely by the unselfish desire to help someone in need (Batson & Oleson, 1991). This motivation to help can be sufficiently strong that the individual who provides help is sometimes willing to engage in unpleasant, dangerous, and even life-threatening activity (Batson,

Empathy-Altruism Hypothesis The proposal that prosocial behaviour is motivated solely by the desire to help someone in need.

Batson et al., 1995). The feelings of compassion can be sufficiently strong that they outweigh all other considerations (Batson, Klein et al., 1995). The powerful feeling of empathy provides validating evidence to the individual that he or she must *truly value* the other person's welfare (Batson, Turk et al., 1995).

To test this altruistic view of helping behaviour, Batson and his colleagues devised an experimental procedure in which they aroused a bystander's empathy by describing him or her as being either similar to or dissimilar from the victim (see Chapter 7). The bystander was then presented with an opportunity to be helpful (Batson et al., 1983; Toi & Batson, 1982). Each undergraduate research participant was given the role of an "observer" who watched a "fellow student" on a TV monitor as she performed a task while (supposedly) receiving random electric shocks. This fellow student was in fact a research assistant recorded on videotape. After the task was underway, the assistant said that she was in pain and confided that as a child she had had a traumatic experience with electricity. She agreed to continue if necessary, but the experimenter asked whether the observer would be willing to trade places with her or whether they should simply discontinue the experiment. When empathy was low (dissimilar victim and participant), the participants preferred to end the experiment rather than engage in a painful prosocial act. When empathy was high (similar victim and participant), the participants agreed to take the victim's place and receive the shocks. It appears that this altruistic act was motivated solely by empathic concern for the victim. Further, other research indicates that when empathy-based helping is unsuccessful, the helper experiences negative emotion (Batson & Weeks, 1996). In other words, high empathy not only leads to prosocial action because such behaviour feels good, but an unsuccessful attempt to provide help feels bad.

Arguing against this unselfish view of prosocial behaviour, Cialdini and his colleagues (1997) agreed that empathy leads to altruistic behaviour but argued that this only occurs when the participant perceives an overlap between self and other. If another person overlaps oneself—in effect, is part of one's own self-concept—then a helpful participant is simply helping himself or herself. These investigators presented evidence that without this feeling of oneness, empathic concern does *not* increase helping. Batson and his colleagues (1997) responded with additional evidence indicating that the perception of overlapping is *not* necessary—empathy leads to helping even in the absence of oneness.

Negative-State Relief: Helping Can Reduce Your Own Negative Affect

Cialdini and colleagues own explanation of prosocial behaviour is known as the negative-state relief model (Cialdini, Baumann, & Kenrick, 1981). In other words, prosocial behaviour can act as a self-help undertaking to reduce one's negative affect. Research shows that it doesn't matter whether the bystander's negative emotions were aroused before the emergency arose or were aroused by the emergency itself. That is, you might be upset about receiving a bad grade or about seeing an injured stranger. In either instance, you may engage in a prosocial act primarily in order to improve your own mood (Dietrich & Berkowitz, 1997; Fultz, Schaller, & Cialdini, 1988). In such situations, sadness leads to prosocial behaviour, and empathy is not a necessary component (Cialdini et al., 1987).

More generally, research indicates that our current affective state has an impact on our willingness to help. We may avoid helping if it will worsen our mood and will be more likely to help if it will raise our mood (e.g., Cunningham, et al., 1990; Rosenhan, Salovey, & Hargis, 1981). The negative-state relief model concerns itself with our desire to avoid negative affect. The next model, in contrast, focuses on a desire to experience positive affect.

Empathic Joy: Helping Can Lead to the "Helper's High"

It is generally true that it feels good to have a positive impact on other people. The emotion that is elicited by performing a prosocial act is sometimes labelled *helper's high*—a feeling of calmness, self-worth, and warmth (Luks, 1988). It can literally be better to give than to receive. Helping can thus be explained on the basis of the **empathic joy hypothesis** (Smith, Keating, & Stotland, 1989). From this perspective, a helper responds to the needs of a victim because he or she wants to feel good about accomplishing something.

One implication of this formulation is that it is crucial for the person who helps to know that his or her actions have a positive impact on the victim. It is argued that if helping were based entirely on empathy, feedback about its effect would be irrelevant. Is that accurate? To find out, Smith, Keating, and Stotland (1989) asked research participants to watch a videotape in which a female student said she might drop out of college because she felt isolated and distressed. After they watched the videotape, the participants were given the opportunity to offer advice. Some were told that they would receive feedback about the effectiveness of their advice, and others were told that they would not be told what the woman decided to do. The woman was described as either similar to a participant (high empathy) or dissimilar (low empathy). Under these conditions, empathy alone was not enough to bring about a prosocial response. Rather, empathy *and* feedback about one's impact were required.

In each of the three theoretical models that have just been described—(1) empathy–altruism hypothesis, (2) negative-state relief model, and (3) empathic joy hypothesis—affective state is a crucial element. That is, prosocial behaviour involves changes in affect. People are assumed to engage in helpful behaviour either because of feelings of concern for another or because it results in improved mood. Depending on the specific circumstances, each of the three models can make accurate predictions about how people will respond.

There is, however, a fourth explanation of prosocial behaviour that approaches the question in an entirely different way—perhaps the tendency to help others is based on genetics rather than emotion.

Evolutionary Origins of Prosocial Behaviour: Genetic Determinism

Evolutionary ideas about the origins of prosocial behaviour rest on notions of *kin selection*—an extension of Darwin's theory of natural selection. Hamilton (1964) suggested that individuals can maximize reproductive success not only *directly*, through their own efforts to reproduce, but also *indirectly*, through helping genetic kin to reproduce. People who are altruistic to their genetic relatives (siblings, cousins, nephews, etc.) increase the chance that the genes they both share will be represented in subsequent generation. If those shared genes include an inherited tendency to be altruistic, then this characteristic could increasingly become part of our human nature.

The **genetic determinism model** is based on this more general theory of human behaviour (Pinker, 1998). Evolutionary psychologists stress that we are not conscious of responding to genetic influences—we simply do so because we are built that way (Rushton, 1989b). In effect, they assume that humans are programmed to help just as they are programmed with respect to prejudice (Chapter 5), attraction, mate selection (Chapter 6), aggression, and other behaviours.

One implication of kin selection theory is that humans are more likely to help out those who share their genes. An extension of this idea comes from *genetic similarity theory* (discussed in Chapter 5), which suggests that we recognize those who share our genes in the general population by their visual similarity to ourselves (Rushton,

Empathic Joy Hypothesis The proposal that prosocial behaviour is motivated by the positive emotion a helper anticipates experiencing as a result of having a beneficial impact on the life of someone in need.

Genetic Determinism Model The proposal that behaviour is driven by genetic attributes that evolved because they enhanced the probability of transmitting one's genes to subsequent generations.

■ Parental Sacrifice as Genetic Selfishness?

FIGURE 8.6 Every day parents help out their children and in the long term they are often willing to sacrifice their own needs in order that their children do well. But can this altruism be explained as "self-ishness" at the genetic level? Are parents merely motivated by an unconscious desire to ensure the continuation of their genes?

Russell, & Walls, 1984) and that we will be selectively helpful to such people. Thus, instinctively each individual organism is fundamentally motivated to live long enough to reproduce, *or* to enhance the reproductive odds of another individual whose genetic makeup is similar to his or her own (Browne, 1992). Studies on nonhuman animal species indicate that the greater the genetic similarity between two individual organisms, the more likely it is that one will help the other when such help is needed (Ridley & Dawkins, 1981). Such behaviour has been described as the result of the "selfish gene" (Dawkins, 1976)—see Figure 8.6.

A slightly different approach that stems from kin selection was offered by Burnstein, Crandall, and Kitayama (1994). They argued that natural selection would favour those who helped *relatives* who were young enough *to reproduce*. Helpfulness to a close relative is perceived as rational, ethical, and a matter of obligation—but, this is true only if helping would affect survival or reproductive success (Kruger, 2001) and only if the individual feels emotionally close to the relative (Korchmaros & Kenny, 2001). Burnstein and his colleagues conducted a series of studies based on hypothetical decisions about who should be helped. As predicted on the basis of genetic similarity, research participants were more likely to help a close relative than either a distant relative or a nonrelative. And as predicted on the basis of reproductive ability, more help was offered to young relatives than to old ones—for example, more help was given to a female relative young enough to bear children than to a female relative past menopause.

In a review of the altruism literature, Buck and Ginsberg (1991) concluded that there is no evidence of a gene that determines prosocial behaviour. Among humans, however, and among other animals as well (de Waal, 1996), there *are* genetically based abilities to communicate emotions and to form social bonds. It may be these inherited capacities that increase the odds that one person will help another when problems arise. In effect, humans are inherently sociable and capable of empathy. When people interact with each other in social relationships, "they are always prosocial, usually helpful, and often altruistic" (Fiske, 1991, p. 209).

What can we conclude about the motive to help others? Certainly, prosocial behaviour is in the range of human capabilities and may, therefore, have a genetic basis. However, the complex conditions and influences that lead to its occurrence preclude this being a simple preprogrammed or instinctive response. Clearly our prosocial capacities are influenced by many factors, as shown in this section. It seems quite possible, when these are taken into account, that we respond to the needs of others on the basis of a variety of motives—some selfish, some altruistic, some related to evolved tendencies, some apparently unrelated. Further, different individuals in different situations may well be helpful for quite different reasons. *Regardless of the underlying reason for any specific prosocial response, it can be agreed that one very positive aspect of human behaviour is that we frequently are willing to help those in need.*

KEY POINTS

- The *empathy–altruism* hypothesis proposes that, because of empathy, we help those in need simply because it feels good to do so.

- The *negative-state relief model* proposes that people help other people in order to relieve and make less negative their own emotional discomfort.

- The *empathic joy hypothesis* bases helping on the positive feelings of accomplishment that arise when the helper knows that he or she was able to have a beneficial impact on the person in need.

- The *genetic determinism model* traces prosocial behaviour to the process of kin selection—to the extent that prosocial acts increase the odds of that person's genes being transmitted to future generations. As a result, they become part of our biological heritage.

Further Determinants of Helping Behaviour: Internal and External Influences

Prosocial behaviour can occur beyond the emergency situation. We help each other out when we give money to charity, arrange to help a friend move house, lend notes to a classmate, and so on. In none of these situations is there the time pressure or the intensity that an emergency involves. In this section we will examine additional influences on prosocial behaviour, both internal to the actor and external in the situation. Internal influences considered are our *attributions* about the victim's need, and dispositional or *personality* factors. External determinants are the immediate influence of others as *role models*, *characteristics of the victim*, and the long-term influence of our *culture*—whether this is rural versus urban, regional, or national culture.

Attributions of Responsibility: Assessing the Victim

In non-emergency situations the potential helper often has time to assess the object of his or her behaviour—the person in need of help. These cognitive evaluations can interact with, or sometimes produce, an emotional response that will, in turn, determine helping.

If you were taking a walk and came across a man lying unconscious by the curb, your tendency to help or not help would be influenced by all of the factors we have discussed earlier—from the presence of other bystanders to empathy. But let's add another element to this situation. Would you be more willing to help the man if his clothes were stained and torn and he clutched a wine bottle in his hand, or if his clothes were neat and clean and he had a bruise on his forehead? The odds are that you would be *less* strongly motivated to help the badly dressed man with the wine. Why? Despite the fact that both of these strangers seem to need assistance, you would be more likely to act if you did not make the attribution that the man was *personally responsible for his difficulty.* In general, if the victim is perceived to be the cause of the problem, people are less motivated to help; in fact, they are likely to respond with the emotion of disgust and be unwilling to help, because, after all, "the victim is to blame" (Weiner, 1980). Help is much more likely if the problem is believed to be caused by *circumstances beyond the victim's control.* As shown in Figure 8.7, a model formulated by Weiner (1980) proposes that we respond with disgust to a victim who is responsible for the problem, and that this reaction does not motivate helping. When the victim is not responsible for the problem, we respond with empathy, which motivates a helpful response.

The general tendency is to attribute more personal responsibility for misfortunes to those who are different from ourselves than to those who are similar. Consider the crime of rape. Most sexual assaults are committed by men, and most of the victims are women. Because of this gender difference in perpetrators and victims, women perceive themselves as similar to the person who is attacked, while men perceive themselves as

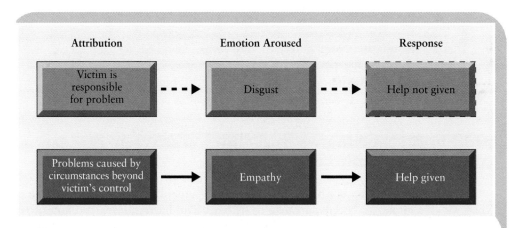

■ Who Is Responsible for the Victim's Plight?

FIGURE 8.7 Weiner's (1980) attributional analysis of helping behaviour suggests that perceptions of the cause of the victim's problems have different effects on the emotions aroused by the situation. If the victim is believed to be responsible for the problem, disgust is aroused and help is not given. If, in contrast, the problem is attributed to external circumstances, empathy is aroused and help is given.

similar to the person who commits the crime (Bell, Kuriloff, & Lottes, 1994). Further, the more similar a woman feels to the female victim, the *less* she blames the victim for the attack. In contrast, the more similar a man feels to the accused rapist, the *more* he blames the victim for what happened. Because of these different attributions, women are motivated to help those assumed to be innocent rape victims, and men are more willing to help those perceived to be falsely accused of the crime.

Even very religious individuals may refrain from helping if they attribute responsibility to the victim (Campbell, 1975). If the victim is perceived as one who violated your religious values (e.g., drinking alcohol), you are less likely to help. In Canada, Jackson and Esses (1997) studied religious fundamentalists whose values were violated by the "immoral" sexual behaviour of homosexuals and single mothers. When gay men and unwed mothers were described as having employment problems, the fundamentalists believed that such individuals should not receive help, but, rather, that they should change their lifestyles. In response to victims who did not behave in a way that violated their religious values (strangers simply described as Native Canadians or students), those with employment problems were perceived as free of blame and deserving of aid.

Research indicates the importance of understanding the role of attributions of responsibility in prosocial behaviour. It appears that if individuals are different from or disliked by you, or they challenge your values, then you will be less willing to offer them help. And this can be justified by believing that somehow they are more responsible for their predicament.

Dispositional Differences in Prosocial Behaviour: The Altruistic Personality

While changing emotions and cognitions may have a temporary impact on prosocial behaviour, researchers have long sought to discover the enduring characteristics that comprise the prosocial or **altruistic personality**. Table 8.1 shows some of the major variables that have been considered, and we will describe related research below.

Research on the Altruistic Personality

An attempt to identify the altruistic personality was undertaken by Bierhoff, Klein, and Kramp (1991). These investigators selected several personality variables identified in previous prosocial research and administered measures to assess their levels in two groups of German citizens. The first group consisted of men and women who had been at the scene of an accident and administered first aid before an ambulance arrived. The second group consisted of the control subjects who reported witnessing an automobile accident but provided no help to the victims. These two groups were matched with respect to sex, age, and social status. This work demonstrated the importance of the five factors in Table 8.1. These factors distinguished the first, prosocial group from the less helpful accident witnesses.

These five characteristics of the altruistic personality were confirmed in another study of people who helped a quite different kind of victim. Oliner and Oliner (1988) obtained personality data on people throughout Europe who were actively involved in rescuing Jews from the Nazis during World War II. Those who bravely defied the authorities and protected Jews were found to be remarkably similar to those who provided first aid to accident victims.

Altogether, people with an altruistic personality have a strong sense of internal control, a high belief in a just world, and a sense of duty, and they tend to show empathy and concern for others, rather than an egocentric concern for the self. How would you rate yourself on these five dimensions?

Altruistic Personality
The combination of dispositional variables that make an individual more likely to engage in altruistic behaviour. Included are an empathic self-concept, belief in a just world, feelings of social responsibility, internal locus of control, and low egocentrism.

In an attempt to identify the factors that make up the altruistic personality, investigators compared citizens who witnessed a traffic accident and provided first aid to the victim with citizens who witnessed such an accident and did not provide first aid. As indicated here, five personality characteristics were found to differentiate the two groups. Together these characteristics identify altruistic individuals.

TABLE 8.1 Aspects of the Altruistic Personality

Personality Characteristics of Those Who Offered Assistance	Description
Higher empathy	*Empathy* is the ability to take another person's perspective and to feel or imagine the other's emotions and cognitions.
Internal locus of control	The belief that one can control one's own outcomes: that is, choose to behave in ways that maximize good outcomes and minimize bad ones. Those with an *external locus of control* believe that they are at the mercy of external and uncontrollable factors and that their own chosen behaviour has little effect on outcomes.
Belief in a just world	Perceive the world as a fair and predictable place in which people get what they deserve. This belief leads to the conclusion that not only is helping those in need the right thing to do, but the person who helps will actually benefit from doing so.
Socially responsible	Are interested in public matters and involved in the community; feel a sense of duty. Believe each person is responsible for helping those in need.
Low egocentrism	Are not self-absorbed and competitive.

Source: Based on data in Bierhoff, Klein, & Kramp, 1991.

KEY POINTS

- Attributions of *responsibility* can determine emotion and prosocial behaviour. We are more likely to help if we attribute the problem to circumstances beyond the victim's control and if our values are not threatened by the victim.
- The *altruistic personality* consists of empathy, internal locus of control, belief in a just world, high social responsibility, and low egocentricity.

Role Models: Providing Helpful Cues

If you are out shopping and pass someone collecting money to help the homeless, provide warm coats for needy children, buy food for those in poverty, or whatever, do you reach in your pocket or purse to make a contribution? One determinant of your behaviour is whether you see someone else contribute. People are much more likely to donate money if they observe others doing so (Macauley, 1970). Even the presence of paper money and coins in the collection box acts as an encouragement to a charitable response.

The presence of fellow bystanders who fail to respond to an emergency inhibits helpfulness, as we have seen. In an analogous way, the presence of a helpful bystander provides a *role model* and encourages helpfulness. This modelling effect was shown in a field experiment in which a female confederate was parked by the side of a road with a flat tire. Male motorists were much more likely to stop and help if (several minutes earlier) they had observed another woman with car trouble receiving help (Bryan & Test, 1967).

The positive effect of models is not limited to real-life encounters. Television is found to influence viewers in various ways, and altruism is one of them. In a study of the effects of TV, investigators showed six-year-olds an episode of *Lassie* that contained a rescue scene, an episode of the same program unrelated to prosocial behaviour, or a humorous segment of *The Brady Bunch* (Sprafkin, Liebert, & Poulous, 1975). Children exposed to the rescue were more likely to help in a subsequent play session. Other investigators have found that when preschool children are exposed to prosocial programs such as *Mister Dressup* or *Sesame Street* (see Figure 8.8), they are more likely to behave in an altruistic way than children who have not watched such shows (Forge & Phemister, 1987). These studies consistently indicate that television can exert a very positive influence on the development of prosocial responses.

Of course, for most children their first prosocial models are their parents. As research on the altruistic personality has found, those with the strongest prosocial tendencies often have parents who were altruistic and involved in the community (e.g., Oliner & Oliner, 1988).

■ The Impact of a Prosocial Model

FIGURE 8.8 Investigators have found that when preschool children are exposed to prosocial programs such as *Mister Dressup*, they are more likely to behave in an altruistic way than children who have not watched such shows.

Who Needs Help? Characteristics of the Victim

Research consistently shows that a similar victim is more likely to receive help than a dissimilar one (Clark et al., 1987; Dovidio & Morris, 1975; Hayden, Jackson & Guydish, 1984), thus supporting evolutionary predictions. You will recall that similarity almost always has a positive influence on attraction (see Chapter 6), and research also indicates that we are more likely to help those that we like or are attracted to. So a physically attractive victim receives more help that an unattractive one (Benson, Karabenick, & Lerner, 1976).

If you are prejudiced against a particular group, there is a decrease in the likelihood of you helping one of its members. For example, Shaw, Borough, and Fink (1994) found that a homosexual stranger in need received less help than a heterosexual stranger, although the two were in exactly the same position and for the same reason. In a method called the "wrong number technique," a male research assistant dialled random telephone numbers from a pay phone. When the call was answered, he pretended he had called the wrong number and just used up his last quarter. He explained that he had a flat tire and asked if the person who answered could call his boyfriend (in the homosexual condition) or girlfriend (in the heterosexual condition) to say that he would be late for the celebration of their first anniversary. Most people (over 70 percent) called the "girlfriend" of the man in distress but few (less than 35 percent) called the "boyfriend" of the man in distress.

Research has consistently shown that men are very likely to provide help to women (Latané & Dabbs, 1975; Piliavin & Unger, 1985). How can such findings be explained? Helpful men are puzzling, because adult women are higher in empathy than men, and the same is true for young girls versus young boys (Shigetomi, Hartmann, & Gelfand, 1981).

One possibility lies in Step 4 of the decision-making model. Many emergency situations require certain skills and knowledge (e.g., changing a flat tire or determining what is wrong with an automobile engine) or a level of strength and special training (e.g., overpowering an attacker or ripping a seat belt out of a car) that have traditionally been associated with men rather than women. Perhaps it is for this reason that a female motorist in distress by the side of the road receives more offers of assistance than a male or a male–female couple in the same predicament (Pomazal & Clore, 1973; Snyder, Grether, & Keller, 1974). Also, the motorists who stop to provide help are most often young males who are driving alone.

The motivation for providing such help may not be entirely prosocial or altruistic, however. For one thing, men stop to help an attractive woman more frequently than to help an unattractive one (West & Brown, 1975). It seems possible, then, that the motivation is primarily romantic or sexual. Przybyla (1985) found that men who had just seen an erotic tape were more helpful to female laboratory assistants than to male assistants who had the same problem with dropped papers. Note also that viewing or not viewing an erotic tape had no effect on the helping behaviour of women in response to representatives of either gender.

However, more recent research among police officers suggests that both genders may show a prosocial bias towards the opposite sex. Koehler and Willis (1994) investigated whether police officers in two dozen municipal police departments reacted more helpfully to members of the opposite sex. They suggest that issuing a warning is a more prosocial response than issuing a traffic ticket. Their overall finding was that both male and female officers were more likely to issue traffic tickets to drivers of the same gender than to drivers of the opposite gender. (ie, as opposed to a warning)

Cultural Context: Regional and Societal Differences in Prosocial Behaviour

People are often quite convinced that those who live in one region of a country are more helpful than those in another, or that country-folk are more kind and considerate than city-folk. And if you were raised in one of these contexts you probably support this belief. The source of, for example, a rural–urban discrepancy is often thought to be differences in cultural values. Similarly, it is also true that some nationalities have more prosocial reputations than others. Social psychology has investigated these questions, and an answer can be provided, at least to the rural–urban issue, though not to the issues of societal or national differences.

Rural versus Urban Helping

Although cultural diversity is most often studied with respect to racial, ethnic, or national differences, place of residence can also be an important determinant of human behaviour. If you have ever spent much time in a large city and/or in a small town, do you believe that interpersonal interactions and interpersonal behaviour may be affected by such settings?

Milgram (1970) suggested that the external demands of an urban environment involve *stimulus overload* for city dwellers (see Figure 8.9). For example, crowded cities are noisier than small towns—filled with the sounds of traffic, sirens, and squealing brakes (Cooke, 1992). And inevitably, people in a city come into contact with more people (including more strangers) each day than people in a less crowded community. The best way to survive in such an environment is to screen out nonessential stimuli and go on about one's own business. The larger the city, the

■ Stimulus Overload in Large Cities

FIGURE 8.9 Research has shown that people in large cities are less helpful than people in smaller communities. One explanation stresses *stimulus overload*—the fact that city dwellers are faced with too much stimulation and learn to screen out much of the noise and bustle around them.

faster pedestrians walk—much like the seminary students rushing between campus buildings. Even those who commute from suburbia to the city behave differently in the two locations (Sadalla, Sheets, & McCreath, 1990; Walmsley & Lewis, 1989).

An expected consequence of stimulus overload is a general disregard for others, especially strangers. As a result, as Levine and colleagues (1994) predicted, helpfulness should decrease. These researchers obtained relevant data on prosocial behaviour in 36 small, medium, and large cities across the United States. They measured several different forms of helping, which included informing a stranger that he or she had dropped a pen, assisting a person in a leg brace pick up magazines when they slipped to the sidewalk, making change for a quarter, helping a blind person cross the street, picking up and mailing a stamped letter that apparently had been lost, and per capita charitable contributions to the United Way. A strong negative relationship was found between these combined indicators of prosocial acts and population density (Levine et al., 1994). That is, the greater the number of people living in a given locality, the less helpful the residents were.

Earlier research also supported the generalization that city dwellers are less friendly and less helpful to strangers than are small-town residents (Korte, 1980, 1981; Krupat & Guild, 1980). And the relationship between population and helpfulness exists not only in Canada (e.g. Rushton, 1978) but all over the world (e.g., Amato, 1983; Yousif & Korte 1995). Clearly, our surroundings can influence the decisions that are essential to prosocial actions.

Cross-Cultural Comparisons

A (nonscientific) test of helping behaviour conducted by *Reader's Digest* provides some interesting comparisons for Canadians (reported in the *Globe and Mail*, February 19, 1997). Ten wallets, each containing $50 cash, were dropped in 12 Canadian cities and the number returned intact to their owners was tracked. Toronto, Canada's largest city, had the lowest return rate. Only four of the ten wallets were returned. Moncton had the greatest honesty rate of 100 percent. Charlottetown ranked second with eight wallets returned. Seven wallets were returned in Vancouver and Winnipeg; six in Montreal, Calgary, Saskatoon, Whitehorse, Val D'Or, Quebec, and St. John's; and five in Halifax. Women were more likely to return the wallets (73 percent) than men (56 percent). In comparison to previous tests conducted in other countries, Canada's return rate of 64 percent was slightly lower than Britain (65 percent) and the United States (67 percent) and higher than Asia (57 percent) and Europe (58 percent).

The focus of cross-cultural comparisons of prosocial behaviour has been on societies that differ in individualism versus collectivism (see Smith & Bond, 1999). At the individualistic extreme of the spectrum, values stress that each person strives to be a self-contained unit and seeks success and recognition on the basis of individual achievement. It's every man for himself, every woman for herself. In contrast, collectivistic societies stress interlocking family-like connections in which individuals depend on one another, sharing both hardship and success. It's one for all and all for one. Given such differences in outlook, differences in help-seeking behaviour might well be expected.

However, the picture that emerges is somewhat more complex. In general, the demand to be prosocial to those in the in-group may be greater in collective cultures, but this may not be true where helping strangers is concerned (see Smith & Bond, 1999). It appears that helping a stranger depends upon the culture's evaluation of the person in need of help and the local social norms: for example, whether the stranger is seen as threatening in that particular culture, or of high or low status, and so on. However, one study that compared large cities in 18 countries found that those in the large cities of wealthy countries were less likely to give help to strangers than those in similar-sized cities in poorer countries (Norenzayan & Levine, 1994).

When it comes to *help-seeking* behaviour, the picture seems clearer—those raised more collectively find it easier to ask for help. In one study carried out in Israel (Nadler, 1986), those raised in the more communal setting, in a *kibbutz*, were much more likely to seek help from others than those raised in the more individualistic setting of a large city in the same country. Why should this be so? In the communal setting of a kibbutz, people would expect to be dependent on one another and help seeking would be a normative way to cope with problems. Those living in a city, however, would view self-reliance as important and would be more reluctant to turn to others for help (Nadler, 1986).

KEY POINTS

- Exposure to prosocial models in real life and in the media has a positive effect on prosocial acts.
- Help is more likely to be given to those who are similar to oneself and by men to women more often than vice versa.
- The culture context can influence prosocial behaviour. Research shows higher levels of helping in rural than urban settings. Pressure to be helpful to others in your in-group may be greater in collectivistic cultures but this does not necessarily extend to helping a stranger. Help seeking is more likely among individuals familiar with a communal experience than among those with an individualistic background.

Sources of Aggression: Theories about Its Nature and Causes

While humans have the capacity to help, we also have the capacity to harm. And as with prosocial behaviour, social psychologists have wanted to know *why*. What causes human beings to harm each other? What makes them turn, with brutality unmatched by even the fiercest of predators, against their fellow human beings? Scholars and scientists have pondered such questions for centuries, with the result that many contrasting explanations for the paradox of human violence have been proposed. Here, we'll examine several that have been especially influential.

The Evolution of Aggression: A Part of Human Nature?

The oldest and probably best-known explanation for human aggression is the view that human beings are somehow "programmed" for violence by their very nature. Interestingly, in a different form, that is the focus of a recent social psychological perspective on aggression—that of *evolutionary social psychology*.

Such theories suggest that human violence arises from built-in (i.e., inherited) tendencies to aggress against others. The most famous early supporter of this idea was Sigmund Freud, who held that aggression stems mainly from a powerful *death wish* (thanatos), possessed by all persons. According to Freud, this instinct is initially aimed at self-destruction but is soon redirected outward, toward others.

Another view, much more closely related to today's evolutionary approach, was proposed by Konrad Lorenz, a Nobel Prize-winning scientist. Lorenz (1966, 1974), a zoologist, proposed that aggression springs mainly from an inherited *fighting instinct* that human beings share with many other species. This instinct developed during the course of evolution because it yielded important benefits for the species. For example, fighting serves to disperse populations over a wide area, thus ensuring maximum use of available natural resources. Further, because it is often closely related to mating, fighting helps to ensure that only the strongest and most vigorous individuals will pass on their genes to the next generation.

Modern Evolutionary Approaches

Originating in the 1970s with the field of sociobiology (e.g., Dawkins, 1976; Wilson, 1975), the modern *evolutionary social psychology* approach to aggression suggests that since aggression aids the males of many species in obtaining mates, principles of natural selection will, over time, favour increasing levels of aggression, at least among males. While sociobiologists initiated this view as applied to many animal species, modern evolutionary social psychology focuses on human beings, suggesting that our aggressive capacities have also evolved in the context of natural selection.

The modern evolutionary approach to aggression has often focused on extreme manifestations of aggression, particularly on interpersonal violence. For example, two long-term proponents of evolutionary psychology, Martin Daly and Margo Wilson at McMaster University, have examined patterns of homicide and demonstrated that victim–killer relations often follow evolutionary predictions: that is, homicide is much less likely to occur between those who share genetic material than those who don't (e.g., Daly & Wilson, 1982, 1988, 1999). They also coined the term the young male syndrome to refer to the fact that young males are more likely to be involved in violence and risk-taking generally than older males or females (Wilson & Daly, 1985).

From the evolutionary perspective, this syndrome is explained as stemming from the greater competitiveness of males as they vie with each other for available mates. As discussed in Chapter 6, females make the greater *parental investment* in reproduction (e.g., they carry, give birth, and feed the infant) and because of this, Trivers (1972) suggests, females have evolved to be more cautious in choosing a mate. Males, on the other hand, will have evolved to compete with each other for the resources necessary to attract females. Thus, young males, who generally have few resources, will tend to be in conflict and to perpetrate violence upon other young males, their major source of competition.

Christian Mesquida and Neil Wiener (1996) of York University have taken this idea and extended it to apply to the ultimate manifestation of our aggression—warfare. However, their emphasis is not so much on inter-male violence as on *male collective violence*. They suggest that "the relative number of young males in a given population… is likely to influence political affairs and lead to collective violence" (Mesquida & Wiener, 1996, p. 249). If a society has a large proportion of young males, there will be a larger number who fail to acquire substantial resources and successfully mate. These young men may be able to achieve their evolutionary goals if they participate in collective aggression to attain resources. For example, an uprising or revolution could result in a redistribution of resources from older to younger generations within a society, or cross-border warfare might extend the resource base. In support of this contention, Mesquida and Weiner (1996) examined United Nations' data for 88 countries and found a positive correlation between the proportion of young males (aged 15–29 years) and the severity of collective violence in that society.

These findings fit with those of Daly and Wilson and other researchers who show a connection between the level of young males in society and many kinds of violent behaviour (e.g., Cohen & Land, 1987; Hilton, Harris, & Rice, 2000). Internationally, commentators have remarked on the high number of male adolescents who are

Young Male Syndrome The fact that young males are more likely to be involved in violence (as both victim and perpetrator) than older males or females.

■ The Young Male Syndrome in Collective Violence

FIGURE 8.10 The evolutionary perspective has suggested that the young male syndrome (the greater involvement of young males in violence) occurs because of their inherent tendency to compete with each other for the resources needed to attract a mate. Taking this idea further, Mesquida and Wiener (1996) have suggested that the likelihood of collective unrest in a society will increase as the proportion of young males in the population increases. This photograph shows adolescent males taking part in a political uprising in Liberia. Could their involvement stem, at least in part, from evolved tendencies?

involved in warfare, particularly in developing countries (see Figure 8.10). The evolutionary approach suggests that, in part, their involvement may stem from genetically programmed tendencies to compete for resources.

Until a few years ago, few social psychologists accepted the notion of "instincts" as a major factor in human aggression. Among the many reasons for their objections to such ideas were these: (1) Human beings aggress against others in many different ways—everything from ignoring target persons or spreading false rumours about them to the kind of brutal acts that are often reported on the evening news. (2) The frequency of aggressive actions varies tremendously across human societies—being as much as 50 times more common in some societies than in others (e.g., Fry, 1998). Social psychologists asked, "How can aggressive behaviour be determined by genetic factors if such huge differences exist?"

Reasons why aggression is not solely evolutionary

On the basis of these and other considerations, social psychologists have generally downplayed the role of genetic and biological factors in human aggression, though accepting that they might influence aggression in other species. However, with the advent of modern evolutionary approaches, this situation has changed considerably. Modern evolutionary theorists and researchers, unlike their earlier counterparts, seldom suggest that evolved tendencies are the sole cause of aggression in human beings; rather, they see such tendencies as *interacting* with other factors, both environmental and internal, that can facilitate or inhibit aggression (e.g., Daly & Wilson, 1999). And today, social psychologists, while continuing to view the phenomenon of aggression as complex and influenced by many factors, are generally willing to accept that evolution may have laid the groundwork for our capacity for harm.

KEY POINTS

- Early instinct theories suggest that aggression stems largely from innate urges or tendencies, such as a death wish.
- Among modern evolutionary approaches, the *young male syndrome*—the preponderance of young males involved in violence—is seen as derived from evolved competition between males for reproductive success.
- While social psychologists have not endorsed a simple instinct theory, they do recognize the potential role of evolution in human aggression.

Drive Theories: The Motive to Harm Others

When social psychologists rejected the instinct views of aggression proposed by Freud and Lorenz, they countered with an alternative of their own: the view that aggression stems mainly from an externally elicited *drive* to harm others. This approach is reflected in several different **drive theories** of aggression (e.g., Berkowitz, 1989; Feshbach, 1984). These theories propose that external conditions—especially *frustration*—arouse a strong motive to harm others. This aggressive drive, in turn, leads to overt acts of aggression (see Figure 8.11)

By far the most famous of these theories is the well-known **frustration–aggression hypothesis** (Dollard et al., 1939). According to this view, frustration leads to the arousal of a drive whose primary goal is that of harming some person or object—primarily the perceived cause of frustration (Berkowitz, 1989). In its original form, this hypothesis made the sweeping assertion that frustrated persons always engage in some type of aggression and that all acts of aggression, in turn, result from frustration. The central role assigned to frustration by this hypothesis has turned out to be largely false: frustration is only one of many different causes of aggression, and a fairly weak one at that.

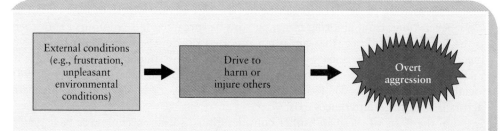

■ Drive Theories of Aggression: Motivation to Harm Others

FIGURE 8.11 *Drive theories* of aggression suggest that aggressive behaviour is pushed from within by drives to harm or injure others. These drives, in turn, stem from external events such as frustration. Such theories are no longer accepted as valid by most social psychologists, but one such view—the famous *frustration–aggression hypothesis*—continues to influence modern research.

Moreover, aggression stems from many causes others than frustration. Along these lines, Berkowitz (1989, 1993) has proposed a revised version of the frustration–aggression hypothesis that seems consistent with a large amount of evidence about the effects of frustration. According to this view, frustration is an unpleasant experience, and it may lead to aggression largely because of this fact. In other words, frustration sometimes produces aggression because of a basic link between negative affect (unpleasant feelings) and aggressive behaviour—a relationship that has been confirmed in many studies (e.g., da Gloria et al., 1994).

We should add that frustration *can* serve as a powerful determinant of aggression under certain conditions—especially when it is viewed as illegitimate or unjustified (e.g., Folger & Baron, 1996). That is, a person has been blocked from achieving a desired outcome for reasons that are perceived as unfair. Further, some aspects of the original frustration–aggression theory have received support in recent research (e.g., the suggestion that aggression toward a source of anger may be displaced to other, innocent targets; Marcus-Newhall et al., 2000). In this way, although the original ideas have been shaped by research, drive theories have had a lasting impact on the study of human aggression.

Modern Theories of Aggression: Taking Account of Learning, Cognitions, Mood, and Arousal

Unlike earlier views, modern theories of aggression (e.g., Anderson, 1997; Berkowitz, 1993; Zillmann, 1994) do not focus on a single factor as the primary cause of aggression. Rather, they draw on advances in many fields of psychology in order to gain added insight into such behaviour. While no single theory includes all the elements that social psychologists now view as important, one approach—the **general affective aggression model**, proposed by Anderson (Anderson, 1997; Anderson et al., 1996)—provides a good illustration of the breadth and sophistication of these new perspectives. It incorporates suggestions from drive theories (e.g., the frustration–aggression hypothesis), cognitive theory (e.g., Berkowitz, 1993), and from *social learning theory*'s view that aggression can be learned by exposure to aggressive models (Bandura, 1973).

According to this theory (known as the *GAAM* for short), aggression is triggered by a wide range of *input variables*—aspects of the current situation and/or tendencies individuals bring with them to a given situation. Variables falling into the first category (the current situation) include frustration, some kind of attack from another person (e.g., an insult), exposure to *aggressive models* (other persons behaving aggressively), the presence of cues associated with aggression (e.g., guns or other weapons), and virtually anything that causes individuals to experience discomfort—everything from uncomfortably high temperatures to a dentist's drill, or even an extremely dull lecture. Variables in the second category (*individual differences*) include traits that predispose individuals toward aggression (e.g., high irritability), certain attitudes and beliefs about violence (e.g., believing that it is acceptable and appropriate), values about violence (e.g., the view that it is a "good" thing—perhaps that it shows an individual's worth or masculinity), and specific skills related to aggression (e.g., knowing how to fight, knowing how to use various weapons).

According to the GAAM, these situational and individual difference variables can then lead to overt aggression through their impact on three basic processes: *arousal*—they may increase physiological arousal or excitement; *affective states*—they can arouse hostile feelings and outward signs of these (e.g., angry facial expressions); and *cognitions*—they can induce individuals to think hostile thoughts or bring hostile memories to mind. Depending on individuals' *appraisals* (interpretations) of the current situation and on possible restraining factors (e.g., the presence of police or the

General Affective Aggression Model (GAAM) A modern theory of aggression suggesting that aggression is triggered by a wide range of input variables; these influence arousal, affective stages, and cognitions.

■ The GAAM: One Modern Theory of Human Aggression

FIGURE 8.12 As shown here, the general affective aggression model suggests that human aggression stems from many different factors. A wide range of input variables influence cognitions, affect, and arousal, and these internal states plus other factors determine whether, and in what form, aggression occurs.

Source: Based on suggestions by Anderson, 1997.

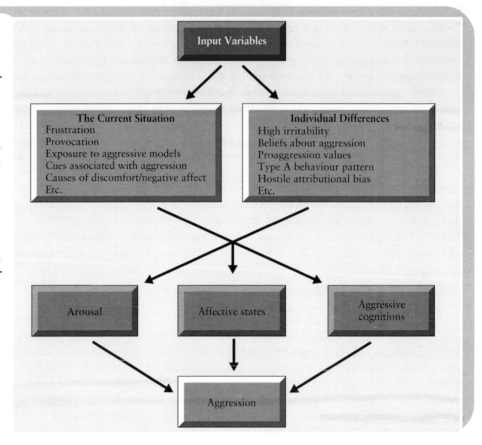

threatening nature of the intended target person), aggression either occurs or does not occur. See Figure 8.12 for an overview of the GAAM.

Modern theories like the GAAM are, admittedly, much more complex than the early ones offered by Freud and Lorenz, or even the famous frustration–aggression hypothesis (Dollard et al., 1939). But, they are also supported by a growing body of evidence (e.g., Lieberman & Greenberg, 1999), and are much more likely to provide an accurate and complete picture of the origins of human aggression—and that, of course, is what science is all about.

KEY POINTS

- *Drive theories* suggest that aggression stems from externally elicited drives to harm or injure others. The *frustration–aggression hypothesis* is the most famous example of such theories.

- Contrary to the frustration–aggression hypothesis, not all aggression stems from frustration, and frustration does not always lead to aggression. Frustration is a strong elicitor of aggression only under certain limited conditions.

- Modern theories of aggression such as the *general affective aggression model* (GAAM) recognize the importance of learning, various eliciting input variables, cognitions, individual tendencies, and affective states.

Further Determinants of Aggression: Internal and External Influences

Think back to the last time you lost your temper. What made you "lose your cool"? Chances are quite good that your anger, and any subsequent aggression, stemmed from the actions of another person together with difficulties of the situation. Aggression often stems from various social conditions that either initiate its occurrence or increase its intensity, as the GAAM suggests. Many factors play a role in this regard and we will examine several of these in more detail below.

Heightened Arousal: Emotion, Cognition, and Aggression

Suppose that you are driving to the airport to meet a friend. On the way there, another driver cuts you off and you almost have an accident. Your heart pounds wildly and your blood pressure shoots through the roof; but, fortunately, no accident occurs. Now you arrive at the airport. You park and rush inside. When you get to the security check, an elderly man in front of you sets off the buzzer. He becomes confused and can't seem to understand that the security guard wants him to empty his pockets. You are irritated by this delay. In fact, you begin to lose your temper and mutter—not too softly— "What's wrong with him? Can't he get it?"

Now for the key question: Do you think that your recent near miss in traffic may have played any role in your sudden surge of anger? Could the emotional arousal from that incident have somehow transferred to the scene inside the airport? Growing evidence suggests that it could (Zillmann, 1988, 1994). Under some conditions, heightened arousal—whatever its source—can enhance aggression in response to provocation, frustration, or other factors. In fact, in various experiments, arousal stemming from such varied sources as participation in competitive games (Christy, Gelfand, & Hartmann, 1971), vigorous exercise (Zillmann, 1979), and even some types of music (Rogers & Ketcher, 1979) has been found to increase subsequent aggression. Why is this the case? A compelling explanation is offered by **excitation transfer theory** (Zillmann, 1983, 1988).

Excitation Transfer Theory A theory suggesting that arousal produced in one situation can persist and intensify emotional reactions occurring in subsequent situations.

This theory suggests that because physiological arousal tends to dissipate slowly over time, a portion of such arousal may persist as a person moves from one situation to another. In the example above, some portion of the arousal you experienced because of the near miss in traffic may still be present as you approach the security gate in the airport. When you encounter a minor annoyance at the gate, that arousal intensifies your emotional reactions to the annoyance. The result: you become enraged rather than just mildly irritated. Excitation transfer theory further suggests that such effects are most likely to occur when the persons involved are relatively unaware of the presence of *residual arousal*—a common occurrence, as small elevations in arousal are difficult to notice (Zillmann, 1994). Excitation transfer theory also suggests that such effects are likely to occur when the persons involved recognize their residual arousal but attribute it to events occurring in the present situation (Taylor et al., 1991). In the airport incident, for instance, your anger would be intensified if you recognized your feelings of arousal but attributed them to the elderly man's actions (see Figure 8.13).

Sexual Arousal and Aggression: Emotional and Cognitive Links

Are sexual arousal and aggression somehow linked? Freud felt that they were, and suggested that the desire to hurt or be hurt by one's lover is often a normal part of sexual relations. Whether this is true or not, there is indeed some evidence for important links between sexual arousal—or even, as we will soon see, merely being exposed to

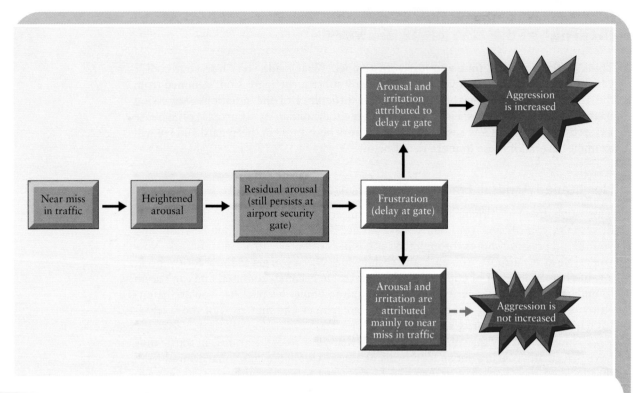

- Excitation Transfer Theory

FIGURE 8.13 Excitation transfer theory suggests that arousal occurring in one situation can persist and intensify emotional reactions in later, unrelated situations. Thus the arousal produced by a near miss in traffic can intensify feelings of annoyance stemming from delays at an airport security gate.

Source: Based on suggestions by Zillmann, 1988, 1994.

sex-related words—and subsequent aggression. Let's take a closer look at this intriguing research.

Extensive research findings suggest that the relationship between sexual arousal and aggression is *curvilinear* in nature. Mild sexual arousal reduces aggression to a level below that shown in the absence of such arousal, while higher levels of arousal actually increase aggression above this level. Why is this so? One explanation is provided by the following *two-component model* (Zillmann, 1984).

According to this theory, exposure to erotic stimuli produces two effects: It increases *arousal* and it influences current *affective states*—negative or positive moods or feelings. Whether sexual arousal will increase or reduce aggression, then, depends on the overall pattern of such effects. Mild erotic materials generate weak levels of arousal but high levels of positive affect—most people enjoy looking at them. As a result, aggression is reduced. In contrast, explicit sexual materials generate stronger levels of arousal, but also higher levels of negative affect—many people find some of the acts shown to be unpleasant or even repulsive. As a result, such materials may increase aggression. The findings of several studies support this two-factor theory (e.g., Ramirez, Bryant, & Zillmann, 1983), so it appears to provide a useful explanation for the curvilinear relationship between sexual arousal and aggression.

In addition to these affective or emotional links between sexual arousal and aggression, however, more recent research suggests that there may be cognitive links, too. Do you remember the principle of *priming,* which we discussed in Chapters 2 and 5? This suggests that specific stimuli (or primes) may activate cognitive processes related to them and so influence our thinking and judgments.

Mussweiler and Forster (2000) conducted a study in which both women and men were exposed either to neutral prime words (e.g., "clock," "roof") or sex-related prime words (e.g., "skin," "bed"). Then, both women and men were given a chance to throw darts either at a photo of a human face or at physical objects (e.g., a vase). The authors predicted that when exposed to sex-related words, men would throw more darts at the human face, while this would not be true for women. They reasoned that in our society sex and aggression are more linked for males than for females and, therefore, thoughts of aggression might be primed by sex-related words for male subjects but not for females. Results supported their hypothesis. The results of a follow-up study that used somewhat different procedures indicated that these effects occurred only if the target was a female; males primed with sex-related words aggressed more than males primed with neutral words, but only against a woman's photo. Women showed no differences of this kind.

These results suggest that the link between sex and aggression may be more complex than was initially believed. Not only does sexual arousal influence aggression through the generation of positive and negative affect (i.e., moods or feelings); in addition, exposure to sex-related stimuli may activate schemas or other mental frameworks that can, in turn, influence overt behaviour toward specific targets. If these findings remind you of the general affective aggression model (GAAM) we described earlier in this chapter, you are right on track: as this model suggests, in order to fully understand human aggression, we must take careful account of a wide range of factors—social, affective, cognitive, and personal. We have already discussed variables relating to the first three categories, so we turn next to *personal* causes of aggression—traits and characteristics of individuals that can influence when, where, and toward whom they choose to aggress.

Dispositional Influences on Aggression: Aggressive Personality Factors

Are some persons "primed" for aggression by their personal characteristics? Informal observation suggests that this is so (see Figure 8.14). Some individuals rarely lose their tempers or engage in aggressive actions, but others seem to be forever losing it, with potentially serious consequences. In this section we will consider several personal traits or characteristics that seem to play an important role in aggression.

The Type A Behaviour Pattern: Why the A in Type A Could Stand for Aggression

Do you know anyone you could describe as (1) extremely competitive, (2) always in a hurry, and (3) especially irritable and aggressive? If so, this person shows the characteristics of what psychologists term the Type A behaviour pattern (Glass, 1977; Strube, 1989). At the opposite end of the continuum are persons who do not show these characteristics—individuals who are *not* highly competitive, who are not always fighting the clock, and who do *not* readily lose their temper; such persons are described as showing the Type B behaviour pattern.

Given the characteristics mentioned above, it seems only reasonable to expect that Type A's would tend to be more aggressive than Type B's in many situations. And in fact, the results of several experiments indicate that this is actually the case

Type A Behaviour Pattern A pattern consisting primarily of high levels of competitiveness, time urgency, and hostility.

Type B Behaviour Pattern A pattern consisting of the absence of characteristics associated with the Type A behaviour pattern.

■ Personality and Aggression

FIGURE 8.14 Are some persons primed for aggression by their own personalities? Research findings agree with this cartoon in suggesting that this is so.

"What are you doing outside of coach?"

(Baron, Russell, & Arms, 1985; Carver & Glass, 1978). For example, consider a study by Berman, Gladue, and Taylor (1993). These researchers exposed young men known to be Type A or Type B to increasing provocation from a stranger. As part of the experimental procedure, subjects were required to choose a level of electric shock to be delivered to this person. Another feature of the study involved measurement of participants' testosterone level; as we pointed out before, testosterone is an important sex hormone, found in much higher levels in males than in females. Results indicated that during the competitive task, Type A's who also had a high level of testosterone set the highest level of shocks for their opponent. In addition, Type A's with high testosterone levels were much more likely than other participants to use the highest shock setting available. These findings indicate that two different personal characteristics—the Type A behaviour pattern and testosterone level—both play a role in determining aggressive behaviour.

Additional findings indicate that Type A's are truly hostile people: they don't merely aggress against others because this is a useful means for reaching other goals, such as winning athletic contests or furthering their own careers. Rather, they are more likely than Type B's to engage in what is known as **hostile aggression**—aggression in which the prime objective is inflicting harm on the victim (Strube et al., 1984). In view of this fact, it is not surprising to learn that Type A's are more likely than Type B's to engage in such actions as child abuse and spouse abuse (Strube et al., 1984). In contrast, Type A's are not more likely to engage in **instrumental aggression**—aggression performed primarily to attain other goals aside from harming the victim, goals such as control of valued resources or praise from others for behaving in a "tough" manner.

Hostile Aggression Aggression in which the prime objective is to harm the victim, as opposed to aggression whose prime objective is some other purpose.

Instrumental Aggression Aggression in which the primary objective is not harm to the victim but attainment of some other goal, such as access to valued resources.

Narcissism, Ego-Threat, and Aggression: On the Dangers of Wanting to Be Superior

Do you know the story of Narcissus? He was a character in Greek mythology who fell in love with his own reflection in the water and drowned trying to reach it. His name has now become a synonym for excessive self-love—for holding an over-inflated view of one's own virtues or accomplishments. Research findings indicate that this trait may be linked to aggression in important ways. Specifically, studies by Bushman and Baumeister (1998) suggest that persons high in narcissism (ones who agree with such items as "If I ruled the world it would be a much better place" and "I am more capable than other people") react with exceptionally high levels of aggression to slights from others—feedback that threatens their inflated self-image. Why? Because such persons have nagging doubts about the accuracy of their inflated egos and so react with intense anger toward anyone who threatens to undermine them. This tendency to be aggressive may be one reason why their attempts at impression management ultimately fail, as we saw in Chapter 7.

KEY POINTS

- *Excitation transfer theory* and research shows that heightened arousal can increase aggression if it persists beyond the situation in which it was induced and is falsely interpreted as anger.

- Mild levels of sexual arousal reduce aggression, while higher levels increase such behaviour. Males and females are differently affected by sex-related primes.

- Persons showing the *Type A* behaviour pattern are more irritable and more aggressive than persons with the *Type B* behaviour pattern.

- Persons high in *narcissism* (ones who hold an over-inflated view of their own worth) react with exceptionally high levels of aggression to feedback from others that poses a threat to their egos.

Evaluating Others' Behaviour: Provocation and Attribution

Suppose that one day, another shopper in a supermarket bumped you with her cart. Suppose she then remarked, "Out of my way, stupid!" How would you react? Probably with anger, and perhaps with some kind of retaliation. You might make a biting remark such as "What's wrong with you—are you nuts?" Alternatively, you might, if you were angry enough, push *your* cart into hers, or even into her!

This incident illustrates an important point about aggression: Often, it is the result of physical or verbal **provocation** from others. When we are on the receiving end of some form of aggression from others, we rarely turn the other cheek. Instead, we tend to reciprocate, returning as much aggression as we have received—or perhaps even slightly more, especially if we are certain that the other person *meant* to harm us (Dengerink, Schnedler, & Covey, 1978; Ohbuchi & Kambara, 1985). Such effects are demonstrated very clearly by a study conducted by Chermack, Berman, and Taylor (1997).

In this study, participants competed with an opponent on a competitive reaction-time task devised by Stuart Taylor—commonly called the *Taylor Aggression Paradigm*. On each trial, the participant and his opponent (who was not really there) set a level of shock the loser—the person slower to respond—would receive after that

Provocation
Actions by others that are perceived as acts of aggression deriving from hostile intentions.

trial. The shocks were set by means of ten buttons on the equipment and could range in intensity from ones that could not be felt to ones that participants found painful. Prior to each reaction-time trial, participants learned what level of shock had been set for them by their opponent. In one condition (low provocation), the opponent chose button two on all occasions. In another condition (high provocation), he gradually raised the level of shocks he set for the participant from two to nine. (Needless to say, participants were warned about the possibility of receiving actual shocks during the informed consent procedures.)

As you can see from Figure 8.15, participants' aggression was strongly influenced by the level of provocation they received. In the low-provocation condition, they set relatively low shocks for their opponent and did not increase these over time. In the high-provocation condition, they set higher shocks (except in the first block of trials), and they raised these dramatically over time. The findings also illustrate the "and then some" effect mentioned above: even in the low-provocation condition, participants set a slightly higher level of shocks for their opponent than they received.

A related tendency may potentially play an important role in the interpretation of others' behaviour: the tendency to perceive hostile intent in others even when it is totally lacking. Presumably, the stronger this tendency—known as **hostile attributional bias**—the greater individuals' likelihood of engaging in reactive aggression in response to provocation from others.

Evidence that this is actually the case has been provided by several studies (Dodge, Murphy, & Buchsbaum, 1984). For example, in one of these studies, Dodge and colleagues (1990) examined the relationship between hostile attributional bias and aggression among a group of male adolescents confined to a maximum-security prison for juvenile offenders. These young men had been convicted of a wide range of violent crimes, including murder, sexual assault, kidnapping, and armed robbery. The

Hostile Attributional Bias The tendency to perceive others' actions as stemming from hostile intent when these actions are ambiguous.

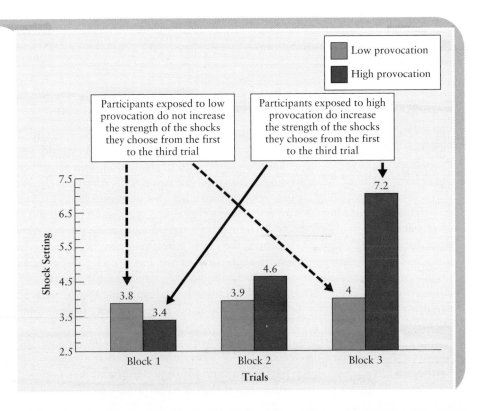

■ Effects of Provocation on Aggression

FIGURE 8.15 Research participants who were strongly provoked by another person directed much more aggression against this person than did participants who were not strongly provoked, and also increased their aggression over time from Block 1 to Block 3 of the trials. Those who were weakly provoked did not increase aggression in this way.

Source: Based on data from Berman, Chermack, & Taylor, 1997.

researchers found that hostile attributional bias among these men was related to the number of interpersonally violent crimes they had committed and to trained observers' ratings of the prisoners' tendencies to engage in reactive aggression in response to provocation.

In short, the tendency to perceive malevolence or malice in the actions of others, even when it doesn't really exist, is an important trait—one that can exacerbate the effect of others' provocation.

Gender and Aggression: Are There Real Differences?

Are males more aggressive than females? Folklore suggests that they are, and research findings suggest that in this case such informal observation is correct: when asked whether they have ever engaged in any of a wide range of aggressive actions, males report a higher incidence of many aggressive behaviours than do females (Harris, 1994, 1997). On close examination, however, the picture regarding gender differences in aggression becomes more complex. On the one hand, males are generally more likely than females both to perform aggressive actions and to be the targets of such behaviour (Bogard, 1990; Harris, 1992, 1994). Further, this difference seems to persist throughout the lifespan, occurring even among people in their 70s and 80s (Walker, Richardson, & Green, 1999). On the other hand, however, the magnitude of these gender differences appears to vary greatly across situations.

First, gender differences in aggression are much larger in the absence of provocation than in its presence. In other words, males are significantly more likely than females to aggress against others when these persons have not provoked them in any manner (Bettencourt & Miller, 1996). But in situations where provocation is present, and especially when it is intense, females may be just as aggressive as males.

Second, the size—and even the direction—of gender differences in aggression seem to vary greatly with the *type* of aggression in question. Research findings indicate that males are more likely than females to engage in various forms of *direct* aggression—actions that are aimed directly at the target and which clearly stem from the aggressor (e.g., physical assaults, pushing, shoving, throwing something at another person, shouting, making insulting remarks) (Bjorkqvist et al., 1994). However, females are more likely to engage in various forms of *indirect* aggression—actions that allow the aggressor to conceal his or her identity from the victim. Such actions include spreading vicious rumours about the target person, gossiping behind this person's back, telling others not to associate with the intended victim, making up stories to get the victim in trouble, and so on. Research findings indicate that females' greater tendencies to engage in indirect aggression are present among children as young as eight and increase through age 15 (Bjorkqvist et al., 1992; Osterman et al., 1998), and they seem to persist into adulthood as well (Bjorkqvist, Osterman, & Hjelt-Back, 1994; Green, Richardson, & Lago, 1996). Further, these tendencies have been observed in several different countries—Finland, Sweden, Poland, and Italy (Osterman et al., 1998)—and so appear to be quite general in scope. In sum, gender differences with respect to aggression exist, but they are smaller and more complex in nature than common sense might suggest.

Before concluding this discussion, we should make one final point: Men and women also differ considerably with respect to one other kind of aggression—*sexual coercion*. Such behaviour involves words and deeds designed to overcome a partner's objections to engaging in sexual behaviour, and they can range from verbal tactics such as false statements of love to threats of harm and actual physical force. As we noted earlier, males are far more likely to engage in such behaviour than are females (e.g., Mussweiler & Forster, 2000). Further, findings reported by Hogben and his colleagues (Hogben et al., 2001) indicate that this difference may stem, at least in part, from greater acceptance by males than females of the idea that aggression is a legitimate and acceptable form of behaviour. Specifically, Hogben and associates (2001) found that the more strongly males endorsed such beliefs, the greater their tendency to engage in sexual coercion; in contrast, this was not the case for females.

KEY POINTS

- Response to *provocation* from others is a powerful elicitor of aggression. We rarely turn the other cheek; rather, we match—or slightly exceed—the level of aggression we receive from others.

- A tendency to exhibit the *hostile attributional bias* leads people to attribute others' actions to hostile intent even when this is not so. As a result, they are more aggressive than persons low in this characteristic.

- Overall, males are more aggressive than females, but this difference tends to disappear in the face of strong provocation. Males are more likely to use direct forms of aggression, but females are more likely to use indirect forms of aggression.

Situational Determinants of Aggression: Alcohol Consumption and Exposure to Violent Media

While aggression is often strongly influenced by internal emotional and cognitive processes and by personality characteristics, it is also affected by factors relating to the situation or context in which it occurs. Here, we'll examine two of the many *situational factors* that can influence aggression: alcohol consumption and exposure to violent media. Research on the first of these topics has continued for many years and provides a clear illustration of how social psychologists make progress in understanding complex topics, so we'll examine it in the following Canadian Research: On the Cutting Edge section.

Canadian Research: On the Cutting Edge

Alcohol and Aggression: The Effects Depend on Sex and Predisposition

It is widely believed that some persons, at least, become more aggressive when they consume alcohol. This idea is supported by the fact that bars and nightclubs are frequently the scenes of violence. It is also supported by systematic research into the link between alcohol and aggression (Bushman & Cooper, 1990). Pihl and associates at McGill University have made a made major contributions to our understand-

ing of the effects of alcohol, as well as the nature of alcoholism, over two decades. A number of studies have clearly shown that alcohol consumption increases the likelihood of aggressive behaviour. For example, in one study, men who had strong or weak tendencies to aggress consumed substantial doses of enough to make them legally drunk—and were then provoked using the *Taylor Aggression Paradigm* described

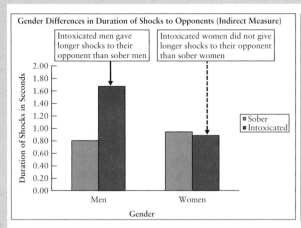

Gender Differences in Duration of Shocks to Opponents (Indirect Measure)

Intoxicated men gave longer shocks to their opponent than sober men

Intoxicated women did not give longer shocks to their opponent than sober women

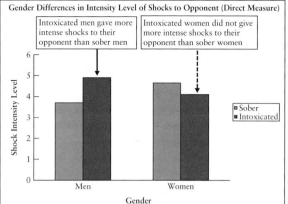

Gender Differences in Intensity Level of Shocks to Opponent (Direct Measure)

Intoxicated men gave more intense shocks to their opponent than sober men

Intoxicated women did not give more intense shocks to their opponent than sober women

■ The Impact of Alcohol on Aggression for Men and Women

FIGURE 8.16 When men who were drunk were provoked, they responded with increased aggression compared to men who were sober. However, this did not occur for women—those who were drunk showed levels of aggression at or slightly below the levels of sober women.

above. (Needless to state, participants in such research are always warned in advance that they may be receiving alcoholic beverages, and only those who consent to such procedures actually take part.)

Those who had consumed alcohol were found to behave more aggressively, and to respond to provocations more strongly, than those who did not consume alcohol. And this was true regardless of whether the man was an aggressive individual normally—subjects who normally had few aggressive tendencies showed levels of aggression that were close to those with strong aggressive tendencies when both were intoxicated (Pihl, Lau, & Assaad, 1997).

Another intriguing question examined by these researchers is whether there are sex differences in aggressive response to alcohol (Hoaken & Pihl, 2000). Again using the Taylor Aggression Paradigm, male and female subjects from 18 to 30 years old, who were intoxicated or sober, were provoked by their opponent in a competitive game. Two measures of subjects' aggression were the intensity and the duration of shocks delivered.

Based on previous research (Giancola & Zeichner, 1995), it was hypothesized that female aggression would be greater for the more *indirect* measure of aggression (duration of the shock) than for the more direct measure (intensity of the shock). Figure 8.16 shows the results.

While alcohol increased aggression for males, it did not do so for females using either measure of aggression. Further, there was no evidence of increased aggression using the more indirect measure. In this study, women showed considerable levels of direct aggression (level of shock intensity) compared to both sober and intoxicated men.

These findings, and those of other studies (e.g., Giancola, 2002; Giancola & Zeichner, 1995), suggest that the alcohol–aggression relationship may differ for men and women. Why this occurs is, at present, unclear. In sum, research to date indicates that alcohol can indeed be one situational factor contributing to the occurrence of aggression, but this is more likely to occur for men, particularly when there is a predisposition to aggression.

Exposure to Media Violence: The Effects of Witnessing Aggression

List several films you have seen in recent months. Now, answer the following question: How much aggression or violence did each of these contain? How often did characters in these movies hit, shoot at, or otherwise attempt to harm others? Unless you have chosen very carefully, you probably recognize that many of the films you have seen contain a great deal of violence—much more than you are ever likely to see in real life (Reiss & Roth, 1993; Waters et al., 1993).

Media Violence
Depictions of violent actions in the mass media.

This fact raises an important question that social psychologists have studied for decades: Does exposure to media violence increase aggression among children or adults? Literally hundreds of studies have been performed to test this possibility, and the results seem clear: *Exposure to media violence may indeed be one factor contributing to high levels of violence in countries where such materials are viewed by large numbers of persons* (e.g., Anderson, 1997; Berkowitz, 1993; Paik & Comstock, 1994; Wood, Wong, & Cachere, 1991). Many kinds of evidence lend support to this conclusion. For example, in *short-term laboratory experiments,* children or adults have viewed either violent films and television programs or nonviolent ones; then, their tendency to aggress against others has been measured. In general, the results of such experiments have revealed higher levels of aggression among participants who viewed the violent films or programs (e.g., Bandura, Ross, & Ross, 1963; Geen, 1991b).

Other and perhaps more convincing research has employed *longitudinal* procedures, in which the same participants are studied for many years (e.g., Huesmann & Eron, 1984, 1986). Results of such research, too, are clear: the more violent films or television programs participants watched as children, the higher their levels of aggression as teenagers or adults—for instance, the higher the likelihood that they have been arrested for violent crimes. Such findings have been replicated in many different countries—Australia, Finland, Israel, Poland, and South Africa (Botha, 1990). Thus, these findings appear to hold across different cultures.

While these longitudinal studies have been carefully conducted, it's important to remember that they are still only correlational in nature. As we noted in Chapter 1, the fact that two variables are correlated does *not* imply that one necessarily causes the other. However, when the results of these studies are combined with the findings of short-term laboratory experiments, a strong case for the suggestion that exposure to media violence is one potential cause of human aggression does seem to emerge.

But why, you may be wondering, do these effects occur? A number of possibilities exist. First, individuals may simply learn new ways of aggressing from watching television programs and films—ways they would not have imagined before. "Copycat crimes," in which a violent crime reported in the media is then copied by different persons in distant locations, suggest that such effects are real.

Another effect of watching media violence involves what is known as *desensitization effects*. After viewing many vivid scenes of violence, individuals become hardened to the pain and suffering of other persons: they experience less emotional reaction to such cues than was originally true (e.g., Baron, 1974a), and this may lessen their own restraints against engaging in aggression.

Research indicates that a third effect may occur as well: watching scenes of violence may serve to "prime" hostile thoughts, so that these come to mind more readily—they become more accessible to conscious thought. This, in turn, can increase the likelihood that a person will engage in overt aggression (Anderson, 1997). Because repeated exposure to media violence may strengthen such priming effects over time, the impact of watching violence may be cumulative—and even more important than was previously assumed.

Because exposure to media violence may have harmful effects on society, why, you may be wondering, is there so much of it on television and in films? One answer is that the advertisers who pay for these programs believe that "violence sells"—it is one way to increase audience size. While this may be true, findings reported by Bushman (1998) suggest that media violence may actually backfire from the point of view of increasing the sales of products advertised on such shows. He found that audiences who watch violent programs are significantly *less* likely to remember the content of commercials shown during these programs than are audiences who watch nonviolent programs. Apparently, violent images on the television screen trigger memories of other violent scenes, and such thoughts distract viewers from paying attention to commercials. These findings suggest that sponsoring violent television programs is not just questionable from a moral point of view; it may also make little economic sense for sponsors!

Culture and Aggression: The Social Context of Violence

Earlier we called attention to the existence of variations in the levels of aggression around the world. A recent study comparing violent crime across 11 Western nations provides ample evidence of such differences. For example, the reports of criminal victimization due to violent offences (robbery, assault, and sexual assault) vary from 8 percent of the population in England and Wales, 7 percent in the United States, 6 percent in Canada, Finland, the Netherlands, and Sweden, to the lowest level of 3 percent in Northern Ireland. Homicide rates also vary, though they show a different pattern— see Figure 8.17. Moreover, the rate of violence within a given culture can change drastically over time as social conditions change (e.g., Robarchek & Robarchek, 1997).

Most cultural values include the abhorrence of violence. So what accounts for the massive differences we can see in the levels of aggression, violent crime, and homicide?

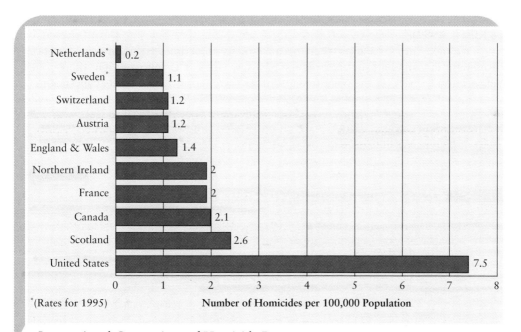

* (Rates for 1995) **Number of Homicides per 100,000 Population**

■ International Comparison of Homicide Rates

FIGURE 8.17 This figure illustrates that levels of violence, as indicated by homicide rates, can vary tremendously across different cultures. In the context of Western nations, as shown here, the United States stands out with a rate of 7.5 homicides per 100,000 of the population. In the context of the world as a whole, the United States is not one of the highest—Colombia at 70.9 in 1995 takes that honour. However, what is really remarkable worldwide is the tremendous variation in homicide rates between even geographically adjacent nations. Note that Canadian rates are less than a third of those in the United States.

Source: Statistics Canada, 1998, Juristat, Catalogue No. 85-002, Vol. 18, No. 6.

Cultural norms about the appropriateness of aggression do vary and that will have an impact on expectations as far as violence is concerned. For example, in _cultures of honour_ there are strong norms condoning violence as a means of responding to an affront to one's honour. Research has shown that a job applicant, who admitted having been in prison because he killed someone who grossly undermined his honour, had more positive responses in the South and West United States where such norms are more prevalent than in the North (Cohen & Nisbett, 1997). But in order to explain variation in violent crime, a web of economic, political, and socio-historical factors also need to be taken into account. We will discuss psychological evidence related to one cultural and political issue—gun control—in Chapter 10.

In short, culture does seem to play an important role in aggression. Growing evidence suggests that it determines not only the rate of violence but also the forms violence generally takes and the targets selected. A group of researchers (Ostermann et al., 1994) investigated cultural differences in aggression in eight-year-old children in several different cultural and ethnic groups. They found that African-American children were more aggressive (both in self-ratings and ratings by peers) than Caucasian-American, Polish, and Finnish children. Such findings have been attributed to differences in childrearing practices (Kumagai, 1983; Osterwell and Nagano-Nakamura, 1992). These studies emphasize the importance of cultural values and beliefs in determining aggression in society. Contrasting beliefs about aggression influence childrearing practices in various cultures, and these, in turn, help to explain why cultural differences in the rate and intensity of many forms of aggression tend to persist over time (Fraczek & Kirwil, 1992).

We next turn to a topic that, because of its sometimes-tragic impact, has been prominent in Canadian society over the past few years. The following On the Applied Side section focuses on the phenomenon of _bullying_—its origins and its prevention.

On the **Applied Side**

Bullying: Singling Out Others for Repeated Abuse

Over the last few years a number of teenagers in Canada have killed themselves, leaving suicide notes that spoke of relentless bullying as the cause. In March 2000 Hamed Nastoh jumped from the Pattullo Bridge in Surrey, in November of the same year Dawn-Marie Wesley hanged herself at her home in Mission, and in April 2002 Emmet Fralick shot himself at home in Halifax. All three were 14 years old and the victims of bullying—repeated aggression in a context in which they had less power or prestige than the persons who aggressed against them — other members of their peer group (Olweus, 1993). And

Bullying A pattern of behaviour in which one individual is chosen as the target of repeated aggression by one or more others; the target person (the victim) generally has less power than those who engage in aggression (the bullies).

these tragic examples weren't isolated cases. In one Canadian survey, 15 percent of children in elementary and middle school reported that they had been bullied "more than once or twice" over a six-week period (Pepler et al., 1997). While the court system has begun to prosecute the young bullies for criminal harassment, extortion, and assault (as occurred with both Dawn-Marie Wesley's and Emmet Fralick's tormentors), it has become evident that we need to understand and combat this problem on a much larger scale.

Bullying has been studied primarily as something that occurs among children and teenagers; however, it is also common in other contexts, such as workplaces and prisons. Indeed, recent findings indicate that fully 50 percent of persons in prison are exposed to one or more episodes of bullying each week (Ireland & Ireland, 2000). Because most research has focused on bullying among children, though, we will focus on this work here. Two basic questions have been considered in research on bullying among children: (1) what are the characteristics of bullies and victims—in other words, why do some persons become bullies and others victims, while still others are not involved in bullying; and (2) what steps can be taken to reduce or prevent bullying?

The Characteristics of Bullies and Victims

Perhaps we should start with two basic facts. First, research on bullying indicates that relatively few children are purely victims or purely bullies; rather, a larger number play both roles: they bully some people and are bullied, in turn, by others (e.g., see Figure 8.18; Vermande et al., 2000). Second, bullying seems to be common all around the globe, from Australia to Finland and from Japan to Canada (Smith & Brain, 2000; Smorti, Menesini & Smith, 2003).

But now, returning to the central question, what, specifically, has research on bullying discovered about the characteristics of bullies and their victims? First, that they differ in their perceptions of the social world. For instance, bullies tend to perceive others as acting the way they do because they are that kind of person or because they intended to act in the way they did (Smorti & Ciucci, 2000). In contrast, victims tend to perceive others as acting as they do at least in part because they are responding to external events or conditions, including how others have treated *them*. What this implies is that bullies may be more likely than victims to fall prey to the *hostile attributional bias* described earlier in this chapter. So, in a sense, they strike at others repeatedly because they perceive them to be potentially dangerous and wish to subdue such opponents in advance.

Additional findings indicate that while bullies and victims are not easy to differentiate in terms of specific characteristics, children who play both roles (*bully/victims*, as they are often termed) do differ from children who are not involved in bullying. Such bully/victims are lower in self-esteem, lower in the belief that they can control their own outcomes, and higher in Machiavellianism—a tendency to adopt a ruthless, manipulative approach to dealing with other persons (e.g., Mynard & Joseph, 1997; Andreou, 2000). As one researcher (Andreou, 2000, p. 54) puts it, "These children believe that they live in a world in which they can be either bullies or victims, and they choose to be both to be consistent with their low self-esteem and their Machiavellian strategy for dealing with other people."

Finally, we should note that bullies and bully/victims seem to be less effective in coping with stress than are other children, especially those not involved in bullying. Bullies and bully/victims are more likely to respond to stress with aggression (lashing out at someone physically

■ Bullying: All Too Common in Many Schools

FIGURE 8.18 *Bullying*—repeated assaults by one or more persons against a target person who is weaker or lower in power—is very common among children. Research findings indicate that it can have devastating effects on the victims, and on the bullies, too.

or verbally) or by engaging in self-destructive behaviours (doing something dangerous, smoking, taking drugs). In contrast, children not involved in bullying are more likely to react to stress in more adaptive ways, for instance, by distracting themselves (taking their minds off the stress by engaging in hobbies or exercise). Overall, then, it seems fair to say that children who become bullies or bully/victims have a more negative view of the world than other children and show personal characteristics that may interfere with their personal happiness and adjustment.

Reducing the Occurrence of Bullying: Some Positive Steps

Bullying can have devastating effects on its victims. As mentioned earlier, there have been several cases in which children who are bullied repeatedly and brutally by their classmates have actually committed suicide (O'Moore, 2000). These distressing facts lead to the following question: What can be done to reduce or even eliminate bullying? Many research projects—some involving the entire school systems of several countries—have been conducted to find out, and the results have been at least moderately encouraging.

First, it appears that students themselves can be every effective in reducing bullying. When children are trained to intervene rather than to simply stand by when bullying occurs, the incidence of such behaviour can be substantially reduced (e.g., Cowei, 2000). However, it appears that girls are more willing to intervene than are boys, who tend to perceive bullying as part of being masculine: "real" boys can both take it and dish it out. Special efforts may be necessary, therefore, to induce boys as well as girls to intervene when bullying occurs.

Teachers, too, can play a very helpful role in reducing bullying. One recent project conducted in Ireland (O'Moore, 2000) indicates that teachers often do not fully grasp the importance of low self-esteem in bullying, so programs designed to call this point to the attention of teachers can be very useful. Once they understand that bullies as well as victims suffer from low self-esteem, teachers can take steps to enhance children's feelings of self-worth, and this, in turn, can be a very useful initial step toward reducing bullying.

Additional projects carried out in the Netherlands (e.g., Limper, 2000) and in Norway (e.g., Roland, 2000) have enlisted the aid of parents (through parents associations) and the help of outside experts such as psychologists and professors to reduce bullying. In these programs, efforts are made to change the entire school environment so that it is clear to students, teachers, and parents alike that bullying is *not* a normal part of growing up and is *not* to be tolerated. For example, in the Netherlands, the following points have been stressed:

1. Bullying must been seen to be a problem by all involved parties—teachers, parents, and students.
2. If bullying occurs, teachers must draw attention to it and take an unequivocal stand against it.
3. Students must be provided with direct means for dealing with bullying—they must be told precisely what to do and whom to see when bullying occurs.
4. If a teacher or school refuses to address the problem, then an outside expert must be called in to help.

The effects of programs emphasizing such steps are encouraging and suggest that when concerted action is taken, bullying can indeed be reduced.

KEY POINTS

- The effects of alcohol on aggression differs for males and females.
- Exposure to media violence has been found to increase aggression among viewers. This occurs because of several factors, such as the priming of aggressive thoughts and a weakening of restraints against aggression.
- Research indicates wide cultural variation in the levels of violence and aggression. Cultural norms about aggression vary and may be related to childrearing practices.
- *Bullying*, repeated aggression against an individual with less power, often occurs among school children. Research has identified characteristics of bullies and their victims and indicated that programs designed to reduce bullying can be very effective.

The Prevention and Control of Aggression: Some Useful Techniques

If there is one idea in this chapter we hope you'll remember in the years ahead, it is this: aggression, whether it takes the form of bullying or any one of its manifestations, is not an inevitable or unchangeable form of behaviour. On the contrary, because it stems from a complex interplay of external events, cognitions, and personal characteristics, it can be prevented or reduced. In this final section we'll consider several additional procedures that, when used appropriately, can be effective in this regard.

Punishment: An Effective Deterrent to Violence?

Throughout history, most societies have used **punishment** as a means of deterring human violence. Nations have established harsh punishment for such crimes as murder, sexual assault, and assault. Are such tactics effective? Will the threat of severe punishment actually prevent individuals from engaging in aggressive acts in the first place? The pendulum of scientific opinion on this issue has swung back and forth for decades. At present, however, the weight of existing evidence seems to suggest that if used in an appropriate manner, punishment can be an effective deterrent to violence. In order for it to succeed, however, several conditions must be met (Baron & Richardson, 1994; Bower & Hilgard, 1981).

> **Punishment**
> Procedures in which aversive consequences are delivered to individuals each time they engage in specific actions. Under appropriate conditions, punishment can serve as an effective deterrent to human aggression.

What conditions must be met for punishment to succeed? Four are most important:

1. It must be *prompt*—it must follow aggressive actions as quickly as possible.
2. It must be *certain*—the probability that it will follow aggression must be very high.
3. It must be *strong*—strong enough to be highly unpleasant to potential recipients.
4. It must be perceived by recipients as *justified* or deserved.

Unfortunately, of course, these conditions are often the ones lacking from the criminal justice systems of many nations. The delivery of punishment for aggressive actions is often delayed for months or even years; the magnitude of punishment itself is variable from one locale to another; and it is well known that many violent crimes go unpunished—no one is ever apprehended, tried, or convicted of them. In view of these facts, it is hardly surprising that punishment has often seemed to fail as a deterrent to violent crime. The dice, so to speak, are heavily loaded against the possibility of its succeeding. However, if these conditions were changed, the potential impact of punishment might well be enhanced.

Learning Not to Be Aggressive

Interventions based on social learning theory suggest that if we learn aggressive behaviour, it can be unlearned, or perhaps, not taught at all.

One approach is to use modelling to a constructive end by exposure to *nonaggressive models*. If exposure to aggressive actions by others in the media or in person can increase aggression, it seems possible that exposure to *nonaggressive* behaviour might produce opposite effects. In fact, the results of several studies indicate that this is so (e.g., Baron, 1972b; Donnerstein & Donnerstein, 1976). When individuals who have been provoked are exposed to others who either demonstrate or urge restraint, the tendency of potential aggressors to lash out is reduced. These findings suggest that it may be useful to place restrained, nonaggressive models in tense and potentially dangerous situations. Their presence may well tip the balance against overt violence.

Techniques of *social skills training* can also be useful in decreasing aggression. Many people don't know how to respond to provocations from others in a way that will soothe these persons rather than annoy them. They don't know how to make requests, or how to say no to requests from others, without making people angry. Persons lacking in basic social skills seem to account for a high proportion of violence in many societies (Toch, 1985), so equipping such persons with improved social skills may go a long way toward reducing aggression. This can be done by watching other persons (social models) demonstrate both effective and ineffective behaviours (Schneider, 1991). Such gains can be obtained through just a few hours of treatment (Bienert & Schneider, 1993), so this approach is practical and cost-effective as well as successful.

Catharsis: Does Getting It Out of Your System Really Help?

Does somehow blowing off steam really help individuals get rid of—or at least control—their aggressive impulses? The belief that such activities are effective in this

Catharsis Hypothesis The view that providing angry persons with an opportunity to engage in vigorous but noninjurious activities will reduce their level of emotional arousal and lower their tendencies to aggress against others.

respect is very widespread. Many persons accept some version of what psychologists describe as the catharsis hypothesis (Dollard et al., 1939)—the idea that participation in activities that allow individuals to vent their anger and hostility in some relatively safe way will actually reduce later aggression.

Is this hypothesis valid? Existing evidence offers a mixed picture (Feshbach, 1984; Geen, 1991b). On the one hand, participation in various activities that are not harmful to others (e.g., vigorous physical activity, shouting obscenities into an empty room) can reduce emotional arousal stemming from frustration or provocation (Zillmann, 1979). On the other hand, such effects appear to be temporary. Arousal stemming from provocation may reappear as soon as individuals remember the incidents that made them angry (Caprara et al., 1994).

What about the idea that performing "safe" aggressive actions reduces the likelihood of more harmful forms of aggression? The results of research on this issue are even less encouraging. Overt physical aggression, it appears, is not reduced by (1) watching scenes of media violence (Geen, 1978), (2) attacking inanimate objects (Bushman, Baumeister, & Stack, 1999; Mallick & McCandless, 1966), or (3) aggressing verbally against others. Indeed, some findings suggest that aggression may actually be *increased* by these activities. For instance, Bushman, Baumeister, and Stack (1999) recently found that hitting a punching bag increased rather than reduced aggression. And in related research, Bushman (2001) found that research participants who thought about someone who had angered them while hitting a punching bag became *angrier* and behaved more aggressively than participants who thought about becoming physically fit while punching the bag.

In short, contrary to popular belief, catharsis does *not* appear to be a very effective means for reducing aggression. Participating in "safe" forms of aggression or merely in vigorous, energy-draining activities may produce temporary reductions in arousal; but feelings of anger may quickly return when individuals meet, or merely think about, the persons who previously annoyed them. For this reason, catharsis may be less effective in producing lasting reductions in aggression than is widely believed.

Cognitive Interventions: Apologies and Overcoming Cognitive Deficits

Suppose that you are standing at the counter in a store, waiting your turn. Suddenly, another customer walks up and starts to place an order. You are beginning to get angry when this person turns toward you, notices you, and quickly apologizes. "I'm so sorry," he says. "I didn't see you. You were here first." How do you react? Probably, your anger will dissipate; you may even smile at this person in appreciation for his courtesy. This incident suggests that apologies—admissions of wrongdoing that include expressions of regret and requests for forgiveness—often go a long way toward defusing aggression. Research findings support this conclusion: apologies (e.g., Ohbuchi, Kameda, & Agarie, 1989) and excuses that make reference to factors beyond the excuse-giver's control, are quite effective in reducing aggression by persons who have been provoked in some manner (e.g., Baron, 1989b; Weiner et al., 1987). So if you feel that you are making another person angry, apologize without delay. The trouble you will save makes it quite worthwhile to say "I'm sorry."

Apologies Admissions of wrongdoing that include expressions of regret and requests for forgiveness.

Other cognitive mechanisms for reducing aggression relate to the fact that when we are very angry, our ability to think clearly—for instance, to evaluate the consequences of our own actions—may be sharply reduced. In addition, as noted recently by Lieberman and Greenberg (1999), we may adopt modes of thought in which we process information in a quick and impetuous manner, thus increasing the chances that we will "lash out against" someone else—including other persons who are not the cause of our annoyance or irritation. This phenomenon is known as *displaced aggression*—aggression is directed against innocent victims rather than the persons who provoked us or caused our discomfort (Lieberman & Greenberg, 1999; Tedeschi & Norman, 1985; Pedersen, Gonzales, & Miller, 2000). Any procedures that serve to overcome such cognitive deficits, therefore, may help reduce overt aggression (Zillmann, 1993). One such technique involves *preattribution*—attributing annoying actions by others to unintentional causes before the provocation actually occurs. For example, before meeting with someone you know can be irritating, you could remind yourself that she or he doesn't mean to make you angry—it's just the result of an unfortunate personal style. Another technique involves preventing yourself (or others) from dwelling on real or imagined wrongs. You can accomplish this by distracting yourself in some way—for instance, by watching an absorbing movie or television program or working on complex puzzles. Such activities allow for a cooling-off period during which anger can dissipate. They also help to re-establish cognitive controls over behaviour—controls that help to hold aggression in check.

KEY POINTS

- *Punishment* can be effective in reducing aggression, but only when it is delivered in accordance with specific principles.

- The *catharsis hypothesis* appears to be mainly false. Engaging in vigorous activities may produce reductions in arousal, but these are only temporary. Similarly, engaging in apparently "safe" forms of aggression does not reduce aggressive tendencies.

- Aggression can also be not learned or it can be reduced by exposure to nonaggressive models and training in social skills.

- Aggression can be reduced by *apologies*—admissions of wrongdoing that include requests for forgiveness—and by engaging in activities that distract attention away from causes of anger.

Ideas To Take With You

Being a Responsive Bystander

In this chapter you have read examples of real and staged emergencies. In your own life you undoubtedly have in the past and will in the future come across numerous unexpected situations in which your help is badly needed. How you decide to respond is obviously up to you, but at least consider the following suggestions that might be useful in assisting you to make an informed decision.

Pay Attention to What Is Going On around You.
In our everyday lives we often think more about ourselves (our plans, worries, expectancies, etc.) than about our surroundings. For many reasons, we would do well not only to stop and smell the roses, but also to stop and pay attention. Remember the seminary students who were behind schedule and in such a hurry that they ignored a man who appeared to have collapsed in a doorway? There are often other things worth thinking about and observing beyond yourself.

If You See Something Unusual, Consider More than One Alternative.

The crying child might be unhappy about not getting a second piece of candy, but she also might be the target of abuse. The man who is running down the street might be a jogger, but he might also be a thief. The smoke you smell might be burnt toast, but it might indicate that the building is on fire. The idea is not to panic or jump to conclusions, but rather to consider various possibilities. Seek additional evidence. Is someone hitting the child? Is the running man carrying a large bag? Is there smoke coming out of the basement? Most unexpected events of this sort are probably easily explained and of little importance, but you need to be alert to the possibility that in rare instances there may really be an emergency.

Consider Yourself to Be as Responsible as Anyone Else for Responding.

No, it's not really your special responsibility, but think of it as everyone's responsibility. I (Donn Byrne) was once in a multiplex movie theatre in a mall, and when it was time for the film to begin, nothing happened. A roomful of people sat in their seats and stared at a blank screen. This seemed ridiculous to me, so I left my seat, went to the refreshment counter, and asked the person selling the popcorn to inform someone that the movie had not begun on screen 12. She told the manager, someone pushed the right button, and the movie began. This was a very mild emergency, and I didn't expect a medal; but the same general principle applies to serious situations as well as to trivial ones. If you let the unresponsiveness of others be your guide, you are acting as foolishly as they are.

Be Willing to Act.

It is not reasonable simply to react to what others do and never to act on your own. If you are afraid of what other people might think of you and of being evaluated negatively, just remember that others are as uncertain and confused as you may be. It may feel cool to stand back and do nothing, but it often is actually the stupid choice. What if the worst possible thing occurs—that is, what if you make an honest mistake and look foolish? It's not the end of the world, and you will probably never see these people again anyway. Do what you think is the right thing to do.

Summary

- The purest form of *prosocial behaviour* is *altruism,* which contrasts with *aggression.* (p. 281)

Bystander Response to an Emergency

- The *bystander effect* occurs in part because of *diffusion of responsibility.* (p. 282)
- Bystanders go through five steps when deciding whether to help. (p. 284)

Prosocial Motivation: Why Do People Help?

- The *empathy–altruism* hypothesis proposes that empathy is crucial to prosocial behaviour. (p. 289)

- The *negative-state relief model* proposes that people help to relieve their own negative emotions. (p. 290)
- The *empathic joy hypothesis* bases helping on feelings of accomplishment that bring joy to the helper. (p. 291)
- The *genetic determinism model* traces prosocial behaviour to the processes of evolution and kin selection. (p. 291)

Further Determinants of Helping Behaviour: Internal and External Influences

- Attributions of *responsibility* can determine emotion and prosocial behaviour. (p. 293)
- Those with an *altruistic personality* are more likely to help. (p. 295)

- Exposure to prosocial models increases prosocial acts. (p. 295)
- Characteristics of the victim (similarity and gender) can influence helping behaviour. (p. 298)
- The culture context (rural versus urban, collectivistic versus individualistic) can influence prosocial behaviour. (p. 299)

Sources of Aggression: Theories about Its Nature and Causes

- Early *instinct theories* suggest that aggression stems largely from innate tendencies. (p. 301)
- Modern evolutionary approaches have suggested that the evolution of aggression derives from its contribution to reproductive success. (p. 302)
- *Drive theories*, such as the *frustration–aggression hypothesis,* suggest that aggression stems from externally elicited drives to harm others. (p. 304)
- Modern theories such as the *general affective aggression model* (GAAM) recognize the importance of many factors as influencing aggression. (p. 305)

Further Determinants of Aggression: Internal and External Influences

- *Excitation transfer theory* suggests that heightened arousal, including sexual arousal, can influence aggression. (p. 307)
- *Type A* individuals are more aggressive than *Type B* individuals. (p. 309)

- High *narcissism* is also a predictor of higher levels of aggression. (p. 311)
- Response to *provocation* from others is a powerful elicitor of aggression. (p. 311)
- The *hostile attributional bias* leads people to attribute others' actions to hostile intent. (p. 312)
- Greater male aggression compared to females tends to disappear in the face of strong provocation. (p. 313)
- The effects of alcohol on aggression differ for males and females. (p. 314)
- Exposure to *media violence* has been found to increase aggression among viewers. (p. 315)
- Research indicates wide cultural variation in the levels of violence and aggression. (p. 317)
- *Bullying*, repeated aggression against an individual with less power, often occurs among school children. (p. 318)

The Prevention and Control of Aggression: Some Useful Techniques

- Under certain conditions *punishment* can be effective in reducing aggression. (p. 321)
- The *catharsis hypothesis* suggests engaging in vigorous activities may produce reductions in arousal. (p. 321)
- Aggression can be reduced by various methods derived from social learning approaches. (p. 321)
- Aggression can be reduced by *apologies* and by distraction from causes of anger. (p. 322)

For More Information

Shroeder, D. A., Penner, L. A., Dovidio, J. F., & Piliavin, J. A. (1995). The social psychology of helping and altruism: Problems and puzzles. New York: McGraw-Hill.

This is the first text devoted entirely to the topic of prosocial behaviour. The authors cover much of the material discussed in Chapter 8, plus such topics as the developmental aspects of helping, cooperation, and collective helping. They also present an integrative conceptual framework based on affect and cognition, and make suggestions for future research.

Baron, R. A., & Richardson, D. R. (1994). Human aggression (2nd ed.). New York: Plenum.

A broad introduction to current knowledge about human aggression. Separate chapters examine the biological, social, environmental, and personal determinants of aggression. Additional chapters examine the development of aggression and the occurrence of aggression in many natural settings.

Moeller, T. G. (2001). Youth aggression and violence: A psychological approach. Mahwah, NJ: Erlbaum.

This book examines the causes of aggression by young persons in schools and other settings. It considers the genetic and biological underpinnings of such aggression, family and social factors, and examines the findings of current research employing a wide range of methods. This is a very timely book on an important topic closely related to issues examined in this chapter.

Weblinks

www.bfskinner.org
B. F. Skinner Foundation

www.trauma-pages.com
David Baldwin's Trauma Information Pages

CHAPTER NINE

Groups and Individuals: The Consequences of Belonging

Groups: Their Nature and Function
How Groups Function: Roles, Status, Norms, and Cohesiveness

How Groups Affect Individual Performance: Facilitation or Social Loafing?
Social Facilitation: Performance in the Presence of Others/Social Loafing: Letting Others in the Group Do the Work

Decision Making by Groups: How It Occurs and the Pitfalls It Faces
The Decision-Making Process: How Groups Attain Consensus/The Nature of Group Decisions: Moderation or Polarization?/Decision Making by Groups: Some Potential Pitfalls

Coordination in Groups: Cooperation or Conflict?
Cooperation: Working with Others to Achieve Shared Goals/Conflict: Its Nature, Causes, and Effects/Resolving Conflicts: Some Useful Techniques

Perceived Fairness in Groups: Getting What We Deserve—or Else!
Judgments of Fairness: Outcomes, Procedures, and Courtesy/Reactions to Perceived Unfairness: Tactics for Dealing with Injustice

SPECIAL SECTIONS

Canadian Research: On the Cutting Edge
Commitment to the Group: Continued Loyalty in Times of Change

Cornerstones
Performance in the Presence of Others: The Simplest Group Effect?

On the Applied Side
Reaching the Verdict They Want: Biased Processing in Juries

■ What Makes a Group a Group?

FIGURE 9.1 In order for two or more persons to be termed a group, several criteria must be met. The left photo shows an actual social group; the right photo shows a mere collection of individuals who are not part of a group.

During the course of our lives, all of us belong to many different groups, some we choose and others that are chosen for us. For example, membership in cultural, gender, or family groups is seldom voluntary: we are born into such groups and raised within them. However, later in life we often choose to join various groups: clubs, political parties, groups of friends, or work groups. Once people belong to a number of groups, whether involuntarily or by choice, they are subject to a wide variety of forces and processes and, as we'll soon see, the effects of such membership can be profound.

To provide you with an overview of the scope and magnitude of *group influence*—the effects of group membership on individual behaviour—we'll focus on five topics. First, we'll consider the basic *nature of groups*: what they are and how they influence their members. Second, we'll examine the impact of groups on individual *task performance*—how our performance on various tasks can be affected by our working with others or, in some cases, merely by others' presence on the scene. Third, we'll consider *decision making* in groups, focusing on the potential benefits and costs of this process. Fourth, we'll turn to the question of what might be termed *coordination* within groups—the extent to which individuals pool their efforts and work together toward goals (i.e., cooperate with one another) or, instead, choose to work against one another in what is known as *conflict*. Finally, we'll examine the question of *fairness* in groups—the extent to which individuals believe that they are being treated fairly or unfairly, and the impact of such beliefs on their behaviour. Another important topic closely related to group functioning, *leadership*, is discussed in Chapter 10.

Groups: Their Nature and Function

Look at the photos in Figure 9.1. Which shows a group? Probably you would identify the one on the left as a group but the one on the right as a mere collection of persons.

Group A collection of persons who are perceived to be bonded together in a coherent unit to some degree.

Why? Because, implicitly, you already accept a definition of the term **group** close to the one adopted by social psychologists: A collection of persons who are perceived to be bonded together in a coherent unit to some degree (e.g., Dasgupta, Banaji, & Abelson, 1999; Lickel et al., 2000). Social psychologists refer to this property of groups as *entiativity*—the extent to which a group is perceived as being a coherent entity (Campbell, 1958). Entiativity varies greatly, ranging from mere collections of people who happen to be in the same place at the same time but have little or no connection with one another, to highly intimate groups such as our family or persons with whom we have romantic relationships. So clearly, some groups are much closer to our conception of what a group is like than others. But what determines whether, and to what extent, we perceive several persons as forming a coherent group? This question has received growing attention from researchers in recent years, and a clear answer has begun to emerge. For instance, consider research on this issue by Lickel and his colleagues (Lickel et al., 2000).

These researchers presented the names of 40 different kinds of groups (e.g., sports teams, the audience at a movie) to research participants and asked them to rate each on several dimensions, including these: the extent to which it is a coherent unit (entiativity), how important it is to group members, how much group members interact with one another, the extent to which they share common goals and common outcomes, how similar they are to one another, and how long these groups are likely to last. In addition, participants were asked to place the groups into *categories*—clusters of groups that seem to go together.

As shown in Table 9.1, participants perceived the groups as differing greatly in terms of entiativity: some (e.g., families, rock bands, close friends) were rated as being very high on this dimension, while others (e.g., plumbers, people at a bus stop) were perceived as very low in this respect. Perhaps more important, other findings indicated that several factors influenced these ratings: the degree to which group members interacted with one another (this was the strongest predictor of ratings of entiativity), the group's importance to members, the extent to which members shared outcomes and common goals, and their similarity to each other. The higher groups were on these dimensions, the more they were seen as forming coherent entities. Other findings indicated that four distinct types of group emerged from participants' efforts to divide them into categories: *intimacy groups* (family, two people in a romantic relationship), *task-oriented groups* (e.g., committees, work groups), *social categories* (e.g., women, Americans), and *weak social relationships or associations* (e.g., people who live in the same neighbourhood, people who enjoy classical music). To test the generality of these findings, Lickel and his colleagues (2000) then repeated this study in another country—Poland. Results were virtually identical, so it appears that at least in two different cultures, the factors that lead individuals to perceive groups as forming coherent units (i.e., as being high in entiativity) are very much the same.

Additional research indicates that judgments concerning a group's entiativity exert important effects on how we think about such groups—for instance, our overall impression of the group (e.g., Susskind et al., 1999) and the attributions we make about it (e.g., Yzerbyt et al., 1998). Indeed, judgments concerning a group's entiativity, once made, seem to influence our processing of information about the group at an implicit (nonconscious) level of thought. For instance, when we perceive a group as being high in entiativity, we tend to compare the members with each other to a greater extent than is true for groups low in entiativity (Pickett, 2001). And such comparisons seem to occur implicitly, without conscious thought or intention. Clearly, then, entiativity is a key dimension from the point of view of understanding precisely what constitutes a group and how being part of a group can influence our behaviour.

Participants in a recent study rated some groups as much higher on entiativity—being a coherent entity. Ratings could range from 1 to 9.

TABLE 9.1 Entiativity of Various Groups

Groups	Entiativity Ratings
Members of a professional sports team	8.27
Members of a family	8.16
Members of a rock band	8.16
Friends who do things together	7.75
Members of an orchestra	7.21
Members of a labour union	6.89
Women	5.16
People who live in the same neighbourhood	4.78
Teachers	4.70
People attending an athletic contest	3.69
People in line at a bank	2.40

Source: Based on data from Lickel et al., 2000.

How Groups Function: Roles, Status, Norms, and Cohesiveness

That groups often exert powerful effects upon their members is obvious and will be a basic theme of this chapter. Before turning to group influence, however, we should address a basic issue: How, precisely, do groups affect their members? A complete answer to this question involves many processes we have already examined in this book, including conformity, persuasion, and attraction. In addition, four aspects of groups themselves play a key role in this regard: *roles, status, norms,* and *cohesiveness.*

Roles: Differentiation of Functions within Groups

Think of a group to which you belong or have belonged—anything from the Scouts to a professional association. Now consider this question: did everyone in the group act in the same way or perform the same functions? Your answer is probably *no*. Different persons performed different tasks and were expected to accomplish different things for the group. In short, they played different **roles**. Sometimes roles are assigned; for instance, a group may select different individuals to serve as its leader, treasurer, or bouncer. In other cases individuals gradually acquire certain roles without being formally assigned to them. Regardless of how roles are acquired, people often *internalize* them; they link their roles to key aspects of their self-perceptions and self-concept (see Chapters 2 and 4). When this happens, a role may exert profound effects on a person's behaviour, even when she or he is not in the group. For instance, a professor, used to lecturing to students, may lecture his or her family when at home—something the authors have each been accused of doing!

Roles The set of behaviours that individuals occupying specific positions within a group are expected to perform.

Roles help to clarify the responsibilities and obligations of group members, so in this respect they are very useful. They do have a downside, though. Group members sometimes experience *role conflict*—stress stemming from the fact that roles they play within different groups are somehow at odds with each other. For instance, the parents of young children often experience conflict between their role as *parent* and their role as *student* or *employee*, and this can be highly stressful for them (Williams et al., 1992).

Status: The Prestige of Various Roles

Status refers to social standing or rank within a group; and even today, a time when there is a strong tendency to downplay such differences in many settings, status distinctions continue to exist and to influence individual behaviour. Different roles or positions in a group are often associated with different levels of status, and people are often extremely sensitive to this fact. Why? Because status is linked to a wide range of desirable outcomes—everything from salary and "perks" to first choice among potential romantic partners (Buss, 1993). For this reason, groups often use status as a means of influencing the behaviour of their members: only "good" members—ones who follow the group's rules—receive high status.

Evolutionary psychologists attach considerable importance to status, noting that in many different species, including our own, high status confers important advantages on those who possess it. Specifically, high-status persons have greater access than lower status persons to key resources relating to survival and reproduction, such as food and access to mates. For instance, throughout human history, and in many different societies, high-status males have had access to a larger number of potential mates. As a result, some theorists contend, evolution has favoured stronger motivation for status among men than among women. And in fact, men tend to score higher on measures of status motivation than do women (e.g., Pratto, 1996). Whether this is due to evolutionary pressures or other factors, of course, is unclear, but there seems little doubt that high status brings important rewards for persons of both genders, so it is not surprising that people seek to gain it. In short, status is one of the rewards that groups offer members, and as such may be one factor in group influence.

How, precisely, do people acquire high status? As noted by Buss (1998), sheer size may play some role—taller men have an edge. For instance, presidents and heads of large corporations tend to be taller than average (e.g., Gillis, 1982). Whether this advantage of being tall will fade as women move increasingly into such high-status positions remains to be seen, but at least for men, "bigger" does seem to be "better" where status is concerned.

Factors relating to individuals' behaviour, too, play a role in acquiring status. Recent research by Tiedens (2001), for instance, suggests that people can sometimes boost their status through intimidation—by appearing angry and threatening. In one intriguing study, Tiedens (2001) showed that those who watched President Clinton (when giving grand jury testimony about his affair with Monica Lewinsky) responding angrily expressed higher approval of him than when he was sad. Several other studies offered additional support for the suggestion that displays of anger can boost one's status. For instance, in another study, participants (employees of a software company) rated each other in terms of how frequently they each expressed several emotions, including anger and sadness. These ratings were then related to several measures of status in the company—the number of previous promotions they had received, current salary, and predictions of future promotions by the manager. Results indicated that the frequency of sadness was not related to any of these measures, but frequency of expressing anger was strongly related to all three. In other words, the more often employees expressed anger, the higher their current and future predicted status.

Of course, there may be important limits to these findings: Too much anger may reduce rather than increase status, and calm anger may be more effective than overt rage. But overall, Tiedens's (2001) findings suggest that expressing anger may be one means of acquiring status in at least some groups.

Norms: The Rules of the Game

Earlier we alluded to a third factor responsible for the powerful impact of groups on their members: rules, or **norms**, established by groups to tell their members how they are supposed to behave. We discussed social norms in detail in Chapter 7; here, we simply want to note again that norms often exert powerful effects on behaviour. Moreover, as mentioned above, adherence to norms is often a necessary condition for gaining status and other rewards controlled by groups.

Norms Rules within a group indicating how its members should (or should not) behave.

Cohesiveness: The Force That Binds

Consider two groups. In the first, members like one another very much, strongly desire the goals their group is seeking, and feel that they could not possibly find another group that would better satisfy their needs. In the second, the opposite is true: members don't like one another very much, don't share common goals, and are actively seeking other groups that might offer them a better deal. Which group will exert stronger effects on the behaviour of its members? The answer is obvious: the first. The reason for this difference involves what social psychologists describe as **cohesiveness**— all the forces that cause members to remain in the group, including factors such as liking for the other members and the desire to maintain or increase one's status by belonging to the "right" groups (Festinger et al., 1950). At first glance, it might seem that cohesiveness would involve primarily liking between individual group members. However, recent evidence suggests that it involves *depersonalized attraction*—liking for other group members stemming from the fact that they belong to the group and embody or represent its key features, quite apart from their traits as individuals (Hogg & Haines, 1996).

Cohesiveness All forces acting on group members to cause them to remain part of a group; including mutual attraction, interdependence, shared goals, and so on.

Several factors influence cohesiveness, including (1) status within the group (Cota et al., 1995)—cohesiveness is often higher for high- than for low-status members; (2) the effort required to gain entry into the group—the greater these costs, the higher the cohesiveness (see our discussion of *dissonance theory* in Chapter 4); (3) the existence of external threats or severe competition—such threats increase members' attraction and commitment to the group; and (4) size—small groups tend to be more cohesive than large ones.

In sum, several aspects of groups—roles, status, norms, and cohesiveness—determine the extent to which the groups can, and do, influence their members' behaviour. Another facet of the importance of a group to its members derives from their own commitment. Just as we saw (in Chapter 6) that commitment in interpersonal relationships may enhance the longevity of a marriage or friendship, organizational commitment may determine how well an individual functions within the group and whether he or she remains loyal to its aims. This important aspect of group functioning will be explored in the following Canadian Research: On the Cutting Edge section.

Canadian Research: On the Cutting Edge

Commitment to the Group: Continued Loyalty in Times of Change

An individual's sense of commitment to the group and its aims is one of the factors that determines his or her willingness to work and contribute towards group goals, as we will discuss later in the chapter. John Meyer and colleagues (Allen & Meyer, 1998; Meyer & Herscovitch, 2001) at the University of Western Ontario have developed a model to describe what they term **organizational commitment**—the extent to which individual members of an organization feel emotional attachment, continued dependence, and moral obligation towards their group or organization.

In this *three-component model* (shown in Figure 9.2) organizational commitment consists of three components that singly or together can contribute to an individual's level of commitment. *Affective commitment* is the emotional attachment, identification, and involvement with the organization. The more the group contributes to the individual's sense of worth, social enjoyment, and personal fulfillment, the greater the feeling of affective commitment. *Continuance commitment* is an individual's dependence on the organization for valued

> **Organizational Commitment** The extent to which individual members of an organization feel emotional attachment, continued dependence, and moral obligation towards their group or organization.

assets such as money or status in the community. The more the retention of valued assets is contingent upon belonging to the organization, the greater the perceived costs of discontinued membership. Finally, *normative commitment* is an individual's sense of moral obligation to remain in the group. The strength of this component will be influenced by cultural and social experiences that emphasize the importance of responsibility to the group or organization, as well as any sense of obligation to reciprocate benefits received from membership.

This description of commitment in a group context also has many parallels with the model of interpersonal commitment mentioned in Chapter 6—the *investment model of commitment*. In a way very similar to an interpersonal relationship, the stronger the organizational commitment the more an individual will work for the group and the less likely he or she is to leave. Further, the loss of membership in a work group can sometimes be as devastating as the loss of a close relationship. For example, being laid off from a job or profession to which one is strongly committed can lead to depression and a loss of identity.

In the last two decades there have been many mergers and downsizing of corporations and government offices. What happens to organizational commitment when rapid change in organizations occurs?

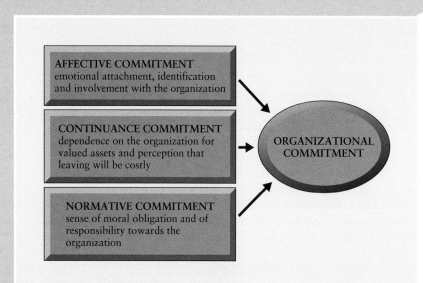

■ A Model of Organizational Commitment

FIGURE 9.2 The three-component model of organizational commitment suggests that *affective commitment, continuance commitment,* and *normative commitment* all contribute towards an individual's continued sense of loyalty and willingness to work for an organization, as well as lessening the likelihood that the individual will try to leave.

Source: Based on Allen & Meyer, 1998.

Allen and Meyer (1998) point out the difficulty of maintaining organizational commitment in times of change because very often the basis of the relationship between member and organization, or between employee and employer is fundamentally changed. For instance, if the nature of a person's job is changed—more work is put on their desk or their work relationships are disrupted due to downsizing—this may alter *affective commitment*. If the perceived benefits of employment lessen as job security decreases, then *continuance commitment* may alter. Finally, the sense of moral obligation may be damaged, lessening *normative commitment*. This is particularly likely to occur if the person feels that the organization has violated the *psychological contract*—not held up its end of the bargain.

In one study of nurses with extensive experience—an average 24 years of work within their organization—Herscovitch and Meyer (2002) examined responses to organizational change as a function of nurses' levels of commitment. Specifically, they measured affective, continuance, and normative commitment to organizational change. When nurses' behavioural support for real changes in their workplace was measured, the researchers found that the *affective* and, to a lesser extent, the *normative* components of commitment were most predictive of willingness to work towards that change, as shown in Figure 9.3. Nurses

who felt emotionally involved and valued the changes at work (affective commitment), and who felt a moral obligation to cooperate (normative commitment), were more likely to show behavioural support for workplace changes: that is, they were more willing to make efforts and sacrifices in order to achieve that change. The degree of dependence on the job (continuance commitment) was not as good a predictor of such cooperation with change.

We can perhaps conclude that when change is about to occur in an organization, it is important that employees feel a sense of emotional attachment and moral obligation to their workplace. How could an employer ensure that this was the case? What appears to be crucial to both affective and normative commitment to an employer is a sense that the organization has treated its members with *fairness* and *support* during the process of change (Meyer & Allen, 1997). In such situations where an employer has, for example, kept employees informed about pending changes, explained why jobs are being restructured, offered retraining to those who will lose their jobs, included employees in the decision-making process, and so on, then a higher level of commitment is maintained despite the insecurity (DeNisi, 1991; Meyer et al., 1998). As we will see later in this chapter, such behaviour is characteristic of attempts to maintain *interpersonal justice*.

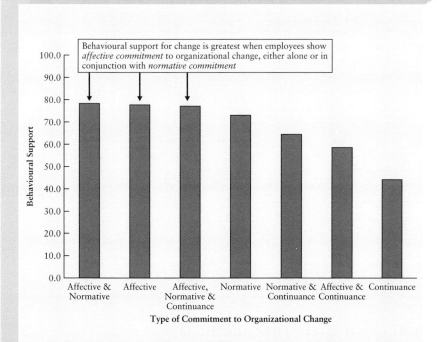

■ Organizational Commitment and Supporting Change

FIGURE 9.3 Nurses who had faced organizational changes in their jobs and showed *affective commitment* to change in their organization (either alone or in conjunction with normative commitment) were more likely to have shown cooperation with the changes in their workplace.

Source: Based on Herscovitch & Meyer, 2002.

How Groups Affect Individual Performance: Facilitation or Social Loafing?

Sometimes, when we perform a task, we work totally alone—for instance, studying alone in your room. In many other cases, even if we are working on a task by ourselves, other people are present—for instance, studying in a crowded library. In still other cases, we work on tasks together with other persons, as part of a task-performing group. What are the effects of other persons on our performance in these various settings? The answer seems to vary as a function of our relationship with these other persons. If others are simply present but not working with us, one set of effects occurs. If, instead, they are working with us as part of a group or team, another set occurs. Let's take a closer look at both situations.

Social Facilitation: Performance in the Presence of Others

Imagine that you are a young athlete—an ice-skater, for example—and that you are preparing for your first important competition. You practise your routines alone for several hours each day, month after month. Finally, the big day arrives and you skate out onto the ice in a huge arena filled with the biggest crowd you've ever seen. How will you do? Better or worse than when you practised alone? This was one of the first topics ever studied in social psychology, so before we turn to modern findings concerning this issue, let's consider some very early research on it by Floyd Allport (1920), whose early and influential work is described in the Cornerstones section below.

Cornerstones

Performance in the Presence of Others: The Simplest Group Effect?

Social psychology was literally struggling for its existence as an independent field when Floyd Allport decided to study what, in his opinion, was a very basic question: What are the effects of working on a task in the presence of other persons who are working on the same, or even a different, task—persons who are not competing with each other? Allport felt that this was an important question and—more to the point—one that would allow the new field to replace speculation with scientific data. To study the effects of the presence of others on task performance, he used several different, but related, methods.

In one study, for example, he asked participants to write down as many associations as they could think of for words printed at the top of an otherwise blank sheet of paper (e.g., "building," "laboratory"). The participants were allowed to work for three one-minute periods, and they performed this task both alone and in the presence of two other persons. Results were clear: 93 percent of the participants produced more associations when working in the presence of others than when working alone.

Allport was encouraged by these findings but realized that in many cases, participants could think of more words than they could actually list. This, he reasoned, might be affecting the results. To eliminate this problem, he asked participants to write down every third or every fourth word they thought of—not all of them. Again results indicated that performance was increased in the presence of others. But still Allport was not satisfied: he wondered whether the same effect would be found with a more complex task—one requiring high levels of thought. To find out, he asked participants to read short passages from ancient Roman authors, then to write down all the arguments they could think of that would tend to *disprove* the points made in these passages. Again, they performed this task while alone and while in the presence of several other persons; and once more, results indicated that performance was increased when individuals worked in groups. Not only did participants come up with more arguments—the quality of these ideas was better, too (see Figure 9.4).

Allport's research paved the way for the study of what soon came to be known in social psychology as **social facilitation**. Early researchers defined this term as improvements in performance produced by the mere presence of others, either as audience or as co-actors—persons performing the same task but independently (e.g., students taking an exam in the same room). As we'll soon see, the concept of social facilitation turned out to be premature: the presence of others does not always enhance performance, and social psychologists now understand why this is so. There can be little doubt, however, that although some of his conclusions were later modified, Allport's early studies were, in many ways, a model for the young field of social psychology—a model still reflected in its scientific orientation today.

Social Facilitation Effects upon performance resulting from the presence of others.

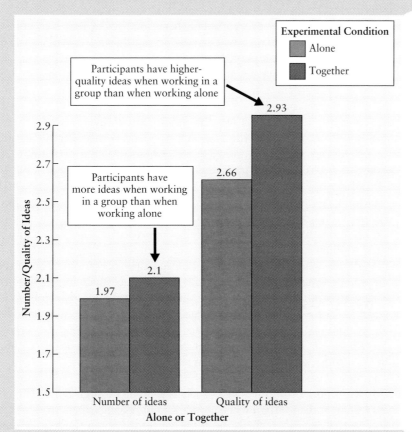

■ Effects of Co-actors on Cognitive Performance

FIGURE 9.4 Not only did participants in Allport's (1920) research think of more arguments when they worked in the presence of others; the quality of these arguments was better, too. On the basis of such findings, social psychologists concluded-in error, as it turned out-that the presence of other persons usually facilitates task performance.

Source: Based on data from Allport, 1920.

The Presence of Others: Is It Always Facilitating?

Allport's research and that conducted by other early social psychologists (e.g., Triplett, 1989) seemed to indicate that the presence of others is a definite plus—it improves performance on many different tasks. As the volume of research on this topic increased, however, puzzling findings began to appear: sometimes the presence of others facilitated performance, but sometimes it produced the opposite effect (Pessin, 1933). So social facilitation did not always help performance. Why? Why did the presence of others sometimes enhance but sometimes reduce performance? This question remained largely unanswered until the mid-1960s, when a famous researcher, Robert Zajonc, offered an insightful answer.

The Drive Theory of Social Facilitation: Other Persons as a Source of Arousal

Imagine that you are performing some task alone. Then several other people arrive on the scene and begin to watch you intently. Will your pulse beat quicker because of this audience? Informal experience suggests that it may—that the presence of other persons in the form of an interested audience can increase our activation or arousal. Zajonc suggested that this fact might provide the solution to the social facilitation puzzle. Here's why.

When arousal increases, our tendency to perform *dominant responses*—the ones we are most likely to perform in a given situation—also rises. Such dominant responses, in turn, can be correct or incorrect for that situation. If this is so, then it follows logically that if the presence of an audience increases arousal, this factor will *improve* performance when our dominant responses are correct ones, but may *impair* performance when such responses are incorrect (see Figure 9.5).

Another implication of Zajonc's reasoning, which is known as the **drive theory of social facilitation** because it focuses on arousal or drive, is this: The presence of others will improve individuals' performance when they are highly skilled at the task in question (because in this case their dominant responses will tend to be correct) but will interfere with individuals' performance when they are not highly skilled—for instance, when they are learning to perform a task. (Under these conditions, their dominant responses will probably *not* be correct.)

Many studies soon provided support for Zajonc's theory. Individuals were more likely to perform dominant responses in the presence of others than when alone, and their performance on various tasks was either enhanced or impaired depending on whether these responses were correct or incorrect in each situation (e.g., Geen, 1989; Zajonc & Sales, 1966).

Additional research raised an important question, however: Does social facilitation stem from the *mere physical presence of others*? Or do other factors, such as concern over others' evaluations of us, also play a role? Support for the latter conclusion was provided by the findings of several ingenious studies indicating that social facilitation effects occurred only when individuals believed that their performance could be observed and evaluated by others (e.g., Bond, 1982). For instance, such effects did not occur if the audience was blindfolded or showed no interest in watching (Cottrell et al., 1968). Such findings led some researchers to suggest that social facilitation actually stems either from **evaluation apprehension**—concern over being judged by others (which is often arousing)—or from concerns over *self-presentation*—making a good impression on others, a topic we discussed in Chapter 7.

Reasonable as these suggestions seem, they don't apply in all cases. For example, animals (even cockroaches!) perform simple tasks such as running through a maze better when in the presence of an audience than when alone (Zajonc, Heingartner, & Herman, 1969). It would seem weird to suggest that insects are concerned about the impressions

Drive Theory of Social Facilitation A theory suggesting that the mere presence of others is arousing and increases the tendency to perform dominant responses.

Evaluation Apprehension Concern over being evaluated by others. Such concern can increase arousal and so contribute to social facilitation.

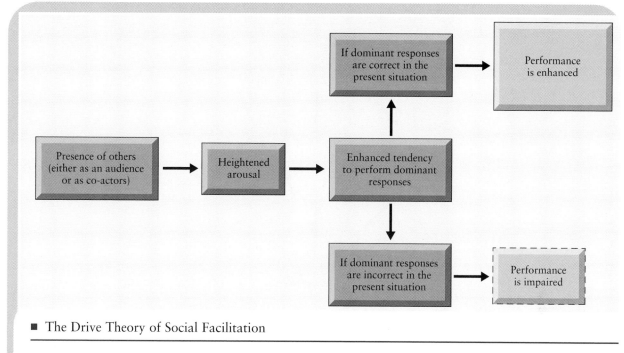

■ The Drive Theory of Social Facilitation

FIGURE 9.5 According to the drive theory of social facilitation (Zajonc, 1965), the presence of others increases arousal, and this in turn increases the tendency to perform dominant responses. If dominant responses are correct, performance is enhanced; if they are incorrect, performance is impaired.

they make on others, so these findings are not compatible with the suggestion that social facilitation stems solely from evaluation apprehension or self-presentation concerns. What's the final answer? Read on for one possibility.

Distraction–Conflict Theory: A Possible Resolution

Distraction–Conflict Theory A theory suggesting that social facilitation stems from the conflict produced when individuals attempt simultaneously to pay attention to other persons and to the task being performed.

The apparent answer is provided by a theory known as **distraction–conflict theory**, proposed by Robert S. Baron and his colleagues (yes, a different Robert Baron from the one who is writing these words). This theory, like Zajonc's view, assumes that audiences and co-actors both increase arousal. It also suggests, however, that such arousal stems from conflict between two competing tendencies: (1) the tendency to pay attention to the task being performed, and (2) the tendency to direct attention to the audience or co-actors. Such conflict is arousing; and this, in turn, increases the tendency to perform dominant responses (see Figure 9.6). If these responses are correct, performance is enhanced; if they are incorrect, performance is impaired (e.g., Baron, 1986; Sanders, 1983).

Several findings offer support for this view. For example, audiences produce social facilitation effects only when directing attention to them conflicts in some way with task demands (Groff, Baron, & Moore, 1983). When paying attention to an audience does not conflict with task performance, social facilitation fails to occur. Similarly, individuals experience greater distraction when they perform various tasks in front of an audience than when they perform them alone (Baron, Moore, & Sanders, 1978). Finally, when individuals have little reason to pay attention to others present on the scene—for instance, when these persons are performing a different task—social facilitation fails to occur; but when they have strong reasons for paying attention to others, social facilitation occurs (Sanders, 1983).

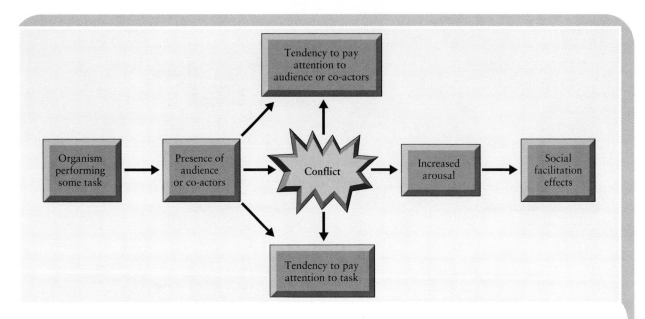

■ The Distraction-Conflict Theory

FIGURE 9.6 According to this theory, the presence of an audience or co-actors increases arousal by inducing conflicting tendencies to (1) pay attention to the audience and (2) pay attention to the task being performed. This arousal, in turn, increases the tendency to perform dominant responses. This theory helps explain why animals as well as human beings show social facilitation effects.

One major advantage of distraction–conflict theory is that it can explain why animals, as well as people, are affected by the presence of an audience. Because animals, too, can experience conflicting tendencies to work on a task *and* pay attention to an audience, they should also be susceptible to social facilitation. A theory that can explain similar patterns of behaviour among organisms ranging from cockroaches through human beings is powerful indeed, and worthy of very careful attention. So distraction–conflict theory—although it may not provide a complete or final answer to the question "Why does social facilitation occur?"—clearly represents a major step toward this goal and remains social psychology's best answer to the persistent puzzle of social facilitation.

KEY POINTS

- The mere presence of other persons either as an audience or as co-actors can influence our performance on many tasks. Such effects are known as *social facilitation*.
- The *drive theory of social facilitation* suggests that the presence of others is arousing and can either increase or reduce performance, depending on whether dominant responses in a given situation are correct or incorrect.
- The *distraction–conflict theory* suggests that the presence of others is arousing because it induces conflicting tendencies to focus on the task being performed and on an audience or co-actors. This theory helps explain why social facilitation occurs for animals as well as people.

Social Loafing: Letting Others in the Group Do the Work

Suppose that you and several other people are helping a friend to move. In order to lift the heaviest pieces of furniture, you join forces, with each person lending a hand. Will all of the people helping exert equal effort? Probably not. Some will take as much of the load as possible, while others will simply hang on, appearing to help without really doing much.

This pattern is quite common in situations where groups of person perform what are known as **additive tasks**—tasks in which the contributions of each member are combined into a single group product. On such tasks, some persons work hard while others goof off, doing less than their share, and less than they might do if they were working alone. Social psychologists refer to such effects as **social loafing**—reductions in motivation and effort when individuals work collectively in a group, compared to when they work individually or as independent co-actors (Karau & Williams, 1993).

That social loafing occurs has been demonstrated in many experiments. In one of the first, for example, Latané, Williams, and Harkins (1979) asked groups of male students to clap or cheer as loudly as possible at specific times, supposedly so that the experimenter could determine how much noise people make in social settings. They performed these tasks in groups of two, four, or six persons. Results were clear: Although the total amount of noise rose as group size increased, the amount produced *by each participant* dropped. In other words, each person put out less and less effort as group size increased. Such effects are not restricted to simple and seemingly meaningless situations like this; on the contrary, they appear to be quite general in scope and occur with respect to many different tasks—cognitive ones as well as ones involving physical effort (Weldon & Mustari, 1988; Williams & Karau, 1991). Moreover, social loafing appears in both genders, and among children as well as adults. The only exception to the generality of such effects seems to be a cultural one: social loafing effects don't seem to occur in *collectivistic cultures*, such as those in many Asian countries—cultures where the collective good is more highly valued than individual accomplishment or achievement (Earley, 1993). In such cultures, in fact, people seem to work *harder* when in groups than they do when alone—sometimes termed *social striving* to contrast with social loafing. So, as we've noted repeatedly, cultural factors sometimes play a very important role in social behaviour

Aside from this important exception, however, social loafing appears to be a pervasive fact of social life. If this is indeed true, then two important questions arise: *Why* do such effects occur? And what steps can be taken to reduce their occurrence?

The Collective Effort Model: An Expectancy Theory of Social Loafing

Many different explanations for the occurrence of social loafing have been proposed. For example, one view—*social impact theory*—related social loafing to a topic we examined in Chapter 8, *diffusion of responsibility* (Latané, 1981). According to social impact theory, as group size increases each member feels less and less responsible for the task being performed. The result: each person exerts decreasing effort on it. In contrast, other theories have focused on the fact that in groups, members' motivation decreases because they realize that their contributions can't be evaluated individually—so why work hard? (Harkins & Szymanski, 1989). Perhaps the most comprehensive explanation of social loafing offered to date, however, is the **collective effort model** (**CEM**) proposed by Karau and Williams (1993).

These researchers suggest that we can understand social loafing by extending a basic theory of individual motivation—*expectancy–valence theory*—to situations involving group performance. Expectancy–valence theory suggests that individuals will work hard on a given task only to the extent that the following conditions exist: (1) They believe that working hard will lead to better performance (*expectancy*); (2) they believe that better performance will be recognized and rewarded (*instrumentality*); and (3) the rewards available are ones they value and desire (*valence*). In other words, individuals working alone will exert effort only to the extent that they perceive direct links between hard work and the outcomes they want.

According to Karau and Williams (1993), these links often appear weaker when individuals work together in groups than when they work alone. First, consider *expectancy*—the belief that increased effort will lead to better performance. This may be high when individuals work alone, but lower when they work together in groups, because people realize that other factors aside from their own effort will determine the group's performance; for instance, the amount of effort exerted by other members. Similarly, *instrumentality*—the belief that good performance will be recognized and rewarded—may also be weaker when people work together in groups. They realize that valued outcomes are divided among all group members, and that as a result they may not get their fair share given their level of effort. Because there is more uncertainty about the links between how hard people work and the rewards they receive, social loafing occurs; and within the framework of the collective effort model, this is not surprising. After all, when individuals work with others, the relationship between their own performance and rewards is more uncertain than when working alone.

Is the collective effort model accurate? To find out, Karau and Williams performed a meta-analysis of dozens of studies of social loafing. The CEM makes several predictions concerning the conditions under which social loafing should be most and least likely to occur. For example, it predicts that social loafing will be weakest (1) when individuals work in small rather than large groups; (2) when they work on tasks that are intrinsically interesting or important to them; (3) when they work with respected others (friends, teammates, etc.); (4) when they perceive that their contributions to the group product are unique or important; (5) when they expect their co-workers to perform poorly; and (6) when they come from cultures that emphasize group effort and outcomes rather than individual outcomes (Asian cultures versus Western ones, for instance). The results of the meta-analysis offered support for all these predictions. In other words, social loafing was weakest (and strongest) under conditions predicted by the theory. In addition, it was found that social loafing was a very reliable and pervasive effect: it occurred across many different studies conducted with many different kinds of participants and many different kinds of tasks.

Reducing Social Loafing: Some Useful Techniques

Unfortunately, the conditions for social loafing exist in many settings where groups of persons work together—for instance, in many manufacturing plants, government offices, and even student groups. Social loafing has the effect of disrupting group morale, because some members, at least, will feel that they are being taken advantage of by others. If social loafing poses a threat to performance in many settings, the next question is obvious: What steps can be taken to reduce it? Research findings offer some useful suggestions.

First, and most obvious, groups can devise ways to make the output or effort of each participant readily identifiable (e.g., Williams, Harkins, & Latané, 1981). Under these conditions, people can't sit back and let others do their work, so social loafing is in fact reduced. Second, groups can reduce social loafing by increasing members' commitment to successful task performance (Brickner et al., 1986).

Pressures toward working hard will then serve to offset temptations to engage in social loafing. Third, groups can diminish social loafing by increasing the apparent importance or value of a task (Karau & Williams, 1993). Fourth, social loafing declines when individuals view their contributions to the task as unique rather than merely duplicating those of others (Weldon & Mustari, 1988). And finally, social loafing can be reduced through the strengthening of group cohesiveness—a factor we discussed earlier. For a summary, see Figure 9.7.

There are some situations where the conditions that reduce social loafing occur spontaneously. For example, in the summer of 2003 firefighters converged on the cities of Kelowna and Cranbrook in British Columbia to combat the extensive fires that were threatening those communities. There was no doubt about the need for help, the importance of their task and their commitment to it. As a result, people in that region still remember the tremendous and concerted efforts that were made by these firefighters that year.

The Ideas to Take with You feature at the end of the chapter provides practical suggestions on how you can both benefit from social facilitation and protect yourself against social loafing by others.

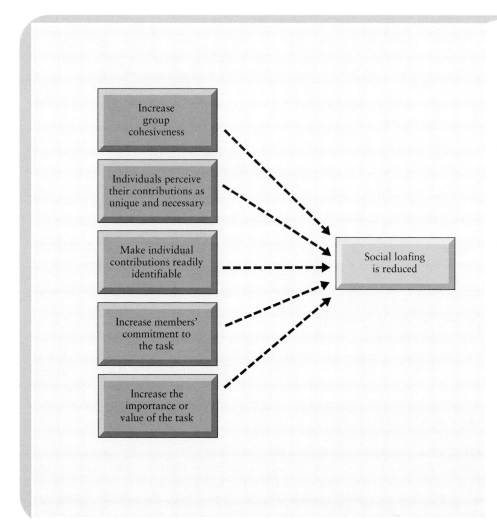

■ Reducing Social Loafing

FIGURE 9.7 When a group is cohesive, when its members believe that their contribution is necessary and can be identified, when they are committed to what they believe is an important task, then social loafing is unlikely to occur. Research shows that introducing these conditions *can* sharply reduce social loafing—the tendency of group members to "goof off" at the expense of others.

Decision Making by Groups: How It Occurs and the Pitfalls It Faces

Decision Making The process of combining and integrating available information in order to choose one out of several possible courses of action.

Groups are called upon to perform many tasks—everything from conducting surgical operations through harvesting the world's crops. One of the most important activities they perform, however, is **decision making**—combining and integrating available information in order to choose one out of several possible courses of action. Governments, large corporations, military units, sports teams—virtually all social entities entrust key decisions to groups. Why? While many factors play a role, the most important seems to be this: Most people believe that groups usually reach better decisions than individuals. After all, it is reasoned, they can pool the expertise of their members and avoid extreme courses of action.

Are such beliefs accurate? Do groups really make better or more accurate decisions than individuals? In their efforts to answer this question, social psychologists have focused on three major topics: (1) How do groups actually make decisions and reach consensus? (2) Do decisions reached by groups differ from those reached by individuals? (3) What accounts for the fact that groups sometimes make truly disastrous decisions—ones so bad it is hard to believe they were actually reached?

The Decision-Making Process: How Groups Attain Consensus

When a group first begins to discuss an issue, its members rarely voice unanimous agreement. Rather, the members come to the decision-making task with different information and so support a wide range of views (e.g., Larson, Foster-Fishman, & Franz, 1998; Gigone & Hastie, 1997). After some period of discussion, however, they usually reach a decision. This is not always the case—for example, juries become "hung," and other decision-making groups, too, may deadlock. In most cases, though, some decision is reached. Is there any way of predicting this final outcome? In short, can we predict the decision a group is likely to reach from information about the views initially held by its members? Growing evidence suggests that we can (e.g., Kerr & MacCoun, 1985; Kaplan & Miller, 1987).

Social Decision Schemes Rules relating the initial distribution of member views to final group decisions.

Social Decision Schemes: Blueprints for Decision

To summarize some very complex findings in simple terms, it appears that the final decisions reached by groups can often be predicted quite accurately by relatively simple rules known as **social decision schemes**. These rules relate the initial distribution of member views or preferences to the group's final decisions. For example, one scheme—the *majority-wins rule*—suggests that in many cases the group will opt for whatever position is initially supported by a majority of its members (e.g., Nemeth et al., 2001). According to this rule, discussion serves mainly to confirm or strengthen the most popular view. In contrast, a second decision scheme—the *truth-wins rule*—indicates that the correct solution or decision will ultimately come to the fore as its correctness is recognized by a growing number of members. A third decision scheme, adopted by many juries, is the *two-thirds majority rule*. Here, juries tend to convict defendants if two-thirds of the jurors initially favour this decision (Davis et al., 1984). Finally, some groups seem to follow a *first-shift rule*. They tend, ultimately, to adopt a decision consistent with the direction of the first shift in opinion shown by any member.

Surprising as it may seem, the results of many studies indicate that these straightforward rules are quite successful in predicting even complex group decisions. Indeed, they have been found to be accurate in this regard up to 80 percent of the time (e.g., Stasser, Taylor, & Hanna, 1989). Thus, they seem to provide important insights into how groups move toward consensus: apparently, it seems, in accordance with straightforward decision rules that can predict the final outcome with surprising accuracy.

Normative and Informational Influence in Groups: Influencing Each Other's Views

Many studies indicate that, in general, decision-making groups move toward consensus; indeed, as we'll see below, this strong tendency to seek uniformity or agreement is one of the potential dangers of decision making by groups. But how, precisely, do members influence each other so that the group moves toward such consensus? The answer seems to be through the two kinds of influence we described in Chapter 7: *normative social influence* and *informational social influence*. Normative social influence is based on our desire to be liked or accepted, and groups certainly use this tactic to influence disagreeing members to go along. Similarly, groups also employ informational social influence, which is based on our desire to be right—to hold the correct views. Many studies in which decision-making groups have been carefully observed indicate that both forms of social influence are used by members to bring "mavericks" (disagreeing members) into line (e.g., Kaplan, 1989; Kelley et al., 1997; Larrey & Paulus, 1999). Moreover, this appears to be true in a wide range of decision-making groups, ranging from juries to cabinet-level groups in governments. In short, there is no real mystery as to why groups move toward the position adopted by the majority of their members initially; they attain consensus through reciprocal social influence among their members.

The Nature of Group Decisions: Moderation or Polarization?

Truly important decisions are rarely left to individuals. Instead, they are usually assigned to groups—and highly qualified groups at that. Even total dictators usually consult with groups of skilled advisers before taking major actions. As we noted earlier, the major reason behind this strategy is the belief that groups are far less likely than individuals to make serious errors—to rush blindly over the edge. Is this really true?

Research on this issue has yielded surprising findings. Contrary to popular belief, a large body of evidence indicates that groups are actually more likely to adopt extreme positions than individuals making decisions alone. In fact, across many different kinds of decisions and in many different contexts, groups show a pronounced tendency to shift toward views more extreme than the ones with which they initially

Group Polarization
The tendency of group members to shift toward more extreme positions than those they initially held as a result of group discussion.

began (Burnstein, 1983; Lamm & Myers, 1978). This phenomenon is known as **group polarization,** and its major effects can be summarized as follows: Whatever the initial leaning or preference of a group prior to its discussions, it is strengthened during the group's deliberations. The result: Not only does *the group* shift toward more extreme views—individual members, too, often show such a shift—see Figure 9.8. (The term *group polarization* does not refer to a tendency of groups to split apart into two opposing camps or poles; on the contrary, it refers to a strengthening of the group's initial preferences.)

Why does this effect occur? Two major factors seem to be involved. First, it appears that *social comparison*—a process we examined earlier—plays an important role. Everyone wants to be "above average," and where opinions are concerned, this implies holding views that are "better" than those of other group members. What does "better" mean? This depends on the specific group: Among a group of liberals, "better" would mean "more liberal." Among a group of conservatives, it would mean "more conservative." Among a group of racists, it would mean "even more bigoted." In any case, during group discussions, at least some members discover (to their shock!) that their views are *not* "better" than those of most other members. The result: after comparing themselves with these persons, they shift to even more extreme views, and the group polarization effect is off and running (Goethals & Zanna, 1979).

A second factor involves the fact that, during group discussion, most arguments presented are ones favouring the group's initial leaning or preference. As a result of hearing such arguments, persuasion occurs (presumably through the *central route* described in Chapter 4), and members shift, increasingly, toward the majority view. These shifts increase the proportion of arguments favouring this view, and, ultimately, members convince themselves that this is the "right" view and shift toward it with increasing strength. Group polarization results from this process (Vinokur & Burnstein, 1974).

■ Group Polarization: Its Basic Nature

FIGURE 9.8 As shown here, *group polarization* involves the tendency for decision-making groups to shift toward views that are more extreme than the ones with which they initially began, but in the same general direction. Thus, if groups start out slightly in favour of one view or position, they often end up holding this view more strongly or extremely after deliberations. The shift toward extremity can be quite dangerous in many settings.

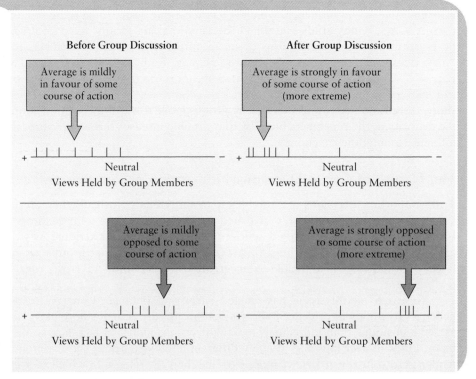

Regardless of the precise basis for group polarization, it definitely has important implications. The occurrence of polarization may lead many decision-making groups to adopt positions that are increasingly extreme, and therefore increasingly dangerous. In this context, it is chilling to speculate about the potential role of such shifts in disastrous decisions by political, military, or business groups that should, by all accounts, have known better—for example, the decision by the hardliners in the now-vanished Soviet Union to stage a coup to restore firm communist rule, or the decision by Apple computer *not* to license its software to other manufacturers (a decision that ultimately cost it most of its sales). Did group polarization influence these and other disastrous decisions? It is impossible to say for sure, but research findings suggest that this is a real possibility.

Decision Making by Groups: Some Potential Pitfalls

The tendency of many decision-making groups to drift toward polarization is a serious factor that can interfere with their ability to make accurate decisions. Unfortunately, this is not the only process that can exert such negative effects. Several others, too, seem to emerge out of group discussions and can lead groups into disastrous courses of action (Hinsz, 1995). Among the most important of these are (1) *groupthink*, (2) biased processing of information by group members, and (3) groups' seeming inability to share and use information held by some but not all of their members.

Groupthink: When Too Much Cohesiveness Is a Dangerous Thing

Earlier, we suggested that tendencies toward group polarization may be one reason why decision-making groups sometimes go off the deep end, with catastrophic results. However, another and even more disturbing factor may also contribute to such outcomes. This is a process known as **groupthink**, a mode of thinking by group members in which concern with maintaining group consensus—or *concurrence seeking*—overrides the motivation to evaluate all potential courses of action as accurately and realistically as possible (Janis, 1982). A decision-making group will close ranks, cognitively, around a decision, assume that the group can't be wrong, that all members must support the decision strongly, and that any information contrary to it should be rejected. Historically a number of high-powered group decisions, from the decision to launch the ill-fated space shuttle *Challenger* in the United States to the devising of the Meech Lake Accord in Canada, can be seen as influenced by the process of groupthink (Baron, Byrne, & Watson, 1997; Janis, 1982).

Groupthink The tendency of members of highly cohesive groups to seek consensus or concurrence so strongly that they ignore information inconsistent with their views and often make disastrous decisions.

Once a decision-making group develops this collective state of mind, it appears, it becomes unwilling—even, perhaps, *unable*—to change its course of action, even if external events suggest very strongly that the original decision was a poor one. In fact, according to Janis (1982), the social psychologist who originated the concept of groupthink, norms soon emerge in the group that actively prevent its members from considering alternative courses of action. The group is viewed as being incapable of making an error, and anyone with lingering doubts is quickly silenced, both by group pressure and by his or her own desire to conform.

Why does groupthink occur? Research findings (e.g., Kameda & Sugimori, 1993; Tetlock et al., 1992) suggest that two factors may be crucial. The first is a very high level of *cohesiveness* among group members who are similar in background, interests, and values and so tend to like each other very much. The second is the kind of emergent group norms mentioned above—norms suggesting that the group is both infallible and morally superior, and that because of these factors there should be no further discussion of the issue at hand; the decision has been made, and the only task now is to support it as strongly as possible. According to Janis this process is most likely to occur when decision makers are under pressure and isolated from outside input (Janis, 1982). The result: the group shifts from focusing on making the best decision possible to focusing on maintaining a high level of consensus and achieving a decision at all costs, with truly disastrous effects.

Biased Processing of Information in Groups

While groupthink is a dramatic process, other more subtle but equally costly sources of bias exist in decision-making groups. One of the most important of these is the tendency for such groups to process available information in a biased manner. Groups, like individuals, are not always motivated to maximize accuracy; on the contrary, they are often motivated to find support for the views they initially favour. In other words, they act more like "intuitive lawyers," searching for evidence that supports their case (initial preferences) than as "intuitive scientists," seeking truth and accuracy (e.g., Baumeister & Newman, 1994). Such tendencies do not always stem from the selfish pursuit of self-interest; rather, they may derive from adherence to values or principles that are generally accepted in society and viewed in a positive light. A clear illustration of this kind of potential clash between positive values and accuracy in decision making occurs in juries—especially those concerned with settling civil suits in which one side seeks damages from the other. Research investigating this problem is described in the following On the Applied Side section.

On the **Applied Side**

Reaching the Verdict They Want: Biased Processing in Juries

Following legal rulings sometimes appears to clash with natural justice. How will juries cope when faced with such dilemmas? Research seems to suggest that they may bias their processing of information to fit with their own, but not the legal system's, view of justice.

An example is when juries in civil suits where damages are claimed are instructed by the judge to follow one of three legal rules: *comparative negligence*—reduce the award sought by the plaintiff in proportion to the extent the plaintiff was negligent (responsible for the harm she or he suffered); *contributory negligence*—award the plaintiff *no damages* if she or he was negligent to any extent; *strict liability*—award *full damages* to the plaintiff if the defendant was negligent to any extent. As we will discuss further in the following section, only the first of these rules is consistent with *distributive justice*—it provides damages proportionate to the negligence of each party. The other rules, although often used in legal proceedings, violate this common-sense rule of justice.

Taking account of this fact, Sommer, Horowitz, and Bourgeois (2001) predicted that juries would engage in biased processing of information in order to adhere to distributive justice, even if instructed

by a judge to follow the other two rules. To test this prediction, they conducted a study in which participants listened to an audiotape of a civil trial in which a plaintiff was suing an automobile manufacturer for $1 million in damages; the case involved a faulty fuel filter that caused a gas tank to explode, resulting in the death of the plaintiff's wife. In three different conditions, jurors were told to follow each of the rules above in making their decisions. Sommer, Horowitz, and Bourgeois (2001) reasoned that jurors would engage in biased processing of information concerning the trial in order to adhere to distributive justice. Thus, for example, they would discuss more pro-plaintiff evidence under the contributory negligence rule (which strongly favours the defendant) than under the strict liability rule (which strongly favours the plaintiff). As you can see from Figure 9.9, this is precisely what happened. Other measures indicated that jurors did actually engage in biased processing of available evidence in order to obtain the decisions they wanted—ones consistent with the principle of distributive justice.

These findings and those of related research (e.g., Frey, Schulz-Hardt, & Stahlberg, 1996) indicate that

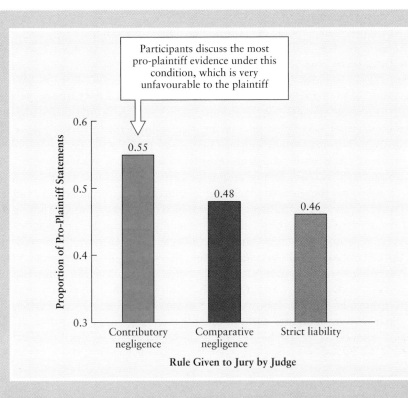

Participants discuss the most pro-plaintiff evidence under this condition, which is very unfavourable to the plaintiff

Proportion of Pro-Plaintiff Statements

- Contributory negligence: 0.55
- Comparative negligence: 0.48
- Strict liability: 0.46

Rule Given to Jury by Judge

■ Biased Processing and Group Decisions

FIGURE 9.9 Mock jurors told to follow legal rules in deciding a damage case engaged in biased processing in order to ignore these rules and adhere to the principle of distributive justice (fairness). Specifically, they discussed more pro-plaintiff evidence under the contributory negligence rule (which strongly favours the defendant) than under the strict liability rule (which strongly favours the plaintiff).

Source: Based on data from Sommer, Horowitz, & Bourgeois, 2001.

juries and other decision-making groups do indeed engage in biased processing. In other words, they process available information in ways that allow them to reach the decisions they want! Jury biases will be discussed further in Chapter 10, when we examine social psychological aspects of the legal system.

Why Groups Often Fail to Share Information Unique to Each Member

A third potential source of bias for decision-making groups involves the fact that contrary to what common sense suggests, such groups do not always pool their resources—share information and ideas that are unique to each member. In fact, research on this issue (Gigone & Hastie, 1993, 1997; Stasser, 1992) indicates that such pooling of resources or information may be the exception rather than the rule. When groups discuss a given issue and try to reach a decision about it, they tend to discuss information shared by most if not all members, rather than information that is known to only one or a few. The result: the decisions they make tend to reflect the shared information (e.g., Gigone & Hastie, 1993). This is not a problem if such information points to the best decision. But consider what happens when information pointing to the best decision is *not* shared by most members. In such cases, the tendency of group members to discuss mainly the information they all already possess may prevent them from reaching the best decision.

Disturbingly, research findings suggest that this tendency is strong indeed. For instance, even with respect to medical diagnoses, which can involve life-and-death decisions, teams of interns and medical students discussed more shared than unshared information during group discussions. However, the more they pooled *unshared* information (information known, initially, to only some members), the more accurate were the groups' diagnoses (e.g., Larson et al., 1998; Winquist & Larson, 1998).

Improving Group Decisions

Groupthink, biased processing, discussing information already known to all the members—these are discouraging barriers to effective decision making by groups. Can these potential pitfalls be overcome? Many studies have addressed this issue, and together, they do point to some promising techniques. Several of these involve encouraging dissent, because doing so may slow the rapid movement of groups toward consensus. One such approach is the **devil's advocate technique** (e.g., Hirt & Markman, 1995), in which one group member is assigned the task of disagreeing with and criticizing whatever plan or decision is under consideration. This tactic often works because it induces members to think carefully about the decision toward which they are moving.

Another approach involves calling in outside experts who offer their recommendations and opinions on the group's plans (e.g., Janis, 1982). Recent studies suggest that most effective of all may be **authentic dissent**, in which one or more group members actively disagree with the group's initial preference without being assigned this role. For instance, a study by Nemeth and her colleagues (2001) found that authentic dissent was more likely to encourage original thinking by group members, greater consideration of alternative views, and more attitude change away from the group's initial position than was the devil's advocate approach. In any case, it is clear that decision making by groups *can* be improved; however, active steps must be taken to achieve this goal. Left to their own devices, and without outside intervention, groups often do slip easily into the mental traps outlined here—often with disastrous results.

Devil's Advocate Technique A technique for improving the quality of group decisions in which one group member is assigned the task of disagreeing with and criticizing whatever plan or decision is under consideration.

Authentic Dissent A technique for improving the quality of group decisions in which one or more group members actively disagree with the group's initial preference without being assigned this role.

KEY POINTS

- It is widely believed that groups make better decisions than individuals. However, research findings indicate that groups are often subject to *group polarization effects*, which lead them to make more extreme decisions than individuals.
- In addition, groups often suffer from *groupthink*—when a desire to achieve consensus takes precedence over reaching the right decision.
- Groups often engage in biased processing of information in order to reach the decisions they initially prefer, or to adhere to general values such as the principle of *distributive justice*.
- Groups often fail to share important information and to pool their resources.
- Group decision-making can be improved through the use of methods such as the *devil's advocate technique* and *authentic dissent*.

Coordination in Groups: Cooperation or Conflict?

In Chapter 8 we explored the subject of *prosocial behaviour*—actions that benefit others but have no obvious or immediate benefits for the persons who perform them. Although prosocial behaviour is far from rare, another pattern—one in which helping is mutual and both sides benefit—is even more common. This pattern is known as **cooperation** and involves situations in which group members work together to attain shared goals. Cooperation can be highly beneficial; indeed, through this process, groups can attain goals that their individual members could never hope to reach by themselves. Surprisingly, though, cooperation does not always develop. Frequently, persons belonging to a group try to coordinate their efforts but somehow fail in this attempt.

Cooperation Behaviour in which group members work together to attain shared goals.

Even worse, group members may perceive their respective personal interests as incompatible, with the result that instead of working together and coordinating their efforts, they work *against* each other—often producing negative results for both sides. This state of affairs, known as **conflict**, can be defined as a process in which individuals or groups perceive that others have taken or will soon take actions incompatible with their own interests. Conflict is indeed a process; for, as you probably know from your own experience, it has a nasty way of escalating—starting, perhaps, with simple mistrust, and quickly moving through a spiral of anger, resentment, and actions designed to harm the other side. When conflict is carried to extremes, the ultimate effects can be very harmful to both sides.

In one sense, cooperation and conflict can be viewed as falling on opposite ends of a continuum relating to *coordination*—the extent to which individuals in groups work together or against one another. We'll now take a closer look at the nature of both of these processes as well as at some of the factors that influence their occurrence.

Conflict A process in which individuals or groups perceive that others have taken or will soon take actions incompatible with their own interests.

Cooperation: Working with Others to Achieve Shared Goals

That cooperation can be highly beneficial is obvious. So why, you may be wondering, don't group members always coordinate their activities so that all can benefit? One answer is straightforward: Some goals that people seek simply can't be shared. Several people seeking the same job, promotion, or romantic partner can't combine forces to attain their goals: the desired outcome is available to only one person in each case, so cooperation is not possible. In such cases conflict may quickly develop, as each person attempts to optimize his or her own outcomes (Tjosvold, 1993).

In many other situations, however, cooperation *could* develop but does not. Why? The answer seems to involve a number of different factors that together serve to tip the balance either toward or away from the kind of coordination that cooperation requires.

The Nature of Cooperation: Dealing with Social Dilemmas

Many situations, in which cooperation could potentially develop but does not, can be described as ones involving **social dilemmas**; these are situations in which each person can increase his or her individual gains by acting in a certain way, but if all (or most) persons act that same way, the outcomes experienced by all are reduced (Komorita & Parks, 1994). As a result, the persons in such situations must deal with *mixed motives*; there are reasons to cooperate (to avoid negative outcomes for all), but also reasons to *defect*—to do what is best for oneself. After all, if only one or a few persons engage in such behaviour, they will benefit while the others will not. A classic illustration of this kind of situation, and one in which it is reduced to its simplest form, is known as the *prisoner's dilemma* (see Figure 9.10).

Social Dilemmas Situations in which each person can increase his or her individual gains by acting in one way, but if all (or most) persons do the same thing, the outcomes experienced by all are reduced.

Here, there are two persons, and each can choose either to cooperate or to compete. If both cooperate, then they both experience large gains. If both compete, each person experiences much smaller gains, or actual losses. The most interesting pattern occurs if one chooses to compete while the other chooses to cooperate. In this case, the first person experiences much larger gains than the second, trusting one. This situation is called the "prisoner's dilemma" because it reflects a dilemma faced by two suspects who have been caught by police. Assume that the police do not have enough evidence to convict either person. If both stick to their stories (i.e., they both cooperate), they will be set free or receive a very short sentence for a minor crime. If both confess, they will both be convicted and receive stiff sentences. If one confesses (i.e., turns states' evidence) but the other does not, the police will have enough evidence to convict both, but the person who confesses will receive a lighter sentence because of the help she or he has given. As you can see, this situation captures the essence of many social dilemmas:

■ The Prisoner's Dilemma: To Cooperate or Compete—That Is the Question!

FIGURE 9.10 In the prisoner's dilemma, a simple form of social dilemma, two persons can choose either to cooperate or to compete with one another. If both choose to cooperate, each receives a very favourable outcome. If both choose to compete, each receives a negative outcome. If one chooses to compete while the other chooses to cooperate, the first person receives a much better outcome than the second person. Research findings indicate that many factors influence the choices people make in this kind of mixed-motive situation.

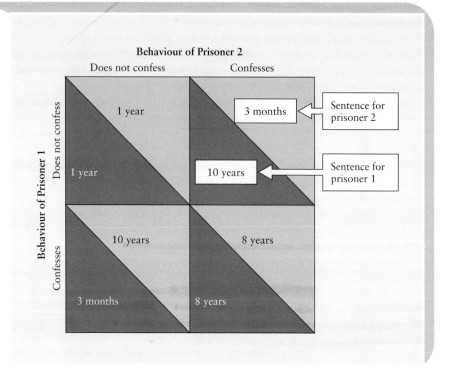

each suspect experiences pressures both to cooperate and to compete. Social psychologists have used this type of situation, or ones very much like it (simulated, of course!), to examine the factors that tip the balance toward trust and cooperation or mistrust and competition (e.g., Insko et al., 2001). The findings of such research indicate that many factors play a role in whether cooperation or competition develops.

Factors Influencing Cooperation: Reciprocity, Personal Orientations, and Communication

While many different factors determine whether individuals will choose to cooperate with others in situations involving the mixed motives generated by social dilemmas, among the most important are tendencies toward *reciprocity*, *personal orientations* towards cooperation, and *communication*.

Reciprocity is probably the most obvious of these factors. Throughout life, we tend to follow this principle, treating others very much as they have treated us (e.g., Pruitt & Carnevale, 1993). In choosing between cooperation and competition, too, we seem to adopt this general rule. When others cooperate with us and put their selfish interests aside, we usually respond in kind. In contrast, if they defect and pursue their own interests, we generally do the same (Kerr & Kaufman-Gilliland, 1994).

Evolutionary psychologists have noted that this tendency to adopt reciprocity where cooperation is concerned is not restricted to human beings; it has been observed among other species, too (e.g., bats and chimpanzees; Buss, 1999). This, in turn, raises an intriguing question: because "cheaters" (those who do not return cooperation after receiving it) often gain an advantage, how could a strong tendency toward reciprocity have evolved? One possible answer is provided by the theory of *reciprocal altruism* (e.g., Cosmides & Tooby, 1992). This theory suggests that by sharing resources such as food, organisms increase their chances of survival, and thus the likelihood that they will pass their genes on to the next generation. Further, they tend to share in such a

Reciprocity A basic rule of social life suggesting that individuals tend to treat others as these persons have treated them.

way that the benefits are relatively great for the recipients of such cooperation while the costs are relatively minimal to the provider. For instance, if one hunter has more meat than he and his family can eat, while another is starving, the costs to the first for sharing are minimal, while the gains to the second are great. When the situation is reversed, cooperation will again benefit both parties and increase their chances of survival. In contrast, organisms that act in a purely selfish manner do not gain such benefits.

A second factor that exerts strong effects on cooperation is *personal orientation* toward such behaviour. Think about the many people you have known during your life. Can you remember ones who strongly preferred cooperation—people who could be counted on to work together with other group members in almost every situation? In contrast, can you remember others who usually preferred to pursue their own selfish interests and could *not* be relied on to cooperate?

You probably have little difficulty in bringing examples of both types to mind, for large individual differences in the tendencies to cooperate exist. Such differences, in turn, seem to reflect contrasting perspectives toward working with others—perspectives that individuals carry with them from situation to situation, even over relatively long periods of time (e.g., Knight & Dubro, 1984). Specifically, research findings indicate that individuals can possess any one of three distinct orientations toward situations involving social dilemmas: (1) a *cooperative* orientation, in which they prefer to maximize the joint outcomes received by all the persons involved; (2) an *individualistic* orientation, in which they focus primarily on maximizing their own outcomes; or (3) a *competitive* orientation, in which they focus primarily on defeating others—on obtaining better outcomes than other persons do (DeDreu & McCusker, 1997; Van Lange & Kuhlman, 1994). These orientations exert strong effects on how people behave in many situations, so they are an important factor in whether cooperation does or does not develop.

The Discontinuity Effect: Why Groups Are More Competitive than Individuals

So far, we have focused on cooperation between individuals. But this is not the only situation that exists where cooperation is concerned. Groups, too, can choose to cooperate or compete with each other. Research findings indicate, however, that such *intergroup cooperation* may be difficult to achieve. Specifically, many studies have found evidence for a *discontinuity effect*—a greater tendency for groups than individuals to compete in mixed-motive situations of the type discussed above (e.g., the prisoner's dilemma; e.g., Insko et al., 2001; Schopler et al., 2001).

Why is this so? Insko and colleagues (2001) point to three factors that may play a role. First, people tend to distrust other groups more than other persons; in fact, they expect individuals to cooperate with them, but they are much less optimistic about receiving such treatment from groups. Second, when groups act in a selfish, competitive manner, their members can convince each other that this is appropriate; individuals, in contrast, must handle such selfishness without social support. Third, individuals know that they are readily identifiable to their opponents; members of groups, in contrast, can enjoy a degree of anonymity. Evidence for the influence of all of these factors exists, so it appears that the tendency for groups to be more competitive than individuals stems from several factors (e.g., Schopler & Insko, 1999). For instance, consider one study conducted by Insko and his colleagues (Insko et al., 2001).

In this experiment, participants played a prisoner's dilemma game either as individuals or as three-person groups. Half were led to believe that they would make the choice to cooperate or compete with their opponent only once, while others were led to believe that they would make this choice a number of times. Insko and his colleagues (2001) predicted that when groups anticipated continuing interactions, they would become less competitive because a longer-term orientation would work against the three factors mentioned above—distrust, social support for acting in a purely selfish manner, and reduced

■ Reducing the Discontinuity Effect: The Potential Benefits of a Long-Term Orientation

FIGURE 9.11 When participants expected to interact with their opponents repeatedly, both individuals and groups showed reduced tendencies to compete. However, these reductions were much larger for groups. These findings are consistent with theoretical explanations for the discontinuity effect—why groups are more competitive than individuals.

Source: Based on data from Insko et al., 2001.

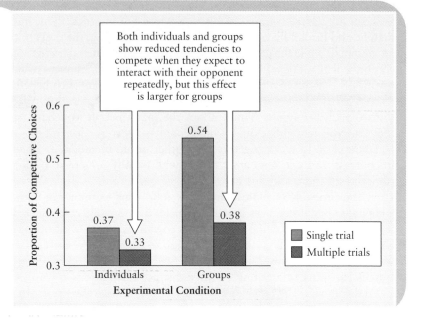

Both individuals and groups show reduced tendencies to compete when they expect to interact with their opponent repeatedly, but this effect is larger for groups

identifiability. In contrast, because individuals already show a much higher level of cooperation, this factor would not influence their choices concerning cooperation or competition to as large a degree. As you can see from Figure 9.11, this is precisely what happened: groups showed a much lower tendency to make a competitive choice when they anticipated multiple contacts with their opponent, while individuals showed a much smaller reduction.

In sum, cooperation can occur between groups as well as within them, and research findings confirm what is apparent in the social world around us: intergroup cooperation may be even harder to attain, for several reasons, than intragroup cooperation.

KEY POINTS

- *Cooperation*—working together with others to obtain shared goals—is a common aspect of social life.
- However, cooperation does not develop in many situations in which it is possible. One reason is that such situations often involve *social dilemmas*, in which overall joint gains can be increased by cooperation but individuals can increase their own gains by defection.
- Several factors influence whether cooperation occurs in such situations. These include strong tendencies toward *reciprocity*, personal orientation toward cooperation, and communication.
- Evolutionary psychologists suggest that our tendency to reciprocate may result from the fact that organisms that cooperate are more likely to survive and reproduce than organisms that do not.
- The *discontinuity effect* refers to the fact that groups are more likely to compete with one another than are individuals. In short, intergroup cooperation may be more difficult to attain than intragroup cooperation.

Conflict: Its Nature, Causes, and Effects

If prosocial behaviour and cooperation constitute one end of the coordination dimension—a dimension describing how individuals and groups work together—then *conflict* lies at or near the other end. As we noted earlier, conflict is a process in which one individual or group perceives that others have taken or will soon take actions incompatible with that individual's or group's own interests. The key elements in conflict are summarized in Figure 9.12.

Conflict is, unfortunately, an all-too-common part of social life, and it can be extremely costly to both sides. What factors cause individuals and groups to enter into this seemingly irrational process? And, perhaps even more important, what can be done to reduce such behaviour? These are the questions that social psychologists have addressed in their research.

Major Causes of Conflict

Our definition of conflict emphasizes the existence—and recognition—of incompatible interests. And indeed, incompatible interests constitute the defining feature of conflicts. Interestingly, though, conflicts sometimes fail to develop even though both sides have incompatible interests; and in other cases, conflicts occur even though the two sides don't really have opposing interests—they may simply *believe* that these exist (e.g., DeDreu & Van Lang, 1995; Tjosvold & DeDreu, 1997). Clearly, then, conflict involves much more than opposing interests. In fact, a growing body of evidence suggests that *social* factors may play a role as strong as or even stronger than incompatible interests in initiating conflicts.

One social factor that plays a role in this respect consists of what have been termed *faulty attributions*—errors concerning the causes behind others' behaviour (e.g., Baron, 1989b). When individuals find that their interests have been thwarted, they generally try to determine why this occurred. Was it bad luck? A lack of planning on their part? A lack of needed resources? Or was it due to intentional interference by another person or group? If they conclude that the latter is true, then the seeds for an

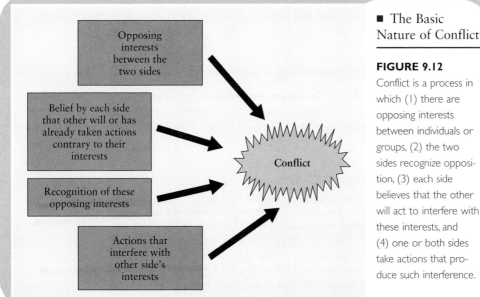

■ The Basic Nature of Conflict

FIGURE 9.12

Conflict is a process in which (1) there are opposing interests between individuals or groups, (2) the two sides recognize opposition, (3) each side believes that the other will act to interfere with these interests, and (4) one or both sides take actions that produce such interference.

intense conflict may be planted—*even if other persons actually had nothing to do with the situation*. In other words, erroneous attributions concerning the causes of negative outcomes can and often do play an important role in conflicts, and sometimes cause conflicts to occur when they could readily have been avoided. (See Chapter 8 for a related discussion on the effects of the *hostile attributional bias*.)

Another social factor that seems to play an important role in conflict is what might be termed *faulty communication*. For example, a phenomenon known as *transparency overestimation*—the belief that your goals and motives are more clearly recognized by your opponents than is actually true (Vorauer & Claude, 1998)—can escalate antagonisms. Imagine that a conflict is building, for instance, and one side makes a move towards compromise, overestimating how obvious this move is to the opposition. The opposition in fact fails to recognize it and continues with threats. The compromisers can often end up angrier than they were originally because now they believe their "olive branch" has been rejected. Another is example is "helpful" criticism. Have you ever been on the receiving end of harsh criticism—criticism you felt was unfair, insensitive, and not in the least helpful? The results of several studies indicate that feedback of this type, known as *destructive criticism*, can leave the recipient hungry for revenge—and so set the stage for conflicts that, again, do not necessarily stem from incompatible interests (e.g., Baron, 1990a; Cropanzano, 1993).

A third social cause of conflict involves the tendency to perceive our own views as objective and as reflecting reality, but those of others as biased by their ideology (e.g., Keltner & Robinson, 1997; Robinson et al., 1995). Research findings indicate that this tendency is stronger for groups or individuals who currently hold a dominant or powerful position (Keltner & Robinson, 1997). This, in turn, often leads to what is known as the *status quo bias*—a tendency for powerful groups defending the current status quo to be less accurate at intergroup perception than the groups that are challenging them. For instance, they perceive their position as much more reasonable or objective than it is.

Finally, personal traits or characteristics, too, seem to play a role in conflict. For example, as mentioned in Chapter 8, *Type A* individuals—ones who are highly competitive, always in a hurry, and relatively irritable—tend to become involved in conflicts more often than calmer and less irritable *Type B* persons (Baron, 1989a).

So where does all this leave us? With the conclusion that conflict, like cooperation, has many different roots. It does *not* stem solely from opposing interests. On the contrary, it often derives from social factors—long-standing grudges or resentment, the desire for revenge, inaccurate social perceptions, poor communication, and similar factors.

Resolving Conflicts: Some Useful Techniques

Because conflicts are often very costly, the persons involved usually want to resolve them as quickly as possible. What steps are most useful for reaching this goal? While many strategies may succeed, two seem especially useful—bargaining and superordinate goals.

Bargaining: The Universal Process

By far the most common strategy for resolving conflicts is **bargaining** or negotiation (e.g., Pruitt & Carnevale, 1993). In this process, opposing sides exchange offers, counteroffers, and concessions, either directly or though representatives. If the bargaining process is successful, a solution acceptable to both sides is attained and the conflict is resolved. If, instead, bargaining is unsuccessful, costly deadlock may result and the conflict may intensify. What factors determine which of these outcomes occurs? As you can probably guess, many play a role.

Bargaining (Negotiation) A process in which opposing sides exchange offers, counteroffers, and concessions, either directly or through representatives.

First, and perhaps most obviously, the outcome of bargaining is determined, in part, by the specific tactics adopted by the bargainers. Many of these are designed to accomplish a key goal: to reduce the opponent's *aspirations* so that this person or group becomes convinced that it cannot get what it wants and should, instead, settle for something more favourable to the other side. Tactics for reducing opponents' aspirations include (1) beginning with an extreme initial offer—one that is very favourable to the side proposing it; (2) the "big lie" technique—convincing the other side that one's break-even point is much higher than it is so that they offer more than would otherwise be the case (e.g., a used car salesperson may claim that she will lose money on the deal if she lowers the price, when in fact this is false) and (3) convincing the other side that you have an "out"—that if they won't make a deal with you, you can go elsewhere and get even better terms (Thompson, 1998).

Do these tactics seem ethical to you? This is a complex question on which individuals may well differ, but social psychologists who have conducted research on this question (Robinson et al., 1998) have found that there is general agreement that four types of tactics are questionable from an ethical standpoint: (1) *attacking an opponent's network*—manipulating or interfering with an opponent's network of support and information; (2) *false promises*—offering false commitments or lying about future intentions; (3) *misrepresentation*—providing misleading or false information to an opponent; and (4) *inappropriate information gathering*—collecting information in an unethical manner (e.g., through theft, spying, etc.). These tactics are measured by a questionnaire known as the *Self-reported Inappropriate Negotiation Strategies Scale* (or SINS for short).

Perhaps more interesting than the fact that such tactics exist is the finding that, depending on their role as a negotiator, individuals find them more or less acceptable. At first glance, you might expect that aggressive negotiators intent on winning might view such tactics as more appropriate than will negotiators who adopt a more defensive posture. In fact, though, exactly the opposite seems to be true. Negotiators who must defend themselves against opponents they view as unprincipled and aggressive actually rate various tactics such as those listed above as *more* acceptable (e.g., Ford & Blegen, 1992). Why? Apparently because they feel that they have to do whatever they can to defend against the harsh assaults they fully expect to follow.

Clear evidence for the effects of negotiators' roles on their perceptions of the appropriateness of questionable negotiating tactics has been provided by Garcia, Darley, & Robinson (2001). These researchers asked both lawyers for the defence and for the prosecution to rate the appropriateness of various tactics measured by SINS. Participants (actual lawyers) rated the appropriateness of these kinds of tactics both in the abstract and in response to their use by an opponent (i.e., how appropriate is it for you to use these tactics if they have been used by your opponent?). Garcia, Darley, & Robinson (2001) predicted that public defenders would rate the tactics as more appropriate than would district attorneys, and that both groups would rate these tactics as more appropriate in response to their use by an opponent. Results confirmed both hypotheses (see Figure 9.13).

A second, and very important, determinant of the outcome of bargaining involves the bargainers' overall *orientations* toward the process (Pruitt & Carnevale, 1993). People taking part in negotiations can approach such discussions from either of two distinct perspectives. They can view the negotiations as "win-lose" situations, in which gains by one side are necessarily linked with losses for the other. Or they can approach negotiations as potential "win–win" situations, in which the interests of the two sides are not necessarily incompatible and in which the potential gains of both sides can be maximized.

■ Negotiating Tactics in the Courtroom: Which Are Acceptable?

FIGURE 9.13 Negotiators often use tactics that are questionable from the standpoint of being ethical. Surprisingly, negotiators who play a defensive role, such defence lawyers in the court system, view such tactics as more appropriate than do negotiators who play an offensive, aggressive role, such as prosecutors.

Not all situations offer the potential for win–win agreements; but many conflicts that at first glance seem to involve head-on clashes do in fact provide such possibilities. If participants are willing to explore all options carefully, they can sometimes attain what are known as *integrative agreements*—ones that offer greater joint benefits than simple compromise (in which all differences are split down the middle). For example, suppose that two cooks are preparing recipes that call for an entire orange, and they have only one orange between them. What should they do? One possibility is to divide the orange in half. That leaves both with less than they need. Suppose, however, that one cook needs all the juice and the other needs all the peel. Here, a much better solution is possible: they can share the orange, each using the part she or he needs. Many techniques for attaining such integrative solutions exist; a few of these are summarized in Table 9.2.

Superordinate Goals: "We're All in This Together"

As we saw in Chapter 5, individuals often divide the world into two opposing camps— "us" and "them." They perceive members of their own group (us) as quite different from, and usually better than, people belonging to other groups (them). These tendencies to magnify differences between one's own group and others and to disparage outsiders are very powerful and often play a role in the occurrence and persistence of conflicts. Fortunately, they can be countered through the induction of **superordinate goals**— goals that both sides seek and that tie their interests together rather than driving them apart (e.g., Sherif et al., 1961; Tjosvold, 1993). Mediators in a dispute will often look

Superordinate Goals
Goals that both sides to a conflict seek and that tie their interests together rather than driving them apart.

Many different strategies can be useful in attaining integrative agreements—ones that offer better outcomes than simple compromise. A few of these are summarized here.

TABLE 9.2 Tactics for Reaching Integrative Agreements

Tactic	Description
Broadening the pie	Available resources are increased so that both sides can obtain their major goals.
Nonspecific compensation	One side gets what it wants; the other is compensated on an unrelated issue.
Logrolling	Each party makes concessions on low-priority issues in exchange for concessions on issues it values more highly.
Bridging	Neither party gets its initial demands, but a new option that satisfies the major interests of both sides is developed.
Cost cutting	One party gets what it desires, and the costs to the other party are reduced in some manner.

for such goals in order to overcome a competitive or a win-lose orientation on the part of negotiators.

In sum, resolution of conflict can sometimes be achieved through bargaining and the introduction of superordinate goals, though there are many potential pitfalls along the way.

KEY POINTS

- *Conflict* is a process that begins when individuals or groups perceive that others' interests are incompatible with their own.
- Conflict can also stem from social factors such as faulty attributions, poor communication, the tendency to perceive our own views as objective, and personal traits.
- Conflict can be reduced in many ways, but the tactics of bargainers and their overall orientations are important in reaching integrative agreements. Also, *superordinate goal* induction is effective.

Perceived Fairness in Groups: Getting What We Deserve—or Else!

Have you ever been in a situation in which you felt that you were getting less than you deserved from some group to which you belonged—less status, less approval, less pay? If so, you probably remember that your reactions to such *perceived unfairness* were most likely very strong, and not at all pleasant. Perhaps you experienced anger, resentment, and powerful feelings of injustice (e.g., Cropanzano, 1993; Scher, 1997). If you did, you may also recall your strong desire to change things. Social psychologists have recognized such effects for many years and have conducted many studies to understand (1) the factors that lead individuals to decide they have been treated fairly or unfairly, and (2) what they do about it—their efforts to deal with perceived unfairness (e.g., Adams, 1965). We'll now consider both questions.

Judgments of Fairness: Outcomes, Procedures, and Courtesy

One major circumstance that leads individuals to perceive that they are being treated unfairly is an imbalance between the *contributions*, or inputs, individuals make to a relationship or group and the *outcomes* they receive in return—their share of available rewards (Adams, 1965). In general, we expect these to be *proportional* to those of others in the group: the more a person contributes, the larger the share of available reward that person should receive. Thus if someone who makes a large contribution to a group receives a lion's share of the rewards, while someone who makes a small contribution receives a much smaller share, everything is fine: contributions and outcomes are in balance, and we perceive that fairness or *equity* exists. However, when there is a perceived imbalance in contributions and subsequent rewards—for example, when someone's contributions are perceived to be large and yet the rewards are small—an experience of *inequity* or unfairness results. A large body of research findings indicate that in fact, we do base many of our judgments of fairness on this kind of cognitive equation (see Figure 9.14). We compare the ratio of our inputs and outcomes to those of other persons to determine whether we are being treated fairly. Social psychologists refer to this as **distributive justice**—whether individuals feel they are receiving a fair share of available rewards proportionate to their contributions to the group or any social relationship.

Distributive Justice
The fairness of the distribution of available rewards or resources among group members.

■ Distributive Justice: Deciding Whether We Have Received Our Fair Share

FIGURE 9.14 In order to determine whether they have received a fair share of available rewards, individuals compare the ratio of their own contributions and outcomes with other persons' ratios. If these are roughly in balance, then they perceive that equity—fairness—exists (top panel). If they are out of balance, then they perceive that inequity—unfairness—exists.

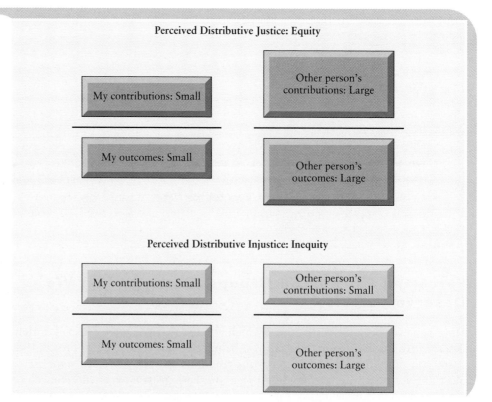

Two more points are worth carefully noting. First, judgments about distributive justice are very much in the eye of the beholder; *we* do the comparing and *we* decide whether our share of available rewards is fair relative to that of other group members (Greenberg, 1990). Second, we are much more sensitive about receiving *less* than we feel we deserve than about receiving *more* than we feel we deserve. In other words, the *self-serving bias* we described in Chapter 2 operates strongly in this context (Greenberg, 1996).

Procedural and Interpersonal Justice: Why Procedures and Courtesy Matter, Too

In addition to concern over how much we receive relative to others, we are also interested in (1) the procedures followed in the allocation of available rewards—**procedural justice**; and (2) the considerateness and courtesy shown to us by the parties responsible for dividing the available rewards—**interpersonal (or interactional) justice** (Folger & Bies, 1989; Shapiro, Buttner, & Barry, 1995).

Procedural Justice
The fairness of the procedures used to allocate available rewards among group members.

Interpersonal (or Interactional) Justice
Courtesy and consideration shown to group members by those responsible for distributing rewards; an important factor in perceived fairness.

What factors influence judgments concerning procedural justice? Ones such as these: (1) the *consistency* of procedures—the extent to which they are applied in the same manner to all persons; (2) *accuracy*—the extent to which procedures are based on accurate information about the relative contributions of all group members; and (3) *opportunity for corrections*—the extent to which any errors in distributions can be adjusted; (4) *bias suppression*—the extent to which decision makers avoid being influenced by their own self-interest; and (5) *ethicality*—the extent to which decisions are made in a manner compatible with ethical and moral values held by the people affected.

Evidence that such factors really do influence our judgments concerning procedural justice has been obtained in many studies (e.g., Brockner et al., 1994; Leventhal, Karuza, & Fry, 1980). For instance, in one recent investigation, Magner and colleagues (2000) asked property owners in a medium-sized city to rate the extent to which their taxes were determined through fair procedures. Results indicated that ethicality, accuracy, and bias suppression were important factors in taxpayers' decisions about procedural justice: the more these factors were present, the more the people perceived the process of setting each person's taxes to be fair.

Turning to *interactional justice,* two factors seem to play a key role in our judgments about how we have been treated: (1) the extent to which we are given clear and rational reasons for *why* rewards were divided as they were (Bies, Shapiro, & Cummings, 1988); and (2) the courtesy and sensitivity with which we are informed about these divisions (e.g., Greenberg, 1993b). Have we been treated with the respect that we deserve? Or have the people in charge of distributing rewards acted in a high-handed, insensitive manner? These are the kind of questions we ask ourselves in deciding whether we have been treated in an interpersonally fair manner.

Are any of these types of justice more important than the others? Although you might guess that we would pay more attention to the rewards we receive (i.e., distributive justice) than to procedures or courtesy, a growing body of evidence suggests that this is not necessarily so—we also care quite strongly about both procedures and courtesy (e.g., Brockner & Wiesenfeld, 1996; Greenberg & Alge, 1997).

In sum, we judge fairness in several different ways—in terms of the rewards we have received (distributive justice), the procedures used to reach these divisions (procedural justice), and the style in which we are informed about these divisions (interpersonal, or interactional, justice). All three forms of perceived justice can have strong effects on our behaviour, and in this way, can influence the functioning of groups to which we belong.

Reactions to Perceived Unfairness: Tactics for Dealing with Injustice

If *dissonance* is unpleasant (see Chapter 3), then *inequity*—the perception that one has been cheated or shortchanged by others—is downright obnoxious. As we noted earlier, most people react quite strongly to such treatment. But what, precisely, do they do? What steps do they take to restore fairness, or at least to reduce perceptions of unfairness? Here are some of the most important strategies that people adopt.

Individuals who perceive their situation as one of *distributive injustice* often attempt to restore fairness through a number of tactics. Most important are attempts at *changing the balance of contributions and outcomes* for themselves or others. For example, they may reduce contributions or demand larger rewards. If this does not work, they may take more drastic actions, such as leaving the group altogether. All these reactions are readily visible in workplaces—settings where judgments concerning fairness play a key role. Employees who feel that they are being underpaid may come in late, leave early, or do less on the job. In addition, they may request more benefits— higher pay, more vacation, and so on. If these tactics fail, they may protest, join a union and go out on strike, or (ultimately) quit and look for another job.

Such reactions are also visible in intimate relationships: when members of a couple feel that they are being treated unfairly by their spouse or significant other (e.g., they have to do more than their share of the housework), they often react with anger and resentment, and they may take steps to change the situation (e.g., Sprecher, 1992). This can range from direct requests to their partner to deciding to leave the relationship for another. Interestingly, recent findings indicate that perceived unfairness not only may lead to marital distress, it may be a result of it. In a carefully conducted longitudinal study, Grote and Clark (2001) asked married couples to rate their marital satisfaction, their marital conflict, and the perceived fairness of division of household tasks at three different times: while the wife was pregnant, six months after their child was born, and 12 to 15 months after their child was born. Results indicated that the more conflict couples reported before the child was born, the greater their perceptions of unfairness at the later times (after the child was born). These findings occurred for both genders but were, not surprisingly, somewhat stronger for women, who, in fact, do more than half of the household chores in most couples. These results suggest that when couples are getting along well and conflict is low, they do *not* pay much attention to unfairness, even if it exists. But when conflict is high, their attention is focused on unfairness, and this, in turn, may serve to intensify conflict still further (see Figure 9.15). In sum, perceived unfairness can be the result of marital conflict as well as a cause of such difficulties for couples.

When unfairness relates primarily to procedures (*procedural justice*) or a lack of courtesy (*interpersonal justice*), individuals may adopt different tactics. Procedures are often harder to change than specific outcomes, because they frequently go on behind closed doors and may depart from announced policies in many ways. Similarly, changing the negative attitudes or personality traits that lie behind inconsiderate treatment by bosses, professors, or other reward allocators is a difficult if not impossible task. The result? Individuals who feel that they have been treated unfairly in these ways often turn to more *covert techniques* to even the score. For instance, a growing body of evidence suggests that feelings of procedural or interpersonal unfairness lie behind many instances of employee theft and sabotage (e.g., Greenberg & Scott, 1996).

Finally, individuals who feel that they have been treated unfairly but conclude that there is little they can do about it may cope with the situation simply by *changing their perceptions*. They may conclude, in short, that they are being treated fairly— because, for instance, other persons who receive larger rewards somehow *deserve* this special treatment by virtue of possessing something "special": extra talent, greater experience, a bigger reputation, or some other special qualities. In such cases, individuals who feel that they cannot eliminate unfairness can at least cope with it and reduce the discomfort it produces, even though they may continue to be treated unfairly by others.

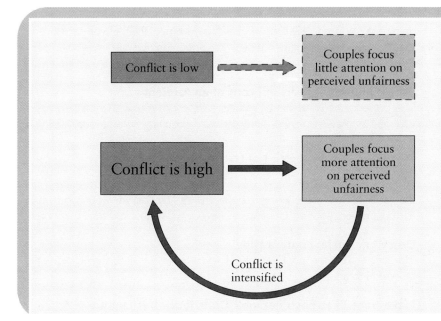

■ The Role of Perceived Unfairness in Intimate Relationships

FIGURE 9.15 When conflict is low, couples do not seem to focus much attention on perceived unfairness. When conflict is high, however, they do, and the resulting perceptions of unfair treatment may further intensify such conflict.

Source: Based on data and suggestions from Grote & Clark, 2001.

KEY POINTS

- Individuals wish to be treated fairly by the groups to which they belong. Fairness can be judged in terms of outcomes (*distributive justice*), in terms of procedures (*procedural justice*), or in terms of courteous treatment (*interpersonal justice*).
- When individuals feel that they have been treated unfairly, they often take steps to restore fairness.
- These steps include moderating their contributions, demanding greater rewards, protesting, engaging in covert actions such as employee theft or sabotage, and/or changing their own perceptions about fairness.
- In intimate relationships, conflict can lead to increased feelings of unfair treatment, and this, in turn, can further intensify conflict.

Ideas to Take With You

Maximizing Your Own Performance

Social facilitation effects seem to occur because the presence of others is arousing. Arousal increases our tendency to perform dominant responses. If these are correct for the situation, our performance is improved; if they are incorrect, our performance is impaired. This analysis leads to several practical suggestions.

Study Alone, but Take Tests in the Presence of Others.
If you study alone, you'll avoid the distraction caused by other persons and so will learn new material more efficiently. If you have studied hard, your

dominant responses will probably be correct ones; so when you take a test, the increased arousal generated by other persons will improve your performance.

Work on Simple Tasks in Front of an Audience.
The presence of an audience will increase your arousal and thus enhance your ability to exert physical effort on tasks requiring pure physical effort.

Minimizing Social Loafing by Others

Social loafing occurs when persons working together put out less effort than they would if they were working alone. This can be costly to you if you work hard but others goof off. Here are some ways you can avoid such outcomes.

Don't Let Social Loafers Hide!
Make sure that the contribution of each member of the group can be assessed individually.

Make Sure That Each Person's Contribution Is Unique.
Every group member's contribution should be unique—not identical to that of others. In this way, each person can be held personally responsible for what he or she produces, and assessment of individual contribution is easier.

Increase Commitment.
Try to work only with people who are committed to the group's goals. If you cannot choose your group members, use other means of increasing commitment. These can be informal, such as ensuring that each member contributes to group plans and agrees in front of other group members to accomplish certain tasks; or formal, such as drawing up a "group contract" clearly outlining expectations of each person in the group and getting all group members to sign it.

Summary

Groups: Their Nature and Function
- A *group* is a collection of persons perceived to form a coherent unit to some degree. (p. 328)
- Groups influence their members' *roles, status, norms,* and *cohesiveness.* (p. 329)
- Organizational commitment can be particularly important when there are changes in working conditions. (p. 332)

How Groups Affect Individual Performance: Facilitation or Social Loafing?
- Social facilitation is the influence of others on an individual's task performance. (p. 334)

- The *drive theory of social facilitation* suggests the mere presence of others is arousing and can either increase or reduce performance. (p. 336)
- The *distraction–conflict theory* suggests that the presence of others is arousing because it induces conflicting tendencies to focus on the task and on an audience. (p. 337)
- *Social loafing* is the reduced output by group members when working together on a task. (p. 339)
- The *collective effort model* (CEM) states that social loafing occurs because in groups there are often weaker links between individuals' efforts and their outcomes. (p. 339)
- Groups can reduce social loafing in several ways. (p. 340)

Decision Making by Groups: How It Occurs and the Pitfalls It Faces

- *Group polarization* effects can lead groups to make more extreme decisions than individuals. (p. 343)
- *Groupthink*—when a desire to achieve consensus takes precedence over reaching the right decision—can lead to unwise decisions by groups. (p. 345)
- Groups often engage in biased processing of information. (p. 346)
- Groups often fail to share important information and to pool their resources. (p. 347)
- Group decision-making can be improved through the use of methods such as the *devil's advocate technique* and *authentic dissent*. (p. 348)

Coordination in Groups: Cooperation or Conflict?

- *Cooperation* is working together with others to obtain shared goals. (p. 348)
- In situations that involve *social dilemmas*, cooperation can be more difficult to achieve. (p. 349)

- Several factors influence whether cooperation occurs in such situations. (p. 350)
- The evolutionary theory of reciprocal altruism suggests that our tendency to *reciprocate* may have evolved. (p. 350)
- The discontinuity effect refers to the fact that groups are more likely to compete with one another than are individuals. (p. 351)
- *Conflict* occurs when we perceive that others' interests are incompatible with our own. (p. 353)
- A number of factors cause or increase conflict. (p. 353)
- Conflict can be reduced through *bargaining* and introducing *superordinate goals*. (p. 356)

Perceived Fairness in Groups: Getting What We Deserve—or Else!

- Fairness can be judged in terms of *distributive justice*, *procedural justice*, or *interpersonal justice*. (p. 358)
- Perception of injustice often leads to attempts to restore fairness. (p. 359)
- Perceived unfairness in intimate relationships increases when conflict is high. (p. 359)

For More Information

Foddy, M., Smithson, M., Schneider, S., & Hogg, M. A. (Eds.). (2000). *Resolving social dilemmas: Dynamic, structural, and intergroup aspects.* Philadelphia: Psychology Press.

In this book, experts on social dilemmas—and on cooperation and competition—discuss the nature of such situations and techniques for resolving them in a way that maximizes the outcomes of all persons concerned. This is an excellent source to consult if you'd like to know more about how people behave in situations involving conflicting pressures to cooperate and compete.

Thompson, L. (1998). *The mind and heart of the negotiator.* Upper Saddle River, NJ: Prentice Hall.

In this well-written and relatively brief book, a noted researcher describes the nature of negotiation from the perspective of modern social psychology. The roles of various cognitive processes and biases, perceived fairness, past experience, and group processes are all described. An excellent source to consult if you'd like to know more about bargaining.

Witte, E., & Davis, J. H. (Eds.). (1996). *Understanding group behaviour: Consensual action by small groups.* Hillsdale, NJ: Erlbaum.

Noted experts summarize existing knowledge about many aspects of group behaviour. The sections on decision making are especially interesting, and expand greatly upon the information on this topic presented in this chapter.

Weblinks

www.trinity.edu/~mkearl/socpsy-8.html
Collective Behavior and the Social Psychologies of Social Institutions

www.communitypsychology.net
Community Psychology Net

CHAPTER TEN

Applied Social Psychology:
Health, Work and Legal Applications

Applying Social Psychology to Health Issues
Responding to Health-Related Information/The Effects of Stress on Health/Coping with Stress

Applying Social Psychology to the World of Work: Job Satisfaction, Prosocial Behaviour, and Leadership
Job Satisfaction: Attitudes about Work/Prosocial Behaviour at Work: Organizational Citizenship Behaviour/Leadership: Patterns of Influence within Groups

Social Psychology and the Legal System
Before the Trial Begins: Effects of Police Procedures and Media Coverage/The Eyewitness/The Central Participants in a Trial: Some Effects of Defendants and Jurors

SPECIAL SECTIONS

CORNERSTONES
Second Language Learning and Bilingualism: The Contribution of Wallace Lambert

ON THE APPLIED SIDE
The Weapons Effect: A Social Psychological Perspective on the Impact of Firearms

In this final chapter we come full circle by emphasizing, as we did in Chapter 1, the importance of **applied social psychology**—the use of social psychological principles and research methods in real-world settings to solve a variety of individual and societal problems (Weyant, 1986). We are also looking back to the beginning of modern social psychology with Kurt Lewin's *action research* in the 1940s and '50s. He emphasized how practical social psychology can be when applied to social problems and we end the book by reiterating that point with this applied chapter.

Applications of social psychology have expanded tremendously in recent years and the fact that social psychology can be applied to so many areas is a mark of its growing strength and relevance. Many of the Canadian social psychologists mentioned throughout this book are involved in applying their ideas and research to social problems. Perhaps the most famous of the early applied studies in Canadian social psychology comes from the work of Wallace Lambert at McGill University. The following Cornerstones section describes his examination of second language learning and bilingualism—a topic very central to Canadian identity.

Applied Social Psychology
Psychological research and practice in real-world settings, directed toward the understanding of human social behaviour and the attempted solution of social problems.

Cornerstones

Second Language Learning and Bilingualism: The Contribution of Wallace Lambert

Second language learning and bilingualism have been particularly important issues in Canada's bilingual society. It is not surprising, therefore, that Canadian researchers were pioneers in this area and remain on the forefront of research today. The most notable of these researchers is Wallace Lambert of McGill University, whose work has extended over 30 years.

Canada became an officially bilingual country in 1969 when the Official Languages Act was endorsed by Parliament, giving equal status to the English and French languages. Currently, 85 percent of the population can speak English, 31 percent can speak French, and 18 percent are English-French bilingual (Statistics Canada, 2002). This latter figure represents a 45 percent increase since the 1950s in the proportion of the population who are bilingual (Harrison & Marmen, 1994).

One reason for this increase may be the growth of French immersion programs for non-Francophone children. These programs were initiated in Quebec in 1965, when the Protestant School Board of Montreal launched the "St. Lambert Project" for children of Anglophone and immigrant parents. Wallace Lambert and his colleagues investigated the children's progress, and the results of their research have guided the introduction of French immersion programs since that time (Genesee, 1984; Lambert & Tucker, 1972). Children in the project were taught entirely in French from kindergarten to Grade 2. The English language was introduced for half-hour periods during Grade 2 and

the proportion of the curriculum taught in English was gradually increased until by Grade 7 this included about half of the classes. The progress of these mostly Anglophone children was compared with that of Anglophone children taught in English and Francophone children taught in French.

Parents at that time, as now, had many questions about the effects of French immersion. For example, does being initially taught exclusively in French create deficits in English language proficiency? Would problems arise if children were taught a particular subject (e.g., history or mathematics) in French originally and then had to switch to English? Results of Lambert's research were encouraging. Children in the St. Lambert project achieved a level of spoken French far superior to that of Anglophone children in conventional French-as-a-second-language programs, though they did not quite achieve the proficiency of native French speakers. Further, their written and oral skills in English were as good as those of the children taught in English (Lambert, 1974). There was also no deficit shown if children were tested in English on a subject that they had studied in French. In fact, the overall results of the St. Lambert project, and subsequent research into similar programs, tend to confirm that early French immersion produces no detrimental effects on English language development or progress of other academic subjects, while French language progress is much enhanced (Genesee & Gandara, 1999).

Beyond the academic effects of acquiring a second language, Lambert was interested in the *social* implications of such bilingualism for the individual and for group relations. For example, the St. Lambert project found that the children involved had a more positive attitude to Francophones than conventionally educated Anglophone children. However, later research suggested that this more positive attitude may not last into adulthood (Genesee & Gandara, 1999).

Lambert also suggested (1978; Lambert & Taylor, 1984) that second language acquisition may have different implications for a majority and a minority individual. The acquisition of a second language is mostly beneficial for persons who belong to the majority group in a particular society, enhancing their academic, employment, and social opportunities. Lambert termed this *additive bilingualism*. However, there may be some sense of personal and social loss involved in second language acquisition (usually the language of the majority) for the minority individual. Lambert termed this *subtractive bilingualism*. Minority individuals may, for instance, find themselves drawn increasingly to participate in the majority culture and communicate in that language, with consequent losses of their own culture and sense of social identity. For example, Bourhis's (1990) research examined communication in the bilin-

gual New Brunswick civil service. Anglophones are a majority in that context and tend to be of higher status. He found that Francophones were much more likely to switch to English when addressed in that language by an Anglophone colleague than a fully bilingual Anglophone was to switch to French when addressed in that language. Ultimately, the outcome of subtractive bilingualism can be the loss of a language, as has happened with some of Canada's Aboriginal languages. In Quebec, the controversial language laws were designed to prevent this type of loss (see Figure 10.1).

Lambert's body of work has combined theoretical and applied research in addressing social problems: a true example of Lewin's *action research*. As Lewin suggested (1948), social psychologists can also be agents of social change. Building on the pioneering research described above, Canadian social psychologists continue to investigate the social psychology of language, studying, for example, its importance to intergroup relations and cross-cultural communication (Bourhis, 1984; Genesee & Bourhis, 1988; Clement, Baker & MacIntyre, 2003) or to individual social identity and acculturation (Clément, 1987; Young & Gardner, 1990).

■ Attempts to Prevent the Erosion of the French Language in Quebec

FIGURE 10.1 Awareness of the tendency for majority-group languages to prevail and minority-group languages to erode, has led successive governments in Quebec to institute educational programs and policies designed to prevent bilingualism from being *subtractive*.

Because of the tremendous expansion of *applied social psychology* in the years since Wallace Lambert carried out his classic research, no one chapter can possibly represent the breadth of this exciting work. What we do provide, however, are selections from three major applied areas. The first two of these sections (applications related to *health* and to *work* issues) are well-established disciplines with extensive literatures; the last section (applications to the *legal system*) provides a sample of a more recent, but rapidly developing, applied topic. These three topics will give you an idea of the exciting work being carried out in today's "action research."

KEY POINTS

- Applied social psychology involves research and practice directed towards understanding and solving social problems.
- The research of Wallace Lambert is a classic example of applied research. He investigated the academic and social impact of bilingualism and second language learning.

Applying Social Psychology to Health Issues

Health and illness tend to be thought of in terms of physical processes that are dealt with exclusively by the medical profession. However, it is now increasingly clear that psychological factors affect all aspects of our physical well-being (Rodin & Salovey, 1989; Rabasca, 2000). As a result, investigators interested in **health psychology** focus on the psychological processes affecting the development, prevention, and treatment of physical illness (Glass, 1989). Let's consider a number of ways in which social psychological research has been applied to health.

Health Psychology The study of the effects of psychological factors in the development, prevention, and treatment of physical illness.

Responding to Health-Related Information

If headlines were our main source of knowledge, we would live in constant fear of SARS, AIDS, mad cow disease, flesh-eating bacteria, and new viruses from monkeys that turn our insides into spaghetti. In contrast to the headlines, a Health Canada report on the health of Canadians paints a positive picture (Health Canada, 2000). Life expectancy in Canada has reached an all-time high of 81.4 years for women and 75.7 years for men; ranking in the top three in the world. There has also been a decline in the infant mortality rate. Further improvements relevant to health include the first-ever decline in the incidence of cancer, as well as decreased use of drugs and cigarettes; even the accidental death rate is declining (Easterbrook, 1999).

But it is often difficult to know how to respond to health information in the media. As well as frightening headlines, we also regularly receive very positive news indicating that medical science is on the brink of preventing or curing cancer, diabetes, and other dreaded diseases (e.g., Lemonick & Park, 2001). And our cognitive biases, namely the tendency to use the *availability heuristic* (discussed in Chapters 2) may make us either over- or underestimate the threat of disease. How do we decide to accept or reject health information?

Factors Determining Whether We Accept or Reject Health Information

An important factor in whether we accept or reject health information is the affective nature of health warnings. Experts often present data about disease prevention in an emotion-arousing manner in the hope that fear will motivate us to do the right thing. One difficulty with this approach is that people often reject as "untrue" a health message that arouses anxiety. The rejection acts to reduce our anxiety and thus makes it unnecessary for us to change our behaviour (Liberman & Chaiken, 1992). Information about something as frightening as breast cancer, for example, can activate defence mechanisms that interfere with women's attending to, remembering, and/or acting on relevant information about the importance of early detection (Millar, 1997).

One common way to deal with threatening information actually increases the odds that the person will engage in behaviour involving health risks. Consider a situation in which unmarried individuals are contemplating sexual intercourse. Among many factors to consider are the threat of disease and the threat of unwanted pregnancy. Such considerations create anxiety. One "remedy" for anxiety is alcohol. Whenever people drink alcohol, anxiety is decreased—but so is cognitive capacity. The resulting *alcohol myopia* (Steele & Josephs, 1990) causes people to focus on the immediate cues in the environment and to forget about the long-term consequences. This can lead to risky behaviour if, for example, the immediate environment provides cues suggesting the desirability of having intercourse and fails to suggest the potential negative consequences of failure to use condoms (MacDonald, Zanna, & Fong, 1996; MacDonald et al., 2000). In this way, drinking can lead to unsafe sex, as well to other risky behaviours such as unsafe driving.

While a negative message may evoke anxiety and avoidance, health messages can be *positively framed*, suggesting that altered behaviour will result in a gain. Positive framing is most effective in motivating *preventive* behaviour, whereas a *negatively framed* message, suggesting a loss from failing to act, is best for motivating *detection* behaviour (Rothman et al., 1999). This difference was demonstrated in research focusing on dental messages. A positive dental pamphlet—"People who use a mouth rinse daily are taking advantage of a safe and effective way to reduce plaque accumulation"—heightened interest in using a plaque-fighting mouth rinse. In contrast, a negative dental pamphlet— "Failing to use a disclosing rinse before brushing limits your ability to detect areas of plaque accumulation"—heightened interest in using a plaque-detecting rinse.

People who ignore various health messages often have a sense of *unrealistic optimism* or an *optimistic bias*. There's no reason to alter your behaviour if you are convinced that bad things are not going to happen to you. With unrealistic optimism, you feel free to drive while intoxicated, eat as much saturated fat as you like, and go bungee jumping (Helweg-Larsen & Shepperd, 2001; Middleton, Harris, & Surman, 1996).

Risky behaviour can also occur in a limited specific situation. Would you drink from a stranger's water bottle? The answer seems to depend on whether you are challenged to do so and whether you are concerned about how you are viewed by others. Martin and Leary (1999) designed an unusual experiment in which a research participant was asked to drink three mildly unpleasant liquids, after which another participant (actually a research assistant) offered a partially empty bottle of water from his backpack to wash out the bad taste. (Though it was made to appear that the assistant had been drinking from the bottle, actually only clean, non-used bottles were used.) The assistant either offered the bottle in a nonchallenging way—"That stuff must have tasted pretty nasty. Do you want a drink of my water?" In the challenging condition, he said the same thing and added, "...if you're not worried about drinking out of the same bottle as me." A questionnaire measured *social-image concern*—the degree to which participants were concerned about how other people assess them. As shown in Figure 10.2, those in the high image concern group drank more than those in the low image concern group, and those who were challenged drank more than those who were not challenged. You can see that risky health behaviour was a function of situational factors (challenge or no challenge) and dispositional factors (concern with self-image). Now that you have this information, how would you answer the question "Would you drink from a stranger's water bottle?"

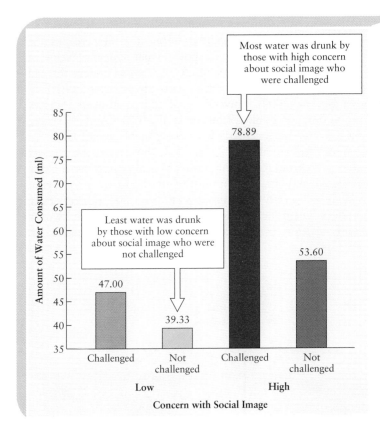

Most water was drunk by those with high concern about social image who were challenged

Least water was drunk by those with low concern about social image who were not challenged

47.00

39.33

78.89

53.60

Amount of Water Consumed (ml)

Challenged | Not challenged | Challenged | Not challenged

Low | High

Concern with Social Image

■ Taking a Health Risk: Challenge and Concern about Social Image

FIGURE 10.2 The amount of water consumed when drinking from a stranger's water bottle was affected by whether or not this behaviour had been challenged and whether the research participant was high or low in concern about social image. Those who were challenged drank more, and those high in social image concern also drank more.

Source: Based on data in Martin & Leary, 1999.

The Effects of Stress on Health

During World War II, psychologists became increasingly interested in stress and its impact on cognition, overt behaviour, and health (Lazarus, 1993; Somerfield & McCrae, 2000). **Stress** is defined as any physical or psychological event that is perceived as a potential threat to physical or emotional well-being. Among university and college students, the resulting distress often includes anxiety and depression, which may, in turn, lead to alcohol abuse and eating problems (Oliver et al., 1999). **Coping** refers to the way in which people deal with threats and with their emotional consequences (Taylor, Buunk, & Aspinwall, 1990; Tennen et al., 2000). Of special interest is the effect of stress on health.

The Relationship between Stress and Illness

Research consistently indicates that as stress increases, depression and illness become more likely. And we encounter a great many sources of stress. For example, university and college students experience stress caused by such factors as low grades, the ups and downs of romantic and sexual relationships, and living in a new environment (Gall, Evans, & Bellrose, 2000). Common everyday hassles include arguing with loved ones (Chapman, Hobfoll, & Ritter, 1997; Foxhall, 2001) or living under crowded conditions (Evans, Lepore, & Schroeder, 1996), commuting in heavy traffic (Weinberger, Hiner, & Tierney, 1987), and dealing with environmental noise (Evans, Bullinger, & Hygge, 1998). Increases in such stressors are associated with an increased probability of developing a cold or flu and sometimes with the development of more serious conditions such as heart disease (Foxhall, 2001).

Stress Any physical or psychological event perceived as being able to cause us harm or distress.

Coping Responding to stress in a way that reduces the threat and its effects; includes what a person does, feels, or thinks in order to master, tolerate, or decrease the negative effects of a stressful situation.

Being the victim of a natural disaster such as a tornado or a man-made disaster such as a terrorist attack is obviously stressful, and a major component is the perception of oneself as vulnerable and threatened by the inability to control what happens (Weinstein et al., 2000). Even indirect exposure to the September 11, 2001, terrorist attacks through the media was associated with symptoms of post-traumatic stress disorder (PTSD) among school children (Saylor, et al., 2003), university and college students (Harvey, DeRoma, Saylor, & Politano, 2002), and adults (Schuster, et al., 2001). And effects can continue long after a disaster has ended, particularly with direct involvement.

How, exactly, could stress result in illness? In general, those who are stressed report a negative affective state, aches and pains, and more physical symptoms of illness (Affleck et al., 1994; Brown & Moskowitz, 1997); but the effects of stress go beyond that. As outlined in Figure 10.3, Baum (1994) proposes both direct and indirect effects of stress. There are indirect effects when the emotional turmoil (depression and worry) caused by stress interferes with health-related behaviours such as seeking medical care

■ Stress and Illness: Direct and Indirect Effects

FIGURE 10.3 It has long been known that as stress increases, the likelihood of illness also increases. The mechanisms underlying this relationship are gradually beginning to be understood. It appears that stress has indirect effects (it leads to behavioural changes) as well as direct physiological effects.

Source: Based on material in Baum, 1994.

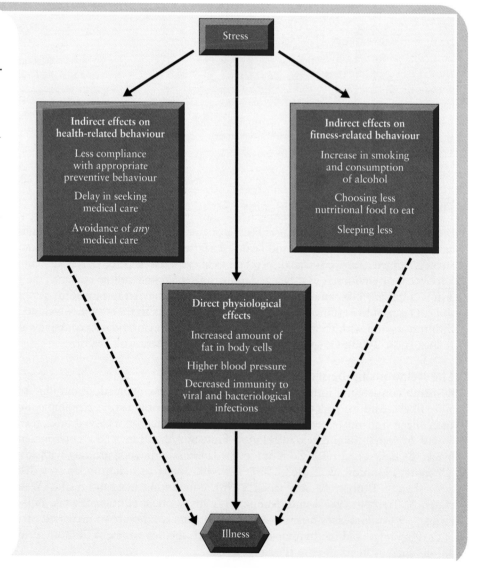

or eating a balanced diet (Whisman & Kwon, 1993; Wiebe & McCallum, 1986). There are also direct physiological effects in that stress delays the healing process in wounds, has adverse effects on the endocrine system, and causes the body's immune system to function less well (Kiecolt-Glaser et al., 1998; Stone et al., 1987).

Findings of a direct link between psychological responses and the body's defence against disease has led to the development of the field of **psychoneuroimmunology**. This interdisciplinary approach explores the relationships among stress, emotional and behavioural reactions, and the body's immune system (Ader, 2001). For example, Jemmott and Magloire (1988) obtained samples of students' saliva, which contains *secretory immunoglobulin A*, the body's primary defence against such infections. The level of this substance was found to drop during final exams and then to rise again when exams were over. In a work setting, parallel findings indicate that the immune system suffers when projects turn out badly, especially for workers who blame themselves for what went wrong (Schaubroeck, Jones, & Xie, 2001). The psychological–physiological connection works in both directions. Not only is there an effect of psychological variables on the immune system, but the activation of the immune system alters neural activity and thus affects behaviour, mood, and cognitive functioning (Maier & Watkins, 2000).

Psychoneuroimmun-ology The research field that explores the relationships among stress, emotional and behavioural reactions, and the immune system.

Individual Differences in Vulnerability to Stress

Given the same objectively stressful conditions, some people experience more negative emotional reactions than others and are thus more likely to get sick. For example, men who are perfectionists ("I feel that I must do things perfectly, or not do them at all") are more depressed than nonperfectionists when stress is high (Joiner & Schmidt, 1995).

Though genetic factors explain some of the differences in the effects of stress (Kessler et al., 1992), Friedman, Hawley, and Tucker (1994) present evidence from a large number of studies indicating a difference between **disease-prone personalities** and **self-healing personalities**. Those who are disease-prone respond to stressful situations with negative emotions and unhealthy behaviour patterns, and the result is illness and a shorter life span. For a self-healing person, in contrast, stress is unpleasant, but it is perceived as something to be managed. Healthy behaviour is maintained, and illness is either avoided or of brief duration. There is a general tendency for such individuals to be enthusiastic about life, emotionally balanced, alert, responsive to others, energetic, curious, secure, and constructive. Such individuals have also been described as expressing *subjective well-being* and as being *optimistic*. They express gratitude when others help them and forgiveness when others do them harm. They benefit from interpreting daily life in positive terms, being strongly involved in their work and their leisure activities, feeling a sense of purpose in their lives, and anticipating a positive future (Myers & Diener, 1995; Segerstrom et al., 1998; Vaillant, 2002).

Disease-Prone Personalities Personality characterized by negative emotional reactions to stress, ineffective coping strategies, and unhealthy behaviour patterns; often associated with illness and a shortened life span.

Self-Healing Personalities Personality characterized by effective coping with stress; self-healing individuals are balanced, energetic, responsive to others, and positive about life.

Earlier in this book, we encountered similar descriptions of those with a secure attachment style (Chapter 6) and those with an altruistic personality (Chapter 8). A combination of such characteristics seems to promote positive behaviour and serve as a protection against the negative effects of stress. Table 10.1 summarizes many of the personality differences between those who are most disease-prone and those who are self-healing.

Note that a long, happy life is most likely to occur among people with this positive outlook, along with a lifestyle that includes exercise, an interest in continued learning, and the avoidance of cigarette smoking, alcohol abuse, and obesity (Vaillant, 2002).

A somewhat different personality pattern (*Type A*)—associated with coronary disease—was described in Chapter 8. Type A individuals, compared with the more placid Type B individuals, are more hostile, have higher blood pressure (Contrada, 1989), and are twice as likely to develop heart disease (Weidner, Istvan, & McKnight, 1989).

Stress often results in illness, but some individuals are far more vulnerable than others. As indicated in the table, differences in vulnerability are associated with a variety of personality differences

TABLE 10.1 Vulnerability to Stress: Self-Healing Personality versus Disease-Prone Personality.

	Self-Healing Personality	Disease-Prone Personality
Behavioural Tendencies	• avoids interpersonal conflicts • nonperfectionist • extroverted • completes school assignments on time	• gets into interpersonal conflicts • perfectionist • introverted • procrastinates
Expectancies and Beliefs	• positive bias in interpreting stressful events • internal locus of control • believes in a just world • high self-efficacy • optimistic • approaches goals, focusing on positive outcomes	• negative bias in interpreting stressful events • external locus of control • does not believe in a just world • low self-efficacy • pessimistic • avoids goals, focusing on negative outcomes
Personal Characteristics	• not neurotic • well adjusted • high self-esteem • independent • accessible attitudes—knows his or her likes and dislikes	• neurotic • maladjusted • low self-esteem • dependent • inaccessible attitudes—unsure of his or her likes and dislikes

Sources: Amirkhan, Risinger, & Swickert, 1995; Bandura, 1993; Birkimer, Lucas, & Birkimer, 1991; Bernard & Belinsky, 1993; Bolger & Zuckerman, 1995; Booth-Kewley & Vickers, 1994; Bornstein, 1995; Campbell, Chew, & Scratchley, 1991; Dykema, Bergbower, & Peterson, 1995; Elliot & Sheldon, 1998; Fazio & Powell, 1997; Gunthert, Cohen, & Armeli, 1999; Hemenover, 2001; Joiner & Schmidt, 1995; Tice & Baumeister, 1997; Tomaka & Blascovich, 1994.

Coping with Stress

Each of us inevitably encounters stressful situations throughout life. Beyond those fortunate enough to have self-healing personalities, what kind of strategies can be developed to help deal with stress? We will briefly describe some of the most effective.

Increasing Physical Fitness

Fitness Being in good physical condition as indicated by endurance and strength.

It should not come as a surprise to learn that eating nutritious foods, getting enough sleep, and engaging in regular exercise results in increased **fitness**—that is, being in good physical condition as indicated by endurance and strength. Even 15 to 20 minutes of aerobic exercise (jogging, biking, swimming, dancing, etc.) each day or every other day increases fitness. Just one hour a week spent walking cuts the rate of heart disease in half (Lee et al., 2001). The result of being fit is a sense of well-being and self-efficacy (see Chapter 4), along with the perception of being able to handle stress (Brown, 1991; Jessor, Turbin, & Costa, 1998; Rudolph & Kim, 1996; Winett, 1998).

Overeating, eating less nutritious food, and becoming overweight constitute a special set of problems that undermine fitness. In the past, because food supplies were scarce and unpredictable, humans and other animals evolved to eat as much as possible whenever food was available (Pinel, Assanand, & Lehman, 2000). The excess was stored in the body as a buffer against starvation whenever food became difficult to obtain. Though overeating was adaptive for our ancestors, most of us who live in the industrialized world are surrounded by a wide variety of readily available, good-tasting food containing many more calories and much more fat and sugar than we need. For most people, overeating in the twenty-first century is not at all adaptive, but the fight to maintain an optimal weight is a difficult one because we are genetically programmed to eat too much. To establish different eating habits, the best approach is to begin in infancy with breast-feeding rather than formula from a bottle (O'Neil, 1999) and to continue throughout childhood with a balanced diet at home and in school (Berger, 1999). In adulthood, those who avoid becoming overweight are healthier and have a longer life span (Calle et al., 1999).

Almost everyone should be able to become fit, but most of us do not. To change from being a "couch potato" to someone with a better diet, an adequate amount of sleep, and regular exercise requires strong motivation, continuing commitment, and the ability to regulate one's own behaviour (Mullan & Markland, 1997; Schwarzer, 2001).

Coping Strategies: Positive Emotions and Regulatory Control

Compas and his colleagues (1991) proposed that *coping*, or responding effectively to stress, involves a two-level process. The first level involves *emotion-focused coping*—attempts to reduce the negative emotional response elicited by the threat and to increase positive affect (Folkman & Moskowitz, 2000a, 2000b; Stanton et al., 2000). Even if the threat is still there, we prefer to feel less anxious and less angry, and we seek ways to increase our positive feelings. At the second level is *problem-focused coping*, which involves an attempt to deal with the threat itself and to gain control of the situation (see Figure 10.4).

At the first level, a useful emotion-focused strategy for coping with stress is to discover how to create positive affect for oneself. People who are able to regulate their emotions seek ways to experience positive, happy feelings and an optimistic outlook despite negative events (Chang, 1998; Mayer & Salovey, 1995). Those who seldom laugh respond to increases in stress with greater negative affect, but those who laugh the most do not (Kuiper & Martin, 1998). In one study of long-term responses to the 9-11 tragedy, those who were able to generate more positive emotions had greater resilience and developed fewer depressive symptoms (Fredrickson, Tugade, Waugh, & Larkin, 2003). Other effective aids to positive feelings range from enjoyable work (Csikszentmihalyi & LeFevre, 2000), to experiencing love (J. Levin, 2000), or seeking comfort in religion and spirituality (George et al., 2000; Seybold & Hill, 2001). Any activity that helps improve one's mood seems able to counteract the negative effects of stress.

At the second level, one problem-focused strategy is successful *regulatory control*—the processes that enable an individual to guide his or her goal-directed activities over time and across situations. For example, seeking out more positive events (such as a family gathering or spending time with friends) when you are under stress actually enhances the immune system (Stone, Neal, et al., 1994). Further, a *decrease* in positive events has a negative effect on health similar to that of an *increase* in negative events (Goleman, 1994). Regulatory control includes holding positive beliefs (Reed & Aspinwall, 1998), engaging in constructive behaviour (Fabes & Eisenberg, 1997), giving up short-term pleasures to gain long-term satisfactions (Mayer & Salovey, 1995), and having positive expectations about the future—a feeling of hope (Chang & DeSimone, 2001; Snyder, 2000).

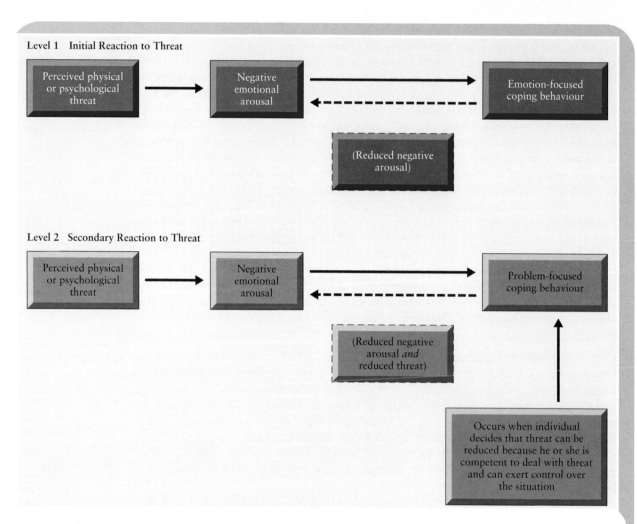

Level 1   Initial Reaction to Threat

Perceived physical or psychological threat → Negative emotional arousal → Emotion-focused coping behaviour

(Reduced negative arousal)

Level 2   Secondary Reaction to Threat

Perceived physical or psychological threat → Negative emotional arousal → Problem-focused coping behaviour

(Reduced negative arousal *and* reduced threat)

Occurs when individual decides that threat can be reduced because he or she is competent to deal with threat and can exert control over the situation

■ Responding to Threat: Focus on Emotions, Then Focus on Problem

FIGURE 10.4 We respond to threat in two ways. The initial reaction is an emotional one (Level 1), and we must cope with our feelings of distress—emotion-focused coping. If the threat cannot be reduced in any way, emotional coping is all that can be done. If the threat can be modified or removed, however, it is possible to cope with the problem itself (Level 2)—problem-focused coping.

Source: Based on information in Compas et al., 1991.

Seeking Social Support

Social Support The physical and psychological comfort provided by a person's friends and family members.

Social support—the physical and psychological comfort provided by other people (Sarason, Sarason, & Pierce, 1994)—is beneficial in times of stress, and it is effective regardless of the kind of coping strategies that are used (Frazier et al., 2000). In part, just being with those you like seems helpful. As you might also guess on the basis of attraction research (in Chapter 6), people who desire social support tend to turn to others who are similar to themselves (Morgan, Carder, & Neal, 1997) and those with secure attachment styles are better able to seek, and more likely to receive, social support from others (Davis, Morris, & Kraus, 1998; Mikulincer & Florian, 1995). Further, women are more likely than men to give and to receive social support (Barbee et al., 1993; Porter, Marco et al., 2000).

People are better able to avoid illness in response to threat (and to recover from any illness that develops) if they interact with others rather than remaining isolated (Roy, Steptoe, & Kirschbaum, 1998). The negative effects of workplace stress can be lessened when an employee is given support by co-workers or by the organization (Shinn et al., 1993). During the Gulf War, Israeli military personnel and civilians who exhibited a *secure attachment style* (see Chapter 6) were best able to seek and to receive the benefits of social support (Mikulincer & Florian, 1995). Students whose attachment style is secure report the most social support, and those who are fearful and avoidant report the least (Davis, Morris, & Kraus, 1998). The positive effects of social support noted in research include fewer sports injuries among youngsters (Smith, Smoll, & Ptacek, 1990), feelings of well-being during pregnancy (Zachariah, 1996), lower stress and less postpartum depression among new mothers (Collins et al., 1993; Logsdon, Birkimer, & Barbee, 1997), and decreased risk of heart disease among the elderly (Uchino, Kiecolt-Glaser, & Cacioppo, 1992).

Different amounts of social support are available in different ethnic groups (Gamble & Dalla, 1997). For example, Mexican-American families report larger support networks than Anglophone families. The importance of social support is one explanation of the finding that people who attend weekly religious services live longer than people who do not (Crumm, 1998). Among African-Americans, this difference is remarkable in that those involved in religious activity live about 14 years longer than those who are not involved.

What is it about social support that makes it helpful? One reason for the positive effects is the benefit of communicating one's problems to others. Simple though this may sound, talking about stress tends to reduce one's negative feelings and the incidence of both major and minor health problems (Clark, 1993). In one experimental test of this proposition (Lepore, 1997), students scheduled to take graduate entrance exams were asked to write either about their feelings or about a trivial topic; only those who wrote about their feelings experienced decreased depression (also see Greenberg & Stone, 1992; Hughes, Uhlmann, & Pennebaker, 1994; Pennebaker, 1997). Strangely enough, even writing about an imaginary traumatic experience resulted in fewer illnesses in research participants during the subsequent four weeks, compared to a control group that didn't write about such an event (Greenberg, Wortman, & Stone, 1996). When people suppress their thoughts in order to avoid negative emotions, the immune system is adversely affected (Petrie, Booth, & Pennebaker, 1998). It appears that confession is not only good for the soul, but good for the body as well (Emmons & Colby, 1995; Pennebaker & Graybeal, 2001). However, this is only true if you are at ease with being emotionally expressive to others (Katz & Campbell, 1994) and can be sure of a supportive response from others (Holahan et al., 1997).

KEY POINTS

- *Health psychology* studies the effects of psychological factors on physical illness.
- We receive health-related information on a daily basis, and all of us need to remain informed and willing to change our minds in response to new findings.
- *Stress* is defined as any event that is perceived as a potential source of physical or emotional harm. It can have both direct and indirect effects on the probability of illness.
- *Psychoneuroimmunology* explores the relationships among stress, emotional and behavioural reactions, and the immune system.

- A wide variety of dispositional differences are associated with the ability to resist the negative effects of stress (the *self-healing personality*) as opposed to the tendency to be badly affected by stress (the *disease-prone personality*).

- Effective strategies for *coping* with stress can be *emotion-focused* or *problem-focused* and include increasing one's physical fitness, encouraging *positive affect*, and *regulatory control* of thoughts and activities.

- *Social support* is the physical and psychological comfort provided by others. It is beneficial in times of stress and is related to lower levels of illness.

Applying Social Psychology to the World of Work: Job Satisfaction, Helping, and Leadership

What single activity fills more of most persons' time than any other? For most people the answer is provided by a single word: work. And we don't work alone; on the contrary, most of us work together with other persons in what, from the point of view of social psychology, are social situations. It's not surprising, then, that the principles and findings of social psychology have often been applied to the task of understanding what goes on in work settings. These findings have been put to use in work settings by social psychologists themselves, and by **industrial/organizational psychologists**—psychologists who specialize in studying all aspects of behaviour in work settings, including work settings in many different cultures (e.g., Johns & Xie, 1998; Murnighan, 1993). Similarly, many findings of social psychology have been adapted and put to practical use by persons in management, especially in a field known as **organizational behaviour**—which, as its name suggests, studies human behaviour in organizations (e.g., Greenberg & Baron, 2002).

In this section we'll consider some of the contributions made by social psychology in this respect. Specifically, we'll examine three major topics: *job satisfaction*—employees' attitudes toward their jobs; *organizational citizenship behaviour*—prosocial behaviour (e.g., helping) at work; and *leadership*—the process through which one member of a group, its leader, influences other members to work toward attaining shared group goals (e.g., Yukl, 1994).

Industrial/Organizational Psychologists Psychologists who study all aspects of behaviour in work settings.

Organizational Behaviour A field of study that examines human behaviour in organizations

Job Satisfaction: Attitudes about Work

As we saw in Chapter 3, we are rarely neutral in response to the social world. On the contrary, we hold strong attitudes about many aspects of it. Jobs are no exception to this rule. If asked, most persons can readily report their attitudes toward their jobs, and also toward the organizations that employ them. Attitudes concerning one's own job or work are generally referred to by the term **job satisfaction** (e.g., Wanous, Reichers, & Hudy, 1997), while attitudes toward one's company are known as *organizational commitment* (e.g. Allen & Meyer, 1991; Meyer et al., 1998)—see our discussion of that topic in Chapter 9.

Job Satisfaction Attitudes concerning one's job or work.

Factors Affecting Job Satisfaction

Despite the fact that many jobs are repetitive and boring in nature, surveys involving literally hundreds of thousands of employees conducted over the course of several decades point to a surprising finding: most people indicate that they are quite satisfied with their jobs (e.g., Page & Wiseman, 1993), though wide range of job satisfaction levels do exist. A key question, then, is: what factors influence such attitudes? Research on this issue indicates that two major groups of factors are important: *organizational factors* related

■ Organizational Factors in Job Satisfaction

FIGURE 10.5 How an organization treats its employees is an important factor in their job satisfaction. Clearly, the organization shown here is not interested in generating high levels of job satisfaction among its workers!

to a company's practices or the working conditions provided (see Figure 10.5), and *personal factors* related to the traits of individual employees.

The organizational factors that influence job satisfaction contain few surprises: people report higher satisfaction when they feel that the reward systems in their companies are fair (when raises, promotions, and other rewards are distributed fairly—see Chapter 9); when they like and respect their bosses and believe these persons have their best interests at heart; when they can participate in the decisions that affect them; when the work they perform is interesting rather than boring and repetitive; and when they are neither *overloaded* with too much to do in a given amount of time nor *underloaded* with too little to do (e.g., Callan, 1993; Melamed et al., 1993; Miceli & Lane, 1991). Physical working conditions also play a role: when they are comfortable, employees report higher job satisfaction than when they are uncomfortable (e.g., too hot, too noisy, too crowded; Baron, 1994).

Turning to personal factors, both seniority and status are important. The longer people have been in a given job and the higher their status, the greater their satisfaction (Zeitz, 1990). Similarly, the greater the extent to which jobs are closely matched to individuals' personal interests, the greater their satisfaction (Fricko & Beehr, 1992). In addition, certain personal traits are closely related to job satisfaction. For instance, research findings indicate that differences in what have been termed *core self-evaluations*—individuals' basic assessment about themselves and their self-worth—may play a key role (see Chapter 4) (e.g., Judge, Locke, & Durham, 1997). Such core self-evaluations involve four basic factors: self-esteem, generalized feelings of self-efficacy, locus of control (people's beliefs about their ability to influence their own outcomes), and emotional stability. As you would probably guess, persons with positive core self-evaluations tend to express higher job satisfaction than do those with negative core self-evaluations in many different settings (Judge et al., 1998). Additional evidence indicates that this may be so because persons high in core self-evaluations (i.e., persons who hold a favourable view of themselves and their own abilities) tend to hold more complex, challenging jobs. Such jobs, in turn, offer more autonomy and variety in the tasks they involve (more favourable *job characteristics*), and this, in turn,

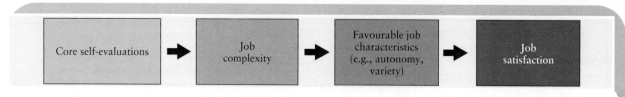

■ Core Self-Evaluations: An Important Determinant of Job Satisfaction

FIGURE 10.6 Persons who are high in their core self-evaluations—their basic assessment of themselves and their own self-worth—report higher job satisfaction than do persons low in core self-evaluations. Recent findings (e.g., Judge, Bono, & Locke, 2000) suggest that this is because persons high in core self-evaluations select more complex jobs. Such jobs offer more favourable characteristics (e.g., they are more challenging, provide more autonomy). These favourable characteristics, in turn, lead to high levels of job satisfaction.

leads to high job satisfaction, as can be seen in Figure 10.6. Research by Judge, Bono, and Locke (2000) provides clear support for this reasoning, so it does appear that core self-evaluations are an important factor in job satisfaction.

 At first glance, the really surprising results in this area are those indicating that job satisfaction may actually have an important genetic component—and that as a result, individuals have a tendency to express either relatively high or relatively low levels of job satisfaction *no matter where they work*. The first research pointing to such conclusions was conducted by Arvey and his colleagues (1989) in the 1980s. They found that the level of job satisfaction reported by identical twins who had been raised apart correlated significantly, and that these correlations were higher than was true for unrelated pairs of individuals. Remember that identical twins share the same genetic makeup, which unrelated individuals, of course, do not. Further, additional findings indicated that as much as 30 percent of variation in job satisfaction from one person to another may stem from genetic factors! While these findings remain somewhat controversial (e.g., Cropanzano & James, 1990), they have been replicated in other studies (e.g., Keller et al., 1992). As we discussed in Chapter 3, it may be that basic tendencies to experience positive or negative affect are inherited and such tendencies would influence feelings about our work.

Although these same results remain somewhat controversial (e.g., Cropanzano & James, 1990), they have been replicated in other studies (e.g., Keller et al., 1992). Thus, it appears that job satisfaction my stem, at least in part, from genetic factors. How can such effects occur? One possibility involves genetically influenced differences in *affective temperament* (e.g., Weiss & Cropanzano, 1996). In other words, genetic factors influence temperament—general tendencies to be upbeat, positive, and happy at one extreme versus depressed, negative, and unhappy at the other. Differences in temperament do indeed seem to stem, at least in part, from genetic factors, and are visible even in very young infants (e.g., Lemery et al., 1999). Such differences may influence how individuals experience emotionally significant events at work (e.g., praise or criticism from one's boss; an argument with a co-worker), and such contrasting experiences, in turn, may affect job satisfaction. Though this explanation remains speculative in nature, additional studies indicate that attitudes toward work are highly stable over time, even when individuals change jobs. Persons who express high levels of satisfaction in one job at a given time are likely to express high levels of satisfaction in a different job at a later time (Steel and Rentsch, 1997). These results, and those of similar studies (e.g., Gerhart, 1987) don't in any way imply that job satisfaction can't be changed—it can. But together, these findings indicate that, as we saw in Chapter 3, changing strongly held attitudes is always a challenging task for those who want to produce such shifts.

The Effects of Job Satisfaction on Task Performance: Weaker than You Might Guess

Are happy workers—people who like their jobs—productive workers? Common sense seems to suggest that they would be, but it's important to remember that job satisfaction is a kind of attitude. And, as we noted in Chapter 3, attitudes are not always strong predictors of overt behaviour. Thus, you should not be surprised to learn that although job satisfaction is related to performance in many jobs, this relationship is relatively weak—correlations in the range of 0.15 to 0.20 (e.g., Judge, 1993; Tett & Meyer, 1993).

Why isn't this relationship stronger? Because several factors may tend to weaken or moderate the impact of job satisfaction on performance. First, if the job is very rigidly structured and absolutely the same level of performance is demanded of the worker (as in assembly-line work), then there is little room for changes in job performance and, therefore, job satisfaction cannot have any influence. Second, there are many additional factors (other than job satisfaction) that can also determine performance: working conditions, the availability of required materials and tools, the extent to which the task is structured, and so on. In many cases, the effects of these factors may be more important than job satisfaction in determining performance. For instance, even employees who love their jobs can't do their best work if the environment in which they work is too hot, too cold, or too noisy. Finally, it is possible that positive attitudes toward one's job—or toward co-workers or the entire organization—may be reflected primarily in forms of behaviour unrelated to performance (e.g., Keller, 1997), for instance, through praising the company to people outside it, conserving its resources, or helping other co-workers. Such actions can have very beneficial effects on an organization, so let's take a closer look at them now.

Prosocial Behaviour at Work: Organizational Citizenship Behaviour

In Chapter 8, we examined many aspects of *prosocial behaviour*—helpful actions that benefit others but have no obvious benefits for the persons who perform them. As we saw in that chapter, prosocial behaviour stems from many different factors and can yield a wide range of effects. That prosocial actions occur in work settings, too, is obvious: employees often help each other with difficult tasks and sometimes even volunteer to do more than is required for their jobs. Research on prosocial behaviour in work settings, therefore, has focused on two important questions: What forms of prosocial behaviour do employees show? And what factors encourage or discourage such behaviour? Let's see what research on these questions has revealed.

While various terms have been used to describe prosocial behaviour in work settings (e.g., Van Dyne & LePine, 1998), most researchers refer to such behaviour as **organizational citizenship behaviour (OCB)**—defined as prosocial behaviour occurring within an organization that may or may not be rewarded by the organization (e.g., Organ, 1997). The fact that such behaviour is not automatically or necessarily rewarded (e.g., through a bonus or a raise in pay) is important, because it suggests that OCB is performed voluntarily, often without any thought of external reward for doing so (see Figure 10.7). Thus, it does indeed qualify as prosocial behaviour according to the definition noted above.

Organizational Citizenship Behaviour (OCB) Prosocial behaviour occurring within an organization that may or may not be rewarded by the organization.

The Nature and Basis for Organizational Citizenship Behaviour

How do individuals working in an organization seek to help one another? Research findings suggest that they do so in many different ways, and that these actions can be directed at helping either other persons (*individual OCB*) or their organization (*organizational OCB*). Examples of individual OCB include helping others who have a

■ Organizational Citizenship Behaviour: Prosocial Behaviour at Work

FIGURE 10.7 Prosocial behaviour at work takes many different forms and can be directed toward other employees or toward the organization itself.

heavy workload, volunteering to do things that are not required, and always being on time and refraining from taking unnecessary breaks. Examples of organizational OCB include "saying positive things about the organization to persons outside it," "attending functions that are not required," and "reading—and paying attention to—memos concerning new company policies or procedures" (Bettencourt, Gwinner, & Meuter, 2001; Skarlicki & Latham, 1997).

What factors lead individuals to engage in various forms of organizational citizenship behaviour? One noted factor is employees' perceptions of the *breadth of their jobs*—what behaviours are required and which are voluntary. The more broadly employees define their jobs, the more likely they are to engage in instances of OCB (Morrison, 1994; Van Dyne & LePine, 1998). This is because the individual with a broader definition will be more willing to take on extra tasks to help another person.

A second factor that you may not be surprised to hear is important to OCB seems to be employees' *perceptions of justice* (Aryee & Chay, 2001) and *organizational commitment* (Randall, Fedor, & Longenecker, 1990), as described in Chapter 9. For example, Aryee and Chay (2001) studied union members and found that perceptions by the members that they were being treated fairly by the union strongly predicted behaviours designed to help it (organizational OCB) and other members (individual OCB). But this was especially true when participants in the study also perceived that the union actively supported them (e.g., cared about their well-being) and was instrumental in helping them reach important goals (e.g., improving working conditions, improving job security).

Finally, research findings indicate that employees do not always engage in OCB without any hope of reward for doing so. On the contrary, growing evidence suggests that managers often take subordinates' willingness to engage in OCB into account when making decisions about their raises and promotions (e.g., Podsakoff, MacKenzie, & Hui, 1993). In other words, managers take note of employees' willingness to be good team players and tend to reward such behaviour. An intriguing study by Hui, Lam, and Law (2000) indicates that employees are well aware of this fact and often engage in OCB as a means of gaining desirable outcomes, such as a promotion.

In their study, Hui, Lam, and Law (2000) asked tellers at a large international bank to rate the extent to which they believed that their chances of promotion would be higher if they engaged in OCB (e.g., volunteered for things that are not required, helped others who had heavy workloads). At the same time, the tellers' supervisors also rated the extent to which the subordinates engaged in OCB. These initial ratings were made three months prior to a decision concerning the tellers' promotions. Three months after this decision, managers again rated the tellers' tendencies to engage in OCB. Hui, Lam, and Law (2000) predicted that the greater the tellers' tendencies to engage in OCB, the more likely they would be to receive a promotion, and that the more strongly the tellers believed that OCB was instrumental to promotion, the more they would engage in such behaviour. Both predictions were supported by the findings. In addition, and most interesting of all, Hui, Lam, and Law (2000) also predicted that employees who perceived OCB as instrumental to their promotion would be more likely to show an actual *drop* in such behaviour after receiving a promotion; in contrast, they predicted that such a drop would not occur among tellers who did not perceive OCB as instrumental for promotion or who were not promoted. As you can see in Figure 10.8, this is precisely what happened: among tellers who were promoted, those who believed that engaging in OCB was important to gaining this reward showed a substantial drop in OCB after receiving the promotion. Other tellers did not show a similar pattern. These findings indicate that OCB at work is often *not* pure altruism. On the contrary, many employees recognize that engaging in OCB will boost their image and further their careers.

In sum, as is true of prosocial behaviour in other settings, individuals' tendencies to engage in such actions at work are influenced by several different factors. To the extent that these are present, OCB will be a frequent occurrence in an organization; to the extent these factors are lacking, such behaviour will occur at a lower rate.

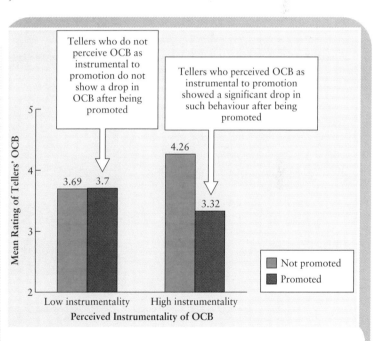

■ Evidence That Employees Sometimes Engage in OCB in Order to Gain Promotion

FIGURE 10.8 Tellers in a large bank who believed that engaging in OCB would increase their chances of promotion actually showed a drop in such behaviour after gaining the promotion they sought. In contrast, tellers who did not perceive OCB as instrumental in gaining promotion or who were not promoted did not show a similar decline in their willingness to help others.

Source: Based on data from Hui, Lam, & Law, 2000.

Leadership The process through which one member of a group (its leader) influences other group members toward attainment of shared group goals.

Leader The group member who exerts the greatest influence within the group.

Great Person Theory A view of leadership suggesting that great leaders possess certain traits that set them apart from most human beings, traits that are possessed by all such leaders no matter when or where they lived.

Leadership: Patterns of Influence within Groups

Research on leadership has long been part of social psychology, but it is also an applied topic studied by other fields as well (e.g., Bass, 1998). We could easily devote an entire chapter to this topic, so to hold the length of this discussion within bounds, we'll focus on the following topics: (1) why some individuals, but not others, become leaders; (2) contrasting *styles* of leadership; and (3) the nature of *charismatic* and *transformational* leadership.

But what is **leadership**? To a degree, it's like love: easy to recognize, but hard to define (see Chapter 6). However, psychologists generally use this term to mean the process through which one member of a group (its leader) influences other group members toward attainment of shared group goals (Yukl, 1994). In other words, being a leader involves influence—a **leader** is the group member who exerts most influence within the group.

Who Becomes a Leader? The Role of Traits and Situations

Are some people born to lead? Common sense suggests that this is so. Famous leaders such as Alexander the Great, Queen Elizabeth I, and more recently, Pierre Trudeau—see Figure 10.9—seem to differ from ordinary people in several respects. Such observations led early researchers to formulate the **great person theory** of leadership—the

■ The Great Person Theory of Leadership

FIGURE 10.9 According to the great person theory, all great leaders share certain traits that set them apart from other persons, and they possess these traits no matter where or when they lived. Research findings offer little support for this view, but research does suggest that leaders differ from other persons with respect to certain traits.

Queen Elizabeth I

Pierre Elliot Trudeau

Alexander the Great

view that great leaders possess certain traits that set them apart from most human beings, traits that are possessed by all such leaders, no matter when or where they lived.

Currently, leadership is seen as a product of many factors. However, recent research has shown that leaders often possess special qualities (Kirkpatrick & Locke, 1991). They rate higher than most people on the following traits: *drive*—the desire for achievement coupled with high energy and resolution; *self-confidence*; *creativity*; and *leadership motivation*—the desire to be in charge and exercise authority over others. Perhaps the most important single characteristic of leaders, however, is a high level of *flexibility*—the ability to recognize what actions or approaches are required in a given situation and then to act accordingly (Zaccaro, Foti, & Kenny, 1991).

So, can we conclude that some persons are more suited for leadership than others? Research suggests that, to some extent, the answer is yes—persons who possess certain traits, such as those listed above, are more likely to become leaders and to succeed in this role than are persons who do not possess these traits or who possess them to a lesser degree. It is also clear, however, that leaders do *not* operate in a social vacuum. On the contrary, different groups, facing different tasks and problems, seem to require different types of leaders, or at least leaders who demonstrate contrasting styles (House & Podsakoff, 1994; Locke, 1991). So traits, while they do indeed matter where leadership is concerned, are only part of the total picture. With this thought in mind, let's take a closer look at precisely *how* leaders lead—the contrasting styles they can adopt.

How Leaders Lead: Contrasting Styles and Approaches

All leaders are definitely not alike. They may share certain traits to a degree, but they differ greatly in terms of personal style or approach to leadership (e.g., George, 1995; Peterson, 1997). While there are probably as many different *styles* of leadership as there are leaders, research on leader behaviour or style suggests that, in fact, most leaders can be placed along a small number of dimensions relating to their overall approach to leadership. Two such dimensions emerged in very early research on leadership (e.g., Weissenberg & Kavanagh, 1972) and have been repeatedly confirmed. The first is known as **initiating structure** (or *production orientation*). Leaders high on this dimension are primarily concerned with getting the job done. They engage in actions such as organizing work, urging subordinates to follow the rules, setting goals, and making leader and subordinate roles explicit. In contrast, leaders low on this dimension engage in such actions to a lesser degree.

The second dimension is known as **consideration** (or *person orientation*). Leaders high on this dimension focus on establishing good relations with their subordinates and on being liked by them. They engage in such actions as doing favours for subordinates, explaining things to them, and watching out for their welfare. Leaders low on this dimension, in contrast, do not really care how well they get along with their subordinates. (See Figure 10.10 for an overview of these two basic dimensions of leader behaviour.)

Is either of these two styles superior? Not really. Both offer a mixed pattern of advantages and disadvantages. High consideration (high concern for people) can result in improved group morale, but because such leaders do not like to tell subordinates what to do or give them negative feedback, efficiency sometimes suffers. In contrast, when leaders are high on initiating structure, efficiency may be high but subordinates may conclude that the leader does not really care about them. As a result, their commitment to the organization may suffer. Overall, though, it appears that leaders who are high on both dimensions may have an edge in many situations. In other words, leaders who are concerned with establishing good relations with their subordinates *and* with maintaining efficiency and productivity may often prove superior to leaders showing other patterns of behaviour.

Two additional dimensions of leader behaviour that have been uncovered by careful research involve the extent to which leaders make all the decisions themselves or allow

Initiating Structure A key dimension of leader behaviour. Leaders high on this dimension are primarily concerned with getting the job done (that is, with production); also known as *production-orientation*.

Consideration A key dimension of leader behaviour; also known as *person-orientation*. Leaders high on this dimension focus on establishing good relations with their subordinates and on being liked by them.

■ Leader Behaviour:
Two Basic Dimensions

FIGURE 10.10 The behaviour of leaders has been found to vary along the two dimensions shown here: *consideration*, which involves concern for people and good relations with them, and *initiating structure*, which involves concern for production and task completion. Any given leader can be high or low on each of these dimensions.

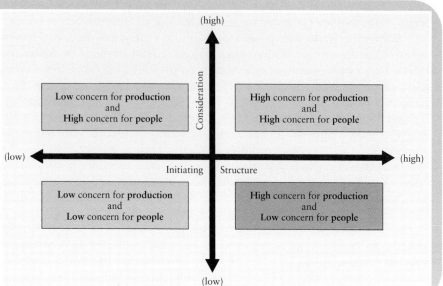

participation by group members (an *autocratic-participative* dimension), and the extent to which leaders try to run the show by closely directing the activities of all group members (a *directive-permissive* dimension) (Muczyk & Reimann, 1987; Peterson, 1997). If you think back over your own experiences, you can probably recall leaders who were high or low on both of these dimensions. Research shows that many employees dislike the micromanagement of leaders who are autocratic or directive because it suggests that their manager has no confidence in them. However, being high or low on each of these dimensions is not necessarily good or bad from the point of view of leader effectiveness—it depends on the situation. For instance, under emergency conditions, when decisions have to be made quickly, an autocratic style may be helpful; under more relaxed conditions, though, most persons prefer participative leaders who let them have input into the decision-making process. The same is true for the directive-permissive dimension; when subordinates are new at their jobs, they need direction from the leader; once they have mastered their jobs, though, it is usually better for the leader to take a step back and leave them alone.

Transformational or Charismatic Leaders: Leaders Who Change the World

Have you ever seen films of Pierre Trudeau? John F. Kennedy? Nelson Mandela? Martin Luther King, Jr.? If so, you may have noticed that there seemed to be something special about these leaders. As you listened to their speeches, you may have found yourself being moved by their words and stirred by the vigour of their presentations. You are definitely not alone in such reactions: these leaders exerted powerful effects on many millions of persons and, by doing so, changed their societies. Leaders who accomplish such feats are termed **charismatic leaders** (or, sometimes, *transformational* leaders; House & Howell, 1992; Kohl, Steers, & Terborg, 1995).

What characteristics make certain leaders charismatic? Research has indicated that personality plays a part (e.g., Barrick & Mount, 1991). For instance, in one large-scale investigation, Judge and Bono (2000) had hundreds of persons who were participating in community leadership programs complete questionnaires designed to measure their standing on each of five personality dimensions. Results indicated that three of these were most important to transformational leadership: *agreeableness*—the tendency to be kind, gentle, trusting, and trustworthy—was strongly related to such leadership;

Charismatic Leaders
Leaders who exert exceptionally powerful effects on large numbers of followers or on entire societies; also known as *transformational leaders*.

extraversion—the tendency to be outgoing, assertive, and active; and *openness to experience*—the tendency to be creative, imaginative, and perceptive.

Further, while there is still discussion in this area, most researchers would generally agree (e.g., Bass, 1985; Judge & Bono, 2000) that transformational leaders have the following core characteristics: (1) *idealized influence*—they serve as a charismatic role model to followers (i.e., they show charisma); (2) *intellectual stimulation*—they stimulate creativity among followers by questioning assumptions and the status quo; (3) *individual consideration*—they pay attention to and support the individual needs of followers; and (4) *inspirational motivation*—they articulate a clear, inspiring vision to followers. One way they do this is to engage in a special kind of *framing* that adds extra meaning and purpose to the goals and actions of a group (Conger, 1991). As one expert in this area puts it, charismatic leaders somehow "make ordinary people do extraordinary things" (Conger, 1991). Of course, this may not always be towards positive ends, as the influence of Adolf Hitler or some cult leaders attests.

Finally, researchers agree that transformational leaders are often masters of *impression management*, a process we described in Chapter 7. When this skill is added to the traits and behaviours mentioned above, the ability of such leaders to influence large numbers of followers loses some of its mystery. Transformational leaders produce the profound effects they do because they possess characteristics that, together, arm them with an impressive personal style-one that many people find hard to resist.

Cultural Differences in Leadership: North American and Asian CEOs

Are the kinds of leadership processes we have described above universal—present in all cultures? Or does leadership operate differently in different cultures? In the twenty-first century, it seems more and more evident that in economic terms we are globally interdependent: an economic downturn in of one part of the world will have a negative impact on other parts of the world. With such interdependence it becomes increasingly important that the leaders of business understand each other. However, significant differences have been noted in the style of such leaders in different countries (Bhagat, Kedia, Crawford, & Kaplan, 1990; Kotter, 1982).

When comparing leadership in Asian and North American corporations, researchers point to *cultural values* as the source of leadership differences (see Chapter 3 for a discussion of cultural values). For example, Doktor (1990) notes that business leaders in Japan and Korea perceive that what affects one part of society may well affect other parts as well—in line with the collectivism of the culture, they emphasize the *interdependence* of different segments of society. Thus, they view their corporate decisions in a broad context that takes account of the decisions' consequences for other segments of society outside the business community. In North America, in contrast, decisions tend to be viewed in a somewhat narrower context, which focuses on a company and its goals. How do these contrasting cultural values influence the leadership style of Asian and North American CEOs? Doktor contends that because Japanese and Korean managers consider the broader context of their actions and decisions, they feel more strongly than North American CEOs that these should not be rushed.

In support of these contentions, Doktor carried out a comparative study of the heads of major companies in the United States, Japan, Korea, and Hong Kong (1990). He found that while CEOs in each country spent about the same proportions of their days working alone (25 percent) and working in groups (75 percent), the duration of each task they performed varied greatly. In the United States, almost 50 percent of all tasks were of short duration (completed in only nine minutes or less). In contrast, the percentage of short tasks in Japan and Korea was much lower (10 percent and 14 percent, respectively). The percentage for Hong Kong, where cultural values are a mix between the traditional Chinese values and Western individualism, was in between these two.

A second cultural value that has been considered important is *power distance*, referring to the extent of hierarchical status-differences in a society—see Chapter 3. Those nations that score highly on Hofstede's measure of power distance also tend to be high in collectivism (Hofstede, 1983). In such cultures, there tends to be a strictly maintained hierarchy, which limits communication between those at different levels of a society or organization. For example, Smith and colleagues (1999) found that leaders in high power distance cultures did not refer to subordinates when making decisions or resolving group problems. Similarly, in a survey of the attitudes of pilots and flight attendants from eight nations, Merrit and Helmreich (1996) found that subjects from Asian nations endorsed autocratic leadership styles, with *top-down* communication and decision making (communication and decisions come from the leaders to the followers rather than the reverse). However, in many collective cultures there are also mechanisms whereby members can contribute to the leader's decisions through participating in collective consultations (Smith & Bond, 1998).

One study of attitudes to leadership styles in electronic plants in the United States, Mexico, Japan, Taiwan, and Korea (Howell, et al., 1997) found that subjects from all five nations positively rated leaders who were supportive and made rewards contingent on performance. However, directive leadership was more positively rated in Mexico, Korea, and Taiwan than in the United States and Japan, and participative leadership was endorsed only by those in the United States. This and similar studies (see Smith & Bond, 1999) suggest that the relationship between leaders and their groups will vary in subtle ways among nations that we consider collectivistic. We cannot assume a uniform leadership style.

So even today, when modern technology dictates the form of many business practices, cultural differences can and do play a key role in shaping the actions and perceptions of business leaders. As T. Fujisawa, the cofounder of Honda Corporation, once put it, "Japanese and American management are 95 percent the same—and differ in all important respects." We might add that those differences can be traced, to an important degree, to differences in cultural values.

KEY POINTS

- People spend more time at work than in any other single activity. Because they often work with others, the findings and principles of social psychology help to explain behaviour in work settings.

- Job satisfaction is an individual's attitude toward her or his job. Job satisfaction is influenced by organizational factors, such as working conditions and the fairness of reward systems, and personal factors such as seniority, status, and specific personality traits. Research suggests that job satisfaction is often highly stable over time for many persons and that it may be influenced by genetic factors.

- The relationship between job satisfaction and task performance is relatively weak, partly because many factors other than work-related attitudes influence performance.

- Individuals often engage in prosocial behaviour at work, known as *organizational citizenship behaviour* (OCB). OCB is influenced by several factors, including job satisfaction, the extent to which employees feel they are being treated fairly by their organization, organizational commitment, and the extent to which they define their job responsibilities broadly.

- *Leadership* refers to the process through which one member of a group (its leader) influences other group members toward the attainment of shared group goals.

- Although the *great person theory* of leadership is no longer supported, research findings suggest that leaders do indeed have special traits.

- Leaders vary with respect to their behaviour or style. Classic research in social psychology suggested that leaders vary in terms of two basic dimensions: *consideration* and *initiating structure*. In addition, leaders vary along two other key dimensions: autocratic–participative and directive-permissive.

- *Transformational (charismatic) leadership* exerts profound effects on followers and often changes their societies. Research suggests that it is associated with certain personality characteristics (agreeableness, extroversion, and openness to experience) and stems from certain behaviours by leaders, such as stating a clear vision, inspirational motivation and framing, and possessing a strong personal style.

- Cross-cultural research suggests that major differences between leaders in Asian and North American corporations stem from differences in cultural values such as the extent to which *interdependence* of the corporation and society is recognized and *power-distance*.

Social Psychology and the Legal System

If the real world matched our ideals, the judicial process would provide an elaborate and totally fair set of procedures that ensured objective, unbiased, and consistent decisions about violations of criminal and civil laws. Our legal and judicial system ordinarily strives to live up to that ideal—not to leave justice to the arbitrary whims of legal professionals or to chance. Yet research in **forensic psychology** (psychology specifically concerned with legal issues) repeatedly indicates that the human participants in the process do not always function according to rational guidelines (Davis, 1989). Social psychologists have provided a considerable body of evidence indicating that when people interact, their behaviour and their judgments are affected by attitudes, cognitions, and emotions that may be biased, irrational, and unfair. And those same factors are equally relevant when people evaluate and interact in the justice system. Research in the area of forensic psychology has expanded tremendously in the past decade (e.g., Gudjonsson & Haward, 1998; Loftus, 1992). We will concentrate on examining four of the major figures in the justice system: (1) the media and public opinion; (2) police procedures; (3) eyewitnesses; (4) the defendant.

Forensic Psychology
Psychological research and theory that deals with the effects of cognitive, affective, and behavioural factors on legal processes.

Before the Trial Begins: Effects of Police Procedures and Media Coverage

Long before a criminal case reaches a courtroom, two major factors influence both the testimony that will eventually be presented and the pretrial attitudes of the jurors: (1) how the police deal with witnesses and suspects, and (2) how information about the case is presented in the media.

Police Procedures

Long before a case reaches a courtroom, it is the job of the police to investigate and accumulate evidence that will be presented during a trial. Social psychological factors can influence the success of this process, as police interact with and question the suspects and eyewitnesses.

Research indicates that most people are very likely to obey the law and to accept the outcomes of legal procedures so long as they believe that the laws and the procedures are fair and just (Miller & Ratner, 1996; Tyler et al., 1997). Each individual's beliefs are based in part on personal experiences with the legal system, and such experiences begin with the police. In both the United Kingdom and North America, most citizens agree that police investigators should stress an *inquisitorial approach*—a search for the truth—rather than an *adversarial approach*—an attempt to prove guilt (Williamson, 1993). In the United Kingdom, legislation was passed to provide training for police officers in an effort to persuade them to conduct interviews in a cooperative way—simply investigating the facts. One reason for such legislation is that court rulings on both sides of the Atlantic consistently agree that confessions obtained by means of coercive confrontation are unreliable and inadmissible (Gudjonsson, 1993).

Does police behaviour actually conform to the guidelines preferred by the public and mandated by the courts? To answer that question, a Scotland Yard study was designed to determine exactly how British detectives go about the interrogation process (Williamson, 1993). Observations were made of actual interactions between detectives and suspects, and the officers were found to differ in their goals and in their style. Despite the new training that stressed fact-finding to obtain evidence, many of the detectives remained oriented toward obtaining a confession. Beyond differing in their goals, detectives also differed in their style—they were either friendly and cooperative or angry and confrontational. When the detectives were classified with respect to their goals and their styles, as shown in Figure 10.11, they were split about fifty-fifty with respect to seeking evidence versus seeking a confession, but 70 percent were found to employ a cooperative approach rather than a confrontational one. Some observers believe, however, that most law officers actually do seek confessions but have learned to limit such questioning to times when their behaviour is not being observed or recorded (Moston & Stephenson, 1993).

Whatever the style of interrogation, its impact on the person being questioned is increased by the physical setting of the questioning (Schooler & Loftus, 1986; Smith & Ellsworth, 1987). It is not surprising that investigators much prefer to conduct a formal investigation in an intimidating location such as police headquarters rather than in nonthreatening surroundings such as the suspect's home or place of work. Both the setting and the authority of the questioner (a government representative) reinforce the ordinary citizen's belief that whoever is asking the questions is an expert possessing detailed

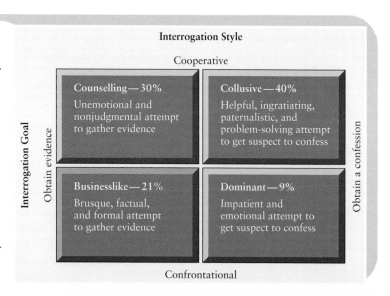

■ Evidence versus a Confession; Cooperation versus Confrontation

FIGURE 10.11 Police interrogations can be classified according to the goal of the questioning (to obtain evidence or to obtain a confession) and the style of the person asking the questions (cooperative or confrontational). In a British study, about half of the detectives were oriented toward obtaining facts and half toward obtaining a confession. With respect to style, however, over two-thirds engaged in cooperative behaviour and less than a third in confrontational behaviour.

Source: Based on data from Williamson, 1993.

knowledge of the case (Gudjonsson & Clark, 1986) and should not be opposed. In effect, the individual finds himself or herself as the target of social influence procedures designed to obtain compliance or even obedience, as described in Chapter 7.

Under these circumstances, three factors operate to encourage compliant and obedient responding. The witness usually feels (1) some *uncertainty* about the "right" answers, (2) some degree of *trust* in the officer asking the questions, and (3) an unspoken *expectation* that he or she is supposed to know the answer. As a result, rather than saying "I don't know" or "I don't remember" or "I'm not sure," most people tend to provide answers, at least tentative ones. Such answers are often provided by the use of **leading questions**. This type of questioning *leads* the witness towards a particular answer—one that the interrogator implies that he or she expects (e.g., Smith & Ellsworth, 1987). And once a person provides an answer, he or she is inclined to accept its accuracy, especially if the interrogator provides immediate reinforcement with a nod or by saying "good," or the like. One result is that the person being questioned can honestly believe and even "remember" the details of something that never happened.

Interrogators need not resort to heavy-handed methods to elicit testimony or confession (Kassin & McNall, 1991). A "soft-sell" technique can produce the same ends. For example, in interacting with a suspect, an interrogator can *minimize* the strength of the evidence and the seriousness of the charge, implying that punishment will be mild or seeming to blame the victim for what happened. Kassin and McNall (1991) point out, however, that although this soft-sell technique may seem to be noncoercive, it is simply a less obvious way to elicit compliance. In effect, the suspect confesses after being lulled into a false sense of security.

The use of social influence techniques to elicit confessions sometimes goes a step beyond the soft sell; for example, deceit, such as lying to a suspect about evidence, can be used. Kassin examined the power of *deceit* in obtaining a false confession (e.g., Kassin & Kiechel, 1996). From his review of such techniques, Kassin (1997) concludes that the criminal justice system currently does not provide adequate protection to the innocent person who becomes a suspect and that confessions obtained by means of manipulative procedures should not be considered credible.

Media Publicity

On a regular basis, daily newspapers, radio and television news programs, and sometimes magazines and books devote a lot of space to information about crimes, accidents, and lawsuits, especially if they are dramatic or unusual or involve famous people (Barnes, 1989; Henry, 1991). One of the potentially negative aspects of a free press in this instance is that public opinion (including the opinion of individuals who might later be jurors) can be affected by how such news is presented. In Canada, the details of cases or evidence are sometimes suppressed by the courts if their publication might detract from a fair trial. An example is the ban on reporting of evidence during Karla Homolka's manslaughter trial to prevent biasing a future jury during the subsequent murder trial of her husband, Paul Bernardo. There were objections by Canadian media to those restrictions. It has been said, only half jokingly, that the United States sequesters a jury after the trial begins, but Canada "sequesters" the public beforehand (Farnsworth, 1995). The crucial task for research has been to document how potential jurors are affected by exposure to media publicity.

In research on two highly publicized cases involving defendants accused of distributing marijuana and a defendant charged with murdering a police officer, Moran and Cutler (1991) surveyed potential jurors. They found in each instance that the more knowledge people had about the details of the case, the more blame they placed on those arrested for the crimes. The investigators also found that knowledge of the crimes was

Leading Questions Questions that are worded so as to suggest and elicit answers that the interrogator expects.

unrelated to whether the respondents believed they could make impartial judgments. Given people's mistaken faith in their own lack of bias, Judge O'Connell (1988) suggests that asking potential jurors whether they can be fair and impartial is as useless as asking a person who is a practising alcoholic if he or she has the drinking under control.

Not only does media publicity affect people's judgment about a specific case, but media information also has more general effects. For example, when people are exposed to descriptions of very serious crimes, they then view other crimes and other offenders more harshly than if they have not had such exposure (Roberts & Edwards, 1989)—this would appear to be a *priming effect* (see Chapter 2). Presumably, they interpret all crime more negatively because of exposure to a few serious cases.

Media reportage of crime also appears to influence the public's perception of the *prevalence* of crime. Anthony Doob of the University of Toronto's Centre of Criminology has been investigating such issues for many years (e.g., Doob & Macdonald, 1979; Roberts & Doob, 1990). Statistics for 2001 show that crime rates in Canada, including those for violent crime, have been falling over the past decade, with the homicide rate at its lowest since 1968 (Statistics Canada, 2001).

Despite this good news, many Canadians feel unsafe in their own neighbourhoods. An international survey of criminal victimization in 1998 in eleven industrialized countries (Besserer, 1998) asked individuals how safe they felt "walking alone in your area after dark." Canada was one of the three countries with the lowest ratings. Further, a Canadian victimization survey reported that 46 percent of Canadians believed that the level of crime has increased in the past five years, and this was during a period when it was actually declining (Gartner & Doob, 1994).

Why should our perceptions be so at odds with reality? Doob's research indicates that media publicity may be at fault insofar as it tends to overrepresent violent crime, as well as report it inadequately (Doob, 1985; Roberts & Doob, 1990). For example, Doob found that over 50 percent of newspaper crime reporting in Canada concerned violent crime (1985), though it is in fact a small percentage of all crime. Further, 95 percent of the public cite the news media as the principle source of information about criminal cases (Roberts & Doob, 1990). The *availability heuristic* clearly applies here (see Chapter 2)—when we make assumptions about the crime rate and its dangers, we are relying on the biased information that is available to us.

One place where media publicity has certainly played a role in public opinion is in the issue of gun control. Beyond media effects, however, does the widespread availability of firearms in our society have an impact on crime? We will examine this controversial subject in the following On the Applied Side section.

On the **Applied Side**

The Weapons Effect: A Social Psychological Perspective on the Impact of Firearms

In February 2000, a boy in first grade took a gun to school and shot a six-year-old classmate. This was perhaps the most shocking in a series of incidents in recent years of students arming themselves and killing others at school. The majority of the incidents we have heard about took place in the United States. But in Taber, Alberta, a 14-year-old boy shot and killed another student in school and might have gone on to kill more if not disarmed. One of the major questions raised by these incidents is whether the widespread availability of firearms contributes to such violence. When this is suggested, it is sometimes countered with the National Rifle Association slogan: "Guns don't kill people, people kill people." What does research suggest?

The first source of information comes from social psychological experiments examining what has been termed the *weapons effect* (the stimulating effect of the mere presence of a gun or other weapon on aggressive impulses).

A noted authority on aggression research, Leonard Berkowitz, conducted the original experiment demonstrating the weapons effect (Berkowitz & Lepage, 1967). Subjects were initially angered by both a series of mild but annoying electric shocks and a negative evaluation delivered by another subject (actually an experimenter). They were then given the opportunity to reciprocate and were taken into a laboratory where the shocking apparatus was located. Researchers varied whether or not subjects were simultaneously exposed to violent weapons. In one condition, a shotgun and a revolver were on the table beside the shocking apparatus, in a second condition there were sports racquets, and in the control condition there was nothing at all. The experimenter appeared surprised to see the objects on the table and pushed them aside in a matter-of-fact way, explaining that another experimenter must have left them there. Berkowitz predicted that the presence of the weapons, even though they were not relevant to the subjects' task, would facilitate aggression. Results supported this hypothesis: subjects exposed to the firearms delivered significantly more shocks than those in the other two conditions. The weapons effect has been replicated many times and in a number or countries including Sweden, Belgium, and Italy (see Berkowitz, 1993).

A second body of research consists of correlational studies from a wide variety of disciplines examining the relationship between firearms availability and violence of various kinds. This research relates crime statistics to levels of gun ownership or the restrictiveness of gun laws. A number of reviews of this complex literature exist (Cukier, 1998; Gabor, 1994; Lester, 1984). To summarize from these, the strongest relationship appears to be between firearms availability and homicide rates in general, and with rates of homicide using firearms in particular. Many studies have shown that the greater the availability of firearms, the higher the homicide rate (e.g., Cook, 1979, 1987; Killias, 1993; Lester, 1991). Figure 10.12 shows an example of this relationship for four English-speaking countries taken from a recent international study of firearms regulation (United Nations, 1998).

There is heated debate about interpretation of this correlational research (e.g., Kleck, 1991; Lott, 1998; Mundt, 1990, 1993) and some studies do not find the relationships mentioned above—they suggest that gun control will have little impact on crime (e.g., Kleck, 1991; Mauser, 1996, cited in Cukier, 1998). Further, some research demonstrates a *deterrent effect* of gun availability (Kleck, 1991, 1988). For example, John Lott (1998), in his book *More Guns, Less Crime* provides data suggesting that as gun laws become less restrictive (and guns become more available), violent crimes decrease, particularly robbery and homicide. This and most studies showing a deterrent effect come from the United States and use data from within that country only (Gabor, 1994).

Among methodological problems raised by critics of the deterrent effect research (e.g., Hemenway, 1998; Gabor, 1994; Webster, Vernick, Ludwig, & Lester, 1997), a major limitation is a lack of variation in levels of firearms availability. Since firearms are so widely available in the United States, there is insufficient opportunity to examine whether the absence of firearms is associated with lower levels of violence. For this we need to turn to international data such as that shown in Figure 10.12. Firearms are much less prevalent in other Western countries and so is violent crime, and homicide in particular (United Nations, 1998). Also, deterrent effects appear to be temporary and disappear when long-term trends are examined (McDowall, et al., 1989, 1991).

In summary, there is substantial research supporting the view that increased firearms availability can contribute to rates of homicide—though this research is not without its detractors. A final question that these data raise is: If greater firearms availability contributes to higher homicide rates, what are the mechanisms through which this could occur?

Beyond the obvious fact that guns are by nature more lethal than knives or clubs (Cook, 1987), two important social psychological processes may be at work (Berkowitz, 1993).

First, the social learning view might suggest that the more firearms available, the greater the opportunity for modelling their use. For example, the string of school student shootings may be what are termed "copycat" crimes—that is, modelled on each other. The incident in Taber, Alberta, occurred not long after a highly publicized case at Columbine High School in Colorado where 12 students and a teacher were killed. Modelling from films or video games has been suggested as a factor influencing the two teenaged boys who committed those murders. And parental modelling may have contributed to the actions of the first grade boy who killed the six-year old—his father had been prosecuted for gun-related offences (*Globe & Mail*, March 1, 2000, p. A8).

Second, the existence of a weapons effect undermines the assertion that "Guns don't kill people, people kill people." This phenomenon suggests that the greater the availability of guns, the more violence will be triggered. Berkowitz (1993) has explained the weapons effect as occurring because a gun acts as an **aggressive cue**-a stimulus that past experience has taught us is associated with aggression. Such cues work to increase the likelihood of impulsive aggression

Aggressive Cue
An environmental cue that has become associated with violence and has the effect of intensifying or activating impulsive aggression.

(rather than premeditated or deliberate aggression) by raising emotional arousal and increasing cognitive priming related to aggression. These notions are incorporated in the GAAM theory of aggression (see Chapter 8). Many aggressive cues exist in our environments but guns are particularly associated with extreme aggression—killing. As Berkowitz put it, "Guns not only permit violence, they can stimulate it as well. The finger pulls the trigger, but the trigger may also be pulling the finger" (1968, p. 22).

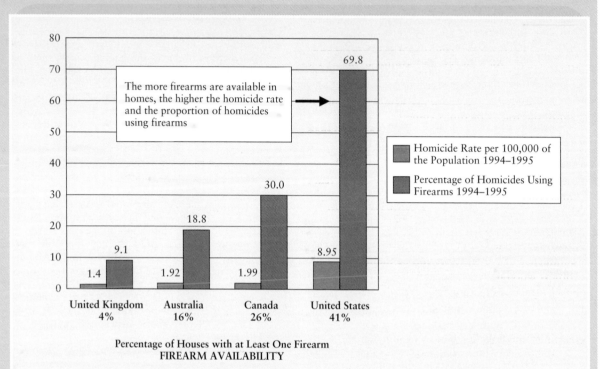

The more firearms are available in homes, the higher the homicide rate and the proportion of homicides using firearms

Homicide Rate per 100,000 of the Population 1994–1995

Percentage of Homicides Using Firearms 1994–1995

Percentage of Houses with at Least One Firearm
FIREARM AVAILABILITY

■ The Relationship between Firearm Availability and Homicide in Four English-Speaking Countries

FIGURE 10.12 Correlational research relating firearms and violence finds the strongest relationship between homicide rates and availability of firearms. As shown, firearms are available in only 4 percent of the homes in the United Kingdom but in 41 percent of homes in the United States. The homicide rate in 1994 was six times higher in the U.S. than in the U.K., and the proportion of firearms used in homicides was almost eight times higher.

Source: Adapted from United Nations International Study on Firearm Regulation, 1998.

The Eyewitness

Eyewitness Accuracy and Memory

Each year in courtrooms, witnesses present crucial evidence concerning many suspects (Goldstein, Chance, & Schneller, 1989). This testimony has a major impact on jurors, even though eyewitnesses are frequently wrong (Wolf & Bugaj, 1990). Altogether, jurors are most convinced by such characteristics as speaking style (speaking without hesitation in long elaborate sentences and without contradictions), inclusion of many details, and age (children are believed less than adults; Bell & Loftus, 1988; Leippe, Manion, & Romanczyk, 1992; Whitley & Greenberg, 1986). The more nervous the witness appears, the less accurate he or she is perceived to be (Bothwell & Jalil, 1992).

Because the events that are witnessed are almost always totally unexpected, of brief duration, and stressful (Hosch & Bothwell, 1990), even the most honest, intelligent, and well-meaning person may be inaccurate when asked to recall the details of a past event or to identify a suspect. Studies of mistakes (wrongful convictions) indicate that inaccurate eyewitness identification is the single most important reason that innocent defendants are convicted (Wells, 1993; Wells, Luus, & Windschitl, 1994).

Many factors have been found to affect the accuracy of witnesses in laboratory studies (Wells & Luus, 1990). For example, accuracy decreases if there is a weapon in the suspect's hand (Tooley et al., 1987) or if the suspect and the witness belong to different racial or ethnic groups (Platz & Hosch, 1988). Yuille and Tollestrup of the University of British Columbia found that eyewitnesses who had been drinking alcohol were less accurate than sober eyewitnesses in recalling the details of a staged theft, but they were equally able to recognize the thief's picture (Yuille & Tollestrup, 1990). Other research has shown that real-life witnesses have a higher level of accuracy than is usually found in laboratory studies or simulations, perhaps because the real-life events of a crime are more important to witnesses (Yuille, 1983; Yuille & Cutshall, 1986). Such findings highlight the need for confirmation of laboratory results through studying real criminal cases. In general, such replication is crucial to the validity of the findings of forensic psychology and to the confidence that the legal system can have in psychological experts (Ogloff & Cronshaw, 2001).

When giving testimony, a witness's certainty is found to be unrelated to his or her accuracy (Bothwell, Deffenbacher, & Brigham, 1987). In fact, one study demonstrated that the confidence of eyewitnesses can be manipulated (Luus & Wells, 1994). For instance, an eyewitness who falsely identifies a suspect can become highly confident if positive feedback is given by the investigating detective—"Another witness picked out the same one you did." This confidence remains high (a *perseverance effect*) even if the choice is later discredited.

Remembering Past Events

You may have heard of "recovered memories": instances in which an adult, often during therapy, suddenly remembers a traumatic past event, most often centring on having been the victim of sexual abuse. More women than men report such memories, possibly because more young girls than young boys are sexually abused in childhood. Several recent celebrity autobiographies contain such accounts. However, some commentators have emphasized that such memories can be inaccurate (Humphreys, 1998).

At present, debate over **repressed memory** (totally forgetting a traumatic incident or incidents) has generated polarized opinions and strong emotions (Dineen, 1998; Pope, 1996). There is a conflict between (1) those who believe that victims accurately recall previously forgotten traumatic events, and that events relating to child molestation should be prosecuted (Brown, 1997); and (2) those who believe that false recovered memories are subtly encouraged by well-meaning therapists and others. They inadvertently engage in "memory-recovery" practices, leading suggestible clients to remember events that did not actually occur (Frank, 1996; Lindsay, 1998; Loftus, 1998).

Repressed Memory
A form of psychogenic amnesia: forgetting the details of a traumatic event in order to protect against the anxiety and fear associated with that event.

Considering how easy it is to encourage false confessions and false memories about a very recent event, false memories of events in the distant past should be at least as easy to create and perhaps more so. Indeed, a number of researchers have demonstrated that it is not difficult to create false childhood memories among adult subjects (DuBreuil, Garry, & Loftus, 1998; Loftus, 1997; Loftus, Coan, & Pickrell, 1996; Pezdek, Finger, & Hodge, 1997).

Studies of other types of traumatic experiences that result in memory loss (e.g., automobile accidents, natural disasters, combat, attempted suicide, and the death of a parent are some examples) can be informative (Arrigo & Pezdek, 1997). This research indicates that sometimes memory of trauma is quite accurate and sometimes quite false. These findings suggest that recovered memories of childhood sexual abuse are also sometimes true and sometimes not, and that it would be extremely useful to develop ways to differentiate accurate memories from inaccurate ones (Poole & Lindsay, 1998). Further, recent research shows that some people are more easily led to false memories than are others, and some are better at leading another person to have such memories than are others (Porter, Birt, et al., 2000). As one example, the creation of a false memory is facilitated when the participant is low in extraversion and the interviewer is high in extraversion. Based on a review of the literature, Stephen Porter and colleagues at Dalhousie (Porter, Campbell, Birt, & Woodworth, 2003) have formulated guidelines for forensic professionals when evaluating allegations that involve memory of events long past. These are shown in Table 10.2.

When evaluating allegations involving memory of long-past events, Porter and colleagues recommend four guidelines for forensic professionals in psychology and the law. Evaluation should focus on the context of memory recall or disclosure, the content of memory, the individual's susceptibility to memory distortion, and the presence of corroborative evidence. It is emphasized that tools are available for measuring some of these factors (e.g., dissociative tendencies and historical memory content) and that a well-trained psychologist should perform such assessments.

TABLE 10.2 Guidelines for Evaluation of Historical Memory for Criminal Incidents

	Evaluation of	**Less Credibility**	**More Credibility**
Guideline 1	The context of memory recall or disclosure	If suggestive therapeutic or interview techniques (e.g., hypnosis or guided imagery) have been used to help the recall process.	If memories are recovered in a spontaneous manner and in the absence of secondary gains.
Guideline 2	The content of memory	If the memory was not recalled for an extended period of time and later recovered, particularly when suggestive techniques were used in the recovery.	If the memory has been continuously held. Usually, historical memory is vivid for the central details, while more peripheral information (times, dates, locations) become somewhat distorted.
Guideline 3	Individual characteristics	The individual has greater susceptibility to suggestion and a tendency towards dissociation; is highly imaginative and is introverted.	The individual is less susceptible to suggestion or dissociation; is less imaginative and more extraverted.
Guideline 4	Corroboration	Lack of supporting information, or information that refutes historical memories.	Information that supports the historical memory from potential witnesses or official records.

Source: Based on information in Porter et al., 2003.

Increasing the Accuracy of Witnesses

Despite the possibility for errors, you should not conclude that eyewitnesses are always wrong; often they are extremely accurate (Yuille & Cutshall, 1986). In addition, many attempts have been made to find ways of increasing the accuracy of witnesses. In Munsterberg's (1907) early research, he turned to hypnosis as a possible solution, but gave it up when he discovered the ease with which false memories can be suggested.

One target for improvement has been the police line-up in which witnesses examine several individuals (the suspect plus several nonsuspects) and try to identify the one who is guilty. Wells and Luus (1990) suggest that a line-up is analogous to a social psychological experiment in which the police officer as experimenter is testing a hypothesis about who is the perpetrator. Based on this analogy, it follows that police officers can improve the accuracy of line-ups by following well-established experimental procedures that provide safeguards against contaminated data. In line-ups as well as in experiments, it is crucial to avoid biasing the data, or giving clues to expectations and so forth. For example, with a **blank-line-up control** procedure, a witness is first shown a line-up containing only innocent nonsuspects (Wells, 1984). If the witness fails to identify any of them, there is increased confidence in his or her accuracy. If an innocent person is identified, the witness is informed and then cautioned about the danger of making a false identification; this improves witness accuracy when actual line-ups are presented.

Other factors that can influence eyewitness accuracy were revealed in a study by Kassin and his colleagues (2001). Sixty-four psychologists who were experts on this topic were asked for their opinions of crucial factors affecting eyewitness accuracy. Eighty percent of them agreed on the effects of each of the phenomena that are indicated in Table 10.3. You can see that accuracy is impaired, for example, when the witness

Blank-Line-up Control A procedure in which a witness is shown a police line-up that does not include a suspect; this helps police to determine the accuracy of the witness and to emphasize the importance of being cautious in making a positive identification.

A group of 64 psychologists with courtroom experience were asked their opinions about factors affecting eyewitness testimony. There was 80 percent agreement among these experts with respect to 15 factors that influence accuracy, including the ones shown here.

TABLE 10.3 Factors That Influence Eyewitness Accuracy

Factor	Effect on Accuracy of Eyewitness
Mug shot-induced bias	Exposure to mug shots of a suspect increases the likelihood that the witness will later choose that suspect in a line-up.
Postevent information	Eyewitness testimony about an event often reflects not only what the witness actually saw, but information he or she obtained later on.
Alcoholic intoxication	Alcoholic intoxication impairs an eyewitness's later ability to recall persons and events.
Cross-race bias	Eyewitnesses are more accurate when identifying members of their own race than members of other races.
Weapon focus	The presence of a weapon impairs an eyewitness's ability to accurately identify the perpetrator's face.
Child suggestibility	Young children are more vulnerable than adults to interviewer suggestion, peer pressures, and other social influences.

Source: Based on information in Kassin et al., 2001.

experiences a high level of stress during the event, when a weapon was present, when only one person is asked to be identified (a show-up) rather than selected out of a group of people (a line-up), and when members of a line-up are fairly similar to one another in appearance.

The Central Participants in a Trial: Some Effects of Defendants and Jurors

Characteristics of Defendants

If you think of a defendant as a stranger at a party and a juror as someone who encounters and evaluates this stranger, you should be able to think of many social psychological factors that might determine how the juror would react to the defendant. Especially important are nonverbal communication and attribution (Chapter 2); prejudice and discrimination (Chapter 5); impression formation and impression management (Chapters 6 and 7), and interpersonal attraction (Chapter 6). Such matters should, of course, be irrelevant when we judge the guilt or innocence of someone accused of committing a crime, but they nevertheless do influence the outcomes of both real and simulated trials (Dane, 1992).

Research consistently indicates that attractive defendants are treated better than unattractive ones in gaining acquittals, receiving light sentencing, eliciting sympathy of the jury, and being considered not dangerous, according to studies conducted in Canada (Esses & Webster, 1988) and in the United States (Stevens, 1980; Wuensch, Castellow, & Moore, 1991; Castellow, Wuensch, & Moore, 1990). This *attractiveness effect* is stronger with serious but nonfatal crimes such as burglary, and with female defendants (Quigley, Johnson, & Byrne, 1995)—see Figure 10.13. Because lawyers are aware of this attractiveness bias, they advise their clients to do everything possible to improve their appearance before entering the courtroom.

The defendant's gender and socioeconomic status can sometimes affect judicial decisions (Mazella & Feingold, 1994): being female and of high socioeconomic status is usually an advantage. However, in a mock trial, Cruse and Leigh (1987) presented

■ The Impact of Physical Attractiveness on Legal Outcomes

FIGURE 10.13 Research shows that more attractive individuals tend to be treated more leniently in the legal system, especially if they are female. However, this advantage tends to decrease when fatality is involved in the crime. Given that often we believe that "what is beautiful is also good," would the attractiveness of this person influence your judgment of her during a trial?

jurors with testimony in an assault case in which either a male or a female defendant was alleged to have cut a victim with a kitchen knife. In this case, the woman was judged guilty more often. The researchers suggest that stabbing someone with a knife was a masculine behaviour—a woman "shouldn't act that way." In other words, she violated expectancies based on gender roles, making her behaviour seem more heinous.

The defendant's ethnicity and race also influence the outcome. Defendants whose testimony is in another language that must be translated are judged more guilty than when the same testimony is originally given in English (Stephan & Stephan, 1986). The police forces of a number of major Canadian cities have had internal inquiries into charges of biased treatment or brutality towards Asian, African, or Aboriginal Canadians. The Royal Commission of Inquiry into the wrongful conviction for murder of Donald Marshall, a Micmac Indian, identified racist attitudes of the police and other officials as one of the causes of this injustice. Further, Aboriginal people are disproportionately represented in the Canadian prison population, accounting for less than 3 percent of the population as a whole, but for 20 percent of provincial prison admissions and 12 percent of federal admissions (Menzies, 1999). After reviewing their treatment at many levels of the judicial process, Pontin and Kiely suggest that "Aboriginal people are victims of a discriminatory criminal justice system" (Pontin & Kiely, 1997, p. 155). In the United States, African-American defendants are more likely to be convicted than white defendants, and are more likely to receive a prison sentence (Stewart, 1980) or the death penalty (Sniffen, 1991). A study of American trials also indicated that 11.1 percent of criminals (regardless of race) who kill a white victim receive a death sentence, while only 4.5 percent of those who kill a black victim are sentenced to die (Henderson & Taylor, 1985). Research into the O. J. Simpson case showed that public opinion was split along racial lines: white Americans believed overwhelmingly in his guilt, while black Americans were equally sure of his innocence (Graham, Weiner & Zucker, 1997; Toobin, 1995).

Characteristics of Jurors

Jurors also differ in the way they process information, and these differences can lead to incompetent decisions. For example, about a third of those chosen as jurors have already made up their minds about the trial by the time the opening arguments are made. As the trial progresses, 75 to 85 percent begin to favour one side over the other, and this bias affects how subsequent evidence is processed (Carlson & Russo, 2001). Once a juror's bias is established, a guilty or a not-guilty schema is formed, and all of the evidence and testimony that follows is either (1) interpreted so as to fit the schema or (2) ignored if it absolutely doesn't fit (Kuhn, Weinstock, & Flaton, 1994).

Jurors whose minds are made up are very certain about their beliefs, give extreme verdicts, and are responsible for hung juries, because they resist changing their minds. In contrast, the most competent jurors process trial information by constructing at least two alternate schemas so that each bit of evidence can fit into one schema or the other.

Various decisions made by jurors are associated with specific personality dispositions and specific attitudes and beliefs. Some of these dispositional effects are summarized in Table 10.4.

Altogether, research on the legal system provides evidence that judicial fairness and objectivity often fail because of quite common human characteristics. The increased use of technology such as videotaped testimony, computer animation, and simulations in the courtroom (Carpenter, 2001) quite possibly will only add to problems with objectivity. The total elimination of biases in the courtroom is a laudable goal, but it may not be a reachable one.

Various attitudes, beliefs, and personality dispositions of jurors have been found to be related to the decisions that those jurors make. A few of the findings are summarized here.

TABLE 10.4 Juror Characteristics as Predictors of Juror Decisions

Juror Characteristic	Juror Decision
Leniency Bias (assumption that the defendant is also a victim)	*Epistemic Understanding* (ability to differentiate whether a claim makes sense and whether it is true)
Less likely to vote guilty (MacCoun & Kerr, 1988)	Tendency to understand that a fact and an opinion differ and that a claim represents a theory that must be substantiated by evidence (Kuhn, 2001)
Authoritarianism (tendency to hold authoritarian beliefs and attitudes)	*Negative Attitude about Psychiatry*
More likely to vote guilty (Narby, Cutler, & Moran, 1993) and to react to all offences as serious and deserving punishment (Feather, 1996)	Less likely to accept testimony about defendant's mental state (Cutler, Moran, & Narby, 1992)
Attributional Complexity (preference for complex over simple explanations)	*Entity Theorists* (those who believe that traits are fixed and unchangeable)
Less likely to vote guilty and to consider external causes for defendant's behaviour (Pope & Meyer, 1999)	More likely to rely on cues they believe to indicate character, such as the defendant's clothing (Gervey et al., 1999)

KEY POINTS

- *Forensic psychology* studies psychological factors that influence the legal system.
- Most people would prefer police to search for the truth rather than attempt to prove guilt, but both interrogation approaches are common.
- For a variety of reasons, it is not uncommon for an innocent person to confess to a crime and even to believe himself or herself to be guilty.
- Extensive media coverage of crime leads to misperceptions about its frequency, but the coverage occurs because people find it interesting.
- Social psychology has studied the importance of *aggressive cues*, such as guns, as contributors to the level of violence. These findings have implications for the issue of gun or firearms control.
- *Eyewitnesses* to a crime often make mistakes. One serious and controversial legal problem is the recovery of *repressed memories* of past criminal events.
- Based on research, guidelines for evaluation of recovered memories by professionals have been proposed.
- A variety of procedures such as the *blank-line-up control* have been developed to help ensure greater accuracy.

- Defendants' physical and social characteristics can influence legal outcomes: Racial similarity or dissimilarity of defendants and jurors can have a major impact on the final verdict in a trial.
- A juror's response to the evidence and to the defendant depends on his or her affective evaluations, cognitive processing, and various personality characteristics.

Ideas to Take with You

Don't Rush to Judgment

Whether as a potential juror or as an official member of a jury, you will be exposed to a great deal of information, many arguments, and diverse facts about any given crime and about the suspected criminal. Even if you are simply a member of the general public with no formal role to play, it is still important that you keep in mind some of the issues involved in reaching valid conclusions about legal matters. If you are actually a member of a jury, your open-mindedness can have a huge impact on the defendant's life.

Remember: When a Suspect Is Arrested, This Does Not Automatically Indicate Guilt.
When you hear the details of a brutal crime and then learn on TV or in the newspapers that a suspect has been arrested, don't assume that the crime is necessarily solved or that the arrested individual had been found guilty. Before guilt or innocence is determined, there must be an indictment, a trial, the presentation of evidence for and against the defendant, a consideration of precise legal issues, and an attempt by the jury to reach consensus. The most reasonable position to take is that either the prosecution or the defence might be correct, so you would be wise to construct two alternative schemas for yourself—one in which you store all of the information indicating guilt and one in which you store all of the information indicating innocence. Wait until all the facts are in before deciding which schema makes more sense.

Separate Attraction from Judgments Based on Evidence.
It is probably not possible to enter any situation with a totally objective, open mind. Remember, research findings suggest that we automatically respond to stimuli with relatively positive or relatively negative attitudes. The best we can do is to separate how much we like the defendant from what we know on the basis of testimony and physical evidence. No matter how you feel about the individual's appearance, ethnic background, political views, sexual orientation, or whatever else, the question is not how much you like him or her but whether or not the bulk of the evidence indicates guilt beyond a reasonable doubt. In everyday life, we often blur the distinction between attraction toward someone and factual knowledge about that person. In the courtroom, it is crucial that such distinctions be made.

Don't Let Your Opinion be Swayed by Emotional Appeals.
We all know that the prosecutor and the defence lawyer have very specific and quite different scenarios to "sell." Each side wants to convince the onlookers

that there is only one version of the truth; and each side will try to appeal to your feelings, your prejudices, your patriotism, or whatever else might be effective in convincing you. Again, your task is not to deny the disgust you may feel about a brutal crime or the sympathy you may feel toward an innocent citizen who has been dragged into court and accused unfairly of committing a criminal act. Both feelings are reasonable. The question, however, is once again a matter of what is indicated by the evidence and what is prescribed as legally relevant. The courtroom is clearly a place where it is important to separate emotional processes from cognitive ones; indeed, our system of law is based on the assumption that regular citizens have the ability to do this.

Summary

● *Applied social psychology* involves research and practice directed towards understanding and solving social problems. (p. 365)
● Research by Lambert on bilingualism is a classic example of applied research. (p. 365)

Applying Social Psychology to Health Issues

● *Health psychology* studies the effects of psychological factors on physical illness. (p. 367)
● The acceptance of health-related information depends upon a number of factors. (p. 368)
● *Stress* is defined as any event that is perceived as a potential source of physical or emotional harm. (p. 369)
● *Psychoneuroimmunology* explores the relationships among stress, emotional and behavioural reactions, and the immune system. (p. 371)
● A number of dispositional differences are associated with the response to stress. (p. 371)
● Strategies for *coping* with stress include *emotion-focused* or *problem-focused* strategies. (p. 372)
● *Social support* can be beneficial in times of stress and is related to lower levels of illness. (p. 374)

Applying Social Psychology to the World of Work: Job Satisfaction, Helping, and Leadership

● The findings and principles of social psychology help to explain behaviour in work settings. (p. 376)
● *Job satisfaction* is an individual's attitude toward her or his job and is influenced by a variety of factors. (p. 376)
● Job satisfaction and task performance are not strongly related. (p. 376)
● *Organizational citizenship behaviour* (OCB) involves prosocial behaviour at work. OCB is influenced by several factors. (p. 379)

● *Leadership* refers to one member of a group influencing other group members toward the attainment of shared group goals. (p. 381)
● The *great person theory* of leadership suggests that leaders have special traits. (p. 382)
● Leaders vary with respect to their behaviour or style. (p. 383)
● *Transformational (charismatic) leadership* exerts profound effects on followers and often changes their societies. (p. 384)
● Cross-cultural research suggests there are major differences between leaders in Asian and North American corporations. (p. 385)

Social Psychology and the Legal System

● *Forensic psychology* studies psychological factors that influence the legal system. (p. 387)
● Police procedures during investigation and interrogation can influence outcomes. (p. 387)
● The style of questioning, such as *leading questions*, can produce inaccurate witness reports and induce innocent persons to confess to a crime. (p. 388)
● Extensive media coverage leads to misperceptions about the legal system. (p. 389)
● The relationship between firearms availability and violence has been widely studied, including the importance of *aggressive cues*. (p. 390)
● *Eyewitnesses* to a crime often make mistakes. (p. 392)
● One issue is the credibility of *repressed or recovered memories* of past criminal events. (p. 393)
● Accuracy of witnesses can be improved through procedures such as the *blank-line-up control*. (p. 395)
● Defendants' physical and social characteristics can influence legal outcomes. (p. 396)
● A juror's response to the evidence depends upon a number of personal and situational factors. (p. 397)

For More Information

Le Fanu, J. (2000). *The rise and fall of modern medicine*. New York: Carroll and Graf.

This is an interesting book that deals with medical knowledge past and present, demonstrating the way in which medical beliefs and medical decisions have been shaped by cultural beliefs as much as by science. Much of this material (especially the portion dealing with current medical practices) may be controversial, but it is consistently intriguing.

Radley, A. (1994). *Making sense of illness: The social psychology of health and disease*. Thousand Oaks, CA: Sage.

This book cuts across the field of health psychology, sociology, and medicine to describe the importance of psychological factors in responding to stress, coping with acute and chronic health problems, and behaving in ways that promote good health and prevent disease.

Greenberg, J., & Baron, R. A. (2002). *Behavior in organizations* (8th ed). Upper Saddle River, NJ: Prentice-Hall.

This book provides a broad overview of our knowledge about behaviour in work settings. Many of the topics covered represent applications of social psychology to issues relating to organizations.

Amsterdam, A. G., & Bruner, J. (2000). *Minding the law*. Cambridge, MA: Harvard University Press.

In this collaborative effort by a lawyer and a psychologist, the way that cognitive processes influence judicial decision making is described in detail. They use actual court cases as examples of how psychological phenomena can shape the judicial process.

Weblinks

www.ncela.gwu.edu/ncbepubs/symposia/first/ issues-ref.htm
"Issues in Foreign Language and Second Language Education" by Wallace Lambert (Proceedings of the First Research Symposium on Limited English Proficient Student Issues, 1990)
www.carleton.ca/~rthibode/activism.html
Activism and Psychology home page, Carleton University

www.westview.abelgratis.com/topics/culture/ biasinhealth.html
"Optimistic Bias in Perceiving Physical and Mental Health Risks" by Berger, Magnuson, Maxwell, Tubbs, Miami University, Ohio

References

Adams, J. S. (1965). Inequity in social exchange. In L. Berkowitz (Ed.), *Advances in experimental social psychology* (Vol. 2, pp. 267–299). New York: Academic Press.

Adams, M. (1997). *Sex in the snow: Canadian social values at the end of the millennium.* Toronto: Viking Penguin.

Ader, R. (2001). Psychoneuroimmunology. *Current Directions in Psychological Science, 10,* 94–98.

Adorno, T. W., Frenkel-Brunswick, E., Levinson, D. J., & Sanford, R. H. (1950). *The authoritarian personality.* New York: Harper & Row.

Affleck, G., Tennen, H., Urrows, S., & Higgins, P. (1994). Person and contextual features of daily stress reactivity: Individual differences in relations of undesirable daily events with mood disturbance and chronic pain intensity. *Journal of Personality and Social Psychology, 66,* 329–340.

Ajzen, I. (1987). Attitudes, traits, and actions: Dispositional prediction of behavior in personality and social psychology. In L. Berkowitz (Ed.), *Advances in experimental social psychology* (Vol. 20). San Diego, CA: Academic Press.

Ajzen, I. (1991). The theory of planned behavior: Special issue: Theories of cognitive self-regulation. *Organizational Behavior and Human Decision Processes, 50,* 179–211.

Ajzen, I., & Fishbein, M. (1980). *Understanding attitudes and predicting social behavior.* Englewood Cliffs, NJ: Prentice-Hall.

Alagna, F. J., Whitcher, S. J., & Fisher, J. D. (1979). Evaluative reactions to interpersonal touch in a counseling interview. *Journal of Counseling Psychology, 26,* 465–472.

Albarracin, D., & Wyer, R. S., Jr. (2000). The cognitive impact of past behavior: Influences on beliefs, attitudes, and future behavioral decisions. *Journal of Personality and Social Psychology, 79,* 5–22.

Alexander, M. J., & Higgins, E. T. (1993). Emotional trade-offs of becoming a parent: How social roles influence self-discrepancy effects. *Journal of Personality and Social Psychology, 65,* 1259–1269. Allen, N.J., & Meyer, J.P. (1990). The measurement and antecedents of affective, continuance, and normative commitment to the organization. *Journal of Occupational Psychology, 63,* 1–18.

Allport, F. H. (1920). The influence of the group upon association and thought. *Journal of Experimental Psychology, 3,* 159–182.

Allport, F. H. (1924). *Social psychology.* Boston: Houghton Mifflin.

Allport, G.W. (1954). *The nature of prejudice.* Reading, MA: Addison-Wesley.

Altemeyer, B. (1981). *Right-wing authoritarianism.* Winnipeg: University of Manitoba Press.

Altemeyer, B. (1988). *Enemies of freedom.* San Francisco: Jossey-Bass.

Altman, I & Taylor, D.A. (1973). *Social penetration: The development of interpersonal relationships.* New York: Holt, Rinehart & Winston.

Amato, P.R. (1983). Helping behavior in urban and rural settings: Field studies based on a taxonomic organization of helping episodes. *Journal of Personality and Social Psychology, 45,* 571–586.

Amirkhan, J. H., Risinger, R. T., & Swickert, R. J. (1995). Extraversion: A "hidden" personality factor in coping? *Journal of Personality, 63,* 189–212.

Andersen, B. L., & Cyranowski, J. M. (1994). Women's sexual self-schema. *Journal of Personality and Social Psychology, 67,* 1079–1100.

Andersen, B. L., Cyranowski, J. M., & Espindle, D. (1999). Men's sexual self-schema. *Journal of Personality and Social Psychology, 76,* 645–661.

Anderson, C. A. (1997). Effects of violent movies and trait hostility on hostile feelings and aggressive thoughts. *Aggressive Behavior, 23,* 161–178.

Anderson, C. A., Anderson, K. B., & Deuser, W. E. (1996). A general framework for the study of affective aggression: Tests of effects of extreme temperatures and of viewing weapons on hostility. *Personality and Social Psychology Bulletin, 22,* 366–376.

Anderson, C. A., Bushman, B. J., & Groom, R. W. (1997). Hot years and serious and deadly assault: Empirical tests of the heat hypothesis. *Journal of Personality and Social Psychology, 73,* 1213–1223.

Anderson, P. B., & Aymami, R. (1993). Reports of female initiation of sexual contact: Male and female differences. *Archives of Sexual Behavior, 22,* 335–343.

Andreoletti, C., Zebrowitz, L. A., & Lachman, M. E. (2001). *Personality and Social Psychology Bulletin, 27,* 969–981.

Andreou, E. (2000). Bully/victim problems and their association with psychological constructs in 8- to 12-year-old Greek schoolchildren. *Aggressive Behavior, 26,* 49–58.

Archer, J. (1996). Sex differences in social behavior: Are the social role and evolutionary explanations compatible? *American Psychologist, 51,* 909–917.

Argyle, M. (1988). *Bodily communication.* New York: Methuen

Armitage, C. J., & Conner, M. (2000). Attitudinal ambivalence: A test of three key hypotheses. *Personality and Social Psychology Bulletin, 26,* 1421–1432.

Armstrong, P. (1996). From caring and sharing to greedy and mean? In A. Lapierre, P. Savard, & P. Smart (Eds.), *Language, culture and values in Canada at the dawn of the twenty-first century.* Ottawa: Carleton University Press.

Aron, A., & Henkemeyer, L. (1995). Marital satisfaction and passionate love. *Journal of Social and Personal Relationships, 12,* 139–146.

Aron, A., & Westbay, L. (1996). Dimensions of the prototype of love. *Journal of Personality and Social Psychology, 70,* 535–551.

Aron, A., Aron, E. N., & Allen, J. (1998). Motivations for unreciprocated love. *Personality and Social Psychology Bulletin, 24,* 787–796.

Aron, A., Dutton, D. G., Aron, E. N., & Iverson, A. (1989). Experiences of falling in love. *Journal of Social and Personal Relationships*, 6, 243–257.

Aronoff, J., Woike, B. A., & Hyman, L. M. (1992). Which are the stimuli in facial displays of anger and happiness? Configurational bases of emotion recognition. *Journal of Personality and Social Psychology*, 62, 1050–1066.

Aronson, E. (1999). *The social animal*. (8th ed.). New York: Worth.

Aronson, E., Bridgeman, D. L., & Oeffner, R. (1978). Interdependent interactions and prosocial behavior. *Journal of Research and Development in Education*, 12, 16–27.

Aronson, E., Fried, C., & Stone, J. (1991). Overcoming denial: Increasing the intention to use condoms through the induction of hypocrisy. *American Journal of Public Health*, 18, 1636–1640.

Arriaga, X. B., & Agnew, C. R. (2001). Being committed: Affective, cognitive, and conative components of relationship commitment. *Personality and Social Psychology Bulletin*, 27, 1190–1203.

Arriaga, X. B., & Rusbult, C. E. (1998). Standing in my partner's shoes: Partner perspective taking and reactions to accommodative dilemmas. *Personality and Social Psychology Bulletin*, 24, 927–948.

Arrigo, J. M., & Pezdek, K. (1997). Lessons from the study of psychogenic amnesia. *Current Directions in Psychological Science*, 6, 148–152.

Arvey, R. D., Bouchard, T. J., Jr., Segal, N. L., & Abraham, L. M. (1989). Job satisfaction: Genetic and environmental components. *Journal of Applied Psychology*, 74, 187–192.

Aryee, S., & Chay, Y. W. (2001). Workplace justice, citizenship behavior, and turnover intentions in a union context: Examining the mediating role of perceived union support and union instrumentality. *Journal of Applied Psychology*, 86, 154–160.

Asch, S. E. (1951). Effects of group pressure upon the modification and distortion of judgment. In H. Guetzkow (Ed.), *Groups, leadership, and men*. Pittsburgh, PA: Carnegie.

Asch, S. E. (1956). Studies of independence and conformity: A minority of one against unanimous majority. *Psychological Monographs*, 70 (Whole no. 416).

Ashmore, R. D., Solomon, M. R., & Longo, L. C. (1996). Thinking about fashion models' looks: A multidimensional approach to the structure of perceived physical attractiveness. *Personality and Social Psychology Bulletin*, 22, 1083–1104.

Aspinwall, L. G. (1998). Rethinking the role of positive affect in self-regulation. *Motivation and Emotion*, 22, 1–32.

Atwood, M. (1982). *Second words: Selected critical prose*. Boston: Beacon Press.

Aune, R. K., & Basil, M. D. (1994). A relational obligations approach to the foot-in-the-mouth effect. *Journal of Applied Social Psychology*, 24, 546–556.

Averill, J. R., & Boothroyd, P. (1977). On falling in love: Conformance with romantic ideal. *Motivation and Emotion*, 1, 235–247.

Azar, B. (1997a, November). Defining the trait that makes us human. *APA Monitor*, 1, 15.

Baccman, C., Folkesson, P., & Norlander, T. (1999). Expectations of romantic relationships: A comparison between homosexual and heterosexual men with regard to Baxter's criteria. *Social Behavior and Personality*, 27, 363–374.

Baer, D. (1999). Educational credentials and the changing occupational structure. In J. Curtis, E. Grabb, & N. Guppy (Eds.), *Social inequality in Canada: Patterns, problems, and policies* (2nd ed., pp. 92–106). Scarborough, Ont.: Prentice Hall.

Baize, H. R., Jr., & Schroeder, J. E. (1995). Personality and mate selection in personal ads: Evolutionary preferences in a public mate selection process. *Journal of Social Behavior and Personality*, 10, 517–536.

Baker, R. R., & Bellis, M. A. (1995). *Human sperm competition*. London: Chapman & Hall.

Baldwin, D. A. (2000). Interpersonal understanding fuels knowledge acquisition. *Current Directions in Psychological Science*, 9, 40–45.

Banaji, M., & Hardin, C. (1996). Automatic stereotyping. *Psychological Science*, 7, 136–141.

Bandura, A. (1973). *Aggression: A social learning analysis*. Englewood Cliffs, NJ: Prentice-Hall.

Bandura, A. (1993). Self-efficacy mechanisms in psychobiological functioning. *Stanford University Psychologist*, 1, 5–6.

Bandura, A. (1997). *Self-efficacy: The exercise of control*. New York: Freeman.

Bandura, A. (1999). A sociocognitive analysis of substance abuse: An agentic perspective. *Psychological Science*, 10, 214–216.

Bandura, A. (2000). Exercise of human agency through collective efficacy. *Current Directions in Psychological Science*, 9, 75–78.

Bandura, A., Ross, D., & Ross, S. (1963). Imitation of film-mediated aggressive models. *Journal of Abnormal and Social Psychology*, 66, 3–11.

Banner, L.W. (1983). *American beauty*. Chicago: The University Press.

Barbee, A. P., Cunningham, M. R., Winstead, B. A., Derlega, V. J., Gulley, M. R., Yankeelov, P. A., & Druen, P. B. (1993). Effects of gender role expectations on the social support process. *Journal of Social Issues*, 49, 175–190.

Bargh, J. A. (1997). The automaticity of everyday life. In R. S. Wyer Jr. (Ed.), *Advances in social cognition* (Vol. 10). Mahwah, NJ: Erlbaum.

Bargh, J. A., & Pietromonaco, P. (1982). Automatic information processing and social perception: The influence of trait information presented outside of conscious awareness on impression formation. *Journal of Personality and Social Psychology*, 43, 437–449.

Bargh, J. A., Chen, M., & Burrows, L. (1996). Automaticity of social behavior: Direct effects of trait construct and stereotype activation on action. *Journal of Personality and Social Psychology*, 71, 230–234.

Barnes, F. (1989). Fearless leader. *New Republic*, 201(22), 11–13.

Baron, R. A., Byrne, D., & Watson, G. (1998). *Exploring social psychology: Second Canadian edition*. Scarborough, Ont.: Allyn & Bacon.

Baron, R. A. (1972). Reducing the influence of an aggressive model: The restraining effects of peer censure. *Journal of Experimental Social Psychology, 8,* 266–275.

Baron, R. A. (1974). Aggression as a function of victim's pain cues, level of prior anger arousal, and exposure to an aggressive model. *Journal of Personality and Social Psychology, 29,* 117–124.

Baron, R. A. (1989a). Applicant strategies during job interviews. In G. R. Ferris & R. W. Eder (Eds.), *The employment interview: Theory, research, and practice* (pp. 204–216). Newbury Park, CA: Sage.

Baron, R. A. (1989b). Personality and organizational conflict: The Type A behavior pattern and self-monitoring. *Organizational Behavior and Human Decision Processes, 44,* 281–297.

Baron, R. A. (1990). Attributions and organizational conflict. In S. Graham & V. Folkes (Eds.), *Attribution theory: Applications to achievement, mental health, and interpersonal conflict* (pp. 185–204). Hillsdale, NJ: Erlbaum.

Baron, R. A. (1994). The physical environment of work settings: Effects of task performance, interpersonal relations, and job satisfaction. In M. Staw & L. L. Cummings (Eds.), *Research in organizational behavior* (Vol. 16, pp. 1–46). Greenwich, CT: JAI Press.

Baron, R. A. (1997). The sweet smell of helping: Effects of pleasant ambient fragrance on prosocial behavior in shopping malls. *Personality and Social Psychology Bulletin, 23,* 498–503.

Baron, R. A., & Richardson, D. R. (1994). *Human aggression* (2nd ed.). New York: Plenum.

Baron, R. A., Markman, G. D., & Hirsa, A. (2001). Perceptions of women and men as entrepreneurs. Evidence for differential effects of attributional augmenting. *Journal of Applied Psychology, 86,* 923–929.

Baron, R. A., Russell, G. W., & Arms, R. L. (1985). Negative ions and behavior: Impact on mood, memory, and aggression among Type A and Type B persons. *Journal of Personality and Social Psychology, 48,* 746–754.

Baron, R. S. (1986). Distraction-conflict theory: Progress and problems. In L. Berkowitz (Ed.), *Advances in experimental social psychology,* Vol. 20. New York: Academic Press.

Baron, R. S., Moore, D., & Sanders, G. S. (1978). Distraction as a source of drive in social facilitation research. *Journal of Personality and Social Psychology, 36,* 816–824.

Baron, R. S., Vandello, U. A., & Brunsman, B. (1996). The forgotten variable in conformity research: Impact of task importance on social influence. *Journal of Personality and Social Psychology, 71,* 915–927.

Barrett, L., Dunbar, R.I.M., & Lycett, J. (2002). *Human evolutionary psychology.* Houndsmill, Basingstoke: Palgrave.

Barrett, L. F., Lane, R. D., Sechrest, L., & Schwartz, G. E. (2000). Sex differences in emotional awareness. *Personality and Social Psychology Bulletin, 26,* 1027–1035.

Barrett, S.R. (1987). *Is God a racist? The right wing in Canada.* Toronto: University of Toronto Press.

Barrick, M. R., & Mount, M. K. (1991). The Big Five personality dimensions and job performance: A meta-analytic analysis. *Personnel Psychology, 44,* 1–26.

Bartholomew, K. (1990). Avoidance of intimacy: An attachment perspective. *Journal of Social and Personal Relationships, 7,* 147–178.

Bartholomew, K. (1993). From childhood to adult relationships: Attachment theory and research. In S.W. Duck (Ed.), *Understanding relationship processes 2: Learning about relationships* (pp. 30–32). London: Sage.

Bartholomew, K., & Horowitz, L.M. (1991) Attachment styles among young adults: A test of a four-category model. *Journal of Personality and Social Psychology, 61,* 226–244.

Bass, B. I. (1998). *Leadership* (2nd ed.). New York: Free Press.

Bass, B. M. (1985). *Leadership and performance beyond expectations.* New York: Free Press.

Batson, C. D., & Oleson, K. C. (1991). Current status of the empathy–altruism hypothesis. In M. S. Clark (Ed.), *Prosocial behavior* (pp. 62–85). Newbury Park, CA: Sage.

Batson, C. D., & Weeks, J. L. (1996). Mood effects of unsuccessful helping: Another test of the empathy–altruism hypothesis. *Personality and Social Psychology Bulletin, 22,* 148–157.

Batson, C. D., Batson, J. G., Todd, R. M., Brummett, B. H., Shaw, L. L., & Aldeguer, C. M. R. (1995). Empathy and the collective good: Caring for one of the others in a social dilemma. *Journal of Personality and Social Psychology, 68,* 619–631.

Batson, C. D., Duncan, B. D., Ackerman, P., Buckley, T., & Birch, K. (1981). Is empathic emotion a source of altruistic motivation? *Journal of Personality and Social Psychology, 40,* 290–302.

Batson, C. D., Early, S., & Salvarani, G. (1997). Perspective taking: Imagining how another feels versus imagining how you would feel. *Personality and Social Psychology Bulletin, 23,* 751–758.

Batson, C. D., Klein, T. R., Highberger, L., & Shaw, L. L. (1995). Immorality from empathy-induced altruism: When compassion and justice conflict. *Journal of Personality and Social Psychology, 68,* 1042–1054.

Batson, C. D., O'Quin, K., Fultz, J., Vanderplas, M., & Isen, A. M. (1983). Influence of self-reported distress and empathy on egoistic versus altruistic motivation to help. *Journal of Personality and Social Psychology, 45,* 706–718.

Batson, C. D., Turk, C. L., Shaw, L. L., & Klein, T. R. (1995). Information function of empathic emotion: Learning that we value the other's welfare. *Journal of Personality and Social Psychology, 68,* 300–313.

Baum, A. (1994). Behavioral, biological, and environmental interactions in disease processes. In S. Blumenthal, K. Matthews, & S. Weiss (Eds.), *New research frontiers in behavioral medicine: Proceedings of the national conference* (p. 62). Washington, DC: NIH Publications.

Baumeister, R. F., Twenge, J. M. Nuss, C. K. (2002). Effects of Social Exclusion on Cognitive Processes: Anticipated Aloneness Reduces Intelligent Thought. *Journal of Personality and Social Psychology, 83,* 817–827

Baumeister, R. F., & Leary, M. R. (1995). The need to belong: Desire for interpersonal attachments as a fundamental human motivation. *Psychological Bulletin, 117,* 497–529.

Baumeister, R. F., & Newman, L. S. (1994). Self-regulation of cognitive inference and decision processes. *Personality and Social Psychology Bulletin, 20,* 3–19.

Baumeister, R. F., Catanese, K. R., & Vohs, K. D. (2001). Is there a gender difference in strength of sex drive? Theoretical views, conceptual distinctions, and a review of relevant evidence. *Personality and Social Psychology Review, 5,* 242–273.

Baumeister, R. F., Chesner, S. P., Sanders, P. S., & Tice, D. M. (1988). Who's in charge here? Group leaders do lend help in emergencies. *Personality and Social Psychology Bulletin, 14,* 17–22.

Baumeister, R. F., Wotman, S. R., & Stillwell, A. M. (1993). Unrequited love: On heartbreak, anger, guilt, scriptlessness, and humiliation. *Journal of Personality and Social Psychology, 64,* 377–394.

Baumrind, D. (1985). Research using intentional deception: Ethical issues revisited. *American Psychologist, 40,* 165–174.

Beaman, A. I., Cole, M., Preston, M., Klentz, B., & Steblay, N. M. (1983). Fifteen years of the foot-in-the-door-research: A meta-analysis. *Personality and Social Psychology Bulletin, 9,* 181–186.

Beaton, A., Tougas, F., & Joly, S. (1996). Neosexism among male managers: Is it a matter of numbers? *Journal of Applied Social Psychology, 26,* 2189–2203.

Beckwith, J. B. (1994). Terminology and social relevance in psychological research on gender. *Social Behavior and Personality, 22,* 329–336.

Bednar, R.L., Wells, M.G., & Peterson, S.R. (1989). *Self-esteem: Paradoxes and innovations in clinical theory and practice.* Washington, DC: American Psychological Association.

Bell, B. E., & Loftus, E. F. (1988). Degree of detail of eyewitness testimony and mock juror judgments. *Journal of Applied Social Psychology, 18,* 1171–1192.

Bell, S. T., Kuriloff, P. J., & Lottes, I. (1994). Understanding attributions of blame in stranger rape and date rape situations: An examination of gender, race, identification, and students' social perceptions of rape victims. *Journal of Applied Social Psychology, 24,* 1719–1734.

Bem, S. L. (1974). The measurement of psychological androgyny. *Journal of Consulting and Clinical Psychology, 42,* 155–162.

Bem, S. L. (1975). Sex role adaptability: One consequence of psychological androgyny. *Journal of Personality and Social Psychology, 31,* 634–643.

Bem, S. L. (1981). Gender schema theory: A cognitive account of sex typing. *Psychological Review, 88,* 354–364.

Bem, S. L. (1983). Gender schema theory and its implications for child development: Raising gender-aschematic children in a gender schematic society. Science: *Journal of Women in Culture and Society, 8,* 598–616.

Bem, S. L. (1995). Dismantling gender polarization and compulsory heterosexuality: Should we turn the volume down or up? *Journal of Sex Research, 32,* 329–334.

Benson, P. L., Karabenick, S. A., & Lerner, R. M. (1976). Pretty pleases: The effects of physical attractiveness, race, and sex on receiving help. *Journal of Experimental Social Psychology, 12,* 409–415.

Berger, A. (1999, July 20). An early start for healthier habits. *New York Times,* F7.

Berkowitz, L. (1968). Impulse, aggression and the gun. *Psychology Today, 2 (4),* 18–22.

Berkowitz, L. (1989). Frustration-aggression hypothesis: Examination and reformulation. *Psychological Bulletin, 106,* 59–73.

Berkowitz, L. (1993). *Aggression: Its causes, consequences, and control.* Philadelphia: Temple University Press.

Berkowitz, L. (in press). Affect, aggression, and antisocial behavior. In R. J. Davidson, K. Scherer, & H. H. Goldsmith (Eds.), *Handbook of affective sciences.* New York: Oxford.

Berkowitz, L., & LePage, A. (1967). Weapons as aggression-eliciting stimuli. *Journal of Personality and Social Psychology, 7,* 202–207.

Berman, M., Gladue, B., & Taylor, S. (1993). The effects of hormones, Type A behavior pattern and provocation on aggression in men. *Motivation and Emotion, 17,* 125–138, 182–199.

Bernard, L. C., & Belinsky, D. (1993). Hardiness, stress, and maladjustment: Effects on self-reported retrospective health problems and prospective health center visits. *Journal of Social Behavior and Personality, 8,* 97–110.

Berry, D. S., & Hansen, J. S. (1996). Positive affect, negative affect, and social interaction. *Journal of Personality and Social Psychology, 71,* 796–809.

Berry, J. W., & Kalin, R. (1995). Multicultural and ethnic attitudes in Canada: An overview of the 1991 national survey. *Canadian Journal of Behavioural Science, 27,* 301–320.

Berry, J. W. (1967). Independence and conformity in subsistence-level societies. *Journal of Personality and Social Psychology, 7,* 415–418.

Berry, J. W. (1969). On cross-cultural comparability. *International Journal of Psychology, 4,* 119–28.

Berry, J. W. (1976). *Human ecology and cognitive style: Comparative studies in cultural and psychological adaptation.* New York: Sage/Halsted.

Berry, J. W. (1978). Social psychology: Comparative, societal and universal. *Canadian Psychological Review, 19,* 93–104.

Berry, J. W. (1989). Imposed etics–emics–derived etics: The operationalisation of a compelling idea. *International Journal of Psychology, 24,* 721–735.

Berry, J.W. (1999). Intercultural relations in plural societies. *Canadian Psychology, 40,* 12–21.

Berry, J.W. (1999). Intercultural relations in plural societies. *Canadian Psychology, 40,* 12–21.

Berry, J. W., & Annis, R. C. (1974) Ecology, culture and psychological differentiation. *International Journal of Psychology, 9,* 173–193.

Berry, J. W., Kalin, R., & Taylor, D. M. (1977). *Multiculturalism and ethnic attitudes in Canada.* Ottawa: Supply and Services Canada.

Berry, J. W., Kim, U., Minde, T., & Mok, D. (1987). Comparative studies of acculturative stress. *International Migration Review, 21,* 491–551.

Berry, J. W., Poortinga, Y. H., & Pandey, J. (Eds.). (1997). *Handbook of cross-cultural psychology: Volume 1.* (2nd ed.) Needham Heights, MA: Allyn & Bacon.

Berry, W. (1993). *Sex, economy, freedom, and community.* New York: Pantheon.

Berscheid, E., Snyder, M., & Omoto, A. M. (1989). The Relationship Closeness Inventory: Assessing the closeness of interpersonal relationships. *Journal of Personality and Social Psychology, 57,* 792–807.

Bersoff, D. (1987). Social science data and the Supreme Court: Lockhart as a case in point. *American Psychologist, 42,* 52–58.

Besserer, S. (1998). Criminal victimization: An international perspective. *Juristat, 18* (6). Ottawa: Statistics Canada

Betancourt, B. A., & Miller, N. (1996). Gender differences in aggression as a function of provocation: A meta-analysis. *Psychological Bulletin, 119,* 422–447.

Betsch, T., Plessner, H., Schwieren, C., & Gutig, R. (2001). I like it but I don't know why: A value-account approach to implicit attitude formation. *Personality and Social Psychology Bulletin, 27,* 242–253.

Bettencourt, L. A., Gwinner, K. P., & Meuter, M. L. (2001). Comparison of attitude, personality, and knowledge predictors of service-oriented organizational citizenship behaviors. *Journal of Applied Psychology, 86,* 29–41.

Bhagat, R, S., Kedia, B. L., & Harveston, P. D. (2002). Cultural variations in the cross-border transfer of organizational knowledge: An integrative framework. *Academy of Management Review, 27,* 204–221.

Bibby, R. W. (1990). *Mosaic Madness.* Toronto: Stoddart.

Bibby, R. W. (1995). *The Bibby report: Social trends Canadian style.* Toronto: Stoddart.

Bickman, L. D. (1975). Personality constructs of senior women planning to marry or to live independently after college. Unpublished doctoral dissertation, University of Pennsylvania.

Bickman, L. D. (1975). *Personality constructs of senior women planning to marry or to live independently after college.* Unpublished doctoral dissertation, University of Pennsylvania.

Bienert, H., & Schneider, B. H. (1993). Diagnosis-specific social skills training with peer-nominated aggressive-disruptive and sensitive-isolated preadolescents. *Journal of Applied Developmental Psychology, 26,* 182–199.

Bierhoff, H. W., Klein, R., & Kramp, P. (1991). Evidence for the altruistic personality from data on accident research. *Journal of Personality, 59,* 263–280.

Bies, R. J., Shapiro, D. L., & Cummings, L. L. (1988). Causal accounts and managing organizational conflict: Is it enough to say it's not my fault? *Communication Research, 15,* 381–399.

Birkimer, J. C., Lucas, M., & Birkimer, S. J. (1991). Health locus of control and status of cardiac rehabilitation graduates. *Journal of Social Behavior and Personality, 6,* 629–640.

Birnbaum, G. E., Orr, I., Mikulincer, M., & Florian, V. (1997). When marriage breaks up—does attachment style contribute to coping and mental health? *Journal of Social and Personal Relationships, 14,* 643–654.

Birt, C. M., & Dion, K. L. (1987). Relative deprivation theory and responses to discrimination in a gay male and lesbian sample. *British Journal of Social Psychology, 26,*139–145.

Bissoondath, N. (1994). *Selling Illusions.* Toronto: Penguin.

Bissoondath, N. (2002). *Selling illusions : the cult of multiculturalism in Canada.* Revised and updated. Toronto: Penguin.

Bjorkqvist, K., Lagerspetz, K. M. J., & Kaukiainen, A. (1992). Do girls manipulate and boys fight? Developmental trends in regard to direct and indirect aggression. *Aggressive Behavior, 18,* 117–127.

Bjorkqvist, K., Osterman, K., & Hjelt-Back, M. (1994). Aggression among university employees. *Aggressive Behavior, 20,* 173–184.

Blanck, P. D., & Rosenthal, R. (1992). Nonverbal behavior in the courtroom. In R. S. Feldman (Ed.) et al., *Applications of nonverbal behavioral theories and research.* (pp.89–115). Hillsdale, NJ: Lawrence Erlbaum.

Blaney, P. H. (1986). Affect and memory: A review. *Psychological Bulletin, 99,* 229–246.

Blascovich, J., Spencer, S. J., Quinn, D., & Steele, C. (2001). African Americans and high blood pressure: The role of stereotype threat. *Psychological Science, 12,* 225–229.

Blascovich, J., Wyer, N. A., Swart, L. A., & Kibler, J. L. (1997). Racism and racial categorization. *Journal of Personality and Social Psychology, 72,* 1364–1372.

Bobo, L. (1983). Whites' opposition to busing: Symbolic racism or realistic group conflict? *Journal of Personality and Social Psychology, 45,* 1196–1210.

Bochner, A. P. (1991). On the paradigm that would not die. In J. A. Anderson (Ed.), *Communication yearbook 14* (pp. 44–491). Newbury Park, CA: Sage.

Bodenhausen, G. V. (1988). Stereotypic biases in social decision making and memory: Testing process models of stereotype use. *Journal of Personality and Social Psychology, 55,* 726–737.

Bodenhausen, G. V., Kramer, G. P., & Susser, K. (1994). Happiness and stereotypic thinking in social judgment. *Journal of Personality and Social Psychology, 66,* 621–632.

Bodi, F. (2003). Al-Jazeera tells the truth about war: My station is a threat to American media control—and they know it. *The Guardian,* March 28, 2003. Guardian Unlimited: Guardian Newspapers Ltd, U.K.. http://www.guardian.co.uk/print/0,3858, 4635417-103677,00.html

Bogard, M. (1990). Why we need gender to understand human violence. *Journal of Interpersonal Violence, 5,* 132–135.

Bolger, N., & Zuckerman, A. (1995). A framework for studying personality in the stress process. *Journal of Personality and Social Psychology, 69,* 890–902.

Bond, C. F. (1982). Social facilitation: A self-presentational view. *Journal of Personality and Social Psychology, 42,* 1042–1050.

Bond, C. F., Jr., & Atoum, A. O. (2000). International deception. *Personality and Social Psychology Bulletin, 26,* 385–395.

Bond, M. H. Leung, K., & Wan, K. C. (1982). The social impact of self effacing attributions: The Chinese case. *Journal of Social Psychology, 118,* 157–166.

Bond, R., & Smith, P. B. (1996). Culture and conformity: A meta-analysis of studies using Asch's (1952b, 1956) line judgment task. *Psychological Bulletin, 119*, 111–137.

Bookwala, J., Frieze, I. H., & Grote, N. K. (1994). Love, aggression and satisfaction in dating relationships. *Journal of Social and Personal Relationships, 11*, 625–632.

Booth-Kewley, S., & Vickers, R. R. Jr. (1994). Associations between major domains of personality and health behavior. *Journal of Personality, 62*, 281–298.

Bornstein, R. F. (1995). Interpersonal dependency and physical illness: The mediating roles of stress and social support. *Journal of Social and Clinical Psychology, 14*, 225–243.

Bornstein, R. F., & D'Agostino, P. R. (1992). Stimulus recognition and the mere exposure effect. *Journal of Personality and Social Psychology, 63*, 545–552.

Bossard, J. H. S. (1932). Residential propinquity as a factor in marriage selection. *American Journal of Sociology, 38*, 219–224.

Bosson, J. K., & Swann, W. B., Jr. (1999). Self-liking, self-competence, and the quest for self-verification. *Personality and Social Psychology Bulletin, 25*, 1230–1241.

Botha, M. (1990). Television exposure and aggression among adolescents: A follow-up study over 5 years. *Aggressive Behavior, 16*, 361–380.

Bothwell, R. K., & Jalil, M. (1992). The credibility of nervous witnesses. *Journal of Social Behavior and Personality, 7*, 581–586.

Bothwell, R. K., Deffenbacher, K. A., & Brigham, J. C. (1987). Correlation of eyewitness accuracy and confidence: Optimality hypothesis revisited. *Journal of Applied Psychology, 72*, 691–695.

Bouchard, T. J., Arvey, R. D., Keller, L. M., & Segal, N. L. (1992). Genetic influences on job satisfaction: A reply to Cropanzano and Hames. *Journal of Applied Psychology, 77*, 89–93.

Bourhis, R.Y. (1984). Cross-cultural communication in Montreal: Two field studies since Bill 101. *International Journal of the Sociology of Language, 46*, 33–47.

Bourhis, R.Y. (1990). Organization communication in bilingual settings: The linguistic work environment survey. In H. Giles, N. Coupland, & J. Coupland (Eds.), *Contexts of accommodation: Developments in applied psycholinguistics*. Cambridge: Cambridge University Press.

Bower, G. H. (1991). Mood congruity of social judgments. In J. P. Forgas (Ed.), *Emotion and social judgments* (pp. 31–55). Oxford: Pergamon Press.

Bower, G. H., & Hilgard, E. R. (1981). *Theories of learning* (5th ed.). Englewood Cliffs, NJ: Prentice-Hall.

Bowlby, J. (1973). *Attachment and loss: Vol. 2 Separation: Anxiety and anger*. New York: Basic Books.

Bowman, M. L. (2003). The diversity of diversity: Canadian-American differences and their implications for clinical training and APA accreditation. *Canadian Psychology, 41*, 230–243.

Branscombe, N. R., & Wann, D. L. (1993). Collective self-esteem consequences of outgroup derogation under identity-threatening and identity-bolstering conditions. *European Journal of Social Psychology*.

Branscombe, N. R., & Wann, D. L. (1994). Collective self-esteem consequences of outgroup derogation when a valued social identity is on trial. *European Journal of Social Psychology, 24*, 641–657.

Brehm, J. W. (1966). *A theory of psychological reactance*. New York: Academic Press.

Brennan, K. A., & Bosson, J. K. (1998). Attachment-style differences in attitudes toward and reactions to feedback from romantic partners: An exploration of the relational bases of self-esteem. *Personality and Social Psychology Bulletin, 24*, 699–714.

Brewer, B. W. (1993). Self-identity and specific vulnerability to depressed mood. *Journal of Personality, 61*, 343–386.

Brewer, M. B. (1986). The role of ethnocentrism in intergroup conflict. In S. Worchel & W.G. Austin (Eds.), *Psychology of intergroup relations* (2nd ed.) (pp. 88–102). Chicago: Nelson-Hall.

Brewer, M. B. (2001). Preface. In Sedikides, C., & Brewer, M. B. (Eds.). *Individual self, relational self, collective self*. Philadelphia: Psychology Press.

Brewer, M. B., Ho, H., Lee, J., & Miller, M. (1987). Social identity and social distance among Hong Kong school children. *Personality and Social Psychology Bulletin, 13*, 156–165.

Brickner, M., Harkins, S., & Ostrom, T. (1986). Personal involvement: Thought-provoking implications for social loafing. *Journal of Personality and Social Psychology, 51*, 763–769.

Bringle, R. G., & Bagby, G. J. (1992). Self-esteem and perceived quality of romantic and family relationships in young adults. *Journal of Research in Personality, 26*, 340–356.

Bringle, R. G., & Winnick, T. A. (1992, October). The nature of unrequited love. Paper presented at the first Asian Conference in Psychology, Singapore.

Brockner, J. M., & Wiesenfeld, B. M. (1996). An integrative framework for explaining reactions to decisions: Interactive effects of outcomes and procedures. *Psychological Bulletin, 120*, 189–208.

Brockner, J., Konovsky, M., Cooper-Schneider, R., Folger, R., Martin, C., & Bies, R. J. (1994). Interactive effects of procedural justice and outcome negativity on victims and survivors of job loss. *Academy of Management Journal, 37*, 397–409.

Brody, L. R., & Hall, J. A. (1993). Gender and emotion. In M. Lewis & J. Haviland (Eds.), *Handbook of emotions* (pp. 447–460). New York: Guilford.

Brooks-Gunn, J., & Lewis, M. (1981). Infant social perception: Responses to pictures of parents and strangers. *Developmental Psychology*, 647–649.

Brown, J. D., & Kobayashi, C. (2002). Self-enhancement in Japan and America. *Asian Journal of Social Psychology, 5*, 145–168.

Brown, J. D., & Kobayashi, C. (2003). Motivation and manifestation: Cross-cultural expression of the self-enhancement motive. *Asian Journal of Social Psychology, 6*, 85–88.

Brown, J. D. (1991). Staying fit and staying well: Physical fitness as a moderator of life stress. *Journal of Personality and Social Psychology, 60*, 555–561.

Brown, J. D., & Rogers, R. J. (1991). Self-serving attributions: The role of physiological arousal. *Personality and Social Psychology Bulletin, 17*, 501–506.

Brown, K. W., & Moskowitz, D. S. (1997). Does unhappiness make you sick? The role of affect and neuroticism in the experience of common physical symptoms. *Journal of Personality and Social Psychology, 72*, 907–917.

Brown, L. S. (1997). The private practice of subversion: Psychology as tikkun olam. *American Psychologist, 52*, 449–462.

Brown, S. L. (1998). Associations between peer drink driving, peer attitudes toward drink, driving, and personal drink driving. *Journal of Applied Social Psychology, 28*, 423–436.

Browne, M. W. (1992, April 14). Biologists tally generosity's rewards. *New York Times*, pp. C1, C8.

Bryan, J. H., & Test, M. A. (1967). Models and helping: Naturalistic studies in aiding behavior. *Journal of Personality and Social Psychology, 6*, 400–407.

Buck, R., & Ginsburg, B. (1991). Spontaneous communication and altruism: The communicative gene hypothesis. In M. S. Clark (Ed.), *Prosocial behavior* (pp. 149–175). Newbury Park, CA: Sage.

Buehler, R., & Griffin, D. (1994). Change-of-meaning effects in conformity and dissent: Observing contrual processes over time. *Journal of Personality and Social Psychology, 67*, 984–996.

Buehler, R., Griffin, D., & MacDonald, H. (1997). The role of motivated reasoning in optimistic time predictions. *Personality and Social Psychology Bulletin, 23*, 238–247.

Buehler, R., Griffin, D., & Ross, M. (1994). Exploring the "planning fallacy": Why people underestimate their task completion times. *Journal of Personality and Social Psychology, 67*, 366–381.

Burger, J. M. (1986). Increasing compliance by improving the deal: The that's-not-all technique. *Journal of Personality and Social Psychology, 51*, 277–283.

Burger, J. M. (1992). *Desire for control: Personality, social, and clinical perspectives*. New York: Plenum.

Burnstein, E. (1983). Persuasion as argument processing. In M. Brandstatter, J. H. Davis, & G. Stocker-Kriechgauer (Eds.), *Human decision processes*. London: Academic Press.

Burnstein, E., Crandall, C., & Kitayama, S. (1994). Some neo-Darwinian rules for altruism: Weighing cues for inclusive fitness as a function of the biological importance of the decision. *Journal of Personality and Social Psychology, 67*, 773–789.

Bushman, B. J. (1984). Perceived symbols of authority and their influence on compliance. *Journal of Applied Social Psychology, 14*, 501–508.

Bushman, B. J. (1988). The effects of apparel on compliance: A field experiment with a female authority figure. *Personality and Social Psychology Bulletin, 14*, 459–467.

Bushman, B. J. (1998). Effects of television violence on memory for commercial messages. *Journal of Experimental Psychology: Applied, 4*, 1–17.

Bushman, B. J. (2001). Does venting anger feed or extinguish the flame? Catharsis, rumination, distraction, anger, and aggressive responding. Manuscript under review.

Bushman, B. J., & Baumeister, R. F. (1998). Threatened egotism, narcissism, self-esteem, and direct and displaced aggression: Does self-love or self-hate lead to violence? *Journal of Personality and Social Psychology, 75*, 219–229.

Bushman, B. J., & Cooper, H. M. (1990). Effects of alcohol on human aggression: An integrative research review. *Psychological Bulletin, 107*, 341–354.

Bushman, B. J., Baumeister, R. F., & Stack, A. D. (1999). Catharsis messages and anger-reducing activities. *Journal of Personality and Social Psychology, 76*, 367–376.

Buss, D. M. (1989). Conflict between the sexes: Strategic interference and the evocation of anger and upset. *Journal of Personality and Social Psychology, 56*, 735–747.

Buss, D. M. (1994). The strategies of human mating. *American Scientist, 82*, 238–249.

Buss, D. M. (1995). Evolutionary psychology: A new paradigm for psychological science. *Psychological Inquiry, 6*, 1–30.

Buss, D. M. (1998). *Evolutionary psychology*. Boston: Allyn and Bacon.

Buss, D. M., & Schmitt, D. P. (1993). Sexual strategies theory: An evolutionary perspective on human mating. *Psychological Review, 100*, 204–232.

Buss, D. M., & Shackelford, T. K. (1997). From vigilance to violence: Mate retention tactics in married couples. *Journal of Personality and Social Psychology, 72*, 346–361.

Buss, D.M. (1999). Human nature and individual differences: The evolution of human personality. In L.A. Pervin, O.P. John, et al. (Eds.), *Handbook of personality theory and research. Second edition*. New York: Guilford Press.

Butler & Geis, D., & Geis, F. L. (1990). Nonverbal affect responses to male and female leaders: Implications for leadership evaluations. *Journal of Personality and Social Psychology, 58*, 48–59.

Butler, A. C., Hokanson, J. E., & Flynn, H. A. (1994). A comparison of self-esteem liability and low trait self-esteem as vulnerability factors for depression. *Journal of Personality and Social Psychology, 66*, 166–177.

Buunk, B. P. (1995). Sex, self-esteem, dependency and extradyadic sexual experience as related to jealousy responses. *Journal of Social and Personal Relationships, 12*, 147–153.

Buunk, B. P., & van der Eijnden, R. J. J. M. (1997). Perceived prevalence, perceived superiority, and relationship satisfaction: Most relationships are good, but ours is the best. *Personality and Social Psychology Bulletin, 23*, 219–228.

Byrne, D. (1992). The transition from controlled laboratory experimentation to less controlled settings: Surprise! Additional variables are operative. Communication Monographs, 190–198.

Byrne, D., & Blaylock, B. (1963). Similarity and assumed similarity of attitudes among husbands and wives. *Journal of Abnormal and Social Psychology, 67*, 636–640.

Byrne, D., & Buehler, R. A. (1955). A note on the influence of propinquity upon acquaintanceships. *Journal of Abnormal and Social Psychology, 51*, 147–148.

Byrne, D., & Clore, G. L. (1970). A reinforcement-affect model of evaluative responses. *Personality: An International Journal, 1*, 103–128.

Byrne, D., & Murnen, S. K. (1988). Maintaining loving relationships. In R. J. Sternberg & M. L. Barnes (Eds.), *The psychology of love* (pp. 293–310). New Haven, CT: Yale University Press.

Byrne, D., & Nelson, D. (1965). Attraction as a linear function of proportion of positive reinforcements. *Journal of Personality and Social Psychology, 1*, 659–663.

Byrne, D., Gouaux, C., Griffitt, W., Lamberth, J., Murakawa, N., Prasad, M. B., Prasad A., & Ramirez, M., III. (1971). The ubiquitous relationship: Attitude similarity and attraction: A cross-cultural study. *Human Relations, 24*, 201–207.

Cacioppo, J. T., Gardner, W. L., & Berntson, G. G. (1999). The affect system has parallel and integrative processing components: Form follows function. *Journal of Personality and Social Psychology, 76*, 839–855.

Caldwell, M.A. & Peplau, L.A. (1982). Sex differences in same-sex friendship. *Sex Roles, 8*, 721–732.

Callan, V. J. (1993). Subordinate manager communication in different sex-dyads: Consequences for job satisfaction. *Journal of Occupational and Organizational Psychology, 66*, 13–27.

Calle, E. E., Thun, M. J., Petrelli, J. M., Rodriguez, M. P. H., & Heath, C. W. (1999). Body-mass index and mortality in a prospective cohort of U.S. adults. *New England Journal of Medicine, 341*, 1097–1105.

Cameron, C. (1977). Sex-role attitudes. In S. Oskamp (Ed.), *Attitudes and opinions* (pp, 339–359). Englewood Cliffs, NJ: Prentice Hall.

Campbell, D. T. (1958). Common fate, similarity, and other indices of the status of aggregates of persons as social entities. *Behavioral Science, 4*, 14–25.

Campbell, D. T. (1975). On the conflicts between biological and social evolution and between psychological and moral tradition. *American Psychologist, 30*, 1103–1126.

Campbell, D. T., & Specht, J. C. (1985). Altruism: Biology, culture, and religion. *Journal of Social and Clinical Psychology, 3*, 33–42.

Campbell, J. D., Chew, B., & Scratchley, L. S. (1991). *Cognitive and emotional reactions to daily events: The effects of self-esteem and self-complexity.*

Cann, A., Calhoun, L. G., & Banks, J. S. (1995). On the role of humor appreciation in interpersonal attraction: It's no joking matter. *Humor: International Journal of Humor Research.*

Caprara, G. V., Barbaranelli, C., Pastorelli, C., & Perugini, M. (1994). Individual differences in the study of human aggression. *Aggressive Behavior, 20*, 291–303.

Carey, M. P., Morrison-Beedy, D., & Johnson, B. T. (1997). The HIV-Knowledge Questionnaire: Development and evaluation of a reliable, valid, and practical self-administered questionnaire. *AIDS and Behavior, 1*, 61–74.

Carlson, K. A., & Russo, J. E. (2001). Biased interpretation of evidence by mock jurors: A meta-analysis. *Journal of Experimental Psychology: Applied, 7*, 91–103.

Carnelley, K. B., Pietromonaco, P. R., & Jaffe, K. (1996). Attachment, caregiving, and relationship functioning in couples: Effects of self and partner. *Personal Relationships, 3*, 257–278.

Carpenter, S. (2001, July/August). They're positively inspiring. *Monitor on Psychology*, 74–76.

Carpenter, S. (2001, March). Fools rush in. *Monitor on Psychology*, 66–67.

Carpenter, S. (2001, October). Technology gets its day in court. *Monitor on Psychology*, 30–32.

Carroll, J. M., & Russell, J. A. (1996). Do facial expressions signal specific emotions? Judging emotion from the face in context. *Journal of Personality and Social Psychology, 70*, 205–218.

Carter, D. B. & McCloskey, L. A. (1984). Peers and the maintenance of sex-typed behavior: The development of children's conceptions of cross-gender behavior in their peers. *Social Cognition, 2*, 294–314.

Carver, C. S., & Glass, D. C. (1978). Coronary-prone behavior pattern and interpersonal aggression. *Journal of Personality and Social Psychology, 376*, 361–366.

Carver, C. S., Reynolds, S. L., & Scheier, M. F. (1994). The possible selves of optimists and pessimists. *Journal of Research in Personality, 28*, 133–141.

Cash, T. F., & Duncan, N. C. (1984). Physical attractiveness stereotyping among black American college students. *Journal of Social Psychology, 122*, 71–77.

Cash, T. F., & Jacobi, L. (1992). Looks aren't everything (to everybody): The strength of ideals of physical appearance. *Journal of Social Behavior and Personality, 7*, 621–630.

Cash, T. F., & Trimer, C. A. (1984). *Sexism and beautyism in women's evaluation of peer performance. Sex Roles, 10*, 87–98.

Caspi, A., Herbener, E. S., & Ozer, D. J. (1992). Shared experiences and the similarity of personalities: A longitudinal study of married couples. *Journal of Personality and Social Psychology, 62*, 281–291.

Caspi, A., Herbener, E. S., & Ozer, D. J. (1992). Shared experiences and the similarity of personalities: A longitudinal study of married couples. *Journal of Personality and Social Psychology, 62*, 281–291.

Castellow, W. A., Wuensch, K. L., & Moore, C. H. (1990). Effects of physical attractiveness of the plaintiff and defendant in sexual harassment judgments. *Journal of Social Behavior and Personality, 5*, 547–562.

Caughlin, J. P., Huston, T. L., & Houts, R. M. (2000). How does personality matter in marriage? An examination of trait anxiety, interpersonal negativity, and marital satisfaction. *Journal of Personality and Social Psychology, 78*, 326–336.

Cervone, D. (1997). Social–cognitive mechanisms and personality coherence: Self-knowledge, situational beliefs, and cross-situational coherence in perceived self-efficacy. *Psychological Science, 8*, 43–50.

Chaiken, A.L. & Derlega, V.J. (1974). Liking for the norm-breaker in self-disclosure. *Journal of Personality, 42*, 117–129.

Chaiken, S., Giner-Sorolla, R., & Chen, S. (1996). Beyond accuracy: Defense and impression motives in heuristic and systematic processing. In P. M. Gollwitzer & J. A. Bargh (Eds.), *The psychology action: Linking motivation and cognition to behavior* (pp. 553–578). New York: Guilford.

Chang, E. C. (1998). Dispositional optimism and secondary appraisal of a stressor: Controlling for confounding influences and relations to coping and psychological and physical adjustment. *Journal of Personality and Social Psychology, 74*, 1109–1120.

Chang, E. C., & DeSimone, S. L. (2001). The influence of hope on appraisals, coping, and dysphoria: A test of hope theory. *Journal of Social and Clinical Psychology, 20*, 117–129.

Chaplin, W. F., Phillips, J. B., Brown, J. D., Clanton, N. R., & Stein, J. L. (2000). Handshaking, gender, personality, and first impressions. *Journal of Personality and Social Psychology, 79*, 110–117.

Chapman, B. (1992). The Byrne-Nelson formula revisited: The additional impact of number of dissimilar attitudes on attraction. Unpublished masters thesis, University at Albany, State University of New York.

Chapman, H. A., Hobfoll, S. E., & Ritter, C. (1997). Partners' stress under-estimations lead to women's distress: A study of pregnant inner-city women. *Journal of Personality and Social Psychology, 73*, 418–425.

Chappell, K. D., & Davis, K. E. (1998). Attachment, partner choice, and perception of romantic partners: An experimental test of the attachment-security hypothesis. *Personal Relationships, 5*, 327–342.

Che-Alford, J., Allan, C., & Butlin, G. (1994). *Families in Canada* (Focus on Canada series). Scarborough, Ont.: Statistics Canada and Prentice Hall Canada.

Cheney, D. L., & Seyfarth, R. M. (1992). Précis of how monkeys see the world. *Behavioral and Brain Sciences, 15*, 135–182.

Chermack, S. T., Berman, M., & Taylor, S. P. (1997). Effects of provocation on emotions and aggression in males. *Aggressive Behavior, 23*, 1–10.

Cheung, S.-K., & Sun, S. Y. K. (2000). Effects of self-efficacy and social support on the mental health conditions of mutual-aid and organization members. *Social Behavior and Personality, 28*, 413–422.

Choi, I., & Nisbett, R. E. (1998). Situational salience and cultural differences in the correspondence bias and actor-observer bias. *Personality and Social Psychology Bulletin, 24*, 949–960.

Christy, C. A., & Voigt, H. (1994). Bystander responses to public episodes of child abuse. *Journal of Applied Social Psychology, 24*, 824–847.

Christy, P. R., Gelfand, D. N., & Hartmann, D. P. (1971). Effects of competition-induced frustration on two classes of modeled behavior. *Developmental Psychology, 5*, 104–111.

Cialdini, R. B. (1994). Interpersonal influence. In S. Shavitt & T. C. Brock (Eds.), *Persuasion* (pp. 195–218). Boston: Allyn & Bacon.

Cialdini, R. B., & Petty, R. (1979). Anticipatory opinion effects. In R. B. Petty, T. Ostrom, & T. Brock (Eds.), *Cognitive responses in persuasion*. Hillsdale, NJ: Erlbaum.

Cialdini, R. B., Brown, S. L., Lewis, B. P., Luce, C., & Neuberg, S. L. (1997). Reinterpreting the empathy–altruism relationship: When one into one equals oneness. *Journal of Personality and Social Psychology, 73*, 481–494.

Cialdini, R. B., Cacioppo, J. T., Bassett, R., & Miller J. A. (1978). A low-ball procedure for producing compliance: Commitment then cost. *Journal of Personality and Social Psychology, 36*, 463–476.

Cialdini, R. B., Kallgren, C. A., & Reno, R. R. (1991). A focus theory of normative conduct. *Advances in Experimental Social Psychology, 24*, 201–234.

Cialdini, R. B., Kenrick, D. T., & Bauman, D. J. (1982). Effects of mood on prosocial behavior in children and adults. In N. Eisenberg-Berg (Ed.), *Development of prosocial behavior*. New York: Academic Press.

Cialdini, R. B., Reno, R. R., & Kallgren, C. A. (1990). A focus theory of normative conduct: Recycling the concept of norms to reduce littering in public places. *Journal of Personality and Social Psychology, 58*, 1015–1026.

Cialdini, R. B., Schaller, M., Houlainham, D., Arps, K., Fultz, J., & Beaman, A. L. (1987). Empathy-based helping: Is it selflessly or selfishly motivated? *Journal of Personality and Social Psychology, 52*, 749–758.

Cialdini, R. B., Vincent, J. E., Lewis, S. K., Catalan, J., Wheeler, D., & Darby, B. L. (1975). Reciprocal concessions procedure for inducing compliance: The door-in-the-face technique. *Journal of Personality and Social Psychology, 31*, 206–215.

Civin, M.A. (1999). On the vicissitudes of cyberspace as potential-space. *Human Relations, 52*, 485–506.

Clark, K., & Clark, M. (1947). Racial identification and racial preferences in Negro children. In T. M. Newcomb & E. L. Hartley, *Readings in social psychology* (pp.169–178). New York: Holt.

Clark, L. F. (1993). Stress and the cognitive-conversational benefits of social interaction. *Journal of Social and Clinical Psychology, 12*, 25–55.

Clark, M. S., Ouellette, R., Powel, M. C., & Milberg, S. (1987). Recipient's mood, relationship type, and helping. *Journal of Personality and Social Psychology, 53*, 94–103.

Clément, R., Baker, S. C. & MacIntyre, P. D. (2003). Willingness to communicate in a second language: The effects of context norms, and vitality. *Journal of Language & Social Psychology, 22*,190–209.

Clément, R. (1987). Second language proficiency and acculturation: an investigation of the effects of language status and individual characteristics. *Journal of Language and Social Psychology, 5*, 271–290.

Cliff, J. E. (1998). Does one size fit all? Exploring the relationship between attitudes toward growth, gender, and business size. *Journal of Business Venturing, 13*, 523–542.

Clore, G. L., Schwarz, N., & Conway, M. (1993). Affective causes and consequences of social information processing. In R. S. Wyer & T. K. Srull (Eds.), *Handbook of social cognition* (2nd ed.). Hilldsale, NJ: Erlbaum.

Cohen, D., & Nisbett, R. E. (1997). Field experiments examining the culture of honor: The role of institutions in perpetuating norms about violence. *Personality and Social Psychology Bulletin, 23*, 1188–1199.

Cohen, L. E., & Land, K. C. (1987). Age structure and crime: Symmetry versus asymmetry and the projection of crime rates through the 1990's. *American Sociological Review, 52*, 170–183.

Collins, M. A., & Zebrowitz, L. A. (1995). The contributions of appearance to occupational outcomes in civilian and military settings. *Journal of Applied Social Psychology, 25*, 129–163.

Collins, N. L. (1996). Working models of attachment: Implications for explanation, emotion, and behavior. *Journal of Personality and Social Psychology, 71*, 810–832.

Collins, N. L., Dunkel-Schetter, C., Lobel, M., & Scrimshaw, S. C. M. (1993). Social support in pregnancy: Psychosocial correlates of Birth outcomes and postpartum depression. *Journal of Personality and Social Psychology, 65,* 1243–1258.

Compas, B. E., Banez, G. A., Malcarne, V., & Worsham, N. (1991). Perceived control and coping with stress: A developmental perspective. *Journal of Social Issues, 47*(4), 23–34.

Condon, J. W., & Crano, W. D. (1988). Inferred evaluation and the relation between attitude similarity and interpersonal attraction. *Journal of Personality and Social Psychology, 54,* 789–797.

Conger, J. A. (1991). Inspiring others: The language of leadership. *Academy of Management Executives, 5*(1), 31–45.

Conner, M. T., & McMillan, B. (1999). Interaction effects in the theory of planned behaviour: Studying cannabis use. *British Journal of Social Psychology, 38,* 195–222.

Connolly, J. A., & Johnson, A. M. (1996). Adolescents' romantic relationships and the structure and quality of their close interpersonal ties. *Personal Relationships, 3,* 185–195.

Constantian, C. (1981). Solitude, attitudes, beliefs, and behavior in regard to spending time alone. Unpublished doctoral dissertation, Harvard University.

Contrada, R. J. (1989). Type A behavior, personality hardiness, and cardiovascular responses to stress. *Journal of Personality and Social Psychology, 57,* 895–903.

Cook, P.J. (1987). Robbery violence. *Journal of criminal Law and Criminology, 78,* 357–376.

Cook, S. W. (1985). Experimenting on social issues: The case of school desegregation. *American Psychologist, 40,* 452–460.

Cooke, P. (1992). Noises out: What it's doing to you. *New York, 25*(4), 28–33.

Cooley, C.H. (1902/1964) *Human nature and the social order.* New York: Schocken Books.

Cooper, A., Gimeno-Gascon, F. J., & Woo, C. (1994). Initial human and financial capital as predictors of new venture performance. *Journal of Business Venturing, 9,* 371–395.

Cooper, J., & Scher, S. J. (1992). Actions and attitudes: The role of responsibility and aversive consequences in persuasion. In T. Brock & S. Shavitt (Eds.), *The psychology of persuasion.* San Francisco: Freeman.

Cooper, J., Fazio, R. H., & Rhodewalt, F. (1978). Dissonance and humor: Evidence for the undifferentiated nature of dissonance arousal. *Journal of Personality and Social Psychology, 36,* 280–285.

Cornwell, B., & Lundgren, D. C. (2001). Love on the Internet: Involvement and misrepresentation in romantic relationships in cyberspace vs. realspace. *Computers in Human Behavior, 17,* 197–211.

Cosmides, L., & Tooby, J. (1992). Cognitive adaptations for social exchange. In J. Barkow, L. Cosmides, & J. Tooby (Eds.), *The adapted mind* (pp. 163–228). New York: Oxford University Press.

Costa, P. T., Jr., Terracciano, A., & McCrae, R. R. (2001). Gender differences in personality traits across cultures: Robust and surprising findings. *Journal of Personality and Social Psychology, 81,* 322–331.

Cota, A. A., Evans, C. R., Dion, K. L., Kilik, L., & Longman, R. S. (1995). The structure of group cohesion. *Personality and Social Psychology Bulletin, 21,* 572–580.

Cottrell, H. B., Wack, K. L., Sekerak, G. J., & Rittle, R. (1968). Social facilitation of dominant responses by the presence of an audience and the mere presence of others. *Journal of Personality and Social Psychology, 51,* 245–250.

Courneya, K. S., & McAuley, E. (1993). Efficacy, attributional, and affective responses of older adults following an acute bout of exercise. *Journal of Social Behavior and Personality, 8,* 729–742.

Cousins, S. D. (1989). Culture and self-perception in Japan and the United States. *Journal of Personality and Social Psychology, 56,* 124–131.

Cowei, H. (2000). Bystanding or standing by: Gender issues in coping with bullying in English schools. *Aggressive Behavior, 26,* 85–98.

Cowley, G. (1996, June 3). The biology of beauty. *Newsweek,* 61–66.

Craik, F. I. M., Moroz, T. M., Moscovitch, M., Stuss, D. T., Winocur, G., Tulving, E., & Kapur, S. (1999). In search of the self: A positron emission tomography study. *Psychological Science, 10,* 26–34.

Cramer, R. E., McMaster, M. R., Bartell, P. A., & Dragna, M. (1988). Subject competence and minimization of the bystander effect. *Journal of Applied Social Psychology, 18,* 1133–1148.

Crandall, C. S. (1988). Social contagion of binge eating. *Journal of Personality and Social Psychology, 55,* 588–598.

Crandall, C. S. (1995). Do parents discriminate against their heavyweight daughters? *Personality and Social Psychology Bulletin, 21,* 724–735.

Crandall, C. S., Tsang, J., & Harvey, R. D. (2000).Group identity-based self-protective strategies: The stigma of race, gender, and garlic. *European Journal of Social Psychology, 30,* 355–381.

Crano, W. D. (1995). Attitude strength and vested interest. In R. E. Petty & J. A. Krosnick (Eds.), *Attitude strength: Antecedents and consequences* (Vol. 4, pp. 131–157). Hillsdale, NJ: Erlbaum.

Crano, W. D. (1997). Vested interest, symbolic politics, and attitude-behavior consistency. *Journal of Personality and Social Psychology, 72,* 485–491.

Crano, W. D., & Prislin, R. (1995). Components of vested interest and attitude-behavior consistency. *Basic and Applied Social Psychology, 17,* 1–21.

Crealia, R., & Tesser, A. (1996). Attitude heritability and attitude reinforcement: A replication. *Personality and Individual Differences, 21,* 803–808.

Creese, G., & Beagan, B. (1999). Gender at work: Seeking solutions for women's equality. In J. Curtis, E. Grabb, & N. Guppy (Eds.), *Social inequality in Canada: Patterns, problems, and policies* (2nd ed., pp. 199–211). Scarborough, ON: Prentice Hall.

Crites, S. L., Jr., Cacioppo, J. T., Gardner, W. L., & Bernston, G. G. (1995). Bioelectrical echoes from evaluative categorization: II. A late positive brain potential that varies as a function of attitude registration rather than attitude report. *Journal of Personality and Social Psychology, 68,* 997–1013.

Crocker, J. (1993). Memory for information about others: Effects of self-esteem and performance feedback. *Journal of Research in Personality, 27,* 35–48.

Crocker, J., & Major, B. (1989). Social stigma and self-esteem: The self-protective properties of stigma. *Psychological Review, 96,* 608–630.

Crocker, J., & Major, B. (1993). When bad things happen to bad people: The perceived justifiability of negative outcomes based on stigma. Unpublished Manuscript.

Crocker, J., Cornwell, B., & Major, B. (1993). *The stigma of being overweight: Affective consequences of attributional.*

Crocker, J., Luhtanen, R., Blaine, B., & Broadnax, S. (1994). Collective self-esteem and psychological well-being among white, black, and Asian college students. *Personality and Social Psychology Bulletin, 20,* 503–513.

Croizet, J. C., & Claire, T. (1998). Extending the concept of stereotype threat to social class: The intellectual underperformance of students from low socioeconomic backgrounds. *Personality and Social Psychology Bulletin, 24,* 588–594.

Cropanzano, R. (Ed.). (1993). *Justice in the workplace* (pp. 79–103). Hillsdale, NJ: Erlbaum.

Cropanzano, R., & James, K. (1990). Some methodological considerations for the behavioral-genetic analysis of work attitudes. *Journal of Applied Psychology, 71,* 433–439.

Crosby, F. (1984). The denial of personal discrimination. *American Behavioral Scientist, 27,* 371–386.

Crosby, F. J. (1982). *Relative deprivation and working women.* Oxford: Oxford University Press.

Crowley, K., Callanan, M. A., Tenenbaum, H. R., & Allen, E. (2001). Parents explain more often to boys than to girls during shared scientific thinking. *Psychological Science, 12,* 258–261.

Crumm, D. (1998, December 11). Keeping the faith may keep mind, body going. Knight Ridder.

Crusco, A. H., & Wetzel, C. G. (1984). The Midas touch: The effects of interpersonal touch on restaurant tipping. *Personality and Social Psychology Bulletin, 10,* 512–517.

Cruse, D., & Leigh, B. S. (1987). "Adam's Rib" revisited: Legal and non-legal influences on the processing of trial testimony. *Social Behavior, 2,* 221–230.

Crutchfield, R. A. (1955). Conformity and character. *American Psychologist, 10,* 191–198.

Csikszentmihalyi, M., & LeFevre, J. (1989). Optimal experience in work and leisure. *Journal of Personality and Social Psychology, 56,* 815–822.

Cukier, W. (1998). Firearms regulation: Canada in the international context. *Health Canada - Chronic Diseases in Canada, 19* (1).

Cunningham, D. R. (1989). Reactions to heterosexual opening gambits: Female selectivity and male responsiveness. *Personality and Social Psychology Bulletin, 15,* 27–41.

Cunningham, M. R., Roberts, A. R., Wu, C.-H., Barbee, A. P., & Druen, P. B. (1995). "Their ideas of beauty are, on the whole, the same as ours": Consistency and variability in the cross-cultural perception of female physical attractiveness. *Journal of Personality and Social Psychology, 68,* 261–279.

Cunningham, M. R., Shaffer, D. R., Barbee, A. P., Wolff, P. L., & Kelley, D. J. (1990). Separate processes in the relation of elation and depression to helping: Social versus personal concerns. *Journal of Experimental Social Psychology, 26,* 13–33.

da Gloria, J., Pahlavan, F., Duda, D., & Bonnet, P. (1994). Evidence for a motor mechanism of pain-induced aggression instigation in humans. *Aggressive Behavior, 20,* 1–7.

Dabbs, J. M., Jr. (1992). Testosterone measurements in social and clinical psychology. *Journal of Social and Clinical Psychology, 11,* 302–321.

Daly, M., & Wilson, M. I. (1982). Homicide and kinship. *American Anthropologist, 84,* 372–378.

Daly, M., & Wilson, M. I. (1999). Human evolutionary psychology and animal behavior. *Animal behavior, 57,* 509–519.

Daly, M., & Wilson, M.I. (1988*). Homicide.* Hawthorne, NY: Aldine de Gruyter.

Damasio, A. R. (1994). *Descartes' error: Emotion, reason and the human brain.* New York: Putnam.

Dana, E. R., Lalwani, N., & Duval, S. (1997). Objective self-awareness and focus of attention following awareness of self-standard discrepancies: Changing self or changing standards of correctness. *Journal of Social and Clinical Psychology, 16,* 359–380.

Dane, F. C. (1992). Applying social psychology in the courtroom: Understanding stereotypes in jury decision making. *Contemporary Social Psychology, 16,* 33–36.

Darley, J. M. (1991). Altruism and prosocial behavior research: Reflections and prospects. In M. S. Clark (Ed.), *Prosocial Behavior* (pp. 312–327). Newbury Park, CA: Sage.

Darley, J. M. (1995). Constructive and destructive obedience: A taxonomy of principal-agent relationships. *Journal of Social Issues, 125,* 125–154.

Darley, J. M., & Batson, C. D. (1973). From Jerusalem to Jericho: A study of situational and dispositional variables in helping behavior. *Journal of Personality and Social Psychology, 27,* 100–108.

Darley, J. M., & Latané, B. (1968). Bystander intervention in emergencies: Diffusion of responsibility. *Journal of Personality and Social Psychology, 8,* 377–383.

Darwin, C. (1871). *The descent of man and selection in relation to sex.* London: Murray.

Darwin, C. (1872). *The expression of emotion in man and animals.* London: Murray.

Dasgupta, N., Banji, M. R., & Abelson, R. P. (1999). Group entiativity and group perception: Association between physical features and psychological judgment. *Journal of Personality and Social Psychology, 75,* 991–1005.

Daubman, K. A. (1993). The self-threat of receiving help: A comparison of the threat-to-self-esteem model and the threat-to-interpersonal-power model. Unpublished manuscript, Gettysburg College, Gettysburg, PA.

Davidson, A. R., & Thompson, E. (1980). Cross-cultural studies of attitudes and beliefs. In H.C. Triandis & R. N. Brislin (Eds.), *Handbook of cross-cultural psychology, Vol. 5,* pp. 25–71. Boston: Allyn & Bacon.

Davie, M. R., & Reeves, R. J. (1939). Propinquity of residence before marriage. *American Journal of Sociology, 44,* 510–517.

Davis, C., Brewer, H., & Weinstein, M. (1993). A study of appearance anxiety in young men. *Social Behavior and Personality, 21,* 63–74.

Davis, J. H. (1989). Psychology and the law: The last 15 years. *Journal of Applied Social Psychology, 19,* 119–230.

Davis, J. H., Tindale, R. S., Naggao, D. H., Hinsz, V. B., & Robertson, B. (1984). Order effects in multiple decisions by groups: A demonstration with mock juries and trial procedures. *Journal of Personality and Social Psychology, 47,* 1003–1012.

Davis, J. L., & Rusbult, C. E. (2001). Attitude alignment in close relationships. *Journal of Personality and Social Psychology, 81,* 65–84.

Davis, M. H., Morris, M. M., & Kraus, L. A. (1998). Relationship-specific and global perceptions of social support: Associations with well-being and attachment. *Journal of Personality and Social Psychology, 74,* 468–481.

Davis, P. J. (1999). Gender differences in autobiographical memory for childhood emotional experiences. *Journal of Personality and Social Psychology, 76,* 498–510.

Dawkins, R. (1976). *The selfish gene.* Oxford: Oxford University Press.

de Waal, F. (1996). *Good natured: The origins of right and wrong in humans and other animals.* Cambridge, MA: Harvard University Press.

de Waal, F. B. M. (2002). Evolutionary psychology: The wheat and the chaff. *Current Directions in Psychological Science, 11,* 187–191.

Dean-Church, L., & Gilroy, F. D. (1993). Relation of sex-role orientation to life satisfaction in a healthy elderly sample. *Journal of Social Behavior and Personality, 8,* 133–140.

Deaux, K. (1993). Commentary: Sorry, wrong number—a reply to Gentile's call. *Psychological Science, 4,* 125–126.

Deaux, K., & Hanna, R. (1984). Courtship in the personals column: The influence of gender and sexual orientation. *Sex Roles, 11,* 363–375.

DeBono, K. G., & Snyder, M. (1995). Acting on one's attitudes: The role of a history of choosing situations. *Personality and Social Psychology Bulletin, 21,* 629–636.

DeDreu, C. K. W., & McCusker, C. (1997). Gain-loss frames and cooperation in two-person social dilemmas: A transformational analysis. *Journal of Personality and Social Psychology, 72,* 1093–1106.

DeDreu, C. K. W., & Van Lange, P. A. M. (1995). Impact of social value orientation on negotiator cognition and behavior. *Personality and Social Psychology Bulletin, 21,* 1178–1188.

DeJong, W., & Musilli, L. (1982). External pressure to comply: Handicapped versus nonhandicapped requesters and the foot-in-the-door phenomenon. *Personality and Social Psychology Bulletin, 8,* 522–527.

Dengerink, H. A., Schnedler, R. W., & Covey, M. X. (1978). Role of avoidance in aggressive responses to attack and no attack. *Journal of Personality and Social Psychology, 36,* 1044–1053.

DePaulo, B. M. (1992). Nonverbal behavior and self-presentation. *Psychological Bulletin, 111,* 230–243.

DePaulo, B. M. (1994). Spotting lies: Can humans learn to do better? *Current Directions in Psychological Science, 3,* 873–886.

DePaulo, B. M., Stone, J. L., & Lassiter, G. D. (1985). Deceiving and detecting deceit. In B. R. Schlenker (Ed.), *The self and social life* (pp. 3230–3370). New York: McGraw-Hill.

Derlega, V.J. & Grzelak, A.L. (1979). Appropriate self-disclosure. In G.J. Chelune (Ed.) *Self-disclosure: Origins, patterns, and implications of openness in interpersonal relationships.* San Francisco: Jossey-Bass.

Desmarais, S., & Curtis, J. (1997). Gender and perceived pay entitlement: Testing for effects of experience with income. *Journal of Personality and Social Psychology, 72,* 141–150.

DeSteno, D. A., Salovey, P. (1994). Jealousy in close relationships: Multiple perspectives on the green-ey'd monster. In A. L. Weber & J. H. Harvey (Eds), *Perspectives on close relationships,* pp. 217–242. Needham Heights, MA: Allyn & Bacon.

Deutsch, F. M., Zalenski, C. M., & Clark, M. E. (1986). Is there a double standard of aging? *Journal of Applied Social Psychology, 16,* 771–785.

Deutsch, M., & Gerard, H. B. (1955). A study of normative and informational social influences upon individual judgment. *Journal of Abnormal and Social Psychology, 51,* 629–636.

Devine, P. G. (1989). Automatic and controlled processes in prejudice: The role of stereotypes and personal beliefs. In A. R. Pratkanis, S. J. Breckler, & A. G. Greenwalt (Eds.), *Attitude structure and function* (pp. 181–212). Hillsdale, NJ: Erlbaum.

Devine, P. G., & Monteith, M. J. (1993). The role of discrepancy-associated affect in prejudice reduction. In D. M. Mackie & D. L. Hamilton (Eds.), *Affect, cognition, and stereotyping: Interactive processes in intergroup perception* (pp. 317–344). Orlando, FL: Academic Press.

Diehl, M., Elnick, A. B., Bourbeau, L. S., & Labouvie-Vief, G. (1998). Adult attachment styles: Their relations to family context and personality. *Journal of Personality and Social Psychology, 74,* 1656–1669.

Diekmann, K. A., Samuels, S. M., Ross, L., & Bazerman, M. H. (1997). Self-interest and fairness in problems of response allocation: Allocators versus recipients. *Journal of Personality and Social Psychology, 72,* 1061–1074.

Diener, E., Wolsic, B., & Fujita, F. (1995). Physical attractiveness and subjective well-being. *Journal of Personality and Social Psychology, 69,* 120–129.

Dietrich, D. M., & Berkowitz, L. (1997). Alleviation of dissonance by engaging in prosocial behavior or receiving ego-enhancing feedback. *Journal of Social Behavior and Personality, 12,* 557–566.

Dijksterhuis, A., & Bargh, J. A. (2001). The perception-behavior expressway: Automatic effects of social perception on social behavior. In: Zanna, M. P. (Ed), *Advances in experimental social psychology, Vol. 33.* San Diego, CA: Academic Press, pp. 1–40.

Dijksterhuis, A., & van Knippenberg, A. (1996). The knife that cuts both ways: Facilitated and inhibited access to traits as a result of stereotype-activation. *Journal of Experimental Social Psychology, 32,* 271–288.

Dijkstra, P., & Buunk, B. P. (1998). Jealousy as a function of rival characteristics: An evolutionary perspective. *Personality and Social Psychology Bulletin, 24,* 1158–1166.

Dijkstra, P., & Buunk, B. P. (2001). Sex differences in the jealousy-evoking nature of a rival's body build. *Evolution and Human Behavior, 22,* 335–341.

Dindia, K., & Allen, M. (1992). Sex differences in self-disclosure: A meta-analysis. *Psychological Bulletin, 112,* 106–124.

Dineen, T., (1998). Sacred cows and straw men. *American Psychologist, 53,* 487–488.

Dion, K. K., & Dion, K. L. (1991). Psychological individualism and romantic love. *Journal of Social Behavior and Personality, 6,* 17–33.

Dion, K. K., & Dion, K. L. (1993). Individualistic and collectivistic perspectives on gender and the cultural context of love and intimacy. *Journal of Social Issues, 49,* 53–69.

Dion, K. K., & Dion, K. L. (1996). Cultural perspectives on romantic love. *Personal Relationships, 3,* 5–17.

Dion, K. K., Berscheid, E., & Hatfield (Walster), E. (1972). What is beautiful is good. *Journal of Personality and Social Psychology, 24,* 285–290.

Dion, K. K., Pak, A. W.-P., & Dion, K. I. (1990). Stereotyping physical attractiveness: A sociocultural perspective. *Journal of Cross-Cultural Psychology, 21,* 158–179.

Dion, K. L. (1975). Women's reactions to discrimination from members of the same or opposite sex. *Journal of Research in Personality, 9,* 294–306.

Dion, K. L. (2002). The social psychology of perceived prejudice and discrimination. *Canadian Psychology, 43,* 1–10.

Dion, K. L., & Dion, K. K. (1987). Belief in a just world and physical attractiveness stereotyping. *Journal of Personality and Social Psychology, 52,* 775–780.

Dion, K. L., Dion, K. K., & Keelan, J. P. (1990). Appearance anxiety as a dimension of social-evaluative anxiety: Exploring the ugly duckling syndrome. *Contemporary Social Psychology, 14,* 220–224.

Dion, K. L., & Earn, B. M. (1975). The phenomenology of being a target of prejudice. *Journal of Personality and Social Psychology, 32,* 944–950.

Dodge, K. A., Murphy, R. R., & Buchsbaum, K. (1984). The assessment of intention-cue detection skills in children: Implications for developmental psychopathology. *Child Development, 55,* 163–173.

Dodge, K. A., Price, J. N., Bachorowski, J. A., & Newman, J. P. (1990). Hostile attributional biases in severely aggressive adolescents. *Journal of Abnormal Psychology, 99,* 385–392.

Doktor, R. H. (1990). *Asian and American CEOs: A comparative study. Organizational Dynamics.* 18(3), 46–56.

Dollard, J., Doob, L., Miller, N., Mowrer, O. H., & Sears, R. R. (1939). *Frustration and aggression.* New Haven: Yale University Press.

Dona, G. (1991). Acculturation and ethnic identity of Central American refugees in Canada. *Hispanic Journal of Behavioral Sciences, 13,* 230–231.

Dona, G., & Berry, J. W. (1994). Acculturation attitudes and acculturative stress of Central American refugees. *International Journal of Psychology, 29,* 57–70.

Donnerstein, E., & Donnerstein, M. (1976). Research in the control of interracial aggression. In R. G. Geen & E. C. O'Neal (Eds.), *Perspectives on aggression.* New York: Academic Press.

Doob, A. N. (1976). Evidence, procedure and psychological research. In G. Bermant, C Nemeth & N Vidmar (Eds.), *Psychology and the law.* Lexington, MA: Lexington Books.

Doob, A. N. (1985). The many realities of crime. In A. N. Doob, & E.L. Greenspan (Eds.), *Perspectives in criminal law.* Aurora, ON: Canada Law Book.

Doob, A. N., & Macdonald, G. E. (1979). Television viewing and fear of victimization: Is the relationship causal? *Journal of Personality & Social Psychology, 37,* 170–179.

Dovidio, J., & Fazio, R. (1991). New technologies for the direct and indirect assessment of attitudes. In J. Tanur (Ed.), *Questions about survey questions: Meaning, memory, attitudes and social interaction* (pp.204–237). New York: Russell Sage.

Dovidio, J. F., & Gaertner, S. L. (1993). Stereotoypes and evaluative intergroup bias. In D. M. Mackie & D. L. Hamilton (Eds.), *Affect, cognition, and stereotyping: Interactive processes in perception.* Orlando, FL: Academic Press.

Dovidio, J., Kawakami, K., Johnson, C., Johnson, B., & Howard, A. (1997). On the nature of prejudice: Automatic and controlled processes. *Journal of Experimental Social Psychology, 33,* 510–540.

Dovidio, J. F., & Morris, W. N. (1975). Effects of stress and commonality of fate on helping behavior. *Journal of Personality and Social Psychology, 31,* 145–149.

Dovidio, J. F., Brigham, J., Johnson, B. & Garerner, S. (1996). Stereotyping, prejudice, and discrimination: Another look. In N. Macrae, C. Stangor, & M. Hwestone (Eds.), *Stereotypes and stereotyping* (pp. 1276–1319). New York: Guilford.

Dovidio, J. F., Evans, N., & Tyler, R. B. (1986). Racial stereotypes: The contents of their cognitive representations. *Journal of Experimental Social Psychology, 22,* 22–37.

Dovidio, J. F., Gaertner, S. L., Isen, A. M., & Lowrance, R. (1995). Group representations and intergroup bias: Positive affect, similarity, and group size. *Personality and Social Psychology Bulletin, 21,* 856–865.

Downey, J. L., & Damhave, K. W. (1991). The effects of place, type of comment, and effort expended on the perception of flirtation. *Journal of Social Behavior and Personality, 6,* 35–43.

Drigotas, S. M., & Rusbult, C. E. (1992). Should I stay or should I go? A dependence model of breakups. *Journal of Personality and Social Psychology, 62,* 62–87.

Drigotas, S. M., Whitney, G. A., & Rusbult, C. E. (1995). On the peculiarities of loyalty: A diary study of responses to dissatisfaction in everyday life. *Personality & Social Psychology Bulletin, 21,* 596–609.

Driscoll, R., Davis, H. E., & Lipetz, M. E. (1972). Parental interference and romantic love: The Romeo and Juliet effect. *Journal of Personality and Social Psychology, 24*, 1–10.

Dubois, D. L., & Tevendale, H. D. (1999). Self-esteem in childhood and adolescence: Vaccine or epiphenomenon? *Applied and Preventive Psychology, 8*, 103–117.

DuBreuil, S. C., Garry, M., & Loftus, E. F. (1998). Tales from the crib. In S. J. Lynn & K. M. McConkey (Eds.), *Truth in memory.* New York: Guilford.

Duck, S., & Barnes, M. H. (1992). Disagreeing about agreement: Reconciling differences about similarity. Communication Monographs, *59*, 199–208.

Duffy, S.M., & Rusbult, C.E. (1986). Satisfaction and commitment in homosexual and heterosexual relationships. *Journal of Homosexuality, 12*, 1–23.

Dunning, D., & Sherman, D. A. (1997). Stereotypes and tacit inference. *Journal of Personality and Social Psychology, 73*, 459–471.

Dutton, D. G., & Aron, A. P. (1974). Some evidence for heightened sexual attraction under conditions of high anxiety. *Journal of Personality and Social Psychology, 30*, 510–517.

Dutton, D. G., Sauders, K., Starzomski, A., & Bartholomew, D. (1994). Intimacy-anger and insecure attachment as precursors of abuse in intimate relationships. *Journal of Applied Social Psychology, 24*, 1367–1386.

Dutton, D. G. (1992). Theoretical and empirical perspectives on the etiology and prevention of wife assault. In R. D. Peters, R. J. McMahon, & V. L. Quinsey (Eds.). *Aggression and violence throughout the life span.* Newbury Park: Sage.

Dykema, J., Bergbower, K., & Peterson, C. (1995). Pessimistic explanatory style, stress, and illness. *Journal of Social and Clinical Psychology, 14*, 357–371.

Eagly, A. H. (1995). The science and politics of comparing women and men. *American Psychologist, 50*, 145–158.

Eagly, A. H., & Chaiken, S. (1998). Attitude structure and function. In G. Lindsey, S. T., Fiske, & D. T. Gilbert (Eds.), *Handbook of social psychology* (4th ed.). New York: Oxford University Press and McGraw-Hill.

Eagly, A. H., & Mladinic, A. (1994). Are people prejudiced against women? Some answers from research on attitudes, gender stereotypes, and judgments of competence. In W. Sroebe & M. Hewstone (Eds.), *European review of social psychology* (Vol. 5, pp. 1–35). New York: Wiley.

Eagly, A. H., & Wood, W. (1999). The origins of sex differences in human behavior: Evolved dispositions versus social roles. *American Psychologist, 54*, 408–423.

Eagly, A. H., Chen, S., Chaiken, S., & Shaw-Barnes, K. (1999). The impact of attitudes on memory: An affair to remember. *Psychological Bulletin, 124*, 64–89.

Eagly, A. H., Kulesa, P., Brannon, L. A., Shaw, K., & Hutson-Comeaux, S. (2000). Why counterattitudinal messages are as memorable as proattitudinal messages: The importance of active defense against attack. *Personality and Social Psychology Bulletin, 26*, 1392–1408.

Eagly, A. H., Makhijani, M. G., & Klonsky, B. G. (1992). Gender and the evaluation of leaders: A meta-analysis. *Psychological Bulletin, 111*, 3–22.

Earley, P. C. (1993). East meets West meets Mideast: Further explorations of collectivistic and individualistic work groups. *Academy of Management Journal, 36*, 319–348.

Earn, B., & Towson, S. (Eds.) (1986). *Readings in social psychology: Classic and Canadian contributions.* Peterborough, ON: Broadview Press.

Easterbrook, G. (1999, January 4 and 11). America the O.K. *The New Republic*, pp. 19–25.

Edwards, K., & Bryan, T. S. (1997). Judgmental biases produced by instructions to disregard: The (paradoxical) case of emotional information. *Personality and Social Psychology Bulletin, 23*, 849–864.

Edwards, K., Heindel, W., & Louis-Dreyfus, E. (1996). *Directed forgetting of emotional and non-emotional words: Implications for implicit and explicit memory processes.* Manuscript submitted for publication.

Edwards, R. (2003). The propaganda war in Iraq. *The Guardian*, March 26, 2003. Guardian Unlimited: Guardian Newspapers Ltd, U.K.. http://media.guardian.co.uk/print/0,3858,4633268-105236,00.html

Eich, E. (1995). Searching for mood dependent memory. *Psychological Science, 6*, 67–75.

Eisenman, R. (1985). Marijuana use and attraction: Support for Byrne's similarity-attraction concept. *Perceptual and Motor Skills, 61*, 582.

Eisenstadt, D., & Leipe, M. R. (1994). The self-comparison process and self-discrepant feedback: Consequences of learning you are what you thought you were not. *Journal of Personality and Social Psychology, 67*, 611–626.

Ekman, P. (1973). Cross-cultural studies of facial expression. In P. Ekman (Ed.), *Darwin and facial expression.* New York: Academic Press.

Ekman, P. (1989). The argument and evidence about universals in facial expressions of emotion. In H. Wagner & A. Manstead (Eds.), *Handbook of psychophysiology: Emotion and social behavior* (pp. 143–164). New York: Wiley.

Ekman, P. A. (1985). *Telling lies.* New York: Norton.

Ekman, P., & Friesen, W. V. (1975). *Unmasking the face.* Englewood Cliffs, NJ: Prentice-Hall.

Elliot, A. J., & Devine, P. G. (1994). On the motivational nature of cognitive dissonance: Dissonance as psychological discomfort. *Journal of Personality and Social Psychology, 67*, 382–394.

Elliot, A. J., & Sheldon, K. M. (1998). Avoidance personal goals and the personality-illness relationship. *Journal of Personality and Social Psychology, 75*, 1282–1299.

Ellsworth, P. C., & Carlsmith, J. M. (1973). Eye contact and gaze aversion in aggressive encounter. *Journal of Personality and Social Psychology, 33*, 117–122.

Emmons, R. A., & Colby, P. M. (1995). Emotional conflict and well-being: Relation to perceived availability, daily utilization, and observer reports of social support. *Journal of Personality and Social Psychology, 68*, 947–959.

Endo, Y., Heine, S. J., & Lehman, D. R. (2000). Culture and positive illusions in close relationships: How my relationships are better than yours. *Personality and Social Psychology Bulletin, 26*, 1571–1586.

Epley, N., & Dunning, D. (2000). Feeling "holier than thou": Are self-serving assessments produced by errors in self- or social prediction? *Journal of Personality and Social Psychology, 79*, 861–875.

Epley, N., & Huff, C. (1998). Suspicion, affective response, and educational benefit as a result of deception in psychology research. *Personality and Social Psychology Bulletin, 24*, 759–768.

Esses, V. M. (1989). Mood as a moderator of acceptance of interpersonal feedback. *Journal of Personality and Social Psychology, 57*, 769–781.

Esses, V. M., & Webster, C. D. (1988). Physical attractiveness, dangerousness, and the Canadian criminal code. *Journal of Applied Social Psychology, 18*, 1017–1031.

Esses, V. M., & Gardner, R.C. (1966). Multiculturalism in Canada: Context and current status. *Canadian Journal of Behavioural Science, 28*, 145–152.

Estrada, C. A., Isen, A. M., & Young, M. J. (1995). Positive affect improves creative problem solving and influences reported source of practice satisfaction in physicians. *Motivation and Emotion, 18*, 285–300.

Ethier, K. A., & Deaux, K. (1994). Negotiating social identity when contexts change: Maintaining identification and responding to threat. *Journal of Personality and Social Psychology, 67*, 243–251.

Evans, G. W., Bullinger, M., & Hygge, S. (1998). Chronic noise exposure and physiological response: A prospective study of children living under environmental stress. *Psychological Science, 9*, 75–77.

Evans, G. W., Lepore, S. J., & Schroeder, A. (1996). The role of interior design elements in human responses to crowding. *Journal of Personality and Social Psychology, 70*, 41–46.

Evans, M. C., & Wilson, M. (1949). Friendship choices of university women students. *Educational and Psychological Measurement, 9*, 307–312.

Exline, R. (1962). Need affiliation and initial communication behavior in problem-solving groups characterized by low interpersonal visibility. *Psychological Reports, 10*, 79–89.

Fabes, R. A., & Eisenberg, N. (1997). Regulatory control and adults' stress-related responses to daily life events. *Journal of Personality and Social Psychology, 73*, 1107–1117.

Farnsworth, C. H. (1995, June 4). Canada puts different spin on sensational murder trial. *Albany Times Union*, pp. E-8.

Fazio, R. H. (1989). On the power and functionality of attitudes: The role of attitude accessibility. In A. R. Pratkanis, S. J. Breckler, & A. G. Greenwald (Eds.), *Attitude structure and function* (pp. 153–179). Hillsdale, NJ: Erlbaum.

Fazio, R. H., & Hilden, L. E. (2001). Emotional reactions to a seemingly prejudiced response: The role of automatically activated racial attitudes and motivation to control prejudiced reactions. *Personality and Social Psychology Bulletin, 27*, 538–549.

Fazio, R. H., & Powell, M. C. (1997). On the value of knowing one's likes and dislikes: Attitude accessibility, stress, and health in college. *Psychological Science, 8*, 430–436.

Fazio, R. H., & Roskos-Ewoldsen, D. R. (1994). Acting as we feel: When and how attitudes guide behavior. In S. Shavitt & T. C. Brock (Eds.), *Persuasion* (pp. 71–93). Boston: Allyn & Bacon.

Fazio, R. H., & Towles-Schwen, T. (1999). The MODE model of attitude–behavior processes. In S. Chaiken & Y. Trope (Eds.), *Dual process theories in social psychology* (pp. 97–116). New York: Guilford.

Fazio, R., Jackson, J., Dunton, B., & Williams, C. (1995). Variability in automatic activation as an unobtrusive measure of racial attitudes: A bona fide pipeline. *Journal of Personality and Social Psychology, 69*, 1013–1028.

Feather, N. T. (1996). Reactions to penalties for an offense in relation to authoritarianism, values, perceived responsibility, perceived seriousness, and deservingness. *Journal of Personality and Social Psychology, 71*, 571–587.

Fein, S., & Spencer, S. J. (1997). Prejudice as self-image maintenance: Affirming the self through derogating others. *Journal of Personality and Social Psychology, 73*, 31–44.

Feingold, A. (1990). Gender differences in the effects of physical attractiveness on romantic attraction: A comparison across five research paradigms. *Journal of Personality and Social Psychology, 59*, 981–993.

Feingold, A. (1992a). Good-looking people are not what we think. *Psychological Bulletin, 111*, 304–341.

Feingold, A. (1992b). Gender differences in mate selection preferences: A test of the parental investment model. *Psychological Bulletin, 112*, 125–139.

Feingold, A. (1994). Gender differences in personality: A meta-analysis. *Psychological Bulletin, 116*, 412–428.

Feldman, S. S., & Nash, S. C. (1984). The transition from expectancy to parenthood: Impact of the firstborn child on men and women. *Sex Roles, 11*, 61–78.

Felmlee, D. H. (1995). Fatal attractions: Affection and disaffection in intimate relationships. *Journal of Social and Personal Relationships, 12*, 295–311.

Felmlee, D. H. (1998). "Be careful what you wish for...": A quantitative and qualitative investigation of "fatal attractions." *Personal Relationships, 5*, 235–253.

Fenigstein, A., & Abrams, D. (1993). Self-attention and the egocentric assumption of shared perspectives. *Journal of Experimental Social Psychology, 29*, 287–303.

Feshbach, S. (1984). The catharsis hypothesis, aggressive drive, and the reduction of aggression. *Aggressive Behavior, 10*, 91–101.

Festinger, L. (1954). A theory of social comparison processes. *Human Relations, 7*, 117–140.

Festinger, L. (1957). *A theory of cognitive dissonance*. Evanston, IL: Row, Peterson.

Festinger, L., & Carlsmith, J. M. (1959). Cognitive consequences of forced compliance. *Journal of Abnormal and Social Psychology, 38*, 203–210.

Festinger, L., Schachter, S., & Back, K. (1950). *Social pressures in informal groups: A study of a housing community*. New York: Harper.

Fincham, F. D. (2003). Marital conflict: Correlates, structure, and context. *Current Directions in Psychological Science, 12*, 23–27.

Fink, B., & Penton-Voak, I (2002). Evolutionary psychology of facial attractiveness. *Current Directions in Psychological Science, 11*, 154–158.

Finn, J. (1986). The relationship between sex-role attitudes and attitudes supporting marital violence. *Sex Roles, 14,* 235–244.

Fisher, H. (1992). *Anatomy of love.* New York: Norton.

Fisher, J. D., & Byrne, D. (1975). Too close for comfort: Sex differences in response to invasions of personal space. *Journal of Personality and Social Psychology, 32,* 15–21.

Fiske, A. P. (1991). The cultural relativity of selfish individualism: Anthropological evidence that humans are inherently sociable. In M. S. Clark (Ed.), *Prosocial behavior* (pp. 176–214), Newbury Park, CA: Sage.

Fiske, S. T. (1993). Social cognition and social perception. In L. W. Porter & M. R. Rosenzweig (Eds.), *Annual Review of Psychology, 44,* 155–194.

Fiske, S. T., & Taylor, S. E. (1991). *Social cognition* (2nd ed.). New York: Random House.

Flory, J. D., Raikkonen, K., Matthews, K. A., & Owens, J. F. (2000). Self-focused attention and mood during everyday social interactions. *Personality and Social Psychology Bulletin, 26,* 875–883.

Folger, R., & Baron, R. A. (1996). Violence and hostility at work: A model of reactions to perceived injustice. In G. R. VandenBos and E. Q. Bulato (Eds.), *Violence on the job: Identifying risks and developing solutions* (pp. 51–85). Washington, DC: American Psychological Association.

Folger, R., & Bies, R. J. (1989). Managerial responsibilities and procedural justice. *Employee Responsibilities and Rights Journal, 2,* 79–90.

Folkman, S., & Moskowitz, J. T. (2000a). Positive affect and the other side of coping. *American Psychologist, 55,* 647–654.

Folkman, S., & Moskowitz, J. T. (2000b). Stress, positive emotions, and coping. *Current Directions in Psychological Science, 9,* 115–118.

Foot, D.K. (1998). *Boom, bust and echo 2000: Profiting from the demographic shift in the new millennium.* Toronto: Macfarlane, Walter & Ross.

Ford, R., & Blegen, M. (1992). Offensive and defensive use of punitive tactics in explicit bargaining. *Social Psychology Quarterly, 55,* 351–362.

Forgas, J. P. (1994). The role of emotion in social judgments: An introductory review and an affect infusion model (AIM). *European Journal of Social Psychology.*

Forgas, J. P. (1995). Mood and judgment: The affect infusion model (AIM). *Psychological Bulletin, 117,* 39–66.

Forgas, J. P., & Fiedler, K. (1996). Us and them: Mood effects on intergroup discrimination. *Journal of Personality and Social Psychology, 70,* 28–40.

Forge, K. L., & Phemister, S. (1987). The effect of prosocial cartoons on preschool children. *Child Study Journal, 17,* 83–88.

Forrest, J. A., & Feldman, R. S. (2000). Detecting deception and judge's involvement; lower task involvement leads to better lit detection. *Personality and Social Psychology Bulletin, 26,* 118–125.

Forston, M. T., & Stanton, A. L. (1992). Self-discrepancy theory as framework for understanding bulimic symptomatology and associated distress. *Journal of Social and Clinical Psychology, 11,* 103–118.

Forsythe, S., Drake, M. F., & Cox, C. E. (1985). Influence of applicant's dress on interviewer's selection decisions. *Journal of Applied Psychology, 70,* 374–378.

Foster, C. A., Witcher, B. S., Campbell, W. K., & Green, J. D. (1998). Arousal and attraction: Evidence for automatic and controlled processes. *Journal of Personality and Social Psychology, 74,* 86–101.

Foster, M. D., & Matheson, K. (1999). Perceiving and responding to the personal/group discrimination discrepancy. *Personality & Social Psychology Bulletin, 25,* 1319–1329.

Foxhall, K. (2001, March). Study finds marital stress can triple women's risk of recurrent coronary event. *Monitor on Psychology,* 14.

Frable, D. E. S. (1993). Dimensions of marginality: Distinctions among those who are different. *Personality and Social Psychology Bulletin, 19,* 370–380.

Fraczek, A., & Kirwil, L. (1992). Living in the family and child aggression: Studies on some socialization conditions of development of aggression. In A. Fraczek & H. Zumkey (Eds.), *Socialization and aggression.* Berlin: Springer-Verlag.

Fraley, R. C., Garner, J. P., & Shaver, P. R. (2000). Adult attachment and the defensive regulation of attention and memory: Examining the role of preemptive and postemptive defensive processes. *Journal of Personality and Social Psychology, 79,* 816–826.

Frank, R. A. (1996). Tainted therapy and mistaken memory: Avoiding malpractice and preserving evidence with possible adult victims of childhood sexual abuse. *Applied & Preventive Psychology, 5,* 135–164.

Frazier, P. A., Tix, A. P., Klein, C. D., & Arikian, N. J. (2000). Testing theoretical models of the relations between social support, coping, and adjustments to stressful life events. *Journal of Social and Clinical Psychology, 19,* 314–335.

Fredrickson, B. L., Tugade, M. M., Waugh, C. E., & Larkin, G. R. (2003). What good are positive emotions in crises? A prospective study of resilience and emotions following the terrorist attacks on the United States on September 11th, 2001. *Journal of Personality and Social Psychology, 84,* 365–376.

Freedman, J. L., & Fraser, S. C. (1966). Compliance without pressure: The foot-in-the-door technique. *Journal of Personality and Social Psychology, 4,* 195–202.

Frey, D., Schulz-Hardt, S., & Stahlberg, D. (1996). Information seeking among individuals and groups and possible consequences for decision making in business and politics. In E. Witte & J. H. Davis (Eds.), *Understanding group behavior: Small group processes and interpersonal relation* (Vol. 2, pp. 211–225). Mahwah, NJ: Lawrence Erlbaum.

Fricko, M. A. M., & Beehr, T. A. (1992). A longitudinal investigation of interest congruence and gender concentration as predictors of job satisfaction. *Personnel Psychology, 45,* 99–117.

Fried, C. B., & Aronson, E. (1995). Hypocrisy, misattribution, and dissonance reduction. *Personality and Social Psychology Bulletin, 21,* 925–933.

Friedman, H. S., Hawley, P. H., & Tucker, J. S. (1994). *Personality, health, and longevity. Current Directions in Psychological Science, 3,* 37–41.

Fritzsche, B. A., Finkelstein, M. A., & Penner, L. A. (2000). To help or not to help: Capturing individuals' decision policies. *Social Behavior and Personality, 28,* 561–578.

Fry, D. P. (1998). Anthropological perspectives on aggression: Sex differences and cultural variation. *Aggressive Behavior, 24,* 81–95.

Fultz, J., Shaller, M., & Cialdini, R. B. (1988). Empathy, sadness, and distress: Three related but distant vicarious affective responses to another's suffering. *Personality and Social Psychology Bulletin, 14,* 312–325.

Furnham, A., Moutafi, J., & Baguma, P. (2002). A cross-cultural study on the role of weight and waist-to-hip ratio on female attractiveness. *Personality and Individual Differences, 32,* 729–745.

Gabor, T. (1994). *The impact of the availability of firearms on violent crime, suicide and accidental death: A review of the literature with special reference to the Canadian situation.* Ottawa: Department of Justice, WD1994–15e.

Gabriel, M. T., Critelli, J. W., & Ee, J. S. (1994). Narcissistic illusions in self-evaluations of intelligence and attractiveness. *Journal of Personality, 62,* 143–155.

Gaertner, S. L., Mann, J. A., Dovidio, J. F., Marrell, A. J., & Pomare, M. (1990). How does cooperation reduce intergroup bias? *Journal of Personality and Social Psychology, 59,* 692–704.

Gaertner, S. L., Mann, J., Murrell, A., & Dovidio, J. F. (1989). Reducing intergroup bias: The benefits of recategorization. *Journal of Personality and Social Psychology, 57,* 239–249.

Gaertner, S. L., Rust, M. C., Dovidio, J. F., Bachman, B. A., & Anastasio, P. A. (1993). The contact hypothesis: The role of a common ingroup identity on reducing intergroup bias. Small Business Research, in press.

Gall, T. L., Evans, D. R., & Bellerose, S. (2000). Transition to first-year university: Patterns of change in adjustment across life domains and time. *Journal of Social and Clinical Psychology, 19,* 544–567.

Gallo, J., & Byrne, D. (2001). *May–December romances in the movies: A cultural influence or a reflection of biological determinants?* Unpublished manuscript, University at Albany, SUNY.

Gallup, G. G. (1994). Monkeys, mirrors, and minds. *Behavioral and Brain Sciences, 17,* 572–573.

Galt, V. (1999). Schools short-change the poor, study says: Low teacher expectations hurt pupil's prospects. *Globe and Mail,* September. pp. A1.

Gamble, W. C., & Dalla, R. L. (1997). Young children's perceptions of their social worlds in single- and two-parent, Euro- and Mexican-American families. *Journal of Social and Personal Relationships, 14,* 357–372.

Gangestad, S. W., & Simpson, J. A. (1993). Development of a scale measuring genetic variation related to expressive control. *Journal of Personality, 61,* 133–158.

Gangestad, S. W., & Simpson, J. A. (2000). The evolution of human mating : Trade-offs and strategic pluralism. *Behavioral and Brain Sciences, 23,* 573–644.

Gangestad, S., & Snyder, M. (1985). On the nature of self-monitoring: An examination of latent causal structure. In P. Shaver (Ed.), *Review of Personality and Social Psychology* (Vol. 6, pp. 65–85). Beverly Hills, CA: Sage.

Garcia, L. T. (1982). Sex role orientation and stereotypes about male-female sexuality. *Sex Roles, 8,* 863–876.

Garcia, S. M., Darley, J. M., & Robinson, R. J. (2001). Morally questionable tactics: Negotiations between district attorneys and public defenders. *Personality and Social Psychology Bulletin, 27,* 731–743.

Gartner, R., & Doob, A. N. (1994). Trends in criminal victimization: 1988–1993. *Juristat, 14,* 1–19.

Geen, R. G. (1978). Some effects of observing violence upon the behavior of the observer. In B. A. Maher (Ed.), *Progress in experimental personality research,* (Vol. 8). New York: Academic Press.

Geen, R. G. (1989). Alternative conceptions of social facilitation. In P. B. Paulus (Ed.), *Psychology of group influence* (2nd ed., pp. 1–37). New York: Academic Press.

Geen, R. G. (1991a). *Human aggression.* Pacific Grove, CA: Brooks/Cole.

Geen, R. G. (1991b). Behavioral and physiological reactions to observed violence: Effects of prior exposure to aggressive stimuli. *Journal of Personality and Social Psychology, 40,* 868–875.

Geertz, C. (1974). "From the native's point of view:" On the nature of anthropological understanding. In R.A. Shweder & R.A. LeVine (Eds.), *Culture theory: Essays on mind, self and emotion.* Cambridge: Cambridge University Press.

Genesee, F. (1984). Beyond bilingualism: Social psychological studies of French immersion programs in Canada. *Canadian Journal of Behavioral Science, 16,* 338–352.

Genesee, F., & Bourhis, R.Y. (1988). *Evaluative reactions to language choice strategies: The role of sociostructural factors.* Language and Communication, 8, 229–250.

Genesee, F., & Gandara, P. (1999).Bilingual education programs: A cross-national perspective. *Journal of Social Issues, 55,* 665–685.

Gentile, D. A. (1993). Just what are sex and gender, anyway? A call for a new terminological standard. *Psychological Science, 4,* 120–122.

George, J. M. (1990). Personality, affect, and behavior in groups. *Journal of Applied Psychology, 75,* 107–116.

George, J. M. (1995). Leader positive mood and group performance: The case of customer service. *Journal of Applied Social Psychology, 25,* 778–794.

George, L. K., Larson, D. B., Koenig, H. G., & McCullough, M. E. (2000). Spirituality and health: What we know, what we need to know. *Journal of Social and Clinical Psychology, 19,* 102–116.

Gerard, H. B., Wilhelmy, R. A., & Conolley, E. S. (1968). Conformity and group size. *Journal of Personality and Social Psychology, 8,* 79–82.

Gerhart, B. (1987). How important are dispositional factors as determinants of job satisfaction? Implications for job design and other personnel programs. *Journal of Personality and Social Psychology, 72,* 366–377.

Gervey, B. M., Chiu, C.-y., Hong, Y.-y., & Dweck, C. S. (1999). Differential use of person information in decisions about guilt versus innocence: The role of implicit theories. *Personality and Social Psychology Bulletin, 25,* 17–27.

Giancola, P. R. (2002). Alcohol-related aggression in men and women: The influence of dispositional aggressivity. *Journal of Studies on Alcohol, 63*, 696–709.

Giancola, P. R., & Zeichner, A. (1995). An investigation of gender differences in alcohol-related aggression. *Journal of studies on Alcohol, 56*, 573–579.

Gibbons, F. X., Eggleston, T. J., & Benthin, A. C. (1997). Cognitive reactions to smoking relapse: The reciprocal relation between dissonance and self-esteem. *Journal of Personality and Social Psychology, 72*, 184–195.

Gigone, D., & Hastie, R. (1993). The common knowledge effect: Information sharing and group judgment. *Journal of Personality and Social Psychology, 65*, 959–974.

Gigone, D., & Hastie, R. (1997). The impact of information on small group choice. *Journal of Personality and Social Psychology, 72*, 132–140.

Gilbert, D. T., & Malone, P. S. (1995). The correspondence bias. *Psychological Bulletin, 117*, 21–38.

Gilbert, D. T., Pelham, B. W., & Srull, D. S. (1988). On cognitive busyness: When person perceivers meet persons perceived. *Journal of Personality and Social Psychology, 54*, 733–740.

Gilbert, L. A. (1993). *Two careers/One family*. Newbury Park, CA: Sage.

Giles, H., Mulac, A., Bradac, J., & Johnson, P. (1986). Speech accommodation theory: The first decade and beyond. *Communication Yearbook, 10*, 8–34.

Gillis, J. S. (1982). *Too small, too tall*. Champaign, IL: Institute for Personality and Ability Testing.

Gilovich, T., & Medvec, V. H. (1994). The temporal pattern to the experience of regret. *Journal of Personality and Social Psychology, 67*, 357–365.

Giner-Sorolla, R., & Chaiken, S. (1994). The causes of hostile media effects. *Journal of Experimental Social Psychology, 30*, 165–180.

Giner-Sorolla, R., & Chaiken, S. (1997). Selective use of heuristic and systematic processing under defense motivation. *Personality and Social Psychology Bulletin, 23*, 84–97.

Glass, S. P., & Wright, T. L. (1992). Justifications for extramarital relationships: The association between attitudes, behaviors, and gender. *Journal of Sex Research, 29*, 361–387.

Glass Ceiling Commission. (1995). *Good for business: Making full use of the nation's human capital*. Washington, DC: Glass Ceiling Commission.

Glass, D. C. (1977). *Behavior patterns, stress, and coronary disease*. Hillsdale, NJ: Erlbaum.

Glass, D. C. (1989). Psychology and health: Obstacles and opportunities. *Journal of Applied Social Psychology, 19*, 1145–1163.

Gleicher, F., Boninger, D., Strathman, A., Armor, D., Hetts, J., & Ahn, M. (1995). With an eye toward the future: Impact of counterfactual thinking on affect, attitudes, and behavior. In N. J. Roses & J. M. Olson (Eds.), *What might have been: the social psychology of counterfactual thinking*. (pp. 283–304). Mahwah, NJ: Erlbaum.

Glick, P., Fiske, S. T., et al. (2000). Beyond prejudice as simple antipathy: Hostile and benevolent sexism across cultures. *Journal of Personality and Social Psychology, 79*, 763–775.

Globe and Mail. (1999). Civil servants win on pay equity. *Globe and Mail*, October 20, pp. A1.

Goethals, G. R., & Zanna, M. P. (1979). The role of social comparison in choice shifts. *Journal of Personality and Social Psychology, 37*, 1469–1476.

Gold, J. A., Ryckman, R. M., & Mosley, N. R. (1984). Romantic mood induction and attraction to a dissimilar other: Is love blind? *Personality and Social Psychology Bulletin, 10*, 358–368.

Goldstein, A. G., Chance, J. E., & Schneller, G. R. (1989). Frequency of eyewitness identification in criminal cases: A survey of prosecutors. *Bulletin of the Psychonomic Society, 27*, 71–74.

Goleman, D. (1994, May 11). Seeking out small pleasures keeps immune system strong. *New York Times*, pp. C1, C15.

Gonnerman, M. E., Jr., Parker, C. P., Lavine, H., & Huff, J. (2000). The relationship between self-discrepancies and affective states: The moderating roles of self-monitoring and standpoints on the self. *Personality and Social Psychology Bulletin, 26*, 810–819.

Goodman, R. (2003). William James. In E. N. Zalta (Ed.), *The Stanford Encyclopedia of Philosophy (Spring 2003 Edition)*. http://plato.stanford.edu/archives/spr2003/entries/james/.

Goodwin, R., & Findlay, C. (1997). "We were just fated together"... Chinese love and the concept of yuan in England and Hong Kong. *Personal Relationships, 4*, 85–92.

Gordin, F. M., Willoughby, A. D., Levine, L. A., Ourel, L., & Neill, K. M. (1987). Knowledge of AIDS among hospital workers: Behavioral correlates and consequences. *AIDS, 1*, 183–188.

Gordon, R. A. (1996). Impact of ingratiation in judgments and evaluations: A meta-analytic investigation. *Journal of Personality and Social Psychology, 71*, 54–70.

Gottlieb, B. H. (1987). Marshalling social support for medical patients and their families. *Canadian Psychology, 28*, 201–217.

Gould, D., & Weiss, M. (1981). Effect of model similarity and model self-talk on self-efficacy in muscular endurance. *Journal of Sport Psychology, 3*, 17–29

Gould, S. J. (1996, September). The Diet of Worms and the defenestration of Prague. *Natural History*, 18–24, 64, 66–67.

Gouldner, A. W. (1960). The norm of reciprocity: A preliminary statement. *American Sociological Review, 25*, 161–179.

Grabb, E., Curtis, J., Baer, D. (2000). Defining moments and recurring myths: Comparing Canadians and Americans after the American revolution. *Canadian Review of Sociology & Anthropology, 37*, 373–420.

Graham, B., & Folkes, V. (Eds.).(1990). *Attribution theory: Applications to achievement, mental health, and interpersonal conflict*. Hillsdale, NJ: Erlbaum.

Graham, J. L. (1985). The influence of culture on the process of business negotiations: an exploratory study. *Journal of International Business Studies, 16*, 81–96.

Graham, S., Weiner, B., & Zucker, G. S. (1997). An attributional analysis of punishment goals and public reactions to O. J. Simpson. *Personality and Social Psychology Bulletin, 23*, 331–346.

Grant, P. (2001, March/April). Face time. *Modern Maturity*, 56–63.

Gray, P. (1993). What is love? *Time, 141*(7), 46–49.

Graziano, W. G., Jensen-Campbell, L. A., & Hair, E. C. (1996). Perceiving interpersonal conflict and reacting to it: The case for agreeableness. *Journal of Personality and Social Psychology, 70,* 820–835.

Green, D. P., Glaser, J., & Rich, A. (1998). From lynching to gay bashing: The elusive connection between economic conditions and hate crime. *Journal of Personality and Social Psychology, 75,* 82–92.

Green, L. R., Richardson, D. R., & Lago, T. (1996). How do friendship, indirect, and direct aggression relate? *Aggressive Behavior, 22,* 81–86.

Greenbaum, P., & Rosenfield, H. W. (1978). Patterns of avoidance in responses to interpersonal staring and proximity: Effects of bystanders on drivers at a traffic intersection. *Journal of Personality and Social Psychology, 36,* 575–587.

Greenberg, J. (1990). Employee theft as a reaction to underpayment inequity: The hidden cost of pay cuts. *Journal of Applied Psychology, 75,* 561–568.

Greenberg, J. (1993b). Stealing in the name of justice: Informational and interpersonal moderators of theft reactions to underpayment inequity. *Organizational Behavior and Human Decision Processes, 54,* 81–103.

Greenberg, J. (1996). *The quest for justice: Essays and experiments.* Thousand Oaks, CA: Sage Publications.

Greenberg, J., & Alge, B. J. (1997). Aggressive reactions to workplace injustice. In R. W. Griffin, A. O'Leary-Kelly, & J. Collins (Eds.), *Dysfunctional behavior in organizations: Vol. 1. Violent behaviors in organizations.* Greenwich, CT: JAI Press.

Greenberg, J., & Baron, R. A. (2002). *Behavior in organizations* (8th ed.). Upper Saddle River, NJ: Prentice-Hall.

Greenberg, J., & Scott, K. S. (1996). Why do workers bite the hands that feed them? Employee theft as social exchange process. In B. M. Staw & L. L. Cummings (Eds.), *Research in organizational behavior* (Vol. 18, pp. 111–156). Greenwich, CT: JAI Press.

Greenberg, J., Pyszcynski, T., & Solomon, S. (1982). The self-serving attributional bias: Beyond self-presentation. *Journal of Experimental Social Psychology, 18,* 56–67.

Greenberg, J., Solomon, S., Pyszczynski, T., Rosenblatt, A., Burling, J., Lyon, D., Simon, L., & Pinel, E. (1992). Why do people need self-esteem? Converging evidence that self-esteem serves an anxiety-buffering function. *Journal of Personality and Social Psychology, 63,* 913–922.

Greenberg, M. A., & Stone, A. A. (1992). Emotional disclosure about traumas and its relation to health: Effects of previous disclosure and trauma severity. *Journal of Personality and Social Psychology, 63,* 75–84.

Greenberg, M. A., Wortman, C. B., & Stone, A. A. (1996). Emotional expression and physical health: Revising traumatic memories or fostering self-regulation? *Journal of Personality and Social Psychology, 71,* 588–602.

Greenwald, A. G., & Banaji, M. R. (1995). Implicit social cognition: Attitudes, self-esteem, and stereotypes. *Psychological Review, 102,* 4–27.

Greenwald, A. G., McGhee, D. E., & Schwartz, J. L. K. (1998). Measuring individual differences in implicit cognition: The implicit association test. *Journal of Personality and Social Psychology, 74,* 1464–1480.

Greenwald, A. G., Spangenberg, E. R., Pratkanis, A. R., & Eskenazi, J., (1991). Double-blind tests of subliminal self-help audiotapes. *Psychological Science, 2,* 119–122.

Greiling, H., & Buss, D. M. (2000). Women's sexual strategies: The hidden dimension of extra-pair mating. *Personality and Individual Differences, 28,* 929–963.

Griffin, D.W., & Bartholomew, K. (1994). The metaphysics of measurement: The case of adult attachment. In D. Perlman & K. Bartholomew (Eds.), *Advances in Personal Relationships, Vol. 5. Attachment processes in adulthood* (pp. 17–52). London: Jessica Kingsley.

Groff, D. B., Baron, R. S., & Moore, D. L. (1983). Distraction, attentional conflict, and drive like behavior. *Journal of Experimental Social Psychology, 19,* 359–380.

Gross, E. F., Juvonen, J., & Gable, S. L. (2002). Internet use and well-being in Adolescence. *Journal of Social Issues, 58,* 75–90.

Grossman, M., & Wood, W. (1993). Sex differences in intensity of emotional experience: A social role interpretation. *Journal of Personality and Social Psychology, 65,* 1010–1022.

Grote, N. K., & Clark, M. S. (2001). Perceiving unfairness in the family: Cause of consequence of marital distress? *Journal of Personality and Social Psychology, 80,* 281–289.

Grote, N. K., Frieze, I. H., & Stone, C. A. (1996). Children, traditionalism in the division of family work, and marital satisfaction: "What's love got to do with it?" *Personal Relationships, 3,* 211–228.

Gudjonsson, G. H. (1993). Confession evidence, psychological vulnerability and expert testimony. *Journal of Community and Applied Social Psychology, 3,* 117–129.

Gudjonsson, G. H. (2003). *The psychology of interrogations and confessions: A handbook.* New York: John Wiley & Sons Ltd.

Gudjonsson, G. H., & Clark, N. K. (1986). Suggestibility in police interrogation: A social psychological model. *Social Behaviour, 1,* 83–104.

Gudykunst, W. B., Gao, G., Schmidt, K. L., et al. (1992). The influence of individualism-collectivism, self-monitoring and predicted-outcome value on communication in in-group and out-group relationships. *Journal of Cross-Cultural Psychology, 23,* 196–213.

Guerrero, L. K. (1998). Attachment-style differences in the experience and expression of romantic jealousy. *Personal Relationships, 5,* 273–291.

Guimond, S., & Dubé-Simard, L. (1983). Relative deprivation theory and the Quebec nationalist movement: The cognitive-emotion distinction and the personal-group deprivation issue. *Journal of Personality and Social Psychology, 44,* 526–535.

Gunthert, K. C., Cohen, L. H., & Armeli, S. (1999). The role of neuroticism in daily stress and coping. *Journal of Personality and Social Psychology, 77,* 1087–1100.

Gur, R. C., Mozley, L. H., Mozley, P. D., Resnick, S. M., Karp, J. S., Alavi, A., Arnold, S. E., & Gur, R. E. (1995). Sex differences in regional glucose metabolism during a resting state. *Science, 267,* 528–531.

Hackel, L. S., & Ruble, D. N. (1992). Changes in the marital relationship after the first baby is born: Predicting the impact of expectancy disconfirmation. *Journal of Personality and Social Psychology, 62,* 944–957.

Hadjistavropoulos T., Malloy, D. C., Sharpe, D., Green, S. M., & Fuchs-Lacelle, S. (2002). The relative importance of the ethical principles adopted by the American Psychological Association. *Canadian Psychology, 43,* 254–259.

Hagborg, W. J. (1993). Gender differences on Harter's Self-Perception Profile for Adolescents. *Journal of Social Behavior and Personality, 8,* 141–148.

Hamilton, D. L., & Sherman, S. J. (1989). Illusory correlations: Implications for stereotype theory and research. In D. Bar-Tal, C. F. Graumann, A. W. Kruglanski, & W. Stroebe (Eds.), *Stereotyping and prejudice: Changing conceptions* (pp. 59–82). New York: Springer-Verlag.

Hamilton, G. V. (1978). Obedience and responsibility: A jury simulation. *Journal of Personality and Social Psychology, 36,* 126–146.

Hamilton, J. C., Falconer, J. J., & Greenberg, M. D. (1992). The relationship between self-consciousness and dietary restraint. *Journal of Social and Clinical Psychology, 11,* 158–166

Hamilton, V. L., & Sanders, J. (1995). Crimes of obedience and conformity in the workplace: Surveys of Americans, Russians, and Japanese. *Journal of Social Issues, 51,* 67–88.

Hamilton, W. D. (1964). The genetical evolution of social behaviour. I and II. *Journal of Theoretical Biology, 7,* 1–52.

Han, S-P., & Shavitt, S. (1994). Persuasion and culture: Advertising appeals in individualistic and collectivistic societies. *Journal of Experimental Social Psychology, 30,* 326–350.

Hansen, C. H, & Hansen, R. D. (1988). Finding the face in the crowd: An anger superiority effect. *Journal of Personality and Social Psychology, 54,* 917–924.

Hansen, T., & Bartsch, R. A. (2001). The positive correlation between personal need for structure and the mere exposure effect. *Social Behavior and Personality, 29,* 271–276.

Harkins, S., & Szymanski, K. (1989). Social loafing and group evaluation. *Journal of Personality and Social Psychology, 56,* 934–941.

Harmon-Jones, E. (2000). Cognitive dissonance and experienced negative affect: Evidence that dissonance increases experienced negative affect even in the absence of aversive consequences. *Personality and Social Psychology Bulletin, 26,* 1490–1501.

Harrigan, J. A., Lucic, K. S., Kay, D., McLaney, A., & Rosenthal, R. (1991). Effect of expresser role and type of self-touching on observers' perceptions. *Journal of Applied Social Psychology, 21,* 585–609.

Harris, M. B. (1994). Gender of subject and target as mediators of aggression. *Journal of Applied Social Psychology, 24,* 453–471.

Harris, M. B., (1992). Sex, race, and experiences of aggression. *Aggressive Behavior, 18,* 201–217.

Harris, M. J., Milich, R., Corbitt, E. M., Hoover, D. W., & Brady, M. (1992). Self-fulfilling effects of stigmatizing information on children's social interactions. *Journal of Personality and Social Psychology, 63,* 41–50.

Harrison, A. A., & Saeed, L. (1977). Let's make a deal: An analysis of revelations and stipulations in lonely hearts advertisements. *Journal of Personality and Social Psychology, 35,* 257–264.

Harrison, B., & Marmen, L. (1994). *Languages in Canada* (Focus on Canada series). Scarborough ON: Statistics Canada and Prentice Hall Canada.

Harvey, C. DeRoma, V., Saylor, C., & Politano, M. (2002). *Indirect exposure to terrorism: An assessment of gender differences in coping styles, PTSD symptoms.* Unpublished manuscript, The Citadel.

Harvey, J. H., & Omarzu, J. (1997). Minding the close relationship. *Personality and Social Psychology Review, 1,* 224–240.

Harvey, J. H., & Weary, G. (Eds.). (1989). *Attribution: Basic issues and applications.* San Diego: Academic Press.

Hassin, R., & Trope, Y. (2000). Facing faces: Studies on the cognitive aspects of physiognomy. *Journal of Personality and Social Psychology, 78, 837–852.*

Hatfield, E. (1988). Passionate and companionate love. In R. L. Sternberg & M. I. Barnes (Eds.), *The psychology of love* (pp. 191–217). New Haven, CT: Yale University Press.

Hatfield, E., & Rapson, R. L. (1992). Similarity and attraction in close relationships. *Communication Monographs, 59,* 209–212.

Hatfield, E., & Rapson, R.L. (1996). *Love and sex: Cross-cultural perspectives.* Needham Heights, MA: Allyn & Bacon.

Hatfield, E., & Sprecher, S. (1986). Measuring passionate love in intimate relations. *Journal of Adolescence, 9,* 383–410.

Hatfield, E., & Walster, G. W. (1981). *A new look at love.* Reading, MA: Addison-Wesley.

Hayden, S. R., Jackson, T. T., & Guydish, J. N. (1984). Helping behavior of females: Effects of stress and commonality of fate. *Journal of Psychology, 117,* 233–237.

Hazan, C., & Shaver, P. R. (1990). Love and work: An attachment-theoretical perspective. *Journal of Personality and Social Psychology, 59,* 270–280.

Hebl, M. R., & Heatherton, T. E. (1998). The stigma of obesity in women: The difference is black and white. *Personality and Social Psychology Bulletin, 24,* 417–426.

Heider, F. (1958). *The psychology of interpersonal relations.* New York: Wiley.

Heilman, D. E., Block, C. J., & Lucas, J. A. (1992). Presumed incompetent? Stigmatization and affirmative action efforts. *Journal of Applied Psychology, 77,* 536–544.

Heinberg, L. J., & Thompson, J. K. (1992). Social comparison: Gender, target importance ratings, and relation to body image disturbance. *Journal of Social Behavior and Personality, 7,* 335–344.

Heine, S.J. (2001). Self as a cultural product: An examination of East Asian and North American selves. *Journal of Personality, 69,* 881–906.

Heine, S.J. (2003). Self-enhancement in Japan? A reply to Brown & Kobayashi. *Asian Journal of Social Psychology, 6,* 75–84.

Heine, S. J., Harihara, M., & Niiya, Y. (2002). Terror management in Japan. *Asian Journal of Social Psychology, 5,* 187–196.

Heine, S. J., & Lehman, D. R. (1995). Cultural variation in unrealistic optimism: Does the West feel more invulnerable than the East. *Journal of Personality and Social Psychology, 68,* 595–607.

Heine, S. J., & Lehman, D. R. (1997). Culture, dissonance, and self-affirmation. *Personality and Social Psychology Bulletin, 23,* 389–400.

Heine, S.J., Lehman, D.R., Markus, H. R., & Kitayama, S. (1999). Is there a universal need for positive self-regard? *Psychological Review, 106,* 766–794.

Heine, S. J., Lehman, D. R., & Peng, K. (2002). What's wrong with cross-cultural comparisons of subjective Likert scales?: The reference-group effect.; *Journal of Personality & Social Psychology, 82,* 903–918.

Helms, A. D. (2001, July 22). With this ring, I thee hyphenate? Knight Ridder.

Helson, R., & Roberts, B. (1992). The personality of young adult couples and wives' work patterns. *Journal of Personality, 60,* 575–597.

Helweg-Larsen, M., & Shepperd, J. A. (2001). Do moderators of the optimistic bias affect personal or target risk estimates? A review of the literature. *Personality and Social Psychology Review, 5,* 74–95.

Hemenover, S. H. (2001). Self-reported processing bias and naturally occurring mood: Mediators between personality and stress appraisals. *Personality and Social Psychology Bulletin, 27,* 387–394.

Hemenway, D. (1998). Survey research and self-defense gun use: An exploration of extreme over estimates. *Journal of Law Criminology.*

Henderson, J., & Taylor, J. (1985, November 17). Study finds bias in death sentence: Killers of whites risk execution. *Albany Times Union,* p. A–19.

Hendrick, C., & Hendrick, S. S. (1986). A theory and method of love. *Journal of Personality and Social Psychology, 50,* 392–402.

Hendrick, C., Hendrick, S. S., Foote, F. H., & Slapion-Foote, M. J. (1984). Do men and women love differently? *Journal of Social and Personal Relationships, 1,* 177–195.

Hendrick, S. S., & Hendrick, C. (1987). Love and sex attitudes and religious beliefs. *Journal of Social and Clinical Psychology, 5,* 391–398.

Hendrick, S. S., Hendrick, C., & Adler, N. L. (1988). Romantic relationships: Love, satisfaction, and staying together. *Journal of Personality and Social Psychology, 54,* 980–988.

Henry, F. & Ginzberg, E. (1985). *Who gets the work: A test of racial discrimination in employment in Toronto.* Toronto: The Urban Alliance on Race Relations and the Social Planning Council of Metropolitan Toronto.

Henry, F. (1978). *The dynamics of racism in Toronto.* Unpublished research report. York University.

Henry, F. (1999). Two studies of racial discrimination in employment. In J. Curtis, E. Grabb, & N. Guppy (Eds.), *Social inequality in Canada: Patterns, problems, and policies* (2nd ed., pp. 226–235). Scarborough, ON: Prentice Hall.

Henry, F., Tator, C., Mattis, W., & Rees, T. (1995). *The colour of democracy: Racism in Canadian society.* Toronto: Harcourt Brace.

Henry, W. A., III. (1991). The journalist and the murder. *Time, 138*(15), 86.

Hense, R., Penner, L., & Nelson, D. (1995). Implicit memory for age stereotypes. *Special Cognition, 13,* 399–415.

Hensley, W. E. (1996). The effect of a ludus love style on sexual experience. *Social Behavior and Personality, 24,* 205–212.

Hepworth, J. T., & West, S. G. (1988). Lynchings and the economy: A time-series reanalysis of Hovland and Sears (1940). *Journal of Personality and Social Psychology, 55,* 239–247.

Herscovitch, L., & Meyer, J. P. (2002). Commitment to organizational change: Extensions of a three-component model. *Journal of Applied Psychology, 87,* 474–487.

Hershberger, S. L., Lichtenstein, P., & Knox, S. S. (1994). Genetic and environmental influences on perceptions of organizational climate. *Journal of Applied Psychology, 79,* 24–33.

Hewstone, M. (1990). The "ultimate attribution error"? A review of the literature on intergroup causal attribution. *European Journal of Social Psychology, 20,* 311–335.

Higgins, E. T. (1987). Self-discrepancy: A theory relating self and affect. *Psychological Review, 94,* 319–340.

Higgins, E. T. (1989). Self-discrepancy theory: What patterns of self-beliefs cause people to suffer? In L. Berkowitz (Ed.), *Advances in experimental social psychology* (Vol. 22, pp. 93–136). San Diego, CA: Academic Press.

Higgins, E. T., & Bargh, J. A. (1987). Social cognition and social perception. In M. R. Rosenszweig & L. W. Porter (Eds.), *Annual review of psychology* (Vol. 38, pp. 369–425). Palo Alto, CA: Annual Reviews Inc.

Higgins, E. T., & King, G. (1981). Accessibility of social constructs: Information processing consequences of individual and contextual variability. In N. Cantor & J. Kihlstrom (Eds.), *Personality, cognition, and social interaction* (pp. 69–121). Hillsdale, NJ: Erlbaum.

Higgins, E. T., Rohles, W. S., & Jones, C. R. (1977). Category accessibility and impression formation. *Journal of Experimental Social Psychology, 13,* 141–154.

Higgins, N. C. & Bhatt, G. (2001). Culture moderates the self-serving bias: Etic and emic features of causal attributions in India and in Canada. *Social Behavior & Personality, 29,* 49–61.

Hill, C. A. (1987). Affiliation motivation: People who need people but in different ways. *Journal of Personality and Social Psychology, 52,* 1008–1018.

Hill, C. A., Blakemore, J. E. O., & Drumm, P. (1997). Mutual and unrequited love in adolescence and young adulthood. *Personal Relationships, 4,* 15–23.

Hilton, N. Z., Harris, G. T., & Rice, M. E. (2000). The functions of aggression by male teenagers. *Journal of Personality and Social Psychology, 79,* 988–994.

Hinkley, K., & Andersen, S. M. (1996). The working self-concept in transference: Significant-other activation and self change. *Journal of Personality and Social Psychology, 71,* 1279–1295.

Hinsz, V. B. (1995). Goal setting by groups performing an additive task: A comparison with individual goal setting. *Journal of Applied Social Psychology, 25,* 965–990.

Hirt, E. R., & Markman, K. D. (1995). Multiple explanation: A consider-an-alternative strategy for debiasing judgments. *Personality and Social Psychology Bulletin, 69,* 1069–1086.

Hirt, E. R., Zillmann, D., Erickson, G. A., & Kennedy, C. (1992). Costs and benefits of allegiance: Changes in fans' self-ascribed competencies after team victory versus defeat. *Journal of Personality and Social Psychology, 61,* 724–738.

Hixon, J. G., & Swann, W. B., Jr. (1993). When does introspection bear fruit? Self-reflection, self-insight, and interpersonal choices. *Journal of Personality and Social Psychology, 64,* 35–43.

Hoaken, P. N. S., & Pihl, R. O. (2000). The effects of alcohol intoxication on aggressive responses in men and women. *Alcohol & Alcoholism, 35,* 471–477.

Hodson, G., & Esses, V. M. (2002). Distancing oneself from negative attributes and the personal/group discrimination discrepancy. *Journal of Experimental Social Psychology, 38,* 500–507.

Hofstede, G. (1980). *Culture's consequences: International differences in work-related values.* Beverly Hills, CA: Sage.

Hofstede, G. (1983). Dimensions of national cultures in fifty countries and three regions. In J. Deregowski, S. Dzuirawiec & R. Annis (Eds.), *Expiscations in cross-cultural psychology.* Lisse, Netherlands: Swets & Zeitlinger.

Hogben, M., Byrne, D., Hamburger, M. E., & Osland, J. (2001). Legitimized aggression and sexual coercion: Individual differences in cultural spillover. *Aggressive Behavior, 29,* 26–43.

Hogg, M. A., & Hains, S. C. (1996). Intergroup relations and group solidarity: Effects of group identification and social beliefs on depersonalized attraction. *Journal of Personality and Social Psychology, 70,* 25–309.

Holahan, C. J., Moos, R. H., Holahan, C. K., & Brennan, P. L. (1997). Social context, coping strategies, and depressive symptoms: An expanded model with cardiac patients. *Journal of Personality and Social Psychology, 72,* 918–928.

Holtgraves, T. (1997). Styles of language use: Individual and cultural variability in conversational indirectness. *Journal of Personality and Social Psychology, 73,* 624–637.

Holtgraves, T. M., & Yang, J. N. (1990). Politeness as universal: Cross-cultural perceptions of request strategies and inferences based on their use. *Journal of Personality and Social Psychology, 59,* 149–160.

Holtzworth-Munroe, A. (2000). A typology of men who are violent toward their female partners: Making sense of the heterogeneity in husband violence. *Current Directions in Psychological Science, 9,* 140–143.

Homer, P. M., & Kahle, L. (1988). A structural equation test of the value-attitude-behavior hierarchy. *Journal of Personality and Social Psychology, 54,* 638–646.

Hornsey, M. J., & Hogg, M. A. (2000). Intergroup similarity and subgroup relations: Some implications for assimilation. *Personality and Social Psychology Bulletin, 26,* 948–958.

Hosch, H. M., & Bothwell, R. K. (1990). Arousal, description and identification accuracy of victims and bystanders. *Journal of Social Behavior and Personality, 5,* 481–488.

House, R. J., & Howell, J. M. (1992). Personality and charismatic leadership. *Leadership Quarterly, 3,* 81–108.

House, R. J., & Podsakoff, P. M. (1994). Leadership effectiveness: Past perspectives and future directions for research. In J. Greenberg (Ed.), *Organizational behavior: The state of the science* (pp. 45–82). Hillsdale, NJ: Erlbaum.

Hovland, C. I., & Sears, R. R. (1940). Minor studies in aggression: VI. Correlation of lynchings with economic indices. *Journal of Psychology, 9,* 301–310.

Hovland, C. I., & Weiss, W. (1951). The influence of source credibility on communication effectiveness. *Public Opinion Quarterly, 1,* 635–650.

Hovland, C. I., Janis, I. L., & Kelley, H. H. (1953). *Communication and persuasion: Psychological studies of one on one.* New Haven, CT: Yale University Press.

Howard, D. J. (1990). The influence of verbal responses to common greetings on compliance behavior: The foot-in-the-mouth effect. *Journal of Applied Social Psychology, 20,* 1185–1196.

Howell, J. P., Dorfman, P. W., Hibino, S., Lee, J. K., & Tate, U. (1997). Leadership in Western and Asian countries: Commonalities and differences in effective leadership processes across cultures. *Leadership Quarterly, 8,* 233–274.

Hoyle, R. H., & Sowards, B. A. (1993). Self-monitoring and the regulation of social experience: A control-process model. *Journal of Social and Clinical Psychology, 12,* 280–306.

Huang, I.-C. (1998). Self-esteem, reaction to uncertainty, and physician practice variation: A study of resident physicians. *Social Behavior and Personality, 26,* 181–194.

Huesmann, L. R., & Eron, L. D. (1984). Cognitive processes and the persistence of aggressive behavior. *Aggressive Behavior, 10,* 243–251.

Huesmann, L. R., & Eron, L. D. (1986). *Television and the aggressive child: A cross-national comparison.* Hillsdale, NJ: Erlbaum.

Hughes, C. F., Uhlmann, C., & Pennebaker, J. W. (1994). The body's response to processing emotional trauma: Linking verbal text with autonomic activity. *Journal of Personality, 62,* 565–585.

Hughes, S. M., & Gallup, G. G. (2003). Sex differences in morphological predictors of sexual behavior: Shoulder to hip and waist to hip ratios. *Evolution and Human Behavior, 24,* 173–178.

Hui, C., Lam, S. S. K., & Law, K. K. S. (2000). Instrumental values of organizational citizenship behavior for promotion: A field quasi-experiment. *Journal of Applied Psychology, 85,* 822–828.

Humphreys, L. G. (1998). A little noticed consequence of the repressed memory epidemic. *American Psychologist, 53,* 485–486.

Humphriss, N. (1989, November 20). Letters. *Time,* p. 12.

Hunter, C. E., & Ross, M. W. (1991). Determinants of health-care workers' attitudes toward people with AIDS. *Journal of Applied Social Psychology, 21,* 947–956.

Huston, T. L., Caughlin, J. P., Houts, R. M., Smith, S. E., & George, L. J. (2001). The connubial crucible: Newlywed years as predictors of marital delight, distress, and divorce. *Journal of Personality and Social Psychology, 80,* 237–252.

Hyde, J. S., & Plant, E. A. (1995). Magnitude of psychological gender differences: Another side to the story. *American Psychologist, 50*, 159–161.

Ickes, W., Reidhead, S., & Patterson, M. (1986). Machiavellianism and self-monitoring: As different as "me" and "you." *Social Cognition, 4*, 58–74.

Insel, T. R., & Carter, C. S. (1995, August). The monogamous brain. *Natural History*, 12–14.

Insko, C. A. (1985). Balance theory, the Jordan paradigm, and the West tetrahedron. In L. Berkowitz (Ed.), *Advances in experimental social psychology*. New York: Academic Press.

Insko, C. A., Schopler, H. J., Gaertner, G., Wildschutt, T., Kozar, R., Pinter, B., Finkel, E. J., Brazil, D. M., Cecil, C. L., & Montoya, M. R. (2001). Interindividual-intergroup discontinuity reduction through the anticipation of future interaction. *Journal of Personality and Social Psychology, 80*, 95–111.

Ireland, C. A., & Ireland, J. L. (2000). Descriptive analysis of the nature and extent of bullying behavior in a maximum security prison. *Aggressive Behavior, 26*, 213–222.

Isen, A. M., & Baron, R. A. (1991). Affect and organizational behavior. In B. M. Staw & L. L. Cummings (Eds.), *Research in organizational behavior* (vol. 15, pp. 1–53). Greenwich CT: JAI Press.

Isen, A. M., & Levin, P. A. (1972). Effect of feeling good on helping: Cookies and kindness. *Journal of Personality and Social Psychology, 21*, 384–388.

Istvan, J., Griffitt, W., & Weidner, G. (1983). Sexual arousal and the polarization of perceived sexual attractiveness. *Basic and Applied Social Psychology, 4*, 307–318.

Ito, T. A., Larsen, J. T., Smith, N. K., & Cacioppo, J. T. (1998). Negative information weighs more heavily on the brain: The negativity bias in evaluative categorizations. *Journal of Personality and Social Psychology, 75*, 887–900.

Izard, C. (1991). *Human emotions* (2nd ed.). New York: Plenum.

Jackson, J. W., & Smith, E. R. (1999). Conceptualizing social identity: A new framework and evidence for the impact of different dimensions. *Personality and Social Psychology Bulletin, 25*, 120–135.

Jackson, L. A., Gardner, P., & Sullivan, L. (1992). Explaining gender differences in self-pay expectations: Social comparison standards and perceptions of fair pay. *Journal of Applied Psychology, 77*, 651–663.

Jackson, L. M., & Esses, V. M. (1997). Of scripture and ascription: The relation between religious fundamentalism and intergroup helping. *Personality and Social Psychology Bulletin, 23*, 893–906.

James, W. (1890). *The principles of psychology* (Vols. 1 and 2). New York: Holt.

Janes, L., & Olson, J. M. (2000). Jeer pressure: The behavioral effects of observing ridicule of others. *Personality and Social Psychology Bulletin, 26*, 474–485.

Janis, I. L. (1954). Personality correlates of susceptibility to persuasion. *Journal of Personality, 22*, 504–518.

Janis, I. L. (1982). *Victims of groupthink* (2nd ed.). Boston: Houghton Mifflin.

Janoff-Bulman, R., & Wade, M. B. (1996). The dilemma of self-advocacy for women: Another case of blaming the victim? *Journal of Social and Clinical Psychology, 15*, 143–152.

Jemmott, J. B., III, & Magloire, K. (1988). Academic stress, social support, and secretory immunoglobulin. *Journal of Personality and Social Psychology, 55*, 803–810.

Jemmott, J. B., III, Ashby, K. L., & Lindenfield, K. (1989). Romantic commitment and the perceived availability of opposite-sex persons: On loving the one you're with. *Journal of Applied Social Psychology, 19*, 1198–1211.

Jessor, R., Turbin, M. S., & Costa, F. M. (1998). Protective factors in adolescent health behavior. *Journal of Personality and Social Psychology, 75*, 788–800.

Jex, S. M., Cvetanovski, J., & Allen, S. J. (1994). Self-esteem as a moderator of the impact of unemployment. *Journal of Social Behavior and Personality, 9*, 69–80.

Jimenez, M. (2003). U.S. view of war is like U.S. coffee: filtered. Two different wars unfold on Western and Arab networks. *National Post*, April 01, 2003. Toronto, Canada: National Post.

Johns, G., & Jia Lin Xie (1998). Perceptions of absence from work: People's Republic of China versus Canada. *Journal of Applied Psychology, 83*, 515–530.

Johnson, B. T. (1994). Effects of outcome-relevant involvement and prior information on persuasion. *Journal of Experimental Social Psychology, 30*, 556–579.

Johnson, C., & Mullen, B. (1994). Evidence for the accessibility of paired distinctiveness in the distinctiveness-based illusory correlation in stereotyping. *Personality and Social Psychology Bulletin, 20*, 65–70.

Johnston, V. S., & Oliver-Rodriguez, J. C. (1997). Facial beauty and the late positive component of event-related potentials. *Journal of Sex Research, 34*, 188–198.

Johnstone, B., Frame, C. L., & Bouman, D. (1992). Physical attractiveness and athletic and academic ability in controversial-aggressive and rejected-aggressive children. *Journal of Social and Clinical Psychology, 11*, 71–79.

Joiner, T. E. Jr., & Schmidt, N. B. (1995). Dimensions of perfectionism, life stress, and depressed and anxious symptoms: Prospective support for diathesis-stress but not specific vulnerability among male undergraduates. *Journal of Social and Clinical Psychology, 14*, 165–183.

Joiner, T. E., Jr. (1994). The interplay of similarity and self-verification in relationship formation. *Social Behavior and Personality, 22*, 195–200.

Joiner, T. E., Jr., Katz, J., & Lew, A. (1999). Harbingers of depressotypic reassurance seeking: Negative life events, increased anxiety, and decreased self-esteem. *Personality and Social Psychology Bulletin, 25*, 630–637.

Jonas, E., Schulz-Hardt, S., Frey, D., & Thelen, N. (2001). Confirmation bias in sequential information search after preliminary decisions: An expansion of dissonance theoretical research on selective exposure to information. *Journal of Personality and Social Psychology, 80*, 557–571.

Jones, E. E. (1979). The rocky road from acts to dispositions. *American Psychologist, 34*, 107–117.

Jones, E. E., & Davis, K. E. (1965). From acts to disposition: The attribution process in person perception. In L. Berkowitz (Ed.), *Advances in experimental social psychology* (Vol. 2, pp. 219–266). New York: Academic Press.

Jones, E. E., & McGillis, D. (1976). Corresponding inferences and the attribution cube: A comparative reappraisal. In J. H. Harvey, W. J. Ickes, & R. F. Kidd (Eds.), *New directions in attribution research* (Vol. 1). Morristown, NJ: Erlbaum.

Jones, E. E., & Nisbett, R. E. (1971). *The actor and the observer: Divergent perceptions of the causes of behavior.* Morristown, NJ: General Learning Press.

Jourard, S.M. (1971). *Self-disclosure.* New York: Wiley.

Jowett, G., & O'Donnell, V. (1999). *Propaganda and persuasion. 3rd edition.* Thousand Oaks, CA: Sage.

Judd, C. M., Ryan, C. N., & Parke, B. (1991). Accuracy in the judgment of in-group and out-group variability. *Journal of Personality and Social Psychology, 61,* 366–379.

Judge, T. A. (1993). Does affective disposition moderate the relationships between job satisfaction and voluntary turnover? *Journal of Applied Psychology, 78,* 395–401.

Judge, T. A., & Bono, J. E. (2000). Five-factor model of personality and transformational leadership. *Journal of Applied Psychology, 85,* 751–765.

Judge, T. A., Bono, J. E., & Locke, E. Q. (2000). Personality and job satisfaction: The mediating role of job characteristics. *Journal of Applied Psychology, 85,* 237–249.

Judge, T. A., Locke, E. A., Durham, C. C., & Kluger, A. N. (1998). Dispositional effects on job and life satisfaction: The role of core evaluations. *Journal of Applied Psychology, 83,* 17–34.

Judge, T. A., Locke, E. Q., & Durham, C. C. (1997). The dispositional causes of job satisfaction: A core evaluation approach. *Research in Organizational Behavior, 19,* 151–188.

Jussim, L. (1991). Interpersonal expectations and social reality: A reflection-construction model and reinterpretation of evidence. *Psychological Review, 98,* 54–73.

Kacmar, K. M., Delery, J. E., & Ferris, G. R. (1992). Differential effectiveness of applicant impression management tactics on employment interview decisions. *Journal of Applied Social Psychology, 22,* 1250–1272.

Kagan, J. (1964). Acquisition and significance of sex-typing and sex-role identity. *Review of Child Development Research, 1.*

Kahn, W., & Crosby, F. (1985). Change and stasis: Discriminating between attitudes and discriminating behavior. *Women and Work: An Annual Review, 1,* 215–238.

Kalichman, S. C., Sarwer, D. B., Johnson, J. R., Ali, S. A., Early, J., & Tuten, J. T. (1993). Sexually coercive behavior and love styles: A replication and extension. *Journal of Psychology & Human Sexuality, 6,* 93–106.

Kalick, S. M., Zebrowitz, L. A., Langlois, J. H., & Johnson, R. M. (1998). Does human facial attractiveness honestly advertise health? Longitudinal data on an evolutionary question. *Psychological Science, 9,* 8–13.

Kalin, R. & Berry, J. W. (1994). Ethnic, and multicultural attitudes. In J. W. Berry & J. Laponce (Eds.), *Ethnicity and culture in Canada: The research landscape* (pp.293–321). Toronto University of Toronto Press.

Kalin, R. & Berry, J. W. (1995). Ethnic and civic self-identity in Canada: Analyses of the 1974 and 1991 surveys. *Canadian Ethnic Studies, 27,* 115.

Kalin, R., & Berry, J. W. (1996). Interethnic attitudes in Canada: Ethnocentrism, consensual hierarchy and reciprocity. *Canadian Journal of Behavioural Science, 28,* 253–261.

Kalin, R., & Berry, J.W. (1982). The social ecology of ethnic attitudes in Canada. *Canadian Journal of Behavioral Science, 14,* 97–109.

Kallen, E. (1995). *Ethnicity and Human Rights in Canada* (2nd ed.) Toronto: Oxford University Press Canada.

Kallgren, C. A., Reno, R. R., & Cialdini, R. B. (2000). A focus theory of normative conduct: When norms do and do not affect behavior. *Personality and Social Psychology Bulletin, 26,* 1002–1012.

Kameda, T., & Sugimori, S. (1993). Psychological entrapment in group decision making: An assigned decision rule and a groupthink phenomenon. *Journal of Personality and Social Psychology, 65,* 282–292.

Kandel, D. B. (1978). Similarity in real-life adolescent friendship pairs. *Journal of Personality and Social Psychology, 36,* 306–312.

Kaplan, M. F. (1989). Task, situational and perceived determinants of influence processes in group decision making. In E. Lawler & B. Markovsky (Eds.), *Advances in group processes* (Vol. 6, pp. 87–1050). Greenwich, CT: JAI.

Kaplan, M. F., & Miller, C. E. (1987). Group decision making and normative versus informational influence: Effects of type of issue and assigned decision rule. *Journal of Personality & Social Psychology, 53,* 306–313.

Karau, S. J., & Williams, K. D. (1993). Social loafing: A meta-analytic review and theoretical integration. *Journal of Personality and Social Psychology, 65,* 681–706.

Karraker, K. H., & Stern, M. (1990). Infant physical attractiveness and facial expression: Effects on adult perceptions. *Basic and Applied Social Psychology, 11,* 371–385.

Kasser, T., & Sharma, Y. S. (1999). Reproductive freedom, educational equality, and female's preference for resource-acquisition characteristics in mates. *Psychological Science, 10,* 374–377.

Kassin, S. M. (1997). The psychology of confession evidence. *American Psychologist, 52,* 221–233.

Kassin, S. M., & Kiechel, K. L. (1996). The social psychology of false confessions: Compliance, internalization, and confabulation. *Psychological Science, 7,* 125–128.

Kassin, S. M., & McNall, K. (1991). Police interrogations and confessions: Communicating promises and threats by pragmatic implication. *Law and Human Behavior, 15,* 233–251.

Kassin, S. M., Tubb, V. A., Hosch, H. M., & Memon, A. (2001). On the "general acceptance" of eyewitness testimony research. *American Psychologist, 56,* 405–416.

Kassin, S. M., & Kiechel, K. L. (1996). The social psychology of false confessions: Compliance, internalization, and confabulation. *Psychological Science, 7,* 125–128.

Katz, D. (1960). The functional approach to the study of attitudes. *Journal of Abnormal and Social Psychology, 70,* 1037–1051.

Katz, I. M., & Campbell, J. D. (1994). Ambivalence over emotional expression and well-being: Nomothetic and Idiographic tests of the stress-buffering hypothesis. *Journal of Personality and Social Psychology, 67,* 513–524.

Kawakami K., & Dividio, J. F. (2001). The reliability of implicit stereotyping. *Personality and Social Psychology Bulletin, 27,* 212–225.

Kawakami K., Dovidio, J. F., Moll, J., Hermsen, S., & Russn, A. (2000). Just say no (to stereotyping): Effects of training in the negation of stereotypic associations on stereotype activation. *Journal and Personality and Social Psychology, 78,* 871–888.

Kawakami, K., Dion, K. L., & Dovidio, J. F. (1998). Racial prejudice and stereotype activation. *Personality and Social Psychology Bulletin, 24,* 407–416.

Keller, L. M., Bouchard, T. J., Jr., Arvey, R. D., Segal, N. L., & Dawis, R. V. (1992). Work values: Genetic and environmental influences. *Journal of Applied Psychology, 77,* 79–88.

Keller, R. T. (1997). Job involvement and organizational commitment as longitudinal predictors of job performance: A study of scientists and engineers. *Journal of Applied Psychology, 82,* 539–545.

Kellerman, J., Lewis, J., & Laird, J. D. (1989). Looking and loving: The effects of mutual gaze on feelings of romantic love. *Journal of Research in Personality, 23,* 145–161.

Kelley, H. H. (1972). Attribution in social interaction. In E. E. Jones et al. (Eds.), *Attribution: Perceiving the causes of behavior.* Morristown, NJ: General Learning Press.

Kelley, H. H., & Michela, J. L. (1980). Attribution theory and research. *Annual Review of Psychology, 31,* 457–501.

Kelly, A. E., & Nauta, M. M. (1997). Reactance and thought suppression. *Personality and Social Psychology Bulletin, 23,* 1123–1132.

Kelman, H. C. (1967). Human use of human subjects: The problem of deception in social psychological experiments. *Psychological Bulletin, 67,* 1–11.

Keltner, D., & Robinson, R. J. (1997). Defending the status quo: Power and bias in social conflict. *Personality and Social Psychology Bulletin, 23,* 1066–1077.

Kendzierski, D., & Whitaker, D. J. (1997). The role of self-schema in linking intentions with behavior. *Personality and Social Psychology Bulletin, 23,* 139–147.

Kenealy, P., Gleeson, K., Frude, N., & Shaw, W. (1991). The importance of the individual in the "causal" relationship between attractiveness and self-esteem. *Journal of Community and Applied Social Psychology, 1,* 45–56.

Kenrick, D. T., Keefe, R. C., Bryan, A., Barr, A., & Brown, S. (1995). Age preferences and mate choice among homosexuals and heterosexuals: A case for modular psychological mechanisms. *Journal of Personality and Social Psychology, 69,* 1166–1172.

Kenrick, D. T., Montello, D. R., Gutierres, S. E., & Trost, M. R. (1993). Effects of physical attractiveness on affect and perceptual judgments: When social comparison overrides social reinforcement. *Personality and Social Psychology Bulletin, 19,* 195–199.

Kenrick, D. T., Neuberg, S. L., Zierk, K. L., & Krones, J. M. (1994). Evolution and social cognition: Contrast effects as a function of sex, dominance, and physical attractiveness. *Personality and Social Psychology Bulletin, 20,* 210–217.

Kenrick, D. T., Sundie, J. M., Nicastle, L. D., & Stone, G. O. (2001). Can one ever be too wealthy or too chaste? Searching for nonlinearities in mate judgement. *Journal of Personality and Social Psychology, 80,* 462–471.

Kenrick, D. T., Sadalla, E. K., & Keefe, R. C. (1998). Evolutionary cognitive psychology: The missing heart of modern cognitive science. In C. Crawford & D. L. Krebs (Eds.), *Handbook of evolutionary psychology* (pp. 485–514). Hillsdale, NJ: Erlbaum.

Kent, G. G., Davis, J. D., & Shapiro, D. A. (1981). Effect of mutual acquaintance on the construction of conversation. *Journal of Experimental Social Psychology, 17,* 197–209.

Kernis, M. H., Paradise, A. W., Whitaker, D. J., Wheatman, S. R., & Goldman, B. N. (2000). Master of one's psychological domain? Not likely if one's self-esteem is unstable. *Personality and Social Psychology Bulletin, 26,* 1297–1305.

Kernis, M. H., Whisenhunt, C. R., Waschull, S. B., Greenier, K. D., Berry, A. J., Herlocker, C. E., & Anderson, C. A. (1998). Multiple facets of self-esteem and their relations to depressive symptoms. *Personality and Social Psychology Bulletin, 24,* 657–668.

Kerr, D. & Ram, B. (1994). *Population dynamics in Canada (Focus on Canada series).* Scarborough, ON: Statistics Canada and Prentice Hall Canada

Kerr, H. L., & MacCoun, R. J. (1985). The effects of jury size and polling method on the process and product of jury deliberations. *Journal of Personality and Social Psychology, 48,* 349–363.

Kerr, N. L., & Kaufman-Gilliland, C. M. (1994). Communication, commitment, and cooperation in social dilemmas. *Journal of Personality and Social Psychology, 66,* 513–529.

Kessler, R. C., Kendler, K. S., Heath, A., Neale, M. C., & Eaves, L. J. (1992). Social support, depressed mood, and adjustment to stress: A genetic epidemiologic investigation. *Journal of Personality and Social Psychology, 62,* 257–272.

Key, W. B. (1973). *Subliminal seduction.* Englewood Cliffs, NJ: Signet.

Kiecolt-Glaser, J. K., Page, G. G., Marucha, P. T., MacCallum, R. C., & Glaser, R. (1998). Psychological influences on surgical recovery: Perspectives from psychoneuroimmunology. *American Psychologist, 53,* 1209–1218.

Kilham, W., & Mann, L. (1974). Level of destructive obedience as a function of transmitter and executant roles in the Milgram obedience paradigm. *Journal of Personality and Social Psychology, 29,* 696–702.

Killeya, L. A., & Johnson, B. T. (1998). Experimental induction of biased systematic processing: The directed through technique. *Personality and Social Psychology Bulletin, 24,* 17–33.

Killias, M. (1993). International correlation between gun ownership and rates of homicide and suicide. *Canadian Medical Association Journal, 148,* 1721–1725.

Kinsella, W. (1994). *Web of hate: Inside Canada's far right network.* Toronto: HarperCollins. Kirby, D. M., & Gardner, R. C. (1973). Ethnic stereotypes: Determinants in children and their parents. *Canadian Journal of Psychology, 27,* 127–143.

Kirkpatrick, S. A., & Locke, E. A. (1991). Leadership: Do traits matter? *Academy of Management Executive, 5*(2), 48–60.

Kitayama, S., & Karasawa, M. (1997). Implicit self-esteem in Japan: Name letters and birthday numbers. *Personality and Social Psychology Bulletin, 23*, 736–742.

Kitayama, S., Markus, H. R., Matsumoto, H., & Norasakkunkit, V. (1997). Individual and collective processes in the construction of the self: Self-enhancement in the United States and self-criticism in Japan. *Journal of Personality and Social Psychology, 72*, 1245–1267.

Kleck, G. (1988). Crime control through the private use of armed force. *Social problems, 35*, 1–21.

Kleck, G. (1991). *Point blank: Guns and violence in America*. Hawthorne, NY: Aldine de Gruyter.

Klein, S. B., & Loftus, J. (1988). The nature of self-referent encoding: The contributions of elaborative and organizational processes. *Journal of Personality and Social Psychology, 55*, 5–11.

Klein, S. B., Loftus, J., & Burton, H. A. (1989). Two self-reference effects: The importance of distinguishing between self-descriptiveness judgments and autobiographical retrieval in self-referent encoding. *Journal of Personality and Social Psychology, 56*, 853–865.

Kleinke, C. L. (1986). Gaze and eye contact: A research review. *Psychological Bulletin, 100*, 78–l00.

Kleinke, C. L., & Dean, G. O. (1990). Evaluation of men and women receiving positive and negative responses with various acquaintance strategies. *Journal of Social Behavior and Personality, 5*, 369–377.

Kline, S. L., Stafford, L., & Miklosovic, J. D. (1996). Women's surnames: Decisions, interpretations and associations with relational qualities. *Journal of Social and Personal Relationships, 13*, 593–617.

Klohnen, E. C., & Bera, S. (1998). Behavioral and experiential patterns of avoidantly and securely attached women across adulthood: A 31-year longitudinal perspective. *Journal of Personality and Social Psychology, 74*, 211–223.

Klohnen, E. C., & Mendelsohn, G. A. (1998). Partner selection for personality characteristics: A couple-centered approach. *Personality and Social Psychology Bulletin, 24*, 268–278.

Knight, G. P., & Dubro, A. (1984). Cooperative, competitive, and individualistic social values: An individualized regression and clustering approach. *Journal of Personality and Social Psychology, 46*, 98–105.

Koehler, J. J. (1993). The base rate fallacy myth. *Psychology, 4*.

Koehler, S. P., & Willis, F. N. (1994). Traffic citations in relation to gender. *Journal of Applied Social Psychology, 24*, 1919–1926.

Koestner, R., Bernieri, F., & Zuckerman, M. (1992). Self-regulation and consistency between attitudes, traits, and behaviors. *Personality and Social Psychology Bulletin, 18*, 52–59.

Kohl, W. L., Steers, R., & Terborg, Jr. (1995). The effects of transformational leadership on teacher attitudes and student performance in Singapore. *Journal of Organizational Behavior, 73*, 695–702.

Kohlberg, L. (1966). A cognitive—developmental analysis of children's sex-role concepts and attitudes. In E. E. Maccoby (Ed.), *The development of sex differences*. Stanford, CA: Stanford University Press.

Kolata, G. (1995, February 28). Man's world, woman's world? Brain studies point to differences. *New York Times*, C1, C7.

Komorita, M., & Parks, G. (1994). Interpersonal relations: Mixed-motive interaction. *Annual Review of Psychology, 46*, 183–207.

Koole, S. L., Dijksterhuis, A., & van Knippenberg, A. (2001). What's in a name: Implicit self-esteem and the automatic self. *Journal of Personality and Social Psychology, 80*, 669–685.

Koole, S. L., & Spijker, M. (2000). Overcoming the planning fallacy through willpower: Effects of implementation intentions on actual and predicted task-completion times. *European Journal of Social Psychology, 30*, 873–888.

Korchmaros, J. D., & Kenny, D. A. (2001). Emotional closeness as a mediator of the effect of genetic relatedness on altruism. *Psychological Science, 12*, 262–265.

Korte, C. (1980). Urban-nonurban differences in social behavior and social psychological models of urban impact. *Journal of Social Issues, 36*, 29–51.

Korte, C. (1981). Constraints on helping in an urban environment. In J. P. Rushton & R. M. Sorrentino (Eds.), *Altruism and helping behavior*. Hillsdale, NJ: Erlbaum.

Kotter, J. (1982). *The general managers*. New York: Free Press.

Kraus, S. J. (1995). Attitudes and the prediction of behavior: A meta-analysis of the empirical literature. *Personality and Social Psychology Bulletin, 21*, 58–75.

Kraut, R., Kiesler, S., Boneva, B., Cummings, J., Helgeson, V., & Crawford, A. (2002). Internet paradox revisited. *Journal of Social Issues, 58*, 49–74.

Kraut, R., Patterson, M., Lundmark, V., Kiesler, S., Mukopadhyay, T., & Scherlis, W. (1998). Internet paradox: A social technology that reduces social involvement and psychological well-being? *American Psychologist, 53*. 1017–1031.

Krosnick, J. A. (1989). Attitude importance and attitude accessibility. *Personality and Social Psychology Bulletin, 15*, 297–308.

Krosnick, J. A., Betz, A. L., Jussim, L. J., & Lynn, A. R. (1992). Subliminal conditioning of attitudes. *Personality and Social Psychology Bulletin, 18*, 152–162.

Krosnick, J. A., Boninger, D. S., Chuang, Y. C., Berent, M. K., & Carnot, C. G. (1993). Attitude strength: One construct or many related constructs? *Journal of Personality and Social Psychology, 65*, 1132–1151.

Krueger, J., & Clement, R. W. (1994). The truly false consensus effect: An ineradicable and egocentric bias in social perception. *Journal of Personality and Social Psychology, 67*, 596–610.

Kruger, D. J. (2001). Psychological aspects of adaptations for kin directed altruistic helping behaviors. *Social Behavior and Personality, 29*, 323–330.

Krupat, E. (1975). *Psychology is social*. Glenview, IL: Scott, Foresman.

Krupat, E., & Guild, W. (1980). Defining the city: The use of objective and subjective measures of community description. *Journal of Social Issues, 36*, 9–28.

Kuhn, D. (2001). How do people know? *Psychological Science, 12*, 1–8.

Kuhn, D., Weinstock, M., & Flaton, R. (1994). How well do jurors reason? Competence dimensions of individual variation in a juror reasoning task. *Psychological Science, 5*, 289–296.

Kuiper, N. A., & Martin, R. A. (1998). Laughter and stress in daily life: Relation to positive and negative affect. *Motivation and Emotion, 22*, 133–153.

Kulik, J. A., Mahler, H. I. M., & Moore, P. J. (1996). Social comparison and affiliation under threat: Effects on recovery from major surgery. *Journal of Personality and Social Psychology, 71*, 967–979.

Kumagai, F. (1983). Filial violence in Japan. *Victimology, 8*, 173–194.

Kunda, Z. (1999). *Social cognition: Making sense of people.* Cambridge, MA: MIT Press.

Kunda, Z., & Oleson, K. C. (1995). Maintaining stereotypes in the face of disconfirmation: Constructing grounds for subtyping deviants. *Journal of Personality and Social Psychology, 68*, 565–579.

Kunda, Z., & Sherman-Williams, B. (1993). Stereotypes and the construal of individuating information. Personality and *Social Psychology Bulletin, 19*, 90–99.

Kurdek, L. A. (1993). Predicting marital dissolution: A 5-year longitudinal study of newlywed couples. *Journal of Personality and Social Psychology, 64*, 221–242.

Kurdek, L. A. (1996). The deterioration of relationships quality for gay and lesbian cohabiting couples: A five-year prospective longitudinal study. *Personal Relationships, 3*, 417–442.

Kurdek, L.A. (1998). Relationship outcomes and their predictors: Longitudinal evidence from heterosexual married, gay cohabiting and lesbian cohabiting couples. *Journal of Marriage and the Family, 60*, 553–568.

Kwan, V. S. Y., Bond, M.H., Boucher, H.C., Maslach, C., & Gan, Y. (2002). The construct of individuation: More complex in collectivist than in individualist cultures. *Personality and Social Psychology Bulletin, 28*, 300–310.

Kwon, Y.-H. (1994). Feeling toward one's clothing and self-perception of emotion, sociability, and work competency. *Journal of Social Behavior and Personality, 9*, 129–139.

La Guardia, J. G., Ryan, R. M., Couchman, C. E., & Deci, E. L. (2000). Within-person variation in security of attachment: A self-determination theory perspective on attachment, need fulfillment, and well-being. *Journal of Personality and Social Psychology, 79*, 367–384.

LaFromboise, T., Coleman, H. L. K., & Gerton, J. (1993). Psychological impact of biculturalism: Evidence and theory. *Psychological Bulletin, 114*, 395–412.

Lambert, A. J. (1995). Stereotypes and social judgment: The consequences of group variability. *Journal of Personality and Social Psychology, 68*, 388–403.

Lambert, W. E. (1967). A social psychology of bilingualism. *Journal of Social Issues, 23*, 91–109.

Lambert, W. E. (1974). The St. Lambert project. In S. T. Carey (Ed.), *Bilingualism, biculturalism and education.* Edmonton: University of Alberta.

Lambert, W. E. (1978). Some cognitive and sociocultural aspects of being bilingual. In J. P. Alatis (Ed.), *International dimensions of bilingual education.* Washington, DC: Georgetown University Press.

Lambert, W. E., & Taylor, D. M. (1984). Language and the education of ethnic minority children in Canada. In R.J. Samuda, J. W. Berry, & M. Laferriere (Eds.), *Multiculturalism in Canada.* Toronto: Allyn & Bacon.

Lambert, W. E., & Tucker, G. R. (1972). *Bilingual education in children: The St. Lambert experiment.* Rowley, MA: Newbury House.

Lambert, W. E., Mermigis, L., & Taylor, D. M. (1986). Greek Canadians' attitudes toward own group and other Canadian ethnic groups: A test of the multiculturalism hypothesis. *Canadian Journal of Behavioral Science, 18*, 35–51.

Lamm, H. & Myers, D. G. (1978). Group-induced polarization of attitudes and behavior. In L. Berkowitz (Ed.), *Advances in experimental social psychology.* New York: Academic Press.

Lamm, H., Wiesmann, U., & Keller, K. (1998). Subjective determinants of attraction: Self-perceived causes of the rise and decline of liking, love, and being in love. *Personal Relationships, 5*, 91–104.

Langer, E. J. (1989). *Mindfulness.* Reading, MA, US: Addison-Wesley.

Langlois, F. H., & Roggman, L. A. (1990). Attractive faces are only average. *Psychological Science, 1*, 115–112.

Langlois, J. H., Ritter, J. M., Roggman, L. A., & Vaughn, L. S. (1991). Facial diversity and infant preferences for attractive faces. *Developmental Psychology, 27*, 79–84.

Langlois, J. H., Roggman, L. A., & Musselman, L. (1994). What is average and what is not average about attractive faces? *Psychological Science, 5*, 214–220.

Lansing, J. B., & Heyns, R. W. (1959). Need affiliation and frequency of four types of communication. *Journal of Abnormal and Social Psychology, 58*, 365–372.

LaPiere, R. T. (1934). Attitude and actions. *Social Forces, 13*, 230–237.

LaPrelle, J., Hoyle, R. H., Insko, C. A., & Bernthal, P. (1990). Interpersonal attraction and descriptions of the traits of others: Ideal similarity, self similarity, and liking. *Journal of Research in Personality, 24*, 216–240.

Larrey, T. S., & Paulus, P. B. (1999). Group preference and convergent tendencies in groups: A content analysis of group brainstorming performance. *Creativity Research Journal, 12*, 175–184.

Larson, J. R. Jr., Christensen, C., Franz, T. M., & Abbott, A. S. (1998). Diagnosing groups: The pooling, management, and impact of shared and unshared case information in team-based medical decision making. *Journal of Personality and Social Psychology, 75*, 93–108.

Larson, J. R., Jr., Foster-Fishman, P. G., & Franz, T. M. (1998). Leadership style and the discussion of shared and unshared information in decision-making groups. *Personality and Social Psychology Bulletin, 24*, 482–495.

Latané, B. (1981). The psychology of social impacts. *American Psychologist, 36*, 343–356.

Latané, B., & Dabbs, J. M., Jr. (1975). Sex, group size, and helping in three cities. *Sociometry, 38,* 180–194.

Latané, B., & Darley, J. M. (1968). Group inhibition of bystander intervention in emergencies. *Journal of Personality and Social Psychology, 10,* 215–221.

Latané, B., & Darley, J. M. (1970). *The unresponsive bystander: Why doesn't he help?* New York: Appleton-Century-Crofts.

Latané, B., & L'Herrou, T. (1996). Spatial clustering in the conformity game: Dynamic social impact in electronic groups. *Journal of Personality and Social Psychology, 70,* 1218–1230.

Latané, B., Williams, K., & Harkins, S. (1979). Many hands make light the work: The causes and consequences of social loafing. *Journal of Personality and Social Psychology, 37,* 822–832.

Latty-Mann, H., & Davis, K. E. (1996). Attachment theory and partner choice: Preference and actuality. *Journal of Social and Personal Relationships, 13,* 5–23.

Lau, S. (1989). Sex role orientation and domains of self esteem. *Sex Roles, 21,* 415–422.

Lauer, J., & Lauer, R. (1985, June). Marriages made to last. *Psychology Today,* 22–26.

Laumann, E. O., Gagnon, J. H., Michael, R. T., & Michaels, S. (1994). *The social organization of sexuality: Sexual practices in the United States.* Chicago: University of Chicago Press.

Lazarus, R. S. (1993). From psychological stress to the emotions: A history of changing outlooks. In L. W. Porter & M. R. Rosenzweig (Eds.), *Annual review of psychology* (Vol. 44, pp. 1–21). Palo Alto, CA: Annual Reviews, Inc.

Leary, M. R., Schreindorfer, L. S., & Haupt, A. L. (1995). The role of low self-esteem in emotional and behavioral problems: Why is low self-esteem dysfunctional? *Journal of Social and Clinical Psychology, 14,* 297–314.

Leary, M. R., Spinger, C., Negel, L., Ansell, E., & Evans, K. (1998). The causes, phenomenology, and consequences of hurt feelings. *Journal of Personality and Social Psychology, 74,* 1225–1237.

Leary, M. R., Tambor, E. S., Terdal, S. K., & Downs, D. L. (1995). Self-esteem as an interpersonal monitor: The sociometer hypothesis. *Journal of Personality and Social Psychology, 68,* 518–530.

Lebra, T. S. (1976). *Japanese patterns of behavior.* Honolulu: University Press of Hawaii.

Lee, I.-M., Rexrode, K. M., Cook, N. R., Manson, J. A. E., Buring, J. E. (2001). Physical activity and coronary heart disease in women: Is "no pain, no gain" passé? *Journal of the American Medical Association, 285,* 1447–1454.

Lee, M. E., Matsumoto, D., Koyayashi, M., Krupp, D., Maniatis, E. F., & Roberts, W. (1992). Cultural influences on nonverbal behavior in applied settings. In R. S. Feldman (Ed.), *Applications of nonverbal behavioral theories and research.* Hillsdale, NJ: Erlbaum.

Lee, Y. T., & Ottati, V. (1993). Determinannts of ingroup and out-group perceptions of heterogeneity: An investigation of Sino-American differences. *Journal of Cross-cultural Psychology, 25,* 146–158.

Lee, Y. T., & Seligman, M. E. P. (1997). Are Americans more optimistic than the Chinese? *Personality and Social Psychology Bulletin, 23,* 32–40.

Leippe, M. R., Manion, A. P., & Romanczyk, A. (1992). Eyewitness persuasion: How and how well do fact finders judge the accuracy of adults' and children's memory reports? *Journal of Personality and Social Psychology, 63,* 181–197.

Lemery, K. S., Goldsmith, H. H., Klinnert, M. D., & Mrazek, D. A. (1999). Developmental models of infant and childhood temperament. *Developmental Psychology, 35,* 189–204.

Lemonick, M. D., & Park, A. (2001, May 28). New hope for cancer. *Time,* 62–69.

Lepore, S. J. (1997). Expressive writing moderates the relation between intrusive thoughts and depressive symptoms. *Journal of Personality and Social Psychology, 73,* 1030–1037.

Lester, D. (1984). *Gun control: Issues and answers.* Springfield, IL: Charles Thomas.

Lester, D. (1991). Are the societal correlates of suicide and homicide rates the same for each lethal weapon? A study of European nations. *European Journal of Psychiatry, 5,* 5–8.

Levenson, R. W., Carstensen, L. L., & Gottman, J. M. (1994). The influence of age and gender on affect, physiology, and their interrelations: A study of long-term marriages. *Journal of Personality and Social Psychology, 67,* 56–68.

Leventhal, G. S., Karuza, J., & Fry, W. R. (1980). Beyond fairness: A theory of allocation preferences. In G. Mikula (Ed.), *Justice and social interaction* (pp. 167–218). New York: Springer-Verlag.

Leventhal, H., Singer, R., & Jones, S. (1965). The effects of fear and specificity of recommendation upon attitudes and behavior. *Journal of Personality and Social Psychology, 2,* 20–29.

Levin, J. (2000). A prolegomenon to an epidemiology of love: Theory, measurement, and health outcomes. *Journal of Social and Clinical Psychology, 19,* 117–136.

Levine, R. V., Martinez, T. S., Brase, G., & Sorenson, K. (1994). Helping in 36 U.S. cities. *Journal of Personality and Social Psychology, 67,* 69–82.

Levine, R.V., Sato, S., Hashimoto, T., & Verma, J. (1995). Love and marriage in eleven cultures. *Journal of Cross-Cultural Psychology, 26,* 554–571.

Levinger, G. (1980). Toward the analysis of close relationships. *Journal of Experimental Social Psychology, 16,* 510–544.

Levy, K. N., Blatt, S. J., & Shaver, P. R. (1998). Attachment styles and parental representations. *Journal of Personality and Social Psychology, 74,* 407–419.

Lewin, K. (1948). *Resolving social conflicts: Selected papers on group dynamics.* New York: Harper & Row.

Lewin, K., Lippitt, R., & White, R. R. (1939). Patterns of aggressive behavior in experimentally created "social climates." *Journal of Social Psychology, 10,* 271–299.

Lewis, M. (1992). Will the real self or selves please stand up? *Psychological Inquiry, 3,* 123–124.

Liberman, A., & Chaiken, S. (1992). Defensive processing of personally relevant health messages. *Personality and Social Psychology Bulletin, 18,* 669–679.

Lickel, B., Hamilton, D. L., Wieczorkowski, G., Lewis, A., Sherman, S. J., & Uhles, A. N. (2000). Varieties of groups and the perception of group entiativity. *Journal of Personality and Social Psychology, 78,* 223–246.

Liden, R. C., & Mitchell, T. R. (1988). Ingratiatory behaviors in organizational settings. *Academy of Management Review, 13,* 572–587.

Lieberman, J. D., & Greenberg, J. (1999). Cognitive-experiential self-theory and displaced aggression. *Journal of Personality and Social Psychology,* in press.

Limper, R. (2000). Cooperation between parents, teachers, and school boards to prevent bullying in education: An overview of work done in the Netherlands. *Aggressive Behavior, 26,* 113–124.

Linden, E. (1992). Chimpanzees with a difference: Bonobos. *National Geographic, 18*(3), 46–53.

Lindsay, D. S. (1998). Recovered memories and social justice. *American Psychologist, 53,* 486–487.

Linville, P. W., & Fischer, G. W. (1993). Exemplar and abstraction models of perceived group variability and stereotypicality. *Social Cognition, 11,* 92–125.

Linville, P. W., Fischer, G. W., & Salovey, P. (1989). Perceived distributions of the characteristics of in-group and out-group members: Empirical evidence and a computer simulation. *Journal of Personality and Social Psychology, 57,* 165–188.

Lippa, R., & Donaldson, S. I. (1990). Self-monitoring and idiographic measures of behavioral variability across interpersonal relationships. *Journal of Personality, 58,* 465–479.

Lipset, S. M. (1990a). *Continental divide: The values and institutions of the United States and Canada.* New York: Routledge.

Lipset, S. M. (1990b). *North American cultures: Values and institutions in Canada and the United States.* Orona, ME: Borderlands.

Lipset, S. M. (2001). Defining moments and recurring myths: A reply. *Canadian Review of Sociology & Anthropology, 38,* 97–100.

Little, A. C., & Hancock, P. J. B. (2002). The role of masculinity and distinctiveness in judgments of human male facial attractiveness. *British Journal of Psychology, 93,* 451–465.

Locke, E. A. (1991). *The essence of leadership.* New York: Lexington Books.

Locke, M. (1995, May 25). Love better with age, study says. *Albany Times Union,* C-5.

Loftus, E. F. (1992). *Witness for the defense.* New York: St. Martin's Press.

Loftus, E. F. (1997). Memory for a past that never was. *Current Directions in Psychological Science, 6,* 60–65.

Loftus, E. F. (1998). The private practice of misleading direction. *American Psychologist, 53,* 484–485.

Loftus, E. F., Coan, J. A., & Pickrell, J. E. (1996). Manufacturing false memories using bits of reality. In L. Reder (Ed.), *Implicit memory and metacognition* (pp. 195–220). Mahwah, NJ: Erlbaum.

Logsdon, M. C., Birkimer, J. C., & Barbee, A. P. (1997). Social support providers for postpartum women. *Journal of Social Behavior and Personality, 12,* 89–102.

Lopez, F. G., Gover, M. R., Leskela, J., Sauer, E. M., Schirmer, L., & Wyssmann, J. (1997). Attachment styles, shame, guilt, and collaborative problem-solving orientations. *Personal Relationships, 4,* 187–199.

Lord, C. G., Ross, L., & Lepper, M. R. (1979). Biased assimilation and attitude polarization: The effects of prior theories on subsequently considered evidence. *Journal of Personality and Social Psychology, 37,* 2098–2109.

Lorenz, K. (1966). *On aggression.* New York: Harcourt, Brace, & World.

Lorenz, K. (1974). *Civilized man's eight deadly sins.* New York: Harcourt, Brace, Jovanovich.

Lott, J.R. (1998). *More guns, less crime.* Chicago: University of Chicago Press.

Luks, A. (1988, October). Helper's high. *Psychology Today,* 39–40.

Lumsdaine, A., & Janis, I. (1953). Resistance to counterpropaganda produced by a one-sided versus a two-sided propaganda presentation. *Public Opinion Quarterly, 17,* 311–318.

Luus, C. A., & Wells, G. L. (1994). The malleability of eyewitness confidence: Co-witness and perseverance effects. *Journal of Applied Psychology, 79,* 714–723.

Lydon, J. E., Meana, M., Sepinwall, D., Richards, N., & Mayman, S. (1999). The commitment calibration hypothesis: When do people devalue attractive alternatives. *Personality and Social Psychology Bulletin, 25,* 152–161.

Lynn, M., & Mynier, K. (1993). Effects of server posture on restaurant tipping. *Journal of Applied Social Psychology, 23.*

Lyubomirsky, S., & Nolen-Hoeksema, S. (1995). Effects of self-focused rumination on negative thinking and interpersonal problem solving. *Journal of Personality and Social Psychology, 69,* 176–190.

Maas, A., & Clark, R. D. III. (1984). Hidden impact of minorities: Fifteen years of minority influence research. *Psychological Bulletin, 95,* 233–243.

Macaulay, J. (1970). A shill for charity. In J. Macaulay & L. Berkowitz (Eds.), *Altruism and helping behavior* (pp. 43–59). New York: Academic Press.

MacCoun, R. J., & Kerr, N. L. (1988). Asymmetric influence in mock jury deliberation: Jurors' bias for leniency. *Journal of Personality and Social Psychology, 54,* 21–33.

MacDonald, T. K., Fong, G. T., Zanna, M. P., & Martineau, A. M. (2000). Alcohol myopia and condom use: Can alcohol intoxication be associated with more prudent behavior? *Journal of Personality and Social Psychology, 78,* 605–619.

MacDonald, T. K., & Ross, M. (1999). Assessing the accuracy of predictions about dating relationships: How and why do lovers' predictions differ from those made by observers? *Personality and Social Psychology Bulletin, 25,* 1417–1429.

MacDonald, T. K., Zanna, M. P., & Fong, G. T. (1996). Decision making in altered states: Effects of alcohol on attitudes toward drinking and driving. *Journal of Personality and Social Psychology, 68,* 973–985.

Mackie, D. M., & Worth, L. T. (1989). Processing deficits and the mediation of positive affect in persuasion. *Journal of Personality and Social Psychology, 57,* 27–40.

MacKinnon, M. (1999). Women gaining ground in work force. *Globe and Mail*, April 19, pp. B1

Macrae, C. N. (1992). A tale of two curries: Counterfactual thinking and accident-related judgments. *Personality and Social Psychology Bulletin*, 18, 84–87.

Macrae, C. N., & Milne, A. B. (1992). A curry for your thoughts: Empathic effects on counterfactual thinking. *Personality and Social Psychology Bulletin*, 18, 625–630.

Macrae, C. N., Bodenhausen, G. V., & Milne, A. B. (1998). Saying no to unwanted thoughts: Self-focus and the regulation of mental life. *Journal of Personality and Social Psychology, 74,* 578–589.

Macrae, C., Bodenhausen, G., & Milne, A. (1995). The dissection of selection in person perception: Inhibitory processes in social stereotyping. *Journal of Personality and Social Psychology,* 69, 397–407.

Magner, N. R., Johnson, G. G., Sobery, J. S., & Welker, R. B. (2000). Enhancing procedural justice in local government budget and tax decision making. *Journal of Applied Social Psychology, 30,* 798–815.

Maheswaran, D., & Chaiken, S. (1991). Promoting systematic processing in low-motivation settings: Effect of incongruent information on processing and judgment. *Journal of Personality and Social Psychology,* 61, 13–25.

Maier, S. F., & Watkins, L. R. (2000). The immune system as a sensory system: Implications for psychology. *Current Directions in Psychological Science,* 9, 98–102.

Maisonneuve, J., Palmade, G., & Fourment, C. (1952). Selective choices and propinquity. *Sociometry,* 15, 135–140.

Major, B., & Adams, J. B. (1983). Roles of gender, interpersonal orientation, and self-presentation in distributive justice behavior. *Journal of Personality and Social Psychology, 45,* 598–608.

Major, B., & Deaux, K. (1982). Individual differences in justice behavior. In J. Greenberg & R. L. Cohen (Eds.), *Equity and justice in social behavior.* New York: Academic Press.

Major, B., Carnevale, P. J. D., & Deaux, K. (1981). A different perspective on androgyny: Evaluations of masculine and feminine personality characteristics. *Journal of Personality and Social Psychology, 41,* 988–1001.

Major, B., Sciacchitano, A. M., & Crocker, J. (1993). In-group versus out-group comparisons and self-esteem. *Personality and Social Psychology Bulletin,* 19, 711–721.

Major, B., Kaiser, C. R., & McCoy, S. K. (2003). It's not my fault: When and why attributions to prejudice protect self-esteem. *Personality & Social Psychology Bulletin, 29,* 772–781.

Mallick, S. K., & McCandless, B. R. (1966). A study of catharsis of aggression. *Journal of Personality and Social Psychology,* 4, 591–596.

Mantell, D. M. (1971).The potential for violence in Germany. *Journal of Social Issues,* 27, 101–112.

Marcus-Newhall, A., Pederson, W. C., Carlson, M., & Miller, N. (2000). Displaced aggression is alive and well: A meta-analytic review. *Journal of Personality and Social Psychology,* 78, 670–689.

Margalit, M., & Eysenck, S. (1990). Prediction of coherence in adolescence: Gender differences in social skills, personality, and family climate. *Journal of Research in Personality, 24,* 510–521.

Markus, H., & Nurius, P. (1986). Possible selves. *American Psychologist, 41,* 954–969.

Markus, H.R., & Kitayama, S. (1991a). Culture and the self: Implication for cognition, emotion, and motivation. *Psychological Review,* 98, 224–253.

Markus, H. R., Mullalluy, P., & Kitayama, S. (1997). Selfways: Diversity in modes of cultural participation. In Neisser, U., & Jopling, D. A., (Eds.), *The conceptual self in context: Culture, experience, self-understanding* (pp.13–61). Cambridge, England: Cambridge University Press.

Martin, C. L. (1987). A ratio measure of sex stereotyping. *Journal of Personality and Social Psychology,* 37, 970—988.

Martin, C. L., & Parker, S. (1995). Folk theories about sex and race differences. *Personality and Social Psychology Bulletin,* 21, 45–57.

Martin, K. A., & Leary, M. R. (1999). Would you drink after a stranger? The influence of self-presentational motives on willingness to take a health risk. *Personality and Social Psychology Bulletin, 25,* 1092–1100.

Martz, J. M., Verette, J., Arriaga, X. B., Slovik, L. F., Cox, C. L., & Rusbult, C. E. (1998). Positive illusion in close relationships. *Personal Relationships,* 5, 159–181.

Maslach, C., Santee, R. T., & Wade, C. (1987). Individuation, gender role, and dissent: Personality mediators of situational forces. *Journal of Personality and Social Psychology,* 53, 1088–1094.

Mathes, E. W., Adams, H. E., & Davies, R. M. (1985). Jealousy: Loss of relationship rewards, loss of self-esteem, depression, anxiety, and anger. *Journal of Personality and Social Psychology,* 48, 1552–1561.

Maugh, T. H., II. (1998, February 21). To keep marriage going, try giving in to your wife. *Los Angeles Times.*

Mayer, J. D., & Hanson, E. (1995). Mood-congruent judgment over time. *Personality and Social Psychology Bulletin,* 21, 237–244.

Mayer, J. D., & Salovey, P. (1995). Emotional intelligence and the construction and regulation of feelings. *Applied & Preventive Psychology,* 4, 197–208.

Mazzella, R., & Feingold, A. (1994). The effects of physical attractiveness, race, socioeconomic status, and gender of defendants and victims on judgments of mock jurors: A meta-analysis. *Journal of Applied Social Psychology,* 24, 1315–1344.

McAdams, D. P. (1979). *Validation of a thematic coding system for the intimacy motive.* Unpublished doctoral dissertation, Harvard University.

McArthur, L. A. (1972). The how and what of why: Some determinants and consequences of causal attribution. *Journal of Personality and Social Psychology,* 22, 171–193.

McCall, M. (1997). Physical attractiveness and access to alcohol: What is beautiful does not get carded. *Journal of Applied Social Psychology,* 23, 453–562.

McCall, M. E., & Struthers, N. J. (1994). Sex, sex-role orientation and self-esteem as predictors of coping style. *Journal of Social Behavior and Personality,* 9, 801–810.

McClure, J. (1998). Discounting causes of behavior: Are two reasons better than one? *Journal of Personality and Social Psychology, 74*, 7–20.

McConnell, A. R., Sherman, S. J., & Hamilton, D. L. (1994). Illusory correlation in the perception of groups: An extension of the distinctiveness-based account. *Journal of Personality and Social Psychology, 67*, 414–429.

McCullough, M. E., Worthington, E. L., Jr., & Rachal, K. C. (1997). Interpersonal forgiving in close relationships. *Journal of Personality and Social Psychology, 73*, 321–336.

McDonald, H. E., & Hirt, E. R. (1997). When expectancy meets desire: Motivational effects in reconstructive memory. *Journal of Personality and Social Psychology, 72*, 5–23.

McDonald, R. D. (1962). *The effect of reward–punishment and affiliation need on interpersonal attraction.* Unpublished doctoral dissertation, University of Texas.

McDowall, D., Wiersema, B., & Loftin, C. (1989). Did mandatory firearm ownership in Kennesaw really prevent burglaries? *Sociology and Sociological Research, 74*, 48–51.

McFarland, C., & Buehler, R. (1995). Collective self-esteem as a moderator of the frog-pond effect in reactions to performance feedback. *Journal of Personality and Social Psychology, 68*, 1055–1070.

McFarland, C., & Buehler, R. (1998). The impact of negative affect on autobiographical memory: The role of self-focused attention to moods. *Journal of Personality and Social Psychology, 75*, 1424–1440.

McGonagle, K. A., Kessler, R. C., & Schilling, E. A. (1992). The frequency and determinants of marital disagreements in a community sample. *Journal of Social and Personal Relationships, 9*, 507–524.

McGowan, S., Daniels, L. K., & Byrne, D. (1999). The Albany Measure of Attachment Style: A multi-item measure of Bartholomew's four-factor model. Manuscript submitted for publication.

McGuire, W. J. (1961). Resistance to persuasion confirmed by active and passive prior refutation of the same and alternate counterarguments. *Journal of Abnormal and Social Psychology, 63*, 326–332.

McGuire, W. J., & McGuire, C. V. (1996). Enhancing self-esteem by directed-thinking tasks: Cognitive and affective positivity asymmetries. *Journal of Personality and Social Psychology, 70*, 1117–1125.

McGuire, W. J., & Papageorgis, D. (1961). The relative efficacy of various types of prior belief-defense in producing immunity against persuasion. *Journal of Abnormal and Social Psychology, 62*, 327–337.

McKenna, K. Y. A., & Bargh, J. A. (2000). Plan 9 from cyberspace: The implications of the internet for personality and social psychology. *Personality and Social Psychology Review, 4*, 57–75.

McKenna, K. Y. A., Green, A. S., & Gleason, M. E. J. (2002). Relationship formation on the internet: What's the big attraction? *Journal of Social Issues, 58*, 9–31.

McNulty, S. E., & Swann, W. B., Jr. (1994). Identity negotiation in roommate relationships: The self as architect and consequence of social reality. *Journal of Personality and Social Psychology, 67*, 1012–1023.

McQuillan, K., & Belle, M. (1999). Who does what? Gender and the division of labour in Canadian households. In J. Curtis, E. Grabb, & N. Guppy (Eds.), *Social inequality in Canada: Patterns, problems, and policies* (2nd ed., pp. 186–198). Scarborough, Ont.: Prentice Hall.

McWhirter, B. T. (1997). A pilot study of loneliness in ethnic minority college students. *Social Behavior and Personality, 25*, 295–304.

Mead, G. H. (1934). *Mind, self and society.* (C. W. Morris, Ed.). Chicago: University of Chicago Press.

Mealey, L., Bridgstock, R., & Townsend, G. C. (1999). Symmetry and perceived facial attractiveness: A monozygotic co-twin comparison. *Journal of Personality and Social Psychology, 76*, 151–158.

Medvec, V. H., & Savitsky, K. (1997). When doing better means feeling worse: The effects of categorical cutoff points on counterfactual thinking and satisfaction. *Journal of Personality and Social Psychology, 72*, 1284–1296.

Medvec, V. H., Madey, S. F., & Gilovich, T. (1995). When less is more: Counterfactual thinking and satisfaction among Olympic athletes. *Journal of Personality and Social Psychology, 69*, 603–610.

Meeus, W. H., & Raaijmakers, Q. A. (1986). Administrative obedience: Carrying out orders to use psychological-administrative violence. *European Journal of Social Psychology, 16*, 311–324.

Melamed, S., Ben-Avi, I., Luz, J., & Green, M. S. (1995). Objective and subjective work monotony: Effects on job satisfaction, psychological distress, and absenteeism in blue-collar workers. *Journal of Applied Psychology, 80*, 29–42.

Mendolia, M., Beach, S. R. H., & Tesser, A. (1996). The relationship between marital interaction behaviors and affective reactions to one's own and one's spouse's self-evaluation needs. *Personal Relationships, 3*, 279–292.

Merritt, A.C., & Helmreich, R. L. (1996). Human factors on the flightdeck: The influence of national culture. *Journal of Cross-Cultural Psychology, 27*, 5–24.

Mesquida, C.G., & Wiener, N.I. (1996). Human collective aggression: A behavioral ecology perspective. *Ethnology and Sociobiology, 17*, 247–262.

Meyer, J.P., Allen, N.J., & Topolnytsky, L. (1998). Commitment in a changing world of work. *Canadian Psychology. 39*, 83–93.

Meyer, J.P., & Allen, N.J. (1997). *Commitment in the workplace: Theory, research, and application.* Thousand Oaks, CA: Sage.

Meyer, J. P., & Herscovitch, L. (2001). Commitment in the workplace: Toward a general model. *Human Resource Management Review, 11*, 299–326.

Miceli, M. P., & Lane, M. C. (1991). Antecedents of pay satisfaction: A review and extension. In K. Rowland & O. R. Ferris (Eds.), *Research in personnel and human resources management* (Vol. 9, pp. 235–309). Greenwich, CT: JAI Press.

Michael, R. T., Gagnon, J. H., Laumann, E. O., & Kolata, G. (1994). *Sex in America: A definitive survey.* Boston: Little, Brown.

Middleton, W., Harris, P., & Surman, M. (1996). Give 'em enough rope: Perception of health and safety risks in bungee jumpers. *Journal of Social and Clinical Psychology, 15*, 68–79.

Mikulincer, M. (1995). Attachment style and the mental representation of the self. *Journal of Personality and Social Psychology, 69,* 1203–1215.

Mikulincer, M. (1998a). Adult attachment style and individual differences in functional versus dysfunctional experiences of anger. *Journal of Personality and Social Psychology, 74,* 513–524.

Mikulincer, M. (1998b). Attachment working models and the sense of trust: An exploration of interaction goals and affect regulation. *Journal of Personality and Social Psychology, 74,* 1209–1224.

Mikulincer, M., & Florian, V. (1995). Appraisal of and coping with a real-life stressful situation: The contribution of attachment styles. *Personality and Social Psychology Bulletin, 21,* 406–414.

Mikulincer, M., Orbach, I., & Iavnieli, D. (1998). Adult attachment style and affect regulation: Strategic variations in subjective self-other similarity. *Journal of Personality and Social Psychology, 75,* 436–448.

Miles, S. M., & Carey, G. (1997). Genetic and environmental architecture of human aggression. *Journal of Personality and Social Psychology, 72,* 207–217.

Milestones. (1989, September 18). *Time,* p. 75.

Milgram, S. (1963). Behavioral study of obedience. *Journal of Abnormal and Social Psychology, 67,* 371–378.

Milgram, S. (1965). Liberating effects of group pressure. *Journal of Personality and Social Psychology, 1,* 127–134.

Milgram, S. (1965). Some conditions of obedience and disobedience to authority. *Human Relations, 18,* 57–76.

Milgram, S. (1970). The experience of living in cities. *Science, 13,* 1461–1468.

Milgram, S. (1974). *Obedience to authority.* New York: Harper.

Millar, M. G. (1997). The effects of emotion on breast self-examination: Another look at the health belief model. *Social Behavior and Personality, 25,* 223–232.

Miller, A. G., McHoskey, J. W., Bane, C. M., & Dowd, T. G. (1993). The attitude polarization phenomenon: Role of response measure, attitude extremity, and behavioral consequences of reported attitude change. *Journal of Personality and Social Psychology, 64,* 516–574.

Miller, D. T., & McFarland, C. (1986). Counterfactual thinking and victim compensation: A test of norm theory. *Personality and Social Psychology Bulletin, 12,* 513–519.

Miller, D. T., & Ratner, R. K. (1996). The power of the myth of self-interest. In L. Montada & M. Lerner (Eds.), *Current societal concerns about justice.* New York: Plenum.

Miller, D. T., & Ross, M. (1975). Self-serving biases in attribution of causality: Fact or fiction? Psychological Bulletin, *82,* 313–325.

Miller, G.F. (1998). How mate choice shaped human nature: A review of sexual selection and human evolution. In C. Crawford & D. L. Krebs (Eds.), *Handbook of evolutionary psychology* (pp. 87–129). Hillsdale, NJ: Erlbaum.

Miller, L. C. (1990). Intimacy and liking: Mutual influence and the role of unique relationships. *Journal of Personality and Social Psychology, 58,* 33–47.

Miller, L.C. (1990). Intimacy and liking: Mutual influence and the role of unique relationships. *Journal of Personality and Social Psychology, 59,* 50–60.

Miller, M. L., & Thayer, J. F. (1989). On the existence of discrete classes in personality: Is self-monitoring the correct joint to carve? *Journal of Personality and Social Psychology, 57,* 143–155.

Miller, N., Maruyama, G., Beaber, R. J., & Valone, K. (1976). Speed of speech and persuasion. *Journal of Personality and Social Psychology, 34,* 615–624.

Miller, R. S. (1991). On decorum in close relationships: Why aren't we polite to those we love? *Contemporary Social Psychology, 15,* 63–65.

Mischel, W. (1967). A social learning view of sex differences in behavior. In E. E. Maccoby (Ed.), *The development of sex differences* (pp. 56–81). London: Tavistock.

Mizokawa, D. T., & Ryckman, D. B. (1990). Attributions of academic success and failure: A comparison of six Asian-American ethnic groups. *Journal of Cross-Cultural Psychology, 21,* 434–451.

Moghaddam, F. M. (1987). Psychology in the three worlds: As reflected by the crisis in social psychology and the move toward indigenous Third World psychology. *American Psychologist, 42,* 912–920.

Moghaddam, F. M. (1990). Modulative and generative orientations in psychology: Implications for Psychology in the three worlds. *Journal of Social Issues, 46,* 21–41.

Moghaddam, F. M., Taylor, D. M., & Wright, S. C. (1993). *Social psychology in cross-cultural perspective.* New York: W. H. Freeman.

Monahan, J. L., Murphy, S. T., & Zajonc, R. B. (2000). Subliminal mere exposure: Specific, general, and diffuse effects. *Psychological Science, 11,* 462–466.

Mondloch, C. J., Lewis, T. L., Budreau, D. R., Maurer, D., Dannemiller, J. L., Stephens, B. R., & Kleiner-Gathercoal, K. A. (1999). Face perception during early infancy. *Psychological Science, 10,* 419–422.

Monsour, M., Betty, S., & Kurzweil, N. (1993). Levels of perspectives and the perception of intimacy in cross-sex friendships: A balance theory explanation of shared perceptual reality. *Journal of Social and Personal Relationships, 10,* 529–550.

Monteith, M. J. (1996). Affective reactions to prejudice-related discrepant responses: The impact of standard salience. *Personality & Social Psychology Bulletin, 22,* 48–59.

Moran, G., & Cutler, B. L. (1991). The prejudicial impact of pretrial publicity. *Journal of Applied Social Psychology, 21,* 345–367.

Moreland, R. L., & Beach, S. R. (1992). Exposure effects in the classroom: The development of affinity among students. *Journal of Experimental Social Psychology, 28,* 255–276.

Moreland, R. L., & Zajonc, R. B. (1982). Exposure effects in person perception: Familiarity, similarity, and attraction. *Journal of Experimental Social Psychology, 18,* 395–415.

Morgan, D. L., & White, R. L. (1993). The structure of the field of personal relationships: Part I. Disciplines. *Personal Relationships Issues, 1,* 2–5.

Morgan, D., Carder, P., & Neal, M. (1997). Are some relationships more useful than others? The value of similar others in the networks of recent widows. *Journal of Social and Personal Relationships, 14,* 745–759.

Morgan, H. J., & Janoff-Bulman, R. (1994). Positive and negative self-complexity: Patterns of adjustment following traumatic versus non-traumatic life experiences. *Journal of Social and Clinical Psychology, 13,* 63–85.

Mori, D. L., & Morey, L. (1991). The vulnerable body image of females with feelings of depression. *Journal of Research in Personality, 25,* 343–354.

Morling, B., Kitayama, S., & Miyamoto, Y. (2002). Cultural practices emphasize influence in the United States and adjustment in Japan. *Personality & Social Psychology Bulletin, 28,* 311–323.

Morojele, N., & Stephenson, G. M. (1994). Addictive behaviors: Prediction of abstinence intentions and expectations in the theory of planned behavior. In D. R. Rutter & L. Quine (Eds.), *Social psychology and health: European perspectives* (pp. 47–70). Aldershot, UK: Avesbury.

Morris, M. W., & Larrick, R. P. (1995). When one cause casts doubt on another: A normative analysis of discounting in causal attribution. *Psychological Review, 102,* 331–335.

Morrison, E. W. (1994). Role definitions and organizational citizenship behavior: The importance of employees' perspective. *Academy of Management Journal, 37,* 1543–1567.

Morrison, H. W. (1954). The validity and behavioral manifestations of female need for affiliation. Unpublished master's thesis, Wesleyan University.

Morrow, G. D., Clark, E. M., & Brock, K. F. (1995). Individual and partner love styles: Implications for the quality of romantic involvements. *Journal of Social and Personal Relationships, 12,* 363–387.

Moscovici, S. (1985). Social influence and conformity. In G. Lindzey & E. Aronson (Eds.), *Handbook of social psychology* (3rd ed.). New York: Random House.

Moskowitz, D. S. (1993). Dominance and friendliness: On the interaction of gender and situation. *Journal of Personality, 61,* 387–409.

Moston, S., & Stephenson, G. M. (1993). The changing face of police interrogation. *Journal of Community and Applied Social Psychology, 3,* 101–115.

Muczyk, J. P., & Reimann, B. C. (1987). The case for directive leadership. *Academy of Management Review, 12,* 637–647.

Mueller, U., & Mazur, A. (1996). Facial dominance of West Point cadets as predictors of later military rank. *Social Forces, 74,* 823–850.

Mugny, G. (1975). Negotiations, image of the other and the process of minority influence. *European Journal of Social Psychology, 5,* 209–229.

Mullan, E., & Markland, D. (1997). Variations in self-determination across the stages of change for exercise in adults. *Motivation and Emotion, 21,* 349–362.

Mullen, B., Brown, R. & Smith, C. (1992). Ingroup bias as a function of salience, relevance, and status: An integration. *European Journal of Social Psychology, 22,* 103–122.

Mundt, R.J. (1990). Gun control and rates of firearms violence in Canada and the United States. *Canadian Journal of Criminology, 35,* 42–47.

Mundt, R.J. (1993). Rejoinder to comments on 'Gun control and rates of firearms violence in Canada and the United States. *Canadian Journal of Criminology, 35,* 42–47.

Munro, G. D., & Ditto, P. H. (1997). Biased assimilation, attitude polarization, and affect in reactions to stereotype-relevant scientific information. *Personality and Social Psychology Bulletin, 23,* 636–653.

Munsterberg, H. (1907). *On the witness stand: Essays in psychology and crime.* New York: McClure.

Murnighan, K. (Ed.). (1993). *Handbook of social psychology in organizations.* Englewood Cliffs, NJ: Prentice Hall.

Murphy, S. T., & Zajonc, R. B. (1993). Affect, cognition, and awareness: Affective priming with suboptimal and optimal stimulus. *Journal of Personality and Social Psychology, 64,* 723–739.

Murray, H. A. (1938/1962). *Explorations in personality.* New York: Science Editions.

Murray, S. L., & Holmes, J. G. (1997). A leap of faith? Positive illusions in romantic relationships. *Personality and Social Psychology Bulletin, 23,* 586–604.

Murray, S. L., Holmes, J. G., & Griffin, D. W. (1996). The benefits of positive illusions: Idealization and the construction of satisfaction in close relationships. *Journal of Personality and Social Psychology, 70,* 79–98.

Murray, S. L., Holmes, J. G., & Griffin, D. W. (2000). Self-esteem and the quest for felt security: How perceived regard regulates attachment processes. *Journal of Personality and Social Psychology, 78,* 478–498.

Murray, S. L., Holmes, J. G., Griffin, D. W., Bellavia, G., & Rose, P. (2001). The mismeasure of love: How self-doubt contaminates relationship beliefs. *Personality and Social Psychology Bulletin, 27,* 423–436.

Mussweiler, T., & Forster, J. (2000). The sex–aggression link: A perception–behavior dissociation. *Journal of Personality and Social Psychology, 79,* 507–520.

Myers, D. G., & Diener, E. (1995). Who is happy? *Psychological Science, 6,* 10–19.

Mynard, H., & Joseph, S. (1997). Bully victim problems and their association with Eysenck's personality dimensions in 8 to 13 year olds. *British Journal of Educational Psychology, 67,* 51–54.

Nadkarni, D. V., Lundgren, D., & Burlew, A. K. (1991). Gender differences in self-depriving behavior as a reaction to extreme inequity. *Journal of Social Behavior and Personality, 6,* 105–117.

Nadler, A. (1986). Help seeking as a cultural phenomenon: Differences between city and kibbutz dwellers. *Journal of Personality and Social Psychology, 51,* 976–982.

Narby, D. J., Cutler, B. L., & Moran, G. (1993). A meta-analysis of the association between authoritarianism and jurors' perceptions of defendant culpability. *Journal of Applied Psychology, 78,* 34–42.

Nemechek, S., & Olson, K. R. (1999). Five-factor personality similarity and marital adjustment. *Social Behavior and Personality, 27,* 309–318.

Nemeth, C. J. (1995). Dissent as driving cognition, attitudes, and judgments. *Social Cognition, 13,* 273–291.

Nemeth, C. J., Connell, J. B., Rogers, J. D., & Brown, K. S. (2001). Improving decision making by means of dissent. *Journal of Applied Social Psychology, 31,* 45–58.

Neuberg, S. L. (1989). The goal of forming accurate impressions during social interactions: Attenuating the impact of negative expectancies. *Journal of Personality and Social Psychology, 56,* 374–386.

Neuberg, S. L., & Newsom, J. T. (1993). Personal need for structure: Individual differences in the desire for simple structure. *Journal of Personality and Social Psychology, 65,* 113–131.

Neuberg, S. L., Smith, D. M., Hoffman, J. C., & Russell, F. J. (1994). When we observe stigmatized and "normal" individuals interacting: Stigma by association. *Personality and Social Psychology Bulletin, 20,* 196–209.

Neumann, R., & Strack, F. (2000). "Mood contagion": The automatic transfer of mood between persons. *Journal of Personality and Social Psychology, 79,* 211–223.

Newby-Clark, I.R., Ross, M., Buehler, R., Koehler, D. J., & Griffin, D. (2000). People focus on optimistic scenarios and disregard pessimistic scenarios while predicting task completion times. *Journal of Experimental Psychology: Applied, 6,* 171–182.

Newcomb, T. M. (1961). *The acquaintance process.* New York: Holt, Rinehart, & Winston.

Nezlek, J. B., & Plesko, R. M. (2001). Day-to-day relationships among self-concept clarity, self-esteem, daily events, and mood. *Personality and Social Psychology Bulletin, 27,* 201–211.

Ng, J. Y. Y., Tam, S. F., Yew, W. W., & Lam, W. K. (1999). Effects of video modeling on self-efficacy and exercise performance of COPD patients. *Social Behavior and Personality, 27,* 475–486.

Niedenthal, P. M., Setterlund, M. B., & Wherry, M. B. (1992). Possible self-complexity and affective reactions to goal–relevant evaluation. *Journal of Personality and Social Psychology, 63,* 5–16.

Nienhuis, A. E., Manstead, A. S. R., & Spears, R. (2001). Multiple motives and persuasive communication: Creative elaboration as a result of impression motivation and accuracy motivation. *Personality and Social Psychology Bulletin, 27,* 118–132.

Nisbett, R. E., Peng, K., Choi, I., & Norenzayan, A. (2001). Culture and systems of thought: Holistic versus analytic cognition. *Psychological Review, 108,* 291–310.

Norenzayan, A., Choi, I., & Nisbett, R. E. (1999). Eastern and Western perceptions of causality for social behavior: Lay theories about personalities and social situations. In D. Prentice & D. Miller (Eds.), *Cultural divides: Understanding and overcoming group conflict.* New York: Sage. pp. 239–272.

Norenzayan, A., & Levine, R. V. (1994). Helping in 18 international cities. Paper presented at the annual meeting of the Western Psychological Association, Kona Hawaii.

Norenzayan, A., & Nisbett, R. E., (2000). Culture and Causal Cognition. *Current Directions in Psychological Science, 9,* 132–135.

O'Connell, P. D. (1988). Pretrial publicity, change of venue, public opinion polls—A theory of procedural justice. *University of Detroit Law Review, 65,* 169–197.

O'Connor, S. C., & Rosenblood, L. K. (1996). Affiliation motivation in everyday experience: A theoretical comparison. *Journal of Personality and Social Psychology, 70,* 513–522.

O'Moore, M. N. (2000). Critical issues for teacher training to counter bullying and victimization in Ireland. *Aggressive Behavior, 26,* 99–112.

O'Neil, J. (1998, December 8). That sly "don't-come-hither" stare. *New York Times,* p. F7.

O'Sullivan, C. S., & Durso, F. T. (1984). Effects of schema-incongruent information on memory for stereotypical attributes. *Journal of Personality and Social Psychology, 47,* 55–70.

Ogloff, J. R. P., & Cronshaw, S. F. (2001). Expert psychological testimony: Assisting or misleading the trier of fact? *Canadian Psychology, 42,* 87–91.

Ohbuchi, K., & Kambara, T. (1985). Attacker's intent and awareness of outcome, impression management, and retaliation. *Journal of Experimental Social Psychology, 21,* 321–330.

Ohbuchi, K., Kameda, M., & Agarie, N. (1989). Apology as aggression control: Its role in mediating appraisal of and response to harm. *Journal of Personality and Social Psychology, 56,* 219–227.

Ohlott, P. J., Ruderman, M. N., & McCauley, C. D. (1994). Gender differences in managers' developmental job experiences. *Academy of Management Journal, 37,* 46–67.

Ohman, A., Lundqvist, D., & Esteves, F. (2001). The face in the crowd revisited: Threat advantage with schematic stimuli. *Journal of Personality and Social Psychology, 80,* 381–396.

Okabe, K. (1987). Indirect speech acts of the Japanese. In D. L. Kincaid (Ed.), *Communication Theory: Eastern and Western Perspectives.* New York: Academic Press.

Oliner, S. P., & Oliner, P. M. (1988). *The altruistic personality: Rescuers of Jews in Nazi Europe.* New York: Free Press.

Oliver, J. M., Reed, C. K. S., Katz, B. M., & Haugh, J. A. (1999). Students' self-reports of help-seeking: The impact of psychological problems, stress, and demographic variables on utilization of formal and informal support. *Social Behavior and Personality, 27,* 109–128.

Oliver, M. B., & Hyde, J. S. (1993). Gender differences in sexuality: A meta-analysis. *Psychological Bulletin, 114,* 29–51.

Olmstead, R. E., Guy, S. M., O'Malley, P. M., & Bentler, P. M. (1991). Longitudinal assessment of the relationship between self-esteem, fatalism, loneliness, and substance use. *Journal of Social Behavior and Personality, 6,* 749–770.

Olweus, D. (1993). *Bullying at school: What we know and what we can do.* Oxford: Blackwell.

Orbell, S., Blair, C., Sherlock, K., & Conner, M. (2001). The theory of planned behavior and ecstasy use: Roles for habit and perceived control over taking versus obtaining substances. *Journal of Applied Social Psychology, 31,* 31–47.

Organ, D. W. (1997). Organizational citizenship behavior: It's construct clean-up time. *Human Performance, 10,* 85–98.

Orive, R. (1988). Social projection and social comparison of opinions. *Journal of Personality and Social Psychology, 54,* 953–964.

Orlofsky, J. L., & O'Heron, C. A. (1987). Stereotypic and nonstereotypic sex role trait and behavior orientations: Implications for personal adjustment. *Journal of Personality and Social Psychology, 52,* 1034–1042.

Osterman, K., Bjorkqvist, K., Lagerspetz, K. M. J., Kaukiainen, A., Landua, S. F., Fraczek, A., & Caprara, G. V. (1998). Cross-cultural evidence of female indirect aggression. *Aggressive Behavior, 24*, 1–8.

Osterman, K., Bjorkqvist, K., Lagerspetz, K. M. J., Kaukianainen, A., Huesmann, L. W., & Fraczek, A. (1994). Peer and self-estimated aggression and victimization in 8-year-old children from five ethnic groups. *Aggressive Behavior, 20*, 411–428.

Osterwell, Z., & Nagano-Hakamura, K. (1992). Maternal views on aggression: Japan and Israel. *Aggressive Behavior, 18*, 263–270.

Ottati, V., Terkildsen, N., & Hubbard, C. (1997). Happy faces elicit heuristic processing in a televised impression formation task: A cognitive tuning account. *Personality and Social Psychology Bulletin, 23*, 1144–1156.

Page, N. R., & Wiseman, R. L. (1993). Supervisory behavior and worker satisfaction in the United States, Mexico, and Spain. *Journal of Business Communication, 30*, 161–180.

Paik, H., & Comstock, G. (1994). The effects of television violence on antisocial behavior: A meta-analysis. *Communication Research, 21*, 516–546.

Pajares, F. (2002). *Biography, chronology, and photographs of William James.* Emory University. http://www.emory.edu/EDUCATION/mfp/ jphotos.html

Pak, A.W., Dion, K. L., & Dion, K. K. (1991). Social-psychological correlates of experienced discrimination: Test of the double jeopardy hypothesis. *International Journal of Intercultural Relations, 15*, 243–254.

Park, J., & Banaji, M. R. (2000). Mood and heuristics: The influence of happy and sad states on sensitivity and bias in stereotyping. *Journal of Personality and Social Psychology, 78*, 1005–1023.

Parks, M. R., & Floyd, K. (1996). Meanings for closeness and intimacy in friendship. *Journal of Social and Personal Relationships, 13*, 85–107.

Parks, M.R., & Floyd, K. (1996). Making friends in cyberspace. *Journal of Communications, 46*, 80–97.

Paulhus, D.L. (1998). Interpersonal and intrapsychic adaptiveness of trait self-enhancement: A mixed blessing? *Journal of Personality and Social Psychology, 74*, 1197–1208.

Paulhus, D. L., Bruce, M. N., & Trapnell, P.D. (1995). Effects of self-presentation strategies on personality profiles and their structure. *Personality and Social Psychology Bulletin, 21*, 100–108.

Paulhus, D.L., Harms, P. D., & Bruce, M. N. (2003). The over-claiming technique: Measuring self-enhancement independent of ability. *Journal of Personality & Social Psychology, 84*, 890–904.

Paulhus, D. L., Martin, C. L., & Murphy, G. K. (1992). Some effects of arousal on sex stereotyping. *Personality and Social Psychology Bulletin, 18*, 325–330.

Pearson, K., & Lee, A. (1903). On the laws of inheritance in man: I. Inheritance of physical characters. *Biometrika, 2*, 357–462.

Pedersen, D. M. (1994). Privacy preferences and classroom seat selection. *Social Behavior and Personality, 22*, 393–398.

Pederson, W. C., Gonzales, C., & Miller, N. (2000). The moderating effect of trivial triggering provocation on displaced aggression. *Journal of Personality and Social Psychology, 78*, 913–947.

Pelham, B. W., & Wachsmuth, J. O. (1995). The waxing and waning of the social self: Assimilation and contrast in social comparison. *Journal of Personality and Social Psychology, 69*, 825–838.

Pennebaker, J. W. (1997). Writing about emotional experiences as a therapeutic process. *Psychological Science, 8*, 162–166.

Pennebaker, J. W., & Graybeal, A. (2001). Patterns of natural language use: Disclosure, personality, and social integration. *Current Directions in Psychological Science, 10*, 90–93.

Peplau, L. A. (2003). Human sexuality: How do men and women differ? Current *Directions in Psychological Science. 12*, 37–40.

Pepler, D. J., Craig, W. M., & Connolly, J. (2002). Bullying, sexual harassment, dating violence and substance use among adolescents. In Wekerle, C., & Wall, A. (Eds.), *The violence and addiction equation: Theoretical and clinical issues in substance abuse and relationship violence,* pp. 153–168. New York: Brunner-Routledge.

Perlini, A. H., & Hansen, S. D. (2001). Moderating effects of need for cognition on attractiveness stereotyping. *Social Behavior and Personality, 29,* 313–322.

Perlini, A. H., Marcello, A., Hansen, S. D., & Pudney, W. (2001). The effects of male age and physical appearance on evaluations of attractiveness, social desirability and resourcefulness. *Social Behavior and Personality, 29,* 277–288.

Perloff, L. S. (1983). Perceptions of vulnerability to victimization. *Journal of Social Issues, 39,* 41–61.

Perloff, L. S., & Fetzer, B. K. (1986). Self-other judgments and perceived vulnerability to victimization. *Journal of Personality and Social Psychology, 50,* 502–510.

Pessin, J. (1933). The comparative effects of social and mechanical stimulation on memorizing. *American Journal of Psychology, 45,* 263–270.

Peterson, R. S. (1997). A directive leadership style in group decision making can be both a virtue and vice: Evidence from elite and experimental groups. *Journal of Personality and Social Psychology, 72,* 1107–1121.

Peterson, R.A., & Jolibert, A.J.P. (1995). A meta-analysis of country-of-origin effects. *Journal of International Business Studies, 26,* 883–900.

Petkova, K. G., Ajzen, I., & Driver, B. L. (1995). Salience of anti-abortion beliefs and commitment to an attitudinal position: On the strength, structure, and predictive validity of anti-abortion attitudes. *Journal of Applied Social Psychology, 25,* 463–483.

Petrie, K. J., Booth, R. J., & Pennebaker, J. W. (1998). The immunological effects of thought suppression. Journal of *Personality and Social Psychology, 75,* 1264–1272.

Pettigrew, T. F. (1969). Racially separate or together? *Journal of Social Issues, 25,* 43–69.

Pettigrew, T. F. (1981). Extending the stereotype concept. In D. L. Hamilton (Ed.), *Cognitive processes in stereotyping and intergroup behavior* (pp. 303–331). Hillsdale, NJ: Erlbaum.

Pettigrew, T. F. (1997). Generalized intergroup contact effects on prejudice. *Personality and Social Psychology Bulletin, 23,* 173–185.

Petty, R. E., & Cacioppo, J. T. (1986). The elaboration likelihood model of persuasion. In L. Berkowitz (Ed.), *Advances in experimental social psychology* (Vol. 19, pp. 123–205). New York: Academic Press.

Petty, R. E., & Cacioppo, J. T. (1990). Involvement and persuasion: Tradition versus integration. *Psychological Bulletin, 107,* 367–374.

Petty, R. E., Cacioppo, J. T., Strathman, A. J., & Priester, J. R. (1994). To think or not to think: Exploring two routes to persuasion. In S. Shavitt & T. C. Brock (Eds.), *Persuasion* (pp. 113–147). Boston: Allyn and Bacon.

Petty, R. J., & Krosnick, J. A. (Eds.). (1995). *Attitude strength: Antecedents and consequences* (Vol. 4). Hillsdale, NJ: Erlbaum.

Pezdek, K., Finger, K., & Hodge, D. (1997). Planting false childhood memories: The role of event plausibility. *Psychological Science, 8,* 437–441.

Phinney, J. S. (1990). Ethnic identity in adolescents and adults: Review of research. *Psychological Bulletin, 108,* 499–514.

Phinney, J. S. (1991). Ethnic identity and self-esteem: A review and integration. *Hispanic Journal of Behavioral Sciences, 13,* 193–208.

Pickett, C. L. (2001). The effects of entiativity beliefs on implicit comparisons between group members. *Personality and Social Psychology Bulletin, 27,* 515–525.

Pierce, C. A. (1992). The effects of physical attractiveness and height on dating choice: A meta-analysis. Unpublished masters thesis, University at Albany, State University of New York.

Pietromonaco, P. R., & Barrett, L. F. (1997). Working models of attachment and daily social interactions. *Journal of Personality and Social Psychology, 73,* 1409–1423.

Pihl, R. O., Lau, M. L., & Assad, J. M. (1997). Aggressive disposition, alcohol, and aggression. *Aggressive Behavior, 23,* 11–18.

Piliavin, J. A., & Unger, R. K. (1985). The helpful but helpless female: Myth or reality? In V. E. O'Leary, R. K. Unger, & B. S. Wallston (Eds.), *Women, gender, and social psychology* (pp. 149–189). Hillsdale, NJ: Erlbaum.

Pinel, J. P. J., Assanand, S., & Lehman, D. R. (2000). Hunger, eating, and ill health. *American Psychologist, 55,* 1105–1116.

Pines, A. (1997). Fatal attractions or wise unconscious choices: The relationship between causes for entering and breaking intimate relationships. *Personal Relationship Issues, 4,* 1–6.

Pines, A., & Aronson, E. (1983). Antecedents, correlates, and consequences of sexual jealousy. *Journal of Personality, 51,* 108–136.

Pinker, S. (1997). *How the mind works.* New York: Harper Collins.

Pinker, S. (1998). *How the mind works.* New York: Norton.

Pinker, S. (2002). *The blank slate: The modern denial of human nature.* New York: Viking Penguin.

Platz, S. G., & Hosch, H. M. (1988). Cross-racial/ethnic eyewitness identification: A field study. *Journal of Applied Social Psychology, 13,* 972–984.

Pleck, J. H., Sonenstein, F. L., & Ku, L. C. (1993). Masculinity ideology: Its impact on adolescent males' heterosexual relationships. *Journal of Social Issues, 49*(3), 11–29.

Pliner, P., Chaiken, S., & Flett, G. L. (1990). Eating, social motives and self-presentation in women and men. *Journal of Experimental Social Psychology, 26,* 240–254.

Podaskoff, P. M., Mackenzie, S. B., & Hui, C. (1993). Organizational citizenship behaviors and managerial evaluations of employee performance: A review and suggestions for future research. In G. R. Ferris (Ed.), *Research in personnel and human resources management* (Vol. 11, pp. 1–40). Greenwich, CT: JAI Press.

Polivy, J., & Herman, C. P. (2000). The false-hope syndrome: Unfulfilled expectations of self-change. *Current Directions in Psychological Science, 9,* 128–131.

Pollock, C. L., Smith, S. D., Knowles, E. S., & Bruce, H. J. (1998). Mindfulness limits compliance with the that's-not-all technique. *Personality and Social Psychology Bulletin, 24,* 1153–1157.

Pomazal, R. J., & Clore, G. L. (1973). Helping on the highway: The effects of dependency and sex. *Journal of Applied Social Psychology, 3,* 150–164.

Pontari, B. A., & Schlenker, B. R. (2000). The influence of cognitive load on self-presentation: Can cognitive busyness help as well as harm social performance? *Journal of Personality and Social Psychology, 78,* 1092–1108.

Poole, D. A., & Lindsay, D. S. (1998). Assessing the accuracy of young children's reports: Lessons from the investigation of child sexual abuse. *Applied & Preventive Psychology, 7,* 1–26.

Pope, J., & Meyer, R. (1999). An attributional analysis of jurors' judgments in a criminal case: A preliminary investigation. *Social Behavior and Personality, 27,* 563–574.

Pope, K. S. (1996). Memory, abuse, and science: Questioning claims about the false memory syndrome epidemic. *American Psychologist, 51,* 957–974.

Porter, L. S., Marco, C. A., Schwartz, J. E., Neale, J. M., Shiffman, S., & Stone, A. A. (2000). Gender differences in coping: A comparison of trait and momentary assessments. *Journal of Social and Clinical Psychology, 19,* 480–498.

Porter, S., Birt, A. R., Yuille, J. C., & Lehman, D. R. (2000). Negotiating false memories: Interviewer and rememberer characteristics relate to memory distortion. *Psychological Science, 11,* 507–510.

Porter, S., Campbell, M. A., & Birt, A. R. (2003). "He Said, She Said": A Psychological Perspective on Historical Memory Evidence in the Courtroom. *Canadian Psychology, 44,* 190–206.

Poulson, R. L., Braithwaite, R. L., Brondino, M. J., & Wuehsch, K. L. (1997). Mock jurors' insanity defense verdict selections: The role of evidence, attitudes, and verdict options. *Journal of Social Behavior and Personality, 12,* 743–758.

Poulson, R. L., Wuensch, K. L., Brown, M. B., & Braithwaite, R. L. (1997). Mock jurors' evaluations of insanity defense verdict selection: The role of death penalty attitudes. *Journal of Social Behavior and Personality, 12,* 1065–1078.

Powell, G. N., & Butterfield, D. A. (1994). Investigating the "glass ceiling" phenomenon: An empirical study of actual promotions to top management. *Academy of Management Journal, 37,* 68–86.

Prager, K. J., & Bailey, J. M. (1985). Androgyny, ego development, and psychosocial crisis. *Sex Roles, 13*, 525–536.

Pratkanis, A. R., & Aronson, E. (1991). *Age of propaganda: The everyday use and abuse of persuasion*. New York: W. H. Freeman.

Pratkanis, A. R., Breckler S. J., & Greenwald, A. G. (Eds.). (1989). *Attitude structure and function*. Hillsdale, NJ: Erlbaum.

Pratkanis, A. R., & Turner, M. E. (1996). Persuasion and democracy: Strategies for increasing deliberative participation and enacting social change. *Journal of Social Issues, 52*, 187–205.

Pratto, F. (1996). Sexual politics: The gender gap in the bedroom, the cupboard, and the cabinet. In D. M. Buss & N. M. Malamuth (Eds.), *Sex, power, conflict: Evolutionary and feminist perspectives* (pp. 179–230). New York: Oxford University Press.

Pratto, F., & Bargh, J. A. (1991). Stereotyping based on apparently individuating information: Trait and global components of sex stereotypes under attentional overload. *Journal of Experimental Social Psychology, 27*, 26–47.

Pratto, F., Stallworth, L. M., Sidanius, J., & Siers, B. (1997). The gender gap in occupational role attainment: A social dominance approach. *Journal of Personality and Social Psychology, 72*, 37–53.

Priester, J. R., & Petty, R. E. (2001). Extending the bases of subjective attitudinal ambivalence: Interpersonal and intrapersonal antecedents of evaluative tension. *Journal of Personality and Social Psychology, 80*, 19–34.

Pruitt, D. G., & Carnevale, P. J. (1993). *Negotiation in social conflict*. Pacific Grove, CA: Brooks/Cole.

Przybyla, D. P. J. (1985). The facilitating effect of exposure to erotica on male prosocial behavior. Unpublished doctoral dissertation, University at Albany, State University of New York.

Puhl, R. M., & Boland, F. J. (2001). Predicting female physical attractiveness: Waist-to-hip ratio versus thinness. *Psychology, Evolution & Gender, 3*, 27–46.

Quigley, B. M., Johnson, A. B., & Byrne, D. (1995, June). *Mock jury sentencing decisions: A meta-analysis of the attractiveness–leniency effect*. Paper presented at the meeting of the American Psychological Society, New York.

Quinn, K. A., Roese, N. J., & Pennington, G. L. (1999). The personal/group discrimination discrepancy: The role of informational complexity. *Personality & Social Psychology Bulletin, 25*, 1430–1440.

Rabasca, L. (2000, October). The internet and computer games reinforce the gender gap. *Monitor on Psychology*, 32–33.

Radecki-Bush, C., Farrell, A. D., & Bush, J. P. (1993). Predicting jealous responses: The influence of adult attachment and depression on threat appraisal. *Journal of Social and Personal Relationships, 10*, 569–588.

Ramirez, J., Bryant, J., & Zillmann, D. (1983). Effects of erotica on retaliatory behavior as a function of level of prior provocation. *Journal of Personality and Social Psychology, 43*, 971–978.

Randall, D. M., Fedor, D. P., & Longenecker, C. O. (1990). The behavioral expression of organizational commitment. *Journal of Vocational Behavior, 36*, 210–224.

Randall, S. (1995). Low fertility in a pastoral population: Constraints or choice? In. R. I. M. Dunbar (Ed.), *Human reproductive decisions: Biological and social aspects*, pp. 279–296. London: MacMillan.

Rands, M., & Levinger, G. (1979). Implicit theories of relationship: An intergenerational study. *Journal of Personality and Social Psychology, 37*, 649–661.

Ratner, C. (1997). *Cultural psychology and qualitative methodology : theoretical and empirical considerations*. New York : Plenum Press.

Raty, H., & Snellman, L. (1992). Does gender make any difference? Common-sense conceptions of intelligence. *Social Behavior and Personality, 20*, 23–34.

Reed, M. B., & Aspinwall, L. G. (1998). Self-affirmation reduces biases processing of health-risk information. *Motivation and Emotion, 22*, 99–132.

Regan, P. C., Snyder, M., & Kassin, S. M. (1995). Unrealistic optimism: Self-enhancement or person positivity? *Personality and Social Psychology Bulletin, 21*, 1073–1082.

Reis, H. T., & Wheeler, L. (1990). Studying social interaction with the Rochester Interaction Record. In M. P. Zanna (Ed.), *Advances in experimental social psychology* (pp.269–318). New York: Academic Press.

Reis, T. J., Gerrard, M. & Gibbons, F. X. (1993). Social comparison and the pill: Reactions to upward and downward comparison of contraceptive behavior. *Personality and Social Psychology Bulletin, 19*, 13–20.

Reiss, A. J., & Roth, J. A. (Eds.). (1993). *Understanding and preventing violence*. Washington, DC: National Academy Press.

Reno, R. R., Cialdini, R. B, & Kalgren, C. A (1993). The transsituational influence of social norms. *Journal of Personality and Social Psychology, 64*, 104–112.

Rensberger, B. (1993, November 9). Certain chemistry between vole pairs. *Albany Times Union*, pp. C–1, C–3.

Rentsch, J. R., & Heffner, T. S. (1994). Assessing self-concept: Analysis of Gordon's coding scheme using "Who am I?" responses. *Journal of Social Behavior and Personality, 9*, 283–300.

Rheingold, H. (1993). *The virtual community: Homesteading on the electronic frontier*. Reading, MA: Addison-Wesley.

Rhodes, G., Sumich, A., & Byatt, G. (1999). Are average facial configurations attractive only because of their symmetry? *Psychological Science, 10*, 52–58.

Rhodes, N., & Wood, W. (1992). Self-esteem and intelligence affect influenceability: The mediating role of message reception. *Psychological Bulletin, 111*, 156–171.

Rhodewalt, F., & Davison, J., Jr. (1983). Reactance and the coronary-prone behavior pattern: The role of self-attribution in response to reduced behavioral freedom. *Journal of Personality and Social Psychology, 44*, 220–228.

Richard, F. D., Bond, C. F., Jr., & Stokes-Zoota, J. J. (2001). "That's completely obvious... and important." Lay judgments of social psychological findings. *Personality and Social Psychology Bulletin, 27*, 497–505.

Richards, Z., & Hewstone, M. (2001). Subtyping and subgrouping: Processes for the prevention and promotion of stereotype change. *Personality and Social Psychology Review, 5,* 52–73.

Ridley, M., & Dawkins, R. (1981). The natural selection of altruism. In J. P. Rushton & R. M. Sorrentino (Eds.), *Altruism and helping behavior*. Hillsdale, NJ: Erlbaum.

Riess, M., & Schlenker, B. R. (1977). Attitude change and responsibility avoidance as modes of dilemma resolution in forced-compliance situations. *Journal of Personality and Social Psychology, 35,* 21–30.

Rind, B. (1996). Effect of beliefs about weather conditions on tipping. *Journal of Applied Social Psychology, 26,* 137–147.

Rind, B., & Bordia, P. (1996). Effect on restaurant tipping of male and female servers drawing a happy, smiling face on the backs of customers' checks. *Journal of Applied Social Psychology, 26,* 218–225.

Riordan, C. A. (1978). Equal-status interracial contact: A review and revision of a concept. *International Journal of Intercultural Relations, 2,* 161–185.

Robarchek, C. A., & Robarchek, C. J. (1997). Waging peace: The psychological and sociocultural dynamics of positive peace. In A. W. Wolfe, & H. Yang (Eds.), *Anthropological contributions to conflict resolution* (pp. 64–80). Athens, GA: University of Georgia Press.

Robbins, T. L., & DeNisi, A. S. (1994). A closer look at interpersonal affect as a distinct influence on cognitive processing in performance evaluations. *Journal of Applied Psychology, 79,* 341–353.

Roberts, J. V., & Edwards, D. (1989). Contextual effects in judgments of crimes, criminals, and the purposes of sentencing. *Journal of Applied Social Psychology, 19,* 902–917.

Roberts, J.V., & Doob, A.N. (1990). News media influences on public views of sentencing. *Law and Human Behavior, 14,* 451–468.

Robinson, R. J., Lewicki, R. J., & Donahue, E. M. (1998). *Extending and testing a five factor model of ethical and unethical bargaining tactics: Introducing the SINS Scale*. Unpublished manuscript, Harvard University, Business School.

Robinson, R., Keltner, D., Ward, A., & Ross, L. (1995). Actual versus assumed differences in construal: "Naïve realism" in intergroup perception and conflict. *Journal of Personality and Social Psychology, 68,* 404–417.

Rochat, F., & Modigliani, A. (1995). The ordinary quality of resistance: From Milgram's laboratory to the village of Le Chambon. *Journal of Social Issues, 5,* 195–210.

Rodgers, J. L., Billy, J. O. B., & Udry, J. R. (1984). A model of friendship similarity in mildly deviant behaviors. *Journal of Applied Social Psychology, 14,* 413–425.

Rodin, J., & Salovey, P. (1989). Health psychology. In M. R. Rosenzweig & L. W. Porter (Eds.), *Annual review of psychology* (Vol. 40, pp. 533–579). Palo Alto, CA: Annual Reviews.

Rodin, M., & Price, J. (1995). Overcoming stigma: Credit for self-improvement or discredit for needing to improve? *Personality and Social Psychology Bulletin, 21,* 172–181.

Rogers, C. R. (1951). *Client-centered therapy*. Boston: Houghton Mifflin.

Rogers, C. R., & Dymond, R. F. (Eds.). (1954). *Psychotherapy and personality change*. Boston: Houghton Mifflin.

Rogers, R. W. (1980). Subjects' reactions to experimental deception. Unpublished manuscript, University of Alabama, Tuscaloosa.

Rogers, R. W., & Ketcher, C. M. (1979). Effects of anonymity and arousal on aggression. *Journal of Psychology, 102,* 13–19.

Roland, E. (2000). Bullying in school: Three national innovations in Norwegian schools in 15 years. *Aggressive Behavior, 26,* 135–143.

Rose, S. M. (1984). How friendships end: Patterns among young adults. *Journal of Social and Personal Relationships, 1,* 267–277.

Rosenbaum, M. E. (1986). The repulsion hypothesis: On the nondevelopment of relationships. *Journal of Personality and Social Psychology, 51,* 1156–1166.

Rosenhan, D. L., Salovey, P., & Hargis, K. (1981). The joys of helping: Focus of attention mediates the impact of positive affect on altruism. *Journal of Personality and Social Psychology, 40,* 899–905.

Rosenthal, A. M. (1964). *Thirty-eight witnesses*. New York: McGraw-Hill.

Rosenthal, R. (1994). Interpersonal expectancy effects: A thirty year perspective. *Current Direction in Psychological Science, 3,* 176–179.

Rosenthal, R., & Jacobson, L. (1968). *Pygmalion in the classroom: Teacher expectation and student intellectual development*. New York: Holt, Rinehart, & Winston.

Rosenzweig, J. M., & Daley, D. M. (1989). Dyadic adjustment/sexual satisfaction in women and men as a function of psychological sex role self-perception. *Journal of Sex and Marital Therapy, 15,* 42–56.

Ross, L. D. (1977). Problems in the interpretation of 'self-serving' asymmetries in causal attribution: Comments on the Stephan et al. paper. *Sociometry, 40,* 112–114.

Rotenberg, K. J., & Korol, S. (1995). The role of loneliness and gender in individuals' love styles. *Journal of Social Behavior and Personality, 10,* 537–546.

Rothbaum, F., Weisz, J. R., & Snyder, S. S. (1982). Changing the world and changing the self: A two-process model of perceived control. *Journal of Personality & Social Psychology, 42,*5–37.

Rothgerber, H. (1997). External intergroup threat as an antecedent to perceptions of in-group and out-group homogeneity. *Journal of Personality and Social Psychology, 73,* 1206–1212.

Rothman, A. J., & Hardin, C. D. (1997). Differential use of the availability heuristic in social judgment. *Personality and Social Psychology Bulletin, 23,* 123–138.

Rothman, A. J., Martino, S. C., Bedell, B. T., Detweiler, J. B., & Salovey, P. (1999). The systematic influence of gain- and loss-framed messages on interest in and use of different types of health behavior. *Personality and Social Psychology Bulletin, 25,* 1355–1369.

Rotton, J., & Cohn, E. G. (2000). Violence is a curvilinear function of temperature in Dallas: A replication. *Journal of Personality and Social Psychology, 78*, 1074–1081.

Rowe, P. M. (1996, September). On the neurobiological basis of affiliation. *APS Observer*, 17–18.

Roy, M. P., Steptoe, A., & Kirschbaum, C. (1998). Life events and social support as moderators of individual differences in cardiovascular and cortisol reactivity. *Journal of Personality and Social Psychology, 75*, 1273–1281.

Rozin, P. & Nemeroff, C. (1990). The laws of sympathetic magic: A psychological analysis of similarity and contagion. In W. Stigler, R. A. Shweder, & G. Herdt (Eds.), *Cultural psychology: Essays in comparative human development* (pp. 205–232). Cambridge, England: Cambridge University Press.

Rozin, P., Lowery, L., & Ebert, R. (1994). Varieties of disgust faces and the structure of disgust. *Journal of Personality and Social Psychology, 66*, 870–881.

Rubin, J. Z. (1985). Deceiving ourselves about deception: Comment on Smith and Richardson's "Amelioration of deception and harm in psychological research." *Journal of Personality and Social Psychology, 48*, 252–253.

Rubin, Z., Hill, C.T., Peplau, L.A., & Dunkel-Schetter, C. (1980). Self-disclosure in dating couples: Sex roles and the ethic of openness. *Journal of Marriage and the Family, 42*, 305–317.

Rudich, E. A., & Vallacher, R. R. (1999). To belong or to self-enhance? Motivational bases for choosing interaction partners. *Personality and Social Psychology Bulletin, 25*, 1387–1404.

Rudolph, D. L., & Kim, J. G. (1996). Mood responses to recreational sport and exercise in a Korean sample. *Journal of Social Behavior and Personality, 11*, 841–849.

Rule, B. G., & Ferguson, T. J. (1986). The effects of media violence on attitudes, emotions and cognitions. *Journal of Social Issues, 2*, 29–50.

Rule, B. G., & Nesdale, A. R. (1976). Emotional arousal and aggressive behavior. *Psychological Bulletin, 83*, 851–863.

Rule, B. G., & Well, G. L. (1981). Experimental social psychology in Canada: A look at the seventies. *Canadian Psychology, 22*, 69–84.

Rusbult, C. E. (1983). A longitudinal test of the investment model: The development (and deterioration) of satisfaction and commitment in heterosexual involvements. *Journal of Personality and Social Psychology, 45*, 101–117.

Rusbult, C. E., & Martz, J. M. (1995). Remaining in an abusive relationship: An investment model analysis of nonvoluntary dependence. *Personality and Social Psychology Bulletin, 21*, 558–571.

Rusbult, C. E., & Zembrodt, I. M. (1983). Responses to dissatisfaction in romantic involvements: A multidimensional scaling analysis. *Journal of Experimental Social Psychology, 19*, 274–293.

Rusbult, C. E., Martz, J. M., & Agnew, C. R. (1998). The Investment Model Scale: Measuring commitment level, satisfaction level, quality of alternatives, and investment size. *Personal Relationships, 5*, 467–484.

Rusbult, C. E., Morrow, G. D., & Johnson, D. J. (1990). Self-esteem and problem-solving behavior in close relationships. *British Journal of Social Psychology*.

Rusbult, C. E., Van Lange, P. A. M., Wildschut, T., Yovetich, N. A., & Verette, J. (2000). Perceived superiority in close relationships: Why it exists and persists. *Journal of Personality and Social Psychology, 79*, 521–545.

Rushton, J. P. (1978). Urban density and altruism: Helping strangers in a Canadian city, suburb, and small town. *Psychological Reports, 43*, 987–990.

Rushton, J. P. (1989a). Genetic similarity, human altruism, and group selection. *Behavioral and Brain Sciences, 12*, 503–559.

Rushton, J. P. (1989b). Genetic similarity in male friendships. *Ethology and Sociobiology, 10*, 361–373

Rushton, J. P. (1990). Sir Francis Galton, epigenetic rules, genetic similarity theory, and human life-history analysis. *Journal of Personality, 58*, 117–140.

Rushton, J. P., Russell, R. J. H., & Wells, P. A. (1984). Genetic similarity theory: Beyond kin selection. *Behavior Genetics, 14*, 179–193.

Russell, J. A. (1994). Is there universal recognition of emotion from facial expression? A review of the cross-cultural studies. *Psychological Bulletin, 115*, 102–141.

Rusting, C. L., & DeHart, T. (2000). Retrieving positive memories to regulate negative mood: Consequences for mood-congruent memory. *Journal of Personality and Social Psychology, 78*, 737–752.

Ruvolo, A. P., Fabin, L. A., & Ruvolo, C. M. (2001). Relationship experiences and change in attachment characteristics of young adults: The role of relationship breakups and conflict avoidance. *Personal Relationships, 8*, 265–281.

Sadalla, E. K., Sheets, V., & McCreath, H. (1990). The cognition of urban tempo. *Environment and Behavior, 22*, 230–254.

Sadker, M., & Sadker, D. (1994). *Failing at fairness: How America's schools cheat girls*. New York: Charles Scribners Sons.

Safir, M. P., Peres, Y., Lichtenstein, M., Hoch, Z., & Shepher, J. (1982). Psychological androgyny and sexual adequacy. *Journal of Sex and Marital Therapy, 8*, 228–240.

Saki, R. [H. H. Munro]. (1924). Clovis on the alleged romance of business. In *The Square Egg*. New York: Viking.

Salovey, P., & Rodin, J. (1991). Provoking jealousy and envy: Domain relevance and self-esteem threat. *Journal of Social and Clinical Psychology, 10*, 395–413.

Sampson, E. E. (1991). *Social worlds, personal lives*. New York: Harcourt Brace Jovanovich.

Sanchez, J. I., & Fernandez, D. M. (1993). Acculturative stress among Hispanics: a bidimensional model of ethnic identification. *Journal of Applied Social Psychology, 23*, 654–668.

Sanders, G. S. (1983). An attentional process model of social facilitation. In A. Hare, H. Blumberg, V. Kent, and M. Davies (Eds.), *Small groups*. London: Wiley.

Sanna, L. J. (1997). Self-efficacy and counterfactual thinking: Up a creek with and without a paddle. *Personality and Social Psychology Bulletin, 23*, 654–666.

Sanna, L. J., & Pusecker, P. A. (1994). Self-efficacy, valence of self-evaluation, and performance. *Personality and Social Psychology Bulletin, 20*, 82–92.

Sarason, I. G., Sarason, B. R., & Pierce, G. R. (1994). Social Support: Global and relationship-based levels of analysis. *Journal of Social and Personal Relationships, 11,* 295–312.

Sauvé, R. (1994). *Borderlines: What Canadians and Americans should—but don't—know about each other... a witty, punchy and personal look.* Toronto: McGraw-Hill.

Saylor, C. F., Cowart, B. L., Lipovsky, J. A., Jackson, C., & Finch, A. J. (2003). Media exposure to September, 11. *American Behavioral Scientist, 46,* 1622–1642.

Schachter, D. L., & Kihlstrom, J. F. (1989). Functional amnesia. In F. Boller & J. Grafman (Eds.), *Handbook of neuropsychology* (Vol. 3, pp. 209–230). New York: Elsevier.

Schachter, S. (1959). *The psychology of affiliation.* Stanford, CA: Stanford University Press.

Schachter, S. (1964). The interaction of cognitive and physiological determinants of emotional state. In L. Berkowitz (Ed.), *Advances in experimental social psychology* (Vol. 1, pp. 48–81). New York: Academic Press.

Schaubroeck, J., Jones, J. R., & Xie, J. L. (2001). Individual differences in utilizing control to cope with job demands: Effects on susceptibility to infectious disease. *Journal of Applied Psychology, 86,* 265–278.

Scher, A., & Mayseless, O. (1994). Mothers' attachment with spouse and parenting in the first year. *Journal of Social and Interpersonal Relationships, 11,* 601–609.

Scher, S. J. (1997). Measuring the consequences of injustice. *Personality and Social Psychology Bulletin, 23,* 482–497.

Schlenker, B. R. (1980). *Impression management: The self-concept, social identity, and interpersonal relations.* Belmont, CA: Brooks/Cole.

Schneider, B. H. (1991). A comparison of skill-building and desensitization strategies for intervention with aggressive children. *Aggressive Behavior, 17,* 301–311.

Schooler, J. W., & Loftus, E. F. (1986). Individual differences and experimentation: Complementary approaches to interrogative suggestibility. *Social Behaviour, 1,* 105–112.

Schopler, J., & Insko, C. A. (1999). The reduction of the interindividual–intergroup discontinuity effect: The role of future consequences. In M. Foddy, M. Smithson, S. Schneider, & M. Hogg (Eds.), *Resolving social dilemmas: Dynamic, structural, and intergroup aspects* (p. 281–293). Philadelphia: Psychology Press.

Schopler, J., Insko, C. A., Wieslquist, J., Pemberton, M., Witcher, B., Koazr, R., Roddenberry, C., & Wildschut, T. (2001). When groups are more competitive than individuals: The domain of the discontinuity effect. *Journal of Personality and Social Psychology, 80,* 632–644.

Schul, Y., & Vinokur, A. D. (2000). Projection in person perception among spouses as a function of the similarity in their shared experiences. *Personality and Social Psychology Bulletin, 26,* 987–1001.

Schuster, M. A., Stein, B. D., Jaycox, L. H., Collins, R. L., Marshall, G. N., Elliott, M. N., Zhou, A. J., Kanouse, D. E., Morrison, J. L., & Berry, S. H. (2001). A national survey of stress reactions after the September 11, 2001 terrorist attacks. *New England Journal of Medicine, 345,* 1507–1512.

Schwartz, A. E. (1994, December 20). Americans on line seldom fond of disagreement. *Albany Times Union,* p. A–11.

Schwartz, S. H. (1992). The universal content and structure of values: Theoretical advances and empirical tests in 20 countries. In M. Zanna (Ed.), *Advances in experimental social psychology* (Vol. 25, pp. 1–65). New York: Academic Press.

Schwarz, N. (1990). Feelings as information: Informational and motivational functions of affective states. In E. T. Higgins, & R. M. Sorrentino, (Eds.), *Handbook of motivation and cognition: Foundations of social behavior, Vol. 2.* New York: Guilford Press. pp. 527–561.

Schwarz, N., Bless, H., Strack, F., Klumpp, G., Rittenauer-Schatka, G., & Simons, A. (1991b). Ease of retrieval as information: Another look at the availability heuristic. *Journal of Personality and Social Psychology, 61,* 195–202.

Schwarzer, R. (2001). Social–cognitive factors in changing health-related behaviors. *Current Directions in Psychological Science, 10,* 47–51.

Schwarzwald, J., Amir, Y., & Crain, R. L. (1992). Long-term effects of school desegregation experiences on interpersonal relations in the Israeli defense forces. *Personality and Social Psychology Bulletin, 18,* 357–368.

Sears, D. O. (1981). Life stage effects on attitude change, especially among the elderly. In S.B. Kiesler, J.N. Morgan & V.K. Oppenheimer (Eds.), *Aging: Social change* (pp.183–204). New York: Academic Press.

Sears, D. O. (1988). Symbolic racism. In P. A. Katz and D. A. Taylor (Eds.), *Eliminating racism: Profiles in controversy* (pp. 53–84). New York: Plenum.

Sedikides, C., & Brewer, M. B. (Eds.), (2001). *Individual self, relational self, collective self.* Philadelphia: Psychology Press.

Sedikides, C. (1993). Assessment, enhancement, and verification determinants of the self-evaluation process. *Journal of Personality and Social Psychology, 65,* 317–338.

Sedikides, C., & Skowronski, J. J. (1997). The symbolic self in evolutionary context. *Personality and Social Psychology Review, 1,* 80–102.

Sedikides, C., Gaertner, L., & Toguchi, Y. (2003). Pancultural self-enhancement. *Journal of Personality and Social Psychology, 84,* 60–79.

Segall, M. H., Dasen, P.R., Berry, J. W., & Poortinga, Y. H. (1999). *Human behavior in global perspective: An introduction to cross-cultural psychology.* Needham Heights, MA: Allyn & Bacon.

Segerstrom, S. C., Taylor, S. E., Kemeny, M. E., & Fahey, J. L. (1998). Optimism is associated with mood, coping, and immune change in response to stress. *Journal of Personality and Social Psychology, 74,* 1646–1655.

Senecal, C., Vallerand, R. J., & Guay, F. (2001). Antecedents and outcomes of work-family conflict: Toward a motivational model. *Personality and Social Psychology Bulletin, 27,* 176–186.

Seta, C. E., Hayes, N. S., & Seta, J. J. (1994). Mood, memory and vigilance: The influence of distraction on recall and impression formation. *Personality and Social Psychology Bulletin, 20,* 170–177.

Seybold, K. S., & Hill, P. C. (2001). The role of religion and spirituality in mental and physical health. *Current Directions in Psychological Science, 10,* 21–24.

Shackelford, T. K., & Larsen, R. J. (1999). Facial attractiveness and physical health. *Evolution and Human Behavior, 20,* 71–76.

Shapiro, D. L., Buttner, E. H., & Barry, B. (1995). Explanations: What factors enhance their perceived adequacy? Organizational Behavior and Human Decision *Processes, 58,* 346–358.

Shapiro, J. P., Baumeister, R. F., & Kessler, J. W. (1991). A three-component model of children's teasing: Aggression, humor, and ambiguity. *Journal of Social and Clinical Psychology, 10,* 459–472.

Sharpe, D., Adair, J. G., & Roese, N. J. (1992). Twenty years of deception research: A decline in subjects' trust? *Personality and Social Psychology Bulletin, 18,* 585–590.

Sharpsteen, D. J. (1995). The effects of relationship and self-esteem threats on the likelihood of romantic jealousy. *Journal of Social and Personal Relationships, 12,* 89–101.

Sharpsteen, D. J., & Kirkpatrick, L. A. (1997). Romantic jealousy and adult romantic attachment. *Journal of Personality and Social Psychology, 72,* 627–640.

Shaver, P. R., & Brennan, K. A. (1992). Attachment styles and the "big five" personality traits: Their connections with each other and with romantic relationship outcomes. *Personality and Social Psychology Bulletin, 18,* 536–545.

Shaver, P. R., & Hazan, C. (1994). Attachment. In A. L. Weber & J. H. Harvey (Eds.), *Perspectives on close relationships* (pp. 110–130). Boston: Allyn & Bacon.

Shaver, P. R., Papalia, D., Clark, C. L., Koski, L. R., Tidwell, M. C., & Nalbone, D. (1996). Androgyny and attachment security: Two related models of optimal personality. *Personality and Social Psychology Bulletin, 22,* 582–597.

Shaw, J. I., Borough, H. W., & Fink, M. I. (1994). Perceived sexual orientation and helping behavior by males and females: The wrong number technique. *Journal of Psychology and Human Sexuality, 6,* 73–81.

Shaw, R. P., & Wong, Y. (1989). *Genetic seeds of warfare: Evolution, nationalism, and patriotism.* Boston: Unwin Hyman.

Shaywitz, B. A., Shaywitz, S. E., Pugh, K. R., Constable, R. T., Skudlarski, P., Fulbright, R. K., Bronen, R. A., Fletcher, J. M., Shankweiler, D. P., Katz, L., & Gore, J. C. (1995). Sex differences in the functional organization of the brain for language. *Nature,* 373(6515) 607–609.

Sheeran, P., & Abraham, C. (1994). Unemployment and self-conception: A symbolic interactionist analysis. *Journal of Community & Applied Social Psychology, 4,* 115–129.

Sher, J. (1983). *White hoods: Canada's Ku Klux Klan.* Vancouver: New Star Books.

Sherif, M., Harvey, O. J., White, B. J., Hood, W. E., & Sherif, C. W. (1961). *Intergroup conflict and cooperation: The Robbers Cave experiment.* Norman, OK: Institute of Group Relations.

Sherman, S. S. (1980). On the self-erasing nature of errors of prediction. *Journal of Personality and Social Psychology, 16,* 388–403.

Shigetomi, C. C., Hartmann, D. P., & Gelfand, D. M. (1981). Sex differences in children's altruistic behavior and reputations for helpfulness. *Developmental Psychology, 17,* 434–437.

Shinn, M., Morch, H., Robinson, P. E., & Neuner, R. A. (1993). Individual, group and agency strategies for coping with job stressors in residential child care programmes. *Journal of Community and Applied Social Psychology, 3,* 313–324.

Shotland, R. I., & Strau, M. K. (1976). Bystander response to an assault: When a man attacks a woman. *Journal of Personality and Social Psychology, 34,* 990–999.

Showers, C. (1992a). Compartmentalization of positive and negative self-knowledge: Keeping bad apples out of the bunch. *Journal of Personality and Social Psychology, 62,* 1036–1049.

Showers, C. (1992b). Evaluative integrative thinking about characteristics of the self. *Personality and Social Psychology Bulletin, 18,* 719–729.

Showers, C. J., & Kling, K. C. (1996). Organization of self-knowledge: Implications for recovery from sad mood. *Journal of Personality and Social Psychology, 70,* 578–590.

Showers, C. J., & Ryff, C. D. (1996). Self-differentiation and well-being in a life transition. *Personality and Social Psychology Bulletin, 22,* 448–460.

Shweder, R. A. (1990). Cultural psychology: What is it? In J. W. Stigler, R. A. Shweder, & G. Herdt (Eds.), *Cultural psychology: Essays on comparative development* (pp. 1–43). Cambridge: Cambridge University Press.

Shweder, R. A., & Sullivan, M. A. (1993). Cultural psychology: Who needs it? *Annual Review of Psychology, 44,* 497–523.

Sigall, H. (1997). Ethical considerations in social psychological research: Is the bogus pipeline a special case? *Journal of Applied Social Psychology, 27,* 574–581.

Sigelman, C. K., Thomas, D. B., Sigelman, L., & Ribich, F. D. (1986). Gender, physical attractiveness, and electability: An experimental investigation of voter biases. *Journal of Applied Social Psychology, 16,* 229–248.

Sillars, A. L., Folwell, A. L., Hill, K. C., Maki, B. K., Hurst, A. P., & Casano, R. A. (1994). *Journal of Social and Personal Relationships, 11,* 611–617.

Silverstein, R. (1994). Chronic identity diffusion in traumatized combat veterans. *Social Behavior and Personality, 22,* 69–80.

Simmons, C.H., von Kolke, A. & Shimizu, H. (1986). Attitudes toward romantic love among American, German and Japanese students. *Journal of Social Psychology, 126,* 327–336.

Simon, L., Greenberg, J., & Brehm, J. (1995). Trivialization: The forgotten mode of dissonance reduction. *Journal of Personality and Social Psychology, 68,* 247–260.

Simpson, J. A. (1987). The dissolution of romantic relationships: Factors involved in relationship stability and emotional stress. *Journal of Personality and Social Psychology, 53,* 683–692.

Simpson, J. A., Ickes, W., & Blackstone, T. (1995). When the head protects the heart: Empathic accuracy in dating relationships. *Journal of Personality and Social Psychology, 69,* 629–641.

Singh, D. (1993). Adaptive significance of female physical attractiveness: Role of waist-to-hip ratio. *Journal of Personality and Social Psychology, 65*, 293–307.

Singh, D. (1995). Female judgment of male attractiveness and desirability for relationships: Role of waist-to-hip ratio and financial status. *Journal of Personality and Social Psychology, 69*, 1089–1101.

Singh, D., & Luis, S. (1995). Ethnic and gender consensus for the effect of the waist-to-hip ratio on judgments of female attractiveness and desirability for relationships. *Ethology and Sociobiology, 16*, 483–507.

Singh, R., & Tan, L. S. C. (1992). Attitudes and attraction: A test of the similarity-attraction and dissimilarity-repulsion hypotheses. *British Journal of Social Psychology, 31*, 227–238.

Sinha, D. (1988). Indigenisation of psychology in India and its relevance. *The Indian Journal of Social Science, 1*, 77–91.

Sinha, D. (1996). Cross-cultural psychology: The Asian scenario. In J. Pandey, D. Sinha, & D. P. S. Bhawuk (Eds.), *Asian contribution to cross-cultural psychology* (pp. 20–41). Thousand Oaks, CA: Sage.

Sivacek, J., & Crano, W. D. (1982). Vested interest as a moderator of attitude-behavior consistency. *Journal of Personality and Social Psychology, 43*, 210–221.

Skarlicki, D. P., & Folger, R. (1997). Retaliation in the workplace: The roles of distributive, procedural, and interactional justice. *Journal of Applied Psychology, 821*, 434–443.

Smeaton, G., Byrne, D., & Murnen, S. K. (1989). The repulsion hypothesis revisited: Similarity irrelevance or dissimilarity bias? *Journal of Personality and Social Psychology, 56*, 54–59.

Smeaton, G., Rupp, D., Vig, C., & Byrne, D. (1995). The mediating role of similarity assumptions on the effects of attitude similarity and dissimilarity on attraction and repulsion. Unpublished manuscript, University of Wisconsin–Stout, Menomonie.

Smith, P. B., & Schwartz, S. H. (1997). Values. In Berry, J. W., Segall, M. H., & Kagitcibasi, C. (Eds.), *Handbook of cross-cultural psychology*, 2nd edn, Vol. 3. Boston: Allyn & Bacon.

Smith, C. M., Tindale, R. S., & Dugoni, B. L. (1996). Minority and majority influence in freely interacting groups: Qualitative versus quantitative differences. *British Journal of Social Psychology, 35*, 137–149.

Smith, D. E., Gier, J. A., & Willis, F. N. (1982). Interpersonal touch and compliance with a marketing request. *Basic and Applied Social Psychology, 3*, 35–38.

Smith, E. R., Byrne, D., & Fielding, P. J. (1995). Interpersonal attraction as a function of extreme gender role adherence. *Personal Relationships, 2*, 161–172.

Smith, E. R., Byrne, D., Becker, M. A., & Przybyla, D. P. J. (1993). Sexual attitudes of males and females as predictors of interpersonal attraction and marital compatibility. *Journal of Applied Social Psychology, 23*, 1011–1034.

Smith, K. D., Keating, J. P., & Stotland, E. (1989). Altruism reconsidered: The effect of denying feedback on a victim's status to empathetic witnesses. *Journal of Personality and Social Psychology, 57*, 641–650.

Smith, P. B., & Bond, M. H. (1993). *Social psychology across cultures*. Boston: Allyn & Bacon.

Smith, P. B., & Bond, N. H. (1998). *Social psychology across cultures* (2nd ed.). Boston: Allyn & Bacon.

Smith, P. K., & Brain, P. (2000). Bullying in schools; lessons from two decades of research. *Aggressive Behavior, 26*, 1–9.

Smith, R. E., Smoll, F. L., & Ptacek, J. T. (1990). Conjunctive moderator variables in vulnerability and resiliency research: Life stress, social support and coping skills, and adolescent sport injuries. *Journal of Personality and Social Psychology, 58*, 360–370.

Smith, R. H., Kim, S. H., & Parrott, W. G. (1988). Envy and jealousy: Semantic problems and experiential distinctions. *Personality and Social Psychology Bulletin, 14*, 401–409.

Smith, S. S., & Richardson, D. (1985). On deceiving ourselves about deception: Reply to Rubin. *Journal of Personality and Social Psychology, 48*, 254–255.

Smith, V. I., & Ellsworth, P. C. (1987). The social psychology of eyewitness accuracy: Misleading questions and communicator expertise. *Journal of Applied Psychology, 72*, 294–300.

Smorti, A., & Ciucci, E. (2000). Narrative strategies in bullies and victims in Italian schoolchildren. *Aggressive Behavior, 26*, 33–48.

Smorti, A., Menesini, E., & Smith, P. K. (2003). Parents' definitions of children's bullying in a five-country comparison. *Journal of Cross-Cultural Psychology, 34*, 417–432.

Snell, W. E., Jr. (1998). The Relationship Awareness Scale: Measuring relational-consciousness, relational-monitoring, and relational-anxiety. *Contemporary Social Psychology, 18*, 23–49.

Sniffen, M. J. (1991, September 30). Blacks make up 40% of death row. *Albany Times Union*, p. A–3.

Snyder, C. R. (2000). The past and possible futures of hope. *Journal of Social and Clinical Psychology, 19*, 11–28.

Snyder, C. R., & Fromkin, H. L. (1980). *Uniqueness: The human pursuit of difference*. New York: Plenum.

Snyder, M., & Ickes, W. (1985). Personality and social behavior. In G. Lindzey & E. Aronson (Eds.), *The handbook of social psychology* (Vol. 1, 3rd ed., pp. 883–947). New York: Random House.

Snyder, M., & Simpson, J. A. (1984). Self-monitoring and dating relationships. *Journal of Personality and Social Psychology, 47*, 1281–1291.

Snyder, M., Grether, J., & Keller, K. (1974). Staring and compliance: A field experiment on hitchhiking. *Journal of Applied Social Psychology, 4*, 165–170.

Solomon, R. C. (1981, October). The love lost in clichés. *Psychology Today*, pp. 83–85, 87–88.

Somerfield, M. R., & McCrae, R. R. (2000). Stress and coping research: Methodological challenges, theoretical advances, and clinical applications. *American Psychologist, 55*, 620–625.

Sommer, K. L., Horowitz, I. A., & Bourgeois, M. J. (2001). When juries fail to comply with the law: Biased evidence processing in individual and group decision making. *Personality and Social Psychology Bulletin, 27*, 309–320.

Son Hing, L.S., Li, W., & Zanna, M. P. (2002). Inducing hypocrisy to reduce prejudicial responses among aversive racists. *Journal of Experimental Social Psychology, 38*, 71–78.

Sorenson, K. A., Russell, S. M., Harkness, D. J., & Harvey, J. H. (1993). Account-making, confiding, and coping with the ending of a close relationship. *Journal of Social Behavior and Personality, 8*, 73–86.

Sorrentino, R, M., Hewitt, E. C., & Raso-Knott, P. A. (1992). Risk-taking in games of chance and skill: Informational and affective influences on choice behavior. *Journal of Personality & Social Psychology, 62*, 522–533.

Spencer, M. B., & Markstrom-Adams, C. (1990). Identity processes among racial and ethnic minority children in America. *Child Development, 61*, 290–310.

Sprafkin, J. N., Liebert, R. M., & Poulous, R. W. (1975). Effects of a prosocial televised example on children's helping. *Journal of Personality and Social Psychology, 48*, 35–46.

Sprecher, S. (1992). How men and women expect to feel and behave in response to inequity in close relationships. *Social Psychology Quarterly, 55*, 57–69.

Sprecher, S., & Duck, S. (1994). Sweet talk: The importance of perceived communication for romantic and friendship attraction experienced during a get-acquainted date. *Personality and Social Psychology Bulletin, 20*, 391–400.

Stalder, D. R., & Baron, R. S. (1998). Attributional complexity as a moderator of dissonance-produced attitude change. *Journal of Personality and Social Psychology, 75*, 449–455.

Stangor, C., & McMillan, D. (1992). Memory for expectancy-congruent and expectancy-incongruent information: A review of the social and social developmental literatures. *Psychological Bulletin, 111*, 42–61.

Stanton, A. L., Kirk, S. B., Cameron, C. L., & Danoff-Burg, S. (2000). Coping through emotional approach: Scale construction and validation. *Journal of Personality and Social Psychology, 78*, 1150–1169.

Stasser, G. (1992). Pooling of unshared information during group discussion. In S. Worchel, W. Wood, & J. H. Simpson (Eds.), *Process and productivity* (pp. 48–67). Newbury Park, CA: Sage.

Stasser, G., Taylor, L. A., & Hanna, C. (1989). Information sampling in structured and unstructured discussions of three- and six-person groups. *Journal of Personality and Social Psychology, 57*, 67–78.

Statistics Canada (1999). *Annual demographic statistics, 1998*. Ottawa: Statistics Canada Catalogue no. 91–213.

Statistics Canada (1999). *CANSIM Matrix 2*. Statistics Canada Web site.

Statistics Canada (1999). *Census families in private households by family structure, 1991 and 1996 Censuses*. Statistics Canada Web site.

Statistics Canada. (1999). *1996 Census Nation tables*. Statistics Canada Web site.

Statistics Canada, *The Daily* (Thursday July 11, 2002). Changing conjugal life in Canada. Statistics Cananda: http://www.statcan.ca/Daily/English/020711/d020711a.htm

Statistics Canada (2003). *Canada's ethnocultural portrait: The changing mosaic*. http://www.statcan.ca. Steel, R. P., & Rentsch, J. R. (1997). The dispositional model of job attitudes revisited: Findings of a 10-year study. *Journal of Applied Psychology, 82*, 873–879.

Steele, C. M. (1988). The psychology of self-affirmation: Sustaining the integrity of the self. In L. Berkowitz (Ed.), *Advances in experimental social psychology* (pp. 261–302). Hillsdale, NJ: Erlbaum.

Steele, C. M. (1997). A threat in the air: How stereotypes shape the intellectual identities and performance of women and African-Americans. *American Psychologist, 52*, 613–629.

Steele, C. M., & Josephs, R. A. (1990). Alcohol myopia: Its prized and dangerous effects. *American Psychologist, 45*, 921–933.

Steele, C. M., & Lui, T. J. (1983). Dissonance processes as self-affirmation. *Journal of Personality and Social Psychology, 45*, 5–19.

Steele, C. M., Southwick, L., & Critchlow, B. (1981). Dissonance and alcohol: Drinking your troubles away. *Journal of Personality and Social Psychology, 41*, 831–846.

Steele, C. M., Spencer, S. J., & Lynch, M. (1993). Self-image resilience and dissonance: The role of affirmational resources. *Journal of Personality and Social Psychology, 64*, 885–896.

Stephan, W. G. (1985). Intergroup relations. In G. Lindzey & E. Aronson (Eds.), *Handbook of social psychology* (Vol. 2, pp. 599–658). New York: Random House.

Stephan, W. G., & Stephan, C. W. (1988). Emotional reactions to interracial achievement outcomes. *Journal of Applied Social Psychology, 19*, 608–621.

Sternberg, R. J. (1986). A triangular theory of love. *Psychological Review, 93*, 119–135.

Sternberg, R. J. (1988). Triangulating love. In R. J. Sternberg & M. L. Barnes (Eds.), *The psychology of love* (pp. 119–138). New Haven, CT: Yale University Press.

Sternberg, R. J. (1988a). *The triangle of love*. New York: Basic Books.

Stewart, J. E. (1980). Defendant's attractiveness as a factor in the outcome of criminal trials: An observational study. *Journal of Applied Social Psychology, 10*, 348–361.

Stice, E., & Shaw, H. E. (1994). Adverse effects of the media portrayed thin-ideal on women and linkages to bulimic symptomatology. *Journal of Social and Clinical Psychology, 13*, 288–308.

Stiff, J. B., Miller, G. R., Sleight, C., Mongeau, P. J., Gardelick, R., & Rogan, R. (1989). Explanation for visual cue primacy in judgments of honesty and deceit. *Journal of Personality and Social Psychology, 56*, 555–564.

Stiles, W. B., Walz, N. C., Schroeder, M. A. B., Williams, L. L., & Ickes, W. (1996). Attractiveness and disclosure in initial encounters of mixed-sex dyads. *Journal of Social and Personal Relationships, 13*, 303–312.

Stone, A. A., Cox, D., Valdimarsdotti, H., Jandorf, L., & Neale, J. M. (1987). Evidence that secretory IGA antibody is associated with daily mood. *Journal of Personality and Social Psychology, 52*, 988–993.

Stone, A. A., Neale, J. M., Cox, D. S., Napoli, A., Valdimarsdottir, H., & Kennedy-Moore, E. (1994). Daily events are associated with a secretory immune response to an oral antigen in men. *Health Psychology, 13*, 440–446.

Stone, J., Aronson, E., Crain, A. L., Winslow, M. P., T Fried, C. B. (1994). Inducing hypocrisy as a means of encouraging young adults to use condoms. *Personality and Social Psychology Bulletin, 20,* 116–128.

Stone, J., Wiegand, A. W., Cooper, J., & Aronson, E. (1997). When exemplification fails: Hypocrisy and the motives for self-integrity. *Journal of Personality and Social Psychology, 72,* 54–65.

Stradling, S. G., Crowe, G., & Tuohy, A. P. (1993). Changes in self-concept during occupational socialization of new recruits to the police. *Journal of Community & Applied Social Psychology, 3,* 131–147.

Strahan, E. J., Spencer, S. J., & Zanna, M. P. (2002). Subliminal priming and persuasion: Striking while the iron is hot. *Journal of Experimental Social Psychology, 38,* 556–568.

Strauman, T. J., Lemieux, A. M., & Coe, C. L. (1993). Self-discrepancy and natural killer cell activity: Immunological consequences of negative self-evaluation. *Journal of Personality and Social Psychology, 64,* 1042–1052.

Strauman, T.J. (1996). Stability within the self: A longitudinal study of the structural implications of self-discrepancy theory. *Journal of Personality and Social Psychology, 71,* 1142–1153.

Street, R. L., & Buller, D. B. (1987). Nonverbal response patterns in physician-patient interactions: A functional analysis. *Journal of Nonverbal Behavior, 11,* 234–253.

Strickland, B. R. (1992). Women and depression. *Current Directions in Psychological Science, 1,* 132–135.

Stroessner, S. J., Hamilton, D. L., & Mackie, D. M. (1992). Affect and stereotyping: The effect of induced mood on distinctiveness-based illusory correlations. *Journal of Personality and Social Psychology, 62,* 564–576.

Strube, M. J. (1989). Evidence for the Type in Type A behavior: A taxonometric analysis. *Journal of Personality and Social Psychology, 56,* 972–987.

Strube, M., Turner, C. W., Cerro, D., Stevens, J., & Hinchey, F. (1984). Interpersonal aggression and the Type A coronary-prone behavior pattern: A theoretical distinction and practical implications. *Journal of Personality and Social Psychology, 47,* 839–847.

Suls, J., & Rosnow, J. (1988). Concerns about artifacts in behavioral research. In M. Morawski (Ed.), *The rise of experimentation in American psychology* (pp. 163–187). New Haven, CT: Yale University Press.

Sunnafrank, M. (1992). On debunking the attitude similarity myth. Communication Monographs, *59,* 165–179.

Susskind, J., Maurer, K. L., Thakkar, V., Hamilton, D. L., & Sherman, J. (1999). Perceiving individuals and groups: Expectancies, inferences, and causal attribution. *Journal of Personality and Social Psychology, 76,* 181–191.

Sutton, C.D., & Moore, K.K. (1985). Probing opinions: Executive women 20 years later. *Harvard Business Review, 63* (5), 43–66.

Swann, W. B., Jr. (1997). The trouble with change: Self-verification and allegiance to the self. *Psychological Science, 8,* 177–180.

Swann, W. B., Jr., & Gill, M. J. (1997). Confidence and accuracy in person perception: Do we know what we think we know about our relationship partners? *Journal of Personality and Social Psychology, 73,* 747–757.

Swap, W. C. (1977). Interpersonal attraction and repeated exposure to rewarders and punishers. *Personality and Social Psychology Bulletin, 3,* 248–251.

Swim, J. K., Aikin, K. J., Hall, W. S., & Hunter, B. A. (1995). Sexism and racism: Old-fashioned and modern prejudices. *Journal of Personality and Social Psychology, 68,* 199–214.

Tafarodi, R. W. (1998). Paradoxical self-esteem and selectivity in the processing of social information. *Journal of Personality and Social Psychology, 74,* 1181–1196.

Tafarodi, R. W., Kang, S.-J., & Milne, A, B. (2002). When different becomes similar: Compensatory conformity in bicultural visible minorities. *Personality & Social Psychology Bulletin, 28,* 1131–1142.

Tafarodi, R. W., & Vu, C. (1997). Two-dimensional self-esteem and reactions to success and failure. *Personality and Social Psychology Bulletin, 23,* 626–635.

Tafarodi, R. W., Tam, J., & Milne, A. B. (2001). Selective memory and the persistence of paradoxical self-esteem. *Personality and Social Psychology Bulletin, 27,* 1179–1189.

Tajfel, H. (1970). Experiments in intergroup discrimination. *Scientific American, 223* (5), 96–102.

Tajfel, H. (1978). *Differentiation between social groups: Studies in the social psychology of intergroup relations.* London: Academic Press.

Tajfel, H. (1982). *Social identity and intergroup relations.* Cambridge: Cambridge University Press.

Tajfel, H., & Turner, J.C. (1979). An integrative theory of intergroup conflict. In W.G. Austin & S. Worchel (Eds.), *The social psychology of intergroup relations* (pp. 33–47). Monterey, CA: Brooks/Cole.

Takata, T., & Hashimoto, H. (1973). Effects of insufficient justification upon the arousal of cognitive dissonance: Timing of justification and evaluation of task. *Japanese Journal of Experimental Social Psychology, 13,* 77–85.

Tannen, D. (1994). *Talking from 9 to 5.* New York: William Morrow.

Tannen, D. (1995, January 9–15). And rarely the twain shall meet. *Washington Post National Weekly Edition 25.*

Tassinary, L. G., & Hansen, K. A. (1998). A critical test of the waist-to-hip ratio hypothesis of female physical attractiveness. *Psychological Science, 9,* 150–155.

Taylor, D. M. (2002). *The quest for identity: from minority groups to generation Xers.* Westport, Conn.: Praeger.

Taylor, D.M., & McKirnan, D.J. (1984). A five-stage model of intergroup relations. *British Journal of Social Psychology, 23,* 291–300.

Taylor, D.M., & Moghaddam, F.M. (1994). *Theories of intergroup relations: International social psychological perspectives.* Second Edition.New York: Praeger.

Taylor, D.M., Wong-Rieger, D., McKirnan, D.J., & Bercusson, T. (1982). Social comparison in a group context. *Journal of Social Psychology, 117,* 257–259.

Taylor, D. M., Wright, S. C., Moghaddam, F. M., & Lalonde, R. N. (1990). *Personality and Social Psychology Bulletin, 16*, 254–262.

Taylor, P. M, (1995). *Munitions of the mind: A history of propaganda from the ancient world to the present day.* Manchester, England: Manchester University Press.

Taylor, S. E., & Brown, J. D. (1988). Illusion and well-being: A social psychological perspective on mental health. *Psychological Bulletin, 103*, 193–210.

Taylor, S. E., & Brown, J. D. (1994). "Illusion" of mental health does not explain positive illusions. *American Psychologist, 49*, 972–973.

Taylor, S. E., Buunk, B. P., & Aspinwall, L. G. (1990). Social comparison, stress, and coping. *Personality and Social Psychology Bulletin, 16*, 74–89.

Taylor, S. E., Buunk, B. P., & Aspinwall, L. G. (1990). Social comparison, stress, and coping. *Personality and Social Psychology Bulletin, 16*, 74–89.

Taylor, S. E., Helgeson, V. S., Reed, G. M., & Skokan, L. A. (1991). Self-generated feelings of control and adjustment to physical illness. *Journal of Social Issues, 47*, 91–109.

Taylor, S. E., Pham, L. B., Rivkin, I. D., & Armor, D. A. (1998). Harnessing the imagination: Mental stimulation, self-regulation, and coping. *American Psychologist, 53*, 429–439.

Tedeschi, J. T., & Melburg, V. (1984). Impression management and influence in organizations. In S. B. Bacharach & E. J. Lawler (Eds.), *Research in the sociology of organizations* (Vol 3., pp. 31–58). Greenwich, CT: JAI Press.

Tedeschi, J. T., & Norman, N. M. (1985). A social psychological interpretation of displaced aggression. *Advances in Group Processes, 2*, 29–56.

Tennen, H., Affleck, G., Armeli, S., & Carney, M. A. (2000). A daily process approach to coping: Linking theory, research, and practice. *American Psychologist, 55*, 626–636.

Terry, R. L., & Krantz, J. H. (1993). Dimensions of trait attributions associated with eyeglasses, men's facial hair, and women's hair length. *Journal of Applied Social Psychology, 23*, 1757–1769.

Tesser, A. (1993). On the importance of heritability in psychological research: The case of attitudes. *Psychological Review, 100*, 129–142.

Tesser, A., & Martin, L. (1996). The psychology of evaluation. In E. T. Higgins & A. W. Kruglanski (Eds.), *Social psychology: Handbook of basic principles* (pp. 400–423). New York: Guilford Press.

Tesser, A., Martin, L. L., & Cornell, D. P. (1996). On the substitutability of the self-protecting mechanisms. In P. Gollwitzer & J. Bargh (Eds.), *The psychology of action* (pp. 48–68). New York: Guilford.

Tetlock, P. E., Peterson, R. S., McGuire, C., Change, S., & Feld, P. (1992). Assessing political group dynamics: A test of the groupthink model. *Journal of Personality and Social Psychology, 63*, 403–425.

Tett, R. P., & Meyer, J. P. (1993). Job satisfaction, organizational commitment, turnover intention, and turnover: Path analyses based on meta-analytic findings. *Personnel Psychology, 46*, 259–293.

Thompson, J. K., & Tantleff, S. (1992). Female and male ratings of upper torso: Actual, ideal, and stereotypical conceptions. *Journal of Social Behavior and Personality, 7*, 345–354.

Thompson, L. (1998). *The mind and heart of the negotiator.* Upper Saddle River, NJ: Prentice-Hall.

Thompson, M. M., Zanna, M. P., & Griffin, D. W. (1995). Let's not be indifferent about attitudinal ambivalence. In R. E. Petty & J. A. Krosnick (Eds.), *Attitude strength: Antecedents and consequences* (pp. 361–386). Mahwah, NJ: Erlbaum.

Tice, D. M., & Baumeister, R. F. (1997). Longitudinal study of procrastination, performance, stress, and health: The costs and benefits of dawdling. *Psychological Science, 8*, 454–458.

Tice, D. M., Bratslavsky, E., & Baumeister, R. F. (2000). Emotional distress regulation takes precedence over impulse control: If you feel bad, do it! *Journal of Personality and Social Psychology, 80*, 53–67.

Tidwell, M.-C. O., Reis, H. T., & Shaver, P. R. (1996). Attachment, attractiveness, and social interaction: A diary study. *Journal of Personality and Social Psychology, 71*, 729–745.

Tiedens, L. Z. (2001). Anger and advancement versus sadness and subjugation: The effect of negative emotion expressions on social status control. *Journal of Personality and Social Psychology, 80*, 86–94.

Timmers, M., Fischer, A. H., & Manstead, A. S. R. (1998). Gender differences in motives for regulating emotions. *Personality and Social Psychology Bulletin, 24, 974*–985.

Tjosvold, D. (1993). *Learning to manage conflict: Getting people to work together productively.* New York: Lexington.

Tjosvold, D., & De Dreu, C. (1997). Managing conflict in Dutch organizations: A test of the relevance of Deutsch's cooperation theory. *Journal of Applied Social Psychology, 27*, 2213–2227.

Toch, H. (1985). *Violent men* (rev. ed.). Cambridge, MA:

Toi, M., & Batson, C. D. (1982). More evidence that empathy is a source of altruistic motivation. *Journal of Personality and Social Psychology, 43*, 281–292.

Tomaka, J., & Blascovich, J. (1994). Effects of justice beliefs on cognitive appraisal of and subjective, physiological, and behavioral responses to potential stress. *Journal of Personality and Social Psychology, 67*, 732–740.

Toobin, J. (1995, July 17). Putting it in black and white. *New Yorker*, 31–34.

Tooley, V., Brigham, J. C., Maass, A., & Bothwell, R. K. (1987). Facial recognition: Weapon effect and attentional focus. *Journal of Applied Social Psychology, 17*, 845–859.

Tougas, F., Brown, R., Beaton, A.M., & Joly, S. (1995). Neo-sexism: Plus ca change, plus c'est pareil. *Personality and Social Psychology Bulletin, 21*, 842–849.

Tovee, M. J., & Cornelissen, P. L. (2001). Female and male perception of female physical attractiveness in front-view and profile. *British Journal of Psychology, 92*, 391–402.

Towles-Schwen, T., & Fazio, R. H. (2001). On the origins of racial attitudes: Correlates of childhood experiences. *Personality and Social Psychology Bulletin, 27*, 162–175.

Townsend, J. M., & Wasserman, T. (1997). The perception of sexual attractiveness: Sex differences in variability. *Archives of Sexual Behavior, 26*, 243–268.

Trapnell, P. D., & Campbell, J. D. (1999). Private self-consciousness and the five-factor model of personality: Distinguishing rumination from reflection. *Journal of Personality and Social Psychology, 76,* 284–304.

Tremblay, S. (1999). *Crime statistics in Canada, 1998.* Statistics Canada — Catalogue no. 85–002–XIE Vol. 19 no. 9

Triandis, H. C. (1995). *Individualism and collectivism.* Boulder, CO: Westview Press.

Triandis, H.C. (1980). Introduction. In. H.C. Triandis & W.W. Lambert (Eds.) *Handbook of cross-cultural psychology, 1, Perspectives.* Boston: Allyn & Bacon.

Triandis, H.C. (1989) The self and social behavior in different cultural contexts. *Psychological Review, 96,* 506–20.

Trinke, S. J., & Bartholomew, K. (1997). Hierarchies of attachment relationships in young adulthood. *Journal of Social and Personal Relationships, 14,* 603–625.

Triplett, H. (1898). The dynamogenic factors in pace making and competition. *American Journal of Psychology, 9,* 507–533.

Trivers, R. L. (1972). Parental investment and sexual selection. In B. Campbell (Ed.), *Sexual selection and the descent of man: 1871–1971* (pp. 136–179). Chicago: Aldine.

Trope, Y. (1986). Identification and inferential processes in dispositional attribution. *Psychological Review, 93,* 239–257.

Trope, Y., & Liberman, A. (1996). Social hypothesis testing: Cognitive and motivational mechanisms. In E. T. Higgins & A. W. Kruglanski (Eds.), *Social psychology: Handbook of basic principles* (pp. 239–270). New York: Guilford.

Tucker, P., & Aron, A. (1993). Passionate love and marital satisfaction at key transition points in the family life cycle. *Journal of Social and Clinical Psychology, 12,* 135–147.

Turner, J. C., Hogg, M. A., Oakes, P. J., Reicher, S. D., & Wetherell, M. S. (1987). *Rediscovering the social group: A self-categorization theory.* Oxford, England: Blackwell.

Tversky, A., & Kahneman, D. (1973). Availability: A heuristic for judging frequency and probability. *Cognitive Psychology, 5,* 207–232.

Tversky, A., & Kahneman, D. (1982). Judgment under uncertainty: Heuristics and biases. In D. Kahnamen, P. Slovic, & A. Tversky (Eds.), *Judgment under uncertainty* (pp. 3–20). New York: Cambridge University Press.

Tweed, R. G., & Lehman, D. R. (2002). Learning considered within a cultural context: Confucian and Socratic approaches. *American Psychologist, 57,* 89–99.

Twenge, J. M., & Manis, M. M. (1998). First-name desirability and adjustment: Self-satisfaction, others' ratings, and family background. *Journal of Applied Social Psychology, 24,* 41–51.

Tykocinski, O. E. (2001). I never had a chance: Using hindsight tactics to mitigate disappointments. *Personality and Social Psychology Bulletin, 27,* 376–382.

Tykocinski, O. E., & Pittman, T. S. (1998). The consequences of doing nothing: Inaction inertia as avoidance of anticipated counterfactual regret. *Journal of Personality and Social Psychology, 73,* 607–616.

Tyler, T. R. (2002). Is the Internet changing social life? It seems the more things change, the more they stay the same. *Journal of Social Issues, 58,* 195–205.

Tyler, T. R., Boeckmann, R. J., Smith, H. J., & Huo, Y. J. (1997). *Social justice in a diverse society.* Boulder, CO: Westview.

U.S. Department of Justice, Federal Bureau of Investigation (2002). Uniform Crime Reporting: Crime in the United States 2000. http://www.fbi.gov/ucr/cius_00/contents.pdf

U.S. Department of Labor. (1992). *Employment and earnings* (Vol. 39, No. 5: Table A–22). Washington, DC: U.S. Department of Labor.

Uchino, G. N., Kiecolt-Glaser, J. K., & Cacioppo, J. T. (1992). Age-related changes in cardiovascular response as a function of a chronic stressor and social support. *Journal of Personality and Social Psychology, 63,* 839–846.

Udry, J. R. (1980). Changes in the frequency of marital intercourse from panel data. *Archives of Sexual Behavior, 9,* 319–325.

Ullman, C. (1987). From sincerity to authenticity: Adolescents' view of the "true self." *Journal of Personality, 55,* 583–595.

Unger, R. K., & Crawford, M. (1993). Commentary: Sex and gender—The troubled relationship between terms and concepts. *Psychological Science, 4,* 122–124.

United Nations (1998). *International study on firearm regulation.* New York: United Nations.

Vaillant, G. E. (2002). *Aging well.* New York: Little, Brown.

Van Dyne, L., & LePine, J. A. (1998). Helping and voice extra-role behaviors: Evidence of construct and predictive validity. *Academy of Management Journal, 41,* 108–119.

Van Hook, E., & Higgins, E. T. (1988). Self-related problems beyond the self-concept: Motivational consequences of discrepant self-guides. *Journal of Personality and Social Psychology, 55,* 625–633.

Van Lange, P. A. M., & Kuhlman, M. D. (1994). Social value orientation and impressions of partner's honesty and intelligence: A test of the might versus morality effect. *Journal of Personality and Social Psychology, 67,* 126–141.

Van Lange, P. A. M., & Rusbult, C. E. (1995). My relationship is better than—and not as bad as—yours is: The perception of superiority in close relationships. *Personality and Social Psychology Bulletin, 21,* 32–44.

Van Overwalle, F. (1997). Dispositional attributions require the joint application of the methods of difference and agreement. *Personality and Social Psychology Bulletin, 23,* 974–980.

Vanderbilt, A. (1957). *Amy Vanderbilt's complete book of etiquette.* Garden City, NY: Doubleday.

Vanman, E. J., Paul, B. Y., Ito, T. A., & Miller, N. (1997). The modern face of prejudice and structure features that moderate the effect of cooperation on affect. *Journal of Personality and Social Psychology, 73,* 941–959.

Vermande, M. M., van den Oord, E. J. C. G., Goudena, P. P., & Rispens, J. (2000). Structural characteristics of aggressor–victim relationships in Dutch school classes of 4- to 5-year-olds. *Aggressive Behavior, 26,* 11–32.

Vinokur, A., & Burnstein, E. (1974). Effects of partially shared persuasive arguments on group-induced shifts: A group problem-solving approach. *Journal of Personality and Social Psychology, 29,* 305–315.

Vogel, D. A., Lake, M. A., Evans, S., & Karraker, K. H. (1991). Children's and adults' sex-stereotyped perceptions of infants. *Sex Roles, 24,* 605–616.

Vonk, R. (1998). The slime effect: Suspicion and dislike of likeable behavior toward superiors. *Journal of Personality and Social Psychology*, 74, 849–864.

Vonk, R., & van Knippenberg, A. (1995). Processing attitude statements from in-group and out-group members: Effects of within-group and within-person inconsistencies on reading times. Journal of *Personality and Social Psychology*, 68, 215–227.

Vorauer, J. D., & Claude, S. D. (1998). Perceived versus actual transparency of goals in negotiation. *Personality and Social Psychology Bulletin*, 24, 371–385.

Vorauer, J. D., Main, K. J., & O'Connell, G. B. (1998). How do individuals expect to be viewed by members of lower status groups? Content and implications of meta-stereotypes. *Journal of Personality and Social Psychology, 75,* 917–937.

Walker, S., Richardson, D. S., & Green, L. R. (2000). Aggression among older adults: The relationship of interaction networks and gender role to direct and indirect responses. *Aggressive Behavior, 26,* 145–154.

Waller, N. G., Koietin, B. A., Bouchard, T. J., Jr., Lykken, D. T., & Tellegen, A. (1990). Genetic and environmental influences on religious interests, attitudes, and values: A study of twins reared apart and together. *Psychological Science, 1,* 138–142.

Walmsley, D. J., & Lewis, G. J. (1989). The pace of pedestrian flows in cities. *Environment and Behavior, 21,* 123–150.

Walster, E., & Festinger, L. (1962). The effectiveness of "overheard" persuasive communication. *Journal of Abnormal and Social Psychology, 65,* 395–402.

Wan, K.C., & Bond, M.H. (1982). Chinese attributions for success and failure under public and anonymous conditions of rating. *Acta Psychologica Taiwanica, 24,* 23–31.

Wanous, J. P., Reiches, A. E., & Hudy, M. J. (1997). Overall job satisfaction: How good are single-item measures? *Journal of Applied Psychology, 82,* 247–252.

Wardle, J., Bindra, R., Fairclough, B., & Westcombe, A. (1993). Culture and body image: Body perception and weight concern in young Asian and Caucasian British women. *Journal of Community & Applied Social Psychology, 3,* 173–181.

Waters, H. F., Block, D., Friday, C., & Gordon, J. (1993, July 12). Networks under the gun. *Newsweek,* 64–66.

Watson, C. B., Chemers, M. M., & Preiser, N. (2001). Collective efficacy: A multilevel analysis. *Personality and Social Psychology Bulletin, 27,* 1057–1068.

Watson, D., Hubbard, B., & Wiese, D. (2000). Self–other agreement in personality and affectivity: The role of acquaintanceship, trait visibility, and assumed similarity. *Journal of Personality and Social Psychology, 78,* 546–558.

Watts, B. L. (1982). Individual differences in circadian activity rhythms and their effects on roommate relationships. *Journal of Personality, 50,* 374–384.

Wayment, H. A., & Taylor, S. E. (1995). Self-evaluation processes: Motives, information use, and self-esteem. *Journal of Personality, 63,* 729–757.

Wayne, S. J., & Liden, R. C. (1995). Effects of impression management on performance ratings: a longitudinal study. *Academy of Management Journal, 38,* 232–260.

Webster, D. W., Vernick, J. S., Ludwig, J., & Lester, K. J. (1997). Flawed gun policy research could endanger public safety. *American Public Health, 87,* 918–921.

Wegner, D. M., & Bargh, J. A. (1998). Control and automaticity in social life. In D. T. Gilbert, S. T. Fiske, & G. Lindsey (Eds.), *Handbook of social psychology* (4th ed.). New York: McGraw-Hill.

Wegner, D. M., & Gold, D. B. (1995). Fanning old flames: Emotional and cognitive effects of suppressing thoughts of a past relationship. *Journal of Personality and Social Psychology, 68,* 782–792.

Weidner, G., Istvan, J., & McKnight, J. D. (1989). Clusters of behavioral coronary risk factors in employed women and men. *Journal of Applied Social Psychology, 19,* 468–480.

Weigel, F. H., Kim, E. L., & Frost, J. L. (1995). Race relations on prime time television reconsidered: Patterns of continuity and change. *Journal of Applied Social Psychology, 25,* 223–236.

Weigel, R. H., Loomis, J. S., & Soja, M. J. (1980). Race relations on prime time television. *Journal of Personality and Social Psychology, 39,* 884–893.

Weinberger, M., Hiner, S. L., & Tierney, W. M. (1987). In support of hassles as a measure of stress in predicting health outcomes. *Journal of Behavioral Medicine, 16,* 19–32.

Weiner, B. (1980). A cognitive (attribution) emotion-action model of motivated behavior: An analysis of judgments of help-giving. *Journal of Personality and Social Psychology, 39,* 186–200.

Weiner, B. (1985). An attributional theory of achievement motivation and emotion. *Psychological Review, 92,* 548–573.

Weiner, B. (1993). On sin versus sickness: A theory of perceived responsibility and social motivation. *American Psychologist, 48,* 957–965.

Weiner, B. (1995). *Judgments of responsibility: A foundation for a theory of social conduct.* New York: Guilford.

Weiner, B., Amirkhan, J., Folkes, V. S., & Verette, J. A. (1987). An attributional analysis of excuse giving: Studies of a naive theory of emotion. *Journal of Personality and Social Psychology, 52,* 316–324.

Weinstein, N. D. (1982). Unrealistic optimism about susceptibility to health problems. *Journal of Behavioral Medicine, 5.*

Weinstein, N. D. (1984), Why it won't happen to me: Perceptions of risk factors and susceptibility. *Health Psychology, 3,* 431–457.

Weinstein, N. D., Lyon, J. E., Rothman, A. J., & Cuite, C. L. (2000). Changes in perceived vulnerability following natural disaster. *Journal of Social and Clinical Psychology, 19,* 372–395.

Weiss, H. M., & Cropanzano, R. (1996). Affective events theory: A theoretical discussion of the structure, causes, and consequences of affective experiences at work. *Research in Organizational Behavior, 18,* 1–74.

Weissenberg, P., & Kavanagh, M. H. (1972). The independence of initiating structure and consideration: A review of the evidence. *Personnel Psychology, 25,* 119–130.

Weldon, E., & Mustari, L. (1988). Felt dispensability in groups of coactors: The effects of shared responsibility and explicit anonymity on cognitive effort. *Organizational Behavior and Human Decision Processes, 41,* 330–351.

Wells, G. L. (1984). The psychology of lineup identification. *Journal of Applied Social Psychology*, 14, 89–103.

Wells, G. L. (1993). What do we know about eyewitness identification? *American Psychologist*, 48, 553–571.

Wells, G. L., & Luus C. A. E. (1990). Police lineups as experiments: Social methodology as a framework for properly conducted lineups. *Personality and Social Psychology Bulletin*, 16, 106–117.

Wells, G. L., Luus, C. A. E., & Windschitl, P. D. (1994). Maximizing the utility of eyewitness identification evidence. *Current Directions in Psychological Science*, 3, 194–197.

Wells, J. (1997). Stuck on the ladder: Not only is the glass ceiling still in place, but men and women have very different views of the problem. *Maclean's*, October 20, p. 60.

Werner, C. M., Altman, I., & Brown, B. B. (1992). A transactional approach to interpersonal relations: Physical environment, social context, and temporal qualities. *Journal of Social and Personal Relationships*, 9, 297–323.

West, S. G., & Brown, T. J. (1975). Physical attractiveness, the severity of the emergency, and helping: A field experiment and interpersonal simulation. *Journal of Experimental Social Psychology*, 11, 531–538.

Wetsman, A., & Marlowe, F. (1999). How universal are preferences for female waist-to-hip ratios? Evidence from the Hadza of Tanzania. *Evolution and Human Behavior*, 20, 219–228.

Weyant, J. M. (1986). *Applied social psychology*. New York: Oxford University Press.

Wheeler, L., & Kim, Y. (1997). What is beautiful is culturally good: The physical attractiveness stereotype has different content in collectivistic cultures. *Personality and Social Psychology Bulletin*, 23, 795–800.

Whisman, M. A., & Kwon, P. (1993). Life stress and dysphoria: The role of self-esteem and hopelessness. *Journal of Personality and Social Psychology*, 65, 1054–1060.

White, R. K. (1977). Misperception in the Arab–Israeli conflict. *Journal of Social Issues*, 33, 190–221.

Whitley, B. E. Jr. (1993). Reliability and aspects of the construct validity of Sternberg's triangular love scale. *Journal of Social and Personal Relationships*, 10, 475–480.

Whitley, G. E., & Greenberg, M. S. (1986). The role of eyewitness confidence in juror perceptions of credibility. *Journal of Applied Social Psychology*, 16, 387–409.

Wicker, A. W. (1969). Attitudes versus actions: The relationship of verbal and overt behavioral responses to attitude objects. *Journal of Social Issues*, 25, 41–78.

Wiebe, D. J., & McCallum, D. M. (1986). Health practices and hardiness as mediators in the stress-illness relationship. *Health Psychology*, 5, 425–438.

Wiederman, M. W., & Allgeier, E. R. (1996). Expectations and attributions regarding extramarital sex among young married individuals. *Journal of Psychology & Human Sexuality*, 8, 21–35.

Wiener, Y., Muczyk, J. P., & Martin, H. J. (1992). Self-esteem and job involvement as moderators of the relationship between work satisfaction and well-being. *Journal of Social Behavior and Personality*, 7, 539–554.

Wilder, David A. (1984). Intergroup contact: The typical member and the exception to the rule. *Journal of Experimental Social Psychology*, 20, 177–194.

Williams, D. E., & D'Alessandro, J. D. (1994). A comparison of three measures of androgyny and their relationship to psychological adjustment. *Journal of Social Behavior and Personality*, 9, 469–480.

Williams, K. B., Radefeld, P. A., Binning, J. F., & Suadk, J. R. (1993). When job candidates are "hard–" versus "easy-to-get": Effects of candidate availability on employment decisions. *Journal of Applied Social Psychology*, 23, 169–198.

Williams, K. D., & Karau, S. J. (1991). Social loafing and social compensation: The effects of expectations of co-worker performance. *Journal of Personality and Social Psychology*, 61, 570–581.

Williams, K. J., Suls, J., Alliger, G. M., Learner, S. M., & Wan, C. K. (1992). Multiple role juggling and daily mood states in working mothers: An experience sampling study. *Journal of Applied Psychology*, 76, 633–638.

Williams, K., Harkins, S., & Latane, B. (1981). Identifiability as a deterrent to social loafing: Two cheering experiments. *Journal of Personality and Social Psychology*, 40, 303–311.

Williamson, T. M. (1993). From interrogation to investigative interviewing: Strategic trends in police questioning. *Journal of Community and Applied Social Psychology*, 3, 89–99.

Wilson, A. E., & Ross, M. (2000). The frequency of temporal-self and social comparisons in people's personal appraisals. *Journal of Personality and Social Psychology*, 78, 928–942.

Wilson, A. E., & Ross, M. (2001). From chump to champ: People's appraisals of their earlier and present selves. *Journal of Personality and Social Psychology*, 80, 572–584.

Wilson, C. P. (1979). *Jokes: Form, content, use and function*. New York: Academic Press.

Wilson, E. O. (1975). *Sociobiology: The new synthesis*. Cambridge, MA: Harvard University Press.

Wilson, J. P., & Petruska, R. (1984). Motivation, model attributes, and prosocial behavior. *Journal of Personality and Social Psychology*, 46, 458–468.

Wilson, M., Daly, M., Gordon, S., & Pratt, A. (1996). Sex differences in valuations of the environment. *Population and Environment*, 18, 143–159.

Wilson, M. I., & Daly, M. (1985). Competitiveness, risk taking, and violence: The young male syndrome. *Ethology and Sociobiology*, 6, 59–73.

Wilson, T. D., & Kraft, D. (1993). Why do I love thee?: Effects of repeated introspections about a dating relationship on attitudes toward the relationship. *Personality and Social Psychology Bulletin*, 19, 409–418.

Wilson, T. D., & Schooler, J. (1991). Thinking too much: Introspection can reduce the quality of preferences and decisions. *Journal of Personality and Social Psychology*, 60, 181–192.

Winett, R. A. (1998). Developing more effective health-behavior programs: Analyzing the epidemiological and biological bases for activity and exercise programs. *Applied & Preventive Psychology*, 7, 209–224.

Winquist, J. R., & Larson, J. R., Jr. (1998). Information pooling: When it impacts group decision making. *Journal of Personality and Social Psychology, 74*, 317–377.

Witte, E., & Davis, J. H. (Eds.). (1996). *Understanding group behavior: Consensual action by small groups*. Hillsdale, NJ: Erlbaum.

Wolak, J., Mitchell, K. J., Finkelhor, D. (2003). Escaping or connecting? Characteristics of youth who form close online relationships. *Journal of Adolescence, 26*, 105–119.

Wolf, S., & Bugaj, A. M. (1990). The social impact of courtroom witnesses. *Social Behaviour, 5*, 1–13.

Wolfe, S. (1985). Manifest and latent influence of majorities and minorities. *Journal of Personality and Social Psychology, 48*, 899–908.

Wolfgang, A. (1979). The teacher and nonverbal behavior in the multicultural classroom. In A. Wolfang (Ed.), *Nonverbal behavior: Applications and cultural implications*. New York: Academic Press.

Wood, W. (1982). Retrieval of attitude-relevant information from memory: Effects on susceptibility to persuasion on intrinsic motivation. *Journal of Personality and Social Psychology, 42*, 798–810.

Wood, W., Pool, G. J., Leck, K., & Purvis, D. (1996). Self-definition, defensive processing, and influence: The normative impact of majority and minority groups. *Journal of Personality and Social Psychology, 71*, 1181–1193.

Wood, W., Wong, F. Y., & Chachere, J. G. (1991). Effects of media violence on viewers' aggression in unconstrained social interaction. *Psychological Bulletin, 109*, 371–383.

Wortman, C. B., & Linsenmeier, J. A. W. (1977). Interpersonal attraction and techniques of ingratiation in organizational settings. In B. N. Staw & G. R. Salancik (Eds.), *New directions in organizational behavior* (pp. 133–178). Chicago: St. Clair Press.

Wright, R. (1994, November 28). Feminists, meet Mr. Darwin. *The New Republic, 34*, 36–37, 40, 42, 44–46.

Wright, R. (1995, March 13). The biology of violence. *The New Yorker*, 68–77.

Wright, S. C., Aron, A., McLaughlin-Volpe, T., & Ropp, S. A. (1997). The extended contact effect: Knowledge of cross-group friendships and prejudice. *Journal of Personality and Social Psychology, 73*, 73–90.

Wuensch, K. L., Castellow, W. A., & Moore, C. H. (1991). Effects of defendant attractiveness and type of crime on juridic judgment. *Journal of Social Behavior and Personality, 6*, 713–724.

Wyer, R. S. Jr., & Srull, T. K. (Eds.). (1994). *Handbook of social cognition* (2nd ed.) (Vol. 1). Hillsdale, NJ: Erlbaum.

Yang, K.S. (1996). Psychological transformation of the Chinese people as a result of societal modernization. In M.H. Bond (Ed.), *The handbook of Chinese psychology*. Hong-Kong: Oxford University Press.

Yik, M. S. M., Bond, M. H., & Paulhus, D. L. (1998). Do Chinese self-enhance or self-efface? It's a matter of domain. *Personality and Social Psychology Bulletin, 24*, 399–406.

Yoshida, T. (1977). Effects of cognitive dissonance on task evaluation and task performance. *Japanese Journal of Psychology, 48*, 216–223.

Young, M. Y., & Gardner, R. C. (1990). Modes of acculturation and second language proficiency. *Canadian Journal of Behavioral Science, 22*, 59–71.

Yousif, Y., & Korte, C. (1995). Urbanization, culture, and helpfulness: Cross-cultural studies in England and the Sudan. *Journal of Cross-Cultural Psychology, 26*, 474–489.

Yovetich, N. A., & Rusbult, C. E. (1994). Accommodative behavior in close relationships: Exploring transformation of motivation. *Journal of Experimental Social Psychology, 30*, 138–164.

Yu, D. W., & Shepherd, G. H. (1998). Is beauty in the eye of the beholder? *Nature, 396*, 321–322.

Yuille, J. (1993). We must study forensic eyewitnesses to know about them. *American Psychologist, 48*, 572—573.

Yuille, J. C., & Cutshall, J. L. (1986). A case study of eyewitness memory of a crime. *Journal of Applied Psychology, 71*, 291–301.

Yuille, J. C., & Tollestrup, P. A. (1990). Some effects of alcohol on eyewitness memory. *Journal of Applied Psychology, 75*, 268–273.

Yukl, G. (1994). *Leadership in organizations*. Englewood Cliffs, NJ: Prentice-Hall.

Yum, J. O. (2000). The impact of Confucianism on interpersonal relationships and communication patterns in East Asia. In Samovar, L. A., & Porter, R. E. *Intercultural communications: A reader*. Ninth edition. Belmont, CA: Wadsworth.

Zaccaro, S. J., Foti, R. J., & Kenny, D. A. (1991). Self-monitoring and trait-based variance in leadership: An investigation of leader flexibility across multiple group situations. *Journal of Applied Psychology, 76*, 308–315.

Zachariah, R. (1996). Predictors of psychological well-being of women during pregnancy: Replication and extension. *Journal of Social Behavior and Personality, 11*, 127–140.

Zajonc, R. B. (1965). Social facilitation. *Science, 149*, 269–274.

Zajonc, R. B. (1968). Attitudinal effects of mere exposure. *Journal of Personality and Social Psychology Monograph Supplement, 9*, 1–27.

Zajonc, R. B., & Sales, S. H. (1966). Social facilitation of dominant and subordinate responses. *Journal of Experimental Social Psychology, 2*, 160–168.

Zajonc, R. B., Heingartner, A., & Herman, E. M. (1969). Social enhancement and impairment of performance in the cockroach. *Journal of Personality and Social Psychology, 13*, 83–92.

Zammichieli, M. E., Gilroy, F. D., & Sherman, M. F. (1988). Relation between sex-role orientation and marital satisfaction. *Personality and Social Psychology Bulletin, 14*, 747–754.

Zanna, M. P., & Aziza, C. (1976). On the interaction of repression-sensitization and attention in resolving cognitive dissonance. *Journal of Personality and Social Psychology, 44*, 577–593.

Zebrowitz, L. A. (1997). *Reading faces*. Boulder, CO: Westview Press.

Zeitz, G. (1990). Age and work satisfaction in a government agency: A situational perspective. *Human Relations, 43*, 419–438.

Zheng, X., & Berry, J. W. (1991). Psychological adaptation of Chinese sojourners in Canada. *International Journal of Psychology, 26*, 451–470.

Ziller, R. C. (1990). *Photographing the self: Methods for observing personal orientations*. Newbury Park, CA: Sage.

Zillmann, D. (1979). *Hostility and aggression*. Hillsdale, NJ: Erlbaum.

Zillmann, D. (1983). Transfer of excitation in emotional behavior. In J. T. Cacioppo & R. E. Petty (Eds.), *Social psychophysiology: A sourcebook* (pp. 215–240). New York: Guilford Press.

Zillmann, D. (1984). *Connections between sex and aggression*. Hillsdale, NJ: Erlbaum.

Zillmann, D. (1988). Cognition-excitation interdependencies in aggressive behavior. *Aggressive Behavior, 14*, 51–64.

Zillmann, D. (1993). Mental control of angry aggression. In D. M. Wegner & J. W. Pennebaker (Eds.), *Handbook of mental control*. Englewood Cliffs, NJ: Prentice-Hall.

Zillmann, D. (1994). Cognition-excitation interdependencies in the escalation of anger and angry aggression. In M. Potegal & J. F. Knutson (Eds.), *The dynamics of aggression*. Hillsdale, NJ: Erlbaum.

Zimbardo, P. G. (1977). Shyness: What it is and what we can do about it. *Reading*, MA: Addison-Wesley.

Zusne, L., & Jones, W. H. (1989). *Anomalistic psychology: A study of magical thinking* (2nd ed.). Hillsdale, NJ: Erlbaum.

Name Index

Subject Index

Photo Credits